Syngress knows what passing the exam means to you and to your career. And we know that you are often financing your own training and certification; therefore, you need a system that is comprehensive, affordable, and effective.

Boasting one-of-a-kind integration of text, DVD-quality instructor-led training, and Web-based exam simulation, the Syngress Study Guide & DVD Training System guarantees 100% coverage of exam objectives.

The Syngress Study Guide & DVD Training System includes:

- **Study Guide with 100% coverage of exam objectives** By reading this study guide and following the corresponding objective list, you can be sure that you have studied 100% of the exam objectives.

- **Instructor-led DVD** This DVD provides almost two hours of virtual classroom instruction.

- **Web-based practice exams** Just visit us at **www.syngress.com/ certification** to access a complete exam simulation.

Thank you for giving us the opportunity to serve your certification needs. And be sure to let us know if there's anything else we can do to help you get the maximum value from your investment. We're listening.

www.syngress.com/certification

SYNGRESS®

SYNGRESS STUDY GUIDES & DVD TRAINING SYSTEMS

AVAILABLE NOW!
ORDER at
www.syngress.com/certification

SSCP Systems Security Certified Practitioner Study Guide & DVD Training System

The need for qualified information security specialists is at an all-time high. This is the only announced book that shows network and security administrators how to obtain the SSCP certification.

ISBN: 1-931836-80-9
Price: $59.95 USA $92.95 CAN

AVAILABLE NOW!
ORDER at
www.syngress.com/certification

Security+ Study Guide & DVD Training System

The *Security+ Study Guide & DVD Training System* is a one-of-a-kind integration of text, DVD-quality instructor led training, and Web-based exam simulation and remediation. This system gives you 100% coverage of the official CompTIA® Security+ exam objectives plus test preparation software for the edge you need to pass the exam on your first try.

ISBN: 1-931836-72-8
Price: $59.95 USA $92.95 CAN

Watch for our Study Guide and DVD Training Systems for .NET Certification! Coming... May, 2003

AVAILABLE AUGUST 2003!
ORDER at
www.syngress.com/certification

MCSE Installing, Configuring, and Administering Microsoft .NET Server (Exam 70-275) Study Guide & DVD Training System

A fully integrated (Study Guide/Online Exam/DVD) learning system guaranteed to deliver 100% coverage of Microsoft's learning objectives for MCSE Exam 70-275, one of four core requirements for MCSE .NET certification.

ISBN: 1-931836-92-2
Price: $59.95 USA $92.95 CAN

www.syngress.com/certification

SYNGRESS®

SYNGRESS®

COVERS ALL 100% CERTIFIED EXAM OBJECTIVES

MCSE/MCSA
Implementing & Administering Security in a Windows 2000 Network (Exam 70-214)

STUDY GUIDE & DVD TRAINING SYSTEM

Will Schmied
Robert J. Shimonski
Dr. Thomas W. Shinder Technical Editor
Tony Piltzecker Technical Editor

Syngress Publishing, Inc., the author(s), and any person or firm involved in the writing, editing, or production (collectively "Makers") of this book ("the Work") do not guarantee or warrant the results to be obtained from the Work.

There is no guarantee of any kind, expressed or implied, regarding the Work or its contents. The Work is sold AS IS and WITHOUT WARRANTY. You may have other legal rights, which vary from state to state.

In no event will Makers be liable to you for damages, including any loss of profits, lost savings, or other incidental or consequential damages arising out from the Work or its contents. Because some states do not allow the exclusion or limitation of liability for consequential or incidental damages, the above limitation may not apply to you.

You should always use reasonable care, including backup and other appropriate precautions, when working with computers, networks, data, and files.

Syngress Media®, Syngress®, "Career Advancement Through Skill Enhancement®," "Ask the Author UPDATE®," and "Hack Proofing®," are registered trademarks of Syngress Publishing, Inc. "Mission Critical™," and "The Only Way to Stop a Hacker is to Think Like One™" are trademarks of Syngress Publishing, Inc. Brands and product names mentioned in this book are trademarks or service marks of their respective companies.

KEY	SERIAL NUMBER
001	PV43KFU7GY
002	Q29T6CN7VA
003	8C38A9HF5X
004	Z6TN247H9Y
005	7PT5R3T8MS
006	3SHX6BNC4E
007	G8PQND42AK
008	9EU6BKM8D7
009	SU76W4KDFH
010	5BVF397V2Z

PUBLISHED BY
Syngress Publishing, Inc.
800 Hingham Street
Rockland, MA 02370

MCSE Implementing and Administering Security in a Windows 2000 Network Study Guide & DVD Training System

Copyright © 2003 by Syngress Publishing, Inc. All rights reserved. Printed in the United States of America. Except as permitted under the Copyright Act of 1976, no part of this publication may be reproduced or distributed in any form or by any means, or stored in a database or retrieval system, without the prior written permission of the publisher, with the exception that the program listings may be entered, stored, and executed in a computer system, but they may not be reproduced for publication.

Printed in the United States of America

2 3 4 5 6 7 8 9 0

ISBN: 1-931836-84-1

Technical Editor: Thomas W. Shinder M.D and Tony Piltzecker
Technical Reviewer: Robert J. Shimonski
Acquisitions Editor: Jonathan Babcock
DVD Production: Michael Donovan
Cover Designer: Michael Kavish
Page Layout and Art by: Shannon Tozier
Copy Editor: Darlene Bordwell and Judy Edy
Indexer: Rich Carlson

Distributed by Publishers Group West in the United States and Jaguar Book Group in Canada.

Acknowledgments

We would like to acknowledge the following people for their kindness and support in making this book possible.

Karen Cross, Lance Tilford, Meaghan Cunningham, Kim Wylie, Harry Kirchner, Kevin Votel, Kent Anderson, Frida Yara, Jon Mayes, John Mesjak, Peg O'Donnell, Sandra Patterson, Betty Redmond, Roy Remer, Ron Shapiro, Patricia Kelly, Andrea Tetrick, Jennifer Pascal, Doug Reil, David Dahl, Janis Carpenter, and Susan Fryer of Publishers Group West for sharing their incredible marketing experience and expertise.

Duncan Enright, AnnHelen Lindeholm, David Burton, Febea Marinetti, and Rosie Moss of Elsevier Science for making certain that our vision remains worldwide in scope.

David Buckland, Wendi Wong, Daniel Loh, Marie Chieng, Lucy Chong, Leslie Lim, Audrey Gan, and Joseph Chan of Transquest Publishers for the enthusiasm with which they receive our books.

Kwon Sung June at Acorn Publishing for his support.

Jackie Gross, Gayle Voycey, Alexia Penny, Anik Robitaille, Craig Siddall, Darlene Morrow, Iolanda Miller, Jane Mackay, and Marie Skelly at Jackie Gross & Associates for all their help and enthusiasm representing our product in Canada.

Lois Fraser, Connie McMenemy, Shannon Russell, and the rest of the great folks at Jaguar Book Group for their help with distribution of Syngress books in Canada.

David Scott, Annette Scott, Geoff Ebbs, Hedley Partis, Bec Lowe, and Mark Langley of Woodslane for distributing our books throughout Australia, New Zealand, Papua New Guinea, Fiji Tonga, Solomon Islands, and the Cook Islands.

Winston Lim of Global Publishing for his help and support with distribution of Syngress books in the Philippines.

Author

Will Schmied (BSET, MCSE, CWNA, MCSA, Security+, Network+, A+) is a featured writer on Windows 2000 and Windows XP technologies for CramSession.com. He has also authored several works for various Microsoft certification exams. Will provides consulting and training on Microsoft products to small and medium sized organizations in the Hampton Roads, VA area. He holds a bachelor's degree in Mechanical Engineering Technology from Old Dominion University and is a member of the American Society of Mechanical Engineers and the National Society of Professional Engineers. Will currently resides in Newport News, VA with his wife, Allison, and their children, Christopher, Austin, Andrea, and Hannah.

Contributors

Dave Bixler is the Technology Services Manager and Information Security Officer for Siemens Business Systems Inc., one of the world's leading IT service providers, where he heads a consulting group responsible for internal IT consulting, and is also responsible for information security company-wide. Dave has been working in the computer industry for longer than he cares to remember, working on everything from paper tape readers to Windows .NET servers. He currently focuses on Internet technologies, specifically thin client servers, transparent proxy servers, and information security. Dave's industry certifications include Microsoft's MCP and MCSE, and Novell's MCNE.

Martin Grasdal (MCSE+I, MCSE/W2K, MCT, CISSP, CTT, A+), Director of Web Sites and CTO at Brainbuzz.com, has worked in the computer industry for over nine years. He has been an MCT since 1995 and an MCSE since 1996. His training and networking experience covers a broad range of products, including NetWare, Lotus Notes, Windows NT and 2000, Exchange Server, IIS, Proxy Server, and ISA Server. Martin also works actively as a consultant. His recent consulting experience includes contract work for Microsoft as a Technical Contributor to the MCP Program on projects related to server technologies. Martin has served as Technical Editor for several Syngress books, including *Configuring ISA Server 2000: Building Firewalls for Windows 2000* (ISBN: 1-928994-29-6), and *Configuring and Troubleshooting Windows XP Professional* (ISBN: 1-928994-80-6). Martin lives in Edmonton, Alberta, Canada with his wife, Cathy, and their two sons.

Technical Reviewer & Contributor

Robert J. Shimonski (Sniffer SCP, Cisco CCDP, CCNP, Nortel NNCSS, MCSE, MCP+I, Master CNE, CIP, CIBS, CWP, CIW, GSEC, GCIH, Server+, Network+, i-Net+, A+, e-Biz+, TICSA, SPS) is the Lead Network Engineer and Security Analyst for Thomson Industries, a leading manufacturer and provider of linear motion products and engineering. One of Robert's responsibilities is to use multiple network analysis tools to monitor, baseline, and troubleshoot an enterprise network comprised of many protocols and media technologies.

Robert currently hosts an online forum for TechTarget.com and is referred to as the "Network Management Answer Man," where he offers daily solutions to seekers of network analysis and management advice. Robert's other specialties include network infrastructure design with the Cisco and Nortel product line for enterprise networks. Robert also provides network and security analysis using Sniffer Pro, Etherpeek, the CiscoSecure Platform (including PIX Firewalls), and Norton's AntiVirus Enterprise Software.

Robert has contributed to many articles, study guides and certification preparation software, Web sites, and organizations worldwide, including *MCP Magazine*, TechTarget.com, BrainBuzz.com, and SANS.org. Robert's background includes positions as a Network Architect at Avis Rent A Car and Cendant Information Technology. Robert holds a bachelor's degree from SUNY, NY and is a part time Licensed Technical Instructor for Computer Career Center in Garden City, NY teaching Windows-based and

Networking Technologies. Robert is also a contributing author for *Configuring and Troubleshooting Windows XP Professional* (Syngress Publishing, ISBN: 1-928994-80-6) *BizTalk Server 2000 Developer's Guide for .NET* (Syngress, ISBN: 1-928994-40-7), and *Sniffer Pro Network Optimization & Troubleshooting Handbook* (Syngress, ISBN: 1-931836-57-4).

Technical Editors

Thomas W. Shinder M.D. (MVP, MCSE) is a computing industry veteran who has worked as a trainer, writer, and a consultant for Fortune 500 companies including FINA Oil, Lucent Technologies, and Sealand Container Corporation. Tom was a Series Editor of the Syngress/Osborne Series of Windows 2000 Certification Study Guides and is author of the best selling book *Configuring ISA Server 2000: Building Firewalls with Windows 2000* (Syngress Publishing, ISBN: 1-928994-29-6). Tom is the editor of the Brainbuzz.com *Win2k News* newsletter and is a regular contributor to TechProGuild. He is also content editor, contributor, and moderator for the World's leading site on ISA Server 2000, www.isaserver.org. Microsoft recognized Tom's leadership in the ISA Server community and awarded him their Most Valued Professional (MVP) award in December of 2001.

Tony Piltzecker (CISSP, MCSE, CCNA, Check Point CCSA, Citrix CCA, Security+) is author of the *CCSA Exam Cram* and co-author of the *Security+ Study Guide and DVD Training System* (Syngress Publishing, ISBN: 1-931836-72-8). He is a Network Architect with Planning Systems Inc., providing network design and support for federal and state agencies. Tony's specialties include network security design, implementation, and testing. Tony's background includes positions as a senior networking consultant with Integrated Information Systems and a senior engineer with Private Networks, Inc. He holds a bachelor's degree in Business Administration and is a member of ISSA. Tony resides in Leominster, MA with his wife, Melanie, and his daughter, Kaitlyn.

About the Study Guide & DVD Training System

In this book, you'll find lots of interesting sidebars designed to highlight the most important concepts being presented in the main text. These include the following:

- **Exam Warnings** focus on specific elements on which the reader needs to focus in order to pass the exam.

- **Test Day Tips** are short tips that will help you in organizing and remembering information for the exam.

- **Notes from the Underground** contain background information that goes beyond what you need to know from the exam, providing a deep foundation for understanding the security concepts discussed in the text.

- **Damage and Defense** relate real-world experiences to security exploits while outlining defensive strategies.

- **Head of the Class** discussions are based on the author's interactions with students in live classrooms and the topics covered here are the ones students have the most problems with.

Each chapter also includes hands-on exercises. It is important that you work through these exercises in order to be confident you know how to apply the concepts you have just read about.

You will find a number of helpful elements at the end of each chapter. For example, each chapter contains a *Summary of Exam Objectives* that ties the topics discussed in that chapter to the published objectives. Each chapter also contains an *Exam Objectives Fast Track,* which boils all exam objectives down to manageable summaries that are perfect for last minute review. *The Exam Objectives Frequently Asked Questions* answers those questions that most often arise from readers and students regarding the topics covered in the chapter. Finally, in the *Self Test* section, you will find a set of practice questions written in a multiple-choice form similar to those you will encounter on the exam. You can use the *Self Test Quick Answer Key* that follows the *Self Test* questions to quickly determine what information you need to review again. The *Self Test Appendix* at the end of the book provides detailed explanations of both the correct and incorrect answers.

Additional Resources

There are two other important exam preparation tools included with this Study Guide. One is the DVD included in the back of this book. The other is the practice exam available from our website.

- **Instructor-led training DVD provides you with almost two hours of virtual classroom instruction.** Sit back and watch as an author and trainer reviews all the key exam concepts from the perspective of someone taking the exam for the first time. Here, you'll cut through all of the noise to prepare you for exactly what to expect when you take the exam for the first time. You will want to watch this DVD just before you head out to the testing center!

- **Web based practice exams.** Just visit us at www.syngress.com/certification to access a complete Exam Simulation. These exams are written to test you on all of the published certification objectives. The exam simulator runs in both "live" and "practice" mode. Use "live" mode first to get an accurate gauge of your knowledge and skills, and then use practice mode to launch an extensive review of the questions that gave you trouble.

MCSE/MCSA 70-214 Exam Objectives Map and Table of Contents

All of Microsoft's published objectives for the MCSE/MCSA 70-214 Exam are covered in this book. To help you easily find the sections that directly support particular objectives, we've listed all of the exam objectives below, and mapped them to the Chapter number and heading in which they are covered. We've also assigned numbers to each objective, which we use in the subsequent Table of Contents and again throughout the book to identify objective coverage. In some chapters, we've made the judgment that it is probably easier for the student to cover objectives in a slightly different sequence than the order of the published Microsoft objectives. By reading this study guide and following the corresponding objective list, you can be sure that you have studied 100% of Microsoft's MCSE/MCSA 70-214 Exam objectives.

Exam Objective Map

Objective Number	Objective	Chapter Number	Chapter Heading
1	Implementing, Managing, and Troubleshooting Baseline Security		
1.1	Configure security templates.	1	Configuring Basic Windows 2000 Security with Templates
1.1.1	Configure registry and file system permissions.	1	Registry, File System
1.1.2	Configure account policies.	1	Account Policies
1.1.3	Configure audit policies.	1	Local Policies
1.1.4	Configure user rights assignment.	1	Local Policies
1.1.5	Configure security options.	1	Local Policies
1.1.6	Configure system services.	1	System Services
1.1.7	Configure restricted groups.	1	Restricted Groups
1.1.8	Configure event logs.	1	Event Log
1.2	Deploy security templates. Deployment methods include using Group Policy and scripting.	1	Deploying Security Templates Analyzing Your Security Configuration

xi

Objective Number	Objective	Chapter Number	Chapter Heading
1.3	Troubleshoot security template problems. Considerations include Group Policy, upgraded operating systems, and mixed client-computer operating systems.	2	Security Template Application Issues
1.4	Configure additional security based on computer roles. Computer roles include Microsoft SQL Server computer, Microsoft Exchange Server computer, domain controller, Internet Authentication Service (IAS) server, Internet Information Services (IIS) server, and mobile client computer.	2	Configuring Role-Based Server Security
1.5	Configure additional security for client-computer operating systems by using Group Policy.	2	Creating Secure Workstations
2	**Implementing, Managing, and Troubleshooting Service Packs and Security Updates**		
2.1	Determine the current status of service packs and security updates. Tools include MBSA and HFNetChk.	3	Identifying Required Updates
2.2	Install service packs and security updates. Considerations include slipstreaming and using Remote Installation Services (RIS), custom scripts, and isolated networks.	3	Deploying and Managing Updates
2.2.1	Install service packs and security updates on new client computers and servers. Considerations include slipstreaming and using RIS, custom scripts, and isolated networks.	3	Installing Updates on New Computers

Exam Objective Map **xiii**

Objective Number	Objective	Chapter Number	Chapter Heading
2.3	Manage service packs and security updates. Considerations include server computers and remote client computers. Tools include Microsoft Software Update Service, Automatic Updates, and SMS.	3	Deploying and Managing Updates
2.4	Troubleshoot the deployment of service packs and security updates. Typical issues include third-party application compatibility, permissions, and version conflicts.	3	Troubleshooting Update Installations
3	**Implementing, Managing, and Troubleshooting Secure Communication Channels**		
3.1	Configure IPSec to secure communication between networks and hosts. Hosts include domain controllers, Internet Web servers, databases, e-mail servers, and client computers.	6	Deploying and Troubleshooting Windows IP Security
3.1.1	Configure IPSec authentication.	6	Deploying and Troubleshooting Windows IP Security
3.1.2	Configure appropriate encryption levels.	6	Confidentiality
3.1.3	Configure the appropriate IPSec protocol. Protocols include AH and ESP.	6	IPSec Security Services
3.1.4	Deploy and manage IPSec certificates. Considerations include renewing certificates.	4	Certificate Authorities
3.2	Troubleshoot IPSec. Typical issues include IPSec rule configurations, firewall configurations, routers, and authentication.	6	Deploying and Troubleshooting Windows IP Security

Objective Number	Objective	Chapter Number	Chapter Heading
3.3	Implement security for wireless networks.	7	Wireless LAN Security Issues Wireless LAN Security: It's Not Perfect Should You Use Wep? IEEE 802.1x Vulnerabilites Additional Secuirty Measures for Wireless LANs Implementing Wireless LAN Security: Common Best Practices
3.3.1	Configure public and private wireless LANs.	7	Configuring Windows Client Computers for Wireless LAN Security
3.3.2	Configure wireless encryption levels. Levels include WEP and 802.1x.	7	Wired Equivalent Privacy 802.1x Authentication
3.3.3	Configure wireless network connection settings on client computers. Client-computer operating systems include Windows 2000 Professional, Windows XP Professional, and Windows CE 3.0.	7	Configuring Windows Client Computers for Wireless LAN Security
3.4	Configure Server Message Block (SMB) signing to support packet authentication and integrity.	2	Securing Server Message Block Traffic
3.5	Deploy and manage SSL certificates. Considerations include renewing certificates and obtaining self-issued certificates versus public-issued certificates.	8	Configuring Web Site Authentication
3.5.1	Obtain public and private certificates.	4	Requesting a Certificate Exporting and Importing Certificates
3.5.2	Install certificates for SSL.	8	Configuring Web Site Authentication
3.5.3	Renew certificates.	4	Requesting a Certificate Exporting and Importing Certificates

Objective Number	Objective	Chapter Number	Chapter Heading
3.6	Configure SSL to secure communication channels. Communication channels include client computer to Web server, Web server to SQL Server computer, client computer to Active Directory domain controller, and e-mail server to client computer.	8	Configuring Web Site Authentication
4	**Configuring, Managing, and Troubleshooting Authentication and Remote Access Security**		
4.1	Configure and troubleshoot authentication.	8	Configuring User Authentication
4.1.1	Configure authentication protocols to support mixed Windows client-computer environments.	8	Configuring User Authentication
4.1.2	Configure the interoperability of Kerberos authentication with UNIX computers.	8	Configuring Interoperability with UNIX Servers
4.1.3	Configure authentication for extranet scenarios.	8	Authentication for External Users
4.1.4	Configure trust relationships.	8	Configuring Kerberos Trusts
4.1.5	Configure authentication for members of non-trusted domain authentication.	8	Configuring Web Authentication
4.2	Configure and troubleshoot authentication for Web users. Authentication types include Basic, Integrated Windows, anonymous, digest, and client certificate mapping.	8	Configuring Web Authentication
4.3	Configure authentication for secure remote access. Authentication types include PAP, CHAP, MS-CHAP, MS-CHAP v2, EAP-MD5, EAP-TLS, and Multi-factor authentication with smart cards and EAP.	9	Remote Access Authentication Methods Configuring Network Clients for Secure Remote Access

Exam Objective Map

Objective Number	Objective	Chapter Number	Chapter Heading
4.4	Configure and troubleshoot virtual private network (VPN) protocols. Considerations include Internet service provider (ISP), client-computer operating system, Network Address Translation (NAT) devices, Routing and Remote Access server, and firewall server.	9	Configuring a Remote Access Server (RAS) Configuring a Virtual Private Networking (VPN) Server Configuring Network Clients for Secure Remote Access
4.5	Manage client-computer configuration for remote access security. Tools include remote access policy and Connection Manager Administration Kit.	9	Using the Connection Manager Administration Kit (CMAK)
5	**Implementing and Managing a Public Key Infrastructure (PKI) and Encrypting File System (EFS)**		
5.1	Install and configure Certificate Authority (CA) hierarchies. Considerations include enterprise, standalone, and third-party.	4	Installing and Managing Windows 2000 Certificate Authorities
5.1.1	Install and configure the root, intermediate, and issuing CA. Considerations include renewals and hierarchy.	4	Installing and Managing Windows 2000 Certificate Authorities
5.1.2	Configure certificate templates. Considerations include LDAP queries, HTTP queries, and third-party CAs.	4	Configuring Certificate Templates
5.1.3	Configure the publication of Certificate Revocation Lists (CRLs).	4	Configuring Publication of Certificate Revocation Lists (CRLs)
5.1.4	Configure public key Group Policy.	4	Configuring Public Key Group Policy
5.1.5	Configure certificate renewal and enrollment.	4	Requesting a Certificate
5.1.6	Deploy certificates to users, computers, and CAs.	4	Requesting a Certificate Exporting and Importing Certificates

Exam Objective Map   xvii

Objective Number	Objective	Chapter Number	Chapter Heading
5.2	Manage Certificate Authorities (CAs). Considerations include enterprise, stand-alone, and third-party.	4	Installing and Managing Windows 2000 Certificate Authorities
5.2.1	Enroll and renew certificates.	4	Requesting a Certificate
5.2.2	Revoke certificates.	4	Revoking Certificates
5.2.3	Manage and troubleshoot Certificate Revocation Lists (CRLs). Considerations include publishing the CRL.	4	Configuring Publication of Certificate Revocation Lists (CRLs)
5.2.4	Back up and restore the CA.	4	Backing Up and Restoring Certificate Services
5.3	Manage client-computer and server certificates. Considerations include SMIME, EFS, exporting, and storage.	4	Advanced Certificate Management Issues Exporting and Importing Certificates
5.3.1	Publish certificates through Active Directory.	4	Publishing Certificates in Active Directory
5.3.2	Issue certificates using MMC, Web enrollment, programmatic, or auto enrollment using Windows XP.	4	Requesting a Certificate Windows XP auto enrollment
5.3.3	Recover KMS-issued keys.	4	Recovering KMS Issued Keys
5.4	Manage and troubleshoot EFS. Considerations include domain members, workgroup members, and client-computer operating systems.	5	User Operations EFS Architecture and Troubleshooting
6	**Monitoring and Responding to Security Incidents**		
6.1	Configure and manage auditing. Considerations include Windows Events, Internet Information Services (IIS), firewall log files, Network Monitor Log, and RAS log files.	10	Auditing Windows 2000 Auditing IIS Auditing Best Practices
6.1.1	Manage audit log retention.	10	Auditing Best Practices
6.1.2	Manage distributed audit logs by using EventComb.	10	Windows Auditing Tools

Objective Number	Objective	Chapter Number	Chapter Heading
6.2	Analyze security events. Considerations include reviewing logs and events.	10	Auditing Best Practices
6.3	Respond to security incidents. Incidents include hackers, viruses, denial-of-service (DoS) attacks, natural disasters, and maintaining chains of evidence.	11	Security Incidents Malware Issues Incident Response
6.3.1	Isolate and contain the incident. Considerations include preserving the chain of evidence.	11	Chain of Custody
6.3.2	Implement counter measures.	11	Incident Response
6.3.3	Restore services.	11	Incident Response

Contents

Foreword xxxiii

❖ **Part I Implementing, Managing, and Troubleshooting Baseline Security** 1

Chapter 1 Basic Windows 2000 Security: Using Security Templates 3
    Introduction 4
    Windows 2000 Active Directory Review 4
        Introduction to Directory Services 5
        History of the Windows Directory Service 6
        Active Directory Architecture 9
        The X.500 Directory Standard 11
        The Logical Structure of Active Directory 12
            Forests 12
            Trees 13
            Domains 13
            Schema 13
            Global Catalog 14
            Organizational Units 14
            Groups...15
        The Physical Structure of Active Directory 17
            Sites 17
            Domain Controllers 17
            Servers and Workstations 18
            Objects: The Heart of It All 18
        Containers: Odd Men Out 19
    The Basic Windows 2000 Security Tools 20
        Security Configuration Tool Set 20
        Security Templates 21
        Group Policy Security Settings 23
        Security Configuration and Analysis 27
        The Command-Line Tools 30
            Secedit.exe 30
            Gpresult.exe and Gpotool.exe...........................31
        Creating the Security Configuration Tool Set User Interface 31
1.1   Configuring Basic Windows 2000 Security with Templates 32

1.1.2	Account Policies	33
1.1.3/	Local Policies	35
1.1.4/		
1.1.5		
1.1.8	Event Log	42
1.1.7	Restricted Groups	44
1.1.6	System Services	46
1.1.1	Registry	48
1.1.1	File System	50
1.2	Deploying Security Templates	53
	Let's Configure!	54
	Deploying Security via Group Policy	57
	Deploying Security via Scripting	60
1.2	Analyzing Your Security Configuration	63
	Using Security Configuration and Analysis	63
	Examining the Analysis Results	65
	Using Secedit.exe	67
	secedit /analyze	67
	secedit /refreshpolicy	68
	secedit /export	68
	secedit /validate	69
	Areas	69
	Analyzing Security with Secedit.exe	70
	Using Gpresult.exe and Gpotool.exe	71
	Summary of Exam Objectives	73
	Exam Objectives Fast Track	74
	Exam Objectives Frequently Asked Questions	76
	Self Test	77
	Self Test Quick Answer Key	84

Chapter 2 Advanced Security Template and Group Policy Issues 85

	Introduction	86
1.4	Configuring Role-Based Server Security	86
	Securing the Domain	88
	Windows 2000 Domain Controllers	89
	Member Servers	92
	SQL Server 2000	93
	Exchange 2000 Server	97

		Windows 2000 Internet Information Services Servers 99
		Windows 2000 Internet Access Service Servers 106
1.5	Creating Secure Workstations 107	
		Desktop Workstations..107
		Portable Computers 111
1.3	Security Template Application Issues 112	
		Upgrade Installations 112
		Legacy Client Issues 113
		Using Gpresult.exe 114
		Event Log Entries 114
		Last Thoughts on Security Templates 117
3.4	Securing Server Message Block Traffic...................................118	
	Summary of Exam Objectives 120	
	Exam Objectives Fast Track 121	
	Exam Objectives Frequently Asked Questions..........................122	
	Self Test...124	
	Self Test Quick Answer Key 130	

❖ **Part II Implementing, Managing, and Troubleshooting Service Packs and Security Updates** 131

Chapter 3 Identifying, Installing, and Troubleshooting Required Updates 133

	Introduction 134	
2.1	Identifying Required Updates 134	
	Types of Updates 134	
		Service Packs..134
		Hotfixes 135
	Analyzing Your Computers 137	
		Visiting Windows Update 137
		The Microsoft Network Security Hotfix Checker 139
		The Microsoft Baseline Security Analyzer 145
2.2/2.3	Deploying and Managing Updates 152	
2.2.1	Installing Updates on New Computers 155	
		Slipstreaming Installation Media for RIS Deployment.........155
		Scripting Updates 163
		Installing Updates in Isolated Networks 165
	Deployment Updates to Existing Computers 165	
		Windows Update 165
		Windows Update Catalog......................................169

	Software Update Service and Automatic Updates	172
	Systems Management Server	180
	Special Considerations for Updating Servers	181
2.4	Troubleshooting Update Installations	182
	Application Compatibility Issues	182
	Permissions Problems	182
	Version Conflicts	183
	Summary of Exam Objectives	184
	Exam Objectives Fast Track	186
	Exam Objectives Frequently Asked Questions	187
	Self Test	189
	Self Test Quick Answer Key	196

❖ Part III Implementing and Managing a Public Key Infrastructure (PKI) and Encrypting File System (EFS) 197

Chapter 4 Installing, Configuring, & Managing Windows 2000 Certificate Authorities...............................199

	Introduction	200
	Cryptography and You: What is it All About?	200
	Public Key Cryptography	201
	Public Key Functionality	203
	Digital Signatures	203
	Authentication	204
	Secret Key Agreement via Public Key	206
	Bulk Data Encryption without Prior Shared Secrets	206
	Protecting and Trusting Cryptographic Keys	206
	Certificates	207
3.1.4	Certificate Authorities	208
	CA Types	209
	Certificate Hierarchies	211
	Trust and Validation	212
5.1/ 5.1.1/ 5.2	Installing and Managing Windows 2000 Certificate Authorities	212
3.5.1/ 3.5.3/ 5.1.5/ 5.1.6/ 5.2.1	Requesting a Certificate	217

3.5.1/ 3.5.3/ 5.1.6	Exporting and Importing Certificates	222
5.2.2	Revoking Certificates	226
5.1.3/ 5.2.3	Configuring Publication of CRLs	229
5.1.2	Configuring Certificate Templates	231
5.1.4	Configuring Public Key Group Policy	234
	Configuring Automatic Certificate Enrollment	234
	Configuring the Trusted Root CAs	236
5.2.4	Backing Up and Restoring Certificate Services	237
5.3	Advanced Certificate Management Issues	240
5.3.1	Publishing Certificates in Active Directory	241
5.3.3	Recovering Key Management Server Issued Keys	241
5.3.2	Windows XP Auto-enrollment	244
	Summary of Exam Objectives	247
	Exam Objectives Fast Track	249
	Exam Objectives Frequently Asked Questions	253
	Self Test	255
	Self Test Quick Answer Key	261

Chapter 5 Managing and Troubleshooting the Encrypting File System 263

	Introduction	264
	The Role of EFS in a Network Security Plan	265
	Using the Encrypting File System	266
	Encryption Fundamentals	267
	Public Key, or Asymmetric Cryptography	268
	Secret Key, or Symmetric Cryptography	269
	How EFS Works	269
5.4	User Operations	271
	Encrypting a File or Folder	272
	Encrypting a File or Folder on the Local Computer	272
	Encrypting a File or Folder on a Remote Computer	274
	Accessing an Encrypted File	275
	Copying an Encrypted File	276
	Preventing Files from Being Encrypted on a Server	277
	Moving or Renaming an Encrypted File	278
	Sharing an Encrypted File in Windows XP/.NET	278

Decrypting a File 279
Using the Cipher Utility in Windows 2000 280
Encrypting a Directory 282
Employing Recovery Operations 283

5.4 EFS Architecture and Troubleshooting...................................292
EFS Components 292
The Encryption Process 295
The EFS File Information 298
The Decryption Process...300
Troubleshooting EFS 302
Summary of Exam Objectives 304
Exam Objectives Fast Track 305
Exam Objectives Frequently Asked Questions 307
Self Test 310
Self Test Quick Answer Key 316

❖ Part IV: Implementing, Managing, and Troubleshooting Secure Communication Channels 317

Chapter 6 Configuring and Troubleshooting Windows IP Security 319

Introduction 320
The Need for Network Security 321
Snooping 321
Spoofing...322
The TCP/IP Sequence Number Attack 322
Spoofing Tools 322
Password Compromise 323
DoS Attacks 325
TCP SYN Attacks...325
SMURF Attacks 325
Teardrop Attacks 326
Ping-of-Death Attacks 326
MITM Attacks 326
Application-directed Attacks 327
Compromised Key Attacks..327
IP Security Overview 328
Overview of IPSec Cryptographic Services 329
Message Integrity 329
Message Authentication..331

3.1.2	Confidentiality	334
3.1.3	IPSec Security Services	335

        The AH ... 335
        ESP ... 336
        Security Associations and IPSec Key Management
          Procedures ... 337
            Security Associations ... 337
            IPSec Key Management ... 337
    IP Security Management Tools ... 339
        IP Security Policies on Local Machine ... 339
        IP Security Monitor ... 340
        IPSec Policy Agent Service ... 342
        TCP/IP Advanced Options ... 343
        Certificates Snap-In ... 343
        Security Log ... 344
        NetDiag ... 344

3.1/ 3.1.1/ 3.2   Deploying and Troubleshooting Windows IP Security ... 345

    Evaluating Information ... 345
        Evaluating the "Enemy" ... 346
    Determining Required Security Levels ... 347
    Building Security Policies with Customized
      IPSec Consoles ... 347
    Flexible Security Policies ... 349
        Rules ... 352
    Flexible Negotiation Policies ... 355
    Filters ... 356
    Creating a Security Policy ... 358
        Making the Rule ... 359
        Compatibility Notes ... 369
    Troubleshooting IP Security ... 369
Summary of Exam Objectives ... 372
Exam Objectives Fast Track ... 373
Exam Objectives Frequently Asked Questions ... 375
Self Test ... 376
Self Test Quick Answer Key ... 381

Chapter 7 Implementing Secure Wireless Networks 383
Introduction to the Wireless LAN 384
   Benefits of the Wireless LAN..384
      Convenience 384
      Productivity 388
   Wireless LAN Concepts...388
      Communication in a Wireless Network 389
      Wireless Network Architecture....................................392
   IEEE 802.11 Wireless Local Area Networks 394
      IEEE 802.11b 395
      IEEE 802.11a 396
      IEEE 802.11g 396
   802.11 Communication Modes 397

3.3.2   Wired Equivalent Privacy 398
      Creating Privacy with WEP 400
      Authentication 401

3.3.2   802.1*x* Authentication 403
      User Identification and Strong Authentication 405
      Dynamic Key Derivation 405
      Mutual Authentication 406
      Per-Packet Authentication..406

3.3   Wireless LAN Security Issues 407
   Passive Attacks on Wireless Networks 407
      War Driving 408
      Sniffing 412
   Active Attacks on Wireless Networks...............................413
      Spoofing and Unauthorized Access 414
      Denial of Service and Flooding Attacks 416
   Man-in-the-Middle Attacks on Wireless Networks 418
      Network Hijacking and Modification 419
   Jamming Attacks 420

3.3   Wireless LAN Security: It's Not Perfect............................421
      WEP Vulnerabilities 422
      Vulnerability to Plaintext Attacks 422
      Vulnerability of RC4 Algorithm 423
      Stream Cipher Vulnerability 423

3.3   Should You Use WEP? 425
      Security of 64-Bit Versus 128-Bit Keys..........................425

| 3.3 | IEEE 802.1x Vulnerabilities | 426 |

3.3.1/   Configuring Windows Client Computers for
3.3.3   Wireless LAN Security 427
              Windows XP Professional 427
              Windows 2000 Professional 429

3.3   Additional Security Measures for Wireless LANs 431
              Using a Separate Subnet for Wireless Networks 431
              Using VPNs for Wireless Access to Wired Networks 432
              Temporal Key Integrity Protocol 434
              Message Integrity Code 434
              The IEEE 802.11i Standard 435

3.3   Implementing Wireless LAN Security:
      Common Best Practices 436
      Summary of Exam Objectives 439
      Exam Objectives Fast Track 441
      Exam Objectives Frequently Asked Questions 445
      Self Test 446
      Self Test Quick Answer Key 451

❖ Part V Configuring, Managing, and Troubleshooting Authentication and Remote Access Security 453

Chapter 8 Configuring Secure Network and Internet Authentication Methods 455

Introduction 456
Network Authentication in Windows 2000 456
    NTLM 457
    Kerberos 458
Kerberos Overview 459
    Kerberos Concepts 460
        The Authenticator 461
        The KDC 462
        The Session Ticket (ST) 464
        The TGT 466
    Kerberos Authentication across Domain Boundaries 467
    Delegation of Authentication 468
        Proxy Tickets 469
        Forwarded Tickets 469
    Kerberos in Windows 2000 470
        The KDC and Account Database 471

	Kerberos Policy 473
	Delegation of Authentication 474
	Preauthentication 477
	Credentials Cache 478
	DNS Name Resolution 478
	Authorization Data..479
	KDC and Authorization Data 479
	Services and Authorization Data 480
	UDP and TCP Ports 480
4.1.4	Configuring Kerberos Trusts.....................................480
	The Great Link: Kerberos Trusts between Domains 482
	Taking a Shortcut 483
4.1/ 4.1.1	Configuring User Authentication.............................488
4.1.3	Authentication for External Users 488
4.1.2	Configuring Interoperability with UNIX Servers 489
	Using Cleartext Authentication 489
	Using Certificate-based Authentication 489
	Using the Kerberos v5 Protocol 490
	Using NTLM Authentication 490
	Configuring Interoperability with Legacy Windows Clients 490
	Defining LM and NLM Authentication 491
	Using the Directory Services Client................491
	Deploying NTLM Version 2 492
	Making Clients Use NTLMv2 494
4.1.5/ 4.2	Configuring Web Authentication 497
	Using Anonymous Authentication 497
	Using Basic Authentication 497
	Using Digest Authentication 498
	Using Integrated Windows Authentication 500
	Using Client Certificate Mapping 500
	One-to-One Certificate Mapping 501
	Many-to-One Certificate Mapping 501
	Combining Authentication Methods 502
3.5/3.5.2/ 3.6	Configuring Web Site Authentication 502
	Troubleshooting Web Authentication 510

	Summary of Exam Objectives	512
	Exam Objectives Fast Track	513
	Exam Objectives Frequently Asked Questions	517
	Self Test	519
	Self Test Quick Answer Key	525
	Chapter 9 Configuring and Troubleshooting Remote Access and VPN Authentication	**527**
	Introduction	528
4.3	Remote Access Authentication Methods	529
	Point-to-Point Protocol	529
	Password Authentication Protocol	530
	Challenge Handshake Authentication Protocol	530
	Microsoft Challenge Handshake Authentication Protocol	530
	MS-CHAP v2	531
	Extensible Authentication Protocol	532
	EAP-MD5 CHAP	532
	EAP-TLS	532
	EAP and Smartcards/Certificates	533
4.4	Configuring a Remote Access Server	534
	Installing and Configuring the Remote Access Server	535
	Working with RAS Ports	541
4.4	Configuring a Virtual Private Networking Server	546
	Installing and Configuring the VPN Server	547
	Working with VPN Ports	556
	Point-to-Point Tunneling Protocol	556
	Layer 2 Tunneling Protocol	557
	Internet Protocol Security	558
	Configuring L2TP Ports	561
	Configuring Remote Access Policies	562
	Configuring Remote Access Profiles	567
	Dial-in Constraints	567
	IP	568
	Multilink	569
	Authentication	570
	Encryption	570
	Advanced	571
	Remote Access Policy Administrative Models	571
4.3/4.4	Configuring Network Clients for Secure Remote Access	573

4.5	Using the Connection Manager Administration Kit 576	
	Manually Creating the Connections 577	
	Creating a Static Phone Book 578	
	Creating a Dynamic Phone Book................................579	
	Running the CMAK 580	
	Allowing Users to Use the Connection Manager 582	
	Troubleshooting Remote Access Problems 582	
	Problems with a VPN Due to the Internet	
	Service Provider 584	
	Client Computer Operating System Issues 585	
	Network Address Translation Devices 586	
	Routing and Remote Access Server Issues 588	
	Firewall Issues 589	
	Summary of Exam Objectives 591	
	Exam Objectives Fast Track 594	
	Exam Objectives Frequently Asked Questions 596	
	Self Test 598	
	Self Test Quick Answer Key 604	

❖ Part VI Monitoring and Responding to Security Incidents 605

Chapter 10 Configuring and Using Auditing and the Event Logs 607

	Introduction 608	
	Auditing for Increased Security 609	
6.1	Auditing Windows 2000 611	
	Windows 2000 Local Auditing 611	
	Audit Account Logon Events 611	
	Audit Account Management....................................612	
	Audit Logon Events 613	
	Audit Object Events 613	
	Audit Policy Change..613	
	Audit Privilege Use 614	
	Audit Process Tracking 615	
	Audit System Events 616	
	Auditing with Group Policy 620	
	Events to Audit 621	
	Logon Events that Appear in the Event Log....................622	

6.1/	Auditing Best Practices	627
6.1.1/		
6.2		
	Security Analysis	628
	Event Viewer Log Size	629
6.1	Auditing Internet Information Services	630
	Internet Information Services	630
6.1.2	Windows Auditing Tools	633
	The Dump Event Log	634
	EventCombMT	635
	Summary of Exam Objectives	638
	Exam Objectives Fast Track	639
	Exam Objectives Frequently Asked Questions	641
	Self Test	642
	Self Test Quick Answer Key	648

Chapter 11 Responding to and Recovering from Security Breaches 649

	Introduction	650
6.3	Security Incidents	650
	Minimizing Security Incidents	651
	Hackers	655
	Hacker Jargon	655
6.3	Malware Issues	657
	Viruses	658
	Worms	659
	Trojan Horses	659
	Trojan Awareness	663
	Denial of Service	666
	Launching a Distributed DoS	669
6.3/	Incident Response	672
6.3.2/		
6.3.3		
	Defining an Incident Response Plan	672
	Forensics	673
	Conceptual Knowledge	674
	Your Role	675
6.3.1	Chain of Custody	678

Evidence Collection 679
Summary of Exam Objectives 681
Exam Objectives Fast Track 682
Exam Objectives Frequently Asked Questions 683
Self Test 685
Self Test Quick Answer Key 692

❖ Part VII Appendixes 693

Appendix A Utilities for the White Hat 695
Introduction 696
White Hat Vulnerability Testing 698
    LANguard Network Scanner 698
    Network Mapper and Network Mapper for Windows 701
    Ethereal 703
White Hat Protection Tools 705
    SSH 705
    PGP 706
Summary 707

Appendix B Port Numbers and Associated Attacks 709
Introduction 710
Port Numbers 710

Appendix C Self Test Questions, Answers, and Explanations 717

Index 811

Foreword

Congratulations! By picking up this book, you have taken a big step forward in your career. Whether you are an IT guru with years of experience, a neophyte fresh to the exciting world of information technology, or somewhere in the middle, this book will help you get to your destination by providing you with the information and tools you need to take the challenge of a very exciting test: Implementing and Administering Security in a Microsoft Windows 2000 Network.

Computer security seems to be a topic that is forever in the news. Not many a week goes by without some new computer hack, crack, flaw, or vulnerability being discovered and announced. System administrators find themselves on the receiving end of this threat most often—and all of sudden, it seems like that admin is no longer the most powerful person in the organization. The problem is not that Windows 2000 (or Windows XP and Windows .NET Server) is any more a security risk than any other operating system available for use. The problem lies in the fact that the vast majority of publicly accessible computers are running Windows-based operating systems, many of them Windows 2000. This sheer disadvantage (in terms of the number of available targets), combined with the desire of unscrupulous individuals to embarrass admins and Microsoft alike, is what leads to problems. The additional fact that many Windows admins don't really fully understand the criticality of highly secure computers and how to keep them secure only makes the situation that much greater a problem—and that much more attractive an opportunity to people who would seek to gain unauthorized access to a system or network.

Securing a Windows 2000 network does not have to be a difficult process. Microsoft has taken many steps to see to it that you have in your hands as much power as possible to secure your network. That is the good news. To that end, you should be very careful when configuring the security settings for your computers and your entire network. Simply rushing out to enforce a more secure network on your organization is not going to work—you will either find yourself making mistakes (which will often be quite costly), creating new vulnerabilities, or interfering with the daily work routine of your users. It's conceivable that you could even have all three of these issues come biting at your heels all at once. That is the bad news.

But don't fret; all is not lost. With a careful and methodical study of the nuances of Windows 2000 security, you can properly secure your systems and still allow your users' daily work to continue—with minimal negative impact. This book aims not to make you a Windows 2000 security expert but instead to make you into a Windows 2000 administrator who is more aware of the available and necessary options, considerations, and procedures.

This Microsoft Certified Professional (MCP) exam, number 70-214, is an elective exam for the prestigious Microsoft Certified Systems Engineer (MCSE) and Microsoft Certified Systems Administrator (MCSA) certifications. At the time of this exam's release, the Windows 2000 certification track was two years old. The 70-214 exam is a result of the critical need for a security-based examination that verifies an administrator's ability to implement and maintain secure Windows 2000 networks during these two years. It makes sense, after all; you can trace all the existing *design exams* to a corresponding *implementing exam*. In this case, exam 70-214 pairs up with the already existing exam 70-220 (Designing Security for a Microsoft Windows 2000 Network).

What Are the MCSA and MCSE?

It's hard for some of us to believe (or even remember), but the MCP program turned 10 years old in the spring of 2002. From its humble beginnings as not quite an organized system, the Microsoft MCP program has grown into one of the largest and most prestigious information technology certification programs. Microsoft most certainly leads the way in number and subject matter of exams delivered, with one or more exams to fit just about every person. Today, Microsoft has a dozen different IT certification tracks, ranging from networking to office suites. The MCSA and MCSE tracks specifically deal with the networking side of Microsoft's product line.

MCSA Background

Microsoft's newest networking certification track, the Microsoft Certified Systems Administrator, or MCSA, is a little over a year old at the time of this writing. In that year, it has quickly gained popularity as a solid foundation for people who handle day-to-day administration and maintenance of Windows 2000 networks.

Typical duties of the MCSA certified individual include managing, supporting, and troubleshooting daily needs associated with the operation of a Windows 2000 network. Microsoft specifies that an MCSA will typically have 6 to 12 months of hands-on experience managing and supporting workstations and servers in an *existing* Windows 2000 infrastructure. This is a key distinction from the MCSE certification, which may involve designing and implementing a new Windows 2000 infrastructure.

Some typical job titles that MCSAs can have include:

- Systems Administrator
- Network Administrator
- Information Systems Administrator
- Network Operations Analyst
- Network Technician
- Technical Support Specialist

MCSE Background

The Microsoft Certified Systems Engineer, or MCSE, certification has existed for some time now, dating back to the Windows NT 3.51 days and possibly even earlier. The MCSE certification had come under much fire during the Windows NT 4.0 track due to the ease of obtaining it; many people simply memorized the material and took the exams, achieving the MCSE certification without having enough (or in some cases, any) real hands-on experience with the product. Microsoft took great pains when it rolled out the Windows 2000 MCSE track to ensure that it corrected these issues by changing the testing experience. New question types and larger, more complex question banks were implemented in an effort to once again make the MCSE certification meaningful and difficult to attain. From all accounts, it appears that Microsoft's efforts have been largely successful, although no amount of work and planning can stop all individuals who would look to circumvent the system.

The typical duties of the Windows 2000 MCSE certified individual include planning, designing, and implementing Windows 2000 server solutions and architectures. In other words, an MCSE-certified individual should expect to spend more time designing and implementing new solutions than would the MCSA-certified individual. For this reason, the exam requirements for the MCSE certification include three design exams. To this end, Microsoft recommends that the MCSE certified individual have one or more years of real-world, hands-on experience analyzing business and technical requirements to support planning, designing, and implementing solutions capitalizing on Microsoft products and technologies—not including only Windows 2000.

Some typical job titles of MCSEs include:

- Systems Engineer
- Network Engineer
- Systems Analyst
- Network Analyst
- Technical Consultant

The Path to MCSA and MCSE

Security is an extremely important part of administering and designing a Windows 2000 network, and thus this exam can be used as an elective exam for both the MCSE and MCSA certifications.

The MCSA Track

The MCSA track requires a total of four MCP exams or three MCP exams and a combination of two CompTIA exams, as outlined here.

One client operating system exam is required from the following choices:

- Exam *70-210* (Installing, Configuring, and Administering Microsoft Windows 2000 Professional) or Exam *70-270* (Installing, Configuring, and Administering Microsoft Windows XP Professional)

Two core networking exams are required from the following choices:

- Exam *70-215* (Installing, Configuring, and Administering Microsoft Windows 2000 Server) or Exam *70-275* (Installing, Configuring and Administering Microsoft Windows .NET Server)
- Exam *70-218* (Managing a Microsoft Windows 2000 Network Environment) or Exam *70-278* (Managing a Microsoft Windows .NET Server Network Environment)

One elective exam is required from the following choices:

- Exam *70-214* (Implementing and Administering Security in a Microsoft Windows 2000 Network)
- Exam *70-028* (Administering Microsoft SQL Server 7.0) or Exam *70-228* (Installing, Configuring, and Administering Microsoft SQL Server 2000 Enterprise Edition)

- Exam *70-086* (Implementing and Supporting Microsoft Systems Management Server 2.0)
- Exam *70-216* (Implementing and Administering a Microsoft Windows 2000 Network Infrastructure)
- Exam *70-224* (Installing, Configuring, and Administering Microsoft Exchange 2000 Server)
- Exam *70-227* (Installing, Configuring, and Administering Microsoft Internet Security and Acceleration [ISA] Server 2000, Enterprise Edition)
- Exam *70-244* (Supporting and Maintaining a Microsoft Windows NT Server 4.0 Network)

Alternatively, you can substitute one of the following combinations of CompTIA exams for the required elective exam: A+ and Network+ or A+ and Server+. For help in getting your CompTIA certifications put toward your MCSA certification, see the CompTIA Web site at www.comptia.org/certification/mcsa. You can always get the latest news on the MCSA certification track from the Microsoft MCSA Web site, located at www.microsoft.com/traincert/mcp/mcsa/default.asp.

Once you have met all the requirements to achieve MCSA certification, you will usually receive e-mail confirmation of your new MCSA status from Microsoft about 72 hours after successfully completing your last requirements. You can also expect to receive your MCSA welcome kit from Microsoft, confirming your MCSA status, in about six to eight weeks in North America, sometimes longer than that outside North America.

The MCSE Track

The MCSE certification is a premier certification and thus requires a total of seven MCP exams to achieve certification, as outlined here.

One client operating system exam is required from the following choices:

- Exam *70-210* (Installing, Configuring, and Administering Microsoft Windows 2000 Professional) or Exam *70-270* (Installing, Configuring, and Administering Microsoft Windows XP Professional)

Three system networking exams are required from the following choices:

- Exam *70-215* (Installing, Configuring, and Administering Microsoft Windows 2000 Server) or Exam *70-275* (Installing, Configuring, and Administering Microsoft .NET Server)

- Exam *70-216* (Implementing and Administering a Microsoft Windows 2000 Network Infrastructure) or Exam *70-276* (Implementing and Administering a Microsoft .NET Server Network Infrastructure)
- Exam *70-217* (Implementing and Administering a Microsoft Windows 2000 Directory Services Infrastructure) or Exam *70-277* (Implementing and Administering a Microsoft .NET Server Directory Services Infrastructure)

One design exam is required from the following choices:

- Exam *70-219* (Designing a Microsoft Windows 2000 Directory Services Infrastructure)
- Exam *70-220* (Designing Security for a Microsoft Windows 2000 Network)
- Exam *70-221* (Designing a Microsoft Windows 2000 Network Infrastructure)
- Exam *70-226* (Designing Highly Available Web Solutions with Microsoft Windows 2000 Server Technologies)

Two elective exams are required from the following choices:

- Exam *70-214* (Implementing and Administering Security in a Microsoft Windows 2000 Network)
- Exam *70-019* (Designing and Implementing Data Warehouses with Microsoft SQL Server 7.0)
- Exam *70-028* (Administering Microsoft SQL Server 7.0) or Exam *70-228* (Installing, Configuring, and Administering Microsoft SQL Server 2000 Enterprise Edition)
- Exam *70-029* (Designing and Implementing Databases with Microsoft SQL Server 7.0) or Exam *70-229* (Designing and Implementing Databases with Microsoft SQL Server 2000 Enterprise Edition)
- Exam *70-086* (Implementing and Supporting Microsoft Systems Management Server 2.0)
- Exam *70-218* (Managing a Microsoft Windows 2000 Network Environment)
- Exam *70-219* (Designing a Microsoft Windows 2000 Directory Services Infrastructure)
- Exam *70-220* (Designing Security for a Microsoft Windows 2000 Network)
- Exam *70-221* (Designing a Microsoft Windows 2000 Network Infrastructure)

- Exam *70-222* (Migrating from Microsoft Windows NT 4.0 to Microsoft Windows 2000)
- Exam *70-223* (Installing, Configuring, and Administering Microsoft Clustering Services by Using Microsoft Windows 2000 Advanced Server)
- Exam *70-224* (Installing, Configuring, and Administering Microsoft Exchange 2000 Server)
- Exam *70-225* (Designing and Deploying a Messaging Infrastructure with Microsoft Exchange 2000 Server)
- Exam *70-226* (Designing Highly Available Web Solutions with Microsoft Windows 2000 Server Technologies)
- Exam *70-227* (Installing, Configuring, and Administering Microsoft Internet Security and Acceleration [ISA] Server 2000, Enterprise Edition)
- Exam *70-230* (Designing and Implementing Solutions with Microsoft BizTalk Server 2000 Enterprise Edition)
- Exam *70-232* (Implementing and Maintaining Highly Available Web Solutions with Microsoft Windows 2000 Server Technologies and Microsoft Application Center 2000)
- Exam *70-234* (Designing and Implementing Solutions with Microsoft Commerce Server 2000)
- Exam *70-244* (Supporting and Maintaining a Microsoft Windows NT Server 4.0 Network)

You can always get the latest news on the MCSE certification track from the Microsoft MCSE Web site, located at www.microsoft.com/traincert/mcp/mcse/default.asp. Note that although many exams are listed under more than one requirement, you can use any particular exam to fulfill only one requirement. In addition, many exams are either/or, meaning that you can use *either* Exam 70-210 or Exam 70-270 (for example) to fulfill a requirement.

Once you have met all the requirements to achieve MCSE certification, you will usually receive e-mail confirmation of your new MCSE status from Microsoft about 72 hours after successfully completing your last requirements. You can also expect to receive your MCSE welcome kit from Microsoft, confirming your MCSE status, in about six to eight weeks in North America, sometimes longer than that outside North America.

Windows .NET Server 2003

In December 2002, Microsoft announced that the Windows 2000 and Windows .NET Server 2003 tracks would not completely commingle. For currently certified Windows 2000 MCSEs and MCSAs, one or two upgrade exams are required to upgrade to Windows .NET Server 2003 MCSE or MCSA status. At the time of this book's publication, the exact details and exams have not been made public. Check the Microsoft MCSE and MCSA Web sites often to determine the exact changes and new requirements as they are announced.

Registering for Your Exam

MCP exams are administered by two third-party organizations, VUE and Thompson-Prometric. You can register for your exam online or via telephone. At the time of this writing, registration for MCP exams costs $125.00 each, although the prices are periodically adjusted:

- VUE, www.vue.com, (800) 837-8734 (United States and Canada). See www.vue.com/contact/ms for worldwide MCP exam registration phone numbers.

- Thompson-Prometric, www.2test.com, (800) 755-EXAM (United States and Canada). See www.prometric.com/candidates for worldwide MCP exam registration phone numbers.

MCP Status

One last thing that must be mentioned about the certification process is that if this is your first Microsoft MCP exam, you will become a Microsoft Certified Professional (MCP) upon successful completion. You will receive an e-mail confirmation of your new MCP status from Microsoft, usually about 72 hours after successfully completing your exam. You can also expect to receive your MCP welcome kit from Microsoft, confirming your MCP status, in about six to eight weeks in North America, sometimes longer than that elsewhere.

Your Exam Day Experience

If you are unfamiliar with the examination process and format, taking your first MCP exam can be quite an experience. You should plan to arrive at your testing center at least 15 minutes before your scheduled exam start time. Ensure that you bring two forms of identification with you because testing centers are required by the vendor (Microsoft in this case) to verify your identity.

Types of Questions

You should expect to see a variety of question types on this exam because Microsoft tends to use multiple question types to further discourage cheating. Some types of questions that you could encounter are:

- **Multiple choice** This is the standard exam question followed by several answer choices. You will see questions that require only one correct answer and questions that require two or more correct answers. When multiple answers are required, you will be told this in the question, such as "Choose all correct answers" or "Choose three correct answers."

- **Select and place** This type of exam question requires you to select objects and place them into the answer area as specified in the question. You can get a good idea of how select-and-place questions work by visiting the Microsoft Testing Innovations page at www.microsoft.com/traincert/mcpexams/policies/innovations.asp and downloading the select-and-place demo.

- **Hot area** This type of exam question presents a question with an accompanying image and requires you to click the image in a specific location to correctly answer the question. CompTIA regularly uses this type of question on the A+ exams; if you've taken one of those exams, you might already be familiar with this type of question.

The Exam Experience

The exam is delivered via computer. You are allowed to use the Windows calculator at all times during the exam, but all other functions of the testing computer are locked out during the testing process. The testing center will have some means in place to monitor the testing room, either via video camera or one-way mirror glass, to discourage cheating.

Before you actually start the exam, you could be asked to complete one or more short surveys. The time spent completing these surveys is separate from the time you will be allotted to complete the exam itself. If you are not taking the exam in English, you might be entitled to extra testing time, so be sure to talk to the testing center personnel about this issue. You might also be asked to complete one or more surveys following the exam; again, any surveys you are asked to complete will not take away from your exam time.

You will know immediately after the completion of your exam whether or not you have passed and will receive an official score report from the testing center. However, it will take several business days for your online transcript to be updated on Microsoft's

Web site. You can access your online transcript at www.microsoft.com/traincert/mcp/mcpsecure.asp.

Final Thoughts

This exam is one that expects a great deal of background knowledge of Windows 2000 networks and network services. It would be wise to take this exam after completing the core exams (70-210, 70-215, 70-216, and 70-217) as an elective toward your MCSE certification. If you plan to use this exam as an elective toward your MCSA, I would recommend you take it last, only after taking the 70-210, 70-215, and 70-217 exams. Group Policy reigns supreme in Windows 2000, and as such it permeates the content of this exam—regardless of its absence from the official exam objectives page. The profile statement from Microsoft says it all: "Candidates for this exam operate in medium to very large computing environments that use Windows 2000 and Active Directory."

I wish you the best of luck in pursuing your certification goals and thank you for choosing this text to help you take the next step toward those goals. Everyone involved in this project has put their best efforts into creating and delivering a thorough and useful work that not only covers the exam objectives but also provides additional information that we believe will be useful to you to keep your networks secure.

—Will Schmied,
January, 2003

MCSE/MCSA 70-214 Part I

Implementing, Managing, and Troubleshooting Baseline Security

Chapter 1

MCSE/MCSA 70-214

Basic Windows 2000 Security: Using Security Templates

Exam Objectives in this Chapter:

- 1.1 Configure security templates.
- 1.1.1 Configure registry and file system permissions.
- 1.1.2 Configure account policies.
- 1.1.3 Configure audit policies.
- 1.1.4 Configure user rights assignment.
- 1.1.5 Configure security options.
- 1.1.6 Configure system services.
- 1.1.7 Configure restricted groups.
- 1.1.8 Configure event logs.
- 1.2 Deploy security templates. Deployment methods include using Group Policy and scripting.

☑ Summary of Exam Objectives
☑ Exam Objectives Fast Track
☑ Exam Objectives Frequently Asked Questions
☑ Self Test
☑ Self Test Quick Answer Key

Introduction

Security in Windows 2000 is no simple thing; however, it is manageable if taken one step at a time, starting from the bottom up. To that end, in this chapter we look at the first line of defense in making your Windows 2000 network more secure: security templates and Group Policy. This chapter covers a lot of ground, so fasten your seat belts and get ready for the ride! Let's take a look at the topics covered in this chapter:

- A review of the Windows 2000 Active Directory provides the starting point for this chapter and this book. Although this is a security book, not an Active Directory one, a solid Active Directory foundation is required to efficiently administer a Windows 2000 network. Simply put, Active Directory makes Windows 2000 tick, and Windows 2000 relies on Active Directory for all types of things.

- We next examine the basic security tools at your disposal—those that ship with Windows 2000, those that can be found in the Windows 2000 Server Resource Kit, and those that you can get elsewhere.

- Next, we examine how security is configured via templates and Group Policy by taking an item-by-item approach. Each configurable item is presented along with its default setting and usage.

- Once you've gotten your security configured, you will of course want to deploy it, so we walk through the various methods of deploying your security templates and security configurations.

- Lastly, we analyze your security settings using several tools available to you.

Windows 2000 Active Directory Review

In November 1996, Microsoft delivered the first preview of Active Directory for developers at the Professional Developers Conference held in Long Beach, California. At the time, it was merely the directory service that was shipped with Windows NT 5.0, and the preview included many other Windows NT 5.0 features. Many changes have taken place since then. For one, Windows NT 5.0 was renamed Windows 2000, and then it was officially released to the public in February 2000, over three years after its original preview to developers. The change of the name from Windows NT 5.0 to Windows 2000 was a surface change only. Windows 2000 inherits the NT technology legacy from previous versions.

Test Day Tip

Although we spend several pages here presenting (and reviewing) Active Directory, don't get "wrapped around the axle" about the nitty-gritty of Active Directory. This exam is focused on working with security in Windows 2000, and for that you must know Active Directory. Don't worry about being asked very specific questions dealing with the ins and outs of Active Directory; that is the realm of the 70-217 exam.

Introduction to Directory Services

It would be tough to claim that Active Directory is the first directory service ever created. In fact, directory services have been available in a variety of network operating systems (NOSs). Novell's NetWare has used the Novell Directory Service (NDS) for quite some time now. Directory services are used primarily for organizing, locating, and managing network information.

People use directory services without even knowing they are doing so. Because it is used to translate server names to Internet Protocol (IP) addresses, the Domain Name System (DNS) is the most widely used directory service in the world. DNS is rather "usage specific," meaning that it organizes only a limited amount of information about network hosts. DNS stores data about servers, their IP addresses, and services that they offer to the network. Although this is pretty much the extent of DNS, other directory services do not have the same limitations. A directory service can organize all sorts of information about a network. Usually, this information falls into the following categories:

- **Network resources** Servers, printers, and other devices on a network.
- **Network services** Capabilities on the network such as file storage, printing, and e-mail.
- **Network users and groups** Identifiers for users on a network and for groups of users.

As you can see, a directory service organizes the pieces of a network, enabling a way to create relationships between the pieces. The relationships between these pieces are what make the directory service so powerful. For example, in DNS, a DNS client computer can query a DNS server to find out the IP address of a server that it wants to contact. The DNS server receives a hostname query and returns the IP address in short order. More complex relationships can be created in more complex directory services, such as providing access to network resources and services for users who log on as well as providing a controlled security framework for the entire network.

History of the Windows Directory Service

In the not-too-distant past, networks were server centric. Each server had its own security system, which consisted of user accounts, group accounts, and network resources. The server would associate those user accounts to the files, directories, printers, and other services or resources that it had to offer. These associations had a value such that one person could have more access to one network resource than another person, simply due to the rights assigned to user and group accounts. In a way, this server-centric system was one of the first directory services, but one for which the scope existed only on a single server.

Networks first popped up in the military as a method to share data quickly across great distances. They offered a major advantage in times of war. Money was one of the main reasons that networking became prevalent in businesses. Hard drives were extremely expensive, as were printers. Many of the first corporate networks sprang up out of a need to share printers and precious hard-drive space among multiple computers. Soon, these servers' hard drives filled up. They ran out of printer ports. At some point, another server would be added to the network to allow further storage of shared files or to add new printers.

Once an administrator established a server to share files and printers, the administrator was faced with an issue—how to protect sensitive files and printers from unauthorized users while allowing use of the remaining files and printers. In some cases, the administrator wanted to allow some users limited access to a file or a printer. Access rights were added to the system, and users were given specific logon IDs. The server could then easily share files and printers with the correct users, depending on the administrator's configuration.

When a network contained more than one server, administration became difficult. If a user needed to access files or printers residing on two or more servers, that user needed to know how to access each specific server. In addition, the user needed a separate logon ID and password for each server. Some administrators used naming conventions to ensure that a user did not need to have more than one unique logon ID.

Sometimes a network had multiple administrators with different naming conventions, providing users with two or more unique logon IDs. For administrators, it was difficult to keep passwords synchronized, since each server might have a different timing mechanism to enforce password changes. For users, the end result in a multiserver environment was a convoluted and difficult process of remembering the location of resources, remembering the correct logon ID, and remembering the correct current password—all merely to be able to access resources on the network.

Network operating systems soon developed a variety of ways to use a single logon ID and password to access multiple servers. For example, Microsoft Windows NT used a domain architecture. An *NT domain* is a group of Windows NT servers that participate in a single security system listing users, groups, and network resources. It consists of a primary domain controller (PDC), any number of backup domain controllers (BDCs), and any number of member servers and client computers.

The PDC is the security manager of the domain. BDCs maintain a read-only copy of the security database, and the PDC remains the single point of change control. Member servers and client computers contact the domain controller (DC) to access network resources. Because of their membership, a PDC or a BDC in the domain can use the security database to authenticate users to access resources. A member server can use the security database by querying a PDC or BDC. The basic Windows NT domain model is shown in Figure 1.1.

Figure 1.1 A Basic Windows NT Domain

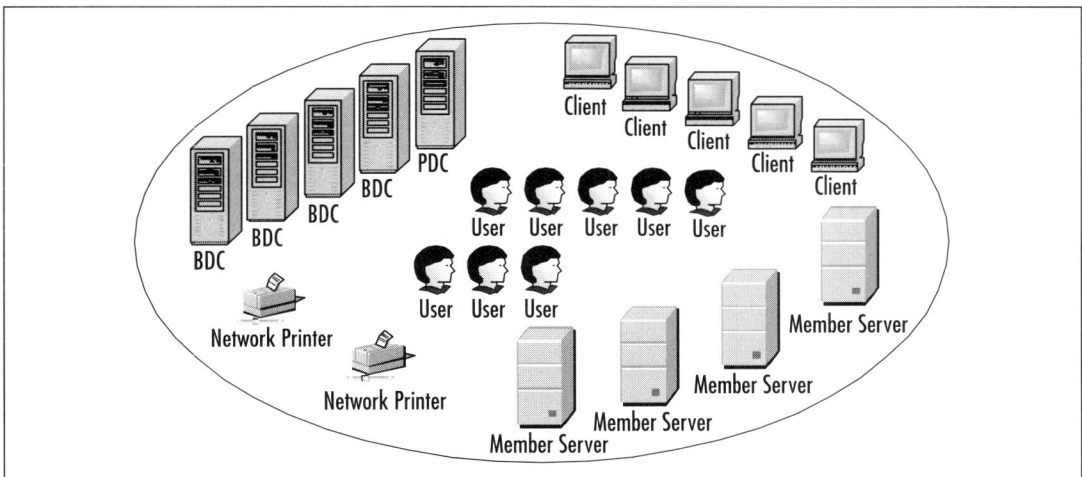

The Windows NT domain was a security boundary, which means that if you needed to separate one security set from another, you needed to have more than one domain. Using trust relationships, you could have multiple domains. A trust relationship is established between two domains. In order to enable users of domain A to access the resources such as the files and printers of domain B, domain B must trust domain A. Drawn in a diagram, this trust relationship is shown as an arrow pointing from the trusting domain to the trusted domain. Microsoft defined various models for a multiple domain structure using Windows NT:

- **Master Domain model** All resource domains trust a single Master Domain that contains all user accounts. This scenario is depicted in Figure 1.2.

Figure 1.2 A Multimaster Windows NT Domain

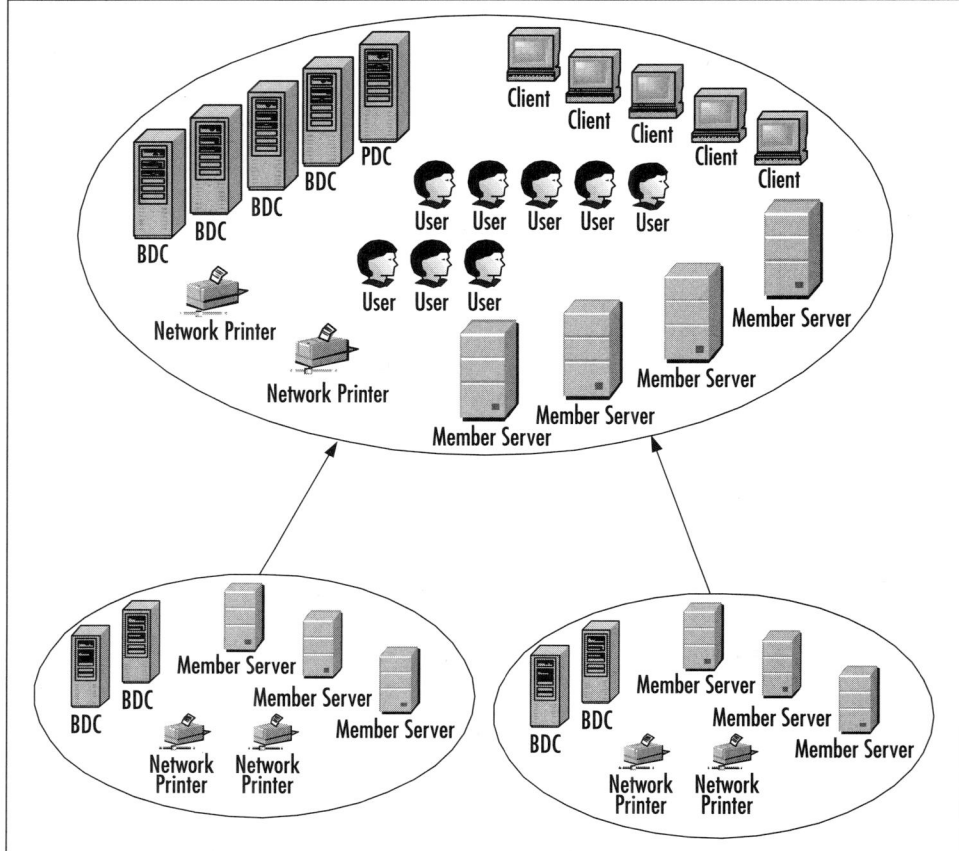

- **Multiple Master Domain model** All resource domains trust all Master Domains. Master Domains contain user accounts. Each Master Domain trusts all other Master Domains.
- **Single Domain model** There is only a single domain that contains all users and resources. There is no trust relationship with other domains.
- **Complete Trust model** All domains trust each other, regardless of whether they contain users, resources, or both.

Windows NT domains contain the rudimentary elements of a directory service. They enable multiple servers to look up information and use it for authenticating users and granting those users access to network resources. Although a domain is effective as a security model for a small or medium-sized organization, it does not have some of the features that a directory service can offer.

An NT domain structure is flat rather than hierarchical like most directory services, which means security cannot be applied at different levels. Since each domain is its own administrative area, the only way to implement distributed administration is to have multiple domains. Legacy NT domains require a significant amount of traffic between clients and the PDC or a BDC. These domains also require the security database to be copied from a PDC to the BDCs on a periodic basis.

This traffic overhead is undesirable over wide area network (WAN) links that might have a limited amount of bandwidth available or that are costly to transmit traffic across. To reduce this overhead, multiple domains can be created such that no domain spans a WAN link. Trust relationships between multiple domains become cumbersome as more domains are added. As a result, trade-offs can be made between WAN performance or administrative needs and domain structures.

The directory services architecture of Windows 2000 was redesigned from the ground up to eliminate the limitations and difficulties found in the Windows NT directory services implementation. Use of the X.500 standard as the basis of Active Directory and implementation of the Lightweight Directory Access Protocol (LDAP) not only ensures that Windows 2000 Active Directory is more robust and user friendly but that it also uses existing and well-known standards that allow it to interact with other directory services and a variety of applications.

Comparing Active Directory to the Windows NT implementation of directory services, it is easy to see that Active Directory offers fully distributed administration via an efficient database that is distributed throughout the network to prevent WAN overhead issues. Let's examine Active Directory in more detail now so we can get a better idea of how it works to not only make using Windows 2000 easier but also to make Windows more secure.

Active Directory Architecture

Active Directory is not automatically part of the Windows 2000 Server installation process, although the capability is available should you need it. When a Windows 2000 Server (any version) is installed as a new install, by default it becomes a member server of a workgroup or domain. (Upgrades are handled differently if a Windows NT PDC or BDC is being upgraded to Windows 2000. In the case of upgrades of an NT PDC or BDC, the installer is prompted to upgrade the domain to Active Directory. If that did not occur, all information from the former domain would be lost.)

Member servers use a security architecture identical to that of the Windows 2000 Professional client workstations, in which they have a flat file local database with a set of local users and groups. This does not allow other servers or workstations to share in that security database. In fact, it hearkens back to the days of a server-centric network. The flat file database allows local users and groups, as well as shared local files and printers, in a server-centric model. Only when a member server or client workstation joins an Active Directory domain can it participate in Active Directory. When a client workstation or member server joins a domain, that server-centric local database remains. However, if a member server is upgraded to a DC, the local database is removed.

When a Windows 2000 server joins an Active Directory domain as a member server, it can communicate with any DC for Active Directory security information. Domains are configured as top-level containers in a tree structure that is created through trust relationships and that uses DNS naming.

Domains sharing a contiguous DNS namespace are organized into domain trees. In a *contiguous namespace*, the domains are linked via the DNS names. For example, a domain named open.com and its subdomain named way.open.com are part of the same contiguous namespace. However, a domain named closed.com is not part of that contiguous namespace and, in fact, forms the basis for another domain tree. There can be multiple domains in Active Directory, either with or without contiguous namespaces. Multiple domains with different namespaces that participate in a single Active Directory commonly are considered a forest of multiple domain trees, as depicted in Figure 1.3. However, it is important to note that a domain on its own can be its own forest.

Figure 1.3 The Windows 2000 Active Directory Domain Model with Forests, Trees, and Organizational Units

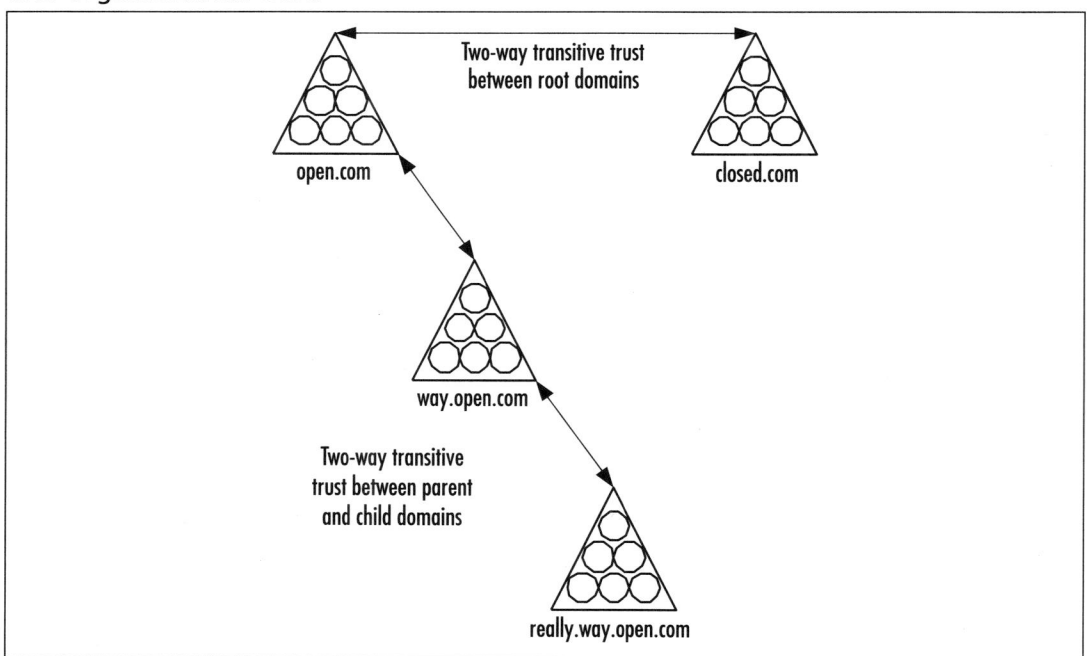

Exam Warning

Bear in mind that although Windows 2000 Active Directory uses the standard DNS namespace, the top-level domain is ignored. In the case of our example domain open.com and its child domain way.open.com, both part of one contiguous namespace. The top-level domain, .com in this case, is ignored by Active Directory due to the way that Microsoft has implemented DNS in Active Directory. The top level of the domain (and the domain name) in this case would be open.

Internal to each domain, Active Directory provides Organizational Units (OUs) to create a tree structure. The OU tree is unique to each domain and completely configurable by an administrator. Within the OU containers, Active Directory enables the administrator to create objects that represent user accounts, network services, and resources such as users, groups, workstations, and printers. The result is a logical structure that can be scaled to any enterprise of any size and organizational formation.

Security is of great concern to companies that connect their private networks to the Internet or to external partners using an extranet solution. The hierarchical structure in Active Directory is a perfect basis for a flexible security service. Active Directory can secure objects using services such as Public Key Infrastructure (PKI) and can even extend to smartcard technologies. The security protocol named after the dog that guards the gates to Hades in Greek mythology, Kerberos, is used for trust relationships and is the default authentication protocol in Active Directory. LDAP can be used over Secure Sockets Layer (SSL), which extends Active Directory security into the Internet.

Some of these types of services integrate as objects, such as PKI certificates, in the authentication process using smartcard technologies and in extended properties of account objects so that they can support extra security requirements. In addition, you can find extensive security administration capabilities in Group Policies implemented within Active Directory.

The Active Directory architecture enables it to become the central authority for authentication and access control to the entire network and even the Internet. Before we move into the topic of using Active Directory to control security in our network, we first need to delve a little deeper into the basics of Active Directory, examining the logical and physical structures of Active Directory as well as the basic Active Directory objects.

The X.500 Directory Standard

Many directory services state that they are X.500 compliant. X.500 is a directory service standard ratified by the International Telecommunications Union (ITU-T) in 1988 and modified in 1993 and 1997. It was intended to provide a means to develop an easy-to-use electronic directory of people that would be available to all Internet users.

The X.500 directory standard specifies a common root of a hierarchical tree. Contrary to its name, the *root* of the tree is depicted at the top level, and all other containers (which are used to create "branches") are below it. There are several types of containers with a specific naming convention. In this naming convention, each portion of a name is specified by the abbreviation of the object type or container it represents. A user has a CN= before the username to represent its "Common Name," a C= precedes a country, and an organization is heralded by an O=. Compared to DNS domain names—for example, host.subdomain.domain—the X.500 version of CN=host/C=US /O=Org appears excessively complicated.

Each X.500 local directory is considered a Directory System Agent (DSA). The DSA can represent either single or multiple organizations. Each DSA connects to the others through a Directory Information Tree (DIT), which is a hierarchical naming scheme that provides the naming context for objects within the directory.

Although Active Directory is derived from the X.500 model, Active Directory does not implement all the X.500 protocols because of the excess overhead involved or the lack of their general usage. Some of the protocols that are not included are:

- Directory Access Protocol (DAP)
- Directory Information Shadowing Protocol (DISP)
- Directory Operational Binding Management Protocol (DOP)
- Directory System Protocol (DSP)

Active Directory does implement LDAP, which affords an effective combination of DAP and DSP features without involving any excess overhead.

The Logical Structure of Active Directory

As we've already briefly outlined, you know that the logical structure of Active Directory works similarly to that of the DNS model. A *forest* is established that forms the organizational boundary. Within that forest, you can then create and populate trees with *domains* and *subdomains*. These domains and subdomains then can be populated with OUs and objects. Additionally, Active Directory's content is controlled by the *schema* and advertised by the *Global Catalog*. Let's take a few minutes to examine each of these logical components in more detail.

Forests

A *forest* is a set of domain trees that share a common schema, configuration, and Global Catalog. The forest usually is referred to by the name of its root domain. It exists as a set of domain trees that trust each other via transitive and hierarchical trust relationships using the default Kerberos security trust model automatically implemented by Active Directory. Figure 1.3 depicts a forest consisting of the open.com and closed.com domain trees. The forest root is the name of the first domain created in it. So if in the example of Figure 1.3 the open.com domain was created first, it would lend its name to the forest as well.

Trees

A *tree* is a hierarchical organization of containers and objects. The tree is similar to the entire file system on a computer's hard drive. The tree has multiple branches created with nested containers. Nested containers are similar to folders in the file system. The ends of each branch are objects that represent users, services, and resources. These objects are analogous to the files inside containers. The *domain tree* is a group of contiguous domains that share a common schema and configuration and are united by trust relationships to create a single namespace. Active Directory can contain one or more trees, which can be depicted via their trust relationships or via their namespace. The open.com tree shown in Figure 1.3 consists of three domains, all of which share the common namespace open.com.

Domains

A *domain* is a group of Windows 2000 computers that participate in the same security subtree. Active Directory consists of one or more domains. Each domain can span both local area network (LAN) and WAN links, depending on the network design and subsequent domain implementation. Multiple domains can exist on the same LAN. When there are multiple domains using different namespaces in Active Directory, it is considered to be a forest of domain trees. This forest must enclose domains that share a common schema and configuration. They produce a GC of users, services, and resources.

Schema

The *schema* defines the types of objects that can be stored in a specific Active Directory. For example, an extremely simple schema might define three object classes as a server, an OU, and a user. Each of these object classes would have attributes such as the server IP address, the OU name, and the user e-mail address. When an actual server, OU, and user object are created, those attributes are given *values*. The value for the server IP address attribute might be 10.10.10.5, the value for the OU name attribute might be HQ, and the value for the user e-mail address attribute might be user@mail.open.com. This concept is summarized in Table 1.1.

Table 1.1 Schema Objects, Attributes, and Values

Object Class	Object	Attribute	Value
Server	Server.open.com	IP address	10.10.10.5
Organizational Unit	CN=HQ	Name	HQ
User	USER	E-mail address	user@mail.open.com

The Active Directory schema can be extended to include additional objects. For example, a backup program that is written to take advantage of Active Directory could add an object class for the backup service and add an attribute to the server object class to enable it as a backup service provider or a backup service requester. The schema must be updated across all the DCs that contain a replica of Active Directory in order for those objects and properties to be recognized and administered from any point in the network.

The Active Directory schema is stored within the directory itself. This reduces the overhead involved with users or applications that run queries on the Active Directory. It also allows the schema to extend dynamically, with immediate access to the new object classes and attributes. The ability to perform schema extensions is protected by access control lists (ACLs) so that only authorized users can extend the schema.

Global Catalog

The Global Catalog (GC) is a listing, or index, of the objects within Active Directory. As an index, the Global Catalog does not contain every value for every property of an object. It contains only enough information to find the object and perhaps a few oft-queried property values.

For example, if all the users in a network query the Active Directory to find their colleagues' telephone extensions, the value of the phone extension property can be placed in the GC to enable quick access to that information. When a property value is not in the GC, there is enough information about the object to locate a replica of the Active Directory partition, which contains the object, without the querying user or application needing to know the location of that object within the Active Directory hierarchy. Of course, the user or application needs to know one or more attributes of the desired object to perform the query.

Organizational Units

OUs are used to organize objects, such as users or computers, into a location for the easier assignment of permissions and privileges. In the Windows NT domain model, this was typically domain with resource domains, which meant the complex establishment of trusts and security between domains. Using OUs does away with all the complex management issues found when using resource domains. Simply place all objects that need the same permission set into an OU and then apply the permissions directly to the OU itself.

OUs make it easy to apply hierarchical security as well, because configurations are inherited by child objects from their parent object. An important fact to consider is that OUs are the smallest items that can receive Group Policy configuration settings. You can further divide objects using groups, but you cannot apply Group Policy to groups, hence you cannot apply enterprise security settings to groups. Figure 1.4 shows how you could divide the closed.com domain into OUs, each for a specific group of objects.

Figure 1.4 Using Organizational Units to Simplify Management

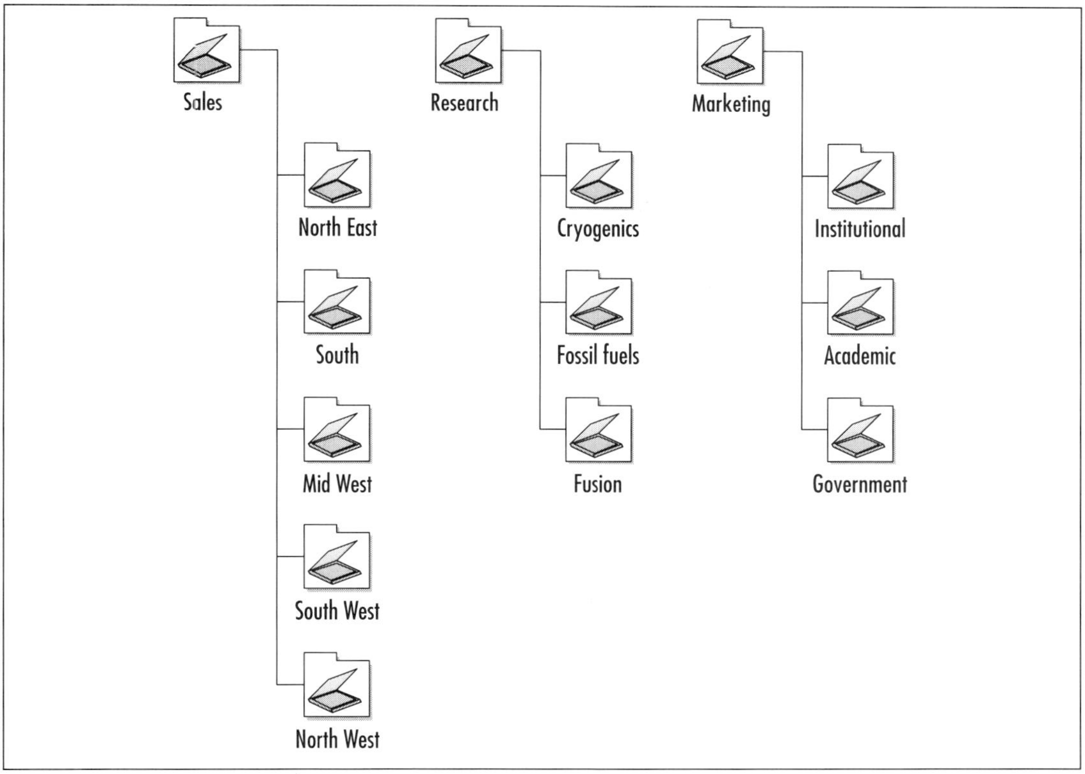

Groups

Groups exist by default on all Windows 2000 installations and are the smallest objects that you can use to apply permission settings to more than one object at a time. You can place user objects, computer objects, and even other group objects inside a group and apply permissions to that group. Groups are typically placed inside OUs so that they can inherit the Group Policy settings.

Figure 1.5 shows the use of groups in one of the OUs in the closed.com domain. Each group contains specific objects that require different security permissions from the other groups.

Figure 1.5 Using Groups to Assign Specific Permissions

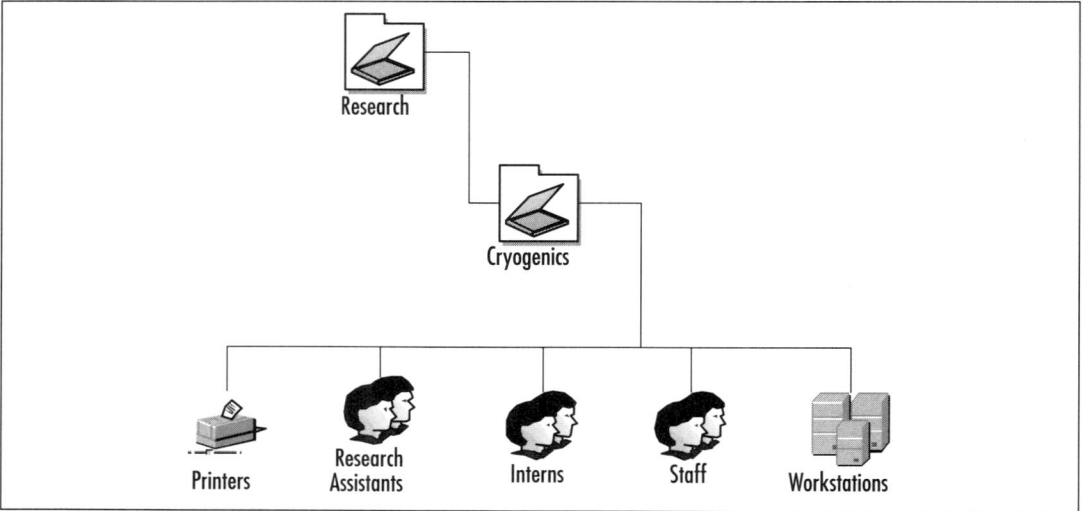

Head of the Class…

Active Directory: It's Just a Big Database

So far in your reading of this chapter, the concept of Active Directory and how it works to keep all parts of a Windows 2000 domain running smoothly might seem a bit overwhelming. Despite all its power, Active Directory is still just a database, much like any other database that you have used in the past.

The differences between the Active Directory database and that database you have at home for your disco record collection is that the Active Directory database is very scalable, is easily configurable via a graphical user interface (GUI) front end, and supports simultaneous access and updating over multiple logical and physical locations. Can your disco record database do all that?

One of the other very important differences between Active Directory and a typical database is that different levels of control can be assigned to various users, such as allowing the help desk the ability to reset user passwords. This feature is called *delegation*, and Active Directory makes it easy for you to delegate almost any common administrative function to a nonadministrative user. For an example of how this works, check out the article *Create a Password Administrator with the Delegation of Control Wizard* at https://www.techrepublic.com/article.jhtml?id= t01320020319WCS01.htm.

The Physical Structure of Active Directory

Armed with your knowledge of the logical structure of Active Directory, you can now start to put some of this information to work looking at Active Directory's physical structure. Things such as sites, DCs, servers, and workstations come into play here; they define the part of Active Directory (and Windows 2000) that you can easily observe without any trouble.

Sites

Think of a *site* as a geographically based location for servers. The official definition of a site is one or more IP subnets that share a fast and reliable connection. It is recommended that a site consist of links with greater than 512 Kbps of available bandwidth. *Available bandwidth* is the amount of bandwidth that is not being used by other network traffic. If a link exists for a T-1 line of 1.54 Mbps, it would appear that it has more than enough bandwidth to meet this recommendation. However, if that T-1 line is saturated with network traffic, it will not be sufficient.

You can configure sites any way you want. If you add IP subnets to one site, you can still move them to their own site later. The nice thing about sites is that they grow and change to match your physical network. Site definition is vague enough to allow a site to encompass WAN links; however, a site is best configured as one that contains only LAN connections that are less likely to become saturated with network traffic. The servers that are placed in a single site are configured automatically for replication to each other. If those servers are connected only with high-speed reliable links, the replication traffic can take advantage of the physical network.

Authentication traffic also takes advantage of site configuration. When a user logs on to Active Directory, the workstation tries to locate servers in the same site as the user first, then tries other servers in other sites. The local site is determined by the IP subnet in which the workstation exists. It looks up a server that is in a site that contains that IP subnet in order to log on. Taking advantage of a physically close server and a fast connection makes the user perceive higher performance from the network.

Domain Controllers

A *domain controller* is the computer (or computers) in a Windows 2000 Active Directory network responsible for managing user access to that network, including logging on, authenticating, and controlling access to network resources. The domain model in Windows NT had one PDC and one or more BDCs, where the PDC was the only DC with a writable copy of the domain database. In Windows 2000 this model is broken because all DCs have a writable copy of the database, and thus all DCs can make changes to this database. In this way, it would seem that all Windows 2000 DCs are created equal, but this is not entirely the case.

The first DC in an organization is automatically assigned the role of the Global Catalog server and the following five other Operations Master roles:

- PDC emulator
- Schema master
- Domain-naming master
- Relative identifier (RID) master
- Infrastructure master

These five roles can be reassigned later as more DCs are added, creating a powerful and robust DC arrangement.

Servers and Workstations

Computer objects are perhaps the most physical items in the entire domain. Users interact with servers and workstations all day, every day. Servers and workstations form the end point in your domain structure.

Objects: The Heart of It All

An *object* is a representation of a user, resource, or service within the Active Directory database. Each object is described by a set of properties, or *attributes*. Each property has a corresponding value. An object typically appears as an icon in a management console, and when you right-click it, you can look at the values of its properties. Some objects do not appear in the various management consoles, because they are not intended to be managed. The basic objects consist of the following:

- Computers
- Users
- Groups
- Shares
- Printers

Of these objects, we have already examined computers and groups; they rightfully appear in more than one part of the Active Directory implementation. Computers are objects in Active Directory and are part of the physical organization of Active Directory. Groups, on the other hand, while objects, are part of the logical organization of Active Directory—the "how it gets organized and implemented" end of business. Users, shares, and printers, on the other hand, are strictly objects and do not really fall into either of the two previously mentioned categories.

Users are the crux of the network. The network exists to serve users' needs, and this service is achieved in a variety of ways, depending on exactly what is needed by whom and where it is needed. Shares and printers, as well as computers, are objects provided to users to enable them to produce a valuable output. Each of these objects can have permissions applied to it, specifying who has what rights to that object. This is a basic part of the Windows 2000 security model.

Containers: Odd Men Out

A *container* is an object in the directory that simply contains other objects. Containers are similar to folders in a file system. Container objects can contain other containers in the same way that a file system folder can contain other folders. A container does not represent any user, service, or resource, but it does have its own attributes and values. Instead, a container is what shapes Active Directory into a tree structure. Both domains and OUs are examples of containers.

Note

For more information Active Directory, consider the following resources:
- *Managing Active Directory for Windows 2000 Server*, Syngress Publishing (ISBN: 1-928994-07-5)
- Active Directory Overview, www.microsoft.com/windows2000/server/evaluation/features/dirlist.asp
- Active Directory Service Overview, www.microsoft.com/windows2000/server/evaluation/business/addatasheet.asp
- Active Directory Design, www.microsoft.com/TechNet/prodtechnol/windows2000serv/training/w2khost/w2ktad.asp

In Active Directory, containers are not security principals. You cannot apply rights to the containers and have those rights flow through to the objects contained within them. Users of Novell Directory Services consider this a limitation to Active Directory, since Novell Directory Services can be configured this way. If you want to have the same functionality with Active Directory, you can mirror the OUs with groups, placing all OU objects within those groups and nesting the groups. It takes some considered planning, especially to ensure that your rights inheritance mirrors your OUs, but the same result can be obtained.

Exam Warning

This exam expects you to have a very solid understanding of Active Directory and Group Policy. This might come as a surprise to many readers, since this understanding is not listed in the exam objectives, but in reality, it is perquisite knowledge for the topics that are covered on this exam. Just the same way IP subnetting never shows up on a Microsoft exam outline but always manages to show up on a test, Active Directory and Group Policy are pivotal to your success on this exam.

The Basic Windows 2000 Security Tools

This section introduces the functions and uses of the Windows 2000 Security Configuration Tool Set. The Tool Set is a response to systems administrators' need for a central, easy-to-use program that easily allows the configuration of domain, OU, and local security within any size Windows 2000 organization. In Windows NT 4.0, configuration of various security parameters required using multiple tools, such as User Manager, User Manager for Domains, Transmission Control Protocol/Internet Protocol (TCP/IP) properties, direct Registry edits, the RAS administrator, and more. The Tool Set makes it possible to configure and manage these security services from a single, centralized interface.

In addition to conveniently bringing together formerly widely disparate programs into a single interface, the Security Configuration and Analysis snap-in allows the administrator to analyze a local machine's current configuration. This analysis can be performed against security templates so that the network manager can compare the present configuration to a proposed ideal configuration, which can then be applied with a couple of simple clicks of the mouse.

The Security Configuration Tool Set comes at an opportune time. Never before has a Microsoft operating system offered the degree of airtight security that Windows 2000 offers. Neither has security been so configurable at such a granular level. The Tool Set allows the administrator to get a handle on configuring and managing the Windows 2000 security scheme.

Security Configuration Tool Set

The Security Configuration Tool Set is a collection of security configuration and management programs included in Windows 2000. The primary goal of each of these components is to make it easier to manage enterprisewide security parameters. The administrator can group the Tool Set components together into a single Microsoft Management Console (MMC) and manage security for the entire enterprise from a central location.

Each component of the Security Configuration Tool Set is integrated into the Windows 2000 security infrastructure. The new Distributed Security Services model, as defined in Windows 2000, requires a central interface to manage an enterprise's complex security requirements. The Tool Set components interact with Active Directory, Kerberos Authentication mechanisms, and Windows 2000 PKI.

The four main components of the Security Configuration Tool Set are:

- Security templates
- Group Policy security configuration objects
- Security Configuration and Analysis snap-in
- Command-line tools

Security Templates

Microsoft provides a full set of templates that conform to a number of common security scenarios. These security templates can be broken into two general categories: default and incremental. The default, or basic, templates are applied by the operating system when a clean install is performed. They are not applied if an upgrade installation is done.

The incremental templates should be applied after the basic security templates have been applied. The incremental template types are compatible (for workstations or servers), secure (workstations, servers, domain controllers), highly secure (workstations, servers, domain controllers), optional components (workstations, servers), and no terminal SID.

If a template name ends in *SV*, it is for a standalone computer or member server (not a domain controller). If a template name ends in *DC*, it is for a domain controller. Template names ending in *WK* are for client computers (workstations). For example, the template basicsv.inf is used to restore a standalone server to the default state of a fresh install; basicwk.inf is used to accomplish the same thing for workstations. Table 1.2 describes the function of these provided templates.

The administrator can save time and effort during an initial rollout by applying these templates to workstations, DCs, and member and standalone servers. Then, as time allows, the administrator can customize and fine-tune security settings for local computers, OUs, or an entire domain. In this chapter, we examine both the application of the initial template and the subsequent fine-tuning configuration of the applied template.

Table 1.2 Windows 2000 Security Templates

Security Level	Template Name	Template Description
Basic	basicwk.inf basicsv.inf basicdc.inf	The basic templates are used to set the initial security configuration of a particular computer. The basic templates can also be used to correct the current configuration on a computer. When a basic template is applied to a computer, the security settings will be rolled back to the installation defaults.

Continued

Table 1.2 Windows 2000 Security Templates

Security Level	Template Name	Template Description
Compatible	compatws.inf	If you do not want your users to have Power User rights but still need them to be able to install and run most legacy applications, the compatible configuration alters the default permissions for the Users group so that legacy applications can run properly. This is not a secure environment; the template creates compatibility by reducing the default security levels on the folders, files, and Registry keys that applications typically access.
Secure	securews.inf securedc.inf	The secure templates increase the level of security for account policy, certain Registry keys, and auditing. Permissions for file system objects are not affected by this configuration. Two secure templates are provided: securedc.inf for DCs and securews.inf for workstations and member servers. The secure templates provide a medium level of security, stricter than the basic templates but not as secure as the highly secure templates.
Highly secure	hisecws.inf hisecdc.inf	Highly secure configurations add security to network communications. IPSec is configured for these machines and is required for communications. Two highly secure templates are provided: hisecdc.inf for domain controllers and hisecws.inf for workstations and member servers. The highly secure templates provide the highest level of preconfigured security available but cause communications problems with legacy clients due the requirement of IPSec for network communications.
Out of box	DC security.inf	The DC security.inf template contains the file and Controller Registry settings initially applied to Windows 2000 Configuration DC during promotion.
	setup security.inf	The setup security.inf template contains the security workstation settings applied to Windows 2000 servers and workstations at the time of installation. For clean installations, these are the same settings as basicsv.inf and basicwk.inf. Unlike basicsv.inf and basicwk.inf, setup security.inf shows the actual values added instead of using variables.

Continued

Table 1.2 Windows 2000 Security Templates

Security Level	Template Name	Template Description
Optional components	ocfiless.inf ocfilesw.inf	These templates improve the local security for optional components such as terminal services and certificate services that are not automatically added to Windows 2000 systems when they are installed.
No terminal server SID	notssid.inf	This template removes the terminal server SID from all Registry and file system objects.

In addition to the templates that ship with Windows 2000, a number of other templates are available from Microsoft as part of the *Security Operations Guide for Windows 2000 Server*, located at www.microsoft.com/technet/security/prodtech/windows/windows2000/staysecure/default.asp. We explore some of these role-specific templates later in Chapter 2.

Exam Warning

You absolutely must have a solid grasp on the purpose and role of each security template that ships with Windows 2000. Key points to keep in mind when working with security templates are which ones are standalone, which ones are incremental, and the basic purpose of each, including the type of computer on which the template is to deployed. *Know those security templates!*

Group Policy Security Settings

Security in Windows 2000 is applied using primarily Group Policies. Group Policy can be applied in an organization at four distinctly different levels, each inheriting the settings from the level above it. Group Policy is applied at the following levels (and in this order):

- **Local** This is Group Policy applied directly to the local computer itself.
- **Site** Site-level Group Policy objects are applied to all objects within that site. Site Group Policy objects (GPOs) overwrite the local GPO. If more than one site-level GPO exists, the administrator can specify the order in which they are applied, thus determining the GPOs that will be overwritten should a conflict occur.
- **Domain** Domain-level GPOs are applied to all objects within the domain and overwrite site-level GPOs. As with site GPOs, the administrator can

specify the order in which domain-level GPOs are applied, should more than one exist.

- **Organizational Unit** OU GPOs are processed last, with the GPO linked to the highest OU processed first, followed by the GPOs linked to each successive child OU. OU GPOs overwrite all GPOs that have come before them and therefore provide the most granular level of security configuration available of all the levels of Group Policy. Again, should more than one OU level GPO exist, the GPOs are processed in the order the administrator specifies.

TEST DAY TIP

You should ensure that you have a complete and total understanding of the four levels at which Group Policy is applied. This understanding should include the order in which the levels are applied. This information will prove valuable for not only this exam, but for just about any Windows 2000 exam you take—not to mention the practical benefit to you in working within your own organization.

You apply security through Group Policy using different tools for each level, as you might expect. At the local level, using the Local Security Settings console (see Figure 1.6) allows you to configure and implement the local GPO. Any changes you make here will be implemented in the local GPO. Note that you could also make these same changes using a local GPO console if you desired from the **Computer Configuration | Windows Settings | Security Settings** node.

Figure 1.6 Using the Local Security Settings Console

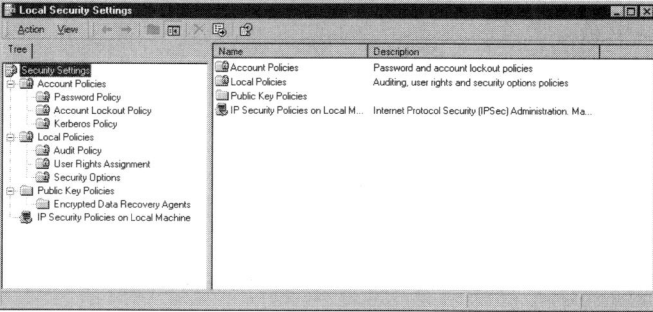

Applying security configurations to the site-level GPO is done using the Active Directory Sites and Services console (see Figure 1.7). Right-click the site name, select **Properties**, change to the **Group Policy** tab of the **Properties** page, and from there you can create or edit Group Policy to apply at the site level. Security settings are not typically applied at the site level, however, which could explain the lack of a tool specifically for this purpose.

Figure 1.7 Accessing Security Configuration Settings at the Site Level

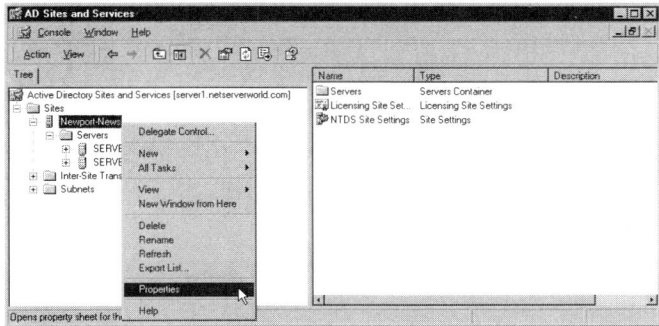

The process of applying security settings at the domain level has been simplified, thanks in part to the existence of the Domain Security Policy console (see Figure 1.8). This console allows you to configure security settings for all objects in the domain, including child domains within that domain. Applying security at the domain is the most common method of Group Policy security application and is discussed further later in this chapter, in the "Configuring Basic Windows 2000 Security with Templates" section.

Figure 1.8 Configuring the Domain-Level Security Policy

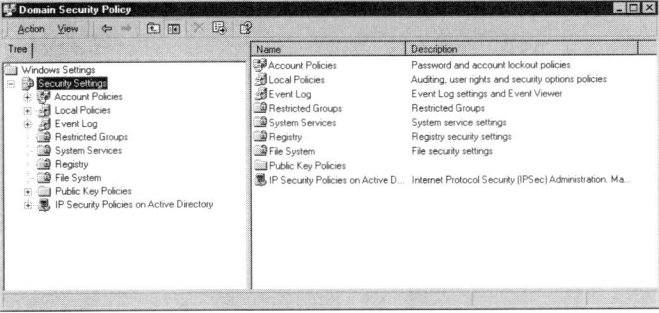

It is of interest that certain security configurations can *only* be made at the domain level, such as those dealing with Account Policies and Registry security. This limitation is due to the fact that Active Directory only allows one domain account policy per domain. For more information this topic (and an exception to the rule), see the Knowledge Base article located at http://support.microsoft.com/default.aspx?scid=KB;en-us;255550.

Alternatively, you can work with domain-level Group Policy from the Active Directory Users and Computers console by right-clicking the domain, selecting **Properties**, and then switching to the Group Policy tab.

Configuring OU Group Policy and security settings requires you to use the Active Directory Users and Computers console, shown in Figure 1.9. To configure settings for a specific OU, right-click it, select **Properties**, change to the **Group Policy** tab, and have at it. As mentioned previously, you can work with domain-level Group Policy security settings by right-clicking the domain and selecting **Properties** (see Figure 1.10).

Figure 1.9 Using the Active Directory Users and Computers Console to Configure Security Settings

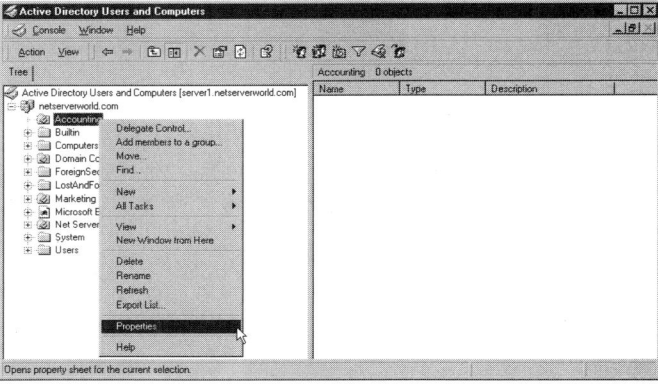

Figure 1.10 Managing Domain Security from Active Directory Users and Computers

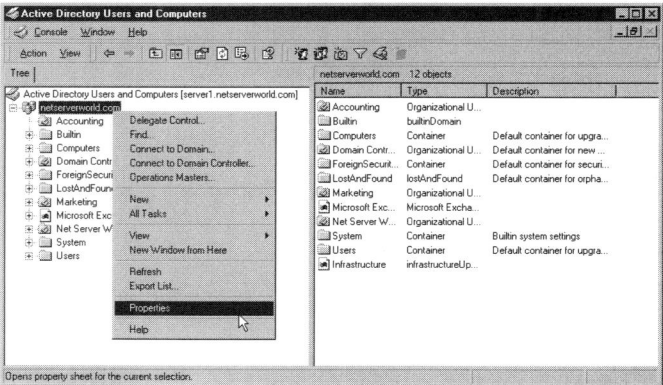

By applying one of the preconfigured templates and then performing customization using the tools outlined here, you can quickly create custom security template solutions that meet your needs without the burden of starting completely from scratch. In the

next section, "Configuring Basic Windows 2000 Security with Templates," we examine each of the major areas that make up a security template.

> **Head of the Class…**
>
> ### Group Policy Security Versus Security Templates
>
> By now it might seem that using Group Policy to configure security settings and using security templates are two ways to accomplish the same task. This is indeed true. The key difference comes when you consider what each was designed for.
>
> Security templates are designed to allow you to quickly apply a preconfigured security solution to a specific computer or group of computers. These templates were designed to be a starting location for further customization. This is where Group Policy comes into play. Should you happen to apply a security template and then later decide you want to further enhance security in a specific area, using one of the aforementioned tools to edit the appropriate Group Policy object is the way to go. In short, look at security templates as a well-defined starting point that can be customized to meet the requirements of the situation by using Group Policy settings.
>
> One key point to remember: Any settings you configure directly in Group Policy cannot be exported into a template for use on another computer. By the same token, settings applied via a template can sometimes be very difficult to remove should you later change your mind about the template application.

Security Configuration and Analysis

The Security Configuration and Analysis console snap-in can be used on a local computer to compare its current security configuration settings to those defined by a template. The template to which you're comparing can be either one of the preconfigured templates supplied with Windows 2000 or a custom-created template that is in use in your organization.

> ### Test Day Tip
>
> The key to working with Security Configuration and Analysis is to never forget that it is used only on the *local* computer, never on a domain or OU scale. This limitation hampers its utility but does not prevent you from using it to develop and deploy robust security templates to your organization on a large scale. Importing templates into a domain or OU is discussed later in this chapter.

Using Security Configuration and Analysis does not cause any settings to be added to the existing security configuration. The Security Configuration and Analysis snap-in database contains the administrator's security preferences. The database is populated with entries derived from security templates. You have the choice to import multiple templates and merge the contents of those templates, or you can import templates in their entirety after the previous database entries have been cleared.

The database is central to the security analysis process. The administrator can initiate a security analysis after configuring the entries in the database to meet the organization's perceived needs. The security analysis compares the settings in the database with the actual settings implemented on the local computer. Individual security settings are flagged by an icon that changes depending on whether the actual security settings are the same as or different from those included in the database. You will also be informed if there are settings that have not been configured at all and thus might require your attention. Figure 1.11 shows the results of a security analysis.

Figure 1.11 The Results of a Security Analysis in the Security Configuration and Analysis Snap-In

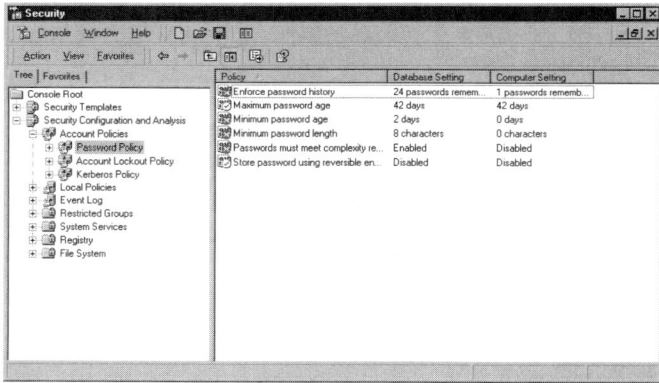

Prior to the security analysis, the administrator configured the preferred security settings in the database. After the database was populated with an ideal security scenario, it was tested against the current machine settings. A green check mark indicates that the current machine settings are the same as those set in the database; a red *X* indicates that there is a conflict; and a generic icon indicates that the setting was not defined in the database. After the analysis is performed, the administrator can make changes to the database as desired and rerun the analysis. When the database matches the precise security configuration required, the administrator can then apply the database settings to the local machine's security policy.

The formulation of a well-planned security policy is a time-consuming process. To add a measure of fault tolerance, the database entries can be exported to a text file, which can be saved for later use on the same machine or applied to another machine, domain, or OU. The exported template is saved as an .inf file and can be imported to other computers, domains, and OUs. In this way, the security parameters can be reproduced exactly from one machine to another.

The following areas can be configured and analyzed using the Security Configuration and Analysis snap-in:

- **Account Policies** The Account Policies node includes those configuration variables that you formerly manipulated in the User Manager for Domains applet in NT 4.0. The two subnodes of the Account Policies node include the Password Policy node and the Account Lockout Policy node. In the Password Policy node, you can set the minimum and maximum password ages and password lengths. The Account Lockout Policy allows you to set lockout durations and reset options.

- **Local Policies** Local policies apply to the local machine. Subnodes of the Local Polices node include Audit Policy, User Rights Policy, and Security Options. Audit and User Rights policies look familiar to users of NT 4.0. The Security Options node offers the administrator many options that formerly were available only by manipulating the Windows NT 4.0 Registry or through the Policy Editor (poledit). Examples include the ability to set the message text and message title during logon, restricting the use of diskettes, and the "Do not display last username at logon" option.

- **Event Log** The Event Log node allows you to configure security settings for the Event Log. These settings include maximum log sizes, configuring guest access to the Event Log, and whether or not the computer should shut down when the security log is full.

- **Restricted Groups** You can centrally control the members of groups. At times, an administrator adds someone temporarily to a group, such as the Backup Operators group, and then neglects to remove that user when the user no longer needs to be a member of that group. These lapses represent a potential hole in network security. You can configure a group membership list in the Restricted Groups node and then configure an approved list of members by reapplying the security template you have created.

- **System Services** You can define the security parameters of all system services in the database via the System Services Node. You can define whether a service startup should be automatic, manual, or disabled. You also can configure which user accounts have access to each service.

- **Registry** The Registry node allows you to set access restrictions on individual Registry keys.

- **File System** The File System node allows you to set folder and file permissions. This is a great aid to the administrator who might have been experimenting with access permissions on a large number of files or folders and then later cannot recall the original settings. You can apply a security template to restore all file and folder permissions to their original settings.

Each of these areas is examined in the next section, "Configuring Basic Windows 2000 Security with Templates." The use and configuration of the Security Configuration and Analysis snap-in is examined later, in the "Analyzing Your Security Configuration" portion of this chapter.

Exam Warning

Knowing and understanding the configurable areas and the roles they play in the overall security process are important for this exam. Don't worry so much about memorizing each configurable item in these areas. (We discuss these items later in this chapter.) You should instead be aware that these different areas exist and what they are used for.

The Command-Line Tools

Although the GUI has replaced the computer tools of old, when all work was done from a text-based command line, command-line tools still play a large role in a network administrator's life. Many jobs have been made easier with the introduction of the functional GUI front for them, whereas others still require the power and control that only the command line can give. Some GUI-based utilities also have command-line alternatives that provide for scripting and automated accomplishment of management tasks. Three tools are presented here: secedit.exe, which comes with Windows 2000, and gpresult.exe and gpotool.exe, which are part of the Windows 2000 Server Resource Kit.

Secedit.exe

The secedit.exe command-line tool offers much of the functionality of the Security Configuration and Analysis snap-in from the command line. This tool allows the administrator to script security analyses for many machines across the enterprise and save the results for later analysis.

The secedit.exe tool's reporting capabilities are limited. Although you can perform a security analysis from the command line, you cannot view the results of the analysis with secedit.exe. You must view the analysis results from the graphic Security Configuration and Analysis snap-in interface.

Additionally, the secedit.exe tool can be used to configure, refresh, and export security settings as well as validate security configuration files. We work with the secedit.exe tool later in this chapter, in the "Analyzing Your Security Configuration" section.

Gpresult.exe and Gpotool.exe

The gpresult.exe and gpotool.exe utilities are part of the Windows 2000 Server Resource Kit. Users without access to the Resource Kit CD can download the utilities from www.microsoft.com/windows2000/techinfo/reskit/tools/default.asp.

The gpresult.exe tool can be used to quickly display the net Group Policy settings for a computer. These settings can be used to help you determine which GPOs have been applied.

The gpotool.exe tool can be used to check the validity of GPOs across multiple domains. This can be helpful in cases in which you are experiencing unexplained difficulties applying Group Policy (i.e., security) settings in your network.

Although neither of these tools is directly related to security, they both have some value to you during times of troubleshooting Group Policy application. Since security settings are commonly deployed via Group Policy, these utilities should be in your toolbox.

Test Day Tip

Don't expect to see any questions about gpresult.exe and gptool.exe on your exam. Information in this chapter pertaining to these two tools is more for your reference, because they can prove to be quite useful when you're trying to track down problems with Group Policy application.

Creating the Security Configuration Tool Set User Interface

Two user interfaces are available to configure system security settings: the graphical interface and the secedit.exe command-line interface. You should do most of your work from the graphical interface—design your security scenarios, test them against extant security settings, and then apply scenarios stored in the security database after testing.

After you customize security scenarios to suit your needs, you can export the scenario to a plaintext file, which you can save for later use. You can edit the exported text file by hand using any available text editor. However, Microsoft recommends that users confine themselves to the graphical interface so as not to introduce random elements into the file's structure and inadvertently corrupt the file contents. Your interaction with the Security Tools set will occur via these interfaces (in order of usage preference):

- Security Configuration and Analysis snap-in
- Group Policy security configuration objects
- The secedit.exe command-line tool

Oddly enough, and despite its power and usefulness, the Security Configuration and Analysis snap-in does not come as a preconfigured MMC console such as the Computer Management or Active Directory Users and Computers consoles. You must create your own custom MMC in order to use the Security Configuration and Analysis snap-in. Exercise 1.01 provides the procedure to create your own "security console."

EXERCISE 1.01

CREATING THE SECURITY CONSOLE

1. Choose **Start | Run**, enter **mmc** in the text box, and click **OK**.
2. From the MMC menu, click **Add/remove snap-in**, and then click the **Add** button.
3. Select and add the following snap-ins:
    - Security Configuration and Analysis
    - Security Templates
4. Click **Close** in the Add Standalone Snap-in window.
5. Click **OK** in the Add/Remove Snap-in window.
6. Save your MMC by clicking the console drop-down menu and choosing **Save As**.
7. In the filename box, type **Security Tool Set** or any other name you want. This step automatically saves your MMC into the Administrative Tools folder.

Configuring Basic Windows 2000 Security with Templates

Armed now with our understanding of how Active Directory works and what tools are available to us as administrators for configuring and implementing basic security measures, we need to now take a look at using the security settings available in the security templates or Group Policy security consoles.

Account Policies

Account Policies define aspects of security that relate primarily to passwords. The Password Policy contains entries related to password aging and password length. The Account Lockout Policy determines how many failed tries a person gets before the account is locked out. The Kerberos Policy applies only to domain logons, since local logons do not use Kerberos. Entries include maximum lifetimes for various tickets, such as user tickets and user renewal. Figure 1.12 shows the expanded Account Policies node. Table 1.3 presents the configurable options available within the Account Policies node.

Figure 1.12 Account Policies

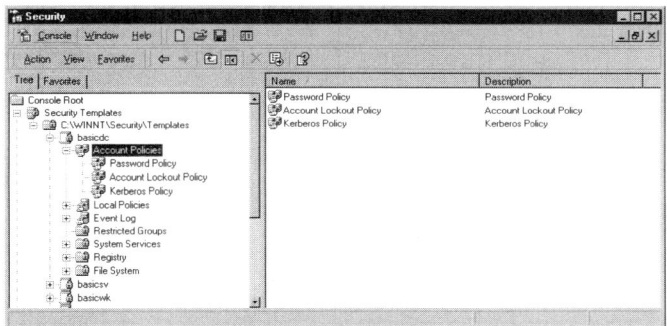

Table 1.3 Account Policies Security Options

Option	Description
Password Policies	
Enforce password history	Remembers users' passwords. Requires that users cannot use the same password again until it has left the password history. Values range from 0 passwords remembered to 24 passwords remembered. The default is 0 passwords remembered.
Maximum password age	Defines the maximum amount of time that a user can keep a password without having to change it. Values range from the password never expires to password expires every 999 days. The default is 42 days.
Minimum password age	Defines the minimum amount of time that a user can keep a password without having to change it. Values range from password can be changed immediately to password can be changed after 998 days. The default is 0 days.

Continued

Table 1.3 Account Policies Security Options

Option	Description
Minimum password length	Defines the minimum number of characters required for a user's password. Value ranges from no password required to at least 14 characters required. The default is 0 characters.
Passwords must meet complexity requirements	Requires that the user's password have a mix of uppercase, lowercase, and numbers. Value is either enabled or disabled. The default is disabled.
Store password using reversible encryption for all users in the domain	Stores a copy of the user's password in Active Directory using reversible encryption. This is required for the message digest authentication method to work. Value is either enabled or disabled. The default is disabled.
Account Lockout Policies	
Account lockout duration	Defines the time in minutes that an account will remain locked out. Value ranges from account is locked out until administrator unlocks it to 99,999 minutes (69 days, 10 hours, and 39 minutes). The default is not defined.
Account lockout threshold	Defines how many times a user can enter an incorrect password before the user's account is locked. Value ranges from the account will not lock out to 999 invalid logon attempts. The default is 5 attempts.
Reset account lockout counter after	Defines how long to keep track of unsuccessful logons. Value ranges from 1 minute to 99,999 minutes. The default is not defined.
Kerberos Policies	
Enforce user logon restrictions	This forces the KDC to validate every request for a session ticket by examining the user rights policy on the target computer to make sure that the user has the right to either log on locally or access the computer across the network. This policy additionally checks to see that the requesting account is still valid. These checks are optional and, when enabled, could result in slower network access to services. The default setting is enabled.
Maximum lifetime for service ticket	Defines the maximum amount of time in minutes that a service ticket is valid. Value ranges from tickets don't expire to 99,999 minutes. The default is 600 minutes (10 hours).

Continued

Table 1.3 Account Policies Security Options

Option	Description
Maximum lifetime for user ticket	Defines the maximum amount of time in hours that a user ticket is valid. Value ranges from tickets don't expire to 99,999 hours. The default is 10 hours.
Maximum lifetime for user ticket renewal	Defines the maximum lifetime of a ticket (Ticket Granting Ticket or session ticket). No ticket can be renewed after this lifetime has passed. The default is seven days.
Maximum tolerance for computer clock synchronization	Specifies the amount of time in minutes that computers' clocks can be skewed. Value ranges from 0 minutes to 99,999 minutes. The default is 5 minutes.

Exam Warning

Password policies can only be set at the domain level. Be attentive to questions that could suggest that policies can be set at the local, site, or OU levels.

Damage & Defense...

Password Age Policies

Although setting a minimum password age is usually a good thing, in at least one instance it can actually provide a security breach in your organization. Say, for example, that you have configured the minimum password age to five days (before a user is allowed to change the password). If that password were compromised, the only way the security breach could be rectified would be through administrator intervention, by resetting the password for the user from Active Directory Users and Computers.

Likewise, setting the minimum password age to 0 days and also configuring 0 password remembered allows users to circumvent the password rotation process by allowing them to use the same password over and over. The key to configuring effective policies, password policies or any other, is to first analyze your needs, then test your configuration, and finally apply it once testing has proved that it meets or exceeds your requirements. Don't be the administrator who mistakenly opens the door to attackers while attempting to secure the network.

Local Policies

Local policies include the Audit Policy, User Rights Assignment, and Security Options. Some Audit Policy selections include auditing logon events, use of user privileges, systems events, and object access. The User Rights Assignment node includes the ability to grant or deny user rights such as the rights to add workstations to the domain, change the system time, log on locally, and access the computer from the network.

The most profound improvements to the program are represented in the Security Options node, where you can make changes that could be made only via direct Registry edits in Windows NT 4.0. Examples of such security options include clearing the pagefile when the system shuts down, message text during logon, number of previous logons kept in cache, and shut down system immediately if unable to log security audits.

Figure 1.13 shows the expanded Local Policies node. Table 1.4 presents the configurable options available within the Local Policies node. The improvements in local policy management are numerous with the addition of the configurable objects available in the Security Options node.

Figure 1.13 Local Policies

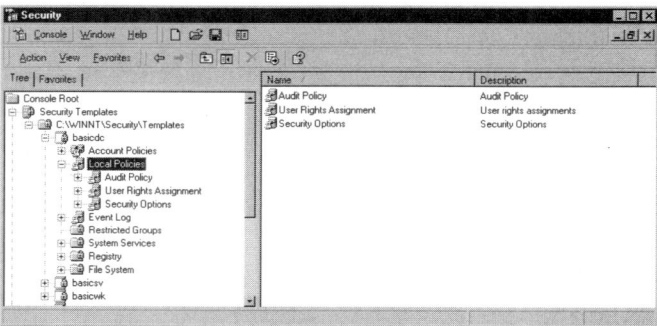

Table 1.4 Local Policies Security Options

Option	Description
Audit Policies	
Audit account logon events	Audits when an account is authenticated to the database. The default is not defined.
Audit account management	Audits when a user account or group is created, deleted, or modified. The default is not defined.
Audit directory service access	Audits when access is gained to an Active Directory object. The default is not defined.
Audit logon events	Audits when a user logs on or off a local computer and when a user makes a network connection to a machine. The default is not defined.
Audit object access	Audits when files, folders, or printers are accessed. The default is not defined.

Continued

Table 1.4 Local Policies Security Options

Option	Description
Audit policy change	Audits when security options, user rights, or audit policies are modified. The default is not defined.
Audit privilege use	Audits when a user right is utilized. The default is not defined.
Audit process tracking	Audits when an application performs an action. The default is not defined.
Audit system events	Audits when a security-related event, such as rebooting the computer, occurs. The default is not defined.
User Rights Assignment	
Access this computer from the network	Allows a user or group to connect to the computer over the network. The default is not defined.
Act as part of the operating system	Allows a process to gain access to resources operating system under any user identity. The default is not defined.
Add workstations to the domain	Allows user or group to add a computer to the domain. The default is not defined.
Back up files and directories	Allows a user or group to bypass file and directory permissions to back up the system. The default is not defined.
Bypass traverse checking	Allows a user or group to pass through directories without having access while navigating an object path in any Windows file system. The default is not defined.
Change the system time	Allows a user or group to set the time for the computer's internal clock. The default is not defined.
Create a pagefile	Allows a user or group to create and change the size of a pagefile. The default is not defined.
Create a token object	Allows a process to create a token to get access to any local resources. The default is not defined.
Create permanent shared objects	Allows a process to create a directory object in the object manager. The default is not defined.
Debug programs	Allows a user or group to attach a debugger to any process. The default is not defined.
Deny access to this computer from the network	Denies the ability to connect to the computer over the network. The default is not defined.
Deny logon as a batch job	Denies the ability to log on using a batch-queue facility. The default is not defined.

Continued

www.syngress.com

Table 1.4 Local Policies Security Options

Option	Description
Deny logon on as a service	Denies the ability to log on as a service. The default is not defined.
Deny logon locally	Denies a user or group the ability to log on to the local machine. The default is not defined.
Enable computer and user accounts to be trusted for delegation	Allows a user or group to set the Trusted for Delegation setting on a user or computer object. The default is not defined.
Force shutdown from a remote system	Allows a user or group to shut down a remote system computer remotely. The default is not defined.
Generate security audits	Allows a process to make entries in the security log. The default is not defined.
Increase quotas	Allows a process to increase the processor quota for any processes to which it has write property access. The default is not defined.
Increase scheduling priority	Allows a process to increase the execution priority for any processes to which it has write property access. The default is not defined.
Load and Unload device drivers	Allows a user or group to install and uninstall Plug and Play device drivers. The default is not defined.
Lock pages in memory	Allows a process to keep data in physical memory. The default is not defined.
Log on as a batch job	Allows a user or group to log on using a batch-queue facility. The default is not defined.
Log on as a service	Allows logging on as a service. The default is not defined.
Log on locally	Allows a user or group to log on to the local machine. The default is not defined.
Manage auditing and security log	Allows a user or group to configure object access auditing. The default is not defined.
Modify firmware environment	Allows changing the system environment values variables. The default is not defined.
Profile single process	Allows a user or group to use performance monitoring tools to monitor the performance of nonsystem processes. The default is not defined.
Profile system performance	Allows a user or group to use performance-monitoring tools to monitor the performance of system processes. The default is not defined.

Continued

Table 1.4 Local Policies Security Options

Option	Description
Remove computer from docking station	Allows a user or group to undock a laptop within Windows 2000. The default is not defined.
Replace a process level token	Allows a process to replace the default token associated with a subprocess that has been started. The default is not defined.
Restore files and directories	Allows a user or group to bypass file and directory permissions when restoring backed-up files and directories. The default is not defined.
Shut down the system	Allows a user or group to shut down the local computer. The default is not defined.
Synchronize directory service data	Allows a process to provide directory synchronization services. The default is not defined.
Take ownership of files or other objects	Allows a user or group to take ownership of any securable system object. The default is not defined.
Security Options	
Additional restrictions for anonymous connections	Adds restrictions for anonymous connections. Choices include none, do not allow enumeration of SAM accounts and share, and no access without explicit anonymous permissions. The default is not defined.
Allow server operators to schedule tasks (domain controllers only)	Gives members of the Server Operators group the right to schedule tasks. The default is not defined.
Allow system to be shut down without having to log on	Enables the shutdown tab on the Ctrl + Alt + Del logon screen. The default is not defined.
Allowed to eject removable NTFS media	Defines the groups that are allowed to eject removable NTFS media. The default is not defined.
Amount of time required before disconnecting session	Defines how long a user can be connected in an idle state before the user is disconnected. The default is not defined.
Audit the access of global system objects	Audits when a system object is accessed. The default is not defined.
Audit use of Backup and Restore privilege	Audits when the Backup and Restore privileges are used. The default is not defined.
Automatically log off users when time expires	Disconnects users who are connected across the network when their time expires. The default setting is disabled.

Continued

Table 1.4 Local Policies Security Options

Option	Description
Automatically log off users when time expires (local)	Disconnects users who are logged in locally when their time expires. The default is not defined.
Clear virtual memory pagefile when system shuts down	Empties the pagefile on shutdown. The default is not defined.
Digitally sign client communications (always)	Requires the computer to sign its communications when functioning as a client, whether or not the server supports signing. Unsigned communications are not allowed. The default is not defined.
Digitally sign client communications (when possible)	Configures the computer to request signed communications when functioning as a client to a server that supports signing. Unsigned communications will be allowed, but they are not preferred. The default is enabled.
Digitally sign server communications (always)	Configures the computer to require that all connecting clients sign their communications. Unsigned communications are not allowed. The default is not defined.
Digitally sign server communications (when possible)	Configures the computer to request that all connecting clients sign their communications. Unsigned communications will be allowed, but they are not preferred. The default is not defined.
Disable Ctrl + Alt + Del requirement for logon	Forces smartcard logon. The default is not defined.
Do not display last user name in logon screen	Does not display the name of the last user to log on to the system. The default is not defined.
LAN Manager authentication level	Controls the level of authentication supported for down-level clients. The default is not defined.
Message text for users attempting to log on	The text to be displayed in a window presented to all users logging on. The default is not defined.
Message title for users attempting to log on	The title of the window presented to all users logging on. The default is not defined.
Number of previous logons to cache (in case domain controller is not available)	Determines how many times users can log on with their cached credentials. The default is not defined.
Prevent system maintenance of computer account password	Prevents the system from changing the computer account password. The default is not defined.

Continued

Table 1.4 Local Policies Security Options

Option	Description
Prevent users from installing printer drivers	Keeps users from installing printers. The default is not defined.
Recovery console: Allow automatic administrative logon	Automatically logs the administrator on with the recovery console administrator account when booting to the recovery console. The default is not defined.
Recovery console: Allow floppy copy and access to all drives and all folders	Allows copying from a diskette when booted into the recovery console. Also allows access to the entire hard drive in recovery mode. The default is not defined.
Rename administrator account	Renames the administrator account to the name specified here. The default is not defined.
Rename guest account	Renames the guest account to the name specified here. The default is not defined.
Restrict CD-ROM access to locally logged on user only	Restricts network access to the CD-ROM. The default is not defined.
Restrict floppy access to locally logged-on user only	Restricts network access to the diskette drive. The default is not defined.
Secure channel: Digitally encrypt or sign secure channel data (always)	Requires the machine to encrypt or sign secure channel data. The default is not defined.
Secure channel: Digitally encrypt secure channel data (when possible)	Configures the machine to encrypt secure channel data when communicating with a machine that supports digital encryption. The default is not defined.
Secure channel: Digitally sign secure channel data (when possible)	Configures the machine to sign secure channel data when communicating with a machine that supports digital signing. The default is not defined.
Secure channel: Require strong (Windows 2000 or later) session key	Requires the use of a Windows 2000 session key. The default is not defined.
Secure system partition (for RISC platforms only)	Secures the system partition. The default is not defined.
Send unencrypted password to connect to third-party SMB servers	Sends a clear text to password to SMB servers that don't support SMB signing. The default is not defined.
Shut down system immediately if unable to log security audits	Shuts down the computer when the security log becomes full. The default is not defined.

Continued

Table 1.4 Local Policies Security Options

Option	Description
Smartcard removal behavior	Determines what will take place when a smartcard is removed from the system. Choices include no action, lock workstation, and force logoff. The default is not defined.
Strengthen default permissions of global system objects (e.g., Symbolic Links)	Strengthens the default permissions of global system objects. The default is not defined.
Unsigned driver installation behavior	Controls what happens when the installation of an unsigned driver is attempted. Choices include silently succeed, warn but allow installation, and do not allow installation. The default is not defined.
Unsigned nondriver installation behavior	Controls what happens when the installation of an unsigned nondriver is attempted. Choices include silently succeed, warn but allow installation, and do not allow installation. The default is not defined.

> **Notes from the Underground…**
>
> ### Brute-Force Attacks
>
> One of the simplest means of gaining access to protected system resources is by a *brute-force attack*, which consists of trying to guess or crack passwords by attempting all possible combinations. Brute-force attacks can be performed by users themselves or by the use of specialized software utilities designed for this purpose. Brute-force hacking differs from dictionary hacking in that dictionary hacking tries to guess passwords by comparing them to a large list of common words and phrases. By configuring for strong passwords, you can defeat dictionary hacking—but protecting against brute-force hacking is nearly impossible.
>
> Your only line of defense when it comes to brute-force attacks (or even social hacking by your own users) comes down to configuring and implementing good auditing policies and also configuring account lockout policies with lockout durations that are appropriate for the sensitivity of the information contained within your network.

Event Log

The Event Log node allows you to configure settings specifically for Event Logs, as shown in Figure 1.14. Event Log Configuration settings allow you to configure the length of time logs are retained as well as the size of the Event Logs. You can also configure that the system should shut down if the security log becomes full. Table 1.5 presents the configurable options available within the Event Log Policies node.

Figure 1.14 Event Log Policies

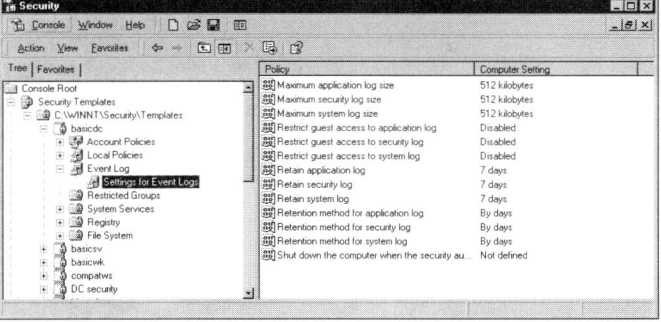

Table 1.5 Event Log Security Options

Option	Description
Maximum Application Log size	Controls how large the Application log can grow. The default is 512 KB.
Maximum Security Log size	Controls how large the Security Log can grow. The default is 512 KB.
Maximum System Log size	Controls how large the System Log can grow. The default is 512 KB.
Restrict guest access to Application Log	Prevents guest access from reading the Application log. The default is disabled.
Restrict guest access to Security Log	Prevents guest access from reading the Security Log. The default is disabled.
Restrict access to System Log	Prevents guest access from reading the System Log. The default is disabled.
Retain Application Log	Tells the Event Log not to overwrite events in the Application Log that are older than the number of days defined. The default is seven days.
Retain Security Log	Tells the Event Log not to overwrite events in the Security Log that are older than the number of days defined. The default is seven days.
Retain System Log	Tells the Event Log not to overwrite events in the System Log that are older than the number of days defined. The default is seven days.

Continued

Table 1.5 Event Log Security Options

Option	Description
Retention method for Application Log	Tells the event log what to do when the Application Log becomes full. Choices include overwrite events by days, overwrite events as needed, and do not overwrite events (clear logs manually). The default is by days.
Retention method for Security Log	Tells the event log what to do when the Security Log becomes full. Choices include overwrite events by days, overwrite events as needed, and do not overwrite events (clear logs manually). The default is by days.
Retention method for System Log	Tells the event log what to do when the System Log becomes full. Choices include overwrite events by days, overwrite events as needed, and do not overwrite events (clear logs manually). The default is by days.
Shut down the computer when the security audit log is full	Instructs the computer to shut down when the Security Log is filled. The default is not defined.

Damage & Defense...

Shutting Out Hackers

Configuring servers to shut down the computer when the Security Log is full makes good sense. If you implement auditing and pay careful attention to the log files, clearing them out every day as required, you can benefit from having Windows automatically shut down a server when its Security Log is full. Common sources of full Security Logs (when carefully tended to by the administrator) usually come from unsuccessful attempts to gain access to the server or gained access to the server that is followed up by privilege use and abuse. Odds are that you've probably got enough information about the nature and source of the attack by the time the server shuts down—why leave it exposed any more than you need to? Of course, this practice requires careful pruning and the daily attention of the administrator. Don't configure this setting if you plan to leave the server to run unattended.

Restricted Groups

The Restricted Groups node lends something new to the security configuration options available in Windows 2000. You can define, as part of security policy, the members of a group. At times, the administrator needs to temporarily add users to groups with a higher classification than the users' typical group memberships. This might be the case when an administrator goes on vacation and another member of the team is assigned full administrative rights.

However, often the "temporary" promotion ends up being an inadvertently permanent one, and the user remains in the Administrators group. Groups can also become members of other groups even though it is not part of the company security plan. By defining Restricted Group membership rules, you can return group membership to that defined by your security policy. Figure 1.15 shows the Restricted Groups node. Exercise 1.02 walks you through configuring restricted groups.

Figure 1.15 The Restricted Groups Node

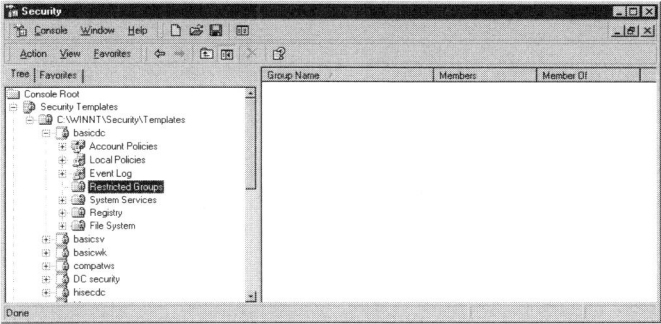

EXERCISE 1.02

CONFIGURING RESTRICTED GROUPS

Navigate to the Restricted Groups section of either your Security Configuration and Analysis snap-in console or the Domain Security Policies console. Then do the following:

1. Right-click **Restricted Groups**, and choose **Add Group** from the context menu. You will see the window shown in Figure 1.16.

   Figure 1.16 The Add Groups Window

   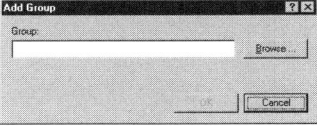

2. You can type the name of the group that you want to restrict, or click **Browse** to pick the group from a list. In this case, click **Browse**. You will see the window shown in Figure 1.17. Select the group that you want to restrict, click **Add**, and then click **OK**.

Figure 1.17 The Select Groups Window

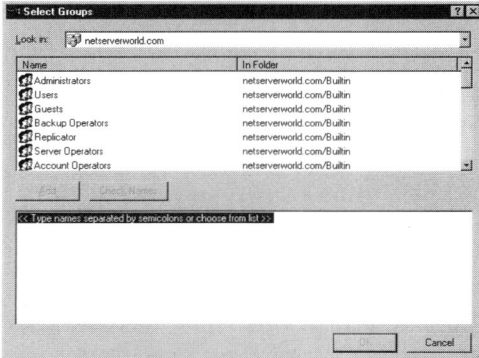

3. Right-click the group you just added from the right pane of the Restricted Groups node, and select **Security**. You will now see the window shown in Figure 1.18.

Figure 1.18 The Configure Membership for Administrators Window

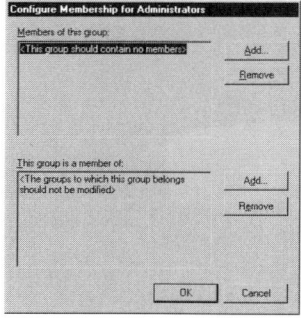

4. In the Configure Membership window, you can restrict the members of your restricted group (in our case, the Administrators group) or you can restrict the other groups of which your restricted group can be a member. Add your restrictions, and click **OK** to save your changes.

System Services

The System Services node allows you to control security and startup policy on all the services defined in the template. Controlling the startup behavior of system services can save the administrator many headaches over time. Consider the situation of users starting up their own RAS or DHCP services haphazardly. This type of situation creates a large security risk for any network.

You can set restrictive networking services startup properties and assign all computers that require certain services to an OU that does have the right to start up particular networking services. Figure 1.19 shows some of the content of the Services node. Exercise 1.03 walks you through configuring System Services Security.

Figure 1.19 Content of the Services Node

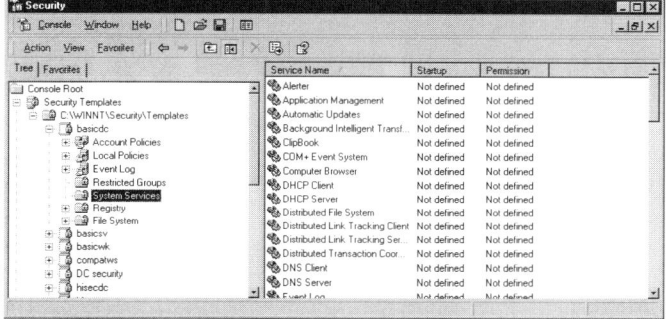

EXERCISE 1.03

CONFIGURING SYSTEM SERVICES SECURITY

1. Navigate to the **System Services** section of either your Security Configuration and Analysis snap-in console or the Domain Security Policies console.

2. Right-click the service that you want to secure, and choose **Security** from the context menu. You will see the Security Policy Setting window shown in Figure 1.20.

Figure 1.20 The Security Policy Setting Window

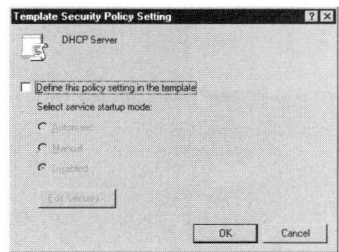

3. In the Security Policy Setting window, check the box next to **Define this policy setting in the template**. After you choose to define the policy, you will immediately be given the window shown in Figure 1.21.

Figure 1.21 Configuring Security for a Service

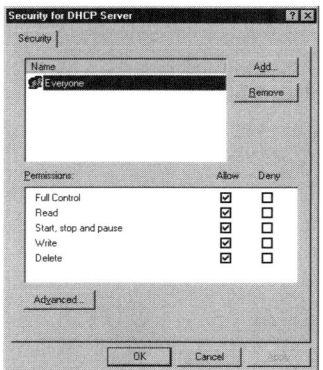

4. Configure the permissions desired, and click **OK** to return to the Security Policy Setting window shown in Figure 1.20.
5. Choose the startup mode for the service, and click **OK** to save your changes.

Registry

Registry keys can also be protected by policy. You can define a security policy for a Registry key or value in the database and then customize the propagation of the setting using the Key Properties dialog box. Exercise 1.04 walks you through configuring Registry security.

EXERCISE 1.04

CONFIGURING REGISTRY SECURITY

1. Navigate to the **Registry** section (see Figure 1.22) of either your Security Configuration and Analysis snap-in console or the Domain Security Policies console.
2. Right-click **Registry** and choose **Add Key** from the context menu. You will see the Select Registry Key window shown in Figure 1.23.

Figure 1.22 The Registry Security Node

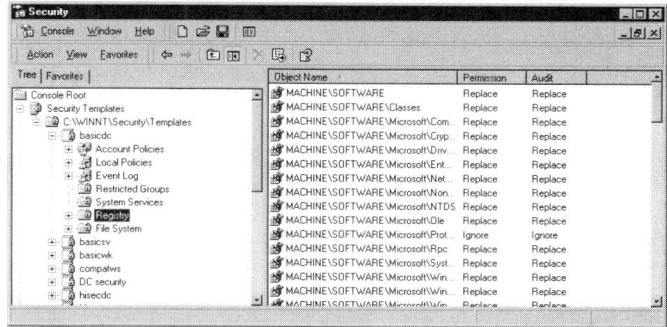

Figure 1.23 The Select Registry Key Window

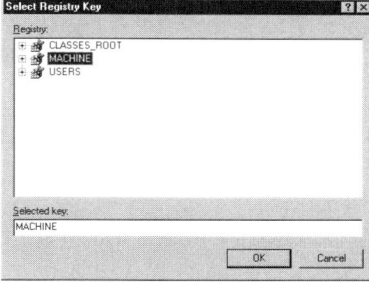

3. Navigate to the key that you want to secure. In this example, we are using the **MACHINE\SOFTWARE** key. Click **OK** to continue.

4. After clicking OK, you will automatically see the Database Security window shown in Figure 1.24. Use this window to choose the permissions that will be assigned to the secured Registry key. After customizing the permissions, click **OK**.

Figure 1.24 The Database Security Window

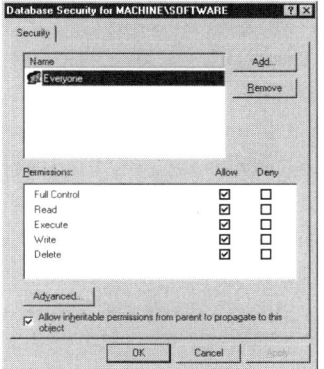

5. Now you see the window shown in Figure 1.25. Use this window to tell Windows what to do with the permissions you set in Step 4. The choices are:

- **Configure the selected key and propagate inheritable permissions to all subkeys.** This will set permissions at the selected key and all keys below it, merging these permissions with whatever permissions are already set at each subkey.

- **Configure the selected key and replace all existing permissions on all subkeys with inheritable permissions.** This will replace the permissions on each subkey with the permissions set at the selected key.

- **Do not allow permissions on this key to be replaced.**

Figure 1.25 The Template Security Policy Setting Window

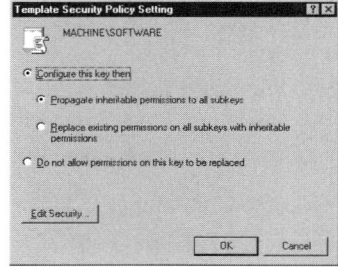

6. Choose one of the settings, and click **OK**.

To edit the Security Policy Setting of an already existing Registry key, simply right-click it and select **Security** to bring up the window shown in Figure 1.25.

File System

The File System Security node allows you to configure NTFS permission for all local drives. It is common for a number of administrators to get into Windows Explorer and customize the NTFS permissions on files and folders throughout the file system. File and folder security should be part of a well-planned and well-implemented security plan.

This security plan can be realized by setting File System Policy in the templates (as shown in Figure 1.26). You can then periodically audit the status of the file system to look for inconsistencies between the plan and the actual state of NTFS permissions in the local environment. Exercise 1.05 walks you through the process of using file system security.

Figure 1.26 The File System Security Node

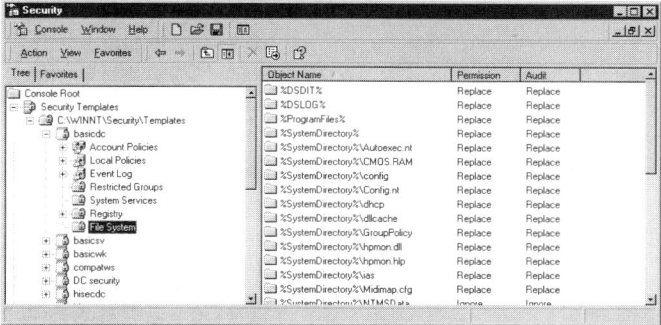

EXERCISE 1.05

CONFIGURING FILE SYSTEM SECURITY

1. Navigate to the **File System** section of either your Security Configuration and Analysis snap-in console or the Domain Security Policies console.

2. Right-click the **File System** node, and select **Add File** from the context menu. You will see the File or Folder window shown in Figure 1.27.

   Figure 1.27 Adding a File or Folder

   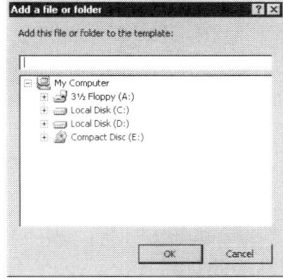

3. Navigate to the file or folder that you want to secure. In this example, we use the root of the C: drive. Click **OK** to continue.

4. After you click **OK**, you will automatically be given the Database Security window shown in Figure 1.28. Use this window to choose the permissions that will be assigned to the secured file or folder. After customizing the permissions, click **OK**.

5. Now that you have set the permissions, you have to tell Windows how to propagate them. Figure 1.29 shows the Template Security Policy Setting window. Use this window to tell Windows what to do with the permissions you just configured. The choices are:

- **Configure this file or folder, then propagate inheritable permissions to all subfolders and files.** This choice sets permissions at the selected file or folder and all subfolders and files below it, merging these permissions with whatever permissions are already set at each subfolder or file.
- **Configure this file or folder then replace existing permissions on all subfolders and files with inheritable permissions.** This choice replaces the permissions on each subfolder and file with the permissions set at the selected file or folder.
- **Do not allow permissions on this file or folder to be replaced.**

Figure 1.28 The Database Security Window

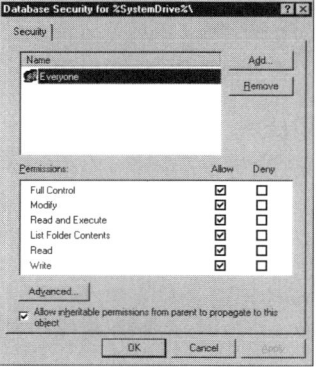

Figure 1.29 The Template Security Policy Window

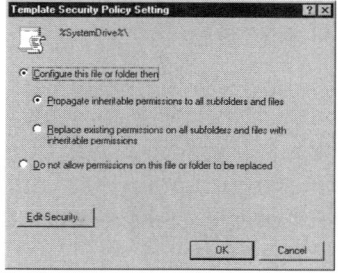

6. Choose the appropriate setting, and click **OK**.

To edit the Security Policy Setting of an already existing File System entry, simply right-click it and select **Security** to bring up the window shown in Figure 1.29.

Deploying Security Templates

Now it's time to deploy our security solution, either by Group Policy and Active Directory or by scripting. If you have worked with Windows NT 4.0 and earlier, you might have had some experience, good and bad, with scripting to set policies and establish environments. With all the improvements and updates in Windows 2000, scripting still remains a viable solution for configuring the environment. Unfortunately, some things can still *only* be done via scripting in Windows 2000 (as in Windows XP and Windows .NET Server), so scripting and command-line management continue to haunt Windows administrators.

So far in this chapter, we have spent a good deal of time discussing the basic tools that we have to work with when configuring Windows 2000 security across our computers and network. Now it's time to get down to the business of deploying our security solution.

Exercise 1.06 walks us through the process of configuring a template to suit our needs. We have already seen how to configure Restricted Groups in Exercise 1.02, Services in Exercise 1.03, Registry Security in Exercise 1.04, and File System Security in Exercise 1.05, but let's step back now and look at configuring some general security options that were presented in the Account Policies, Local Policies, and Event Log Policies sections.

Damage & Defense...

Safety First!

The Security Configuration and Analysis snap-in, Security Templates, the secedit.exe command-line tool, and security extensions to the Group Policy Editor are powerful and efficient tools that allow you to manage and control your organization's security infrastructure. However, as with all the new tools and capabilities of Windows 2000, you should use appropriate caution before employing these tools in a live environment.

Before deployment, be sure to test your security configurations in a lab environment that resembles your live environment as closely as possible.

The secedit.exe command-line tool allows you to schedule regular security audits of local policies on the machines in any domain and OU. By running scripts that call on the secedit.exe program, you can update each computer's personal database with the results of your security analysis. You can then later use the Security Configuration and Analysis snap-in to analyze the results of your automated analysis. Always watch for the effective policy, because it can differ from the policy that you applied to the local machine. Any existing domain or OU security polices that apply to the machine will overwrite local machine policy.

Let's Configure!

The basic process of configuring security settings is the same whether you are configuring them into a security template for analysis, testing, and later application or are applying them directly to your organization via Group Policy at the various levels available to you. For our purposes, we will modify the basicdc.inf template from with the Security Templates snap-in and use this modified template as we go along.

EXERCISE 1.06

CONFIGURING SECURITY TEMPLATES

1. Open your custom security console you created in Exercise 1.01.
2. Navigate to the **basicws.inf** file in the Security Templates snap-in.
3. Enforce strict password policies by double-clicking **Enforce Password History** and configuring it for **18** passwords remembered, as shown in Figure 1.30.

   Figure 1.30 Configuring the Password History Setting

4. Configure account lockout policies by configuring the settings as shown in Figure 1.31.

   Figure 1.31 Configuring Account Lockout Settings

   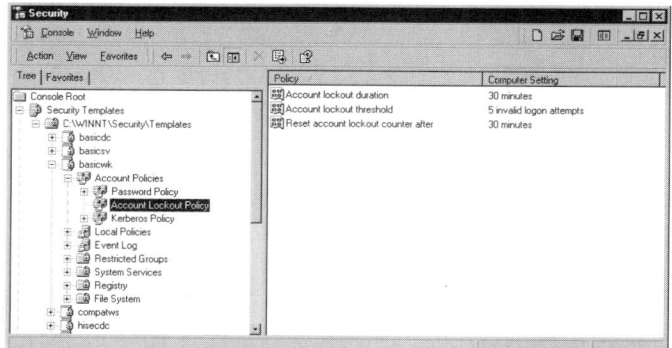

5. Continue to make customizations as desired.
6. When you are done, close out your custom console. You will be prompted to save it; do so.
7. You will be prompted to save changes to your modified security template (see Figure 1.32). Save the changes.

Figure 1.32 Saving Template Changes

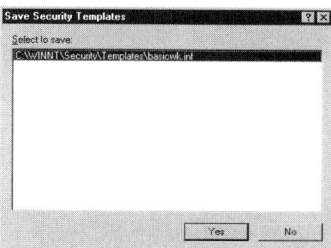

Now that you've got your customized security template, you should take this opportunity to export it. Exporting templates is typically done for one of two reasons: to transfer them over sneaker-net to another computer or to make a copy for safe-keeping in another location. The process to export and import a template is very straightforward and is outlined in Exercise 1.07.

EXERCISE 1.07

IMPORTING AND EXPORTING TEMPLATES

1. Open your Security console and locate the security template you want to export.
2. To export a template, right-click it, and select **Save As**, as shown in Figure 1.33. Be sure to save the template with a descriptive name and in a location you can find later. Note that you can also export a template from the Security Configuration and Analysis snap-in after you have used it to analyze or configure a computer by right-clicking **Security Configuration and Analysis** and selecting **Export Template** (see Figure 1.35).
3. The process to import a saved security template is just as simple. From the Security Templates snap-in, right-click **Security Templates** and select **New Template Search Path** from the context menu, as shown in Figure 1.34. Navigate to the location of your template, and you are in business.

Alternatively, you can use the **Import Template** option from within the Security Configuration and Analysis snap-in (see Figure 1.35).

Figure 1.33 Exporting a Security Template

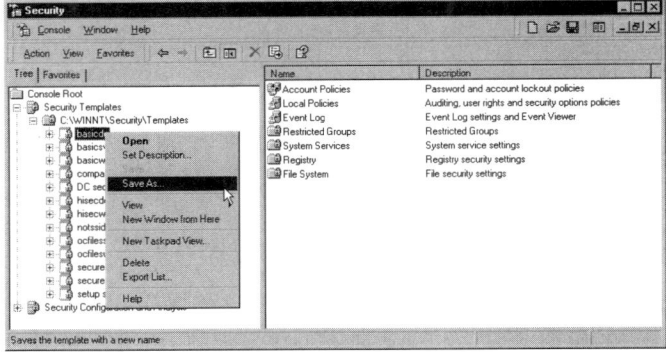

Figure 1.34 Defining a New Template Search Path

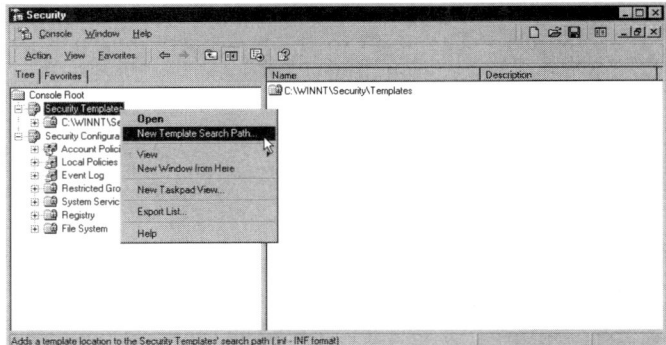

Figure 1.35 Importing Security Templates from Security Configuration and Analysis

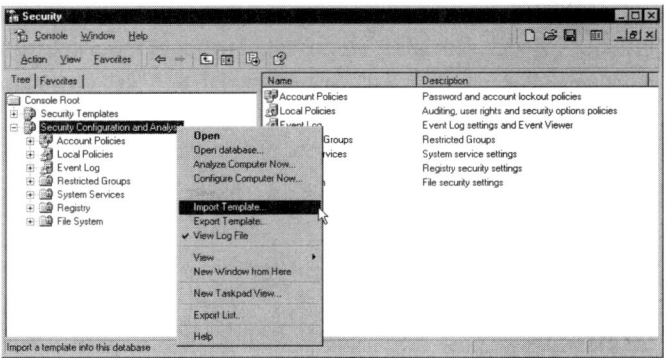

Deploying Security via Group Policy

As useful as is the Security Configuration and Analysis snap-in for configuring local computer security policy, it has major limitation for its use in applying security to higher levels in the organization, such as a domain or OU. The Security Configuration and Analysis snap-in cannot be used to directly apply security settings at these levels, but it can be used to create and test security templates at the local level for deployment at a higher level.

Security policies designed and tested using the Security Configuration and Analysis snap-in can be exported and applied to a domain or OU using the Active Directory Users and Computers console. You can also configure security settings directly in a Group Policy object without using security templates if you desire, but this is not recommended except at the lower levels of your OU structure as you find the need to apply a few specific settings to a specific group of users. Figure 1.36 shows the processing order of Group Policy objects from the local level (first) to the OU level (last).

Figure 1.36 Group Policy Application Order

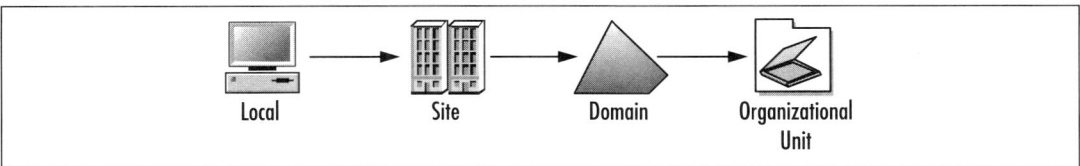

Exercise 1.08 presents the process to import a security template into an OU-level GPO. Exercise 1.09 presents the process to import a security template into a domain-level GPO. After you've imported a template, you can perform further customization if you desire by making edits directly in the Group Policy windows that you will have open while performing Exercise 1.08 and 1.09.

EXERCISE 1.08

IMPORTING SECURITY TEMPLATES AT THE ORGANIZATIONAL UNIT LEVEL

1. Open the **Active Directory Users and Computers** console from the **Administrative Tools** menu. Right-click an organizational unit and select **Properties**.
2. The OU's properties box appears. Click the **Group Policy** tab (see Figure 1.37).

Figure 1.37 The Group Policy Tab of the Organizational Unit Properties Page

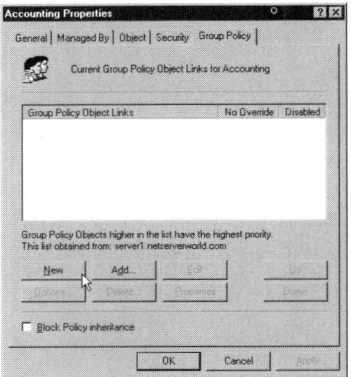

3. Click **New**. Type a name for the Group Policy object. Make sure that the new object is selected, then click **Edit**.

4. Expand **Computer Configuration**, then expand **Windows Settings**. There are two subnodes of Windows Settings: Scripts and Security Templates. Select the **Security Templates** node (see Figure 1.38).

Figure 1.38 Group Policy Security Settings

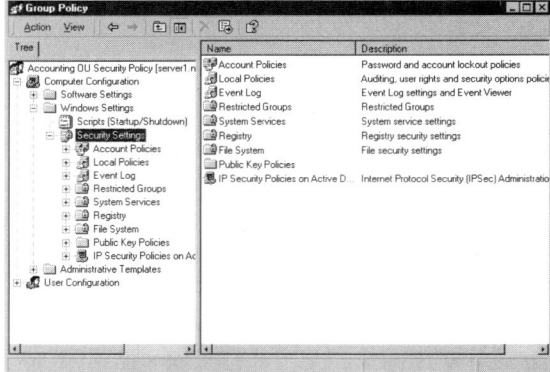

5. Right-click the **Security Settings** node, and select **Import Policy**. Notice that the policies are template files with the .inf extension. You have the option of merging the template's entries into the present OU's security setup, or you can clear the present OU's security settings and have them replaced by the settings in the imported template. Click **Open** to enact the new policy. You are not given the option to test the template settings against the present OU's security configuration. The settings are enabled after you import the policy via the .inf file.

6. Close all windows back to the Active Directory Users and Computers console.

7. To force Group Policy propagation throughout the domain, enter the following command from the command line: **secedit /refreshpolicy machine_policy**.

Now that we've examine how to apply a security template to an OU, let's look next at applying a security template to the domain as a whole. As you will see in Exercise 1.09, the process is fairly similar between the two procedures, with the primary difference being the location at which you import the policy. Furthermore, in most cases you need to allow a longer time for policy replication at the domain level compared with policy replication for those computers in an OU.

EXERCISE 1.09

IMPORTING SECURITY TEMPLATES AT THE DOMAIN LEVEL

1. Open the **Active Directory Users and Computers** console from the Administrative Tools menu. Right-click the domain and select **Properties** (see Figure 1.39).

Figure 1.39 Selecting a Domain for Group Policy Editing

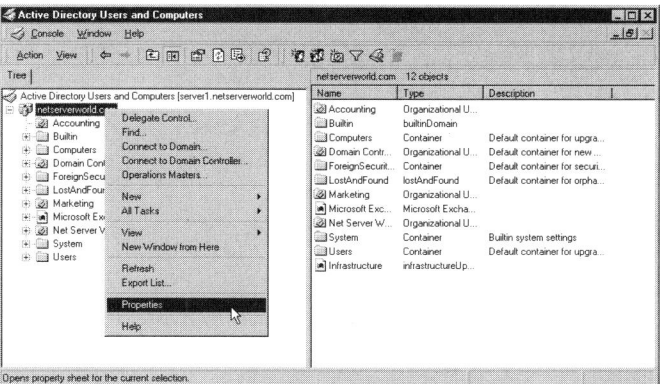

2. The domain's Properties box appears. Click the **Group Policy** tab.
3. Click **New**. Type a name for the Group Policy object. Make sure that the new object is selected, then click **Edit**.

4. Expand **Computer Configuration**, then expand **Windows Settings**. There are two subnodes of Windows Settings: Scripts and Security Templates. Select the **Security Templates** node.

5. Right-click the **Security Settings** node, and select **Import Policy**. Notice that the policies are template files with the .inf extension. You have the option of merging the template's entries into the present OU's security setup, or you can clear the present OU's security settings and have them replaced by the settings in the imported template. Click **Open** to enact the new policy. You are not given the option to test the template settings against the present OU's security configuration. The settings are enabled after you import the policy via the .inf file.

6. Close all windows back to the Active Directory Users and Computers console.

7. To force Group Policy propagation throughout the domain, enter the following command from the command line: **secedit /refreshpolicy machine_policy**.

Deploying Security via Scripting

Using the secedit.exe utility, you can deploy security templates across your network using scripts or batch files should you desire, although you would be better off using the GUI options available to you such as Security Configuration and Analysis or Group Policy. The deployment mode of secedit.exe uses the */configure* switch and is used to configure the target computer's security settings using a stored security template. When used to deploy security templates, secedit has the following syntax:

```
secedit /configure [/DB filename ] [/CFG filename ] [/overwrite][/areas
    area1 area2...] [/log logpath] [/verbose] [/quiet]
```

Modification parameters include the following.

The following command informs secedit.exe which database to apply the security analysis results to:

```
/DB filename
```

This command points to the location of the template that will be applied to the database:

```
/CFG filename
```

This switch causes the current template in the database to be overwritten rather than appended:

```
/overwrite
```

This command allows you to specify a specific security "area" to be configured. The default is all areas:

```
/area area1 area2...
```

The following is the location of the logfile that will be created with details of the security configuration:

```
/log logpath
```

This command provides additional screen and log output:

```
/verbose
```

This command suppresses screen and log output:

```
/quiet
```

The following areas are available for use with the area modifier with the configure switch of secedit:

- **SECURITYPOLICY** Local and domain policy for the system, including account policies, audit policies, and so on.
- **GROUP_MGMT** Restricted group security.
- **USER_RIGHTS** User logon rights and granting of privileges settings.
- **REGKEYS** Registry key security settings.
- **FILESTORE** File system security settings.
- **SERVICES** System services security settings.

Exercise 1.10 outlines using the *secedit* command to deploy a security template to the *local* machine. Using a batch file, you could very easily accomplish this task across multiple computers on your network. For more information on writing and working with scripts in Windows 2000, see the TechNet Script Center at www.microsoft.com/technet/scriptcenter/default.asp.

EXERCISE 1.10

IMPLEMENTING SECURITY TEMPLATES USING SCRIPTING

1. Open a command prompt window by typing **CMD** in the **Run** box and clicking **OK**.
2. From the command prompt, enter the **secedit /configure** command with the required modifiers, such as:

```
secedit /configure /db c:\sectest\2.sdb /cfg C:\WINNT\
    security\templates\securews.inf /log c:\sectest\2apply
        .log /verbose
```

Note that the locations and names are specific to your computer. See Figure 1.40.

Figure 1.40 Performing a Deployment Using *secedit*

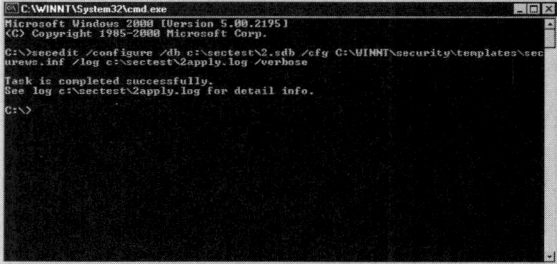

3. Checking the results in **Security Analysis and Configuration** reveals that the settings took (see Figure 1.41), so it works! We cover performing analysis using Security Configuration and Analysis in more detail in the next section.

Figure 1.41 Verifying the Template Deployment was Successful

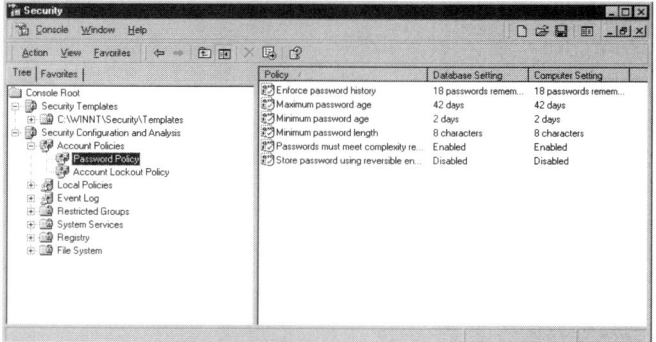

Analyzing Your Security Configuration

After you've carefully configured, tested, and deployed your security solution using security templates and Group Policy, you will want to analyze the security settings from time to time to validate your work and to monitor for changes. Often, changes are made to security settings, such as the temporary promotion of a user to an administrative role, and go unchanged when the situation returns to normal. Other sources of policy change are changes made but not properly documented in your change log or changes made by users who might or might not have a reason to be poking around in your security configuration but either way have found a way to muck it up.

The tools introduced earlier in this chapter come back into play here as you now use them to verify your current settings against your template (ideal) settings. In the next few sections, we examine how the Security Configuration and Analysis snap-in and the command-line tools (secedit.exe, gpresult.exe, and gpotool.exe) can be used as part of a routine check and restore system in order to keep security in your organization where it is supposed to be. A key point to remember as we progress is that the Security Configuration and Analysis snap-in *cannot* be used to examine settings at the domain or organizational level because the snap-in only compares a specific machine's security configuration against a template.

Using Security Configuration and Analysis

One of the most useful features of the Security Configuration and Analysis snap-in is the ability to compare the desired security policies as they are set up in the template with the actual state of the local machine. The administrator is able to glean a tremendous amount of insight regarding the machine's current security configuration using the Analyze feature of the Security Configuration and Analysis snap-in.

Running the analysis is easy. After you import the security settings from the appropriate templates, all you need to do is right-click the **Security Configuration and Analysis** node and select the **Analyze Computer Now** option. Exercise 1.11 walks you through the steps to compare your configured settings against those of a preconfigured template. You need to open an existing database or create a new one in order to perform this analysis. You will test your present security configuration against these entries in the database. If desired, you can apply the settings saved in the database to the computer itself, thus updating the local machine's security configuration.

EXERCISE 1.11

ANALYZING LOCAL SECURITY WITH THE SECURITY CONFIGURATION AND ANALYSIS SNAP-IN

1. Right-click **Security Configuration and Analysis**, and select **Open Database** (see Figure 1.42).

    Figure 1.42 The Open Database Dialog Box

2. If there is already an existing database, you can open that one. If no databases are currently defined, you can create a new one by entering the name of the database in the **File name** box. Then click **Open**.

3. The Import Template dialog box appears (see Figure 1.43). You need to populate the database with security configuration entries. The templates contain this information. Select the template that contains the information that most closely represents the level of security you are interested in (these templates were discussed in Table 1.2), and then click **Open**.

    Figure 1.43 The Import Template Dialog Box

    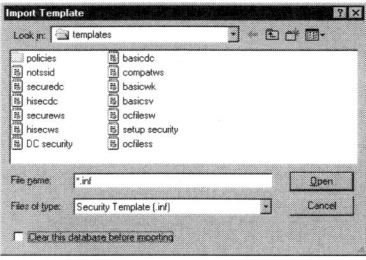

4. In the right pane, you will see instructions on how to analyze or configure your computer. Right-click the **Security Configuration and Analysis** node and select **Analyze Computer Now**. Be careful; if you select Configure Computer Now, it will apply the settings that you have imported into the database to the active security configuration of the computer.

5. After you choose **Analyze Computer Now**, you will be prompted to give a location in which to store the log files. Use the **Browse** button to set the correct location. The default name for the log file is *database_name.log* (where *database_name* is the name of your database). Click **OK** to continue.

6. After you click **OK**, you will be given the Analyzing System Security window shown in Figure 1.44. You can see from this window which component of your system is currently being analyzed. Once this process has finished running, you can see the differences between the template file and your local system.

Figure 1.44 Running the Analysis

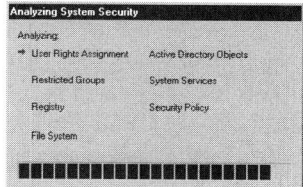

Examining the Analysis Results

After you've performed the analysis, the time-consuming and critically important next step of inspecting the differences comes into play. You need to look through each node of the analysis results and determine if the results agree with your desired settings for the computer. Should you find that the results are not agreeable, you can change the database setting by right-clicking the configuration item and selecting **Security**, as shown in Figure 1.45. The change will then be implemented in the database for further analysis and configuration usage.

Figure 1.45 Changing Settings from within the Database

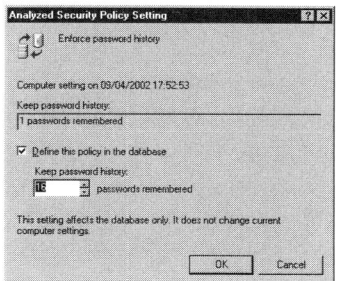

Once all the database settings agree with how you *want* the computer to be, you can apply them by selecting **Configure Computer Now**. Additionally, you can export the template as previously discussed for easy application to other computers in the same role (workstations or member servers and the like).

Figure 1.46 shows the results of our analysis in the Password Policy node where we had previously made some configurations. As you can see, a difference is shown between the database (security template) settings and those currently configured on the local computer. Because we are configuring and testing this template for deployment, this is not a problem in and of itself. Had we found mismatches such as this one during a routine audit of computer security policies, a problem could exist in the organization.

Figure 1.46 Finding Differences in the Password Policies

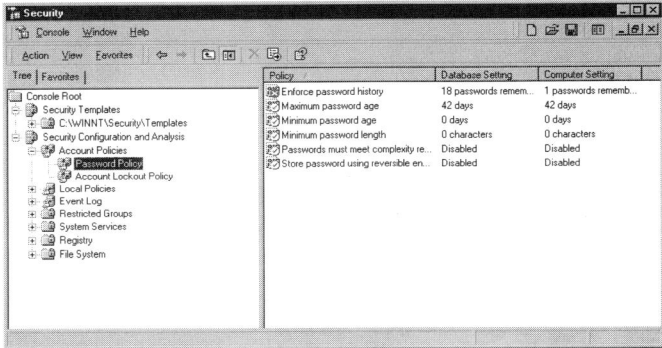

The following icons are used in the analysis output:

- Icons with a green check mark indicate that the database setting and the machine settings are the same.

- Icons with a red *X* indicate that there is a discrepancy between the entry in the database and that of the actual configuration.

- The generic icon means that no setting for that security parameter was set in the database, and thus no analysis was performed.

- Icons with a circled exclamation point or question mark indicate settings that were not analyzed, typically due to not being applicable to the local controller.

In our case, only one setting was different. If this setting was configured correctly (in other words, the way we *want* it to be when applied to the computer), no action is required. However, should we desire, we can edit the database setting as previously discussed to bring it in line with our expectations.

Using Secedit.exe

The secedit.exe command-line interface allows the administrator to:

- Analyze system security
- Configure system security (discussed previously)
- Refresh security settings
- Export security settings
- Validate the syntax of a security template

The *secedit* command has the following high-level syntax:

```
secedit [/analyze] [/configure] [/refreshpolicy] [/export] [/validate]
```

> **TEST DAY TIP**
>
> As far at is pertains to this exam, you should concentrate on understanding how *secedit* can be used to analyze and configure system security. The other functions of *secedit* are not likely to be tested but are valuable information to have at your disposal nonetheless.

secedit /analyze

The */analyze* switch is used to initiate a security analysis and has the following syntax:

```
secedit /analyze [/DB filename ] [/CFG filename ] [/log logpath] [/verbose]
    [/quiet]
```

Modification parameters include the following.

This command informs secedit.exe as to which database to apply the security analysis results to:

```
/DB filename
```

This command points to the location of the template that will be imported into the database for analysis:

```
/CFG filename
```

This is the location of the logfile that will be created from the analysis; the default file is used:

```
/log logpath
```

This command provides additional screen and log output when analysis is carried out:

```
/verbose
```

This prevents any screen or log output:

```
/quiet
```

You can still view the results, however, using Security Configuration and Analysis.

secedit /refreshpolicy

The */refreshpolicy* switch is used to update system security after changes have been made. It has the following syntax:

```
secedit /refreshpolicy {machine_policy | user_policy}[/enforce]
```

Modification parameters include the following.

This command updates the security settings for the local computer:

```
machine_policy
```

This command updates the security settings for the currently logged in local user account:

```
user_policy
```

This command refreshes security settings, even if there have been no changes to the GPO settings:

```
/enforce
```

secedit /export

The */export* switch is used to export the security template currently stored in the database to an .inf file for storage and later use. It has the following syntax:

```
secedit /export [/mergedPolicy] [/DB filename ] [/CFG filename ]
    [/areas area1 area 2...] [/log logPath] [/verbose] [/quiet]
```

Modification parameters include the following.

This command merges and exports domain and local policy security settings into the .inf file:

```
/mergedPolicy
```

This switch informs secedit.exe as to which database to apply the security analysis results to:

```
/DB filename
```

This switch points to the location of the template that will be applied to the database:

`/CFG` *filename*

This switch causes the current template in the database to be overwritten rather than appended:

`/overwrite`

This switch allows you to specify a specific security "area" to be configured. The default is all areas:

`/area` *area1 area2...*

This switch is the location of the logfile that will be created with details of the security configuration:

`/log` *logpath*

This switch provides additional screen and log output:

`/verbose`

This switch suppresses screen and log output:

`/quiet`

secedit /validate

The */validate* switch is used to validate the syntax of a security template before you import it for analysis or configuration of the system. It has the following syntax:

`secedit /validate` *filename*

Modification parameters include the following. The filename of the security template you want to validate:

filename

Areas

The following areas are available for use with the area modifier with the */export* switch of *secedit*:

- **SECURITYPOLICY** Local and domain policy for the system, including account policies, audit policies, and so on.
- **GROUP_MGMT** Restricted group security.

- **USER_RIGHTS** User logon rights and granting of privileges settings.
- **REGKEYS** Registry key security settings.
- **FILESTORE** File system security settings.
- **SERVICES** System services security settings.

Analyzing Security with Secedit.exe

Exercise 1.12 presents the basic process to analyze security on a local computer using the *secedit* command. This process could also be done over the network using scripting. After the analysis is completed, you can either open the database in the Security Configuration and Analysis snap-in to examine the differences or read through the text log itself if you used the */verbose* modifier. Beware—the text file generated using the */verbose* modifier can quickly grow into thousands of lines; the log generated by the example in Exercise 1.12 was 5110 lines long, to be exact!

EXERCISE 1.12

ANALYZING SECURITY WITH SECEDIT.EXE

1. Open a command prompt window by typing **CMD** in the **Run** box and clicking **OK**.
2. From the command prompt, enter the **secedit /analyze** command with the required modifiers such as *secedit /analyze /db c:\sectest\1.sdb /cfg C:\WINNT\security\templates\basicwk.inf /log c:\sectest\1.log /verbose*, where the locations and names are specific to your computer. See Figure 1.47.

Figure 1.47 Performing an Analysis Using *secedit*

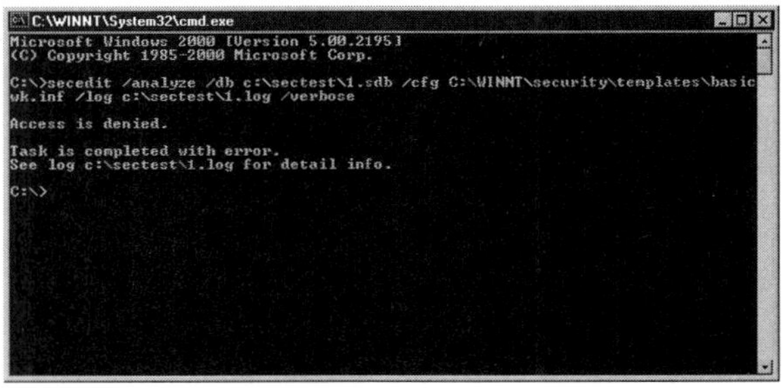

3. You can either view the results in the Security Configuration and Analysis snap-in by opening the database or by viewing the created text log file. Figure 1.48 shows a portion of the text log file indicating a

mismatch in the password history size item. Note that we also saw this in Figure 1.44 when we performed analysis using the GUI—the security template used in the two instances was the same one.

Figure 1.48 Identifying Mismatches in the Text Log Output of *secedit*

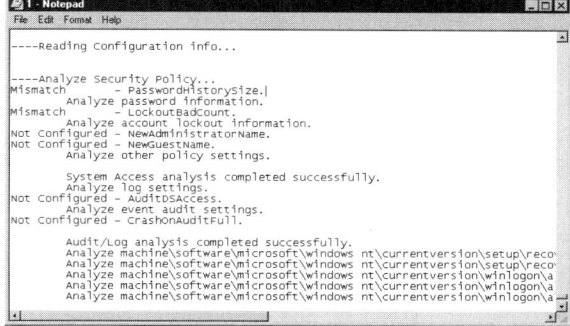

4. You might also find the Windows Grep tool, available for download from www.wingrep.com/, very helpful in searching through your log files. Figure 1.49 shows the output of Windows Grep on our log file.

Figure 1.49 Using Windows Grep to Search the Log File

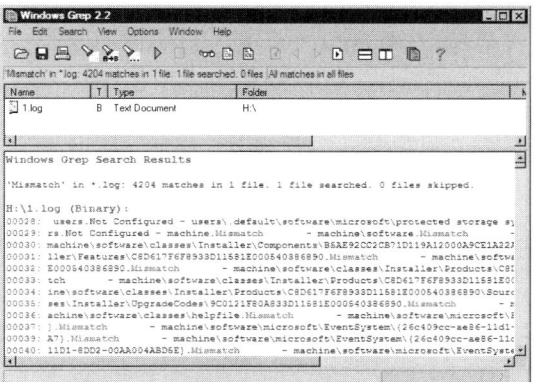

Using Gpresult.exe and Gpotool.exe

These two free utilities are part of the Windows 2000 Resource Kit and can be quite helpful when it comes time to troubleshoot Group Policy application issues. They can be found at www.microsoft.com/windows2000/techinfo/reskit/tools/default.asp.

The gpresult.exe utility can perform the following tasks, plus several others:

- Provide general information about the operating system, currently logged-in user, and computer
- The last time policy was applied and the domain controller that applied policy, for the currently logged-in user and computer
- The complete list of applied Group Policy objects and their details

The gpotool.exe utility can perform the following tasks, plus several others:

- Check Group Policy object consistency
- Check Group Policy object replication
- Display information about a particular Group Policy object, including properties that can't be accessed through the Group Policy snap-in.

TEST DAY TIP

You will not be tested on the gpresult.exe or gpotool.exe tools, but they are useful utilities that should be in your administrative and security toolbox. Should you run into problems with your security configurations that deployed in Group Policy, these utilities should be able to provide you with some insight.

Summary of Exam Objectives

The Security Configuration Tool Set introduces a new and more efficient way to manage security parameters in Windows 2000. Using this new set of configuration and management tools, the administrator can configure and manage the security policies for a single machine or an entire domain or OU. The Tool Set includes the Security Configuration and Analysis snap-in, Security templates, the secedit.exe command-line tool, and the security settings extensions to the Group Policy Editor. You can use these tools together to create and configure security policies for local machines, domains, or OUs.

The Security Configuration and Analysis snap-in allows the administrator to create a database with security configuration entries. These security configuration entries can be used to test against the existing security configuration of a local machine. After the security analysis is complete, the network manager can save the database entries into a text file with the .inf extension. This text file, which is a template consisting of security configuration entries, can be saved or imported in order to define the security definition of another local machine, a domain, or an OU. The security variables in the database can also be applied to the local machine, replacing the current security configuration. The new configuration is applied after the analysis is complete.

Security configuration can be saved as *templates*, which are text files that contain security configuration information. These templates are imported into the Security Configuration and Analysis snap-in database for analysis and application. The Security Configuration and Analysis snap-in cannot be used to configure or analyze security configurations of a domain or OU. At present, there is no way to export extant domain or OU security configurations. However, you can configure the security of a domain or OU via the security settings Group Policy extensions.

The secedit.exe command-line tool allows the administrator to script security analyses, security configurations, security updates, and export of templates. Its functionality is almost equal to that of the Security Configuration and Analysis snap-in, except that you must use the graphical interface to review the results of a security analysis performed by secedit.exe.

An administrator can use the security settings Group Policy extensions to configure domain or OU security policy. In addition, you can import security templates directly into the domain or OU. You should do this with great caution if you have already customized the security settings for a domain or OU. At present, you cannot export the previous settings into a template that might be restored later. However, if the administrator always reconfigures the security parameters of a domain or OU using templates, such templates can always be restored in the future.

Exam Objectives Fast Track

Windows 2000 Active Directory Review

- ☑ Active Directory in an X.500-compatible directory service utilizes the LDAP protocol.
- ☑ Active Directory is organized in a hierarchical structure modeling the Domain Naming System arrangement.
- ☑ Domains at the root of the forest automatically establish two-way transitive trusts between them, unlike previous versions of Windows NT.
- ☑ Child domains and their parent domain automatically establish two-way transitive trusts between them as well.
- ☑ Group Policy applied to an object is processed in the following order (by default): local, site, domain, organizational unit.

The Basic Windows 2000 Security Tools

- ☑ The key components of the Security Configuration tool set are Security templates, Group Policy security configuration objects, the Security Configuration and Analysis snap-in, and command-line tools.
- ☑ The Security Configuration and Analysis snap-in creates, configures, and tests security scenarios. You can create text-based .inf files that contain security settings. You can apply these files to the computer or save them for later use.
- ☑ Microsoft provides templates for configuring security. Default and incremental templates are available. Default templates are applied during a fresh install only. The incremental templates provide additional security above the defaults.
- ☑ Secedit.exe allows us to configure security from the command prompt.
- ☑ The Security Templates snap-in allows us to view and customize the template files stored in %windir%\security\templates.

Configuring Basic Windows 2000 Security with Templates

- ☑ Account policies define password policy, account lockout policy, and Kerberos policy.

- ☑ Local policies include the audit policy, user rights assignment, and security options.
- ☑ Event Log Configuration settings allow you to configure the length of time logs are retained as well as the size of the Event Logs.
- ☑ The Restricted Groups setting configures group membership and group nesting.
- ☑ Registry Policy sets permissions on Registry keys.
- ☑ The File System Security setting configures NTFS permission for all local drives.
- ☑ The System Services setting controls the startup policy for all local services.

Deploying Security Templates

- ☑ The Security Configuration and Analysis snap-in can be used to deploy a security template to a local machine.
- ☑ Security settings can be deployed to a domain or OU via the security settings in a Group Policy object.
- ☑ You can deploy security templates across the network using the secedit.exe tool in a script or batch file.

Analyzing Your Security Configuration

- ☑ Compare security policies in the template with the actual state of the local machine. This practice allows administrators to see the differences before they apply the policy.
- ☑ Use Security Configuration and Analysis to view the results of an analysis in a graphical format.
- ☑ Use the secedit.exe tool to analyze security settings from the command prompt. This tool can be useful if combined with a script or batch file to automatically scan large numbers of computers.
- ☑ After differences in settings have been identified, you can determine the next course of action.

Exam Objectives
Frequently Asked Questions

The following Frequently Asked Questions, answered by the authors of this book, are designed to both measure your understanding of the Exam Objectives presented in this chapter, and to assist you with real-life implementation of these concepts.

Q: Why is Active Directory given so much discussion in this chapter? This isn't a book for an Active Directory exam.

A: True, but this book is intended to be fairly self-standing. Active Directory permeates Windows 2000 through and through, and a basic understanding of it will go a long way toward helping you understand and configure security for a Windows 2000 network.

Q: Can I use the Security Configuration and Analysis snap-in to analyze the security configuration of a domain or OU?

A: Not at this time. This capability should be added in the future. However, at present, you can test scenarios against the current configuration for the local machine.

Q: I would like to use scripts to analyze a number of computers in my domain. What tool would I use to accomplish this task?

A: The secedit.exe command-line tool allows the administrator to analyze a number of machines by creating scripts that can be automated. You can then view the results of the analysis by opening the database file against which the analysis was run.

Q: Why have the changes I made to the security policy on the local computer not taken effect?

A: Effective policy depends on whether a computer is a member of a domain or an OU. Policy precedence flows in the order in which policies are applied. First the local policy is applied, then site policy is applied, then domain policy is applied, and finally OU policy is applied. If there are conflicts among the policies, the last policy applied prevails.

Q: Can I migrate my existing Windows NT 4.0 policies to Windows 2000?

A: No. The NT policies were stored in a .pol file, which included things such as group memberships. There is no way for the Windows 2000 Group Policy Model, which is centered on Active Directory, to interpret the entries in the .pol file. Microsoft recommends configuring the settings in the old .pol files in Active Directory. You can do this easily using the security settings extension to the Group Policy Editor. The Windows NT 4.0 .pol files were created by the System Policy Editor, which used .adm files as templates for the options configured in system policy. These files are compatible with Windows 2000 .adm files. However, you should not import these templates, because you might damage the Registries of client machines. This means that after a Registry setting is set using Windows NT 4.0 .adm files, the setting will persist until the specified policy is reversed or the Registry itself is directly edited.

Self Test

A Quick Answer Key follows the Self Test questions. For complete questions, answers, and epxlanations to the Self Test questions in this chapter as well as the other chapters in this book, see the Self Test Appendix.

Windows 2000 Active Directory Review

1. One of the advantages of Windows 2000 Active Directory over previous versions of Windows NT is that two-way transitive trusts are automatically created between which objects? (Choose all correct answers.)

   A. Between root domains in an Active Directory forest

   B. Between parent domains and child domains

   C. Between child domains at the same level within the tree

   D. Between Windows 2000 and Windows NT 4.0 domains

2. The schema serves what function in Active Directory?

   A. Provides a listing, or index, of all the objects within Active Directory

   B. Defines the types of objects that can be stored in Active Directory

   C. Organizes objects, such as users or computers, into a location designed for easier management and assignment of permissions

   D. Provides for name resolution on the network

The Basic Windows 2000 Security Tools

3. Hannah wants to increase the security on the member servers in her network, but she does not want to interfere with the normal network communications between the servers and other computers on the network. What would be the best security template for her to apply to these member servers?

   A. hisecdc.inf

   B. securews.inf

   C. basicsv.inf

   D. securedc.inf

4. You are the network administrator for a medium-sized company. The HR department has asked you to help interview candidates for the position of assistant security administrator for your Windows 2000 network. During the interview of one of the candidates, you ask the following question: "What can the secedit.exe utility be used for?" What answers do you expect to hear? (Choose all that apply.)

   A. It can be used to list the current Group Policy in effect for a specific user and computer.

   B. It can be used to analyze the security settings of a system.

   C. It can be used to refresh the applied security settings of a system.

   D. It can be used to validate the syntax of chosen security template.

   E. It can be used to edit group membership and permissions for a user or group.

   F. It can be used to remotely monitor privilege use.

   G. It can be used settings.to configure system security

   H. It can be used to export the values stored in a database to a .inf file.

5. Andrew must increase the security on the workstations in his network at any cost, preferably achieving the most secure configuration possible. What would be the best template to apply to his workstations the to provide maximum amount of security, and what negative side effects can he expect to see from the application of the chosen template? (Chose two correct answers.)

   A. hisecdc.inf

   B. securews.inf

   C. basicsv.inf

   D. securedc.inf

   E. hisecws.inf

   F. He should expect no adverse effects to occur except for potentially increased login and logoff times due to extra policy processing invoked by the more secure template

   G. He should expect to lose network connectivity with all other computers that do not support IPSec

   H. He should expect to have to configure Active Directory integrated zones for his DNS servers to support the newly configured workstations

6. You are preparing to deploy some custom security templates across your organization in an effort to increase the overall security of the network. You plan to deploy your security templates via Group Policy. What is the correct processing order for Group Policy in Windows 2000?

   A. Local, domain, site, Organizational Unit

   B. Local, site, domain, Organizational Unit

   C. Site, domain, Organizational Unit, local

   D. Domain, site, Organizational Unit, local

Configuring Basic Windows 2000 Security with Templates

7. Chris wants to configure her network so that users attempting to log on by guessing passwords will be prevented from gaining access to the system. She proposes to perform the following actions. Which actions will have a positive effect on preventing password-guessing users from gaining access to her network? (Choose all that apply.)

    A. Set the Minimum Password Length to 10 characters.

    B. Set the Account Lockout Threshold to 0 invalid login attempts.

    C. Set the Account Lockout Duration to 60 minutes.

    D. Set the Enforce Password History to 25 passwords.

8. Jon, the CTO of your company, asks you what can be done to protect certain areas of the Registry from modification by unauthorized users. What do you tell him?

    A. Use the secedit.exe utility with the /*validate* switch to set security settings on the Registry keys of concern.

    B. Use the regedit application to set security settings on the Registry keys of concern.

    C. Use the Security templates and Security Configuration and Analysis snap-ins to configure, analyze, and implement security settings on the Registry keys of concern.

    D. Use Windows Explorer to mark the Registry files as read only.

    E. Use Windows Explorer to set NTFS permissions on the Registry files so that only authorized users may access them.

9. You want to configure auditing for the workstations in a specific OU in your network. You have opened Security Configuration and Analysis and selected the basicwk.inf template. What section of the template contains the options that you need to configure to enable auditing?

    A. Local Policies

    B. Account Policies

    C. Event Log

    D. Registry

www.syngress.com

Deploying Security Templates

10. Austin has been delegated administrative responsibility for several OUs in his department. How can he most easily make the same changes to the security settings applied to his OUs?

    A. Austin should configure and test a template on a local machine using Security Configuration and Analysis. When he gets the configuration established that he requires, he should export the template and then import it into the specific OU Group Policy objects he is responsible for.

    B. Austin should use the Security Configuration and Analysis snap-in and target it at the specific OU he wants to work with to make the changes.

    C. Austin should edit the Group Policy objects directly for each of the OUs he is responsible for.

    D. Austin should ask a domain administrator to apply the desired settings at the domain level and let them propagate down to his OUs.

11. You have configured and tested two custom security templates for use on your corporate network, corpserver.inf and corpdesktop.inf. Your network is running all Windows 2000 computers and is fragmented into three distinct sections due to the extremely high cost of establishing WAN links between your three geographical locations. You do have dial-up connectivity between the sites using standard plain old telephone service (POTS) lines, but these lines have proven unreliable at best. How can you deploy these templates to the other two sites in your network?

    A. You need to deploy them to two extra domain controllers and then ship one each to your other two sites.

    B. You need to export them from Security Configuration and Analysis and send the .inf files to your other two remote sites. Once there, the other two sites can import them into the required Group Policy object.

    C. You need to establish a Frame Relay connection between all three sites at the same time and push the templates across the WAN link.

    D. You need to make a RDP connection to each domain controller in the remote sites and apply the template to them.

Analyzing Your Security Configuration

12. Andrea is the network administrator of 55 workstations, 10 member servers, and four domain controllers. She would like to perform a security analysis on all her computers without having to physically visit each one. How can Andrea accomplish this task?

    A. This cannot be done at the current time. Andrea will need to sit in front of each machine and use the Security Configuration and Analysis snap-in to perform the analysis.

    B. Andrea can target a remote computer by right-clicking **Security Configuration and Analysis** and selecting **Connect to another computer**.

    C. Andrea can create a script or batch file using the secedit.exe utility with the /*analyze* switch that has an entry for each computer that she wants to analyze.

    D. Andrea can create a script or batch file using the secedit.exe utility with the /*analyze* switch that calls on a prepopulated text file containing the list of computers to be analyzed.

13. Christopher is an assistant network administrator working for Andrea. Christopher has been given the task of examining the results of the *secedit /analyze* script that Andrea ran over the network the previous night. How can Christopher most easily examine the analysis results to determine items that require a follow-up?

    A. Christopher must visit each computer locally and view the database contents using the Security Configuration and Analysis snap-in.

    B. Christopher must use the gpresult.exe tool from the Windows 2000 Resource Kit to be able to easily examine the analysis results.

    C. Christopher can read through the text log from the analysis and identify any mismatches as areas requiring a follow-up.

    D. Christopher can load each database file into the Security Configuration and Analysis snap-in that is running on his computer and identify any mismatches as areas requiring a follow-up.

14. Luanda is attempting to use the Security Configuration and Analysis snap-in to perform an analysis of one of her member servers. The member server is currently configured with the default settings. She wants to compare its settings with those in the securewk.inf security template. What is the correct order of steps to perform the analysis?

    Step 1: Right-click **Security Configuration and Analysis** and select **Analyze computer now**.
    Step 2: Right-click **Security Configuration and Analysis** and select **Open database**.
    Step 3: Select the security template to be used in the analysis.
    Step 4: Select the log file to be used in the analysis.
    Step 5: Right-click **Security Configuration and Analysis** and select **Configure computer now**.
    Step 6: Select the database to be used in the analysis.

    A. 2, 1, 3, 6, 4
    B. 1, 6, 4, 5, 3
    C. 2, 6, 4, 3, 1
    D. 2, 6, 3, 1, 4
    E. 1, 6, 3, 2, 4

15. You have just completed an analysis of your local computer using Security Configuration and Analysis. Looking at the analysis results, you notice several icons have a green check mark on them. You are concerned that your settings do not match those of the template you compared your computer to. What do icons with green check marks mean?

    A. A discrepancy exists between the database settings and the computer setting.
    B. No analysis was performed for this item because it was not configured in the database.
    C. The database setting and the computer setting match.
    D. No analysis was performed for this item because it is not applicable to the computer.

Self Test Quick Answer Key

For complete questions, answers, and epxlanations to the Self Test questions in this chapter as well as the other chapters in this book, see the Self Test Appendix.

1. **A, B**
2. **B**
3. **B**
4. **B, C, D, G, H**
5. **E, G**
6. **B**
7. **A, C, D**
8. **C**
9. **A**
10. **A**
11. **B**
12. **C**
13. **D**
14. **D**
15. **C**

Chapter 2

MCSE/MCSA 70-214

Advanced Security Template and Group Policy Issues

Exam Objectives in this Chapter:

1.3 Troubleshoot security template problems. Considerations include Group Policy, upgraded operating systems, and mixed client-computer operating systems.

1.4 Configure additional security based on computer roles. Computer roles include Microsoft SQL Server computer, Microsoft Exchange Server computer, domain controller, Internet Authentication Service (IAS) server, Internet Information Services (IIS) server, and mobile client computer.

1.5 Configure additional security for client-computer operating systems by using Group Policy.

3.4 Configure Server Message Block (SMB) signing to support packet authentication and integrity.

- ☑ Summary of Exam Objectives
- ☑ Exam Objectives Fast Track
- ☑ Exam Objectives Frequently Asked Questions
- ☑ Self Test
- ☑ Self Test Quick Answer Key

Introduction

You might be tempted to think that after you've deployed your security solution via Group Policy or by using a template, your work is done. Unfortunately, this is not the case. The ground that we covered in Chapter 1 was just the groundwork for much more material to come in this book.

After you've configured a baseline security solution for your network, you might want to go back and take a hard look at the specific roles that each server performs. Different server functions require different security solutions, and in this chapter we take a look at some of the most common server implementations that you can expect to find in your network. You will, of course, want to take the same sort of precautions with your client computers, desktops and portables alike. We will examine the security issues inherent in each of these client computers and what you can do to make them as secure as possible.

After looking at some of the advanced security measures we have at our disposal to create secure servers and clients, we need to address some additional topics associated with using security templates. It's quite possible that you will encounter some problems when attempting to apply a security template to your computers, so we will examine some troubleshooting issues associated with security template deployments. Difficulty in deploying security templates are usually traced to one of two common problems: upgrade installations or legacy clients. We will examine both of these issues in some detail in this chapter. Additionally, we examine the tools with which you can perform troubleshooting of security template deployment.

In the last portion of this chapter, we shift gears somewhat and look at configuring Server Message Block (SMB) traffic for security. Administrators often fail to perform this relatively simple action—more often than not due to lack of knowledge. Configuring for secure SMB communications can help prevent the impersonation of clients and servers, but it has some disadvantages associated with it as well. In this chapter we examine the process and the particulars associated with securing SMB traffic on your network.

Configuring Role-Based Server Security

Configuring server security based on its role has been a topic of great discussion over the past couple of years, although one has to wonder why it took so long to become such an important issue. Not all servers are created equal, and nowhere is this more true than in Windows 2000. It is absolutely critical that you understand not only the functions of your servers but also their vulnerabilities and weaknesses as a result of providing the services that they do.

It has not been uncommon in the last year or two to see almost weekly security bulletins from Microsoft (or more often than not, from an "interested" third party) pointing out a new vulnerability or flaw in some Microsoft product. The most common server products that have been found to have flaws are SQL servers and IIS servers, although almost all the Microsoft Enterprise servers have been found to have some sort of vulnerability or another.

Until recently, you were on your own as to how to lock down a server to make it impervious to attack. All that has changed. Microsoft and several other organizations have taken a very proactive stance toward locking down Microsoft's products. Some of the better and more informative Web sites available to you in your quest to configure effective role-based security can be found at the following sites:

- www.microsoft.com/technet/security/
- http://csrc.nist.gov/itsec/guidance_W2Kpro.html
- http://nsa1.www.conxion.com/win2k/index.html
- www.microsoft.com/technet/security/tools/chklist/w2ksvrcl.asp

Additionally, Microsoft has put together a fairly comprehensive book that includes a good section on configuring role-based security at www.microsoft.com/technet/security/prodtech/windows/windows2000/staysecure/default.asp. Throughout this chapter, we examine some of the templates included in that book and see how they can be used to provide increased, yet still functional, security to your servers.

Test Day Tip

The additional reference material found at these links is not something you will be expected to know come test day. Instead, it is provided for your own reference. Using this extra information, you can better protect your network from attackers.

Note

Learn how and where to get the up-to-date news you need to keep your servers patched. Nothing else you can do will keep your servers safe from newly discovered vulnerabilities and attacks (after you've performed their initial configuration, of course). Be sure to regularly visit www.microsoft.com/technet/security/ to make sure you are abreast of the latest security issues concerning your network.

Securing the Domain

The starting place when it comes to configuring effective role-based server security has to be the domain level. After reading Chapter 1, you should now have a pretty good idea of the types of security settings that you can configure and why you might want to implement each one. In the ideal network environment, the application of security settings (via Group Policy) would look something like the process illustrated in Figure 2.1.

Figure 2.1 Configuring Security for the Enterprise

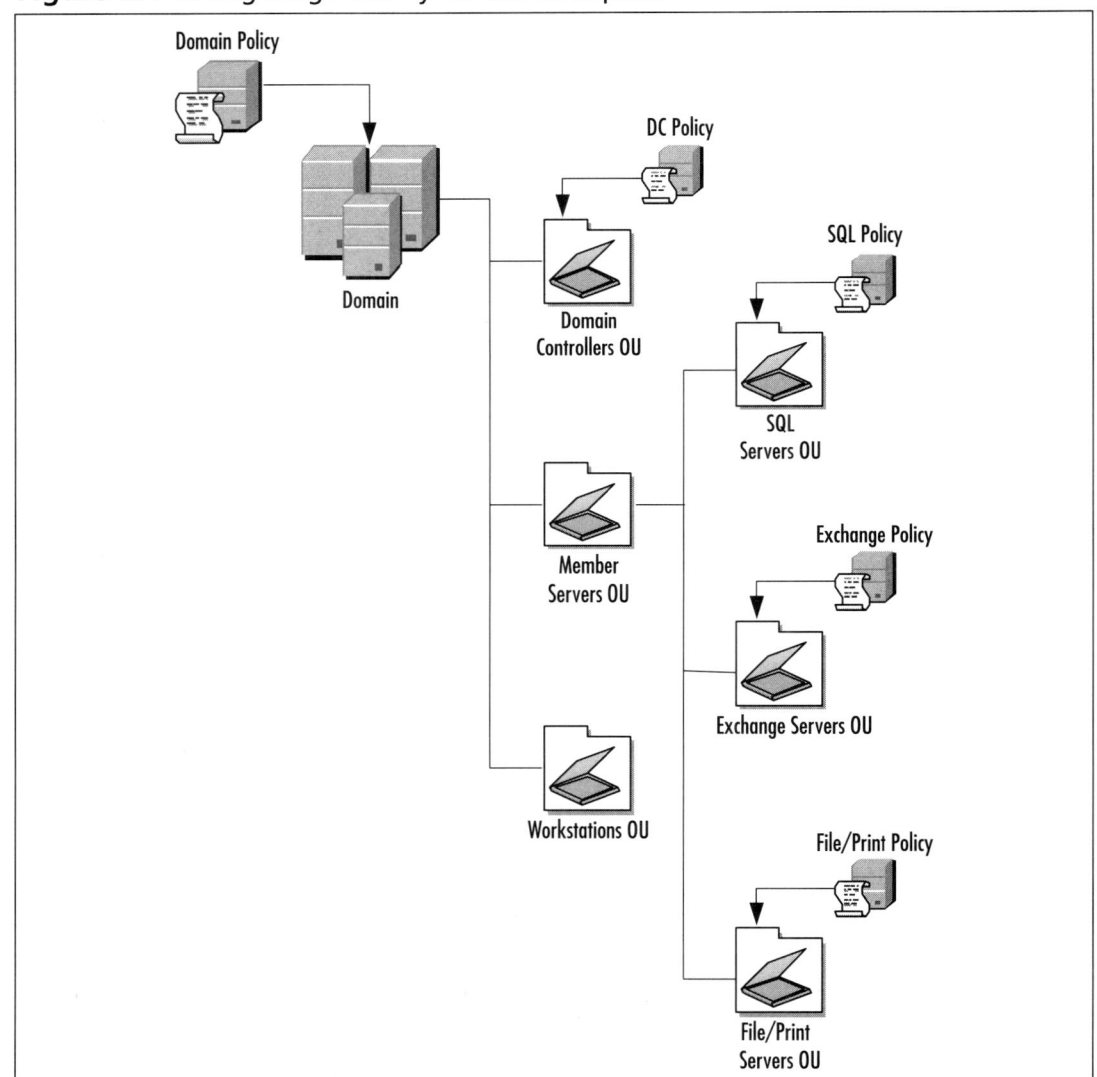

Windows 2000 Domain Controllers

Perhaps the crown jewel of the domain, domain controllers definitely need (and deserve) special treatment when it comes to configuring role-based security. By their very nature, domain controllers have an entirely different set of needs and concerns than any other server on the network. Let's examine some of the concerns associated with domain controllers and then how you can secure them effectively.

By default, when Active Directory is initialized for the first time in your domain, the Domain Controllers OU is created. Active Directory places all domain controllers into this OU, and they should never be moved to any other OU, because very specific ACLs are applied to this OU. Because the Domain Controllers OU (see Figure 2.2) is a top-level OU, it will be unaffected by the policies that we later apply to our member servers. For this reason, domain controllers must have their own specific security policy applied.

Figure 2.2 The Domain Controllers OU

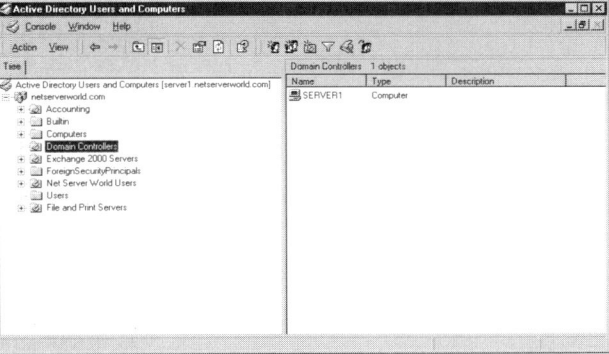

NOTE

You need to be aware of the potential problems that you could run into should you decide to apply the securedc.inf or hisecdc.inf template to your domain controllers if you do not plan properly. You will lose connectivity with legacy clients in your organization that are not using the Directory Services Client (DSClient) software, because they will not be able to use NTLMv2. Furthermore, you could have other issues crop up if you do not plan carefully. *Never* jump into configuration changes on any server, especially your domain controllers, without adequate preparation and a solid backout plan.

By default, the basicdc.inf security template is applied to all domain controllers. In some instances, this basic and low-security template might be adequate to meet an organization's needs, but it is not recommended for the majority of organizations—especially those that have an active connection into their network from the outside, whether via remote access provided to employees or an Internet connection for company and public use.

At a minimum, you should strongly consider applying the securedc.inf security template to your domain controllers by following the steps of Exercise 2.01.

EXERCISE 2.01

SECURING DOMAIN CONTROLLERS

1. From a domain controller, open your Security console that you created in Chapter 1.

2. Using Security Configuration and Analysis, open a new database and import the securedc.inf template.

3. Analyze the domain controller as discussed in Chapter 1 and note the differences, as shown in Figure 2.3. You can perform this process using either Security Configuration and Analysis or secedit.

    Figure 2.3 Inspecting the Changes Before They Are Made

    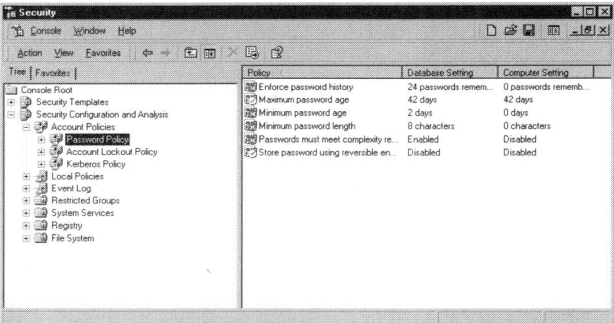

4. Open the **Active Directory Users and Computers** console.

5. Right-click the **Domain Controllers Organizational Unit**. Select **Properties** from the context menu, and switch to the **Group Policy** tab.

6. Create a new **Group Policy Object**, naming it something intuitive such as Secure DC policy.

7. Edit the newly created GPO. Navigate to the **Computer Configuration | Windows Settings | Security Settings node** and right-click it. From the context menu, select **Import Policy**, as shown in Figure 2.4. Select the desired policy—in this case, securedc.inf template.

8. Looking at the settings in the GPO, now you can see that the settings have been loaded into the GPO.

Figure 2.4 Importing the Template

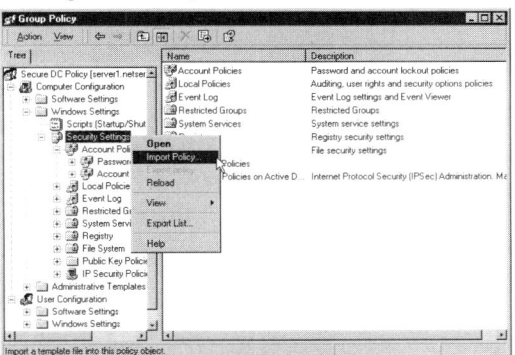

9. Close the **Group Policy** editing window and the **Active Directory Users and Computers** console.
10. To force policy replication immediately, use the **secedit /refreshpolicy machine_policy** command from the command line as discussed previously in Chapter 1. Note that it can take several minutes to several hours for the changes to replicate, depending on the size and complexity of your network.

By applying the securedc.inf template, you made the following changes to the security configuration of the domain controllers in your network:

- Stronger password, account lockout, and auditing settings
- Servers (including domain controllers) configured to ignore LAN Manager responses and to use only NTLMv2 responses
- Users in the domain will not be able to connect to any member server from a client computer using LAN Manager (Windows 9*x* without the Directory Services Client Pack installed)
- SMB packet signing configured, providing a higher level of security

Should you desire to strengthen your domain controller security even further, you can optionally apply the hisecdc.inf security template. As mentioned earlier, the Security Operations for Windows 2000 Server, located at www.microsoft.com/technet/security/prodtech/windows/windows2000/staysecure/default.asp, has some additional configuration changes you can make to domain controllers, including a custom domain controller policy. The same is true for the National Security Agency (Big Brother really *is* watching over your shoulder now!) at http://nsa1.www.conxion.com/win2k/index.html. One last thing you can do to secure your Windows 2000 domain controllers is to ensure that they are always up to date with the latest service packs and hotfixes.

Exam Warning

Pay special attention to the details that you are given to work with during the exam, especially when you have to choose between several similar options or an option that will produce undesired results. You especially need to pay attention when you're applying secure templates to your servers and domain controllers.

Member Servers

Member servers are the most frequently attacked targets on a typical Windows 2000 network. This should come as no surprise when you consider the number of different roles that a member server can play, including, but not limited to:

- SQL server
- Exchange server
- IIS server (Web, FTP, and NNTP)
- File server
- Print server
- RRAS server
- IAS server

The true difficulty in locking down all your servers is in understanding the different nuances and peculiarities associated with each server. Unfortunately gone are the days when one set of configuration settings was good enough and could be applied evenly across the network. Between flaws in the code and malicious attackers seeking to gain entrance through any means possible, your member servers really require the most work of any computers on your network when it comes to protecting them.

Windows 2000 ships with several security templates for workstations, as you saw in Chapter 1. The securews.inf and hisecws.inf templates can be used on member servers of all types (and workstations for that matter) to tighten up the basic security that is installed by default with the basicsv.inf template. However, specific server roles require additional security measures, even beyond using these two incremental security templates. Microsoft has recognized this need and provided additional templates for several different types of member servers, including Exchange servers and IIS servers; the NSA has done the same thing for generic member servers and IAS servers.

SQL Server 2000

The starting point for securing a SQL Server 2000 installation is to ensure that you've got your SQL server up to date with the latest service pack and hotfixes. At the time of this writing, Windows 2000 Service Pack 3 and SQL Server 2000 Service Pack 2 were the latest available. After applying the latest service packs, it is strongly recommended that you download and run the IIS Lockdown tool from www.microsoft.com/Downloads/Release.asp?ReleaseID=33961 and the Microsoft Baseline Security Analyzer (MSBA) from http://support.microsoft.com/default.aspx?scid=kb;en-us;Q320454&sd=tech. No one has publicly released a specific security template for SQL servers, so it's up to you to ensure that you have done all your homework on that front.

Notes from the Underground...

Buffer Overrun Heaven

SQL Server 2000 has become rather famous over the last year or two for the seemingly endless string of buffer overruns it has suffered. A *buffer* in a program is a place that the developer has set aside for the temporary storage of incoming or outgoing data, much like your e-mail in-box. Items come in and then can be distributed as required. A *buffer overrun* occurs when more data is put into a buffer than it was designed to hold. The problem lies in the fact that the extra data will continue to write over the next blocks of memory, erasing the contents that were there. This becomes a security issue when an attacker can successfully deliver a string of data that is sufficiently long to start overwriting memory areas where the program expects to find valid code. Instead, the application unknowingly executes carefully crafted code that the attacker had placed into the server's memory using a buffer overflow.

What makes buffer overflows particularly dangerous and difficult to control? A large application can have literally thousands if not tens of thousands of buffers, and any one of them is subject to a programming error that is just waiting to be exploited.

Exercise 2.02 walks you through the process of running the IIS Lockdown tool on an SQL server; Exercise 2.03 tackles running the MSBA against the SQL server.

EXERCISE 2.02

LOCKING DOWN SQL SERVER WITH THE IIS LOCKDOWN TOOL

1. Download and execute the IIS Lockdown tool locally on the SQL server computer.

2. Click **Next** to dismiss the Wizard opening page.
3. Agree to the license agreement and click **Next** to continue. (You won't be able to continue without agreeing to the license.)
4. Its safe to say that about 99 percent of SQL servers have no need to have IIS services running. Therefore, you can select the **Server that does not require IIS** option from the Select Server Template page as shown in Figure 2.5. Click **Next** to continue.

Figure 2.5 Selecting the Type of Server to Lock Down

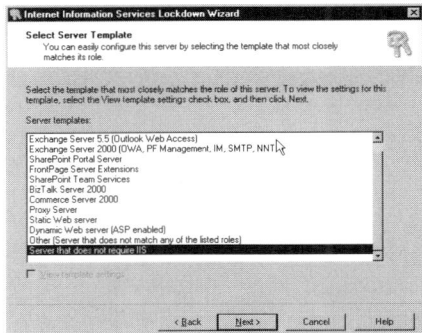

5. On the next page, you will be presented with a summary of the actions to be carried out. In this case, all IIS services will be stopped and disabled on the SQL server. Click **Next** when you are ready to continue.
6. You can watch the progress of the tool, as shown in Figure 2.6.

Figure 2.6 The IIS Lockdown Tool Making Configuration Changes

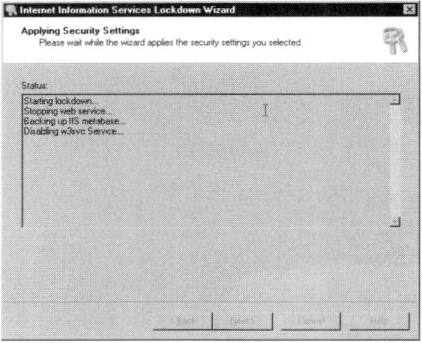

7. After the IIS Lockdown tool has finished, click **Next** and then **Finish** to close the wizard. You have now taken the first step in securing an SQL Server 2000 computer by disabling all IIS services.

After you've done the initial groundwork of running the IIS Lockdown tool against your SQL server, the next thing you should consider doing is to perform a scan of the SQL server using the MBSA tool. The results of the scan will enable you to further harden the server against attacks.

EXERCISE 2.03

HARDENING THE SQL SERVER WITH THE MICROSOFT BASELINE SECURITY ANALYZER

1. Download and install the Microsoft Baseline Security Analyzer onto the SQL server computer. (Alternatively, you can run it from any computer in the domain.)
2. Launch the MSBA tool and click **Scan a computer**.
3. Enter the computer information as required on the **Pick a computer to scan** page (see Figure 2.7) and click **Start scan**. By default, all selectable options are selected, although if you desire, you can deselect them, which will result in a less than optimal scan and is not recommended.

Figure 2.7 Configuring the Scan Parameters

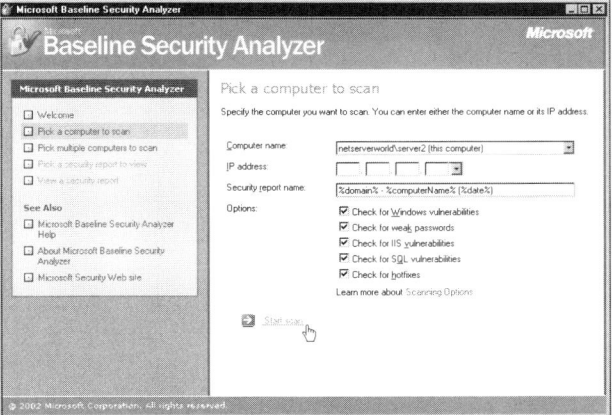

4. The scan can take several minutes to complete, depending on the particular computer being scanned. If you are asked to install any downloads as shown in Figure 2.8, you need to allow the install to proceed in order to complete the scan.
5. When the MBSA tool has finished, you will receive a formatted HTML output like that shown in Figure 2.9. As you can see, we have quite a bit of work to do to harden this server in several categories.

Figure 2.8 Installing Required Updates

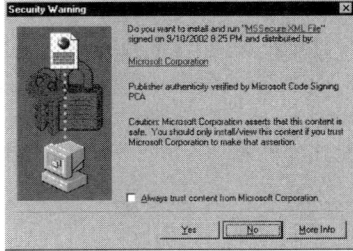

Figure 2.9 Getting the MBSA Scan Results

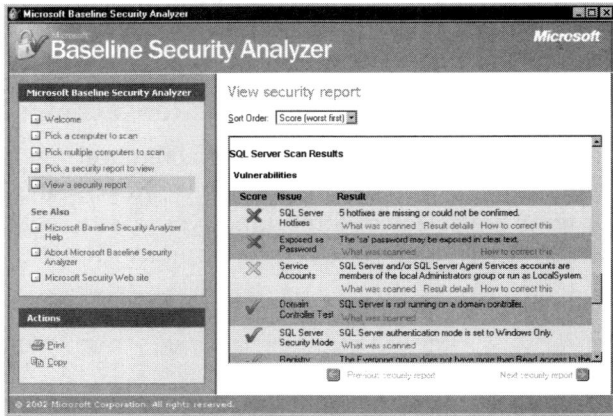

As you can see, the bulk of the process of securing an SQL server is to ensure that it is properly updated in regard to service packs and hotfixes. After this has been done, you can use the IIS Lockdown tool and the MBSA tool to further harden the server. As part of the ongoing maintenance of your SQL servers, you should make a point to run the HFNetChk tool at least weekly. You can get the tool at www.microsoft.com/technet/security/tools/tools/hfnetchk.asp. Exercise 2.04 walks you through using the HFNetChk tool to scan your SQL server.

EXERCISE 2.04

ROUTINE MAINTENANCE WITH THE HFNETCHK TOOL

1. Download and install the HFNetChk from www.microsoft.com/technet/security/tools/tools/hfnetchk.asp onto the SQL server computer.

(Alternatively, you can run it from any computer in the domain if you will be using it as part of a script.)

2. Open a command prompt and change to the location of the extracted HFNetChk files on your computer.
3. Enter the **hfnetchk** command.
4. If you are asked to install any downloads, you need to allow the install to proceed in order to complete the scan.
5. The results are presented on screen as shown in Figure 2.10. Again, we have a lot of work do here. Alternatively, you can save the results of the scan to a text file by using the command **hfnetchk –f filename.txt**. This step can be particularly helpful when you are using the tool as part of a script across several computers.

Figure 2.10 Getting the HFNetChk Results

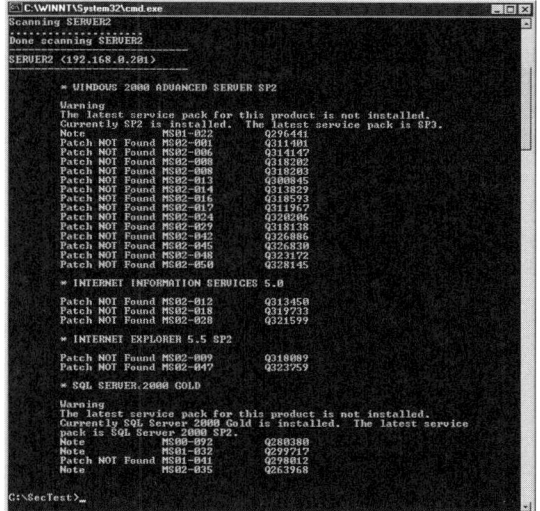

Exchange 2000 Server

The process of securing Exchange 2000 servers is almost identical to that of securing SQL 2000 Server computers. You need to ensure that the most up-to-date service packs and hotfixes are applied to your domain controllers, Exchange 2000 servers, and Global Catalog servers. As of this writing, both Windows 2000 and Exchange 2000 Server are in Service Pack 3. Exchange 2000 Conferencing Server is in Service Pack 2.

After you have applied all required updates and fixes, you should then proceed to follow the same process as outlined for SQL servers: first running IIS Lockdown tool, then running the MBSA tool, and lastly running the HFNetChk tool. The procedures for using the MBSA and HFNetChk tools are identical to those outlined in Exercises 2.3 and 2.4, respectively. Because Exchange 2000 Server makes extensive use of IIS, the process to run the IIS Lockdown tool is different and is discussed in Exercise 2.05.

EXERCISE 2.05

LOCKING DOWN EXCHANGE SERVER WITH THE IIS LOCKDOWN TOOL

1. Download and execute the IIS Lockdown tool locally on the SQL server computer.
2. Click **Next** to dismiss the wizard opening page.
3. Agree to the license agreement and click **Next** to continue. (You won't be able to continue without agreeing to the license.)
4. Select the **Exchange 2000 Server** option from the Select Server Template page, as shown in Figure 2.11. If you want to manually configure the IIS services that get disabled and those that stay available, place a check in the **View template settings** check box. Click **Next** to continue.

Figure 2.11 Selecting the Type of Server to Lock Down

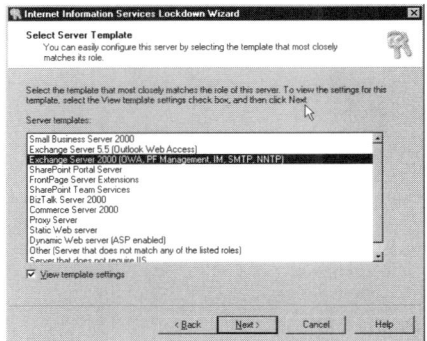

5. On the next page, you be presented with a listing of the services to leave running on the server (see Figure 2.12). The role of the Exchange 2000 server will determine which services you need to leave running. For example, if you do not use newsgroups on your internal network, you can safely disable the NNTP service. If you are not using Outlook Web Access, you can also safely disable the HTTP service. Click **Next** when you are ready to continue.

Figure 2.12 Selecting the Services

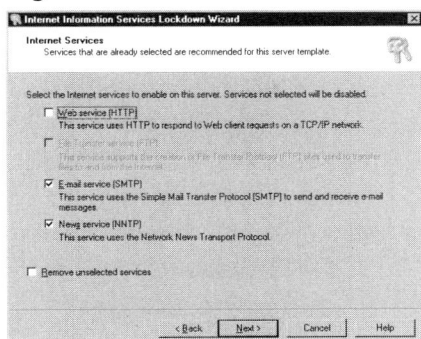

6. Depending on what services you leave running, the next few pages you see will vary. Configure your selections and click **Next** to continue through the pages.

7. After the IIS Lockdown tool has finished, click **Next** and then **Finish** to close the wizard. You have now taken the first step in securing an SQL Server 2000 computer by disabling all IIS services.

Additionally, the Security Operations for Windows 2000 Server, located at www.microsoft.com/technet/security/prodtech/windows/windows2000/staysecure/default.asp, has two customized security policies that you should consider applying to your Exchange 2000 servers. Exchange BackEnd Incremental.inf for back-end Exchange 2000 Servers (the ones not typically requiring HTTP) and OWA FrontEnd Incremental.inf for front-end Exchange 2000 Servers acting as Outlook Web Access servers are provided and should be implemented across all your Exchange 2000 servers as appropriate.

Windows 2000 Internet Information Services Servers

Perhaps the most commonly attacked and the most difficult Windows 2000 member server to secure is the IIS server. Let's face it—whenever you are voluntarily putting information into an untrusted public network like the Internet, you are opening yourself to attacks from all directions. There really is no way to dispute this fact. You can, however, take positive steps toward securing your IIS servers to prevent them from being attacked and compromised, possibly opening the door to the rest of your network.

To start, you should again make a point of ensuring that you have the latest service pack and hotfixes on all IIS servers. After that, you should perform the following sequence of actions, in this order:

1. Run the URLScan tool (see Exercise 2.06). The URLScan tool is an ISAPI filter that is installed at the global level (protecting an entire IIS server) and analyzes HTTP requests as they are received by IIS.
2. Run the IIS Lockdown tool (see Exercise 2.07).
3. Check for any current IIS updates at www.microsoft.com/technet/security/current.asp.
4. Follow the guidelines of the Secure Internet Information Services 5 Checklist at www.microsoft.com/technet/security/tools/chklist/iis5chk.asp (see Exercise 2.08).
5. Run the MBSA tool.
6. Run the HFNetChk tool.

EXERCISE 2.06

LOCKING DOWN IIS SERVERS WITH THE URLSCAN TOOL

1. Download the IIS Lockdown tool to the IIS computer of concern.
2. Open a command prompt and switch to the location of the **iislockd.exe** file.
3. Enter **iislockd /c** to extract the IIS Lockdown files, including the URLScan tool, to the directory of your choosing, as shown in Figure 2.13.

   Figure 2.13 Selecting the Location for the Extracted IIS Lockdown Files

   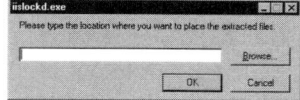

4. Execute the **URLScan tool** from the location to which you extracted it.
5. URLScan will configure your server to be more secure by limiting the types of methods that can be used (such as GET and POST) and the extensions that are allowed and disallowed. The settings are stored in the %windir%\system32\inetsrv\URLScan directory in the urlscan.ini file. A log called urlscan.log is also maintained in that location.
6. Looking at the global properties for the IIS server (see Figure 2.14), you can see the URLScan ISAPI filter is installed with high priority. Note that ISAPI filters installed at the global level, although still applying to all sites on the server, will not be shown in the Properties page for each virtual server.

Figure 2.14 URLScan Is Active and Protecting the IIS Server

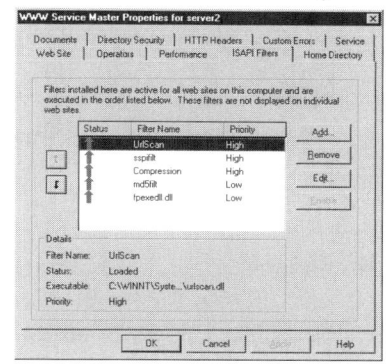

After applying the URLScan ISAPI filter to your IIS server, the next step you need to take is to lock down the IIS server with the IIS Lockdown tool. The procedure to do this task is similar to that of the other servers you might have used IIS Lockdown on, but you should pay attention to some additional configuration options to ensure that you get your IIS server locked down exactly as you need it, with minimal loss of functionality. Exercise 2.07 discusses the procedure to lock down a dynamic (ASP) IIS server using IIS Lockdown.

Damage & Defense...

The Importance of Updating IIS

For several years now, vulnerabilities have been identified in the way that IIS handles Unicode translation. This situation has prompted quite a few security bulletins from Microsoft, yet administrators in many cases simply keep moving along, paying no attention to the problems that exist on their systems. Why do most of the Windows 2000 systems that are compromised get compromised? The reason is failure of administrators and other IT personnel to ensure that their systems are secure and up to date with all required patches and hotfixes.

One of the most famous IIS Unicode exploits was first announced in Security Bulletin MS00-078 and involved the way that IIS interpreted the Unicode equivalents of the forward slash and backslash characters (/ and \). Because IIS did not correctly interpret the Unicode equivalents of these characters, an attack could traverse directories on the server by using the double dot (../). For this reason, an attack could access files stored locally on the server in the context of the IUSR_*computername* account, which is a built-in

Continued

account on IIS servers that is a member of the Everyone and Users groups by default—files that they should not and normally would not be able to access otherwise. By sending a malformed URL to the IIS server, such as http://target/scripts/..%c1%1c../winnt/system32/cmd.exe?/c+dir, an attacker can get out of the Web root directory and modify and delete files on the IIS server and otherwise wreak havoc on the server. In this case, Microsoft released both the URLScan tool and a hotfix that is available at www.microsoft.com/windows2000/downloads/critical/q269862/default.asp. Of course, if you have since applied Service Pack 2 or Service Pack 3, this fix is included.

This type of vulnerability is not the first nor will it be the last to be discovered and exploited in a Windows product. Your best course of action is to always keep up to date on new developments in the security field. The Security Focus Online Web site, at http://online.securityfocus.com/, is a good starting point, as is the NTBugTraq located at www.ntbugtraq.com. Nowhere is it more true that knowledge is power than when we're dealing with computer security.

EXAM WARNING

It's important to understand how URLScan works to protect your IIS servers against many common types of exploits and vulnerabilities. More so, you should understand how to customize a URLScan installation to allow or disallow specific types of traffic as your organizational needs dictate.

EXERCISE 2.07

LOCKING DOWN IIS SERVERS WITH THE IIS LOCKDOWN TOOL

1. Download and execute the IIS Lockdown tool locally on the IIS server computer.
2. Click **Next** to dismiss the Wizard opening page.
3. Agree to the license agreement and click **Next** to continue. (You won't be able to continue without agreeing to the license.)
4. Select the **Dynamic Web Server (ASP enabled)** option from the Select Server Template page, as shown in Figure 2.15. Since we are going to examine all the available options when configuring the server using IIS

Lockdown, place a check in the **View template settings** check box. Click **Next** to continue.

Figure 2.15 Selecting the Type of Server to Lock Down

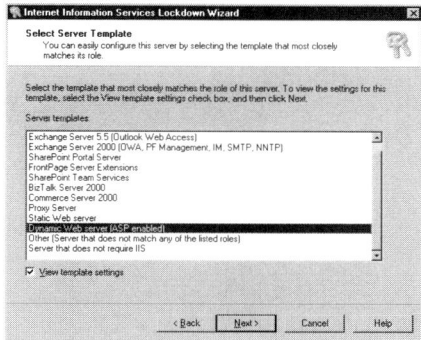

5. On the Internet Services page (see Figure 2.16), you have the option to configure the services that will remain running on the IIS server. In most cases, you only need HTTP, and that is the presumption that we use to continue the rest of the process. After selecting **Web service (HTTP)**, click **Next** to continue.

Figure 2.16 Selecting Services to Remain Enabled

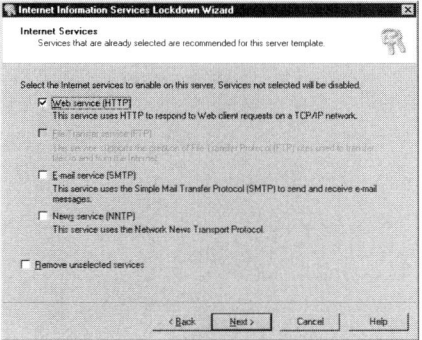

6. On the Script Maps page (see Figure 2.17), you are asked to choose types of scripting you will allow on the IIS server. Since this is a server that has dynamic ASP content, we need to uncheck at least ASP. Other commonly used scripting includes Server Side Includes (SSI) SHMTL, SHTM, and STM. After making your choices, click **Next** to continue.

7. The Additional Security page (see Figure 2.18) presents you with some even more granular configuration options to increase the security of the IIS server. The ones you choose to leave enabled depend on exactly

what you are doing with the IIS server. For example, if you need to allow users to edit and save documents remotely using applications such as Microsoft Word or Microsoft Excel, you would leave WebDAV enabled. After making your choices, click **Next** to continue.

Figure 2.17 Configuring Script Mapping

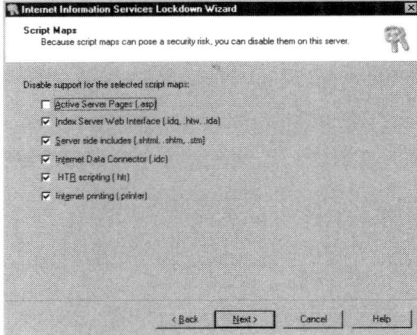

Figure 2.18 Configuring Additional Security Options for the IIS Server

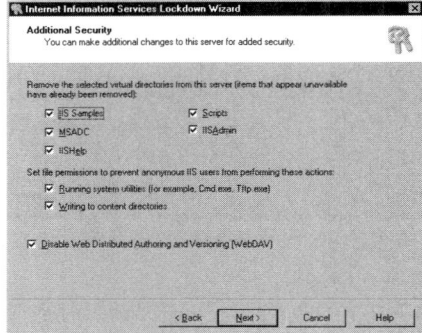

8. The next page, the URLScan page, asks you if you want to install the URLScan ISAPI filter. If you have not already done so (as outlined in the previous exercise), select **URLScan** to be installed. Otherwise, deselect it. After making your choice, click **Next** to continue.

9. The Ready to Apply Settings page (see Figure 2.19) summarizes the choices you have made. If all is well, click **Next** to continue or click **Back** to change the settings you have configured.

10. The Applying Security Settings page informs you as to the progress of the configuration changes. When all the changes have been made, click **Next** to continue. If you want a more detailed report, click the **View Report** button to open the log file.

11. Click **Finish** to close the IIS Lockdown tool.

Figure 2.19 Ready to Apply Settings

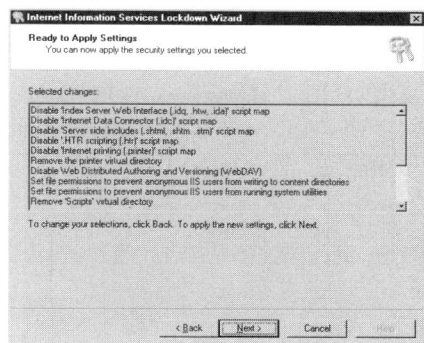

At this time, your IIS server is fairly secure, but more work still remains to be done. You should now check for current (and outstanding) IIS updates that your IIS server might need to have applied. Do this by checking the security homepage on TechNET at www.microsoft.com/technet/security/current.asp. After you've checked the homepage—a task that you should repeat monthly, if not more often—you can move to the next step in the process of locking down your IIS server.

Realizing the strong need for guidance on securing IIS, Microsoft has provided several guides to help you go about getting your IIS server as secure as it can be. The Secure Internet Information Services 5 Checklist at www.microsoft.com/technet/security/tools/chklist/iis5chk.asp is an excellent guide that should be used by any administrator running IIS on a server.

Microsoft has created two customized security templates for IIS servers. The one you use depends on your needs and how your IIS server responds after you've tested the template in a lab environment. The Security Operations for Windows 2000 Server, located at www.microsoft.com/technet/security/prodtech/windows/windows2000/staysecure/default.asp, provides a baseline incremental template called IIS incremental.inf that you might consider applying. Should you find that the settings in this template are not quite secure enough for you, you can find another, more secure template located at http://support.microsoft.com/default.aspx?scid=kb;en-us;Q316347 that Microsoft designed to completely secure IIS servers. Do not apply this template to a domain controller running IIS; unexpected and unwanted things will most certainly happen. In addition, as with all templates and configuration changes, you should first thoroughly test this one in a safe lab environment to determine how your IIS applications will respond once it has been applied.

Test Day Tip

You need not worry about seeing any questions dealing with these custom-created IIS templates or the IIS check list. These resources are provided for your use so that you can lock down your IIS servers as much as possible beyond what is included in Windows 2000 by default.

Head of the Class…

Watch Where You Assign Blame

It really cannot be stressed enough how vulnerable your IIS servers are if you take no proactive action at all. It might not be completely fair to say that Windows 2000 is a hacker's favorite target, but it is not far from the truth. The issue lies not in the fact that Windows 2000 is an inherently insecure operating system, as many would like to believe; all applications, operating systems included, are likely to have flaws and problems. This holds true of Windows, UNIX, Linux, MAC OS, and every other operating system and application in production.

The true problem lies in the fact that many administrators simply do not understand or care to understand the necessity of keeping servers and workstations up to date with new patches and updates as they appear. Some of the fixes are put out because of programming errors that could have been prevented, but a good many of them are released in response to newly discovered attacks and vulnerabilities in the product. No product is perfect, software included, and thus people who have the means and the desire will continue to find ways to penetrate systems. Your job is to stay up to date with the fixes and updates that are issued and ensure that they are tested and deployed in a timely, organized fashion. Anything less equates to sleeping at the wheel.

After you've completed all the previous steps, you are still not quite out of the woods. Now you are in maintenance mode. You should take the time to run the MBSA tool against your IIS server to see if anything has been missed, such as a weak password or a user account that should not be enabled. You'd be amazed at the things that you can miss when configuring an IIS server. Your last, and ongoing, step should be to run HFNetChk against the server to ensure that you really have gotten all the Ts crossed and the Is dotted.

Windows 2000 Internet Access Service Servers

Internet Access Servers (IAS) should be treated the same as most other member servers. You need to look at the same things to maintain the server in its most secure form:

- Up-to-date service packs and hotfixes
- IIS Lockdown tool

- MBSA tool
- HFNetChk tool

>
> **TEST DAY TIP**
>
> You shouldn't expect to receive any specific types of questions dealing specifically with IAS servers on your exam. Rather, you need just to understand the basic concepts that we have been discussing throughout this chapter in regard to the fact that each member server is different from every other member server, and no two member server roles should be approached from the same point of view when it comes to configuring security.

Creating Secure Workstations

Until now we have spent a lot of time looking at how to secure our servers. But what about all those client computers on the network? In this section we examine some of the actions you can take to ensure that your workstations are secure and contribute to the overall security level of your entire network.

Client (workstation) computers can be categorized in two large groups: They are either desktop workstations (and hence not portable) or they are portable (laptop) computers and hence easily removed from the safe confines of your network. Later in this section, we examine extra precautions that can be taken for portable computers.

Desktop Workstations

It should come as no surprise that the first and most important thing you can do to increase the security of desktop clients is to ensure that they are up to date with all required service packs and hotfixes. Chapter 3 examines this process in great detail. Although this might sound like a small matter, don't make the mistake of thinking that it is; once you've identified and downloaded the required updates, you must test them in lab before deploying them.

After the deployment, you must ensure that all updates were received as required and then start the entire process again. There are some means in place (as we discuss in Chapter 3) to make this process an easier one, but none of them ever relieve you, the administrator, of your responsibility to ensure that the required updates are being applied to the appropriate computers.

Both Microsoft and the National Institute of Standards and Technology (NIST) have put forth some guidelines on creating more secure desktop clients. You can view these guidelines at:

- http://csrc.nist.gov/itsec/guidance_W2Kpro.html
- www.microsoft.com/technet/security/tools/chklist/dsktpsec.asp

The NIST information includes a security template that you can apply to your workstations. Alternatively, you can use the securews.inf and hisecws.inf templates included in Windows 2000.

Note
The additional reference material found at these links is not something you will be expected to know about come test day; it is provided for your own reference. Using this extra information, you can best protect your network from attackers.

A full discussion of the multitude of things you can do to secure a workstation is beyond the scope of this chapter, but we do examine a few things you can do in an effort to secure your workstations:

- Apply all required service packs and hotfixes (as previously mentioned).
- Apply a more secure template than the basicwk.inf template.
- Remove the local computer Recovery Agent keys.

We examine the ways to apply service packs and hotfixes in more detail in Chapter 3. Analyzing and configuring computers using the Security Configuration Tool Set was discussed in great detail in Chapter 1. Removing the local computer Recovery Agent keys is fairly straightforward—but it must be done correctly. Removing these keys will prevent users (authorized or not) from being able to use the local computer Recovery Agent to decrypt files that have been encrypted with the Encrypting File System (EFS). Exercise 2.08 presents this process.

EXERCISE 2.08
REMOVING THE LOCAL COMPUTER RECOVERY AGENT KEYS

1. Log into the local computer (not the domain) using the built-in Administrator account—not an account that is a member of the Administrators group.
2. Open the **Local Security Policy** console from the Administrative Tools folder. If the console is missing, enter **secpol.msc** from a command line to open it.

3. Expand the **Public Key Policies** node and open the **Encrypted Data Recovery Agents** folder, as shown in Figure 2.20.

Figure 2.20 Finding the Data Recovery Agent

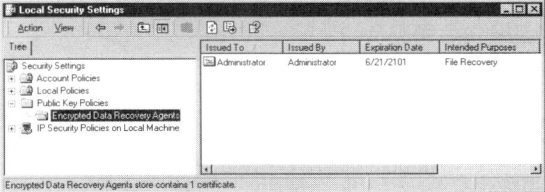

4. Right-click the **Administrator** File Recovery certificate and select **All Tasks | Export** from the context menu, as shown in Figure 2.21.

Figure 2.21 Exporting the Administrator File Recovery Certificate and Keys

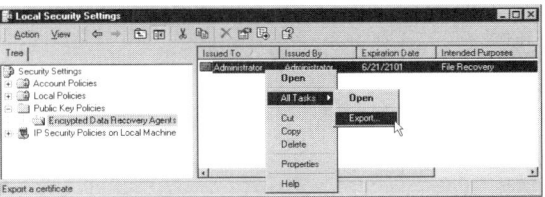

5. Click **Next** to dismiss the Certificate Export Wizard opening page.
6. Select **Yes, export the private key**, and then click **Next** to continue.
7. Select the **Delete the private key if the export is successful** check box to remove the private key (see Figure 2.22). Click **Next** to continue.

Figure 2.22 Deleting the Private Key

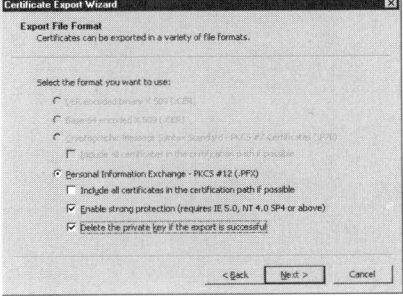

8. Enter and confirm a password that will be used to secure the exported key, and click **Next** to continue.

9. Enter the filename and path for the exported key file to be saved to. Click **Next** to continue.
10. The Completing the Certificate Export Wizard is displayed (see Figure 2.23). Verify that the settings are correct, and click **Finish** to export the certificate and keys to the selected file.

    Figure 2.23 Completing the Certificate Export Wizard Summarizes Your Actions

11. Click **OK** to close the wizard.
12. Restart the computer to complete the process.
13. You should now place the certificate file in a secure location, such as a safe or secure off-site storage facility, to keep it from falling into the wrong hands.

After ensuring that you have done the big three items in desktop security (updates and hotfixes, security templates, and exporting the Recovery Agent certificate), you can begin to look at the other things you can do to keep a workstation secure. Things such as keeping antivirus software up to date and other changes to the operating system, such as those recommended by NIST, can all go a long way toward creating more secure workstations.

 **EXAM WARNING**

Don't worry about the exact particulars of exporting the certificate; you should know where it's done from and why it's done. You should also be able recognize situations, when presented with them, in which you would want to export a certificate and its private keys.

Be aware, though, that no increase in security comes without a corresponding decrease in usability, with the most secure workstations being almost completely unusual. Of course, this type of thought process has been used for many years quite successfully by thin-client workstations that posses almost no capability of their own and instead must rely on a server for almost everything. With careful testing and analysis, you will discover the settings and configuration that provide you the ideal balance between security and usability.

Portable Computers

Portable computers present all the same security problems as desktops—and then some. You, at a minimum, must perform all the same actions for portable computers that you would for desktop computers. You might even want to take your precautions further for your portable computers. A good rule of thumb in seeking to secure portable computers is to limit the amount of sensitive data that they contain. Allow users to place on their portables only what they absolutely must take out of the security of your building. Enforcing the use of EFS on all files on portable computers will also go a long way toward making them more secure. Some other things that you can consider to make your portable computers more secure are:

- Do not save passwords for RAS or VPN connections; make users enter the passwords each time.
- Use the BIOS password so that it must be successfully entered before Windows will even get to the boot sequence.
- Rename the built-in Administrator account and remove it from the Administrators group. (Note that you cannot actually delete this account.)
- Assign very strong passwords to all accounts, especially the account being used for Local Administrative access.

Head of the Class...

Protect That Laptop

Although a discussion of how to do so is beyond the scope of this exam, moving all your portable computer users to Windows XP could prove to be a very good idea. One feature of Windows XP—the ability to encrypt offline folders and files—makes it particularly attractive to portable computer users.

Of course, there are downsides to rolling out Windows XP on portable computers. Windows XP makes it impossible to control many of the properties of wireless LAN cards (known as *profiles*) that you can control in Windows 2000. Windows XP also adds the odd behavior that users can still

Continued

www.syngress.com

> encrypt files on the local computer even after the Data Recovery Agent has been removed—something that is not allowed in Windows 2000. This is not an issue when you have Windows XP computers in a Windows .NET Server 2003 domain, because changes to the Certificate Services in .NET Server 2003 make this change in Windows XP a nonissue.

Obviously, you can do many other things to make more secure portable computers. The bottom line is that you take proactive measures to protect your laptops should they be lost or stolen.

Security Template Application Issues

Troubleshooting security settings can sometimes become a difficult process. Because security settings can be applied by both direct template application and by Group Policy, it is important to accurately determine all Group Policy objects that have been applied to the particular computer of concern. Before we get into looking at some problems and their solutions, remember that security in Windows 2000 depends on Group Policy. Legacy clients that are not receiving Group Policy will require special considerations.

Upgrade Installations

When computers are upgraded from Windows NT 4.0 to Windows 2000, the Windows NT 4.0 Registry and File System ACLs are not changed. This issue can lead to numerous problems when attempting to apply security templates (and several other security configurations) to these upgraded Windows 2000 computers. Fortunately, there is a fairly easy workaround. If you are having a problem with a computer and you know that it was an upgrade installation from Windows NT 4.0, you have two choices:

- Perform a clean installation of Windows 2000, which is always better than upgrading. User files and settings can be migrated using the User State Migration Tool located at www.microsoft.com/windows2000/techinfo/reskit/tools/new/usmt-o.asp.

- Apply the Setup Security.inf security template using the Security Configuration and Analysis snap-in.

Exercise 2.09 walks through the process of applying the Setup Security.inf template to an upgraded Windows NT 4.0 computer to correct the issue with Registry and File System ACLs. After you have applied this template, you should no longer have problems applying security templates unless you have other issues at hand. If all else fails, consider performing a clean installation on upgraded computers to remove this and any other issues the upgrade could cause.

EXERCISE 2.09

APPLYING THE SETUP SECURITY TEMPLATE

1. Create a Security Console, as discussed in Exercise 1.01 of Chapter 1.
2. Right-click **Security Configuration and Analysis** and select **Open database** from the context menu.
3. Enter a name for the database and click **Open**.
4. From the Import Template dialog box, select the **Setup Security.inf** security template, and then click **Open**.
5. Right-click **Security Configuration and Analysis** and select **Analyze computer now** from the context menu.
6. You can now look over the differences between the upgrade computers settings and those of the security template.
7. Make any changes to the settings of the database that you desire.
8. When you are ready to apply the database settings (the values of Setup Security.inf template and any changes you have made) to the upgraded computer, right-click **Security Configuration and Analysis** and select **Configure computer now** from the context menu.

Legacy Client Issues

Legacy clients cannot receive Group Policy settings, and thus they cannot receive the security configurations you have so carefully crafted for them. The most integration that legacy clients can hope to achieve is realized by installing the Directory Services (DS) client. The client for Windows 95 and 98 is located on the Windows 2000 Server CD-ROM in the CLIENTS\WIN9X directory. The client for Windows NT 4.0 can be downloaded from www.microsoft.com/windows2000/server/evaluation/news/bulletins/adextension.asp. The client is neither provided nor supported for Windows Millennium Edition.

Using the DS client, your legacy computer can achieve the following basic Active Directory capabilities:

- Use NTLMv2, which provides for improved security and authentication. This also allows these clients to interact with Windows 2000 computers running a stronger security policy that enforces NTLMv2-only connections.
- The ability to log into the closest Windows 2000 domain controller.
- The ability to change network passwords on any Windows 2000 domain controller.
- The ability to allow access to the Windows 2000 Distributed File System (DFS) fault-tolerant shares specified in Active Directory.

Should you need to apply a security (or any other custom) configuration to your legacy clients, you will need to use System Policies and the System Policy Editor. For more information on creating System Policies for your legacy clients, see http://support.microsoft.com/default.aspx?scid=KB;EN-US;Q318753.

Using Gpresult.exe

You can also use of gpresult.exe tool that comes with the Windows 2000 Resource Kit to gather information on the Group Policy objects that have been applied to a specific computer, the security groups the computer is a part of, and where its security settings are coming from. The gpresult.exe tool can be quite useful in troubleshooting Group Policy issues, but working with it takes some time to get used to—as is true with most command-line tools. You can get the gpresult.exe tool at www.microsoft.com/windows2000/techinfo/reskit/tools/default.asp.

TEST DAY TIP

Although very useful, questions regarding tools from the Resource Kit are not likely to be found on your exam. Does this make learning how to use them less useful? No. These are the tools that you have at your disposal in real life when things go wrong. Just because they're not covered on the test should not weigh heavily in your decision to learn how to work with these tools.

Event Log Entries

By default, the Event Log records errors that occur on your Windows 2000 computers. If you attempt to track down issues with security applications through Group Policy but cannot find any problems, you can configure Active Directory diagnostic event logging to assist you in your search.

By default, only critical or error events are logged in the Event Log. You can, however, change these settings to suit your needs. Doing such requires editing the Registry and is not recommended for those who are unfamiliar with directly editing the Registry. A normal Event Log entry is shown in Figure 2.24. If all is well, this is the only type of entry you ever see in your Event Logs.

Figure 2.24 Event ID 1704: All Is Well

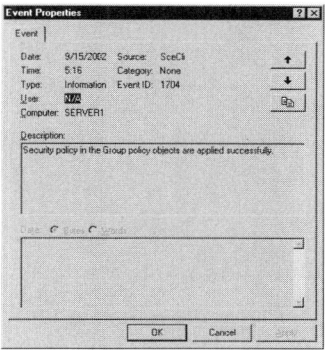

Diagnostic logging of Active Directory events is controlled by the following Registry subkey: HKEY_LOCAL_MACHINE\SYSTEM\CurrentControlSet\Services\NTDS\Diagnostics. Under this subkey, you can configure logging for the following 19 areas:

- Knowledge Consistency Checker (KCC)
- Security events
- ExDS Interface events
- MAPI events
- Replication events
- Garbage collection
- Internal configuration
- Directory access
- Internal processing
- Performance counters
- Initialization/termination
- Service control
- Name resolution
- Backup
- Field engineering

- LDAP interface events
- Setup
- Global Catalog
- Intersite messaging

Each entry can be assigned a value from 0 through 5. The configured value determines the amount of detail that will be logged. The six logging levels are:

- **0 (None)** This is the default level, where only critical events and errors events are logged.
- **1 (Minimal)** You should use this setting to start an investigation into problems you are experiencing.
- **2 (Basic)** This logging level adds more detailed information to the Event Logs but is not as extensive as the next levels.
- **3 (Extensive)** At this level, much logging about an event occurs, such as the steps that are performed to complete a task. This level should be used when you have narrowed down your troubleshooting to a few specific areas.
- **4 (Verbose)** This logging level provides more information than the previous level but not as much as the highest level of logging.
- **5 (Internal)** This logging level records all events. This setting should be used only when you have narrowed down the problem to a specific area, because this level will produce a large number of entries in the Event Log.

Test Day Tip

Don't expect to be tested on low-level diagnostic logging. It is presented here for your reference in the event you should need it if you have problems on your network.

The process of configuring diagnostic logging is presented in Exercise 2.10.

EXERCISE 2.10

ANALYZING SECURITY ISSUES WITH THE EVENT LOGS

1. Open the Registry Editor by clicking **Start | Run** and entering **regedit** in the Run box. Click **OK**.

2. Expand to the following registry key (see Figure 2.25): **HKEY_LOCAL_MACHINE\SYSTEM\CurrentControlSet\Services\NTDS\Diagnostics**

Figure 2.25 Editing the Registry to Increase Logging

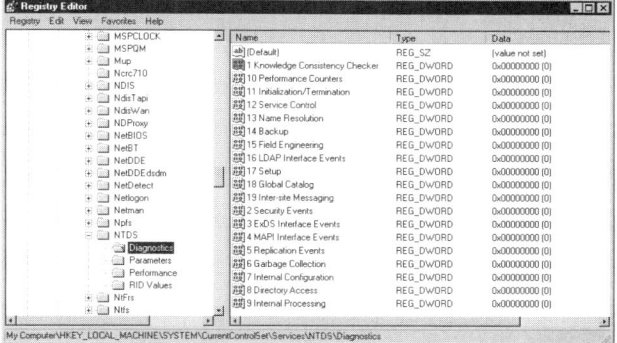

3. To change the logging level for a particular area, double-click the setting and enter the value representing the level of logging you want.
4. Click **File | Exit** to close the Registry Editor after you have completed configuring the settings you require.
5. Monitor the Event Log, looking for entries corresponding to the problem you are trying to track down.

If you need more information on working with the Event Log, see http://support.microsoft.com/default.aspx?scid=kb;en-us;Q302542.

Last Thoughts on Security Templates

Before we move on to the next topic in this chapter, you need to bear in mind two last items concerning security templates when working with them. The first and most important is that you cannot export settings that you have directly configured in a Group Policy object to a template to be applied to other computers. Your best bet is to configure and test templates on a lab computer and then deploy them once you are satisfied they are configured correctly. The second issue that you need to be aware of is that when applied, security templates often make changes that cannot be easily unapplied—meaning that it's not simply a case of installing a software item and then easily uninstalling it. Should you change your mind about the net result after a template has been applied, you could find yourself doing a bit of manual cleanup if you later choose to remove it.

Securing Server Message Block Traffic

The Server Message Block (SMB) authentication protocol provides for mutual authentication, which can help prevent the man-in-the-middle type of attack, and it supports message authentication, which helps prevent message attacks. This security, which is easily configured, is provided by placing a digital signature into each SMB, which is then verified by both the client and the server involved in the communication.

>
>
> **TEST DAY TIP**
>
> Although we discuss the man-in-the-middle attack in more detail in later chapters, a brief explanation is in order here so that you fully understand how securing SMB traffic is something that you want to do. A man-in-the-middle attack occurs when data is intercepted by a third party (an unauthorized attacker), modified, and sent through to the party that was the original recipient. The attacker can thus intercept and modify traffic from both legitimate ends of the connection, in effect driving the connection in the direction he or she wants.

In order for SMB signing to actually work on your network, it must be configured at the same minimum level on both the client and the workstation. You have two basic levels of configuration from which to choose:

- To digitally sign client communication (when possible) and digitally sign server communication (when possible)
- To digitally sign client communication (always) and digitally sign server communication (always)

Table 2.1 presents the default SMB settings that are configured on a server or workstation, depending on the security template that has been implemented on the device.

Table 2.1 SMB Signing Default Settings in Windows 2000 Security Templates

Template	Digitally Sign Client Communication (When Possible)	Digitally Sign Client Communication (Always)	Digitally Sign Server Communication (When Possible)	Digitally Sign Server Communication (Always)
basicdc.inf	Not defined	Not defined	Enabled	Not defined
basicsv.inf	Enabled	Disabled	Disabled	Disabled
basicwk.inf	Enabled	Disabled	Disabled	Disabled
compatws.inf	Not defined	Not defined	Not defined	Not defined
securedc.inf	Enabled	Disabled	Enabled	Disabled

Continued

Table 2.1 SMB Signing Default Settings in Windows 2000 Security Templates

Template	Digitally Sign Client Communication (When Possible)	Digitally Sign Client Communication (Always)	Digitally Sign Server Communication (When Possible)	Digitally Sign Server Communication (Always)
securews.inf	Enabled	Disabled	Enabled	Disabled
hisecdc.inf	Enabled	Enabled	Enabled	Enabled
hisecws.inf	Enabled	Enabled	Enabled	Enabled
setup security.inf	Enabled	Disabled	Disabled	Disabled

If SMB signing is enabled on a server, clients that are also enabled for SMB signing (or require it) will be able to establish a communications session with that server. If SMB signing is required on a server, a client will not be able to establish a session unless the client, at the minimum, has SMB signing enabled.

SMB signing is configured from the **Computer Configuration | Windows Settings | Security Settings | Local Policies | Security Options** node, as shown in Figure 2.26. SMB signing consumes some CPU cycles on any machine on which it is configured. Conservative estimates place this value as high as 15 percent overhead, although the value you can expect to see is largely dependent on the amount of traffic a specific computer receives.

Figure 2.26 Configuring SMB Signing

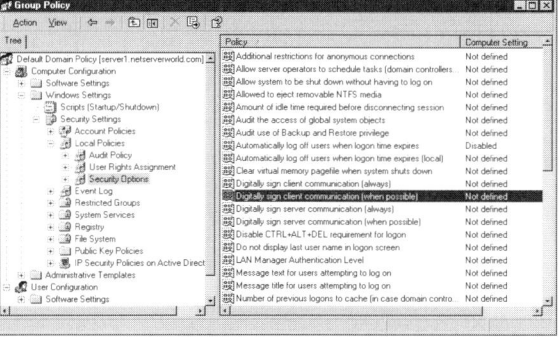

Exam Warning

Make sure that you understand the various configuration options available to you for configuring SMB signing. It's quite easy to get tripped up by not paying attention to what a question is asking when it comes to SMB signing options. You should expect to be asked briefly about SMB signing in some fashion on the exam.

Summary of Exam Objectives

Configuring server security based on its role is a critical step in the security implementation process that you simply cannot overlook. For the longest time, it was simply considered good enough to configure all servers (and most workstations, for that matter) alike when it came to security. This no longer is true.

Fortunately, a number of sources of help are available to you—some from Microsoft, some from respected third parties such as the National Institute of Standards and Technology (NIST) and the National Security Agency (NSA). IIS servers, SQL servers, Exchange servers, IAS servers, file and print servers, and domain controllers all require their own different security configurations. Using specialized security templates (policies) along with hardening tools such as IIS Lockdown, URLScan, the MBSA, and HFNetChk can go a long way toward helping you secure your servers to allow them to perform their functions without leaving them excessively vulnerable to attacks and hostile code implementation.

Desktop workstations and portable client computers also require special security configuration, different from that applied to your servers. Desktop and portable computers should have their Data Recovery Agent certificate and keys removed and placed in a secure storage location, among other things. Implementing specialized (more secure) security templates on these computers is also an option that should be investigated. Of course, keeping all clients up to date with the latest service packs and hotfixes is a critical step in keeping them secure—one that cannot be underestimated. Procuring and deploying updates is discussed in more detail in Chapter 3.

When implementing security in your network, you are likely to run across some problems or issues. Upgraded computers and legacy clients can all lead to problems you were not prepared to deal with. Examining the Event Log and configuring Active Directory diagnostic event logging can help you track down issues with Group Policy applications—and, therefore, security implementation. You also have the gpresult.exe tool at your disposal, which provides a very powerful Group Policy information collection system that can be used from the command line to quickly determine the current state of Group Policy on a target computer.

Although legacy clients cannot receive Group Policy settings, they can still participate in Active Directory in a limited way by use of the Directory Services Client application. Since Group Policy objects are not applied to these clients, you might well want to examine the use of System Policies and the System Policy Editor to configure consistent security and cosmetic settings across these legacy computers.

Server Message Block (SMB) signing can be implemented to prevent the man-in-the-middle attack and message attacks by authenticating both sides of a communications session (server and client) and by also digitally signing the packets. In order for

SMB signing to be effective, both the client and the server must be configured for at least the same minimum setting. Should a server require SMB signing and a client attempting to initiate a connection not at least be enabled for SMB signing, the connection attempt will fail.

Exam Objectives Fast Track

Configuring Role-Based Security

- ☑ Each specific type of Windows 2000 server in your network can, and should be, configured with role-specific security settings. These settings can be implemented in various ways, such as security templates, the IIS Lockdown tool, or the URLScan tool.

- ☑ The IIS Lockdown tool includes a variety of preconfigured templates that can be used to flexibly configure IIS settings on your Windows 2000 servers to prevent them from being easy attack targets.

Creating Secure Workstations

- ☑ Workstations and portable computers should have their Data Recovery Agent certificate and private key exported to a secure location.

- ☑ Portable computers should use the Encrypting File System on all sensitive files. Furthermore, the amount of sensitive material contained on a portable computer should be minimized as much as possible.

Security Template Application Issues

- ☑ Problems with security templates (Group Policy) will usually appear in the Event Log.

- ☑ Logging levels for Directory Service events can be increased to help track down problematic areas with Group Policy.

- ☑ The gpresult.exe tool, available as part of the Windows 2000 Resource Kit, can be used to quickly get extremely detailed information about the security and Group Policy settings in effect on a specific computer.

- ☑ Upgrade installations from Windows NT 4.0 to Windows 2000 can cause problems when applying security templates due to the differences in the

www.syngress.com

Windows NT 4.0 and Windows 2000 Registry and File System ACLs. These are not updated during the operating system upgrade. To remedy this issue, you can either opt to perform a clean install (usually preferred over upgrades) or apply the setup security.inf security template to the upgraded computer using the Security Configuration and Analysis snap-in.

Securing Server Message Block Traffic

- ☑ Server Message Block (SMB) traffic can be digitally signed to prevent man-in-the-middle attacks and message attacks.

- ☑ Both client and server must be configured for at least the same minimum level of SMB signing in order for a session connection attempt to succeed.

- ☑ SMB signing is configured from the **Computer Configuration | Windows Settings | Security Settings | Local Policies | Security Options** node of the Group Policy window. Additionally, you can configure this setting using the various security templates that are provided with Windows 2000.

Exam Objectives Frequently Asked Questions

The following Frequently Asked Questions, answered by the authors of this book, are designed to both measure your understanding of the Exam Objectives presented in this chapter, and to assist you with real-life implementation of these concepts.

Q: How can I apply security settings to my legacy clients?

A: You need to use System Policies with the legacy clients because they cannot use Group Policy objects.

Q: Can't I just configure security settings manually instead of using templates and the other tools available?

A: Yes, you can—it's just not advised that you do it this way. The security templates and tools are provided to make your job easier and to allow you to configure consistent settings across multiple servers.

Q: How does the URLScan ISAPI filter perform its function?

A: The URLScan Security tool inspects all incoming requests to an IIS Web server, allowing only those that comply with the preconfigured rule set to pass. Security of the IIS server is thus increased because it will only respond to valid requests (those that are allowed in the configuration).

Q: Why do I need to export the Data Recovery Agent certificate and private key off my portable computers? If they are lost or stolen, no one will be able to recover any encrypted data without the users' credentials anyway.

A: There are two ways to decrypt EFS encrypted information: using the credentials of the user who encrypted it or using the Data Recovery Agent account, which is the built-in local administrator account by default. Several readily available applications exist that can easily crack passwords in Windows 2000 and, more often than not, the built-in administrative account is the easiest to access. By removing the Data Recovery Agent certificate and private keys, you are giving yourself another layer of security.

Q: What does the Microsoft Baseline Security Analyzer do?

A: The MBSA tool scans the configured computer(s), looking for missing updates, weak passwords, unnecessary user accounts, and various other security concerns. It is used to quickly identify all problematic areas on a computer. After these problems have been corrected, it should be run at least monthly to check for the reoccurrence of any security issues.

Self Test

A Quick Answer Key follows the Self Test questions. For complete questions, answers, and epxlanations to the Self Test questions in this chapter as well as the other chapters in this book, see the Self Test Appendix.

Configuring Role-Based Server Security

1. Chris is having difficulty getting the securews.inf template to apply properly on a client workstation. She suspects that the computer was an upgrade from a previous installation of Windows NT 4.0. What two things can she do to correct this problem?

    A. Perform another upgrade installation of Windows 2000; the first one must not have taken properly.

    B. Apply the setup security.inf template to the computer.

    C. Perform a clean installation of Windows 2000 on the computer.

    D. Enforce the desired security settings using a System Policy.

2. Rob is responsible for six Windows 2000 IIS servers in his organization. What can Rob do to harden his Windows 2000 IIS servers and prevent their vulnerability to attack? (Choose all that apply.)

    A. Use the IIS Lockdown tool to remove unnecessary IIS settings and configuration options.

    B. Use the Movetree tool to set security settings on the IIS server.

    C. Install the URLScan ISAPI filter to prevent certain types of HTTP requests from being served by the IIS server.

    D. Remove his IIS servers from the Active Directory domain and make them standalone member servers.

3. Jeff has just performed a default installation of the URLScan ISAPI filter on his IIS server. Looking at the site that corresponds to his Web site, he cannot see the filter in place. What is the most likely problem?

   A. ISAPI filters are only installed on domain controllers running IIS. Jeff will need to install the ISAPI filter there.

   B. ISAPI filters can only be seen by IIS Admin; Jeff's user account is probably not a member of the IIS Admins group.

   C. Jeff must not have Domain Admin privileges on the network; Domain Admin privileges are required to install any ISAPI filter.

   D. The URLScan ISAPI filter is applied at the global level and is thus not shown at the site level.

4. Andrea is responsible for 25 client workstations and five servers in her Windows 2000 network. Her servers consist of two domain controllers, one Exchange server, and two file and print servers. How many different security configurations should she have on her network, at the minimum?

   A. 30

   B. 5

   C. 4

   D. 2

5. Christopher is making preparations to deploy the hisecdc.inf template to his domain controllers. What things should Christopher do before he deploys this template on his production network? (Choose all that apply.)

   A. Christopher should ensure that he understands the implications and effects of deploying this template on his network.

   B. Christopher should perform a complete backup of his domain controllers.

   C. Christopher should develop a deployment plan that details how the template deployment process will work.

   D. Christopher should write down a list of all administrative usernames and passwords.

6. Crazy Mike, your assistant security administrator, has been given the task of installing the URLScan ISAPI filter on all of your organization's IIS servers. What two ways are available to install the URLScan ISAPI filter?

   A. Extract the URLScan files from the IIS Lockdown Wizard with the **iislockd /c command** and then executing URLScan setup.

   B. Install the URLScan ISAPI filter using the MBSA tool.

   C. Install the URLScan ISAPI filter by downloading it from Windows Update.

   D. Install the URLScan ISAPI filter from within the IIS Lockdown Wizard.

7. You are the network administrator for your organization. You have been charged with creating and implementing a strong network security plan for all your servers and client workstations. How should you go about configuring security for your network? You plan on configuring and testing security templates and their applications in a test environment that mimics your production environment. (Choose all that apply.)

   A. Configure very specific security templates for use on each Organizational Unit that contains a specific group of member servers, such as the Exchange Server OU and the SQL Server OU.

   B. Configure a basic domain-level security template that provides basic security needs such as password and account policies across the entire domain.

   C. Configure a specific security template for the client computers in your network and apply it to a workstation-specific OU, such as Workstations OU.

   D. Configure one security template for all member servers, such as Exchange and SQL servers, and apply it to each OU that contains any of these member servers.

Creating Secure Workstations

8. Lyman has a portable Windows 2000 computer that he travels with to various customer locations and sales presentations. In the event that Lyman's computer is stolen, what can you as the administrator do to prevent someone decrypting his EFS encrypted files?

    A. Remove the Data Recovery Agent certificate from the portable computer.

    B. Do not allow Lyman to place any sensitive information on the portable computer.

    C. Only allow L2TP connections when Lyman dials into the VPN server for remote access.

    D. Force Lyman to use a password that is extremely complex, consisting of numbers, letters, and characters and that is at least 42 characters long.

9. Austin is seeking to export the certificate and private keys for his portable computer to a removable storage medium. When he opens the Local Security Console and starts the procedure to export the certificate and keys, he cannot select the **Yes, export the private key** option because it is grayed out and unavailable for selection. Austin is using the Administrator account. What is the most likely reason for this issue?

    A. He does not have the required permissions because he is not a part of the Administrators group.

    B. He does not have the required permissions because he is not a part of the Domain Admins group.

    C. He is logged into the domain instead of the local computer.

    D. He is logged into the local computer instead of the domain.

10. Matt travels extensively with his Windows 2000 portable computer. What things can you easily do to enhance the security of his portable computer? (Choose all that apply.)

    A. Install Windows 98 on the portable computer.

    B. Remove the default Data Recovery Agent certificate and private key.

    C. Enforce strong passwords for user accounts on the portable computer.

    D. Rename the built-in Administrator account and remove it from the Administrators group.

Security Template Application Issues

11. Hannah is confused as to why the security settings she has configured for the computers in her domain are not being applied to five computers. The five computers are a mixture of Windows NT 4.0 Workstation and Windows 98 clients. What is the most likely reason for this problem?

    A. She has not installed the Directory Services Client onto these five legacy computers.

    B. Legacy computers cannot receive Group Policy object settings. Hannah will need to configure the settings she requires via System Policies.

    C. The computers are not located in the correct Organizational Unit.

    D. The computers are not located in her domain but are in another domain instead.

12. Mei Ling has just applied a new template to her Group Policy object. She then forced Group Policy replication through the domain. What event ID should she hope to see that would indicate that the settings in Group Policy were applied correctly without any problems?

    A. 680

    B. 1704

    C. 612

    D. 520

13. It has been noted in your organization that sometimes problems occur when administrators attempt to apply incremental security templates to Windows 2000 computers that have been upgraded from Windows NT 4.0. What options do you have to remedy this situation so that you can apply the security templates? (Choose all that apply.)

    A. Revert all computers back to Windows NT 4.0.

    B. Perform clean installations of Windows 2000 instead of upgrades.

    C. Apply the Setup Security.inf template to the upgraded computers before attempting to apply any other incremental template.

    D. Remove the default Data Recovery Agent certificate and private key from each upgraded computer.

Securing Server Message Block Traffic

14. Andrea is configuring SMB signing for her network. Which of the following configuration settings will result in client computers being able to connect to servers and use SMB signing? (Choose all that apply.)

    A. Digitally sign client communication (when possible): Not defined
       Digitally sign client communication (always): Not defined
       Digitally sign server communication (when possible): Enabled
       Digitally sign server communication (always): Enabled

    B. Digitally sign client communication (when possible): Enabled
       Digitally sign client communication (always): Enabled
       Digitally sign server communication (when possible): Enabled
       Digitally sign server communication (always): Enabled

    C. Digitally sign client communication (when possible): Disabled
       Digitally sign client communication (always): Enabled
       Digitally sign server communication (when possible): Enabled
       Digitally sign server communication (always): Disabled

    D. Digitally sign client communication (when possible): Disabled
       Digitally sign client communication (always): Disabled
       Digitally sign server communication (when possible): Disabled
       Digitally sign server communication (always): Disabled

15. Bruno is attempting to configure SMB signing for his network servers and clients. Which of the following statements is true about configuring SMB signing?

    A. As long as all computers have the same maximum configuration level assigned, they will be able to communicate securely using SMB.

    B. As long as all computers have the same minimum configuration level assigned, they will be able to communicate securely using SMB.

    C. Servers should be set for Enabled and clients should be set for Not Defined on the Always options to be able to communicate securely using SMB.

    D. Servers should be set for Not Defined and clients should be set for Enabled on the When Possible options to be able to communicate securely using SMB.

Self Test Quick Answer Key

For complete questions, answers, and epxlanations to the Self Test questions in this chapter as well as the other chapters in this book, see the Self Test Appendix.

1. **B, D**
2. **A, C, D**
3. **D**
4. **C**
5. **A, B, C**
6. **A, D**
7. **A, B, C**
8. **A**
9. **C**
10. **B, C, D**
11. **B**
12. **B**
13. **B, C**
14. **B, D**
15. **B**

MCSE/MCSA 70-214
Part II

Implementing, Managing, and Troubleshooting Service Packs and Security Updates

Chapter 3

MCSE/MCSA 70-214

Identifying, Installing, and Troubleshooting Required Updates

Exam Objectives in this Chapter:

2.1 Determine the current status of service packs and security updates. Tools include MBSA and HFNetChk.

2.2 Install service packs and security updates. Consideration include slipstreaming and using Remote Installation Services (RIS), custom scripts, and isolated networks.

2.2.1 Install service packs and security updates on new client computers and servers. Considerations include slipstreaming and using RIS, custom scripts, and isolated networks.

2.3 Manage service packs and security updates. Considerations include server computers and remote client computers. Tools include Microsoft Software Update Service, Automatic Updates, and SMS.

2.4 Troubleshoot the deployment of service packs and security updates. Typical issues include third-party application compatibility, permissions, and version conflicts.

- ☑ Summary of Exam Objectives
- ☑ Exam Objectives Fast Track
- ☑ Exam Objectives Frequently Asked Questions
- ☑ Self Test
- ☑ Self Test Quick Answer Key

Introduction

In a Utopian world, software would be released one time, work perfectly, and offer the absolute best in security and performance. Unfortunately, we live in the real world, and dealing with the seemingly never-ending game of keeping servers and workstations up to date can be a daunting task. To its credit, Microsoft has made some leaps and bounds in the past few years in regard to both initially creating more secure and functional software as well as keeping it that way over its lifetime through service packs and hotfixes.

In this chapter we cover a pretty large amount of ground, looking at keeping your computers up to date (and more important, secure) from the starting point to the ending point in the process. We begin by examining the ways that you, as an administrator, can identify the updates each of your computers will require. Naturally, after you've identified the updates you need, you will want to deploy them to your servers and workstations. Here we look at a variety of deployment methods you can use depending on the situation. Lastly, we examine some potential trouble spots you could encounter and discuss means to deal with them.

Identifying Required Updates

The process of keeping your servers and workstations up to date has to start somewhere—by identifying the updates you need for each of them. Updates typically come in two different varieties: service packs and hotfixes. (Hotfixes are sometimes known by a variety of other names, such as *security hotfix, security fix,* or *update.*) The bottom line is that there are two major types of updates you will need to worry about, differentiated by both size and scope. In the next section we look at the difference between service packs and hotfixes. After we've gotten a good understanding of them and where we can look to find them, we will move on to identifying and procuring required updates.

Types of Updates

As mentioned, you will need to apply two basic types of updates to your network computers over time: service packs and hotfixes. Both can be found at the Windows Update Web site, located at http://windowsupdate.microsoft.com/. They have very different purposes, reliability levels, and application means.

Service Packs

Service packs are large executables that Microsoft issues periodically (usually every 6 to 15 months) to keep the product current and correct problems and known issues. Often service packs include new utilities and tools that can extend a computer's functionality. For example, Windows 2000 Service Pack 3 includes the ability to remove shortcuts to Microsoft middleware products (Windows and MSN Messenger, Outlook Express, and the like) from your computer, if desired. Service packs also include updated drivers and files that have been developed for the product after its initial release. Windows 2000 service packs are all-inclusive and self-executing and typically contain all fixes and previous service packs that have been issued for the product.

> **NOTE**
>
> Although the topic is beyond the scope of this exam, you might be wondering just why Microsoft would willingly allow you to remove shortcuts to its middleware products. This action is a result of the settlement of the Microsoft antitrust lawsuit with the U.S. Department of Justice. You can read more about the settlement terms on Microsoft's Press Pass Web site at www.microsoft.com/presspass/trial/nov02/11-12FinalJudgment.asp.

Perhaps one of the greatest improvements in Windows 2000 service packs is that you can *slipstream* them into the original installation source and create integrated installation media that can be used to install an update to Windows 2000 without the need to subsequently apply the latest service pack. These updated installation sources can be placed back onto a CD-ROM for "sneaker-net" installation methods or can be used for any form of remote installation, including Windows 2000 Remote Installation Services, or for disk cloning.

Although can you get service packs from the Windows Update Web site, the best location to get them is directly from the Microsoft Service Packs page at http://support.microsoft.com/default.aspx?scid=fh;EN-US;sp. From there you will be able to download the service pack without having to install it immediately, as you would if you were using Windows Update.

Hotfixes

Hotfixes, also known as *security fixes, security patches, patches,* or *Quick Fix Engineering*, are small, single-purpose executable files that have been developed to correct a specific critical problem or flaw in a product for which timing is critical. Hotfixes do not typically undergo the same level of testing as service packs do to ensure that they are stable and compatible and do not cause further critical issues. Some hotfixes are not made available to the general public and must be obtained directly from Microsoft Product Support. Others can be found and downloaded from various sources, such as Windows Update, at http://windowsupdate.microsoft.com/ or the TechNET Security page located at www.microsoft.com/technet/security/default.asp.

Hotfixes can be used to correct both client-side and server-side issues. Recently, a pretty even division of client and server hotfixes have been issued as new flaws and weaknesses have been discovered. Perhaps one of the most famous server-side issues that received a hotfix was the Code Red exploitation of IIS servers' indexing service. MS02-018 was issued to correct this problem and stop the propagation of the Code Red worm. You can rely on Windows Update to inform you of missing hotfixes, but you can also use the HFNetChk tool to perform this function for you. The benefit of using HFNetChk is that when it is run against an entire network with a script, it will quickly return the status of all network computers, thus allowing you to determine the computers that require particular hotfixes.

Damage & Defense… Get Those Hotfixes!

Because service packs are only issued once in a long while, hotfixes are going to be your primary means of correcting vulnerabilities and flaws in Windows. You need to make it a regular practice—at least weekly—to check your computers for missing updates. Once you have identified the missing updates, you need to acquire and test them as quickly as you can, but not so quickly that you miss something critical that could cause you new problems down the road. After testing has been completed to your satisfaction, you should take steps to deploy updates as quickly as possible. Sometimes keeping your computers safe from attacks and other vulnerabilities comes down to just a matter of days—perhaps even less. For example, when the Code Red worm struck, it was able to compromise over 250,000 vulnerable systems in less than nine hours. Locating, testing, and deploying required updates as soon as they become available can go great lengths toward keeping your network secure and protected. In the case of the Code Red worm, the vulnerability was known and the fix had been available for some time before the "need" to update and apply fixes and patches was shown to administrators.

EXAM WARNING

As you read this text and through the rest of this chapter, remember the differences between a service pack and a hotfix in terms of what they are designed to do, how they are obtained, and how they are installed. You shouldn't expect to be asked directly what a service pack or hotfix is on the exam, but your understanding of each will be tested in other, more covert, ways.

Analyzing Your Computers

Armed with your basic understanding of the types of updates that are available for Windows 2000, the first step you need to undertake to get your computers up to date (and thus more secure) is to determine their current state. Analyzing your computers can be a very simple task or a difficult one, depending on the size and complexity of your network. If you only are responsible for only five computers and they are all located in the same place, your job will be very easy. If you are responsible for several hundred (or thousand) computers spread out over several geographically distant locations, your job is not going to be so easy. The method you choose to analyze your computers will thus depend largely on these factors:

- How many computers are you responsible for updating?
- Where are your computers located?
- What type of network connectivity do you have between locations?
- Do you have knowledgeable help available to you at all of your locations?

Let's take a look at some of the methods available to analyze your computers, both manually and via automated methods.

Visiting Windows Update

The Windows Update Web site can be a great asset to you if the number of computers to be managed is relatively low—perhaps five or fewer. Since Windows Update requires you to physically be in front of each computer in order to analyze and download the required updates, this method can be both time and bandwidth intensive. Windows Update, however, could be your best option if the number of computers to be updated is few or if a group of computers are not connected to the company network and thus cannot be analyzed via any other method.

Using Windows Update to analyze a computer for required updates is extremely simple, as outlined in Exercise 3.01.

EXERCISE 3.01

DETERMINING THE NEED FOR UPDATING USING WINDOWS UPDATE

1. Click **Start | Windows Update** to open an Internet Explorer window pointed to Windows Update. If the shortcut is missing, you can enter http://windowsupdate.microsoft.com/ into your browser address bar.

The Internet Explorer window shown in Figure 3.1 will appear. If you are asked to download and install anything from Microsoft, accept the download; this is a critical part of the process.

Figure 3.1 The Windows Update Web Site

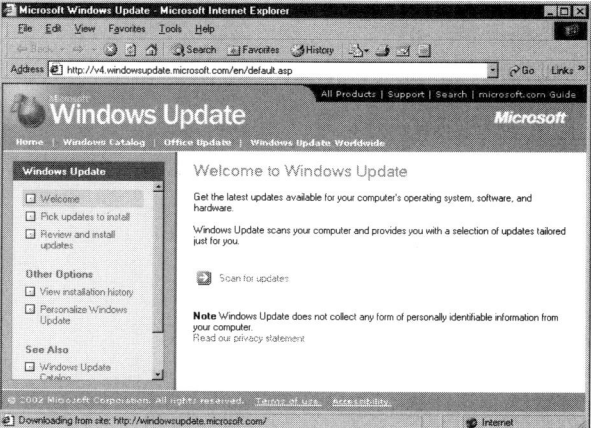

2. Click **Scan for updates** to start the analysis of your computer. After the analysis has completed, you will see the window shown in Figure 3.2.

Figure 3.2 Selecting Required Updates

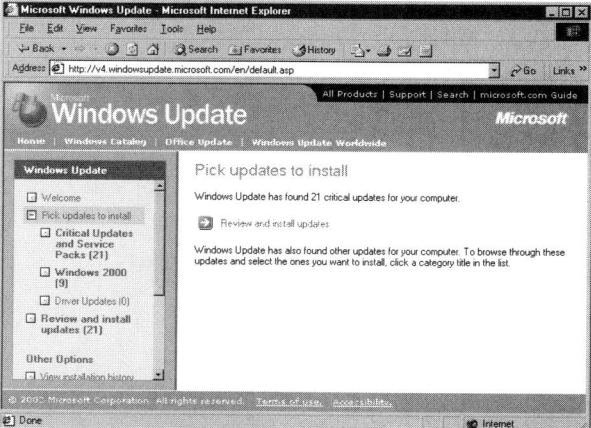

3. You can navigate through the three categories of updates to determine the updates that Windows Update has found your computer needs. The categories are arranged from most important to least important in regard to computer security and safety; this is why drivers are at the bottom of the list.

4. Another useful tool to help you determine what you have previously applied using Windows Update is the View installation option. Clicking **View installation history** changes the display to that shown in Figure 3.3. (Your installed items will likely be different from those shown here.)

Figure 3.3 Checking Previously Installed Updates

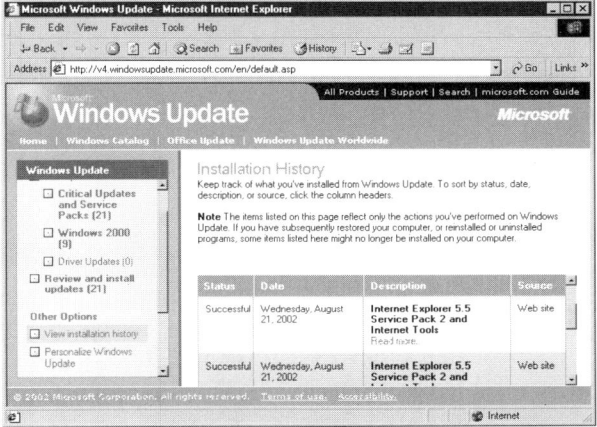

That's all there is to analyzing your computer with Windows Update. Later in this chapter we examine the rest of the steps to use Windows Update to select and install updates onto the local computer.

The next method we examine is the Microsoft Network Security Hotfix Checker, commonly referred to as the *HFNetChk tool*.

The Microsoft Network Security Hotfix Checker

The Microsoft Network Security Hotfix Checker, HFNetChk, is a command-line tool that can be used to quickly analyze one or many computers to determine the installation status of required security patches. Unlike Windows Update, HFNetChk can scan for missing updates from more than one product. Products that HFNetChk currently scans include:

- Windows 2000 Professional, Server, and Advanced Server
- Windows XP Professional
- Windows NT Workstation 4.0, Server 4.0, and Enterprise Edition Server 4.0
- SQL Server 7.0
- SQL Server 2000 Standard and Enterprise Server

- Internet Information Server 4.0
- Internet Information Server 5.0
- Internet Explorer 5.01, 5.01 Service Pack 1, 5.01 Service Pack 2, 5.5, 5.5 Service Pack 1, 5.5 Service Pack 2 for Windows 2000
- Internet Explorer 5.01, 5.01 Service Pack 1, 5.01 Service Pack 2, 5.5, 5.5 Service Pack 1, 5.5 Service Pack 2 for Windows NT 4.0
- Microsoft Data Engine (MSDE) 1.0

When the HFNetChk tool is run, it uses an Extensible Markup Language (XML) file containing information about all available hotfixes as its data source. The XML file contains all pertinent information about each product's hotfixes, such as the security bulletin name and title, and other detailed information about the hotfixes, including the file version, registry keys applied by the hotfix, information about patches that supersede other patches, and various other important types of information about each hotfix.

If the XML file is not found in the directory from which the HFNetChk tool is run or is not specified in the arguments for the HFNetChk tool, it will be downloaded from the Microsoft Web site. The XML file comes in a digitally signed CAB format, and you will be asked to accept the download before the file is downloaded to your computer.

After the CAB file has been downloaded and decompressed, HFNetChk scans the selected computers to determine the operating systems, applications, and service packs you have installed. After this initial scan is completed, HFNetChk parses the XML file to identify any security patches that are required (and not installed) for the configuration of each computer scanned. If a patch is identified as being required but is not currently installed on a computer, HFNetChk returns output informing you so.

By default, HFNetChk only displays those patches and fixes that are necessary to bring your computers up to date. All other nonessential patches are not shown by default. In the event that roll-up packages exist, HFNetChk will not report the individual patches that the roll-up included as being required. When determining the installation status of patch on a computer, HFNetChk evaluates three distinct items: the file version and checksum of every file that is installed by the patch and the Registry key that is installed by the patch. If the Registry key is not found, HFNetChk assumes the patch is not installed. If the Registry key is found, HFNetChk looks for the files that correspond to that patch, comparing the file version and checksum to the XML file. If any one test fails, the output will be that the patch is not installed. You can, however, disable checking Registry keys as part of the analysis process, as we see later in this section.

The basic syntax of the HFNetChk tool is:

```
hfnetchk.exe    [-h hostname] [-i ipaddress] [-d domainname] [-n] [-b]
                [-r range] [-history level] [-t threads] [-o output]
```

```
[-x datasource] [-z] [-v] [-s suppression] [-nosum]
[-u username] [-p password] [-f outfile] [-about]
[-fh hostfile] [-fip ipfile]
```

Table 3.1 provides the function of each of the HFNetChk switches.

Table 3.1 The HFNetChk Switches

Switch	Explanation
-h *hostname*	Specifies the NetBIOS name of the computer to be scanned. If not specified, the default is *localhost*.
-i *ipaddress*	Specifies the IP address of the computer to be scanned. If not specified, the default is the local computer.
-d *domainname*	Specifies the domain name to be scanned. All eligible computers in the domain will be scanned.
-n	Specifies that the local network is to be scanned. All eligible computers on the local network will be scanned.
-b	Compares the current status of fixes to that of a minimum secure baseline standard.
-r *range*	Specifies the inclusive IP address range that is to be scanned in the format *start_IP-end_IP*. For example, 192.168.0.100-192.168.0.199.
-history *level*	Displays an extremely verbose history of hotfixes as follows: 1. Those that are explicitly installed 2. Those that are explicitly not installed 3. Those that are explicitly installed and not installed MSKB Q303215 (located at http://support.microsoft.com/default.aspx?scid=KB;EN-US;Q303215&) has more information on using this switch.
-t *threads*	Specifies the number of threads to be used for executing the scan. The allowable range is from 1 to 128, with the default being 64.
-o *output*	Specifies the desired output format at the completion of the scan. **Tab** outputs in tab-delimited format. **Wrap** outputs in a word-wrapped format. The default setting is *wrap*.
-x *datasource*	Specifies the XML data source containing the hotfix information. By default, this is the mssecure.cab file located at http://download.microsoft.com/download/xml/security/1.0/NT5/EN-US/mssecure.cab. This can be changed to any location on your network and can be an XML filename, compressed XML CAB file, or a URL.
-z	Specifies that Registry checking should not be performed.
-v	Displays all available details for "Patch NOT Found," "WARNING," and "NOTE" messages. When **–o tab** is used, this switch is enabled by default.

Continued

Table 3.1 The HFNetChk Switches

Switch	Explanation
-s *suppression*	Specifies to suppress "NOTE" and "WARNING" messages as follows: 1. Suppress "NOTE" messages only 2. Suppress both "NOTE" and "WARNING" messages The default setting is to show all messages.
-nosum	Specifies that checksum checking is not to be performed. Performing the checksum test can use large amounts of network bandwidth. If speed or bandwidth usage is a concern, using this option speeds up the scan and reduces bandwidth usage. File version checking is still done.
-u *username*	Specifies an optional username to be used to log into remote computers if required in *DOMAIN\Username* format. *CAUTION: This data is sent in clear text across the network!*
-p *password*	Specifies the password to be used with the specified username. *CAUTION: This data is sent in clear text across the network!*
-f *outfile*	Specifies the filename to save the output results to. The default output is to the screen.
-about	Provides information about the version of HFNetChk in use.
-fh *hostfile*	Specifies the file containing a list of NetBIOS computer names to be scanned, one name per line with a maximum of 256 per file.
-fip *ipfile*	Specifies the file containing a list of IP addresses to be scanned, one IP address per line with a maximum of 256 per file.

Exam Warning

Take time to become familiar with the HFNetChk switches. Although you will most likely not be required to regurgitate them in bulk during your exam, you could be presented with one or more questions that will require you to display your understanding of the function of a particular switch and how it will or will not provide the desired solution to the problem at hand.

Exercise 3.02 presents the process to perform a simple network scan, returning the results to a tab-delimited text output file.

EXERCISE 3.02

USING HFNETCHK TO ANALYZE FOR UPDATES

1. Download the HFNetChk tool from www.microsoft.com/downloads/release.asp?releaseid=31154 and to a computer in your network.

2. Extract the files to a location of your choosing by double-clicking the **Nshc332.exe** file. Click **Yes** when asked if you want to install the HFNetChk tool. Click **Yes** again to agree to the license. Enter the location to which you want to extract the files, as shown in Figure 3.4. Click **OK** after entering the location to continue.

   Figure 3.4 Selecting the Extraction Location for the HFNetChk Files

   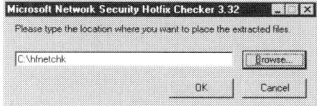

3. Click **OK** after the files are extracted to acknowledge that you know what the HFNetChk tool was designed to do and how to execute it.

4. Open a command prompt and change directories to the location where you placed the extracted HFNetChk files.

5. From the HFNetChk directory, start the analysis process by entering **hfnetchk –v –d domain_name –o tab –f hfnetchk_scan1.txt**. Figure 3.5 shows an example command for a network. Press **Enter** to start the analysis.

   Figure 3.5 Starting the Analysis Process with HFNetChk

   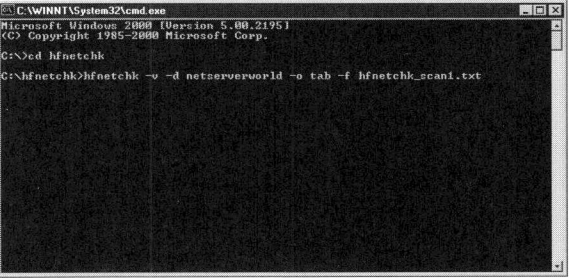

6. You will be asked if you want to install the MSSecureXML file from Microsoft, as shown in Figure 3.6. You must have a copy of the XML file in order for HFNetChk to work. Note that the file is updated regularly as Microsoft posts new fixes and updates, so you might want to

update it each time you run HFNetChk. Click **Yes** to install the XML file and allow the analysis to continue.

Figure 3.6 Getting the XML File

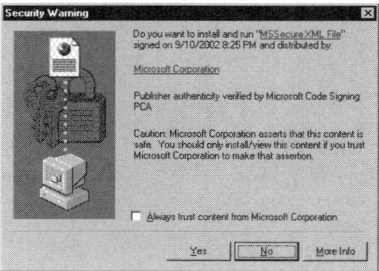

7. Since we have directed the output of the scan to a tab-delimited text file, you should expect to see the output of Figure 3.7 at the conclusion of your scan.

Figure 3.7 The Scan Is Complete

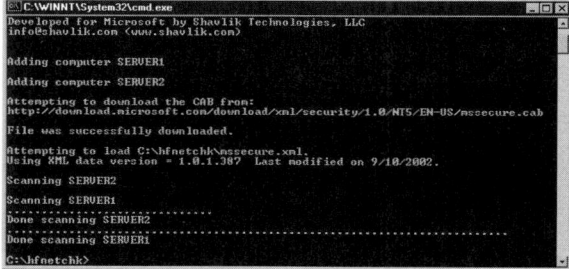

8. An examination of the text output file reveals the situation for our computers. Figure 3.8 shows the tab-delimited file imported into Excel for easier viewing and comparison.

Figure 3.8 The Results of the HFNetChk Analysis

9. Armed with this knowledge, we can now go about getting and installing the required fixes and patches on our computers. That is the topic of the "Deploying and Managing Updates" section later in this chapter.

Even though we performed a relatively simple scan in Exercise 3.2, you can use HFNetChk's various switches to perform very advanced scans on the specific computers of your choosing. By calling the scan from a batch file or script that is scheduled to run weekly, you can easily keep on top of any patches or fixes that your computers require. The only caveat to configuring HFNetChk to run as a scheduled event is that you must specify the location of the XML file—so a small amount of preplanning is required to make it work.

The next method of analyzing computers that we examine is the Microsoft Baseline Security Analyzer tool.

The Microsoft Baseline Security Analyzer

The Microsoft Baseline Security Analyzer (MBSA) is a GUI-based tool that Microsoft developed to detect common security misconfigurations and weaknesses. The MBSA tool can also be used from the command line if desired. The current version of MBSA, version 1.1, can be run on a Windows 2000, Windows XP, or Windows .NET Server computer; it scans for missing hotfixes, weaknesses, and vulnerabilities in the following Microsoft products:

- Windows 2000 Professional, Server, and Advanced Server
- Windows XP Professional
- Windows NT Workstation 4.0, Server 4.0, and Enterprise Edition Server 4.0
- SQL Server 7.0, 7.0 Service Pack 1, 7.0 Service Pack 2, 7.0
- SQL Server 2000 Standard and Enterprise Server
- Internet Information Server 4.0
- Internet Information Server 5.0
- Internet Explorer 5.01 and later
- Office 2000
- Office 2002 (XP)

MBSA uses a modified version of the HFNetChk tool to scan for missing hotfixes, service packs, and other updates. At the completion of the scan, an individual XML output report is created for each computer that has been scanned. This report can be viewed immediately after the completion of the scan or later. When MBSA is executed from the GUI, reports are placed in the SecurityScans folder, which is located in the profile of the user who ran the scan.

For example, if a user named Andrea ran the scan, she could expect to find scan reports located at C:\Documents and Settings\Andrea\SecurityScans or wherever her profile path is pointed. You can use the */f* switch to change the location of the output file when you're running the MBSA tool from the command line.

In Exercise 3.3, we examine how to use the MBSA tool from the GUI to examine a local computer and determine its current status. In Exercise 3.4 we perform the same task, this time from the command line. Using the MBSA tool as part of a script or batch file, you could schedule a regular scan of all your network computers and then examine the results after the scan has completed. You should consider performing a scan such as this one at least once per week as your specific situation dictates.

The basic syntax of the MBSA tool from the command line is:

```
msbacli.exe    [/c domainname\computername] [-i ipaddress] [-d domainname]
               [-r range] [/n IIS] [/n OS] [/n password] [/n SQL]
               [/n hotfix] [/o %domain% - %computername% (%date%)]
               [/e] [/l] [/ls] [/lr report name] [/ld report name]
               [/qp] [/qe] [/qr] [/q] [/f]
```

Table 3.2 details the function of each mbsacli.exe switch.

Table 3.2 The mbsacli.exe Switches

Switch	Explanation
/c *domainname\computername*	Performs a scan on the selected computer.
-i *ipaddress*	Specifies the IP address of the computer to be scanned. If not specified, the default is the local computer.
-d *domainname*	Specifies the domain name to be scanned. All eligible computers in the domain will be scanned.
-r *range*	Specifies the inclusive IP address range that is to be scanned in the format *start_IP-end_IP*—for example, 192.168.0.100-192.168.0.199.
/n IIS	Specifies that IIS checks are to be skipped. The */n* options can be added together, such as /n IIS+OS+SQL.
/n OS	Specifies that operating system checks are to be skipped.

Continued

Table 3.2 The mbsacli.exe Switches

Switch	Explanation
/n password	Specifies that password checks are to be skipped.
/n SQL	Specifies that SQL checks are to be skipped.
/n hotfix	Specifies that hotfix checks are to be skipped.
/e	Lists errors from the latest scan.
/l	Lists all reports available for viewing.
/ls	Lists all reports from the latest scan.
/lr *report name*	Displays an overview of the specified report name.
/ld *report name*	Displays a detailed version of the specified report name.
/qp	Specifies that the progress of the scan is not to be shown.
/qe	Specifies that the error list is not to be shown.
/qr	Specifies that the report list is not to be shown.
/q	Specified that the progress of the scan, the error list, or the report list are not to be shown.
/f	Specifies that output is to be redirected to a file.

Exam Warning

As with the HFNetChk tool, taking some time to become familiar with the switches that can be used with the command-line version of MBSA could help you on exam day. You might be given one or more answers that will require you to know whether or not a particular switch will achieve the desired result.

Exercise 3.03 presents the process to perform a single local computer scan with MBSA from the GUI.

EXERCISE 3.03
USING MBSA TO ANALYZE FOR UPDATES FROM THE GUI

1. Download the Microsoft Baseline Security Analyzer from www.microsoft.com/technet/security/tools/Tools/MBSAhome.asp.
2. Double-click the mbasetup.exe installer. Click **Next** to progress past the first page of the wizard.

3. Accept the license agreement and click **Next** to continue.
4. Enter the requested information as shown in Figure 3.9 and click **Next** to continue.

Figure 3.9 Configuring the Installation of MBSA

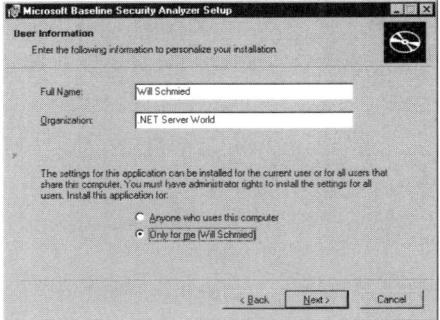

5. On the Destination Folder page, either select a custom installation path or accept the default one and click **Next** to continue.
6. Choose your installation options from the **Choose install options** page and click **Next** to continue.
7. Click Next two more times to start the installation.
8. Click **Finish** to complete the installation process.
9. Launch the newly installed MBSA tool and select **Scan a computer**.
10. On the **Pick a computer to scan** page, configure the computer you want to scan and the scan options you want to use, as shown in Figure 3.10. When you're done, click **Start scan**.

Figure 3.10 Configuring the Local Computer Scan Options

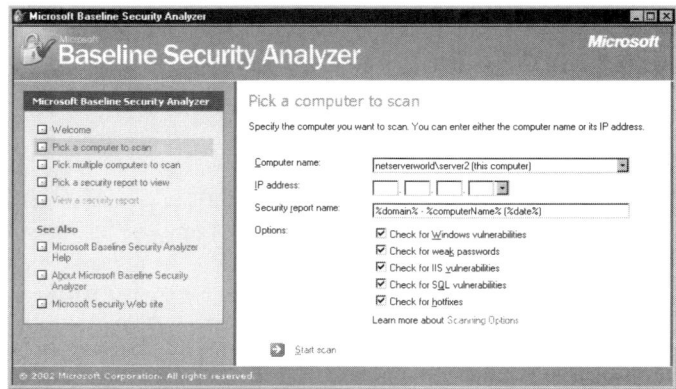

11. You will be asked if you want to install the MSSecureXML file from Microsoft. You must have a copy of the XML file in order for MBSA to work. Note that the file is updated regularly as Microsoft posts new fixes and updates, so you might want to update it each time you run MBSA. Click **Yes** to install the XML file and allow the analysis to continue.

12. After the analysis has been completed, you will receive the results of the scan, as shown in Figure 3.11. It looks as though this server has some serious issues. To examine the specifics of an area, click **Result Details**. The details of the Windows Hotfixes area is shown in Figure 3.12.

Figure 3.11 The MBSA Results

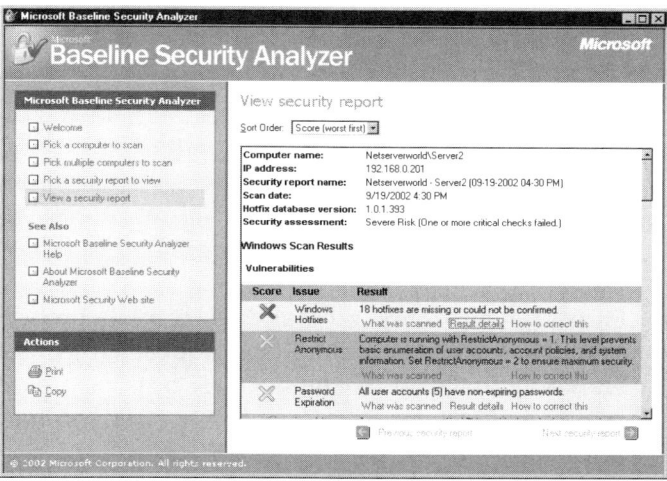

Figure 3.12 Examining Specific Items

13. Armed with this knowledge, we can now go about getting and installing the required fixes and patches on our computers. That is the topic of the "Deploying and Managing Updates" section later in this chapter.

As mentioned previously, you can also run the MBSA tool from the command line, as demonstrated in Exercise 3.04. This method can be useful in working with scripts and batch files, although with the fairly powerful GUI mode available to the MBSA, you might find yourself shying away from using it at the command line in most cases.

EXERCISE 3.04

USING MBSA TO ANALYZE FOR UPDATES FROM THE COMMAND LINE

1. Open a command prompt and change to the location of the MBSA tool. By default, the tool is located in Program Files\Microsoft Baseline Security Analyzer.

2. Enter the following command to scan all computers in the domain: **mbsacli /d domain_name** (see Figure 3.13) or simply enter **mbsacli** to scan only the local machine. Other options are available for scanning, as detailed in Table 3.2. Press **Enter** after you have entered your scan command.

Figure 3.13 Starting an MBSA Scan from the Command Line

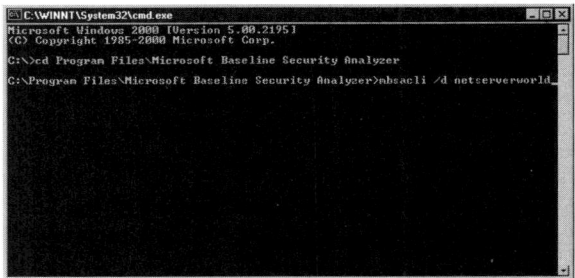

3. You will be asked if you want to install the MSSecureXML file from Microsoft. You must have a copy of the XML file in order for MBSA to work. Note that the file is updated regularly as Microsoft posts new fixes and updates, so you might want to update it each time you run MBSA. Click **Yes** to install the XML file and allow the analysis to continue.

4. After the analysis has been completed, you will receive the results of the scan, as shown in Figure 3.14. You can then open the scan output file in the MBSA GUI version and see exactly what has been found, as shown in Figure 3.15.

Figure 3.14 MBSA Command-Line Scan Is Complete

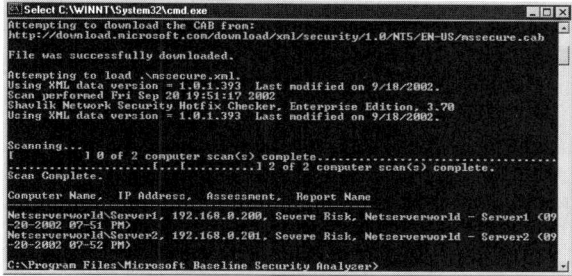

Figure 3.15 Viewing the MBSA Scan Results in the GUI

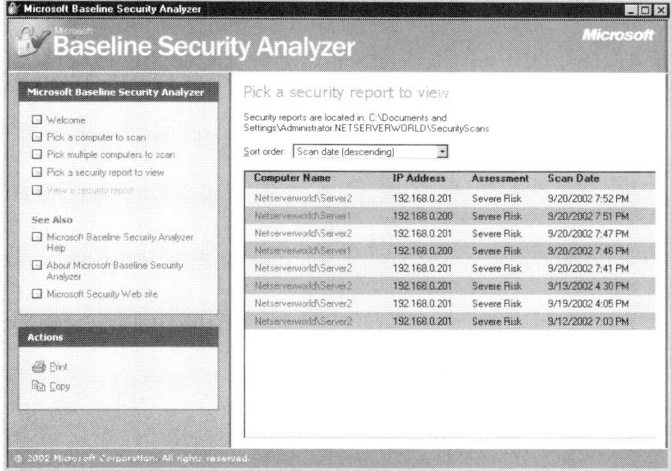

5. Armed with this knowledge, we can now go about getting and installing the required fixes and patches on our computers. That is the topic of the "Deploying and Managing Updates" section later in this chapter.

Notes from the Underground…

You're Not Alone

Don't ever think for a moment that you are the only person who is analyzing your computers for missing updates, weaknesses, and vulnerabilities. Nothing could be further from the truth when it comes to computer networks that have active connections to the Internet.

Worms (such as Code Red, Code Red II, and Nimba) and autorooters (applications that actively scan entire blocks of IP addresses looking for any number of vulnerabilities and weaknesses) are constantly scanning the Internet and all accessible private network computers for targets of opportunity. What exactly makes a target of opportunity? It can be that one misconfigured firewall rule, that one vulnerable service, or even that unsecured Windows 9*x* computer you've got running.

The sad truth is that the odds are greatly in favor of the attacker in this game, because their tools are becoming increasingly simpler and simpler to use while gaining increased power and functionality. A single autorooter might be able to scan dozens of operating systems for thousands of known vulnerabilities across an entire Class B IP block and then automatically attack identified vulnerable systems without any human interaction past clicking *Go* in the GUI. Targets of opportunity, also known as "easy kills," are sought by the vast majority of attackers, but just the same, you could also find yourself under direct attack from a very skilled attacker looking for a specific vulnerability on a specific operating system.

No matter who is scanning and analyzing your computers, whether a beginner script kiddie or an advanced black hat, you are likely being probed and analyzed for vulnerabilities several times per day. If you think that you are safe just by virtue of the number of systems connected to the Internet, nothing could be further from the truth. If you want to get a very good introduction to who these people are and what they can do to your computers, visit the Honeynet Project at http://project.honeynet.org.

Deploying and Managing Updates

Identifying the updates that your computers need might seem like the toughest part of this task; however, that's not the case. Deploying updates, which includes testing them thoroughly before deployment, is in most cases the most time-consuming and problematic part of the update process.

After you have thoroughly tested the updates in a safe environment, usually a lab or an isolated section of the network, you then face the task of actually getting them deployed to the computers that require them. You have a few options available to you when it comes to deployment time, ranging from creating update integrated installation media, using Group Policy and the Remote Installation Service to install updates for you, using other products such as Systems Management Server, or even using scripting.

Of course, all of this assumes that you have actually gone out and gotten the updates you need. You can go about getting the required updates in a variety of ways, some easier than others. How you get the updates you need depends on the method you plan to use to deploy them. The method you use to deploy updates depends on several issues such as whether the computers are new or existing, the physical location of the computers to be updated, and the number of computers to be updated, among other issues.

The most common deployment methods for new computers include slipstreaming and scripting. For existing computers, Windows Update, Software Update Services, Automatic Update, Systems Management Server, scripting, and Group Policy are the more common methods. Of these, Automatic Updates (which has recently replaced the now defunct Critical Notification Service) and Windows Update only apply to the specific computer that they are running on; the rest of the methods can be used to apply fixes and updates to multiple computers.

The Software Update Service is a relatively new service that replaces Windows Corporate Update; however, it only works with Windows 2000, Windows XP, and Windows .NET Servers computers and is not exactly all that intelligent when it comes to applying patches. Systems Management Server (SMS) has been around for quite some time and is due for a new version release, version 2003, in the near future. SMS can be used to deploy all sorts of fixes and updates to all versions of Windows computers.

Scripting can also apply fixes and updates to all versions of Windows computers and is perhaps the best choice when you have a large number of computers requiring the same updates. The same holds true for Group Policy software installation. Of course, there is always good old-fashioned "sneaker-net."

If you need to manually download fixes and patches, you can get them from the following locations:

- For downloading service packs, your best bet is to go straight to the service pack homepage located at http://support.microsoft.com/default.aspx?scid=fh;EN-US;sp.

- For hotfixes and other updates, you have several viable options:
    - You can go directly to the Q article that is listed with the fix. Q articles can be found at http://support.microsoft.com/default.aspx?scid=KB;EN-US;Q*xxxxxx*, where *xxxxxx* is the six-digit Q article number.

- You can look up the specific Security Bulletin that is mentioned at www.microsoft.com/technet/security/bulletin/MS*yy-bbb*.asp, where *yy* is the year and *bbb* is the bulletin number within that year.

- You can visit the Windows Catalog, which replaced the Windows Corporate Update Web site, at http://windowsupdate.microsoft.com/catalog. By working through the options and selecting your operating system and type of downloads you are looking for, you can find most all updates, patches, and hotfixes in one location.

TEST DAY TIP

The download locations presented here are for your own professional knowledge and reference. Don't expect to be tested on them.

Head of the Class…

Test, Backup, Deploy

We cannot stress enough the importance of having a solid, well-documented, and verified update plan for your organization. Consider this scenario: You are the administrator for a small financial organization. Your organization's primary business is that of buying and selling stocks. You, without prior proper planning, apply an untested update to your member servers—the very lifeblood of your custom ASP and SQL financials application. The update causes several of the servers to become unstable because it is conflicting with another previously installed update (which, as you failed to see, the new update's installation notes plainly said to remove before installation). You've now created a problem.

Think that's bad? Wait, it gets worse. You have a pretty good backup plan in place—or so you think. Backups are performed nightly using a well-documented procedure, but no one has ever taken the time to test the plan to see just how well it works. No time is a worse time to test your backup plan than when your mission-critical production servers have been taken down—not by attackers but by the carelessness of the network administrator.

The solution to avoid such a scenario? Test, backup, deploy. Build a small test lab (as large as required and that can be afforded financially) that mimics your actual production environment. If you have Windows 2000 IIS servers and SQL 2000 servers in your production network, you need to duplicate that scenario in the lab. Using Active Directory and Exchange 2000 server? You need to duplicate those as well. Every detail is pertinent and no detail should be ignored, overlooked, or considered superfluous when it comes to building a test lab. Furthermore, the hardware and software configurations used in the production network should be the same ones used in the lab environment.

Continued

> Once you've thoroughly tested a proposed update in your lab, you can take steps to deploy it to your network—but not before performing a backup on the affected systems. Haven't tested your disaster recovery plan lately? You might want to consider doing it now. It's better to find out that it doesn't work when you don't need it to. When you are certain that everything else is ready, then (and only then) can you go forward and deploy the updates. Using this three-step deployment strategy, you will in most cases prevent problems from occurring. You can deal with those that do occur because you now know that your disaster recovery plan works and can be called into action in short order. The bottom line is this: You plan or you pay. Which will you do?

Installing Updates on New Computers

Deploying updates to new computers that are being prepared for installation is the easiest scenario that you can find yourself in. Unfortunately it's also the least likely scenario. But when you need to deploy updates to new computers, you have a couple of good options at your disposal that don't require you to visit each computer and perform the updates manually.

For service pack updates, you can create slipstreamed installation media that incorporate the latest service pack from the very beginning—no time wasted sitting in front of each computer installing the service pack and then waiting for the subsequent restart to confirm that all is well.

For applying the smaller patches, updates, and fixes, you can use a script and the Qchain.exe utility to install them, ensuring that version conflicts and file-locking issues are avoided and you, in the end, get all your updates installed. In some instances you might need to install these updates on computers that are located in isolated networks or are otherwise unavailable for any sort of over-the-network installation. In these cases, you will most likely find yourself visiting each computer with a specially created installation CD or sending the local staff this CD with instructions on its use. We examine each of these scenarios in more detail in the following sections, including several exercises on pulling each of them off successfully.

Slipstreaming Installation Media for RIS Deployment

What's more fun than installing Windows 2000 on 50 new client workstations? Going right behind this installation and installing the latest service pack, of course! In reality, we all know this statement is not exactly the truth, but it does make a good point as to how time-consuming and generally unnerving manually it can be to install an operating system and service pack on new computers.

Fortunately, Windows 2000 provides a solution to the problem of installing an operating system on new computers; it even allows us to ensure that the installation performed is one that is up to date with the latest service pack. Of course, this technology is not new to Windows 2000; it forms one of the cornerstones of Systems Management Server. Additionally, the functionality in Windows 2000 is not as robust as that you will find in Systems Management Server, but overall the Remote Installation Service in Windows 2000 is a fairly simple and foolproof way to perform new operating system installations over the network—all from the comfort of your own desk.

When it comes to deploying service packs to new clients, the method of choice is to slipstream the installation media with the service pack files, thus creating an integrated installation source that contains all the most up-to-date files. To *slipstream* means to place newer files directly over existing files without causing any version conflicts or other issues—something that was a constant source of frustration for Windows NT 4.0 administrators.

All Windows 2000 Service Packs are slipstream ready—meaning that you can extract the service pack files into a directory on your computer that contains the contents of a Windows 2000 Setup CD-ROM. The extracted service pack files simply overwrite the files that currently exist, and you end up with a new, integrated, and updated installation source. The process to slipstream an installation source is discussed in Exercise 3.05.

Exam Warning

The process to slipstream service pack files into an installation source, including all commands issued, is something you should commit to memory. Questions about slipstreaming have an odd tendency to pop up here and there in several of the Windows 2000 MCSE exams.

EXERCISE 3.05

SLIPSTREAMING THE WINDOWS 2000 PROFESSIONAL SOURCE FILES WITH SERVICE PACK 3

1. Create a new folder on your computer to hold the Windows 2000 Professional setup files, such as W2KPRO.

2. Copy the contents of your Windows 2000 Professional Setup CD-ROM to this folder.

3. Create a new folder on your computer to hold the contents of Service Pack 3, such as W2KSP3.

4. Extract Service Pack 3 to this folder by executing the following command at the command prompt: **w2ksp3 –x** (see Figure 3.16).

Figure 3.16 Extracting the Service Pack Files

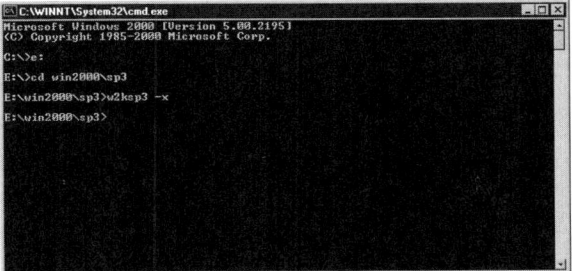

5. After the service pack verifies all files, you will be asked to choose a location to extract them to, as shown in Figure 3.17. Choose the Service Pack folder you created earlier.

Figure 3.17 Entering the Extraction Location

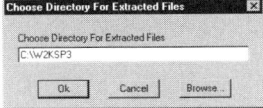

6. After all the service pack files have been extracted, click **OK** to close the extraction window.

7. To slipstream the extracted Service Pack 3 files into the original installation media, enter the following command from the command line: **w2ksp3\i386\update\update.exe -s:c:\w2kpro** (assuming that your folders are located on volume C). After you enter the command, a window like the one shown in Figure 3.18 will open and inform you of the slipstream status.

Figure 3.18 The Integration Process

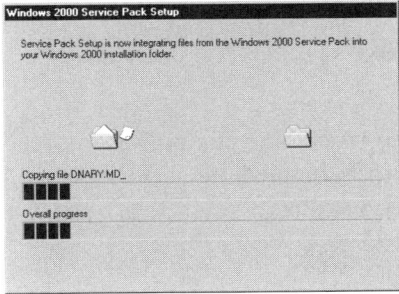

8. When the integration is complete, click **OK** to close the integration window and complete the slipstream process. You now have an integrated Windows 2000 Professional Service Pack installation source.

Of course, now that you have the slipstream installation source, you need to do something with it. You have three options at this point: You can use the Remote Installation Service to install new client systems, you can burn the files to CD-ROM to create an integrated Setup CD-ROM (this will come into play later in this chapter), or you can perform network installations from a file share using the integrated installation files you just created.

Before you can get to work installing Windows 2000 using the Remote Installation Service, you must have the service installed and configured on your network. If you are installing it for the first time, this is an all-in-one process. If you already have it installed, you will be able to skip Exercise 3.06 entirely and create a new installation image as outlined in Exercise 3.7. To use Remote Installation Service, you must have a Windows 2000 Active Directory domain and you must install RIS on a Windows 2000 server, either a member server or a domain controller. For a more in-depth discussion of Windows 2000 RIS, see http://infocenter.cramsession.com/techlibrary/gethtml.asp?ID=1514.

TEST DAY TIP

Don't expect to be tested on the process to install and configure a RIS server in your network. This is outside the domain of this exam. Exercise 3.06 is provided for reference and as a lead-in for Exercise 3.07, which does present some information you could see on this exam.

EXERCISE 3.06

INSTALLING AND CONFIGURING THE REMOTE INSTALLATION SERVICE

1. If you already have RIS configured on your network, you can skip this exercise entirely and instead complete Exercise 3.7. If not, begin the process to install RIS by clicking **Start | Settings | Control Panel | Add/Remove Programs**. Select the **Add/Remove Windows Components** option.

2. From the Windows Component Wizard, select **Remote Installation Services** and click **Next** to continue.

3. The wizard will briefly copy the required files to your Windows 2000 Server in order to support RIS.

4. You might be prompted to provide your Windows 2000 Server Setup CD-ROM or to enter the path to its installation files. Provide the CD-ROM or installation path and click **OK** as required.

5. When the Completing Windows Component Wizard page is shown, click **Finish** to complete the installation of RIS.

6. You will be prompted to restart the server in order to finish the installation process.

7. After the server has restarted, open the **Add/Remove Programs** applet again and click **Add/Remove Windows Components**. You should now see an entry prompting you to configure RIS on the server, as shown in Figure 3.19. Click the **Configure** button to start the RIS Setup Wizard.

Figure 3.19 RIS Awaits Its Configuration…

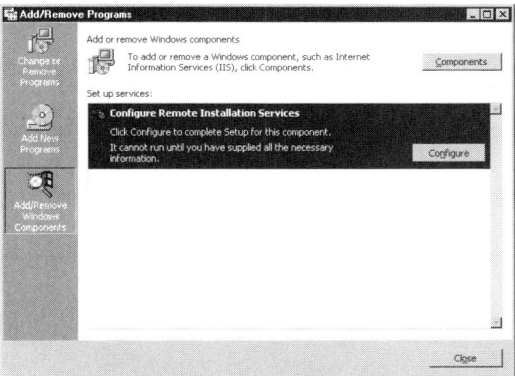

8. Click **Next** to dismiss the opening page of the RIS Setup Wizard.

9. Enter the folder path you want to use as the root for the RIS operating systems and then click **Next** (see Figure 3.20). This is the location at which RIS will store its installation images, so be sure to pick a location that is large enough for the number of installation sources you plan to create—about 250MB for a Windows 2000 installation. A few caveats about the location: It cannot be on a system volume, it must be on an NTFS 5 volume, and it cannot be a DfS share.

Figure 3.20 Selecting the Location for the RIS Root

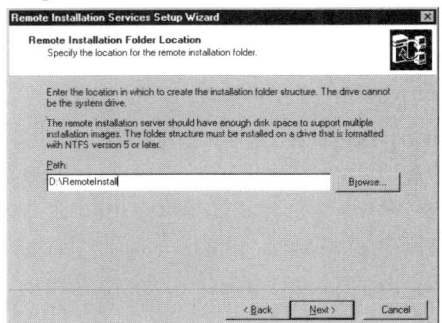

10. On the Initial Settings page, you are asked if you want to start responding to client requests for RIS services at this time. The preferred selection is not to respond to client requests until you have completed configuring and testing the RIS server. To prevent the RIS server from responding to all requests, leave both check boxes unselected and click **Next** to continue.

11. On the Installation Source Files Location page, enter the path to the Windows 2000 Professional installation files, and then click **Next** to continue. Using the location of the files from Exercise 3.5 would give us C:\W2KPRO, for example.

12. On the Windows Installation Image Folder Name page, enter a name for the folder that will store this operating system image, and then click **Next** to continue. In this example, we used **windows2000.pro.sp3** as a folder name.

13. On the Friendly Description and Help Text page (see Figure 3.21), you need to provide a user-friendly name for the RIS image you are creating. Users will see this name on their selection menu when they boot into a RIS installation. After completing this page, click **Next** to continue.

Figure 3.21 Entering a User-Friendly Name and Description for the RIS Image

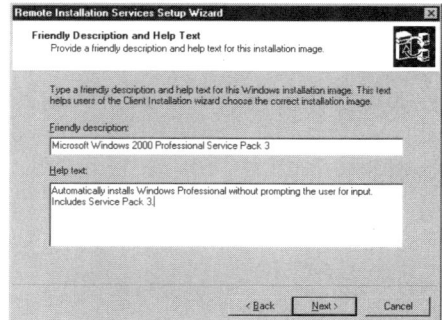

14. On the Review Settings page, you can review the settings that you have configured before creating the RIS image. When you are satisfied with your settings, click **Finish** to complete the RIS server setup and configuration process. You can watch the progress of the operation, as shown in Figure 3.22.

Figure 3.22 Completing the RIS Setup Wizard

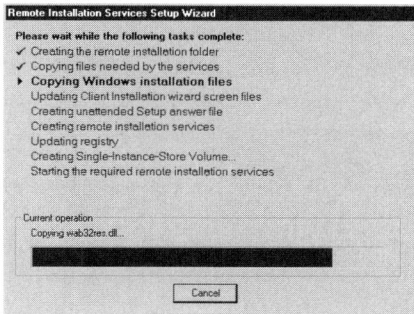

15. When the Wizard has completed, click **Done** to close the RIS Setup Wizard window.
16. If the server you configured for RIS is not already an authorized DHCP server on your network you need to authorize from the DHCP console before it can start servicing client requests. Open the **DHCP** console, right-click in the root of the console, and select **Manage Authorized Servers** from the context menu. This opens the Manage Authorized Servers window, as shown in Figure 3.23.

Figure 3.23 Managing Authorized Servers—Not Just for DHCP Anymore!

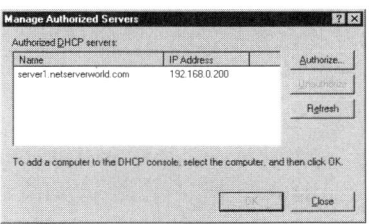

17. Click **Authorize**, enter the IP address or server name for the RIS server, and then click **OK** to authorize the RIS server.
18. You can now perform any further configuration of your RIS server that you would like, including enabling it to respond to client requests and creating additional installation images, by opening the Active Directory Computers and Users console, locating the RIS server, right-clicking it,

and selecting **Properties**. Switch to the **Remote Install** tab and you are in business. For a more detailed discussion of managing RIS, see the tutorial located at http://infocenter.cramsession.com/techlibrary/gethtml.asp?ID=1514.

If you have previously installed and configured a RIS server on your network and only need to create a new installation image for your slipstreamed Windows 2000 Professional Service Pack 3 files, Exercise 3.07 is for you.

EXERCISE 3.07

CREATING A NEW RIS CD-BASED INSTALLATION IMAGE

1. Open the **Active Directory Users and Computers** console. Locate the RIS server of concern and right-click it. Select **Properties** from the context menu.
2. Switch to the **Remote Install** tab and click the **Advanced Settings** button. Switch to the **Images** tab. From here you can view all images hosted on the server.
3. To add a new image, click the **Add** button. This will start the Add Installation Image Wizard. Note that you can only add CD-based imaged from here; you need to run RIPrep to add a new RIPrep installation image.
4. Select **Add A New Installation Image** and click **Next**. Follow through the Add Installation Image Wizard to create the image and its associated answer file.
5. Click **Finish** to complete the Add Installation Image Wizard.

Now that you have an integrated RIS installation image created, you now just need to visit each computer (or have a trained user do it for you) and start the installation process. Your total time in front of each computer will be extremely short compared to the time you would spend if you weren't using a slipstreamed installation source and Remote Installation Services. Using an answer that provides all the required information during the GUI phase of setup, you can even further minimize the time required to perform each installation. Should you need to include fixes, updates, or patches in your installation source, see the tutorial located at http://infocenter.cramsession.com/techlibrary/gethtml.asp?ID=967 for a good walkthrough on how to properly locate them and prepare them for deployment.

Scripting Updates

Individual updates, fixes, and patches can be applied to your new computers quite easily using a script or batch file. Using the Qchain.exe tool, you can safely apply multiple updates, fixes, and patches to a computer without having to restart after each one—a problem that you most often face when attempting to manually install these updates. The Qchain.exe tool, which can be downloaded from www.microsoft.com/downloads/release.asp?ReleaseID=29821, allows you to install multiple updates at one time by preventing file-locking issues and incorrect file versions from being installed.

The following is an example of what could happen if you were to install two hotfixes without using Qchain.exe. When a hotfix is installed, it is placed in the Pending File Rename queue to be replaced *after* the computer has been restarted (hence the reason you must restart the computer following the installation). Because it has been placed in this queue, it is possible that you could potentially perform two updates that both target the same file. Say that you install hotfix 29 and hotfix 65 without restarting the computer in between, and both hotfixes update a specific file called problem_file.exe. Hotfix 29, which was applied first and will be processed first, contains version 3.1.5.33 of problem_file.exe. Hotfix 65, on the hand, contains an older version of the file, version 3.0.2.21. When each of the hotfixes is processed on the subsequent startup, they each (in turn) replace problem_file.exe with their respective versions. The net result is that the hotfix that is processed last will be the "winner," so to speak, in that its version of problem_file.exe will be the one that remains after all updates have been applied. Therein is the crux of the problem.

Using Qchain.exe, you can prevent such problems in most cases. Qchain.exe examines the changes made by each hotfix and applies the most recent file version in the event of a conflict. By doing so, Qchain.exe increases server and workstation uptime by preventing excessive restarts and by preventing file version problems.

If you have five updates to apply, you could use a script as follows to get them installed:

```
@echo off
setlocal
set FIXPATH=the_path_to_the_files
%FIXPATH%\Q123456_w2k_sp2_x86.exe -z -m
%FIXPATH%\Q234567_w2k_sp2_x86.exe -z -m
%FIXPATH%\Q345678_w2k_sp2_x86.exe -z -m
%FIXPATH%\Q456789_w2k_sp2_x86.exe -z -m
%FIXPATH%\Q567890_w2k_sp2_x86.exe -z -m
%FIXPATH%\qchain.exe
```

The *–m* switch turns on quiet mode, suppressing output; the *–z* switch instructs the hotfix executable not to restart after it has run. This script or batch file can then be saved to a network folder and placed in the Startup Scripts folder for a Group Policy object (see Figure 3.24). Figure 3.25 shows the actual directory for the specific GPO to which we have applied this batch file; yours will vary.

Figure 3.24 Placing the Qchain.exe Batch File in the Startup Scripts Folder of the Group Policy Object

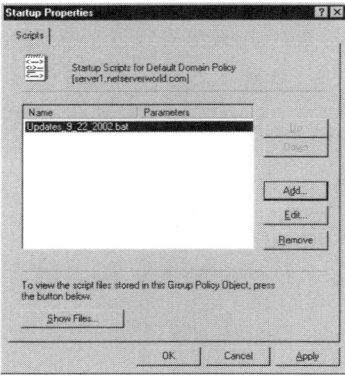

Figure 3.25 Locating the Startup Script Folder

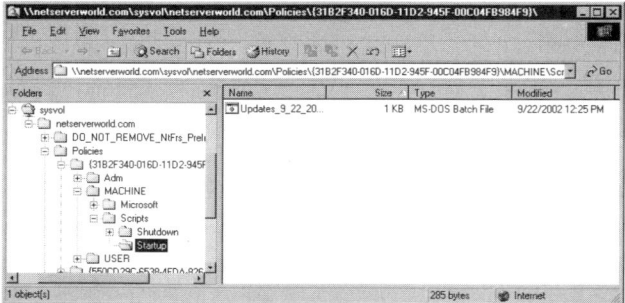

Exam Warning

Ensure that you completely understand the reasons for using Qchain and how it functions to prevent file version problems on your computers as well as increasing computer uptime by requiring only one restart. You should also make sure that you understand the types of updates Qchain is used for and how Qchain is typically used to deploy these updates.

Should you need to apply only one hotfix or update, you can opt to directly apply it or to use a script as discussed here. Scripting using Qchain.exe also works quite well for existing network clients and should be considered for use on them as a first (and preferred) option.

Installing Updates in Isolated Networks

For computers in isolated areas, your installation options are somewhat limited. Your best option in this case is to provide a local administrator or power user with a slipstreamed Windows 2000 Setup CD-ROM that also contains an answer file and any required patches, fixes, or updates that came out after the service pack. See http://infocenter.cramsession.com/techlibrary/gethtml.asp?ID=967 for a good walkthrough on how to accomplish this sort of installation.

Deployment Updates to Existing Computers

Getting updates to your existing computers can be a somewhat more complicated process, depending on the size of your organization, the capacity of your network, and the location of the computers to be upgraded. For existing computers, you can choose from a variety of methods when it comes to deploying updates. Windows Update, the Windows Catalog, Software Update Services, Automatic Updates, and Systems Management Server are among the more common and well-known methods, although more than a handful of available third-party solutions will work, often with better results and easier management.

Windows Update

As we discussed earlier in this chapter, Windows Update is a very simple and easy-to-use method of updating one specific computer at a time. Therein lays its drawback: It can be used to update the local computer and requires that updates be downloaded from Microsoft for that computer. Using Windows Update is a good choice if the number of computers to be updated is relatively small or if you do not have Active Directory in your network. As the number of computers and sites increases, so does your workload, and very quickly Windows Update becomes a solution that is not viable. The exact number of computers at which this breaking point occurs is not fixed and can vary from organization to organization, but a good guideline is 10 computers. If you have 10 computers or fewer in your organization, you can, in most cases, get away with using Windows Update without too much administrative effort. Anything more than 10 and you should consider another means of keeping your computers up to date. Another concern with using Windows Update is that each computer will download the files it requires independently of what any other computer has previously downloaded; this can put quite a hit on your network bandwidth.

Should you need to use Windows Update, the process to scan for required updates was presented earlier in this chapter, in Exercise 3.03. Exercise 3.08 presents the basic process to select and download updates.

TEST DAY TIP

Don't expect to be tested on a large amount of Windows Update knowledge during your exam. Most likely, you will only see to topic referenced lightly. What you need to take away from the discussion in this chapter is what Windows Update does, how it works, and why it is a limited solution not suitable for Enterprise use.

EXERCISE 3.08

UPDATING A SINGLE COMPUTER USING WINDOWS UPDATE

1. After you've completed the Windows Update scan of your computer (refer back to Exercise 3.03), you will now need to select and download updates to be applied to your computer. Some updates are mutually exclusive of all other updates, meaning that they must be downloaded and installed separately from any other updates. Most often, this includes any updates to Internet Explorer, service packs, and any sort of security roll-up.

2. By default, Windows Update automatically places into your download "basket" any items it finds that fall into the Critical Updates and Service Packs category. This does not mean, however, that it can install them all at once or that you must install them at all. To see what items have been identified and selected as Critical Updates or Service Packs, click the **Critical Updates or Service Packs** link to get the page shown in Figure 3.26. Notice that Internet Explorer Service Pack 1 (the first item selected) is one of those items that is mutually exclusive and must be downloaded and installed separately from the rest of the selected items. In this case, you need to either remove all other items from your download list or remove the one specific item. We recommend checking the entire list to make sure that other items are not mutually exclusive and that the list contains only the items you want to download. You can read more about any item by clicking the **Read more** link at the end of the item's description.

Figure 3.26 Examining the Critical Updates and Service Packs List

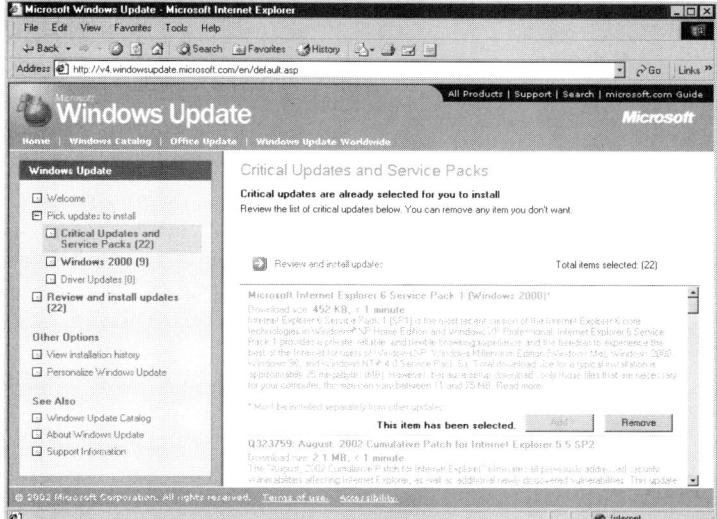

3. The items identified as Windows 2000 updates are not automatically added to your list of selected items, but they might still be useful or needed for your computer. You should examine this list of items by clicking the **Windows 2000** link and adding any updates you ant to have installed to your list.

4. If your scan reveals that you have updated drivers for your computer hardware, they will be listed under **Driver Updates**. You can add any of these updated drivers to your download list as well.

5. Once you have added all the updates that you want to your list (or that you can based on exclusions), click **Review and install updates** to progress to the next step of the Windows Update process (see Figure 3.27).

6. Once again you will have the option to examine the selected updates you have chosen and remove them from your list. Once you are satisfied with your selections, click **Install Now**.

7. You will be presented with a supplemental licensing agreement like the one shown in Figure 3.28. You must click **Accept** to complete the process.

Figure 3.27 Reviewing Selected Updates

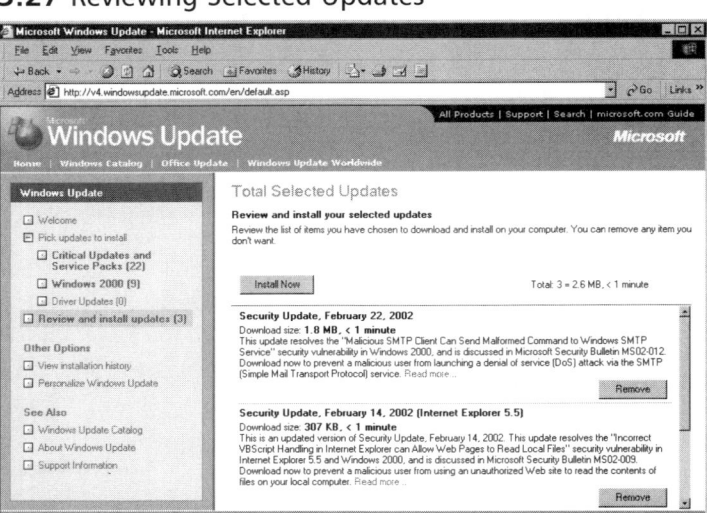

Figure 3.28 Accepting the Licensing Agreement

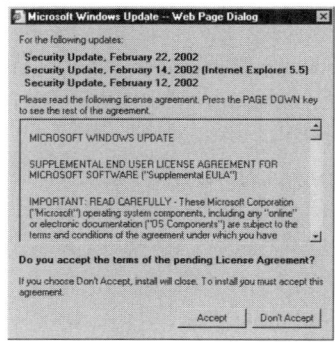

8. Windows Update will now download (see Figure 3.29) and install the selected updates. More often than not, you will be required to restart the computer after the installation to complete the process. Restarting the computer allows files that were in use to be updated. That's all there is to using Windows Update to update a single computer.

Figure 3.29 Windows Update Downloads and Installs the Updates

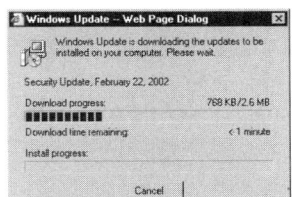

Using Windows Update is a simple, easy way to update a single computer or a few computers. But if you have more than a few computers to update or want to control when and how the updates are applied to your computers, you need to use one of the other methods we discuss in the next few sections.

Windows Update Catalog

The Windows Update Catalog and the Software Update Service have replaced what was once known as Corporate Windows Update. Corporate Windows Update allowed you to browse through all the available updates for your operating system, download the ones you wanted, and then deploy them using any available means such as scripting or Systems Management Server.

Windows Update Catalog pretty much performs the same function as the now defunct Corporate Windows Update site. Software Update Services (SUS) takes the concept a step further by automatically downloading the updates to the SUS server and staging them for you until you are ready to deploy them. We examine Software Update Services next, but for now let's see how the Windows Update Catalog can be used to locate and download updates of our choosing in Exercise 3.09.

EXERCISE 3.09

GETTING UPDATES USING THE WINDOWS UPDATE CATALOG

1. Open Internet Explorer and enter **http://windowsupdate.microsoft.com/catalog** into the address bar. The Windows Update Catalog will open, as shown in Figure 3.30.
2. Click **Find updates for Microsoft Windows operating systems** to start the process of finding updates for your Windows 2000 computers.
3. Choose your operating system from the choices given (see Figure 3.31) to locate all available downloads. If you want to perform an advanced

search and only locate specific items, such as service packs or recommended updates, click **Advanced search options**. After you have configured your search parameters, click **Search** to continue.

Figure 3.30 The Windows Update Catalog

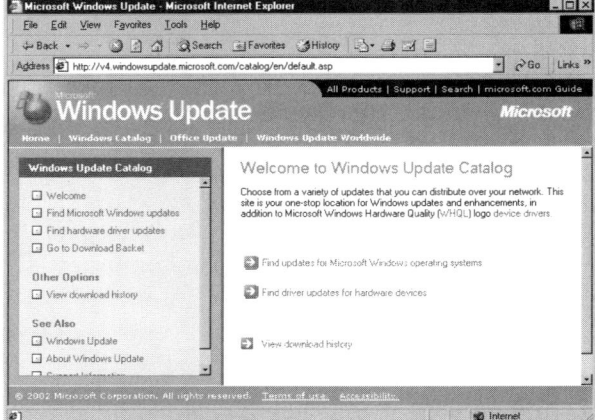

Figure 3.31 Selecting the Search Criteria

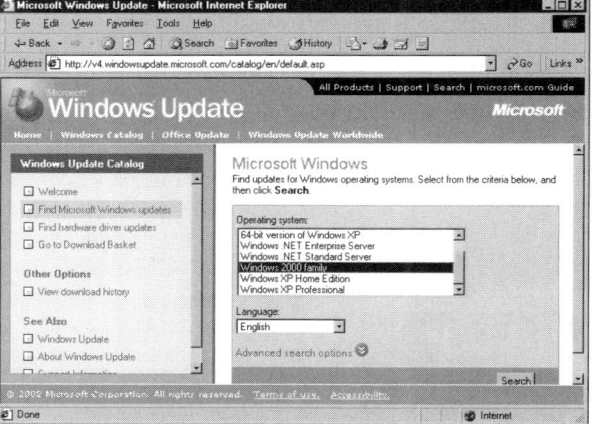

4. Available updates will be enumerated by category in which you have chosen to search. Clicking **Critical Updates and Service Packs** in our case yields the output shown in Figure 3.32.

5. Browse through the listing of updates in order to determine what you need. You can gain more information about a specific update by clicking the **Read more** link within the update's descriptive text. Click **Add** to place an update into your download basket. When you are done selecting updates, click **Go to Download Basket**.

Figure 3.32 Listing the Updates

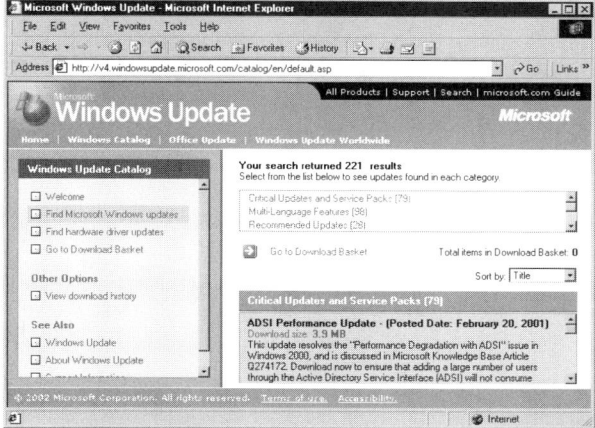

6. The Download Basket (see Figure 3.33) shows all updates that you have chosen to download and allows you to configure a location to which to download the files. When you are ready to download your chosen files, click **Download Now**.

Figure 3.33 Preparing to Download the Selected Update Items

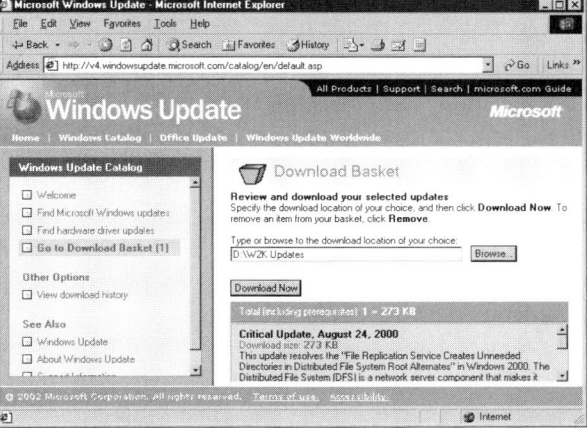

7. When you're prompted to accept the licensing agreement, do so in order to complete the download.

8. Downloaded files can be tracked in the Download History, as shown in Figure 3.34. Now that you've gotten your updates, you can deploy them via your choice of methods.

Figure 3.34 Keeping Track of Downloaded Updates

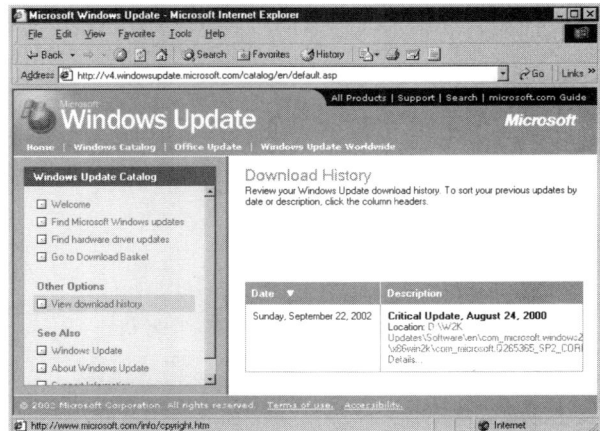

Now let's move on to the Software Update Service, a recent introduction in Windows 2000 that allows you to set up the equivalent of a Windows Update server inside your own intranet.

Software Update Service and Automatic Updates

The Software Update Service is the other half of the replacement for the now defunct Corporate Windows Update. Call it what you will, Software Update Service (when paired with the Automatic Updates client) is really just a Windows Update server that lives inside your private network. As the name of this section implies, it is a two-part process: You must install and configure the SUS in order to get available downloads from Microsoft, and then you must install and configure Automatic Updates so that available updates will be automatically installed on your client computers.

Before you can use SUS or Automatic Updates on your network, you need to download and install the required files. To get the SUS installer file, see www.microsoft.com/windows2000/downloads/recommended/susserver/default.asp. You should also consider downloading a very good SUS Deployment Guide at that location; it is full of excellent tips and best practices that will help you keep your SUS servers running smoothly. The Automatic Updates client can be downloaded from www.microsoft.com/windows2000/downloads/recommended/susclient/default.asp.

Exercise 3.10 walks you through the installation and configuration of your first SUS. It is important to know the restrictions for installing SUS before starting the procedure:

- You must install SUS on a Windows 2000 Server Service Pack 2 (or later) or Windows .NET Server RC1 (or later).

- The server SUS is installed on must be running IIS 5.0 or later.
- The server SUS is installed on must be running Internet Explorer 5.5 or later.
- Software Update Services must be installed on an NTFS 5 partition, and the system partition on the SUS server must also be using NTFS 5.
- SUS cannot be installed on a domain controller.

EXERCISE 3.10

INSTALLING AND CONFIGURING SOFTWARE UPDATE SERVICES

1. Download the SUS package from www.microsoft.com/windows2000/downloads/recommended/susserver/default.asp.
2. Double-click the **SUSSetup.msi** file to begin the installation on your new SUS server.
3. Click **Next** to dismiss the opening page of the wizard.
4. After reading the End User License Agreement, select **I accept the terms in the License Agreement** and click **Next** to continue. You must agree to the terms in order to continue the installation of SUS.
5. From the **Choose setup type** page, click **Custom** in order to see all the configurable options available to you.
6. From the **Choose file locations** page (see Figure 3.35), you can configure the location to place the downloaded updates to instead direct clients to a Microsoft Windows Update server. After making your selections (which you can in most cases leave as the defaults), click **Next** to continue.

Figure 3.35 Selecting File Location Options

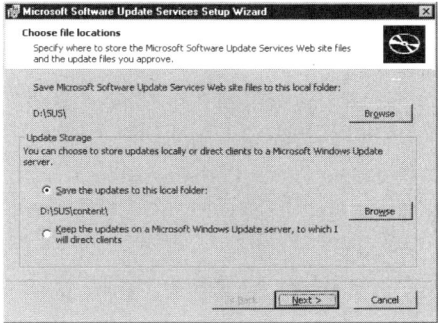

7. From the **Language Settings** page, select the language option that you need. In most cases, you can simply select **English only**. This choice will also reduce the amount of space required for downloaded updates. After selecting your language, click **Next** to continue.

8. On the **Handling new versions of previously approved updates** page (see Figure 3.36), you are asked to make a seemingly small decision, but really it is a critical one. You should always select **I will manually approve new versions of approved updates** in order to avoid any problems with incompatibilities. Once you have adequately tested the newer version, you can turn it loose on the network. After making your selection, click **Next** to continue.

Figure 3.36 Selecting the Installation Method; Be Wary of Allowing Automatic Approvals

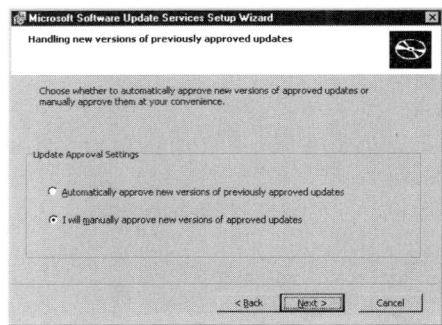

9. The **Ready to install** page provides you with the URL that clients should be targeted toward when configuring the Automatic Updates client. When you are ready to complete the installation of SUS, click **Install**.

10. The setup process will run the IIS Lockdown tool on your Windows 2000 Server in order to secure it as part of its installation process. This includes installing the URLScan ISAPI filter as well.

11. When setup has completed, click **Finish** to close the wizard. You can now administer your SUS server from http://*servername*/SUSAdmin.

12. Open a browser and in the address box, enter the location that corresponds to your SUS server. You should see the SUS server admin page, shown in Figure 3.37.

13. To being, you need to synchronize your server. Click **Synchronize server**. You can, and should, configure a synchronization schedule for your server. You can perform this task by clicking the **Synchronization Schedule** button. This step opens the window shown in Figure 3.38.

Figure 3.37 Administering the SUS Server

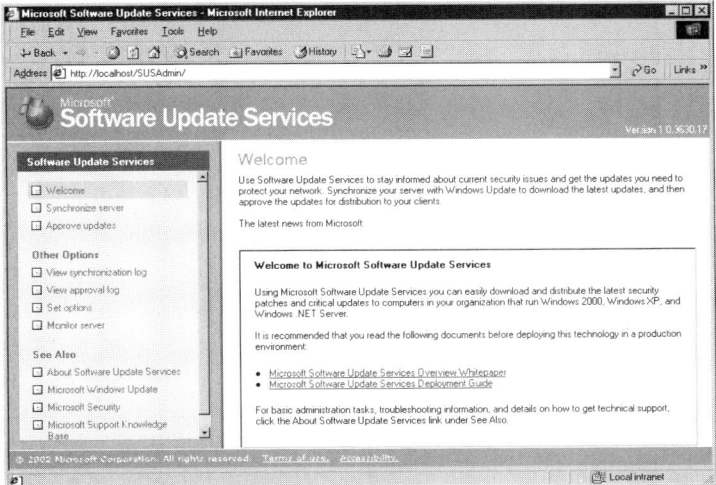

Figure 3.38 Configuring the Synchronization Schedule

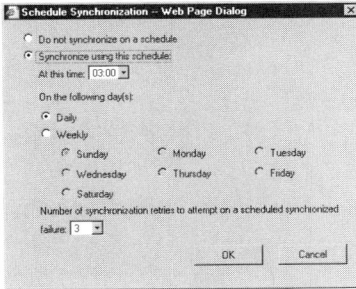

14. If you need to configure options related to a proxy server, click **Set options** from the left pane menu. When you are ready to force a synchronization of your new SUS server to update it, click the **Synchronize Now** button on the **Synchronize server** page.

15. Synchronization will run for some time (as shown in Figure 3.39), depending on the amount of updates that you need.

16. After all updates have been downloaded, click **OK**. You are now prompted to test and approve updates. You can do this at your leisure.

17. When you have tested an update and you are ready to approve it, click **Approve updates** to open the Approve Updates window. Select all updates you are ready to approve (see Figure 3.40) and click **Approve**.

18. You will be asked to verify that the list of updates you are approving is correct, since it will replace the existing approval list. Click **Yes** to allow

the list of approved updates to be made available to Automatic Updates clients.

Figure 3.39 Downloading Required Updates

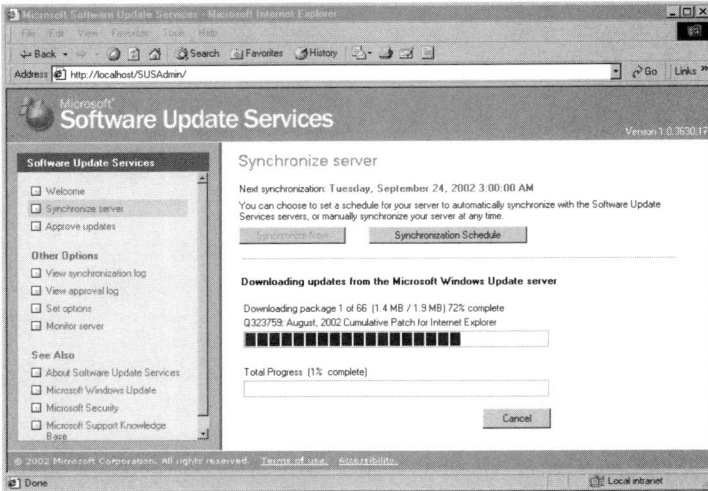

Figure 3.40 Selecting the Approved Updates

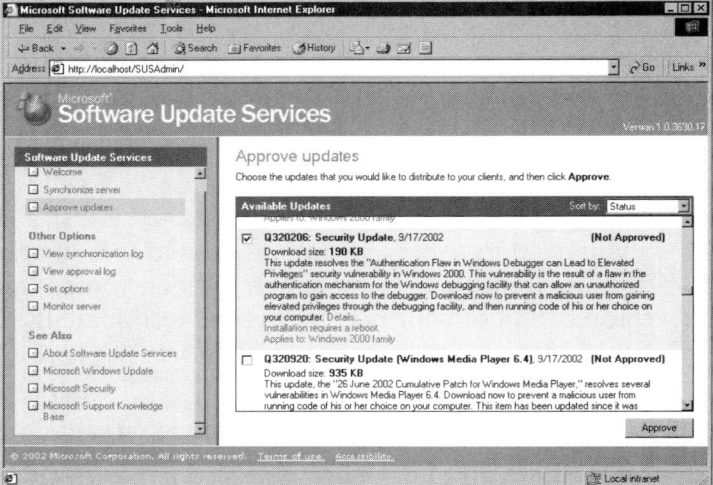

19. You will be presented once again with the familiar supplemental End User License Agreement. Click **Accept** to continue the approval process.

20. Click **OK** when you're informed that the list of updates has been made available to your clients. You have just performed the installation and basic configuration of your first SUS server.

Armed with a functional SUS server, you now need to install the Automatic Updates client software on all your client computers in order for them to take advantage of the service. You can install the Automatic Updates client via any of the traditional methods, including using IntelliMirror and Group Policy, using Systems Management Server (or any other software installation and management application), or by good, old-fashioned sneaker-net.

Since we are only going to install one Automatic Updates client in Exercise 3.11, we will use the sneaker-net method; however, your installation method should be based on the number and location of the client computers on which you want to install the software.

The Automatic Updates client software can be used on the following systems:

- Windows 2000 Professional, Server, or Advanced Server (Service Pack 2 or later). Service Pack 3 includes the Automatic Updates client software.

- Windows XP Home Edition or Professional. Service Pack 1 includes the Automatic Updates client software.

EXERCISE 3.11

INSTALLING AND CONFIGURING THE AUTOMATIC UPDATES CLIENT

1. Download the Automatic Updates client installation package from www.microsoft.com/windows2000/downloads/recommended/susclient/default.asp.

2. Double-click the **WUAU22.msi** file to install the Automatic Updates client. When it completes, you will notice a new applet in the Control Panel (see Figure 3.41).

   Figure 3.41 A New Applet Appears

   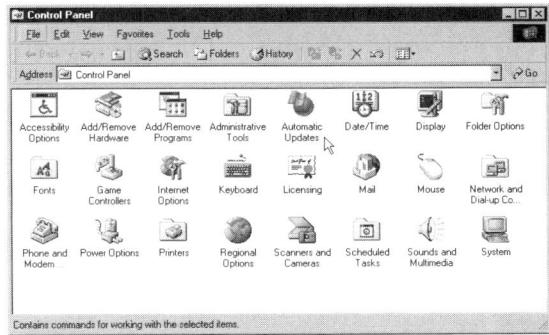

3. By default, the Automatic Updates client is not enabled. If it were (assuming you did no further configuration), it would be able to download updates from the Windows Update server. We are going to configure it to download approved updates from our SUS server instead.

4. Automatic Updates settings for SUS are configured through a special Group Policy administrative template that you must add to the Group Policy object you are editing. Since we are working with one local computer, we will use the Local Group Policy object. However, you can perform this process for any Group Policy object at any level of Active Directory, as you require.

5. Open the Local Group Policy window by typing **gpedit.msc** at the command line.

6. Open the Computer Configuration node, right-click **Administrative Templates**, and select **Add/Remove Templates** from the context menu, as shown in Figure 3.42.

Figure 3.42 Adding a New Template

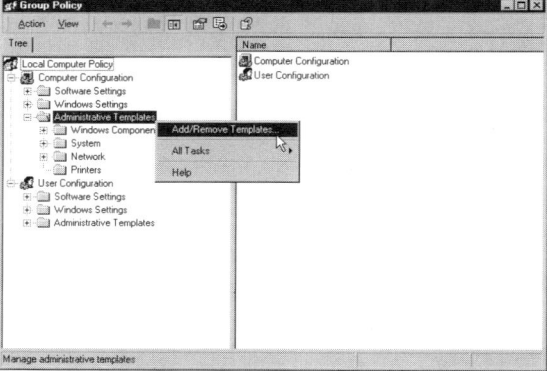

7. Click **Add** and select the **wuau.adm** template, as shown in Figure 3.43. Click **Open**. Click **Close** to close the Add/Remove Templates window.

Figure 3.43 Selecting the New Template

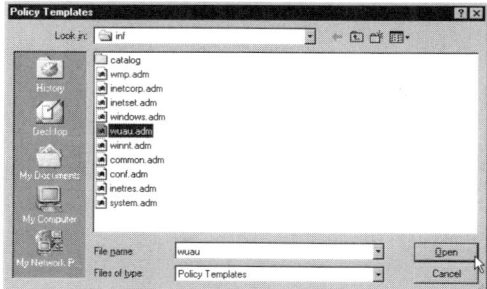

8. Expand the Administrative Templates node to the Windows Updates node.
9. Configure the **Configure Automatic Updates** and **Specify intranet Microsoft update server location** objects to your requirements, as shown in Figures 4.44 and 4.45.

Figure 3.44 Configuring the Configure Automatic Updates Object

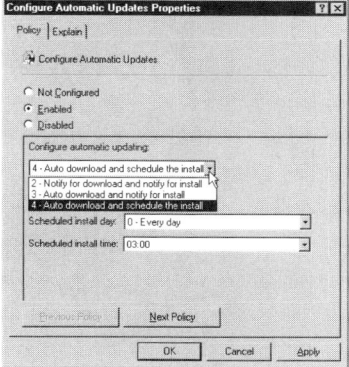

Figure 3.45 Configuring the Specify Intranet Microsoft Update Server Location Object

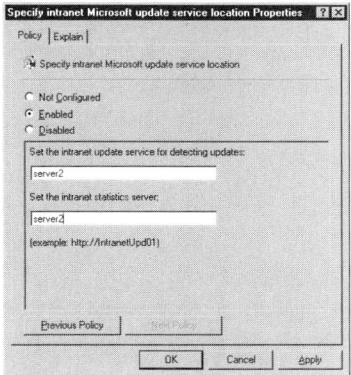

10. After Group Policy has been replicated and taken effect, you will no longer be able to manually control Automatic Updates settings from the Control Panel applet. All available options will be grayed out.
11. Depending on your configuration, updates will either be installed silently according to the configured schedule or will require user intervention to complete the install. In this example, we elected to have updates automatically downloaded and installed. Figure 3.46 shows the result: The

update that was approved (see Figure 3.40) was subsequently installed and now shows up in the Add/Remove Programs listing.

Figure 3.46 Inspecting the Work of the Automatic Updates Service

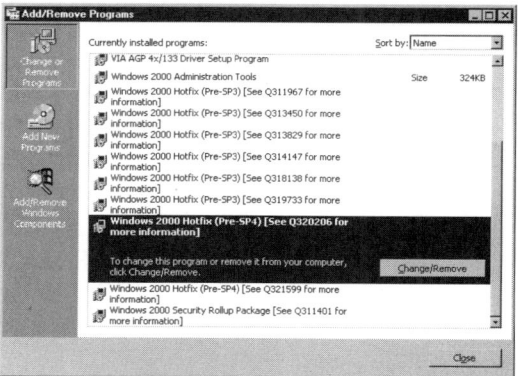

Test Day Tip

Even though it is possible that you will see questions dealing with SUS and the Automatic Updates Client, you should not expect to see detailed installation and configuration questions on the exam. Expect to see questions more along the lines of what SUS and Automatic Updates are, how they work, and what you need to do to get them up and running. Remember, SUS is nothing more than a Windows Update server that you run on your internal network to provide your clients a location to automatically get and install required updates.

Systems Management Server

It is quite likely that in an organization with a well-established software installation and inventory control system, you will instead use some other form of update distribution and installation. Microsoft's Systems Management Server (SMS) is an extremely powerful and popular software management and inventory control application that can be used to install, maintain, and inventory software across most all versions of the Windows operating system. Although a detailed discussion of SMS is beyond the scope of this book, you can find a wealth of information on using SMS to deploy and manage updates on your network at www.microsoft.com/smserver/techinfo/deployment/20/default.asp. SMS 2003 was in beta testing at the time this book went to press and promises to provide more robust Active Directory integration and several other new enhancements. For more information on SMS 2003, see www.microsoft.com/smserver/evaluation/future/default.asp.

Special Considerations for Updating Servers

When you stop to think about it, servers are the life's blood of your network. True, the network exists to provide clients with information and services they need in order to be useful to users, but servers make it all work. The importance of testing, testing, testing, and more testing of any update to be deployed to your servers cannot be emphasized enough. You absolutely must test all updates, no matter how small or seemingly trivial, that will be applied to your servers before they are deployed. After all, you don't want to be known as "*that* admin," do you? You know, the admin who brought the entire company's business to a grinding halt because he failed to adequately test an update before deploying it—oh guess what … the update was not meant for the server it was deployed to, and as a result the server crashed. Too bad that was the Exchange Server. You get the point.

Of course, after testing has been completed to your satisfaction, you are not ready to deploy updates to your servers just yet. You need a well-documented (and approved) upgrade plan that includes a backout plan in the event that things go south in a hurry. Only proceed to install updates after you have been granted approval from your supervisor and the backout plan is well documented. In this way, you provide yourself with an out should things not go according to plan. You also want to ensure that you have a solid, well-tested disaster recovery plan in place. Other solutions such as disk imaging or hot standby systems can also provide some amount of redundancy should things go wrong in a hurry.

The last special precaution that you should take when updating servers is to apply the required updates only to the required servers. Blindly applying all updates to all servers is not only a waste of time and bandwidth, it can also lead to unforeseen problems. Your update plan should be carefully prepared to specify exactly which updates will be applied to which servers in order to prevent this sort of issue. On that note, you might want to apply updates incrementally over a week or two in order to observe how real production servers respond to the update. No matter how much testing you do in the lab, you will never be able to truly recreate the real network conditions that exist in your organization.

Exam Warning

On the exam, just as in real life, pay special attention to any scenarios dealing with performing updates on "critical" or "production" servers.

Troubleshooting Update Installations

From time to time, you might experience problems while updating your computers with the latest hotfix or service pack. When it comes to applying updates to your computers, two universal truths, without a doubt, apply to software installation and update in Windows networks:

- Nothing works correctly every time, no matter how well designed the product.
- If there is an incompatibility issue with an applied update, you will most likely find it—the hard way.

Of course, you can face a host of other issues, but these tend to be the most common that you will see, along with permissions-based problems during upgrade.

Application Compatibility Issues

It is an unfortunate reality that not all software programs that can be run on a Windows 2000 computer are 100-percent compatible with each other. In fact, there are likely cases in which two or more software products should not be run together on the same Windows 2000 computer—ever. Most times you can find out ahead of time about application compatibility issues by visiting the Microsoft Knowledge Base and reading the background information about any update that you are preparing to deploy.

Performing a search against the knowledge base for the application name can also yield some positive results. As a last resort, you should look for available information on the vendor's Web site about compatibility issues. More often than not, vendors make it very clear what combinations of applications you can and cannot use with their products.

Permissions Problems

With very few exceptions, any updates that are installed manually (including Windows Update) require the user to be logged in with local computer Administrative credentials. Members of the Administrators group in Active Directory are, by default, members of every computer's local Administrative group. When updates are being applied by some automated method, such as scripting, SUS, or SMS, the updates are performed using a preconfigured domain account—often invisible even to the administrator.

In the event that you have updates that fail to install due to permissions problems, you need to first determine what method is being utilized to apply the updates. After you have determined the method, you can then go on to examine the account or service account that is being used for the deployment and ensure that it is one that is configured with the correct permissions and is the correct one for the task at hand. Often, installation failures show up in the Event Logs of the local computer and can provide some insight into what went wrong.

Version Conflicts

Without sounding overly optimistic, Windows 2000 really is an intelligent operating system when it comes to keeping its files in order. However, sometimes a version conflict can wreak havoc on your computer. If installing hotfixes or other patches, always use the Qchain.exe tool to prevent version conflicts. In all other cases, always install only one update or hotfix at a time and immediately restart the computer to allow the updates to take effect. Only by using one of these two methods can you ensure that your computers will be protected, for the most part, against version conflicts that arise out of updates gone bad.

Should you fall prey to a version conflict, you might be able to uninstall the suspected culprit update by starting the computer in Safe mode and removing the update using the Add/Remove Programs applet. Severe corruption may require a reinstallation of the operating system and applications—thus providing yet another compelling reason to have in place a well-designed, documented, and tested disaster recovery plan.

Summary of Exam Objectives

Keeping your Windows 2000 computers up to date, and therefore secure, is a big responsibility no matter how many computers you have. The number of computers you have and their geographic locations does become important, however, as you seek to implement a consistent (and usable) change management system on your network.

The first major hurdle that you must cross is to identify any and all required updates for your various computers. How will you accomplish this seemingly unmanageable task? The choice is up to you, but you can use several tools from Microsoft (as well as plenty of others from third parties) to analyze each of your computers and then determine the updates that need to be installed.

Windows Update can be used on a single local computer to quickly create a listing of all missing updates on that computer. If you have only a few computers or you have computers that are separated from the rest of the network, Windows Update could be a viable solution for you. The Microsoft Network Security Hotfix Checker, HFNetChk, is a command-line tool that can be used to quickly and efficiently scan all the computers on your network (or any smaller group) for missing updates. You can save the output results into a tab-delimited text file for later importation into Excel to examine the state of your computers. From this output, you can begin to create an update plan.

You can also use the Microsoft Baseline Security Analyzer, MBSA, in order to help you determine the current needs of your computers. The MBSA can be run from either the GUI or from the command line and includes fairly detailed information about each update that needs to be applied. Be aware, however, that the MBSA tool is primarily concerned with all sorts of security issues that could be occurring on your computers. Items such as weak or blank passwords, for example, will be shown in the MBSA analysis. You will often get more than you bargained for when you use MBSA, which is not a bad thing when it comes to securing your computers.

After identifying the updates you need, the next phase of the update process comes into play: downloading and deploying the updates. Downloading the updates can be done in any number of ways, whether directly from the specific Knowledge Base article discussing a specific issue at hand or by an automated means, such as Windows Update or Software Update Services.

Windows Update, as mentioned previously, is most useful when you have only a small number of computers to update, because it is both time and network resource intensive. Corporate Windows Update has been replaced by two new services: Software Update Services and the Windows Update Catalog. In a sense, Windows Update Catalog functions pretty much identically to the way Corporate Windows Update used to: You select the updates you want to download and then download them to a network location of your choosing.

Software Update Services takes this idea a step further and actually turns an IIS server inside your network into a functioning Windows Update server. SUS can be scheduled to regularly synchronize with Windows Update, ensuring that you always have the most up-to-date fixes and updates available to you. After you have approved an SUS update, it is made available to your Automatic Updates clients in the mode of operation you have configured. The configuration for Automatic Updates is most commonly performed from within Group Policy, whether at the local, domain, site, or OU level, but it can be accomplished by editing the Registry directly if the usage of Group Policy is not desired.

Scripts or batch files can also be used to deploy hotfixes and make a very powerful change management tool when used with the Qchain.exe tool. Qchain.exe acts to ensure that the most up-to-date file versions are maintained on your computer and should be used with all deployments of more than one hotfix. Regardless of how you deploy your hotfixes or the number you deploy, you must always restart the computer to complete the update process and prevent file system version and compatibility issues—problems that Qchain.exe can prevent for you. Alternatively, you can also use dedicated software management packages, such as Systems Management Server or any other third-party application for the deployment of updates on your network.

Although it doesn't happen very often in Windows 2000, you could have some issues after an update has been deployed. Most times you can quickly and safely resolve the problem by uninstalling the update. When asked, always elect to provide for service pack removal at a later date. Most hotfixes and other updates can be removed via the Add/Remove Programs applet with no extra configuration required at the time of installation. Should you not be able to properly start your computer after applying an update, starting in Safe mode and removing the update will usually fix the problem.

Version conflicts can be avoided when performing updates by either installing only one update a time, followed by a restart, or using the Qchain.exe tool to ensure that the correct file versions are installed or maintained on your computer. Permissions (or the lack of proper permissions) will most often cause an update to fail to install properly. This problem can be resolved by verifying the group membership and explicit permissions that have been applied to a specific user or system account. Above all else, a solid and easy-to-use disaster recovery plan is an absolute must when it comes to performing updates to critical production computers. The job you save might be your own.

Exam Objectives Fast Track

Identifying Required Updates

- ☑ The Microsoft Network Security Hotfix Checker, HFNetChk, is a command-line tool that can be used to quickly and efficiently scan all the computers on your network (or any smaller group) for missing updates.

- ☑ The Microsoft Baseline Security Analyzer, MBSA, can also be used to help you determine your computers' current needs. The MBSA can be run from either the GUI or from the command line and includes fairly detailed information about each update that needs to be applied.

- ☑ Single computers or small groups of computers can use Windows Update to identify (and download) required updates.

Deploying and Managing Updates

- ☑ Use the Windows Update Web site to update small groups of computers or computers that are not connected to the main organizational network.

- ☑ Using the Windows Update Catalog, you can select and download the updates of your choosing. You can later deploy them by any means you like, including scripting or manual installation.

- ☑ The Software Update Service and the Automatic Updates client work together to allow you to automatically download updates from the Windows Update servers. No downloaded updates can be installed on a client computer until they have been approved for release by an administrator. Automatic Updates, configured from Group Policy, can then either silently install any approved updates or prompt the computer user for action.

- ☑ Dedicated software management packages, such as Systems Management Server, can also be used to deploy updates to client computers.

- ☑ Take great care in applying updates to servers. Ensure that you have thoroughly tested the update and have a solid backout plan in place before starting to update any server. Update servers in waves to allow you time to observe their performance (in small groups) after they are updated.

www.syngress.com

Troubleshooting Update Installations

- ☑ Always ensure that updates are applied by users with the correct credentials or, if updating by automated means, by a system account with the correct credentials.

- ☑ Use of the Qchain.exe tool can help prevent versioning issues.

- ☑ Should an update have undesirable effects on a computer, you should remove the update from the computer as soon as possible and conduct further testing on it.

- ☑ A solid, proven disaster recovery plan is of critical importance when it's time to upgrade computers. Finding out after the fact that the plan doesn't work is never the right time.

Exam Objectives Frequently Asked Questions

The following Frequently Asked Questions, answered by the authors of this book, are designed to both measure your understanding of the Exam Objectives presented in this chapter, and to assist you with real-life implementation of these concepts.

Q: What happened to the Corporate Windows Update Web site? How am I going to download updates in bulk now?

A: The Corporate Windows Update Web site was replaced in early 2002 by two new services from Microsoft: Software Update Services and the Windows Update Catalog. Of these, the Windows Update Catalog functions in roughly the same manner that the old Corporate Windows Update Web site. You can select updates by operating system and download them to your servers for testing and deployment.

Q: I have a Small Business Server 2000 running for my small company. Can I install the Software Update Services on my server to keep my six computers up to date?

A: No. Because the SBS server would be the domain controller, you cannot install and use SUS on that server. If you placed another member server in the network, you could run SUS from it and keep all the other network computers up to date.

Q: I have installed the Software Update Services on a member server in my company, but my Automatic Updates clients are getting updates that I have not approved. What is wrong?

A: The most likely cause of this issue is that you have not installed the newest version of Automatic Updates (required to function with SUS) and you have not configured the Automatic Updates client behavior in Group Policy to pull updates from your internal servers. Until you configure Automatic Updates from Group Policy, it can (and will) continue to pull downloads from the Windows Update servers.

Q: What makes it unsafe to install multiple hotfixes without restarting the computer after each one?

A: Hotfixes are applied on the subsequent restart of the computer. Should two hotfixes both modify the same file, it is possible that the first one applied could update a file to a newer version, and then the second one applied could overwrite this file with an older version. This can create loss of functionality and system instability. Applying hotfixes with the Qchain.exe utility is the only way to avoid this sort of problem in most cases. (Nothing's perfect—you heard it here first!)

Q: What is the difference between HFNetChk and MBSA?

A: HFNetChk only checks for missing critical updates and service packs; MBSA scans a computer for all sorts of security flaws such as weak or blank passwords and a host of other issues. HFNetChk only runs from the command line, whereas MBSA can be run from the command line or from within the GUI.

Self Test

A Quick Answer Key follows the Self Test questions. For complete questions, answers, and epxlanations to the Self Test questions in this chapter as well as the other chapters in this book, see the Self Test Appendix.

Identifying Required Updates

1. Andrea is responsible for keeping 550 Windows 2000 computers up to date. She would like to determine what, if any, required updates her computers need on a weekly basis. What is the best way for her to go about performing this task with the least administrative effort?

   A. Andrea needs to visit each computer and run HFNetChk locally.

   B. Andrea needs to create a script that runs HFNetChk against her computers and saves the results to a network share for her to examine.

   C. Andrea needs to configure a script that runs Windows Update against each of her computers and provides a text file output.

   D. Andrea needs to keep a log of installed versus required updates for each computer and check the Microsoft Web site weekly, looking for new updates that might be required.

2. Austin is trying to run the MBSA tool on one of his member servers when he is prompted to download and install a strange file claiming to be from Microsoft. What will happen if he rejects the download request for the file MSSecureXML file?

   A. Nothing. The file is optional and not required to complete the scan using MBSA.

   B. Nothing. The download request was obviously a hack attempt from an outside party. Microsoft never needs to download anything to your computer in order to determine its current update status.

   C. Nothing.. The MBSA tool cannot work without the file.

   D. Nothing. As long as Austin knows which updates are and are not installed on his server, MBSA will function properly.

3. Christopher is looking for a tool that can scan all 458 of his network computers from a central location and provide a detailed report of all updates and patches that he needs to apply. He would like to perform this scan with the least amount of administrative effort. What options are available to him? (Choose all correct answers.)

   A. Christopher can use the HFNetChk tool as part of a batch file or script to perform this task.

   B. Christopher can use Software Update Services to perform this task.

   C. Christopher can use the URLScan tool as part of a batch file or script to perform this task.

   D. Christopher can use the MBSA tool from either the command line or the GUI to perform this task.

4. José is creating a script to run the HFNetChk tool on his network to scan for missing updates. What command does he need to use to allow the application to read a text file containing the IP addresses of the computers that he wants to scan?

   A. hfnetchk –h

   B. hfnetchk –i

   C. hfnetchk –fh

   D. hfnetchk –fip

5. Austin has performed several scans of his network using the MBSA tool. Hannah now wants to examine the results of the scans, but she cannot do so. What is the most likely reason for this problem?

   A. Hannah is not a member of the Domain Admins group and thus does not have the proper permissions to access the location to which the scan results have been saved.

   B. Hannah does not have the proper permissions to access files located in Austin's Documents and Settings folder.

   C. Hannah is not connected to the network.

   D. Hannah's computer is not configured to use Kerberos as its authentication protocol.

6. Bruno is responsible for the security of the Windows 2000 computers in his organization. He has several junior administrators who work for him and apply patches and updates to computers as required. What can Bruno do to allow his junior administrators to be able to easily read the MBSA scan results that he generates on a daily basis with the least effort?

   A. Have the junior administrators perform their own MBSA scans. This way, the scan results will be in their Documents and Settings folders.

   B. Run the MBSA tool and elect for the results to be redirected to a location other than the default.

   C. Give the junior administrators the required NTFS permissions to access the scan results in his Documents and Settings folder.

   D. E-mail the MBSA results to all junior administrators daily.

Deploying and Managing Updates

7. Lily is responsible for 20 Windows 2000 computers in her organization. All the computers are on one campus, but they are scattered among four different buildings. Lily is the only network administrator in her company. Her network is a Windows 2000 Active Directory network. What is the easiest way for Lily to keep all her clients updated with the patches and updates they need but not to allow any updates or patches to be issued until she is satisfied that they are stable?

   A. Lily should use Windows Update on each computer locally to download and install the updates her computers need.

   B. Lily should use the Windows Update Catalog to download and install the updates her computers need.

   C. Lily should use Software Update Services and the Automatic Updates client to download and install the updates her computers need.

   D. Lily should download all the updates she needs and create an integrated installation CD-ROM to distribute to each of the four buildings to install the updates on her computers.

8. Hannah needs to locate and download applicable security updates for her network for testing in a lab environment. What are the best ways for her to get these updates as quickly as possible without downloading anything she doesn't want or installing any additional network services? (Choose all that apply.)

    A. Hannah can visit the TechNET security page and download specific updates that she needs.

    B. Hannah can use the Software Update Services to download available updates.

    C. Hannah can use the Windows Update Catalog to download the updates she needs.

    D. Hannah can allow her computers to use Automatic Updates from the Windows Update Web servers.

9. Rick is preparing to install eight hotfixes to his file and print servers. What method should Rick use to ensure that all eight hotfixes get applied correctly and the servers have no stability or compatibility issues after he is done, using the least amount of administrative effort?

    A. Rick should use the Qchain.exe tool in conjunction with a batch file or script to install all eight hotfixes in one shot.

    B. Rick should manually install each hotfix, in order from lowest Q article number to highest Q article number, restarting his server after each one to make sure that version conflicts are prevented.

    C. Rick should manually install all eight hotfixes and then restart his server to ensure that the updates are applied.

    D. Rick should extract all the files from the hotfix executables and then copy these over the existing files on his server.

10. Cindy is trying to install the Software Update Service on her server computer, but the installation keeps failing. What is the most likely reason for this problem?

    A. Cindy's network does not have Active Directory, which is required for SUS to work.

    B. Cindy is attempting to install SUS onto a domain controller, which is not allowed.

    C. Cindy's network has only Windows XP Professional clients. You must have Windows 2000 clients for SUS to install properly.

    D. Cindy does not have Enterprise Admin credentials.

11. Tom has installed and configured the Automatic Updates client on his computer to download updates from an internal server named GREEN42. Automatic Updates was configured to download and install, automatically, any available updates from GREEN42 on a daily basis. After several weeks, Tom noticed that no updates have been applied to his client computer. Given what you know so far, what is the most likely reason that no updates have been received on Tom's computer?

    A. Tom turns his computer off during the update period that has been configured.

    B. GREEN42 is either not running SUS or is not receiving updates from the Windows Update servers.

    C. Tom forgot to accept the supplemental End User License Agreement that is required to make Active Updates function properly.

    D. Tom's copy of Windows 2000 is not properly licensed.

12. Catherine is preparing to deploy Windows 2000 Professional to 75 new workstations in her company. She knows that a new service pack has been made available for Windows 2000, but her Windows 2000 Professional Setup CD-ROM only has Service Pack 1. What is the easiest and fastest way for Catherine to get these 75 new clients installed with Windows 2000 Service Pack 3 without placing an undue strain on the network?

    A. Visit each client, installing Windows 2000 Professional Service Pack 1. After the installation is complete, install Service Pack 3.

    B. Create a slipstreamed installation source using her Windows 2000 Professional Setup CD-ROM and the Service Pack 3 files. Deploy this source to her new clients over the network using the Remote Installation Service.

    C. Use RIS to deploy a Windows 2000 Service Pack 1 image. After this process has been completed, use Group Policy and IntelliMirror to deploy Service Pack 3 using the update.msi file.

    D. Create a slipstream installation source and burn it back to CD-ROM using her Windows 2000 Professional Setup CD-ROM and the Service Pack 3 files. Visit each machine and install Windows 2000 Professional Service Pack 3 from this slipstreamed CD-ROM.

13. Jon is responsible for three client computers that are not part of the corporate network. These computers have Internet connectivity through a broadband DSL connection at their remote site. What is the best way for Jon to keep these three computers up to date without having to travel to this remote location or spend unnecessary money? No users at the remote location are technically competent to perform this task for Jon.

    A. Jon has no other choice but to travel to this location.

    B. Jon should install and configure the Automatic Updates client to get critical updates from the Windows Update servers and automatically install them upon download.

    C. Jon should FTP into the computers and run the HFNetChk tool to check for required updates.

    D. Jon should configure these computers to participate in the corporate network via a leased WAN link.

Troubleshooting Update Installations

14. You are the network administrator of a medium-sized regional organization that has one central office and six field offices spread out over several states. A user in each field office is performing most of the local administrative functions for you, although these users are not as knowledgeable as you would like them to be and sometimes cause problems that you must correct yourself. Yesterday, one of your "assistant administrators" applied several hotfixes to a Windows 2000 server computer in his office. Today you received a phone call from this "assistant administrator" informing you that the power failed in that location overnight and now the Windows 2000 server will not start properly. What do you suspect is the cause of this problem?

    A. The power supply in the server has been damaged.

    B. The user did not properly apply the hotfixes by restarting the server after each one or by using Qchain.

    C. The server was attacked overnight and the Registry has been damaged by the attacker.

    D. The user did not use the HFNetChk tool to determine the hotfixes that were required.

15. Dom, your assistant administrator, has been in the office all night applying hotfixes to your production servers. Now when he restarts them, they all fail to start properly. You quickly determine that the cause of the problem was his lack of using the Qchain utility. Now you have a problem to deal with. Which of the following documents should you consider using at this point?

   A. Network Acceptable Use Policy (AUP)

   B. Server update plan

   C. Network disaster recovery plan

   D. Windows 2000 Resource Kit

Self Test Quick Answer Key

For complete questions, answers, and epxlanations to the Self Test questions in this chapter as well as the other chapters in this book, see the Self Test Appendix.

1. **B**
2. **C**
3. **A, D**
4. **D**
5. **B**
6. **B**
7. **C**
8. **A, C**
9. **A**
10. **B**
11. **B**
12. **B**
13. **B**
14. **B**
15. **C**

MCSE/MCSA 70-214 Part III

Implementing and Managing a Public Key Infrastructure (PKI) and Encrypting File System (EFS)

Chapter 4

MCSE/MCSA 70-214

Installing, Configuring, & Managing Windows 2000 Certificate Authorities

Exam Objectives in this Chapter:

- **3.1.4** Deploy and manage IPSec certificates. Considerations include renewing certificates.
- **3.5.1** Obtain public and private certificates.
- **3.5.3** Renew certificates.
- **5.1** Install and configure Certificate Authority (CA) hierarchies. Considerations include enterprise, standalone, and third-party.
- **5.1.1** Install and configure the root, intermediate, and issuing CA. Considerations include renewals and hierarchy.
- **5.1.2** Configure certificate templates. Considerations include LDAP queries, HTTP queries, and third-party CAs.
- **5.1.3** Configure the publication of Certificate Revocation Lists (CRLs).
- **5.1.4** Configure public key Group Policy.
- **5.1.5** Configure certificate renewal and enrollment.
- **5.1.6** Deploy certificates to users, computers, and CAs.
- **5.2** Manage Certificate Authorities (CAs). Considerations include enterprise, stand-alone, and third-party.
- **5.2.1** Enroll and renew certificates.
- **5.2.2** Revoke certificates.
- **5.2.3** Manage and troubleshoot Certificate Revocation Lists (CRLs). Considerations include publishing the CRL.
- **5.2.4** Back up and restore the CA.
- **5.3** Manage client-computer and server certificates. Considerations include SMIME, EFS, exporting, and storage.
- **5.3.1** Publish certificates through Active Directory.
- **5.3.2** Issue certificates using MMC, Web enrollment, programmatic, or auto enrollment using Windows XP.
- **5.3.3** Recover KMS-issued keys.

Introduction

Organizations today rely on networks for access to information. These range from internal networks to the Internet. Access must be configured to provide information to other organizations that request it. For example, when a person wants to make a purchase, they can quickly check out vendors' prices through their Web pages. To not allow the competition to get ahead of their organization, they must establish their own Web page for the advertising and ordering of their products.

In the past, Windows NT provided user security through account names and passwords. At logon, every user had to submit credentials, which were compared against a server's database for authentication. The matching of the username and password identified the user but failed to identify the corporate server. This environment allowed many Man-in-the-Middle (MITM) attacks. An attacker could configure a server to impersonate the corporate server, thus intercepting the data from the user as well as from the corporate server. With the man in the middle in place, an attacker could grab sensitive data when users sent information to the corporate server. The man in the middle could have access to sensitive information when the server sent the information to the requesting user. The best way to prevent impersonation from occurring on a network is to have both the user and the server verify themselves to each other.

Windows 2000 includes new security features that prevent MITM attacks. The new security features include the components that create the Public Key Infrastructure (PKI). As the name implies, security is based on the use of public key pairs.

Cryptography and You: What is it All About?

The rapid growth of Internet use has given rise to new security concerns. Any company that does not configure a strong security infrastructure is putting the company at risk. An unscrupulous person could, if security were lax, steal information or modify business information in a way that could result in major financial disaster. To protect the organization's information, the man in the middle must be eliminated. Cryptographic technologies provide a way to identify both users and servers during network use.

Test Day Tip

The material presented in this section is all background information designed to enhance your understanding of how the Windows 2000 PKI functions. While you should not expect to be tested on the theory of operations, it is important to understand how it works to effectively configure and administer it.

Public Key Cryptography

Encryption is the process of changing a *cleartext* message into an unreadable form to protect sensitive data. The transformation from the scrambled form, known as *ciphertext*, back to cleartext is called *decryption*.

Cryptography can be dated back to around 2000 B.C. in ancient Egypt. Through time and civilizations, ciphering text played an important role in wars and politics. As modern times provided new communication methods, scrambling information became increasingly more important. World War II brought about the first use of the computer in the cracking of Germany's Enigma code. In 1952, President Truman created the National Security Agency at Fort Meade, Maryland. This agency, which is the center of U.S. cryptographic activity, fulfills two important national functions: it protects all military and executive communication from being intercepted, and intercepts and unscrambles messages sent by other countries.

Three types of cryptographic functions exist. The *hash function* does not involve the use of a key at all, but uses a mathematical algorithm on the data to scramble it. The *secret key* method of encryption, which involves the use of a single key, is used to encrypt and decrypt the information and is sometimes referred to as *symmetric key cryptography*. An excellent example of secret key encryption is the decoder ring you may have had as a child. Any person who obtained your decoder ring could read your "secret" information.

There are basically two types of symmetric algorithms. *Block symmetric* algorithms work by taking a given length of bits known as blocks. *Stream symmetric* algorithms operate on a single bit at a time. One well-known block algorithm is Data Encryption Standard (DES). Windows 2000 uses a modified DES and performs that operation on 64-bit blocks using every eighth bit for parity. The resulting ciphertext is the same length as the original cleartext. For export purposes, the DES is also available with a 40-bit key.

One advantage of secret key encryption is the efficiency with which it takes a large amount of data and encrypts it. Symmetric algorithms can also be easily implemented at the hardware level. The major disadvantage of secret key encryption is that a single key is used for both encryption and decryption. There must be a secure way for the two parties to exchange the one secret key.

In the 1970s, the disadvantage of secret key encryption was eliminated through the mathematical implementation of *public key encryption*. Public key encryption, also referred to as *asymmetric cryptography*, replaced the one shared key with each user's own pair of keys. One key is a *public* key, which is made available to everyone and used for the encryption process only. The other key in the pair, the *private* key, is available only to the owner. The private key cannot be created as a result of the public key's being available.

Data that is encrypted by the public key can only be decrypted using the private key of the pair. It is also possible for the owner to use a private key to encrypt sensitive information. If the data is encrypted using the private key, the public key in that pair of keys is needed to decrypt the data.

The public key is made available to everyone, so a secure key exchange channel is not needed. Figure 4.1 shows the encryption process using the receiver's public key. Bob wants to send Alice a file that is encrypted so only she can access it. Bob encrypts the file with Alice's public key. The encrypted file is sent to Alice. She uses her private key to decrypt the file. As long as Alice's private key is protected, the encrypted data is also protected.

Figure 4.1 Encrypting Data

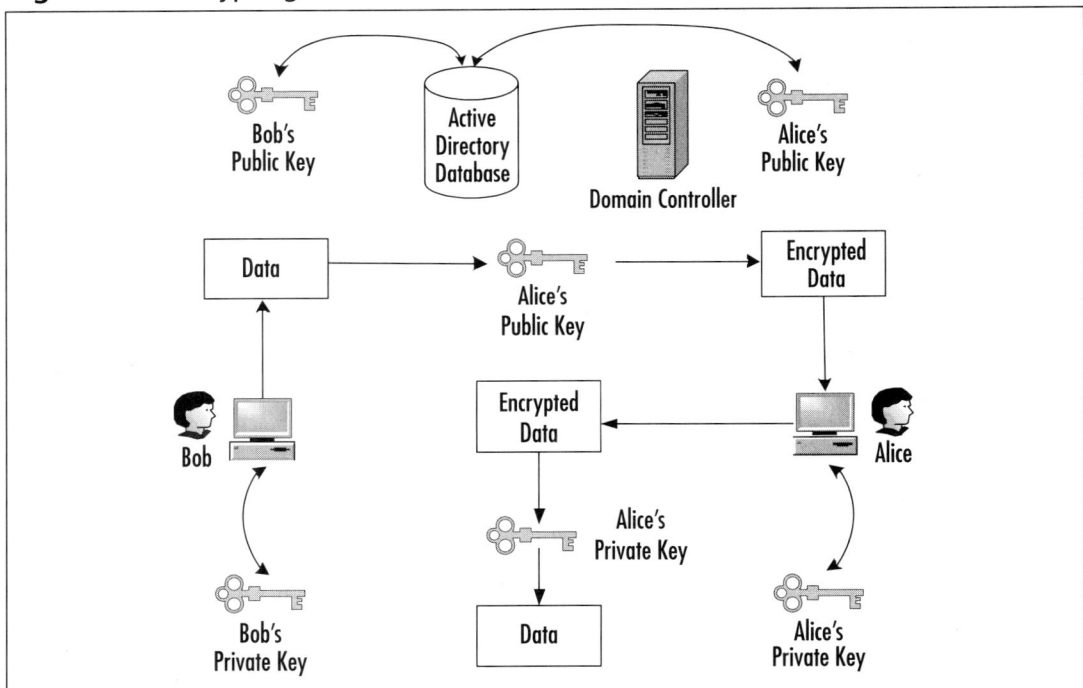

Public key cryptography can do everything secret key cryptography can do, but at a much slower pace. To work around the speed problem of public key encryption, designers often incorporate the two encryption methods together. The designers of Windows 2000 did just that. Any data that requires a fast encryption method is handled by secret key encryption, while the encryption of the secret key itself is handled by public key cryptography. Public key encryption is slow, but because the secret key is small, this method of encryption does not have an impact on the overall process.

Public Key Functionality

Public key cryptography brings major security technologies to the desktop in the Windows 2000 environment. The network is now provided with the capability to allow users to safely do the following:

- Transmit over insecure channels
- Store sensitive information on any commonly used media
- Verify a person's identity for authentication
- Prove that a particular person generated a message
- Prove that the received message was not tampered with in transit

Algorithms based on public keys can be used for all of these purposes. The most popular public key algorithm is the standard RSA, which is named after its three inventors: Rivest, Shamir, and Adleman. The RSA algorithm is based on two prime numbers with more than 200 digits each. A hacker would have to take the ciphertext and the public key and factor the product of the two primes. As computer-processing time increases, the RSA remains secure by increasing the key length, unlike the DES algorithm, which has a fixed key length.

Public key algorithms provide privacy, authentication, and easy key management, but they encrypt and decrypt data slowly because of the intensive computation required. RSA has been evaluated to be from 10 to 10,000 times slower than DES in some environments, which is a good reason not to use public key algorithms for bulk encryption.

Digital Signatures

Forgery is a security issue. When information is sent electronically, no human contact is involved. The receiver wants to know that the person listed as the sender is really the sender and that the information received has not been modified in any way during transit. A hash algorithm is implemented to guarantee the Windows 2000 user that the data is authentic. A hash value encrypted with a private key is called a *digital signature*. Anyone with access to the corresponding public key can verify the authenticity of a digital signature. Only a person with a private key can generate digital signatures. Any modification makes a digital signature invalid.

The purpose of a digital signature is to prevent changes within a document from going unnoticed and also to claim the person to be the original author. The document itself is not encrypted. The digital signature is data sent along with the document that is guaranteed not to be tampered with. A change of any size invalidates the digital signature.

When King Henry II had to send a message to his troops in a remote location, the letter would be sealed with wax, and while the wax was still soft the king would use his ring to make an impression in it. No modification occurred to the original message if the seal was never broken during transit. There was no doubt that King Henry II had initiated the message, because he was the only person possessing a ring that matched the waxed imprint. Digital signatures work in a similar fashion, in that only the sender's public key can authenticate both the original sender and the content of the document.

Digital signatures are generated by a *message digest*, which is a number generated by taking a message and using a hash algorithm. A message digest is regarded as a fingerprint and can range from a 128-bit number to a 256-bit number. A hash function takes variable-length input and produces a fixed-length output. The message is first processed with a hash function to produce a message digest. This value is then signed by the sender's private key, which produces the actual digital signature. The digital signature is then added to the end of the document and sent to the receiver along with the document.

Because the mere presence of a digital signature proves nothing, verification must be mathematically proven. In the verification process, the first step is to use the corresponding public key to decrypt the digital signature. The result produces a 128-bit number. The original message is processed with the same hash function used earlier and results in a message digest. The two resulting 128-bit numbers are then compared, and if they are equal, notification is received of a good signature. If a single character has been altered, the two 128-bit numbers will be different, indicating that a change has been made to the document, which was never scrambled.

Figure 4.2 illustrates the generation of a digital signature. The original message is processed with a mathematical function to generate a message digest. The sender's private key is used to encrypt the message digest, and the final result is a digital signature.

Figure 4.2 Generating a Digital Signature

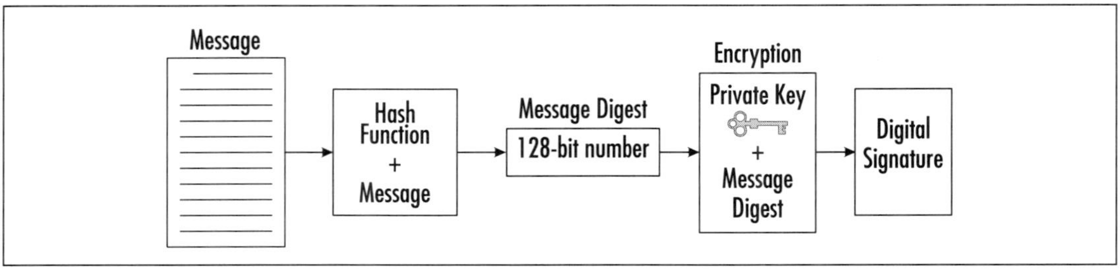

Authentication

Public key cryptography can provide authentication instead of privacy. In Windows 2000, the receiver of the information sends a challenge. The challenge can be implemented one of two ways.

In the first authentication method, a challenge to authenticate involves sending an encrypted challenge to the sender. The challenge is encrypted by the receiver, using the sender's public key. Only the corresponding private key can successfully decode the challenge. When the challenge is decoded, the sender sends the plaintext back to the receiver. This is the proof for the receiver that the sender is truly the sender.

For example, when Alice receives a document from Bob, she wants to authenticate that the sender is really Bob. She sends an encrypted challenge to Bob, using his public key. When he receives the challenge, Bob uses his private key to decrypt the information. The decrypted challenge is then sent back to Alice. When Alice receives the decrypted challenge, she is convinced that the document she received is truly from Bob.

The second authentication method uses a challenge that is sent in plaintext. The receiver, after receiving the document, sends a challenge in plaintext to the sender. The sender receives the plaintext challenge and adds some information before adding a digital signature.

The challenge and digital signature now head back to the sender. The digital signature is generated by using a hash function and then encrypting the result with a private key, so the receiver must use the sender's public key to verify the digital signature. If the signature is good, the original document and sender have at this point been verified mathematically. Figure 4.3 uses Alice and Bob to demonstrate the plaintext challenge.

Figure 4.3 Plaintext Authentication Challenge

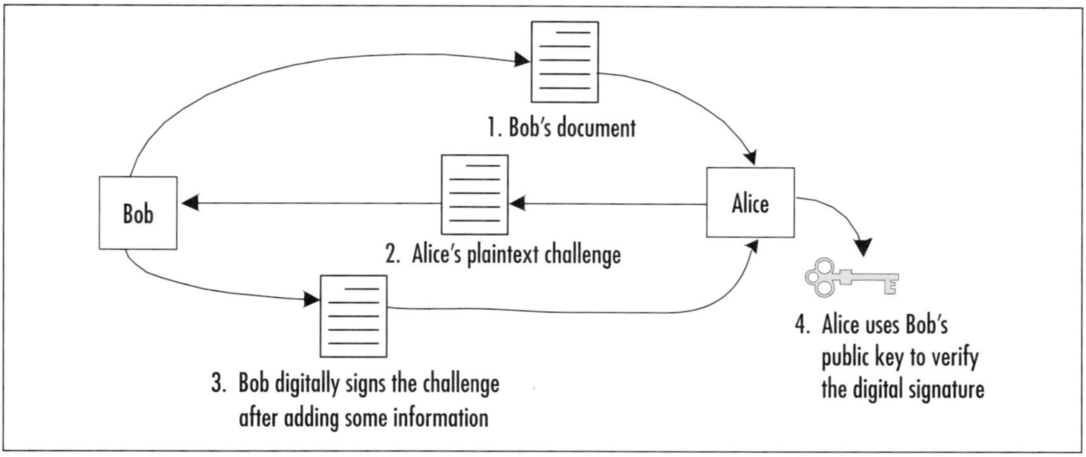

1. Bob's document
2. Alice's plaintext challenge
3. Bob digitally signs the challenge after adding some information
4. Alice uses Bob's public key to verify the digital signature

This type of authentication is referred to as *proof of possession*. The sender must prove they are who they say they are by having the correct corresponding private key. The receiver of the document always starts the process. The document is never encrypted in this authentication process.

Secret Key Agreement via Public Key

The PKI of Windows 2000 permits two parties to agree on a secret key while using nonsecure communication channels. Each party creates half the shared secret key by generating a random number, which is sent to the other party after being encrypted with the other party's public key. Each receiving side then decrypts the ciphertext using a private key, which results in the missing half of the secret key.

By adding both random numbers together, each party has an agreed-upon shared secret key, which can then be used for secure communication even though the secret key was first obtained through a nonsecure communication channel.

Bulk Data Encryption without Prior Shared Secrets

The final major feature of public key technology is that it can encrypt bulk data without generating a shared secret key first. The biggest disadvantage of using asymmetric algorithms for encryption is the slowness of the overall process, which results from the necessary intense computations; the largest disadvantage of using symmetric algorithms for encryption of bulk data is the need for a secure communication channel for exchanging the secret key. The Windows 2000 operating system combines symmetric and asymmetric algorithms to get the best of both worlds at just the right moment.

When large files need to be encrypted, secret key encryption is the quickest method to use. To encrypt such a file, a special session key is created. To protect the session key, which is the secret key needed to decrypt the protected data, the sender quickly encrypts it by using the receiver's public key. This encryption of the session key is handled by asymmetric algorithms, which use intense computation but do not require much time, due to the small size of the session key. The document, along with the encrypted session key, is then sent to the receiver. Only the intended receiver possesses the correct private key to decode the session key, which is needed to decode the actual document. When the session key is in plaintext, it can be applied to the ciphertext of the bulk data, and then it can transform the bulk data back to plaintext.

Protecting and Trusting Cryptographic Keys

When secret key cryptography is implemented, both the sender and the receiver share a key, which they protect and keep private. In some secure fashion, both parties have agreed upon and exchanged this single key, which is used to encrypt and decrypt the data the two parties want to keep secure.

In contrast to secret key cryptography, public key cryptography does not protect all of the involved keys. In public key cryptography, only the private keys are protected; the public keys are shared by the act of publishing them. Because the public key is not protected, in any PKI the sender must be provided with a means to trust the relationship of the public key and its entity.

> ### TEST DAY TIP
> It is sometimes helpful to consider all of the various means in which keys can be transferred amongst users. Smart cards, floppy disks, and other non-traditional means can be used to transfer secret keys without making use of traditional network means.

Unlike secret key cryptography, in which the single key is exchanged by a secure contrived plan, the public key is available without passing any security checkpoints. The public key's availability for public use limits security implementation to protect it. Because public keys are not surrounded by any security measures, a mechanism is needed to ensure that the public key being used is really the entity's public key.

Certificates

Certificates are used to provide the assurance that the public key being used does in fact belong to the entity that owns the corresponding private key. A certificate is a digitally signed statement by its issuer that affirms the validity of both the public key and the subject's identity information. The certificate is the user's guarantee between the public key and the entity holding the corresponding private key. The certificate contains the public key and a complete set of attributes. These attributes may include information about the holder's identity, what the holder is allowed to do, and under what circumstances the certificate is valid. The digital signature ties the attributes and the public key together on the certificate itself. The issuer's signature on the certificate is in effect the guarantee of authenticity.

A real-world example of a certificate is a passport. All passports contain a unique key, the registered passport number from the issuing government. Also included on every passport are the passport holder's full name, date of birth, place of birth, the date of issue, and the expiration date. U.S. passports are issued by the federal government and require a photo identification on the laminated information page. Any country that has agreed to accept these passports trusts that the information on the document is true as long as the passport does not seem to have been illegally altered. This means that foreign countries are relying on the passport's authenticity, just as the user of a public key relies on the issuer's certificate.

The PKI of Windows 2000 supports the International Telecommunication Union (ITU)-T X.509 version 3 standard for certificate creation. This X.509v3 standard defines the format and content of digital certificates. The use of a standard for certification creation allows the exchange of certificates between vendors and ensures true interoperability. X.509v3 certificates contain the information detailed in Table 4.1.

Table 4.1 X.509v3 Certificate Properties

Certificate Field	Description
Version	Provides the version number of the certificate format
Serial Number	Provides the serial number assigned to the certificate the issuing CA assigns the serial number from its unique listing
Algorithm Identifier and Parameters	Lists the signature algorithm and any parameters used by the issuer
Issuer	Provides the name of the CA that issued the certificate
Not Before (Date)	Lists the first date the certificate is to be considered valid
Not After (Date)	Lists the last date the certificate is to be considered valid
Subject Name	Provides identifying information about the person or entity the certificate has been issued to
Subject Public Key Algorithm and Parameters	Lists the algorithm and any parameters used for the subject's public key
Subject Public Key	The actual public key string
Signature	The signature provided by the issuing CA
Issuer Unique ID	An optional field on v2 and later certificates that makes the issuing CA name clearer
Subject unique ID	An optional field on v2 and later certificates that makes the subject name clearer
Extensions	An optional field on v3 and later certificates that specifies custom properties in use

Certificate Authorities

Digital certificates provide a way to validate public keys. By definition, the issuer of a Public Key Certificate is known as a certificate authority (CA). CA's are responsible for validating the identity of a person or organization and for joining that entity with a key pair. The CA stores the public keys and maintains the list of certificates that have been issued.

CA's vary greatly in size. At one end of the spectrum are commercial CAs such as Verisign and GTE Cybertrust, which issue millions of certificates, while at the opposite end are departmental CAs that issue a small number of certificates. Many smaller CAs are known to issue certificates signed by a higher-level CA, which can be inside or outside the organization.

CAs can decide what attributes will be included in the certificates it creates and what method of verification it will implement at the time of creation. Each CA also has the responsibility of validating the identity of a person or organization and associating that entity with the key pair it issued. Users place trust in the CA's ability to distinguish between authorized and unauthorized certificate requests, thus the CA stores and maintains a list of the certificates it has issued. Additionally, every CA has the responsibility of issuing a certificate revocation list (CRL) containing any certificate that has to be revoked. The CRL is published to locations that clients have access to so that they can check the list before any authentication request is approved.

CA Types

CAs provide validation of the entity belonging to the public key, so the administrator must understand the four types of CAs included with the Microsoft Certificate Service:

- Enterprise Root CA
- Enterprise Subordinate CA
- Standalone Root CA
- Standalone Subordinate CA

The Enterprise Root CA is at the top of the PKI. Active Directory is used to verify a certificate requester's identity. Because it is at the top of the PKI, the Enterprise Root CA signs its own CA certificate and then publishes that certificate to every other CA on the network. By signing its own CA certificate, the Enterprise Root CA establishes itself at the top of the CA trust chain. The down side to this arrangement is that since the chain of trust has to start somewhere— in this case, at the Enterprise Root CA—there now exists a weak link in the chain. This is why a third party Trusted Root is sometimes considered for use. Compromise of the Enterprise Root CA will most certainly result in catastrophic effects on the rest of the network if no higher level CA exists.

An Enterprise Root CA uses predefined certificate templates for issuing and requesting certificates. When using certificate templates, the Enterprise Root CA can verify user credentials during certificate enrollment. Each template has an access control list (ACL) that is evaluated at the time the user makes a certificate request to determine if the requester is authorized to receive the template. An example of a template is one created for a smart card logon.

The Enterprise Root CA can be used to issue certificates directly to users, but is generally used to authenticate Enterprise Subordinate CAs, thus authenticating them in the chain of trust. The Enterprise Root CA is integrated with Active Directory, which helps simplify issuing and revoking certificates.

Enterprise Subordinate CAs are available in two different types: intermediate or issuing. All CAs can issue certificates, but the implementation practice in larger organizations is to use issuing certificate subordinate CAs to issue certificates. The issuing CAs issue certificates directly to users that support client services such as smart card logons, the Encrypting File System (EFS), and Internet Protocol (IP) security. The intermediate CA's job is not to issue user certificates but to generate a certificate for issuing CA validation and to provide a link in the chain back to the Root CA. Using a multi-layered CA arrangement can provide redundancy and scalability of a CA implementation. Of course, a smaller organization may not have this type of arrangement and may even only have one CA—the Enterprise Root CA. This results in reduced redundancy, however, as with any time a critical service is placed entirely on one server.

The practical reasons for supporting a model containing multiple CAs include the following:

- **Use** A certificate may be issued for defined purposes such as smart card logons; separation will provide a basis for administering different policies.

- **Geographic** A large organization may have entities at multiple remote sites. The network connections between the multiple sites may require separate issuing CAs.

- **Flexible Configuration** The most important CA is the root, so a company may decide to physically secure the computer by removing it from the network. (See the following Test Day Tip for an example of this.)

- **Shutdown** Multiple CAs enable the administrator to turn off or remove one without having an impact on the CA hierarchy.

- **Organizational Divisions** A large organization may have entities at multiple remote sites. The network connectivity between the multiple sites may require separate issuing CAs.

Test Day Tip

There are some instances where you may have an Active Directory environment and still opt to use a Standalone CA on your network. One example would be a CA that issues code-signing certificates. These certificates must only come from one source (this sole Standalone CA) and users must not be able to request new certificates, which are issued manually by an administrator. This CA must be protected at all costs as it maintains the chain of trust for your code-signing certificates. Make it a Standalone Root CA and place it in a fireproof, waterproof vault when not in use.

Not all Windows 2000 environments use Active Directory, which generates the need for the other two types of CAs. When an environment does not have Active Directory services or is not a member in a Windows 2000 domain, the CAs are referred to as *standalone CAs*. The Standalone Root is at the very top of the certificate structure, but a Standalone Subordinate CA can be an intermediate or issuing CA, much as in the Enterprise environment.

Certificate Hierarchies

As discussed previously, the CA at the very top of a certificate hierarchy is referred to as a *Root CA*. No one within the boundaries of an organization is above the Root CA, so no one within an organization can vouch for its authenticity, and the Root CA typically signs its own certificate. Because the signing of its own identity is not really secure, a third party may sometimes be used to verify a Root CA's certificate; thus, verification of the entire certificate chain is possible outside of the organization's boundaries and up to a publicly available and trusted Root CA.

Any environment can and should have more than one Trusted Root CA. Figure 4.4 shows an environment that contains 106 Trusted Root CA certificates. The Windows 2000 Certificate snap-in not only displays these CA certificates but also includes the expiration date and the intended purpose for each listed CA. From this interface, a user can add or remove a Trusted Root CA. It stands to reason that not all users of digital certificates will use the same Trusted Root CA, thus any number of Trusted Root CA certificates ca be imported into a certificates store (a process which will be examined later in this chapter). By placing these certificates in a certificate store ahead of time (many of which come pre-installed with Windows itself), administrators can quickly verify an issued certificate that is presented to them.

Figure 4.4 Examining the Trusted Root CAs

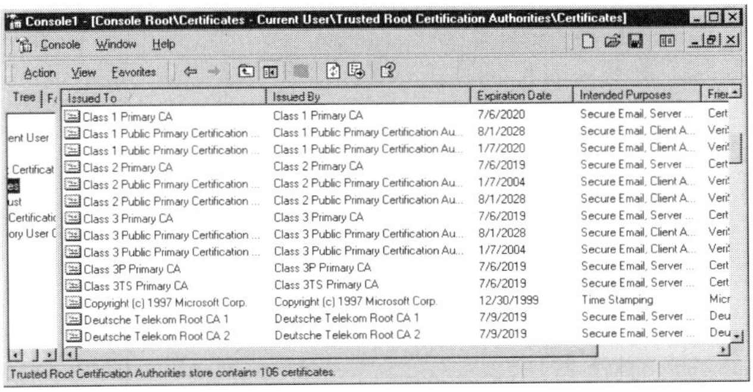

Trust and Validation

When a receiver receives a signed message, the signature is validated through the use of the sender's public key and a mathematical process. The receiver must be sure that the public key truly belongs to the sender; if Bob is the sender, Alice needs proof that it is Bob's public key.

This is where the CA enters the validation process, providing proof that the correct public key was used. Examining the certificate that corresponds to the sender's public key in a CA they trust, allows the recipient to determine the following facts:

- Was the certificate issued by a trusted CA?
- Does the certificate assure a binding between the sender and the sender's public key?
- Does the certificate have a valid signature from its issuer?

The receiver uses the public key of the issuing CA to verify the certificate. The receiver needs to be sure that the public key of the CA used to verify the sender's public key is not an impersonator. This chain reaction of verifying the verifier continues up the CA hierarchical structure. In the final step, a certificate is issued to a CA that the receiver implicitly trusts. This certificate, which does not require authentication, is known as a Trusted Root certificate, because it is at the very top of the key hierarchy and identifies bindings accepted as truthful. When the CA hierarchy is created, the parent-child relationship is established. A user who trusts a particular root certificate implicitly trusts all the certificates issued by that root and its subordinate CAs.

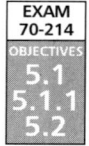

Installing and Managing Windows 2000 Certificate Authorities

Microsoft's PKI consists of the following components:

- **Active Directory** Contains the certificate store for certificates and CRLs
- **Certificate Services** Installed on a Windows 2000 machine to allow it to function as a CA

Microsoft recommends that the necessary domains be created before the needed CAs are set up on the network. Due to the hierarchical structure, the first CA is always the Root CA. The Root CA automatically generates a self-signed CA certificate using its own key pair, as discussed previously, and then generates CA certificates for any of its subordinate CAs as they are subsequently installed.

As with many services, Windows 2000 has a wizard to ease the installation of the certificate service. The wizard walks the installer through the entire process. Preplanning will make the installation run more smoothly. Before installing the Certificate Service, the administrator needs to identify what computer should run the service, considering such factors as current workload, physical security, connectivity, load balancing, and available hardware. The determination of the CA name requires some thought, because all issued certificates are tied to the CA name of the issuing CA. After the CA is created, no rename capability is available. Using the organizational naming convention probably already established for an organization is easiest.

During the Certificate Service installation, a public key pair is generated for the CA that is being created. This key pair is unique to the CA. If an Enterprise CA is being installed, the installation process involves Active Directory, in that a CA object and information about the CA configuration are added to Active Directory.

Before Certificate Services for an Enterprise CA solution can be installed, the administrator must have a properly configured Active Directory environment including Domain Name System (DNS) (which is required for Active Directory). If installing a Standalone CA solution, the administrator may do so with or without an Active Directory environment. To install an Enterprise CA server, the administrator must have administrative rights on the domain controllers, the DNS servers, and the CA server. Computers that have Certificate Services installed on them cannot be renamed, or joined to or removed from a domain after the installation. This makes sense, as performing any of these actions would destroy the CA hierarchy. Exercise 4.01 walks you through the process of installing Certificate Services on a computer.

EXERCISE 4.01

INSTALLING CERTIFICATE SERVICES

1. Click **Start | Settings | Control Panel | Add/Remove Programs**.
2. In the Add/Remove Programs window, click **Add/Remove Windows Components**. This brings up the Windows Components window shown in Figure 4.5.

    Figure 4.5 Adding Windows Components

    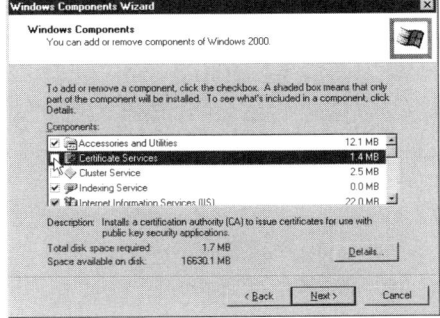

3. Select the check box next to **Certificate Services**. Click **Next** to continue.

4. You will now be presented with the warning shown in Figure 4.6. You cannot change the computer's name or domain membership after Certificate Services are installed. Click **Yes** to continue.

Figure 4.6 Installation Warning Window

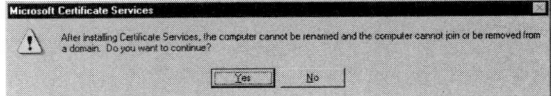

5. Now you have to choose which type of Certificate Server to create. Choose the correct role in Figure 4.7, select the **Advanced Options** check box, and click **Next** to continue.

Figure 4.7 Choosing a Certification Authority Type

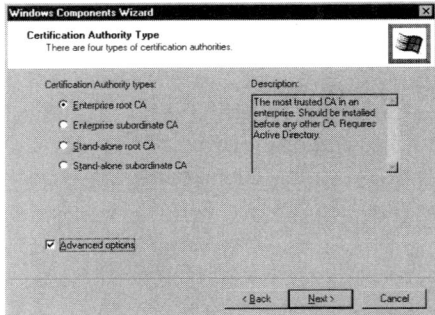

6. Selecting the **Advanced options** check box presents the window shown in Figure 4.8.

Figure 4.8 The Public and Private Key Pair

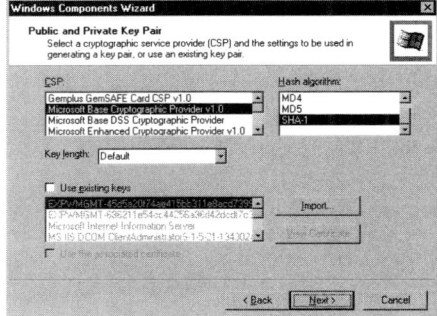

Installing, Configuring, and Managing Windows 2000 Certificate Authorities • Chapter 4 215

7. Select the Cryptographic Service Provider (CSP) and the Hash algorithm to be used. Click **Next**.
8. Figure 4.9 shows the CA Identifying Information window. You must enter a unique name for your CA. This is where you choose how long certificates will be valid—the default is two years. Fill in the needed information and click **Next** to continue.

Figure 4.9 Certification Authority Identifying Information

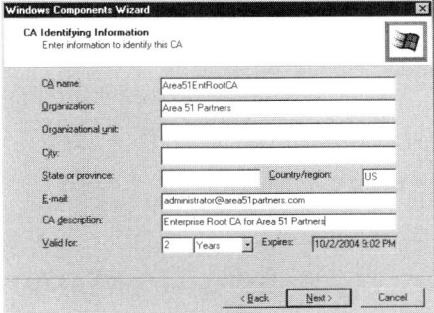

9. You will now be presented with the Data Storage Location window shown in Figure 4.10. Enter the location of the certificate database and the certificate database log. The default is **percentwindir%\system32\certlog**. For fault tolerance, put the database and the log on separate drives. Click **Next** to continue.

Figure 4.10 Selecting Database Storage

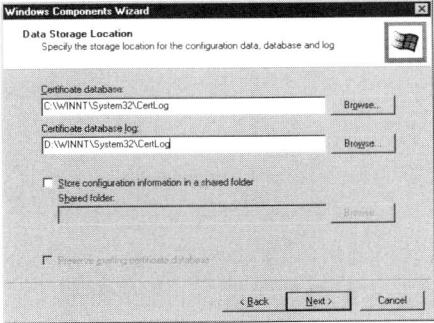

10. If prompted to create a folder, select **Yes**.
11. If the Internet Information Services (IIS) are running on your computer, you will be presented with the window shown in Figure 4.11. IIS must be stopped to allow some of the Certificate Services components to be installed and configured.

www.syngress.com

Figure 4.11 Stopping IIS

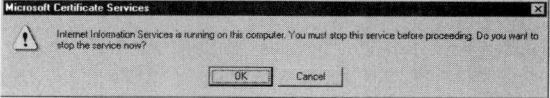

12. Click **OK** to stop IIS from running and continue the install. After this, Certificate Services will be installed and configured on your computer.

13. After setup has finished, you will see the Completing the Windows Components Wizard window. Click **Finish** to accept the changes.

When configuring a complete Windows 2000 CA hierarchy, the first CA is installed as an Enterprise Root CA. The process to install and configure an Enterprise Subordinate CA is almost exactly the same with the differences being that it must be configured to act as a Subordinate CA instead of a Root CA. The process for configuring Standalone Root CA's and Subordinate CA's is also very similar and does not require the presence of Active Directory.

Test Day Tip

It is critical when implementing Certificate Services to understand all of the various CA arrangements that can be configured. Each type of CA has its own strengths and weaknesses, as well as requirements. As is true in most things, there is no one universal solution when it comes to setting up a CA hierarchy—your individual situation will dictate your design. For the test, you need to understand the differences between the types of CAs and their requirements. You can expect to see at least one or more questions on this area in particular.

Once Certificate Services have been installed and configured on a network, it pretty much takes care of itself. Users request certificates using the templates configured to be available and these requests are processed as selected—either automatically approved or placed into a queue for manual approval. There are, however, some additional tasks that need to be completed to keep the CAs operating smoothly.

Exam Warning

Watch out for scenarios that call for code-signing certificates. These always require a trusted, verifiable third-party Root CA such as VeriSign. If you only intend to digitally sign code for distribution within your own internal network, the need for a third-party Root Certificate may not be very strong. If you are distributing applications or ActiveX applets to customers and other users, you must use a third-party Root Certificate to lend trustworthiness and creditability to the certificate you are using to sign the code.

Head of the Class… The Need for Stand-alone CAs

When you think of a stand-alone CA, you probably think of a lot of reasons why not to use it. It does not participate in Active Directory and thus is not nearly as robust or flexible as an Enterprise CA. However, despite its downside, stand-alone CAs have one very important and valuable thing working in their favor: they can be used to issue certificates as required, and then physically removed from the network. The old saying goes, "network security begins with physical security," and it certainly holds true. Being able to remove a CA from the network and place it into a safe, secure location greatly increases its security. Just remember the downside to doing so: clients will not be able to request and automatically receive certificates from a CA that has been removed from the network—an administrator will have to manually issue them and ensure they are delivered to the required location.

NOTE

All of the following examples presume that an Enterprise CA system has been installed.

Requesting a Certificate

It makes sense that the first thing an administrator would want to do after installing and testing a new CA would be to start issuing certificates to their users. They can use the Certificate Request Wizard or the Certificate Services Web page to request a certificate. The wizard is only available when requesting a certificate from an Enterprise CA.

Exercise 4.02 walks you through requesting a certificate with the Certificate Request Wizard via the Certificate snap-in. Exercise 4.03 walks you through requesting a certificate with the Certificate Request Web page.

EXERCISE 4.02

Using the Certificate Request Wizard

You must first create a custom console containing the Certificate snap-in if not already done:

1. Click **Start | Run**.
2. Type **MMC** in the Open line. Click **OK**. This opens a blank MMC.
3. You now need to add the Certificate snap-in. Click on **Console**.
4. Choose **Add/Remove Snap-in** from the pop-up menu.
5. Click **Add**. Choose **Certificates** from the list of available snap-ins (see Figure 4.12). Select **My User Account**.

Figure 4.12 Selecting the Certificates Snap-in

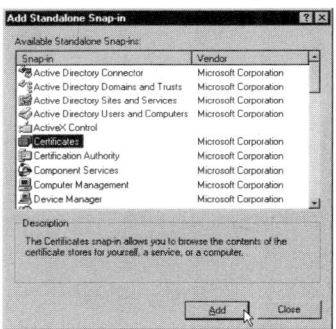

6. Click **Finish**.
7. Click **Close** on the Add Standalone Snap-in window.
8. Click **OK** on the Add/Remove Snap-in window.
   Now you can use your custom console to complete this exercise.
9. Expand **Certificates | Current User**.
10. Expand **Personal**. Right-click on **Certificates** and select **All Tasks | Request New Certificate** from the context menu, as shown in Figure 4.13. This starts the Certificate Request Wizard.
11. Click **Next** to dismiss the opening page of the wizard.
12. You will now be prompted for what type of certificate to request, as shown in Figure 4.14. Choose the correct certificate type (**User** for this example) and click **Next**. If you want to configure advanced options, such as the CSP, select the **Advanced** check box before clicking **Next**.

Figure 4.13 Requesting a Certificate with the Wizard

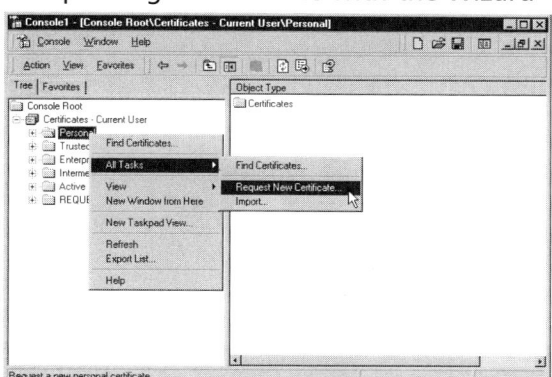

Figure 4.14 Selecting the Certificate Type

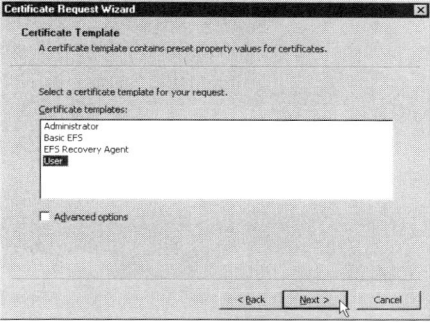

13. Enter a friendly name and description for your certificate, as shown in Figure 4.15, and click **Next** to continue.

Figure 4.15 Entering Details for the Certificate

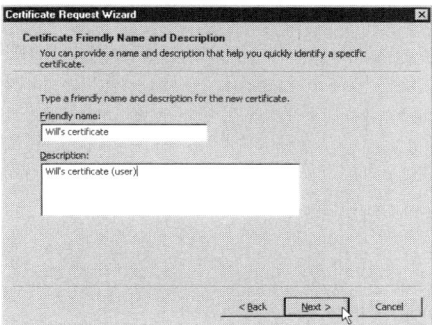

14. Click **Finish** to complete the process. If your request was approved, you will see a window as shown in Figure 4.16. Click **Install Certificate** to install your newly approved certificate.

Figure 4.16 Installing the New Certificate

15. Click **OK** to complete the process.

Now we will examine the process of requesting a new certificate using the Certificate Services Web interface as detailed in Exercise 4.03.

EXERCISE 4.03

USING THE CERTIFICATE SERVICES WEB INTERFACE

1. Open Internet Explorer and enter **http://server_name/certsrv**. This opens the page shown in Figure 4.17.

Figure 4.17 Requesting a Certificate via Web Enrollment

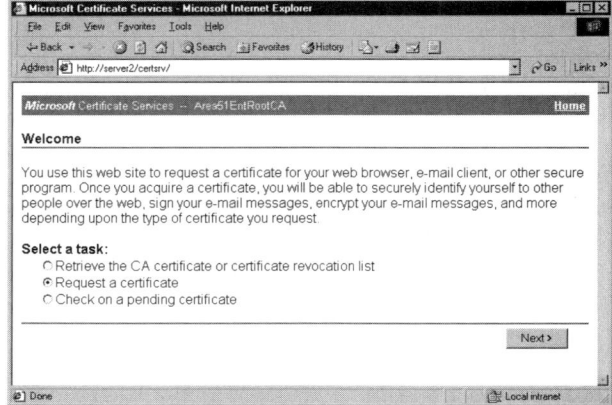

2. Select **Request a certificate** and click **Next**. You can also check on a previous certificate request or view the current CRL from this page if you desire.

3. Select **Advanced request** and click **Next**. This takes you to the page shown in Figure 4.18.

Figure 4.18 Advanced Request Options

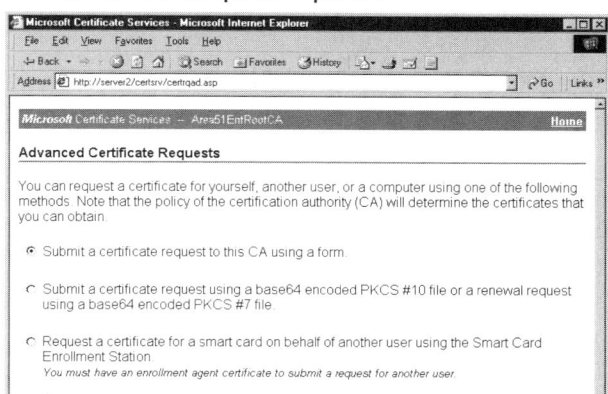

4. Choose **Submit a certificate request to this CA using a form**. Click **Next** to continue. You must next choose a certificate template, as shown in Figure 4.19.

Figure 4.19 Selecting the Template

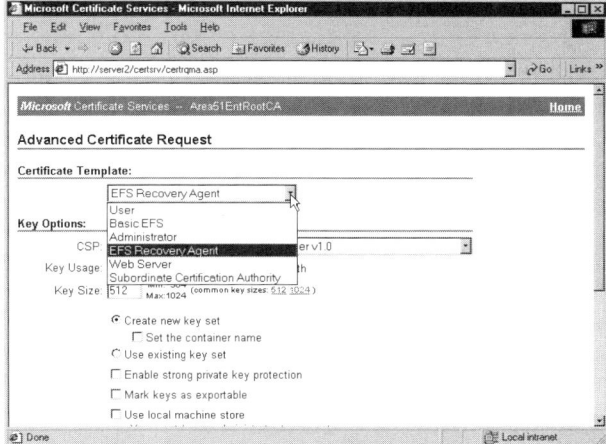

5. Select **EFS Recovery Agent**. Scroll down to the bottom of the page and click **Submit**.

6. You will now be issued the certificate. You must now install the certificate by clicking on the **Install this certificate** link. This installs the certificate and informs you of the fact.

Exam Warning

Remember: if you do not have an Enterprise CA setup you will not be able to use Web Enrollment.

The certificate enrollment used by Microsoft in Windows 2000 is based on the industry standard PKCS-10 and PKCS-7. PKCS-10 is the standard for a certificate request message, and PKCS-7 contains the issued certificate or certificate chain. The Windows 2000 operating system currently supports certificates based on RSA keys and signatures, Diffie-Hellman keys, and Digital Signature Algorithm (DSA) keys and signatures.

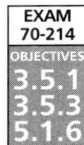

Exporting and Importing Certificates

From time to time it may become necessary to export a certificate and its private key for any number of reasons. Some of the possibilities include Encrypting File System (EFS) recovery (discussed in Chapter 5 in greater detail), backing up a certificate for disaster recovery, or simply moving a certificate from one computer to another. Fortunately, Windows 2000 makes it easy to export a certificate and corresponding private key easily through the Certificates snap-in. If the private key is exported, the information is encrypted as a PKCS-12 (Public Key Cryptography Standards) message to protect it from prying eyes. Exercise 4.04 details the certificate exportation process. Any exported certificate eventually has to be imported, so the importation of certificates is examined in Exercise 4.04. You may also find the need to.Exercise 4.05 details how to import external certificates, such as those from a Trusted Root CA, into a personal certificate store.

EXERCISE 4.04

Exporting a Certificate and a Private Key

1. Expand **Certificates | Current User**.
2. Expand **Personal**.
3. Select **Certificates**.
4. In the details pane (right side) right-click the certificate that you want to export and choose **All Tasks | Export** (see Figure 4.20). This starts the Certificate Export Wizard.
5. Click **Next** to dismiss the opening page of the wizard.

Figure 4.20 Exporting the Certificate

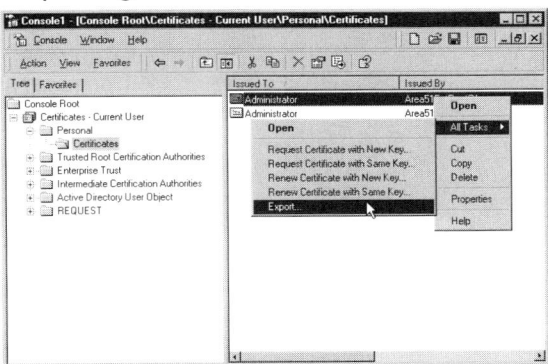

6. As shown in Figure 4.21, choose whether you want to export the certificate with or without its private key. In this example, we will export the certificate and its private key by selecting **Yes, export the private key**. Click **Next** to continue.

Figure 4.21 To Export the Private Key or Not to Export the Private Key

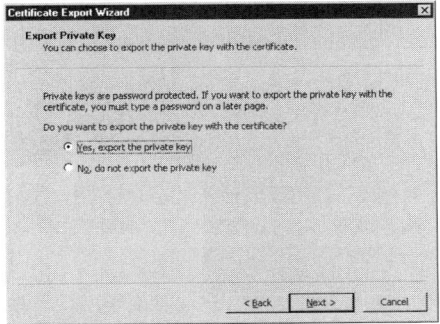

7. From the window shown in Figure 4.22, select the file format that you want to use. In this example, we will be using the PKCS #12 format, as it is the only one that supports exporting the private key. You can also opt to configure more advanced options, such as to include all certificates in the path, enabling strong protection and to delete the private key after successful exportation (this is a good way to prevent the key from being used by any unauthorized personnel). Click **Next** after configuring your options.

8. You will now be prompted for a password to assign to the private key. Enter the password twice and click **Next** to continue.

9. You will now be asked to specify the name and path of the file you want to export. Enter the name and click **Next** to continue.

Figure 4.22 Selecting Certificate Export Options

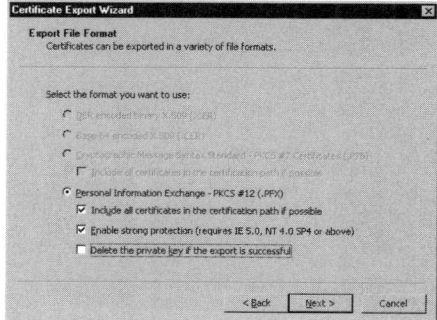

10. Verify that the information is correct and click **Finish** to complete the Certificate Export Wizard. If all is successful, you will be presented with the window shown in Figure 4.23.

Figure 4.23 The Certificate Export was Successfully Completed

11. Click **OK**. The certificate can be found in the location you exported it to. Figure 4.24 shows my exported certificate sitting on the Desktop.

Figure 4.24 The Exported Certificate File

Exam Warning

Pay attention to the question when dealing with exporting certificates to determine whether or not you will need to export the private key as well.

Before doing an export operation of a certificate and its public key pairs, the administrator should look at the CSP being used. When the Microsoft CSP is used, the exporting of key pairs occurs only if the exportable flag CRYPT_EXPORTABLE was set at the time the key was created. Some third-party CSPs may not support the backup and restoration of key pairs and their certificates. If this is the case, only a complete system image backup is possible to provide for restoration of the certificate.

Although Exercise 4.05 examines the importation of a Trusted Root CA certificate, the same process holds true for any certificate you want to import. The main difference is that the process is started from a folder in the certificate store other than the **Trusted Root Certification Authorities**, as shown in Exercise 4.05.

EXERCISE 4.05

IMPORTING A CERTIFICATE FROM A TRUSTED ROOT CA

1. Expand **Certificates | Current User**.
2. Expand **Trusted Root Certification Authorities**. Right-click **Certificate** and choose **Import** from the context menu. This starts the Certificate Import Wizard.
3. Click **Next** to dismiss the first page of the wizard.
4. You will now be asked to select a file to import, as shown in Figure 4.25. Enter or browse to the location of the certificate and then click **Next** to continue.

    Figure 4.25 Selecting the Certificate to Import

    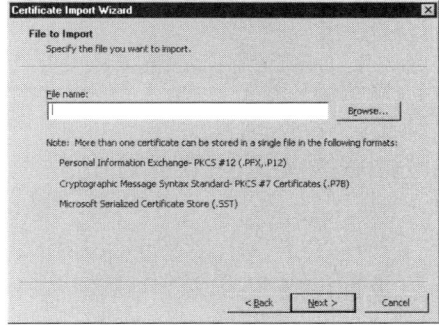

5. Type the password assigned to the file and click **Next** to continue. As shown in Figure 4.26, you may also have additional configurable options. It is always highly recommended to make the private key exportable in case you need to export this certificate and private key later.
6. Choose where to place the certificate and click **Next**.
7. Verify that you have made the correct choices and click **Finish** to complete the wizard.

Figure 4.26 Configuring Advanced Import Options

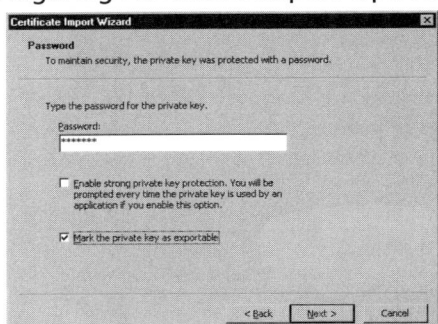

8. You will now be prompted to add the certificate to the Root Store, as shown in Figure 4.27.

Figure 4.27 Adding the Certificate to the Root Store

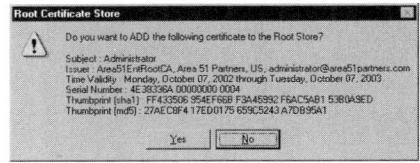

9. Click **Yes**. If the addition is successful, you will be informed of such. Click **OK**.

It is worth mentioning that the Certificate Import Wizard can also be started by double-clicking on an exported certificate file (like the one shown in Figure 4.24). The primary difference in importing a certificate this way is that the administrator will need to specify where to install the certificate at or just allow Windows to handle it automatically.

Revoking Certificates

Certificates tend to be issued with an average lifetime of two or three years. Until they expire, there can be many reasons to cease trusting the credentials. From a security point of view, any of the following circumstances certainly warrant the revoking of a certificate:

- An entity's private key has been compromised
- A project with another organization is completed

- The employee has changed status within the company
- A department is to cease having access to certain information
- The certificate was obtained through forgery

The Windows 2000 public key functions are based on distributed verification, so any revocation of certificates will also be handled in a distributed fashion. There is no need to create a central location for revocation information.

Microsoft designed Windows 2000 revocation around the industry standard CRLs. The Microsoft Enterprise CA publishes the CRLs to Active Directory. From there, domain clients can obtain the information, cache it to the local machine, and then read it from the cache when certificates are verified. Clients can verify certificates when they use a commercial CA or any third-party CA, as long as the published CRL is available over the network. Exercise 4.06 walks you through revoking a certificate and manually publishing a new CRL.

EXERCISE 4.06

REVOKING A CERTIFICATE AND PUBLISHING A CRL

1. Click **Start | Programs | Administrative Tools**.
2. Open **Certification Authority**.
3. Expand the name of your CA.
4. Select **Issued Certificates** (as shown in Figure 4.28).

Figure 4.28 Listing the Issued Certificates

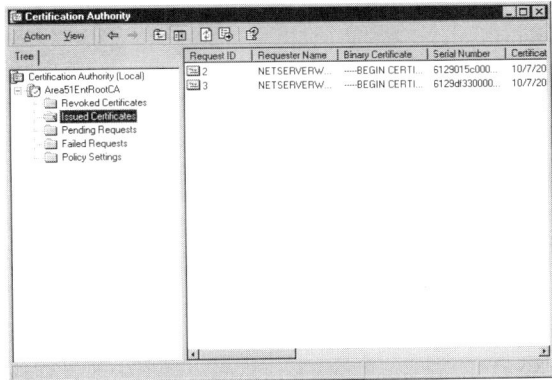

5. In the details pane (right side) right-click the certificate that you want to revoke and choose **All Tasks | Revoke Certificate** from the context menu.

6. You will now be asked (see Figure 4.29) if you are sure that you want to revoke the selected certificate. If you are sure, pick a reason code and click **Yes** to revoke the certificate. You will not be prompted after clicking **Yes**, so be sure that you have the correct certificate and revocation reason. The possible reason codes are the following:
   - Unspecified
   - Key Compromise
   - CA Compromise
   - Change of Affiliation
   - Superseded
   - Cease of Operation
   - Certificate Hold

   Figure 4.29 Selecting the Revocation Reason

   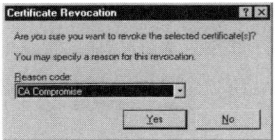

7. To publish a new CRL, right-click on **Revoked Certificates** and choose **All Tasks | Publish** from the pop-up menu. If your CRL has not expired, this gives you the window shown in Figure 4.30.

   Figure 4.30 Manually Publishing a New CRL

   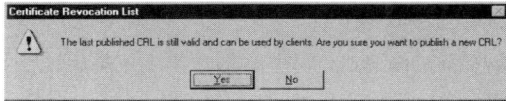

8. Click **Yes** to publish the new CRL.

> **Damage & Defense…**
>
> **Revoke Those Certificates**
>
> Get rid of certificates as soon as you do not need them—having extra certificates in existence only makes your network that much more vulnerable to compromise and attack. If you no longer have a need for a certificate, such as when a user leaves the organization or if a certificate (or CA) has been comprised, you should immediately revoke any and all affected certificates. Do not leave back doors installed that can allow an unauthorized attacker to gain entrance to your network and impersonate an authorized user.
>
> You should also strongly consider manually publishing the Certificate Revocation List (CRL) to your CRL Distribution Points (CDP) any time you find yourself revoking certificates for reasons such as theft, loss, or termination or user or partner contract. Even if you've revoked a certificate, it may be some time until the next CRL publication interval. When the security of your network is at stake, do it right the first time!

Configuring Publication of CRLs

The CRL is a file maintained by each CA that specifies certificates that have not reached their expiration date but are no longer valid for any number of reasons. The CRL provides a critical part of certificate verification by ensuring that a certificate that is presented has not been revoked. CRLs are digitally signed by their respective CA, the same as an issued certificate. Although certificates are immediately added to the CRL when they are revoked, the CRL itself is not published immediately to reflect the changes. Administrators can configure the publication interval for CRLs and the location to which they are published—known as CRL Distribution Points (CDPs). By default, CRLs are published on a one-week interval, but the administrator can configure any value between one hour and 9999 years. CDPs can be configured as Active Directory, Hypertext Transfer Protocol (HTTP), or file-based locations. It is very common to configure multiple CDP methods to ensure that clients can always locate the most current CRL. Exercise 4.07 examines the configuration of the CRL publication interval and the CDP location

EXERCISE 4.07

CONFIGURING CRL PUBLISHING OPTIONS

1. Click **Start | Programs | Administrative Tools**.
2. Open **Certification Authority** and expand the name of your CA.
3. Right-click **Revoked Certificates** and select **Properties** from the context menu. This opens the window shown in Figure 4.31.

Figure 4.31 Configuring the CRL Publication Schedule

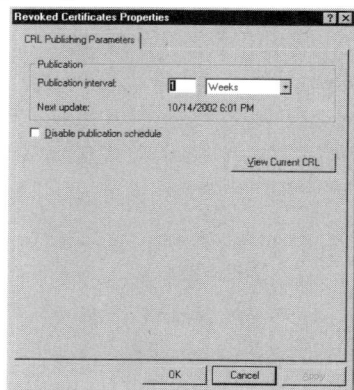

4. Configure the interval of your choosing. If you want to view the current CRL, click **View Current CRL**, which opens a window like that shown in Figure 4.32—of course, your CRL will be different.

Figure 4.32 Viewing the Current CRL

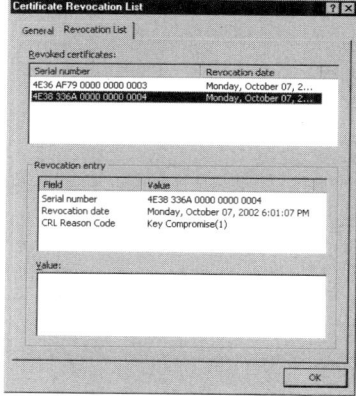

5. After you have configured the CRL publication schedule (or disabled publication by selecting the **Disable publication schedule** checkbox), click **OK** to close out the **Revoked Certificates Properties** window.

6. If you need to change the CRL publication location, you can do so by right-clicking on the CA name and selecting **Properties**. Switch to the **Policy Module** tab and click the **Configure** button. This opens the window shown in Figure 4.33.

Figure 4.33 Configuring the CRL Distribution Points

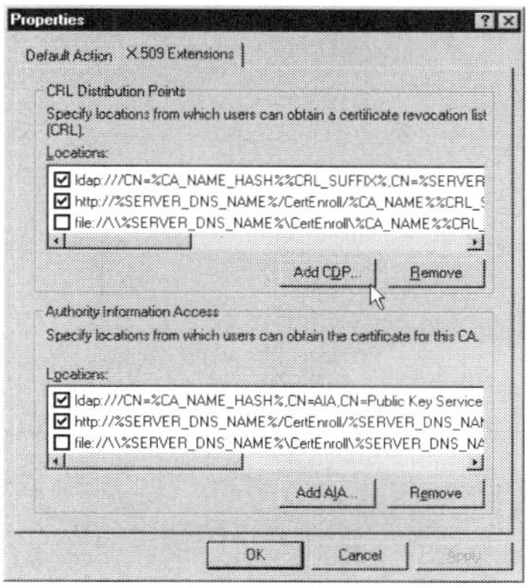

7. Change to the **X.509 Extensions** tab and click **Add CDP**. Enter the URL, file, or Active Directory location you want to publish to and click **OK three times** when you are done.

8. To manually force publish the CRL after you have made the modifications, right-click on the Revoked Certificates folder and select **All Tasks | Publish** from the context menu.

EXAM WARNING

As simple and trivial as it seems, configuring the CRL publication interval and location is very important. You should expect to be tested in some depth about the specifics of these operations.

Configuring Certificate Templates

Certificate templates are used to define policies that control the generation and use of a certificate. A template is identified by a common name that usually associates with the group for which the template was designed, such as the Engineers template or the Developers template.

A template defines components to be incorporated into a certificate, such as :

- Name requirements
- The expiration date

- The CSP
- The public key generation algorithm

The Enterprise CA gets a set of templates with its policy object. The certificate templates available through the Certification Authority Console can be changed, as shown in Exercise 4.08. Table 4.2 lists the types of *user* templates available by default and Table 4.3 lists the types of *machine* templates available by default.

EXERCISE 4.08

SELECTING THE AVAILABLE CERTIFICATE TEMPLATES FOR NEW CERTIFICATE ISSUE

1. Click **Start** | **Programs** | **Administrative Tools**.
2. Open **Certification Authority** and expand the name of your CA.
3. Right-click **Policy Settings**, as shown in Figure 4.34.

    Figure 4.34 Selecting the Certificates to Issue

    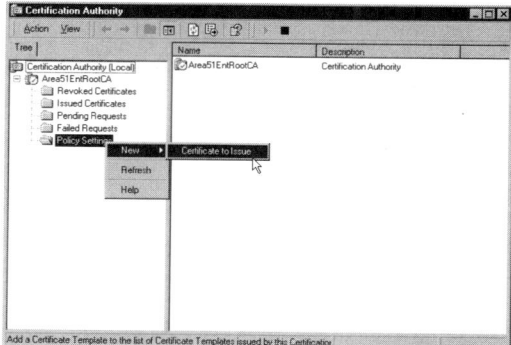

4. Choose **New** | **Certificate to Issue** from the context menu. This gives you the window shown in Figure 4.35.

    Figure 4.35 Adding New Templates

    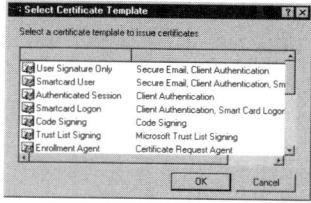

5. Select the certificate template to be available on your CA and click **OK**.

Table 4.2 Templates Available for Users

Template Name	Purposes
Administrator	Code signing, Microsoft trust list signing, EFS, secure e-mail, client authentication
Certification authority	All
ClientAuth	Client authentication
CodeSigning	Code signing
CTLSigning	Microsoft trust list signing
EFS	Encrypting File System
EFSRecovery	File recovery
EnrollmentAgent	Certificate request agent
SmartcardLogon	Client authentication
SmartcardUser	Client authentication, secure e-mail
User	EFS, secure e-mail, client authentication
UserSignature	Secure e-mail, client authentication
Exchange enrollment agent (offline request)	Certificate request agent
Exchange user	Secure e-mail, client authentication
Exchange user signature	Secure e-mail, client authentication

Table 4.3 Templates Available for Machines

Certificate Template Name	Certificate Purposes
Certification authority	All
Domain controller	Client authentication, server authentication
IPSECIntermediateOffline	IP Security
IPSECIntermediateOnline	IP Security
MachineEnrollmentAgent	Certificate request agent
Machine	Client authentication, server authentication
OfflineRouter	Client authentication
SubCA	All
WebServer	Server authentication
Exchange user signature	Secure e-mail, client authentication

Configuring Public Key Group Policy

Windows 2000 fully uses the Kerberos security standard, thus providing single point logons at the enterprise level. Any policy, including the security policy, can be globally established for an entire enterprise, a site, a domain, or an organizational unit. The security policy, once set, would then affect the groups of users or computers defined on the network.

The public key security policy is just one element of the overall Windows 2000 security policy and is a component of the PKI. The security policy is enforced globally, but for ease of administration, it can be centrally defined and managed.

Configuring Automatic Certificate Enrollment

The CA contains numerous properties that are tied to its use. The administrator can use the Microsoft Management Console Certificate snap-in to specify the certificate policy that will control the generation and use of certificates by the CA. When they are specified, the properties restrict when certificates are valid. A user can use the certificate to validate secure mail but may not be allowed to use the certificate's private key for digital signatures. These objects may be restricted in any combination:

- Server authentication
- Client authentication
- Code signing
- E-mail
- IP security end system
- Internet Protocol Security (IPSec) tunnel
- IPSec user
- Timestamping
- Microsoft EFS

To make the PKI transparent to the user, Windows 2000 had to make it possible to support automatic certificate enrollment, which is controlled by certificate types and auto-enrollment objects. Both of these elements are integrated with the group policy object, so they can be defined at the site, the domain, the organizational unit, the computer, or the user level. Exercise 4.09 walks you through configuring automatic certificate enrollment through a group policy object.

EXERCISE 4.09

CONFIGURING AUTOMATIC CERTIFICATE ENROLLMENT

1. Click **Start | Programs | Administrative Tools**.
2. Open **Active Directory Users and Computers**.
3. Right-click on the domain and choose **Properties** from the context menu.
4. Switch to the **Group Policy** tab. Select the Default Domain Policy GPO or any other that you want to work with.
5. Click **Edit**. This opens a window similar to that shown in Figure 4.36.

    Figure 4.36 The Group Policy Editor

    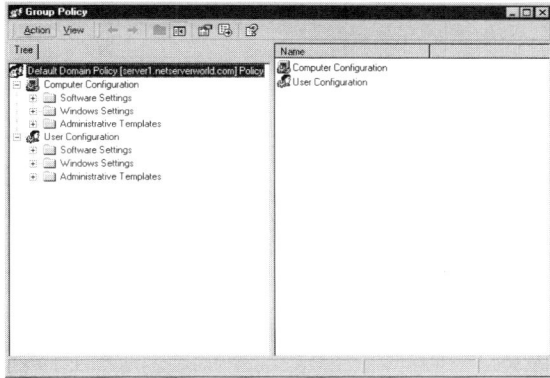

6. Expand the following nodes: **Computer Configuration | Windows Settings | Security Settings | Public Key Policies**.
7. Right-click on **Automatic Certificate Request Settings** (see Figure 4.37) and select **New | Automatic Certificate Request** from the context menu. This opens the **Automatic Certificate Request Setup Wizard**.
8. Click **Next** to dismiss the opening page of the wizard.
9. Choose a certificate template (see Figure 4.38) and click **Next** to continue.
10. Select the CA or CAs that should be used to issue this certificate (only one of the selected CAs will issue any one specific CA) and click **Next** to continue.
11. Click **Finish** to complete the wizard.

Figure 4.37 Configuring Automatic Certificate Enrollments

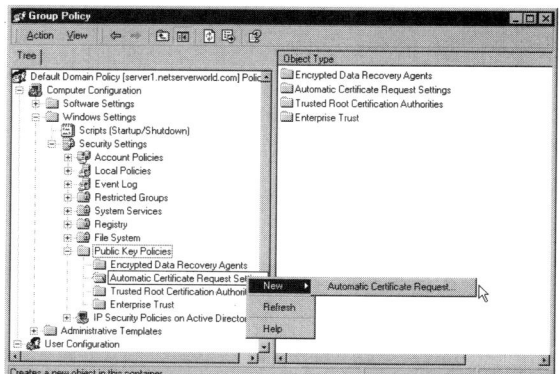

Figure 4.38 Selecting a Template for Use

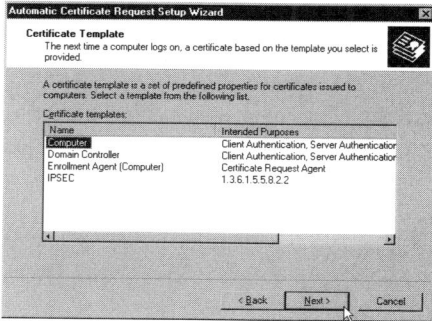

Configuring the Trusted Root CAs

While Figure 4.4 shows how to manage Trusted Root CA certificates from within the Certificate Services snap-in, the changes made there will only apply to the computer they are configured on. To easily make additions to the Trusted Root CAs readily available for the entire domain, the administrator should consider configuring their domain Group Policy Object. To configure Trusted Root CAs using Group Policy, complete the steps outlined in Exercise 4.10.

EXERCISE 4.10

CONFIGURING TRUSTED ROOT CAs

1. Click **Start** | **Programs** | **Administrative Tools**.

Installing, Configuring, and Managing Windows 2000 Certificate Authorities • Chapter 4   237

2. Open **Active Directory Users and Computers**.
3. Right-click on the domain and choose **Properties** from the context menu.
4. Switch to the **Group Policy** tab. Select the Default Domain Policy GPO or any other that you want to work with.
5. Click **Edit**. This opens a window similar to that shown previously in Figure 4.36.
6. Expand the following nodes: **Computer Configuration | Windows Settings | Security Settings | Public Key Policies**.
7. Right-click on **Trusted Root Certification Authorities** (see Figure 4.39) and select **All Tasks | Import** from the context menu. This opens the Certificate Import Wizard.

Figure 4.39 Configuring Trusted Root CAs

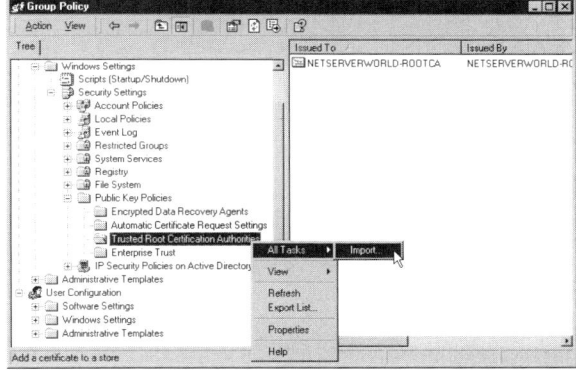

8. Follow the steps in the Certificate Import Wizard to complete the importation process.

EXAM WARNING

You should understand the reason and process behind configuring additional Trusted Root CAs through Group Policy.

Backing Up and Restoring Certificate Services

Microsoft recommends that the entire CA server be backed up. By backing up the system state data on a CA, the administrator will automatically get a backup of the certificate store, the registry, system files, and Active Directory (if the CA resides on a domain controller). Sometimes, the administrator may want to back up just the certificate services portion of the computer without doing a full backup of everything else. Exercise 4.11 walks you through backing up Certificate Services. Backups are only useful if they can be restored. Exercise 4.12 walks you through restoring Certificate Services.

EXERCISE 4.11

BACKING UP CERTIFICATE SERVICES

1. Click **Start | Programs | Administrative Tools**.
2. Open **Certification Authority**.
3. Expand the name of your CA.
4. Right-click your CA and select **All Tasks | Backup CA** from the context menu.
5. Click **Next** to dismiss the opening page of the wizard.
6. You will now be prompted to select the items to be backed up, as shown in Figure 4.40.

   Figure 4.40 Selecting Items to be Backed Up

   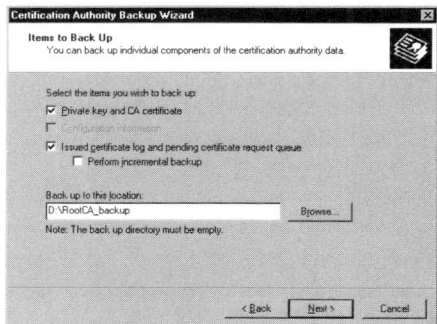

7. Choose what to back up and the backup location and click **Next**.
8. Type in the backup password twice and click **Next**.
9. Click **Finish** to close the wizard.

If you need to restore your Certificate Services backup, proceed as outlined in Exercise 4.12.

EXERCISE 4.12

RESTORING CERTIFICATE SERVICES

1. Click **Start | Programs | Administrative Tools**.
2. Open **Certification Authority**.
3. Expand the name of your CA.
4. Right-click your CA and select **All Tasks | Restore CA** from the context menu. This gives you the notice shown in Figure 4.41.

Figure 4.41 Stopping Certificate Services

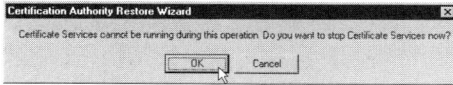

5. Click **OK** to stop Certificate Services from running and start the wizard.
6. Click **Next** to continue. You will now be given the window shown in Figure 4.42.

Figure 4.42 Selecting What to Restore

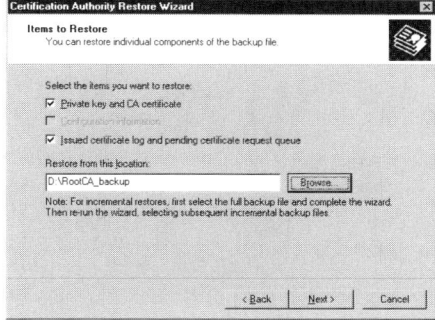

7. Select the items to be restored and the restore file location and click **Next**.
8. You must now enter the password assigned to the restore file. Enter the password and click **Next**.
9. Click **Finish** to complete the wizard.
10. You will now be prompted to restart the certificate services, as shown in Figure 4.43. Click **Yes** to restart the services.

Figure 4.43 Restarting Certificate Services

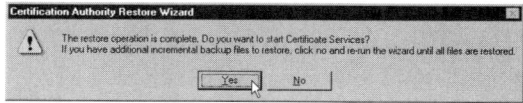

 EXAM WARNING

You should be familiar with the process to back up and restore Certificate Services from the Certification Authority console.

Notes from the Underground...

Nothing in Life Is Perfect

No security method is foolproof, and this includes the use of CAs to verify identity. In early 2001, someone tricked VeriSign into believing that they were a legitimate Microsoft employee and they received two digital certificates from VeriSign to be used for code signing (see www.microsoft.com/technet/security/bulletin/ms01-017.asp). What is even more interesting (or scary, depending on how you look at it) is that this security failure went unnoticed for a month before VeriSign caught onto the problem and revoked the digital certificates.

So, if one of the pioneers in the digital certificate game can be tricked by some slick social engineering into giving out two high-level digital certificates, what are the odds that the same thing might not happen to you on your network? No matter how secure you think you are or how many layers deep your defensive posture is, always remember that an attacker is one step ahead of you…they just do not know it yet. Eventually every system can and will be penetrated if someone tries hard enough and has the capabilities to pull off the attack. This is why "defense in depth" is such a critical concept. The more layers of defense you have in your network, the better your odds are of keeping an attacker out, or at worst, detecting and tracking an attacker should they penetrate your defenses. Never stop thinking you have done enough to protect your network because nothing in life is perfect.

Advanced Certificate Management Issues

After going through all of the previous material, there might still be some advanced issues that you find yourself dealing with at one time or another when working with Certificate Services. These issues are described in the following paragraphs.

Publishing Certificates in Active Directory

By default, all certificates issued by an Enterprise CA are published to Active Directory. If for some reason you need to change the location where certificates are published to, you can do so by modifying the certificate-publishing behavior of the CA, as outlined in Exercise 4.13.

EXERCISE 4.13

SELECTING THE PUBLICATION LOCATION FOR NEW CERTIFICATES

1. Click **Start | Programs | Administrative Tools**.
2. Open **Certification Authority**.
3. Right-click on your CA and select **Properties** from the context menu.
4. Switch to the **Exit Module** tab, select the Exit Module you want to configure, and click **Configure**. This opens the **Properties** page shown in Figure 4.44.

   Figure 4.44 Selecting the Publication Location for New Certificates

   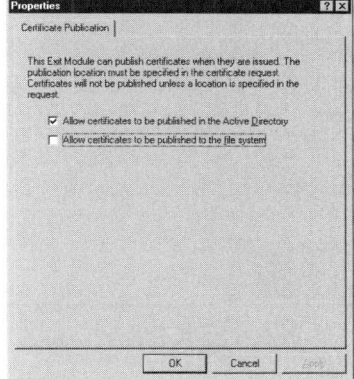

5. Click **OK** twice after making your selections.

Recovering Key Management Server Issued Keys

The Exchange Key Management Server (KMS) makes native use of the Windows 2000 Server Certificate Services, and thus needs no additional CA to perform its duties. The Windows 2000 CAs take care of all certificate issuance and revocation for users enrolled in Advanced Security through KMS, as well as maintaining the CRL and CTL. KMS is flexible and can use any Enterprise CA in an organization in the event that the first CA contacted is busy or unavailable. If you're an Enterprise CA is set up as a subordinate to a trusted third-party CA, such as one provided by VeriSign or Thawte, e-mail users can send messages both inside and outside of the organization using their digital certificates for signing and encryption of the e-mail messages.

KMS actually creates two sets of key pairs when a user is enrolled for Advanced Security:

- The first pair is created by the KMS, and utilized for message encryption.
- The second pair is created by Outlook, and used for digitally signing messages.

The public key created by the KMS is kept in Active Directory and used for decrypting and authenticating incoming messages. The private key created by KMS is kept in an encrypted database maintained by the KMS itself and is only available to its authorized user (the user holding the certificate used to create the key pair). As such, a user may need to recover this private key from time to time. This happens most often when a computer fails or is replaced, thus wiping out the settings that the user had previously configured in Outlook for secure e-mail messaging.

Fortunately, the KMS provides an extremely easy mechanism for recovering lost KMS keys. Exercise 4.14 presents the process for recovering a KMS key and assumes that you have KMS configured and in operation on your network. If not and you would like to read more about using KMS in Exchange 2000, see the article "Key Management Service in Exchange 2000 Server" located at http://msexchange.org/tutorials/Key_Management_Service_In_Exchange_2000_Server.html.

EXERCISE 4.14

RECOVERING A LOST KMS KEY

1. Click **Start | Programs | Microsoft Exchange | System Manager**. This opens the Exchange System Manager (ESM).
2. Expand the organizational node and select the **Advanced Security** node within it. In the right pane of the window, right-click **Key Manager** and select **All Tasks | Recover Keys** from the context menu, as shown in Figure 4.45.
3. Enter your KMS administrative password (not the same as your KMS startup password or your regular Windows network password) as shown in Figure 4.46 and click **OK**.

Figure 4.45 The Exchange System Manager

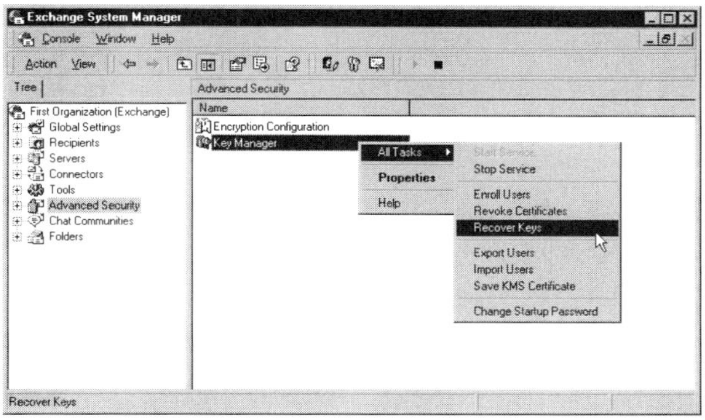

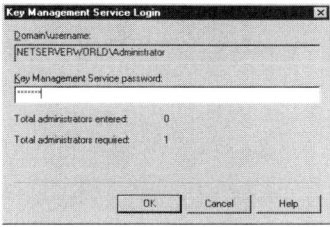

Figure 4.46 Entering the KMS Administrative Password

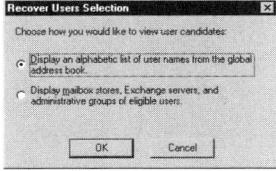

4. Select the method of locating users as shown in Figure 4.47. Click **OK** to continue.

Figure 4.47 Selecting the User Selection Method

5. Select the users you need to recover KMS keys for, and click **Recover** when you have added them all to the right side of the window, as shown in Figure 4.48.
6. Click **OK** to acknowledge the completion of key recovery.
7. Click **Close** to complete the recovery process.
8. Figure 4.49 shows the results of the recovery process—the user is now able to configure e-mail security from within Outlook.

Figure 4.48 Selecting Users for Recovery

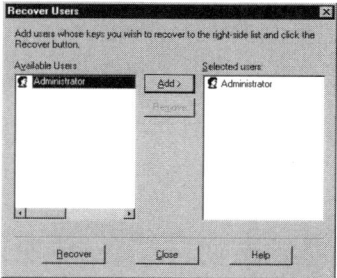

Figure 4.49 Configuring for E-mail Security

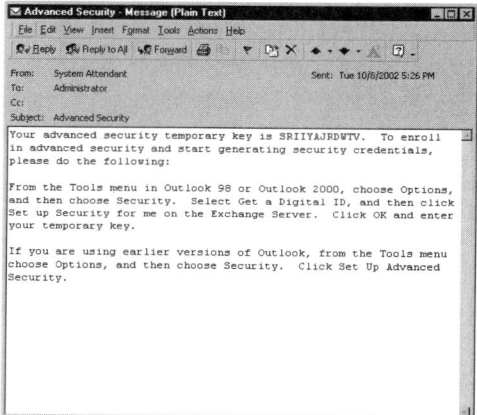

Windows XP Auto-enrollment

EXAM 70-214 OBJECTIVE 5.3.2

One of the new features in Certificate Services in Windows XP and Windows .NET Server 2003 is the concept of auto-enrollment of new certificates and approved renewals. Auto-enrollment is based on a combination of Group Policy settings and Version 2 Certificate template properties, which require Windows XP and Windows .NET Server. This combination provides for Windows XP Professional clients to automatically enroll users with new and newly renewed certificates at every Group Policy refresh (computer startup, user login event, or during a configured Group Policy refresh event).

By providing a means to automatically issue approved certificates and enable PKI-based applications such as EFS, Secure Sockets Layer (SSL), and smart cards, auto-enrollment can greatly reduce the workload incurred in managing a large PKI environment. Certificates are still requested through standard means (via the Microsoft Management Console [MMC] or by using Web Enrollment), but are now automatically installed when the certificate request has been approved and issued. Thus, the user or administrator is no longer required to perform this time-consuming step.

Auto-enrollment is managed via Group Policy and the new Certificate Templates snap-in. For more background information on auto-enrollment, see "Certificate Autoenrollment in Windows XP," located at www.microsoft.com/technet/prodtechnol/ winxppro/maintain/certenrl.asp. Exercise 4.15 walks you through the basic configuration of auto-enrollment. This can be done on a local Windows XP machine via Local Group Policy or on a Windows .NET Server 2003 using Active Directory Users and Computers to edit Group Policy.

EXERCISE 4.15

CONFIGURING AUTO-ENROLLMENT

1. If you are working locally on a Windows XP Professional computer, skip to step 5.
2. On your Windows .NET Server 2003, open the **Active Directory Computers and Users** console.
3. Right-click the site, domain, or Organizational Unit (OU) that you want to configure Group Policy for and click **Properties**.
4. Click the **Group Policy** tab. Select a Group Policy Object to edit and click the **Edit** button. Skip to step 9 to continue this procedure.
5. On a local Windows XP computer, click **Start | Run**. Enter **MMC** into the Run box and click **OK**.
6. From the blank MMC console, click the **File** menu and then click **Add/Remove Snap-in**.
7. In the Add/Remove Snap-in dialog box, click **Add**.
8. In the Add Standalone Snap-in dialog box, click **Group Policy**, and then click **Add**. Select **Local Computer** and click **Finish**.
9. To configure user settings for auto-enrollment, expand the following nodes: **User Configuration | Windows Settings | Security Settings | Public Key Policies** (see Figure 4.50).
10. Right-click the **Autoenrollment Settings** object and select **Properties** from the context menu (see Figure 4.51).
11. If you want to automatically enroll certificates, ensure that the **Enroll certificates automatically** radio button is selected. If you want to further automate certificate processing and provide for automatic renewal, removal, and cleanup of certificates in Active Directory, you should also consider selecting the two checkboxes as well. When you

have configured user auto-enrollment to your satisfaction, click **OK** to close the Properties window.

Figure 4.50 Locating the Auto-enrollment Setting

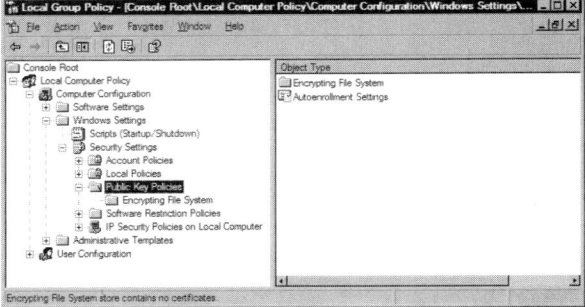

Figure 4.51 Configuring the Auto-enrollment Settings Object

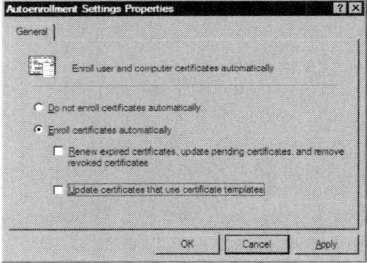

12. If you want to configure auto-enrollment of computer certificates, you can do it from the same location within the Computer Configuration node, as shown in Figure 4.52.

Figure 4.52 Configuring Computer Auto-enrollment

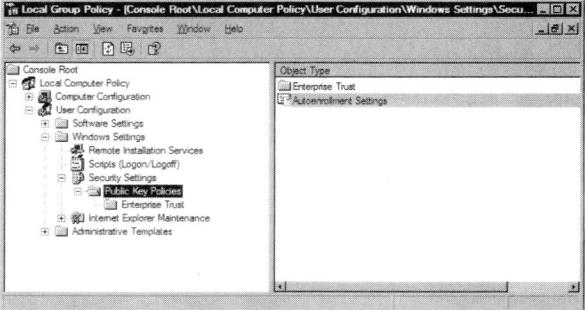

13. Close any open Group Policy windows.

Summary of Exam Objectives

There are three types of cryptographic functions:

- The hash function uses a mathematical algorithm on the data to scramble it.

- The secret key method of encryption uses a single key to encrypt and decrypt information. Secret key encryption quickly encrypts a large amount of data and is sometimes referred to as symmetric key cryptography. The disadvantage of secret key encryption is that a secure method must be in place for the parties to exchange the one secret key.

- The disadvantage of secret key encryption was removed in the 1970s with public key encryption, which is based on the use of key pairs. The public key is made available to everyone, but the private key of the key pair is available only to the owner. Public key encryption is also referred to as asymmetric cryptography. The public key is usually used to encrypt the sensitive data, which means that only the matching private key can decrypt the ciphertext. If a user wants to make information available to everyone with the guarantee that readers are getting information that has not been tampered with, the owner can use the private key to encrypt the data. Under these circumstances the matching public key is needed for the decryption process, and it is available for everyone's use. The disadvantage of public key encryption is that it is slow and therefore cannot protect a large amount of data.

Windows 2000 uses cryptography extensively. A digital signature is a hash value encrypted with a private key. By using the corresponding public key, receivers can be guaranteed that the document contains no modifications and that senders are really who they claim to be. With a digital signature, the document itself is not encrypted. Digital signatures involve the creation of a message digest, which is signed by the sender's private key. A message digest is a 128-bit number generated by hashing the original message.

Public key cryptography can provide authentication instead of privacy. Authentication involves the use of a challenge initiated by the receiver of the data. The challenge can be sent encrypted or in plaintext. Either way, the result is proof for the receiver that the sender is authentic. This type of authentication is referred to as proof of possession. Windows 2000 also uses public key cryptography for bulk data encryption and exchanging a secret key through a nonsecure communication channel.

Certificates are used to provide assurance that the public key used belongs to the entity that owns the corresponding private key. The issuer of a public key certificate is known as a CA. The job of the CA is to validate the identity of a person or organization to the public key. The certificate hierarchy consists of multiple CAs that have trust relationships established between them. The CA at the very top of the certificate hierarchy is referred to as a root. Nothing is above the Root CA, so it simply signs its own certificate. A subordinate is a child to a parent and can take on the role of an intermediate CA or an issuer CA.

A subordinate's certificate is generated by its parent CA. The intermediate CA's purpose is to create certificates for other CAs. The issuer CA is responsible for issuing end entity certificates.

Four types of CAs are available with the Microsoft Certificate Services, which can be broken down into two major categories: Enterprise and Standalone. Enterprise CAs rely on the Active Directory services of the Windows 2000 operating system. The Standalone CA is implemented when Active Directory or membership in a Windows 2000 domain is not available. The four types of CAs are Enterprise Root, Enterprise Subordinate, Standalone Root, and Standalone Subordinate.

The PKI is not a single item but rather a collection of various components working together to allow public cryptography to occur. The main components of the PKI are the following:

- **Active Directory** Policy distribution and certificate publication.
- **Certificate Service** Certificate creation and revocation.
- **Domain Controller/Kerberos Domain Controller** Domain logon.
- **Client** Where most of the activity is initiated.

The Windows 2000 operating system makes many core application services available to domain clients. To use public key encryption, public keys must be generated and then enrolled with a CA. If for some reason a key pair gets lost or corrupted, there must be a way for a client to have key recovery. Keys have an expiration date, so the operating system must include a mechanism for necessary renewal.

Windows 2000 provides core services for domain clients through the PKI. The generation and use of keys is transparent to the user. The PKI is a mechanism for creating, renewing, and revoking keys on an as-needed basis. Generated keys can be automatically enrolled with a CA, and in the event of key corruption, the Windows 2000 PKI makes it possible to recover keys. Because it is possible to log on to Windows 2000 with any computer, the PKI enables clients to use their keys from any network location.

Public key security relies on Trusted Root CA, certificate enrollment and renewal, and smart card logon. The responsibility of the CA is to attest to the public key being used. The top of the hierarchical structure is the Trusted Root CA. Trusted Root CAs are defined through the Certificate snap-in. Administrators must add the appropriate Trusted Root CAs and also remove any Root CAs they do not want to trust.

Certificate templates must be created to define policies that control how to create and then use a certificate. Smart card logon is controlled by the policy that has been established with the user. If the policy is set to enforce smart card logons, the user cannot log on without a smart card and a computer with a smart card reader. If the smart card policy is set to Enabled, password logons are still available.

PKI includes the applications written to support public key encryption. Windows 2000 provides security support for both Transport Layer Security (TLS) and Server Gated Cryptography (SGC). TLS and SGC require both the client and the server to have certificates issued by a CA. Certificate exchanges rely on the use of key pair encryption to end up with a secret session key.

E-mail can be secured by using the Exchange Server and Microsoft Outlook products. The process of digital signatures guarantees both the sender and the message for e-mail. Windows 2000 includes a code-signing technology known as Authenticode, which ensures the integrity and origin of software distribution from vendors over the Internet. The EFS allows any user to encrypt sensitive data by marking the directory or just the individual file for encryption. Windows 2000 also supports smart cards for public key logons.

Exam Objectives Fast Track

Cryptography and You: What is it All About?

- ☑ Encryption is the process of changing a cleartext message into an unreadable form known as ciphertext. Decryption is the process of changing the ciphertext message back to cleartext.

- ☑ Secret key encryption is very efficient at quickly encrypting large quantities of data. Secret key encryption uses a single key for both encryption and decryption.

- ☑ The most popular public key algorithm is the standard RSA, which is named after its three inventors: Rivest, Shamir, and Adleman.

- ☑ Public key algorithms provide better security than secret key encryption, but encrypt and decrypt data more slowly.

- ☑ Digital signatures prevent changes within a document from going unnoticed. They also verify the person to be the original author. Digital signatures do not provide document encryption.

- ☑ Digital certificates provide a way to validate public keys. They assure that public keys belong to the entity that owns the corresponding private key. Certificates provide users with a guarantee between the public key and the entity holding the corresponding private key. The certificate contains the public key and a complete set of attributes.

- ☑ The Microsoft Certificate Service includes four types of CAs: Enterprise Root, Enterprise Subordinate, Standalone Root, and Standalone Subordinate.

- ☑ The Enterprise Root CA is at the top of the PKI. An Enterprise Root CA uses predefined certificate templates for issuing and requesting certificates.

- ☑ PKI is a collection of components that allow public cryptography to occur transparently to clients.

- ☑ The two major services for Window 2000 public key security are the cryptographic service and the certificate management service. The cryptographic service is responsible for key generation, message hashing, digital signatures, and encryption. The certificate management service is responsible for X.509 version 3 digital certificates.

Certificate Authorities

- ☑ Because the Root CA is at the very top of the certificate hierarchy, it signs its own certificate. This is not secure for the Root CA, so a third party is often used to verify a Root CA's certificate.

- ☑ The issuer of a Public Key Certificate is called the CA. Any CA has the responsibility of validating the identity of a person or organization and for associating that entity with the key pair it issued.

- ☑ The Certificate Server Service for Windows 2000 includes the capability to do the following:
    - Issue certificates to users, computers, and services
    - Identify the requesting entity
    - Validate certificate requests, as allowed under the Public Key security policy
    - Support the local enterprises CAs as well as external CAs

Installing and Managing Windows 2000 CAs

- ☑ Active Directory must be properly configured before installing an Enterprise CA. Computers cannot be renamed, joined to, or removed from a domain after installing Certificate Services.

- ☑ For key recovery, a client's private key must be stored where it will always be accessible.

- ☑ A certificate should be valid only for a limited time. Windows 2000 only supports renewal with automatic enrolled certificates. All other certificates must go through a complete certificate enrollment process.

- ☑ Certificates and their properties are stored in certificate stores. Active Directory is the store for an Enterprise CA.

- ☑ Windows 2000 supports roaming users by utilizing roaming profiles and smart cards.

- ☑ The Enterprise CA publishes its CRLs to Active Directory where clients can obtain the information. The CRL is cached to the client's local machine and then read from the cache when certificates are verified.

- ☑ Windows 2000 provides single logons at the enterprise level.

- ☑ CAs are responsible for guaranteeing that a key is valid for a particular user or company. The CAs accomplish this by storing the public key and maintaining a list of issued certificates.

- ☑ The MMC Certificate snap-in is used to specify which CA to trust. Newly created CA's certificates must be added as trusted CAs.

- ☑ Certificate templates define policies that control the generation and use of certificates.

- ☑ Microsoft recommends that you back up your entire CA server by backing up the system state data.

- ☑ Use the CA console to back up and restore Certificate Services without backing up the system state data.

- ☑ Typical tasks involved in managing a CA include requesting certificates, using the Certificate Services Web interface, importing a certificate, and revoking certificates.

- ☑ The CRL lists all revoked certificates and is published to the specified locations on a configured schedule. The CRL can also be manually published by the administrator, if desired.

- ☑ The recommended way to back up a CA is by backing up the entire server, including the system state data.

- ☑ It is possible to back up and restore the CA data only from within the Certification Authority snap-in.

Advanced Certificate Management Issues

- ☑ By default, new certificates are published directly into Active Directory. This can be changed to force certificates to be published into the file system and/or Active Directory, if desired. In 99.999 percent of the cases, it is best to leave the default as is.

- ☑ The public key created by the KMS is kept in Active Directory and used for decrypting and authenticating incoming messages. The private key created by KMS is kept in an encrypted database maintained by the KMS itself and is only available to its authorized user (the user holding the certificate that was used to create the key pair). As such, the need may arise from time to time for a user to recover this private key. This happens most often when a computer fails or is replaced, thus wiping out the settings that the user had previously configured in Outlook for secure e-mail messaging. Fortunately, the KMS provides an extremely easy mechanism to recover these lost KMS keys.

- ☑ Windows XP Certificate auto-enrollment is based on a combination of Group Policy settings and Version 2 Certificate template properties—which requires Windows XP and Windows .NET Server. This combination provides for Windows XP Professional clients to automatically enroll users with new and newly renewed certificates at every Group Policy refresh (computer startup, user login event, or during a configured Group Policy refresh event).

Exam Objectives
Frequently Asked Questions

The following Frequently Asked Questions, answered by the authors of this book, are designed to both measure your understanding of the Exam Objectives presented in this chapter, and to assist you with real-life implementation of these concepts.

Q: What components are needed to build a complete PKI?

A: Five major components are needed to build a PKI. CAs are needed to issue certificates and for certificate revocation lists. The certification publication point, based on any kind of directory service, makes certificates and the CRLs available at any time. Any structure needs some kind of management tool, so a PKI also provides a utility for key and certificate management. The fourth component is the set of well-written applications that make public cryptography transparent to the user when the user has indicated what must be completed. The final component in PKI is hardware that supports cryptographic technologies. The hardware ranges from smart cards used to store secure keys to PCI cards that handle on-board encryption/decryption processing. The fifth component of a complete PKI is completely optional.

Q: What are the primary components of the Windows 2000 PKI?

A: The Microsoft Certificate Services make it possible to create your own CAs and to issue and manage digital certificates. This means that the Microsoft Certificate Service is your CA and management tool. The Active Directory service is your Certificate Publication Point. The third component is the set of well-written applications that work seamlessly with the Windows 2000 PKI, including Microsoft Internet Explorer and the IIS, as well as many third-party vendors. The final primary component of Windows 2000 PKI is a component from the Exchange Server software, the Exchange Key Management Service. The optional hardware support in cryptography is available through the use of smart cards.

Q: Are the security features easy to use?

A: Microsoft has designed the PKI to be easy for everyone to use, from end users to administrators. The PKI components are included with the Windows 2000 operating system, so there is nothing extra to buy or install. Departments can be set up with their own CAs, because the CA software is part of the operating system. The

www.syngress.com

administrator and the end user can use already familiar tools such as the MMC and Internet Explorer to create certificates, view their certificates, view other certificates, validate their authenticity, and set what certificates are authorized to do. By using Internet Explorer, users can access the Microsoft Certificate Service to request that a certificate be created. The Certificate Request Wizard will supply appropriate fields, and the request will automatically be forwarded to the appropriate CA. When the certificate is generated, the public key information is automatically stored in Active Directory, and the private information is delivered to the requester.

Q: For the administrator, how easy is the PKI to maintain?

A: The management of the PKI is a daily task once it is installed. From the Certificate Service and MMC snap-in, the administrator can perform the daily PKI maintenance tasks. Most of the tasks can be completed by merely selecting the appropriate menu item. Normal maintenance includes the following:

- Revoking certificates when necessary
- Defining templates for certificate attributes that will automatically be inherited by newly created certificates
- Viewing the certificates and their properties
- Viewing the properties of a CRL
- Changing group policy settings for users, groups, and computers
- Seeing certificates pending requests
- Viewing failed certificate requests

Q: What does it really mean when people state that you can export DES?

A: In 1996, the U.S. export regulations on cryptography were put under the purview of the Department of Commerce. In the fall of 1998, export restrictions were relaxed. The regulations for exporting cryptographic material and key recovery requirements are as follows:

- The key recovery requirements for export of 56-bit DES and equivalent products are eliminated.
- Export of unlimited strength encryption under license exceptions is now broadened to include others besides the financial industry for 45 countries.

- Export of recoverable products is granted to most commercial firms for a broad range of countries in the major commercial markets, excluding items on the U.S. defense list.
- Export licenses to end users may be granted on a case-by-case basis.

Self Test

A Quick Answer Key follows the Self Test questions. For complete questions, answers, and epxlanations to the Self Test questions in this chapter as well as the other chapters in this book, see the Self Test Appendix.

Cryptography and You: What is it All About?

1. What keys are used in public key encryption and what are their functions? (Choose all that apply.)
   A. A public key that can be used by a sender to encrypt data.
   B. A public key that can be used by a recipient to decrypt data.
   C. A private key that can be used by a recipient to decrypt data.
   D. A private key that can be used by a sender to encrypt data.

2. A digital signature provides what assurance? (Choose all that apply.)
   A. The message has not been tampered with during transit.
   B. The message has been protected from capture during transit.
   C. The message has originated from the sender.
   D. The message has not been delayed during transit.

3. What is used to provide assurance that the public key being used belongs to the entity that owns the corresponding private key?
   A. Active Directory
   B. Digital certificate
   C. Smart card
   D. User name and password

Certificate Authorities

4. What type of CAs does Windows 2000 provide support for? (Choose all that apply.)

    A. Enterprise Root CA

    B. Standalone Root CA

    C. Standalone Subordinate CA

    D. Enterprise Subordinate CA

5. You wish to deploy a certificate services solution for your network, which is not using Active Directory. Your CA will not be required to be on the network continuously, but only for brief periods of time to allow you to issue certificates and publish updated CRLs. You have installed a Trusted Root CA certificate from VeriSign to act as your CA's root. What type of CA should you deploy?

    A. Enterprise Root CA

    B. Standalone Root CA

    C. Standalone Subordinate CA

    D. Enterprise Subordinate CA

Installing and Managing Windows 2000 CAs

6. Ralph is preparing to implement a PKI solution in his small corporate network. He is currently using Windows 2000 Servers and Windows 2000 Professional computers, but has not deployed Active Directory. Ralph does not currently have any plans for an Active Directory deployment and his users are happy in the peer-to-peer workgroup arrangement that they are currently using. The company that Ralph works for is a small software development firm that would like to be able to digitally sign their downloadable applications to assure customers that they are legitimate and valid downloads. What type of Certificate Services solution can Ralph deploy to meet this need without requiring him to spend too much time or money?

A. Ralph should configure his network for Active Directory and issue these code-signing certificates from a newly created Enterprise Root CA.

B. Ralph should configure a Stand-alone Subordinate CA that uses a third-party certificate from VeriSign or Thawte as its root, and issue code-signing certificates with this standalone CA.

C. Ralph should configure his network for Active Directory and create an Enterprise Root and Enterprise subordinate CA. He should then install a trusted Root Certificate on the Enterprise Subordinate CA that comes from a trusted third party such as VeriSign or Thawte, and issue code-signing certificates from the Enterprise Subordinate CA.

D. Ralph should purchase an individual code-signing certificate issued by a trusted third party such as VeriSign or Thawte for each of his code developers, and allow them use these certificates to sign code made available for download.

7. Allison is attempting to install Certificate Services on one of her member servers. She is unable to complete the installation. What are some of the possible reasons for her inability to install Certificate Services? (Choose all that apply.)

A. Allison does not have administrative rights on the domain controllers in her organization.

B. Allison does not have administrative rights on the DNS servers in her organization.

C. Allison does not have administrative rights on the WINS servers in her organization.

D. Allison does not have administrative rights on the computer she is attempting to install Certificate Services onto.

E. Allison does not have administrative rights on the RRAS servers in her organization.

F. Allison does not have administrative rights on the Exchange servers in her organization.

8. Hannah is attempting to install Certificate Services on one of her member servers. From where would Hannah initiate the installation process?

    A. Hannah should issue the certsrv.exe command from the command line to initiate the installation.

    B. Hannah should perform the installation by using the Windows 2000 Setup CD-ROM menu.

    C. Hannah should perform the installation by configuring Certificate Services from the Windows Component Wizard.

    D. Hannah should visit the Windows Update Web site to download and install the required updates to Windows 2000 to support Certificate Services—it is not part of a default installation of Windows 2000.

9. Jon wants to create a trust chain for his Root CA from a third-party CA such as VeriSign or Thawte. How can Jon create this trust chain that starts with the third-party CA, goes next to his Root CA, and then on to his subordinate CAs, which in turn are issuing certificates to users in his network?

    A. Jon will need to purchase a special Root CA server from the third-party company and physically place that in his network.

    B. Jon will need to purchase a certificate from the third-party CA and import it into the trusted root folder of his Root CA. This will make the third-party CA the root of all CAs in his network.

    C. Jon will need to set up a VPN from his network to the third party in order for his Root CA to communicate with their CA's to verify chain of trust.

    D. Jon will need to co-locate his CA in the third-party company's building and issue certificates from it to his subordinate CA's and users.

10. The employees in Christopher's organization routinely access an SSL-secured web site. You would like for their computers to automatically be able to verify the certificate being presented to them instead of being prompted to download and install the other organizations root certificate each time. What can you do? (Choose two correct answers.)

A. Import the Root Certificate into the Trusted Root Certification Authorities folder in the domain Group Policy Object. This will propagate it to all domain computers.

B. Import the root certificate into the Trusted Root Certification Authorities folder in the local computer certificate store for your Root CA.

C. Import the Root Certificate manually into the Trusted Root Certification Authorities folder for each user's personal certificate store.

D. Import the Root Certificate to your domain controller and then export it to a floppy disk for safekeeping.

11. You have recently revoked 14 certificates that were in use in your organization. What would be the next thing you would likely want to do?

A. Perform an incremental backup of your system state data.

B. Publish a new CRL.

C. Renew the CA's certificate.

D. Change the KMS password.

12. Rob is the administrator of a large Windows 2000 PKI implementation, which has several hundred certificates issued and revoked daily. Which of the following presents the best option Rob can perform that will enable his users to always have the most up to date CRL?

A. Configure the CRL publication interval for 30 minutes.

B. Manually publishes the CRL every morning at 9 AM.

C. Configure the CRL publication interval for 60 minutes.

D. Add additional CDPs to the publication list for his CRLs.

13. You want to perform a backup of your Enterprise Root CA server. What methods are available to you to accomplish this task? (Choose all that apply.)

A. Perform a system state backup using the NTBACKUP program.

B. Export all Trusted Root Certificates to removal media.

C. Create a striped disk set on the CA server.

D. Perform a Certificate Services backup from the CA console.

Advanced Certificate Management Issues

14. Andrea is the Exchange administrator for her organization. She is using Exchange 2000 on Windows 2000 and is using the Exchange Key Management Service for advanced e-mail message security. One of her users, George, recently dropped his laptop in the hotel pool while vacationing. George has been issued a new laptop, complete with Windows 2000 and Microsoft Outlook. He would like to be able to continue to use secure e-mail. What can Andrea do to allow him to continue to be able to use secure e-mail functions?

    A. George's KMS private key is tied to his GUID and cannot be recovered without deleting and recreating his user account.

    B. Andrea will need to delete George's Exchange mailbox and create a new one from the Exchange System Manager.

    C. Andrea will need to login to the KMS and perform a key recovery action on George's account. He will receive an e-mail from the Exchange System Attendant providing him with instructions on how to configure for advanced e-mail security.

    D. Andrea will need to contact Microsoft to get the unlock code for the PID used to install Outlook on George's old laptop. Only with this PID can she reassociate his Exchange mailbox to his new laptop and allow him to use secure e-mail functions again.

15. You are the administrator of your organization's small Windows 2000 network. You have just finished configuring a new laptop computer for your CEO who replaced an existing computer. The first time he attempts to digitally sign a message in Outlook, he finds that he does not have the capability to do so. You are using Exchange 2000 as your messaging system and have the Key Management Server in place. What do you need to so that your CEO can digitally sign his e-mail once again? (Choose two answers.)

    A. Use the Key Manager in the ESM.

    B. Open the User Properties page for your CEO in Active Directory Users and Computers.

    C. Recover the lost key and issue your CEO a new enrollment token.

    D. Place a check in the "Password never expires" check box.

Self Test Quick Answer Key

For complete questions, answers, and epxlanations to the Self Test questions in this chapter as well as the other chapters in this book, see the Self Test Appendix.

1. **A, C**
2. **A, C**
3. **B**
4. **A, B, C, D**
5. **C**
6. **B**
7. **A, B, D**
8. **C**
9. **B**
10. **A, B**
11. **B**
12. **C**
13. **A, D**
14. **C**
15. **A, C**

Chapter 5

MCSE/MCSA 70-214

Managing and Troubleshooting the Encrypting File System

Exam Objectives in this Chapter:

5.4 Manage and troubleshoot EFS. Considerations include domain members, workgroup members, and client-computer operating systems.

- ☑ Summary of Exam Objectives
- ☑ Exam Objectives Fast Track
- ☑ Exam Objectives Frequently Asked Questions
- ☑ Self Test
- ☑ Self Test Quick Answer Key

Introduction

Regardless of the efficacy of the barriers that you erect to keep others from accessing or intercepting your sensitive data, you must recognize that your barriers won't always work. Confidential files sometimes fall into the wrong hands. Thus, you need to take additional steps to ensure that when this happens, unauthorized persons will not be able to read the data even though they have it in their possession. That's where encryption comes in.

Data encryption is a concept that predates computers. The art and science of *cryptography* involves hiding or changing information to protect it from unauthorized persons. The word comes from the Greek word for *hidden*, and the ancient Greeks, as well as those in other ancient civilizations, practiced cryptographic techniques when sending important military, political, and personal messages.

Encryption "scrambles" data so that it appears to be gibberish to anyone who doesn't have the means to "unscramble," or *decrypt*, it. All computer data is ultimately sent or stored in binary form (as ones and zeroes). To encrypt the binary data, a mathematical procedure called an *algorithm* (a calculation or formula) is applied, using a variable called the *key*. Methods used to encrypt data are called *ciphers,* and the encrypted form of data is called *ciphertext*. To decrypt data and return it to comprehensible form, the recipient of the data must use the proper key. This might be the same key used to encrypt it (a method called *symmetric encryption*) or it might be a different, mathematically related key (in a method called *asymmetric encryption*).

NOTE

For a fuller discussion of cryptography and encryption as well as other basic security concepts that we have not covered in this book, see Chapter 7 of *Scene of the Cybercrime: Computer Forensics Handbook* by Debra Littlejohn Shinder (Syngress Publishing, Inc., ISBN 1-931836-65-5, 2002).

When we discuss encryption in regard to computer data, we need to make a distinction between two different uses of the technology:

- Encryption of data as it travels across a network
- Encryption of data stored on disk

With the Windows 2000 operating system, Microsoft introduced built-in features to accomplish each of these tasks. Support for the Internet standard Internet Protocol Security (IPSec), which we discuss in Chapter 6, provides encryption for data in transit. In this chapter, we focus on the encryption of data stored on disk as implemented by

Microsoft's Encryption File System (EFS). Remember that prior to Windows 2000, users of Microsoft Windows operating systems had to rely on third-party products to provide encryption of stored data. These products were often very limited, very insecure, and not compatible with each other. Windows 2000 EFS removes the need for these types of products.

Remember, the fact that you might have implemented a firewall (such as ISA Server) and that the Windows NT-based operating systems include mandatory logon and access control for files does not guarantee that your data will be protected from unauthorized eyes. If thieves want to steal your data, they can achieve their goal in many ways. Tools on some other operating systems can access NTFS volumes while bypassing the access control supplied by NTFS. Lack of physical security allows entire portable systems to be stolen easily.

In addition, many laptop and notebook computers now come with removable hard drives. This is great for thieves because they have less contraband to conceal once they've pulled off a theft. The laptop itself still appears on the owner's desk, so a thief has more time to exit a building before any alarms go off. A thief can also disconnect and remove a desktop computer's second hard drive from the premises without being noticed.

To keep your data from being viewed and/or modified by any unauthorized user such as a thief, you should implement file encryption. EFS, which is included in Windows 2000 and improved in Windows XP/.NET, makes this easy. However, in order to take advantage of EFS, you must format the partitions on which it is stored to NTFS. Furthermore, you should know that even if you use these operating systems and use NTFS, no data is encrypted by default. You must explicitly set the encryption property on the files or folders that you want to protect.

In this chapter, we examine the features and architecture of EFS and show you how to use it to provide extra security for your sensitive data.

The Role of EFS in a Network Security Plan

A good network security plan is *multilayered,* just as a good physical security plan includes perimeter control (fencing), external security (guard dogs and security cameras), barriers (locks on doors), internal security (motion detectors and indoor cameras), and object-specific security (safes for valuables). In a network security plan, if your ISA server (or black-box firewall) is analogous to a high, strong fence sitting on the perimeter of the network, you might think of file encryption as a "safe" into which you put specific objects (such as files and folders) to protect them in case someone breaks through all the outer obstacles.

An important part of security planning is determining which assets need the most protection. You'll want to assess the sensitivity and importance of data on a case-by-case basis to decide which files and folders to encrypt. Why not just encrypt the entire contents of the disk and be done with it? Well, that is *not* the best solution, for several reasons:

- Operating system files that must be accessed to use the system cannot be encrypted.
- Data that needs to be compressed cannot be encrypted.
- The encryption/decryption process slows performance somewhat, so taking the performance hit for data that has no need to be encrypted doesn't make sense.
- Encrypted files can only be accessed by the person who encrypted them (in Windows 2000) or persons explicitly added to the access list (in Windows XP/.NET). So files that need to be accessible to many people cannot be encrypted in Windows 2000 and can only be encrypted in Windows XP/.NET with a great deal of work because you'll have to add everyone to the access list.

Another consideration is the fact that encrypting data might in some cases be like putting a red flag on it that announces to the world, "This data is sensitive and important!" If only one file on an entire disk is encrypted, that file will instantly become interesting to any intruder. For this reason, encrypting a number of files instead of only one or two is a good idea. That way, highly sensitive files won't stand out quite so much.

Remember that EFS fills only part of a network's encryption needs. EFS does *not* encrypt data sent across a network. If you attempt to send an EFS encrypted file across a network, someone who intercepts the packet with a protocol analyzer (called a *sniffer*) will be able to read the data. EFS is only intended to protect data on a disk. You should use IPSec to encrypt data to be sent across the network. If data is sensitive enough to be protected while it's stored on disk, it's sensitive enough to be protected when it's transmitted on a network.

Using the Encrypting File System

The Encrypting File System supported in Windows 2000 and XP/.NET is a security feature built into the NTFS file system. In order to encrypt a file (or folder) in any of these operating systems, the file (or folder) must be located on an NTFS 5 volume. NTFS 5 is the version that is created with a Windows 2000 installation. Both public key encryption and secret key encryption (discussed later in this chapter) are implemented within the complete process, so data is encrypted quickly and in such a way that it can stand up against an attack from *cryptanalysts* (people who specialize in analyzing and "breaking" encryption algorithms). U.S. customers who purchase Windows

2000 receive a 56-bit standard DES algorithm for implementation, but U.S. customers can also obtain a 128-bit encryption DES algorithm. Until export approval is received, Microsoft also has a 40-bit DES algorithm for all international customers.

An encrypted file can be read by anyone with a private key that can decrypt the File Encryption Key. In the Windows 2000 implementation of EFS, only the user who encrypted a file and a designated *recovery agent* (usually the network administrator) can decrypt the data. The version of EFS included in Windows XP/.NET adds the capability to share encrypted files with others.

The provision of a recovery agent is important in the implementation of EFS in the business environment. If a user leaves a company or if a user's private key becomes corrupted or is accidentally deleted, the recovery agent can implement data recovery. This might sound like a security weak spot, but data recovery in Windows is not a security weakness.

Microsoft has written code to establish an Encrypted Data Recovery Policy (EDRP), which controls who can recover data if the owner's private key is lost or if an employee leaves the organization. In a workgroup environment, Windows automatically sets up the EDRP on the local machine. In a domain environment, the EDRP is set up in the domain policy by the system administrator, and computers belonging to the domain will receive the EDRP from that location.

If a computer is not a member of a Windows 2000 domain and you force an administrative password change on the user account that was used to encrypt the files, those files become unrecoverable. In a domain environment, you have more recovery options for EFS files.

TEST DAY TIP

If you want to store encrypted files on a remote server, the server must be trusted for delegation. You must be a domain administrator to configure the server as trusted for delegation. This is done through the Active Directory Users and Computers console. For detailed instructions, see Microsoft Knowledge Base article Q307877. Also note that you will not be able to access encrypted files from Macintosh clients.

Encryption Fundamentals

As mentioned previously, encryption is the process of taking a plaintext file and processing it so that the original data is in a new ciphertext (unreadable) format. Typically the encryption process uses an algorithm and a secret value that is referred to as the *key*.

Public Key, or Asymmetric Cryptography

Public key cryptography is designed so that each person in the communication has two keys: a public key and a private key. The two keys are mathematically related, but the private key cannot be discovered by knowing the public key. Table 5.1 identifies the differences between these two keys in typical use.

Table 5.1 Public and Private Keys

Key	Description	Use
Private	Never made known to anyone but the user.	Decryption.
Public	Known worldwide.	Encryption.

Public key cryptography is also known as *asymmetric cryptography* because users employ different keys to encrypt and decrypt a file. Public key-based algorithms usually are highly secure, but they are considered slow. Figure 5.1 illustrates the basic processes of public key encryption and decryption.

Figure 5.1 Public Key Encryption and Decryption

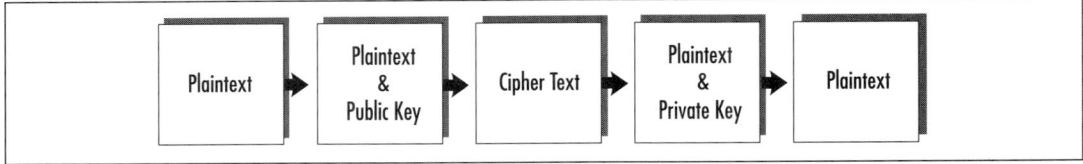

Public Key Cryptography

Public key pairs can be used as described to provide *confidentiality* of data. A message sender uses the recipient's public key to encrypt it, then sends it to the recipient, who uses his or her own private key to decrypt it. Only the private key that belongs to the same key pair as the recipient's public key will work. Another use for public key cryptography is to provide *authentication* of a message sender's identity. For this purpose, the sender encrypts the data with his or her own private key and sends it to the recipient who uses the sender's public key to decrypt it. Because the public key is available to anyone, there is no confidentiality, but because only the private key associated with the sender's public key could have been used to encrypt it (otherwise the public key wouldn't work to decrypt it), the recipient can be assured that the message came from the sender.

Secret Key, or Symmetric Cryptography

Instead of a key pair, *symmetric cryptography* uses a single, shared secret key. The same key is used for both encrypting and decrypting the data.

One popular method of symmetric cryptography is the Data Encryption Standard (DES), which the National Bureau of Standards defined in 1977 for commercial and nonclassified use. Developed by a team of IBM engineers who used their Lucifer cipher and input from the National Security Agency, DES is an encryption algorithm that uses a 56-bit binary number key.

Secret key algorithms are implemented quickly. Because the DES algorithm uses a single key for both encrypting and decrypting data, this security mechanism is weaker in its design than asymmetric methods. Symmetric cryptography requires some mechanism for sharing the secret key, and this requirement exposes it to the possibility of interception. Figure 5.2 illustrates the secret key algorithm method.

Figure 5.2 Secret Key Algorithm

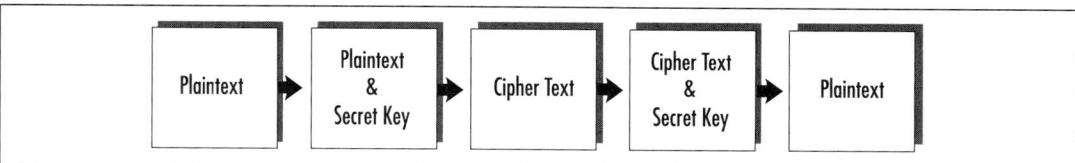

One major difference between symmetric and asymmetric algorithms is the number of keys that are used in the process. Public key algorithms use a key pair, but secret key algorithms use a single key. This major difference can clearly be seen in Figures 5.1 and 5.2.

What the figures do not show is the difference between the two algorithms in terms of the amount of time needed to fully process the encrypting and decrypting of the file. Because of this speed difference, asymmetric algorithms are most useful for small amounts of data. Symmetric algorithms can be used to efficiently encrypt large amounts of data. Public key encryption is a slower-process method than secret key encryption, so the two should be implemented appropriately. The two encryption technologies can be used together for the optimum balance between performance and security.

How EFS Works

Microsoft implements both secret key encryption, which is a faster and less secure process, and public key encryption, which is a slower but more secure process. When the operating system receives a request to encrypt a file, the Encrypting File System generates a random number for the file. This random number is known as the file's *File Encryption Key (FEK)*. With the FEK, a modified DES algorithm, called DESX, is used to generate the encrypted file and store it on disk. The secret key algorithm is being implemented at this point. Figure 5.3 shows a diagram of the EFS encryption process.

Figure 5.3 The EFS Encryption Process

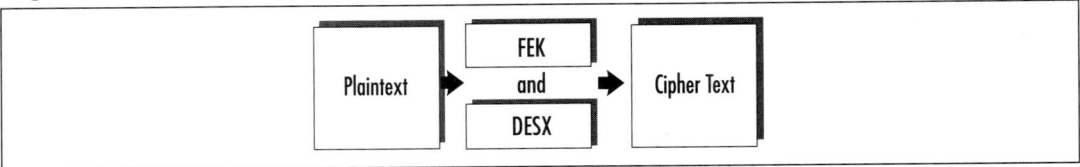

When a file needs to be decrypted, the FEK is used again. If you store the FEK on disk with the file, you have the FEK available for decryption at any time. Anyone who needs to decrypt the file and who has access to it also has access to the file's FEK.

Keeping sensitive data secure is the most important concern, but convenience is also important. Experience shows that when a security process is inconvenient for users, they are less likely to use it. The FEK is stored on disk and is available whenever it is needed, so the process is convenient and quick, but anyone who can get to the file will have available the one item needed for decrypting the file. This means you must address the security of the FEK itself. Secret key encryption is weak in this aspect, but public key encryption can be used here to good effect. Thus, to tighten the FEK's security, you can encrypt it also. This is where public key cryptography comes in.

When a user encrypts a file, the Encrypting File System uses the user's public key to encrypt the FEK. This design prevents users from sharing one decryption key. In Windows 2000, multiple users cannot share encrypted files. The public key encryption method is used only on the small FEK, so the system's performance isn't impacted. The ciphered FEK is stored with the encrypted file. Only the user, with that user's private key, can decrypt the ciphered FEK, which is needed to decrypt the actual file. At this point, both the sensitive data and the FEK are secured. The slow method of public key algorithm is not used on the large file. The final design of file encryption for Windows 2000 allows you to get the best from both encryption worlds.

NOTE

File encryption keys are stored in the nonpaged memory pool. This means the keys will never be in the paging file, which would create a security risk.

Windows XP/.NET enables support for sharing EFS encrypted files among multiple users, without sharing private keys among users. The file must first be encrypted by one user, who can then enable sharing and select the specific users who are to have access to the encrypted file. Any user who has an account on the local machine or in the Active Directory and who has a valid EFS certificate can be added. Each authorized user can then decrypt the file using his or her own private key.

Exam Warning

You might be wondering about the security of temporary files that are used by some programs. Because of the way the NTFS file system works, temp files do not present a security problem. When temp files are created, all the attributes from the original file (including the encryption attribute, if it is present) are copied to the temp files. This means EFS encrypts the temporary copies as well as the original file.

It is for this reason that Microsoft recommends setting the encryption attributes on folders rather than individual files. Keep this in mind when asked about configuring and implementing EFS on your network and during this exam.

Now let's pull all these loose ends together into a clear, precise picture. In the following sections, we look at the "how to" aspects of using EFS to protect your data.

User Operations

The Encrypting File System adds more security to the Windows operating system than ever. This built-in encryption allows any user to protect sensitive data against unauthorized use. This much-needed security feature can be used immediately after operating system installation. The only requirement for EFS is an NTFS partition. No new administrative tasks involving installation and configuration of EFS need to be completed in order for it to work. The user operations that use file encryption are:

- Encrypting a file or folder
- Accessing an encrypted file
- Copying an encrypted file
- Preventing files from being encrypted on a server
- Moving or renaming an encrypted file
- Sharing an encrypted file (in Windows XP/.NET)
- Decrypting a file
- Using the Cipher Utility (in Windows 2000)
- Encrypting a directory
- Employing recovery operations

Encrypting a File or Folder

EFS uses a public key pair and a secret key in the encryption and decryption process. When a user attempts to encrypt a file, the EFS must first determine whether a key pair exists for the user or whether one must be created. If a key pair needs to be created, the generation will occur on a domain controller or on the local computer, depending on the environment, unnoticed by the user.

Other tasks completed by EFS include creating the actual ciphertext file, ciphering the FEK, creating a log, creating a backup file, and deleting the log and backup file used in the encryption process. A great deal of activity takes place in the background, but the user is unaware of it.

In order to manage encrypted file resources, you must first identify the data that needs to be protected and then use one of two methods to let the operating system know where EFS should be implemented. Your choices are:

- The Windows Explorer interface
- The Cipher command-line utility

Encrypting a File or Folder on the Local Computer

An owner can encrypt any folder or file as long as it is stored on an NTFS partition. The easiest way to maintain encrypted files is to first create an encrypted folder in which you plan to store all sensitive data. Marking a directory for encryption has no effect on the listing of the files in the directory when you use the Explorer interface.

You can easily encrypt a folder using the graphical interface. When a folder is created, go to the Advanced Attributes and check **Encrypt contents to secure data**, as shown in Figure 5.4. This sets the encryption bit on the folder.

Figure 5.4 Enabling Encryption

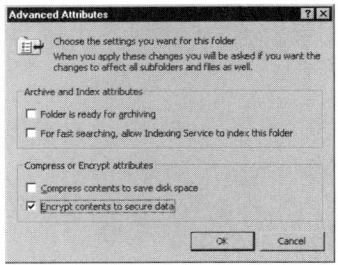

After this bit is set, the directory is marked for encryption. Any newly created file or subdirectory stored in the marked directory from this point on will be encrypted automatically. This makes it easy to encrypt files simply by creating them in or moving them to this folder.

If the directory is marked for encryption and it already contains files and subdirectories, you will receive a dialog box (as shown in Figure 5.5) that allows you to specify how far down in the directory structure encryption should be set.

Figure 5.5 Confirming Attribute Changes

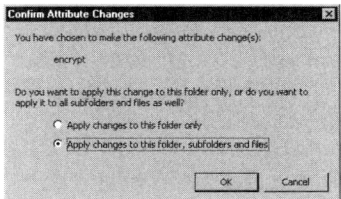

You will see the message box shown in Figure 5.6 while encryption takes place. This message box shows the estimated time required to complete the encryption process.

Figure 5.6 Applying Attributes

TEST DAY TIP

If you create an encrypted folder and another user creates a document in that folder, it will be encrypted using the creator or owner's private key. This means you will not be able to access the document unless (in Windows XP/.NET) the creator/owner has enabled sharing of the encrypted file and added your account to the user access list.

Compressed or system files cannot be encrypted by EFS. Note that EFS encryption is not available until the boot process is completed, which is efficient, considering the complexity of the encryption/decryption process. For this reason, you cannot encrypt the files that are used in the boot process.

The EFS process will fail if you try to encrypt a file that has the system bit set. An attempt to encrypt a system file—that is, a file in which the system attribute is set—produces the message, "An error occurred applying attributes to the file. Access is denied." EFS also will fail if you try to encrypt a file on the root. Encryption can be implemented at both the directory level and the file level. To encrypt a single file on an NTFS partition, follow the steps in Exercise 5.01.

EXERCISE 5.01

ENCRYPTING FILES WITH EFS ENCRYPTION

1. In Windows Explorer, select the file you want to encrypt.
2. Right-click to bring up the **Context** menu, and then select **Properties**.
3. Click **Advanced** on the **General** tab.
4. In the **Advanced Attributes** dialog box, select the check box **Encrypt contents to secure data**, then click **OK**.
5. On the **General** tab, click **OK** or **Apply** to mark the file as encrypted.

Later in this chapter, in the section "Using the Cipher Utility in Windows 2000," we discuss how to use the command-line interface to encrypt and decrypt files and directories.

Encrypting a File or Folder on a Remote Computer

You can encrypt a file or folder on a remote computer that is running NTFS. If the computer is in a domain, however, remote encryption must be enabled by making the remote computer trusted for delegation. Follow the steps in Exercise 5.02 to encrypt a file on a remote machine.

EXERCISE 5.02

ENCRYPTING REMOTE FILES WITH EFS ENCRYPTION

1. Connect to the remote computer through a mapped network drive.
2. Select the file or folder you want to encrypt and right-click it.
3. Click **Properties** in the right context menu.
4. Select the **General** tab, then click the **Advanced** button.
5. Check the **Encrypt contents to secure data** check box.
6. Click **OK**.

Accessing an Encrypted File

Accessing an encrypted file involves no special action by a user. There is no need to explicitly decrypt a file before using it. When the operating system verifies that a user has an acceptable private key, the system automatically decrypts the file so the user can read and/or modify it. The stored file is still encrypted on the disk. When the bytes are moved from the disk into the user's working set, the bytes go through the decryption process. When the user saves the file back to the disk, the file is encrypted again. The encryption and decryption processes are transparent to users.

> **TEST DAY TIP**
>
> If an unauthorized user attempts to open an encrypted file, he or she will receive a message stating that access is denied. An unauthorized user also will not be able to copy or move an encrypted file to a different location on the disk. These events can also indicate that a problem has occurred with an authorized user's certificate, such as certificate expiration or the inability to locate the certificate (logged on locally instead of to the domain or vice versa).

Backing up your encrypted files is important, as with any critical data. In the Windows 2000 and XP/.NET operating systems, just as in earlier versions of Windows NT, a file owner can control access to a file through the use of access permissions. If owners want to remove all access except their own, they can do so by setting NTFS permissions. The fact that only the owner has permission to access a file does not prevent system administrators from backing up the file on a regular basis. Furthermore, any user who belongs to the Backup Operators group has the ability to execute the Backup Utility and back up the file. The Backup Operators group is tied to the Backup Files and Directories user right, which, when it runs the Backup Utility, allows the file to be opened and read. The Backup Files and Directories right contains code that will bypass the normal access control list (ACL).

EFS also provides backup utilities with the ability to back up and restore files in ciphertext format. The backup process will not be able to decrypt the sensitive information nor will it have to decrypt and encrypt during the backing-up operation. The ADVAPI32.DLL library will provide the EFS APIs necessary for access to the encrypted data.

When Windows Backup backs up encrypted files, no special configuration is needed. Members of the Backup Operators group will not have a private key to decrypt the files, so there is no risk that they can read the sensitive data that you have encrypted. Encrypted data is backed up during a backup operation as it exists on disk. The Backup Utility reads and records the ciphertext file without decryption.

Copying an Encrypted File

The *copy* command has been extended in Windows 2000 and later operating systems with two new switches to allow you to export or import an encrypted file. When an encrypted file is copied, the encryption attribute always takes precedence. If either the file you want to copy or the destination directory is encrypted, the resulting new file will be encrypted. This differs from copying files in other circumstances, in which a file always inherits the attributes of the target parent directory. Table 5.2 lists various copying situations and the status of the resulting created files.

Table 5.2 Copying Encrypted Files

Starting Encryption	Copied to	New File Status
Both the directory and file are encrypted	A directory that is not encrypted	Encrypted
Both the directory and file are encrypted	A directory that is encrypted	Encrypted
The directory is encrypted, but the file is not encrypted	A directory that is encrypted	Encrypted
The directory encrypted, but the file is not encrypted	A directory that is not encrypted	Unencrypted
Both the directory and file are unencrypted	A directory that is encrypted	Encrypted
Both the directory and file are unencrypted	A directory that is unencrypted	Unencrypted

---

Damage & Defense...

Encryption Does Not Apply to Diskettes

Be aware that if you copy a file that is encrypted on your hard disk to a medium such as a diskette, which does not support NTFS (or other media formatted in FAT or CDFS, such as a FAT partition on your hard disk or a CD-ROM), the encryption attribute will be lost and the file will be in an unencrypted state on the FAT-formatted media. This can pose a serious security risk. There is *no* warning message that the encryption will be lost when you copy the file. The file is decrypted to make the copy, but this is completely transparent to users.

This can be a problem for users who travel with removable media containing sensitive information. An attacker doesn't even have to brute-force his or her way into a stolen portable computer if they have managed to acquire the diskette or CD that was with it. There are third-party solutions to this problem, such as Pretty Good Privacy (PGP), which can be enacted on files or across an entire disk. Check out PGP at www.pgp.com for more information.

If you copy an encrypted file to a different computer, you'll need to export your EFS certificate and private key to the other computer in order to be able to open the file on the other computer.

Preventing Files from Being Encrypted on a Server

In some circumstances, administrators do not want users to be able to store encrypted files on a file server. A Registry edit can be done on the server to prevent files on the server from being encrypted with EFS. This edit can also prevent encrypted files on a user's local hard disk from being copied to the server in an encrypted state. If a user copies encrypted files to a server that's configured not to store encrypted files, the files will be stored as unencrypted files.

To edit the Registry so that files can't be encrypted on a server, perform the steps of Exercise 5.03.

EXERCISE 5.03

PREVENTING EFS USE ON A SERVER

1. On the **Start** menu, click **Run**.
2. In the **Run** box, type **regedit**. Click **OK**.
3. Navigate to the following Registry key: HKEY_LOCAL_MACHINE\SYSTEM\CurrentControlSet\Control\FileSystem
4. Expand this key and locate the *NtfsEncryptionService* value.
5. Delete this value.

You need to reboot the server before the change takes effect. After you complete the Registry edit, users can only copy their encrypted files to the server in an unencrypted state.

NOTE

Microsoft recommends that you always back up the Registry before making changes to it. See article Q256986 in the Microsoft Knowledge Base for information about how to back up, restore, and edit the Registry. Remember that Registry changes take place immediately; that is, there is no way to undo a change after you've made it (although many changes won't actually take effect until you reboot because that's when the Registry values are loaded by the operating system and/or applications).

Moving or Renaming an Encrypted File

Renaming an encrypted file is no different from renaming a compressed file. The operating system changes the filename but makes no modification to any other fields in the file's header. The fact that the file is encrypted sets an encryption bit in the file's header. Renaming changes the file's name but does not touch the encryption attribute.

When an encrypted file is moved, it retains its encrypted status, regardless of the destination folder if on the same Windows 2000 system and an NTFS partition. When an encrypted file is moved on the same partition, there is no difference to the file other than the resident directory of the file. This is because only the pointer to the file is changed; the file and its attributes are completely untouched.

When the encrypted file is moved to a different NTFS partition, the file is first decrypted and then encrypted before being stored at the new location. When a file or folder is moved to a partition that is not formatted in NTFS, the file or folder loses all NTFS attributes, including the encryption attribute, and is decrypted.

Commonly, users get new workstations due to hardware upgrades, change physical locations in a company, and so forth. In these cases, users' local files are often transferred to new computers. If encrypted files or folders are moved to a new computer, you must export the user's keys and EFS certificate from the old computer and import them to the new computer; otherwise, the user won't be able to access the encrypted files.

Sharing an Encrypted File in Windows XP/.NET

Users of EFS in Windows 2000 found that the feature had a major drawback in some circumstances—specifically, only the user who encrypted a file could access it. It was not possible to allow others to access an encrypted file without the original user having to decrypt it and share it with others in a decrypted state. A major improvement to EFS in Windows XP/.NET is the ability to share access to encrypted files.

In Windows XP/.NET, the original user who encrypts a file can add other user accounts to the list of those who can access the file in its encrypted state. This makes for a higher level of security. Additionally, members of the Administrators group can also add users to the encrypted file.

To allow others to access an encrypted file, follow the steps of Exercise 5.04.

EXERCISE 5.04

ADDING MULTIPLE USERS TO AN ENCRYPTED FILE IN WINDOWS XP

1. In Windows Explorer, right-click the encrypted file that you want to share.

2. Click **Properties**, select the **General** tab, and click **Advanced**.
3. Click **Details**, then click the **Add** button.
4. From the list of users, select the user account with which you want to share access. Click **OK**.
5. Add additional users if you want.
6. Click **OK** to close each dialog box.

Of course, any users that you add to the encrypted file's access list must also have the proper NTFS permissions required to access the file. Encryption and decryption occur transparently, as though the added user were the owner. In addition, remember that you cannot perform this action (adding users) to a folder, only to a file or files.

Decrypting a File

Users never need to explicitly request that a file be *decrypted* as long as only that user needs to access the file (in Windows 2000) or as long as other users who are to have access have been added to the file's properties (in Windows XP/.NET). That does not mean that the decryption process will never occur. The decryption process does occur in two instances:

- EFS goes through the decryption process whenever the file is accessed, but this processing is transparent to the user.
- Decryption occurs when a file's owner decides that the added security method is no longer needed and chooses to set the file's attributes to unencrypted.

When a user wants to read and/or modify the contents of an encrypted file, the operating system decrypts the file as it is moved from the hard drive into physical memory. The file's decryption for use is completely transparent to the user, and the ciphered or encrypted form of the file is still stored on the hard drive. The user does not have to decrypt the file manually before each use. The user works with encrypted files just as he or she works with normal, unencrypted files.

EFS must have the user's private key in order to decrypt the file. If the user does not have a valid private key to the file, the system message "Access is denied" appears, just as when the user does not have the proper permission.

Decryption also occurs if and when a user decides that the encrypted data is no longer sensitive and therefore does not have to be encrypted. The user can then implement the decryption process at the file or directory level. The user can use the Windows Explorer interface to clear the encryption bit, or the user can use the Cipher Utility and execute the appropriate command. When an individual file is selected for decryption, only that file is affected. When the user requests decryption at the directory level, a dialog box appears asking whether the user wants to decrypt all files and subdirectories found within this directory, as shown in Figure 5.7.

Figure 5.7 The Confirm Attribute Changes Dialog Box

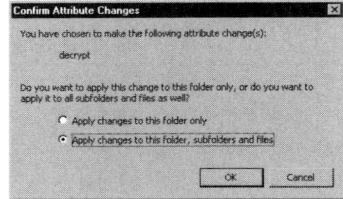

The decryption process at the directory level is exactly like the process for changing permissions at the directory level. To decrypt a file, perform Exercise 5.05.

EXERCISE 5.05

DECRYPTING A FILE

1. Using Explorer, select the encrypted file that you want to now be stored as an unencrypted file.
2. Right-click to bring up the **Context** menu, and select **Properties**.
3. Click **Advanced** on the **General** tab.
4. In the **Advanced Attributes** dialog box, clear the check box to **Encrypt contents to secure data**.
5. Click **OK**.
6. On the **General** tab, click **OK** or **Apply** to mark the file as unencrypted.

Using the Cipher Utility in Windows 2000

Windows 2000 allows users to use file encryption from the command prompt. This can be faster than using the graphical interface when a large number of files are to be encrypted. The command-line utility also provides added functionality (such as the ability to view at one time the encryption status of all files or subdirectories in a specified directory, the ability to force encryption on files that are already encrypted, and so on).

The general format of the Cipher Utility is:

```
cipher  [ /e ]  [ /d ]  [ /s [dir]]  [ /a ]  [ /i ]  [ /f ]  [ /q ]  [filename]
```

When the *cipher* command is executed with no switches or filename, the result is a display of the encryption status of the current directory and any files in the directory. This is useful because users might not readily know which files have been encrypted, since the process during access is transparent. (Another way to determine encryption status is to check the properties of each individual file, but that can be cumbersome.) Table 5.3 identifies each switch of the *cipher* command.

Table 5.3 *Cipher* Command Switches

Switch	Function
/e	Encrypts the specified files. The directory is marked for encryption, so any files or subdirectories created and placed here will be encrypted.
/d	Decrypts the specified files. The directory will be cleared of the encryption attribute so that files added here will not be encrypted.
/a	Performs the specified operation for files and directories.
/s :<dir>	Performs the specified operation on the files in the specified directory and on all subdirectories.
/i	Continues to perform the *cipher* command, even if errors occur, thereby overriding the default behavior in which the *cipher* command stops if an error occurs.
/f	Forces encryption to occur on all specified files, even those that are already encrypted, thereby overriding the default behavior of not encrypting already encrypted files.
/q	Reports only the most essential information.

The *filename* can be replaced with a filename or directory. The *filename* specification allows for wildcard use, thus allowing multiple listings to be affected with a single command execution.

EXAM WARNING

Be sure you know and understand the function of each of the available switches for the *cipher* command. You should expect to be asked at least one question, which could be a bit tricky in its wording, about using *cipher* to work with EFS encrypted files.

Figure 5.8 shows a *cipher* command that was executed with no switches at the root level of the directory structure. Every existing directory is listed, and you can see whether the directory is marked for encryption. The *E* attribute indicates encryption, so, in this example, you can see that Security Files is encrypted. *U* indicates that a directory is unencrypted.

Figure 5.8 Executing the *Cipher* Command with No Switches

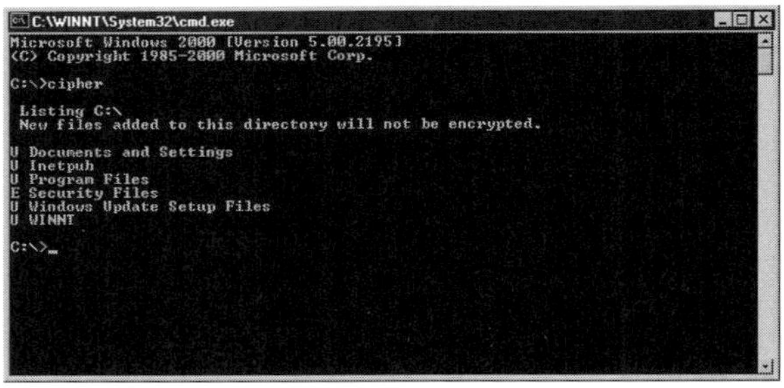

Figure 5.9 shows the result of executing the *cipher* command at the directory level. The directory is marked for encryption, and any new objects stored there will be encrypted. All files and subdirectories are shown, along with their current encryption status. As you might expect, all files in this directory are encrypted. However, a directory could be marked for encryption that contains unencrypted files, as discussed in the next section.

Figure 5.9 Executing the *Cipher* Command at the Directory Level

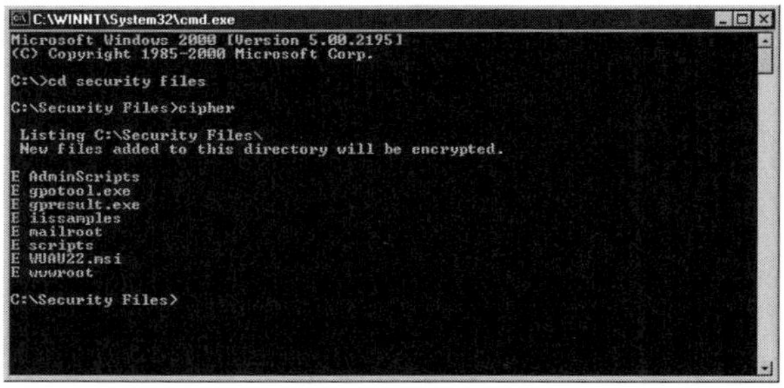

Encrypting a Directory

As mentioned earlier in this chapter, EFS allows encryption to be set at the directory and file levels. When a directory is selected for encryption, what really happens is that any new object placed in the directory—including files and subdirectories—is encrypted. Any current existing file and subdirectory will not be encrypted unless the owner manually sets the encryption bit on the existing object. The best practice is to create a directory, mark it for encryption, and then store all sensitive data in that directory when you work with EFS.

When you modify a directory's attribute to include encryption, the directory itself is not technically encrypted; rather, the directory is *marked* for encryption. This encryption mark controls all the new objects becoming encrypted.

You can also explicitly unencrypt a file in an encrypted directory by unchecking the encryption attribute in its properties or using the *cipher* command.

Employing Recovery Operations

Earlier in the chapter, we mentioned the Encrypted Data Recovery Policy (EDRP). EDRP is part of the local security policy in a workgroup environment or part of the domain security policy for Windows domains. The Security Subsystem in user mode is responsible for enforcing this policy. Users can use file encryption offline, and the Security Subsystem is responsible for caching the EFS policy, much the way logon information is cached on the local machine.

The recovery policy must first be set up by the system administrator. The operating system contains a Recovery Agent Wizard, in which recovery agents are assigned along with their corresponding key pairs. The Microsoft Base Cryptographic Provider is used to create a data recovery file for each recovery agent.

Notes from the Underground...

Watch the Recovery Agents!

Once you start to think about the power of the data recovery agent in Windows 2000, you soon start to realize the importance of planning a good data recovery policy for your organization. Having too many or too few data recovery agents can lead to troubles you would do well to avoid. The worst-case scenario revolves around having more data recovery agents than you need. Let's examine that situation.

Assume that your organization employs EFS on a rather large scale, requiring all users to encrypt all documents. Furthermore, all documents are stored on central file servers that have been delegated for trust. This makes performing backups easier, because all critical files are located on a few centralized file servers. You have three shifts manning your network operations center (NOC) Monday through Friday, with an on-call administrator for the weekends. Since your organization relies so strongly on EFS, you have three data recovery agents per shift, for a total of nine data recovery agents, plus the built-in data recovery agent, which has never been removed. Your organization believes strongly in the diligent use of EFS, but you haven't been able to sell them on strong password requirements or the need for network traffic protection (such as IPSec).

Over the weekend, a member of the cleaning crew has clandestinely planted a rogue wireless access point on your network, connected directly to

Continued

> the network backbone. Your organization does not currently use wireless networking, and thus the existence of the access point goes unnoticed, since it has been cleverly hidden in an out-of-the-way place.
>
> Now the attacker sits in your parking lot (or even further away, depending on the power output of the access point and the gain on his receiving antenna) and sniffs your wired network without any notice by you or your other administrators. Three days later, the attacker manages to capture an administrative username and password from sniffing the network. It just so happens that this administrator has data recovery capability. Now, not only can this attacker gain access to your network (unnoticed most likely until it is too late), he or she can freely decrypt files located on your network file servers and inspect their contents. What's more, the attacker has also been intercepting all EFS-encrypted documents traveling to and from the server, because they have been traveling across the network in cleartext!
>
> A month later, your largest competitor releases a product almost identical to the one you had slated for the following week and dominates the market, shutting your product out of contention for consumer dollars. Coincidence or bad planning?

The default domain recovery policy is configured so that the domain administrator account is the only recovery agent. We recommend that you change this configuration, for two reasons:

- No one should be logging on with the Administrator account (it should be renamed and not in use).
- You need more than one recovery agent for fault-tolerance purposes.

The next two exercises demonstrate the process of adding recovery agents in Windows 2000. Exercise 5.06 walks you through the process of adding a recovery agent for an account that does not already have an EFS recovery certificate. Exercise 5.07 walks you through the process of adding a recovery agent for an account that has an EFS recovery certificate.

EXERCISE 5.06

CREATING A NEW EFS RECOVERY AGENT

1. Open Active Directory Users and Computers (select **Start | Programs | Administrative Tools | Active Directory Users and Computers**), as shown in Figure 5.10.

   Figure 5.10 Active Directory Users and Computers

   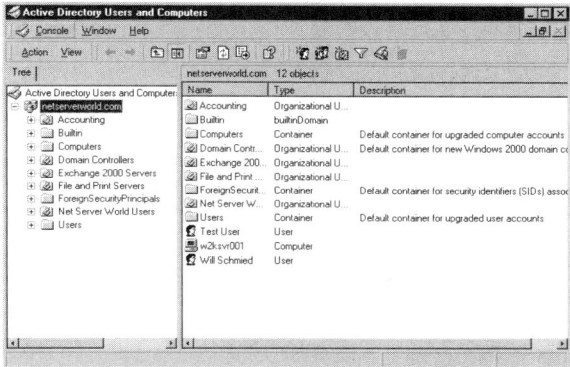

2. Right-click your domain, and choose **Properties**. You will see the window shown in Figure 5.11.

   Figure 5.11 The Group Policy Tab of a Domain's Properties

   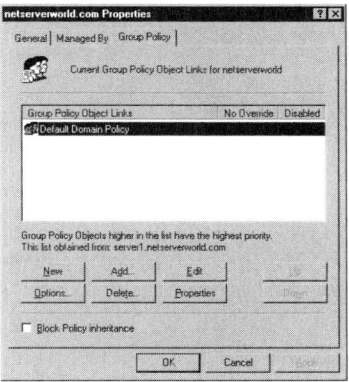

3. Click the **Group Policy** tab.
4. Select **Default Domain Policy**, and click **Edit**. You will see the window shown in Figure 5.12.

Figure 5.12 Editing the Group Policy Object

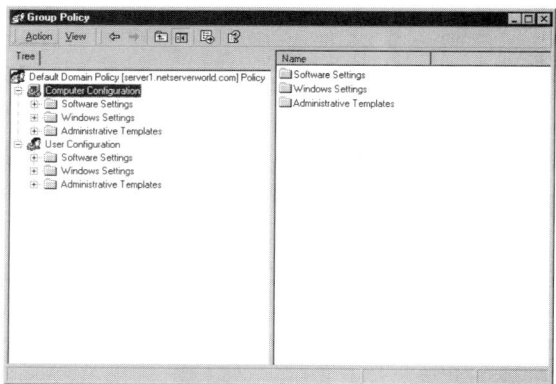

5. Expand **Computer Configuration | Windows Settings | Security Settings | Public Key Policies**.
6. Right-click **Encrypted Data Recovery Agents**, and choose **Create**. This step starts the wizard shown in Figure 5.13.

Figure 5.13 Welcome to the Certificate Request Wizard

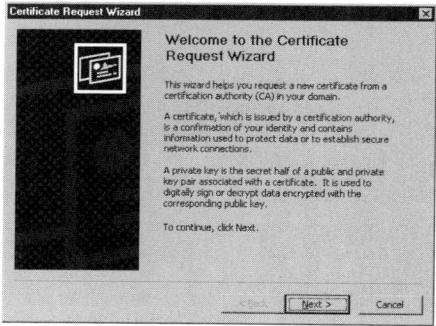

7. Click **Next** to continue the wizard.
8. Figure 5.14 shows the Certificate Template window. This is where you select the type of certificate that you want. Select **EFS Recovery Agent**, and click **Next**. You will see the screen shown in Figure 5.15.
9. Enter a name and description for the certificate, and click **Next**.
10. The Completing the Certificate Request Wizard window displays (see Figure 5.16). Click **Finish** to complete the request process and start installing the new certificate.

Figure 5.14 The Certificate Template Window

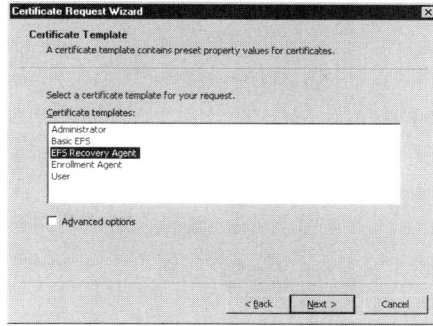

Figure 5.15 The Description Window

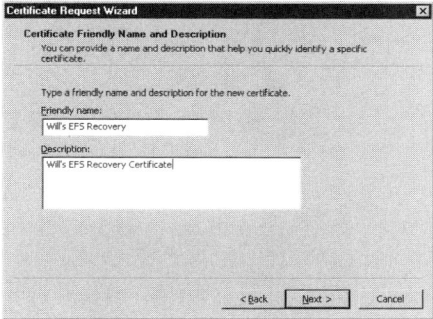

Figure 5.16 Completing the Certificate Request Wizard

11. After requesting the certificate and completing the wizard, you will see the message box shown in Figure 5.17. Click **View Certificate** to look at the new certificate before you install it.

12. Figure 5.18 shows the certificate. Verify that it is for File Recovery. Once the user account has a recovery certificate, that user can be added as a

recovery agent. Note that the certification authority must be configured to issue recovery agent certificates, and the user must have permission to request the certificate.

Figure 5.17 Viewing or Installing a Certificate

Figure 5.18 Viewing an EFS Recovery Certificate

13. Click **OK** to return to the window shown earlier in Figure 5.17.
14. Click **Install Certificate**. You'll see the message box shown in Figure 5.19, indicating that the certificate was installed successfully.

Figure 5.19 The Certificate Request Successful Message Box

Once you've created a new recovery agent certificate, you can complete the process to link the certificate to the user account that you have designated to be the recovery agent by performing the steps outlined in Exercise 5.07. This user should normally be a trusted administrator. Additionally, you will not want to have too many recovery agents—perhaps two per location or site.

EXERCISE 5.07

ADDING AN EFS RECOVERY AGENT

1. Open Active Directory Users and Computers (select **Start | Programs | Administrative Tools | Active Directory Users and Computers**), as shown earlier in Figure 5.10.
2. Right-click your domain, and choose **Properties**, as shown earlier in Figure 5.11.
3. Click the **Group Policy** tab.
4. Select **Default Domain Policy**, and click **Edit** to open the Group Policy Editor, as shown earlier in Figure 5.12.
5. Expand **Computer Configuration | Windows Settings | Security Settings | Public Key Policies**.
6. Right-click **Encrypted Data Recovery Agents**, and choose **Add**. The Add Recovery Agent Wizard shown in Figure 5.20 starts.

Figure 5.20 Welcome to the Add Recovery Agent Wizard

7. Click **Next** to continue the wizard and open the Select Recovery Agents window shown in Figure 5.21.

Figure 5.21 The Select Recovery Agents Window

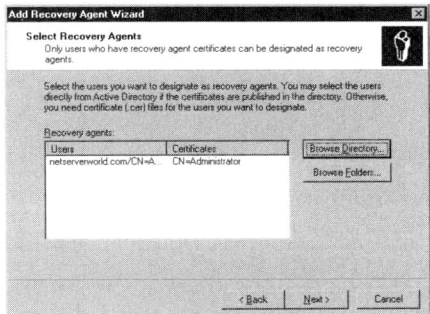

8. In the Select Recovery Agents window, click **Browse Directory** to search Active Directory for recovery agents (see Figure 5.22). Optionally, you could click **Browse Folders** to search for the certificate of your recovery agent.

Figure 5.22 Finding Users to Be Recovery Agents

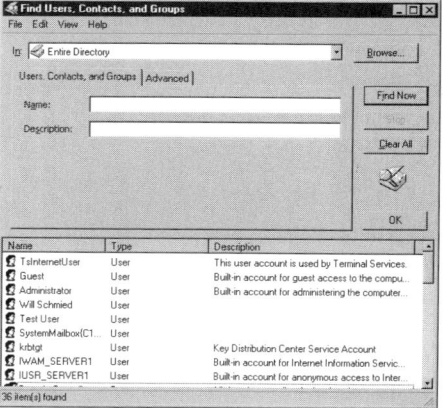

9. After choosing **Browse Directory**, you need to select the users you want to designate as recovery agents. Type the name of the user, and choose **Find Now**. Alternatively, you can click **Find Now** without typing a name to see all users, then select the user from the list and click **OK** to return to the Select Recovery Agents window shown in Figure 5.21.

10. Click **Next** to continue. You will see the Completing the Add Recovery Agent Wizard window shown in Figure 5.23.

Figure 5.23 Completing the Add Recovery Agent Wizard

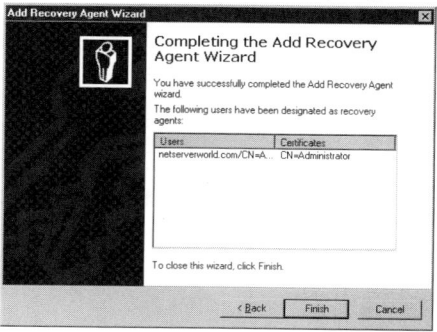

11. Click **Finish** to complete the wizard.

The recommended steps in the recovery of an encrypted file that an owner cannot manipulate are performed by a recovery agent as follows:

1. Assuming that you are the person who will be doing the recovery—that is, you're the recovery agent—use a backup utility to restore a copy of the user's ciphertext file on the computer that has the recovery certificates.
2. Using Explorer, display the encrypted file's properties.
3. On the **General** tab, click **Advanced**.
4. Clear the **Encrypt contents to secure date** check box, which will use your private key to decrypt the file. The decrypted file should now be backed up and restored to the user.

Another method of recovery is to export the recovery agent's recovery certificate to a disk and then import the disk's contents onto the machine that has the encrypted file.

The Windows 2000 operating system also provides a command-line utility, named EfsRecvr, which can be used to recover an encrypted file. If you use the EfsRecvr utility, the same steps should be applied in order to back up the file and restore it on the computer that contains the recovery keys.

The EfsRecvr command-line utility uses this general format:

```
EFSRECVR  [ /S [:dir] ]   [ /I ]  [ /Q ]  [ filename [...] ]
```

Table 5.4 summarizes each of the items in the *EfsRecvr* command line.

Table 5.4 *EfsRecvr* Command-Line Syntax

Item	Function
/S	Recovers the files in the given directory and all subdirectories. The default directory is the current directory.
/I	The recovery process will continue, even if an error occurs. The default behavior is to immediately stop the recovery process if an error occurs.
/Q	Limits the reporting to only essential information needed to load the appropriate keys.
Filename	Specifies a file, directory, or pattern.

EXAM WARNING

Ensure that you know and understand the different ways that you can perform EFS recovery operations as detailed in this chapter. They are, for your review:

- Importing the encrypted files to a recovery computer using your backup utility and then performing the decryption; after the file is

decrypted from Windows Explorer, it can then be copied back to its original location
- Exporting the recovery agent certificate and private key to the location of the encrypted files and then performing the decryption via Windows Explorer
- Opting to use the *EFSRCVR* command instead of the GUI in either of the two previous examples

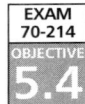

EFS Architecture and Troubleshooting

The EFS components and the encryption process, along with the EFS file information and the decryption process, are involved in EFS file encryption. In the following sections, we examine each of the elements that make up the EFS architecture. After we examine, in depth, the architecture of EFS, we then look at some common troubleshooting issues that you could encounter while deploying and supporting EFS on your network. They're also pretty good stuff to know for the exam!

Test Day Tip

Don't get wrapped around the axle here trying to get every last bit of EFS architectural information down cold. This is not something you should expect to see on the exam, but it is provided for your reference should you desire to gain a deeper understanding of how and why EFS works in Windows 2000.

On the other hand, the troubleshooting guide at the end of this section is extremely valuable and something that you should understand not only for this exam but also for the daily support of your EFS users.

EFS Components

In order to understand the entire encryption/decryption process, you need to look at the operating system architecture. Like its predecessor, Windows NT, the Windows 2000 OS structure contains both user mode and kernel mode. When Microsoft developed its data encryption process, the designers had to decide in which mode the encryption code should run. This decision presented some important considerations.

For example, if data encryption were left in user mode, temporary files that were not encrypted would be created, which would defeat the security objective. On the other hand, applications still run in user mode, so when a user requests encryption using Explorer or the Cipher Utility, the activity must start here. The solution: When EFS is implemented, some of the activity occurs in user mode and some in kernel mode.

In earlier versions of the Windows NT operating system, the Local Security Authority Subsystem (LSASS) was in user mode. With Windows 2000, this subsystem takes on additional tasks and includes some additional functions for the Local Security Authority Server in order for EFS to work properly. The functions are grouped as EFS functions. The NTFS driver, which was introduced in Windows NT 3.1, is in kernel mode. Because users can protect sensitive data only on an NTFS partition, this driver has an active role in the overall encryption process. Figure 5.24 shows both old and new components.

Figure 5.24 EFS Components

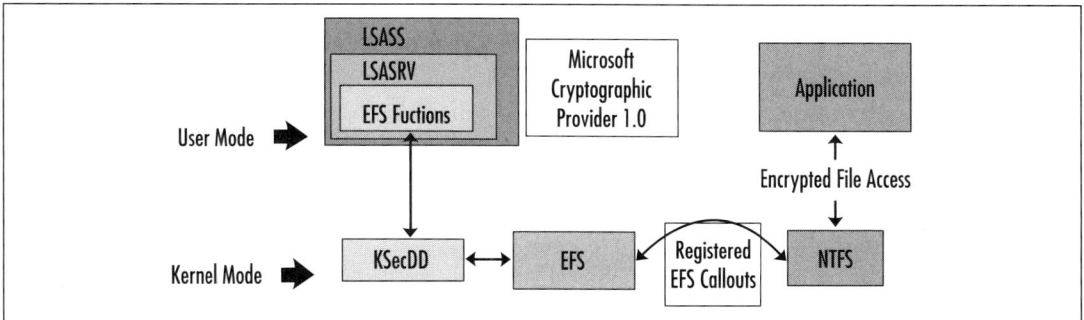

The key components of EFS are:

- **EFS driver** EFS is really a device driver that works in conjunction with the NTFS driver, both of which run in kernel mode. The EFS driver runs on top of NTFS in a layered manner. Whenever a user needs encryption or decryption, the EFS driver works with the cryptography services in Windows 2000 user mode. The EFS communicates with the KsecDD (the security device driver) to request many of the required key management services. When the file system needs to complete an encryption task (which the NTFS driver itself is incapable of performing), the EFS driver takes on the responsibility.

- **EFS File System Runtime Library (FSRTL)** This EFS driver module uses NTFS callouts for tasks such as reading, writing, and opening encrypted files and folders as well as encrypting and decrypting data when it is read from or written to disk. Messages are passed between the EFS driver and the EFS FSRTL via the NTFS file control callouts.

- **KsecDD** This device driver takes the EFS request and "talks" with the Security Subsystem on behalf of the EFS driver. The KsecDD acts as a connection between the needed local procedure call (LPC) calls and the LSASS in user mode.

- **EFS Services** These services are stored in the Local Security Authority Server, which is part of the LSASS. In user mode, the Encrypting File System Services interface with the Microsoft Base Cryptographic Provider 1.0 to provide FEKs and to generate the needed data decryption fields and data recovery fields. The Encrypting File System Service is used to obtain and enforce the encryption data recovery process and to locate the user's key pair when it is needed.

- **Cryptographic Service Provider (CSP)** The Cryptographic Service Provider (CSP) provides the key pairs (public and private key) for EFS users and recovery agents. By default, DESX is the encryption algorithm used by EFS. You can configure Windows XP Pro to use 3DES (a significantly stronger algorithm that provides 128- or 168-bit keys) instead. This is done through Group Policy. Microsoft's base CSP is included with the operating system; Microsoft also provides an enhanced CSP that can be used for EFS encryption. Note that if you enable 3DES for EFS, all new encryption operations (both EFS and IPSec) will use it for encryption.

- **CryptoAPI** This is the application programming interface that allows developers to add cryptography services to the Win32 applications that they write and is used by EFS for all its cryptographic services. Both symmetric and asymmetric cryptographic operations are supported, including key generation, management and exchange, encryption/decryption, hashing, digital signatures, and signature verification.

> **Head of the Class…**
>
> ### The EFS Callback Functions
>
> When the EFS driver initializes, it registers seven EFS callback functions with the NTFS driver. These are the current callback functions:
>
> - *EfsOpenFile* When an application opens an existing file that has EFS attributes, the NTFS driver invokes the EFS callback function *EfsOpenFile*.
>
> - *EfsFilePostCreate* After an NTFS file has created or opened a file for an application, the NTFS driver needs the *EfsFilePostCreate* EFS callback function's help.
>
> - *EfsFileControl* and *EfsFsControl* When a user modifies a file's encryption settings, the NTFS driver makes a request for the EFS callback functions *EfsFileControl* and *EfsFsControl*.
>
> **Continued**

- **EfsRead** When NTFS retrieves data for an application, it petitions EFS for the function named *EfsRead*.
- **EfsWrite** When the user writes information in an encrypted file, the NTFS driver invokes the EFS callback function known as *EfsWrite*, because NTFS cannot encrypt the data itself.
- **EfsFreeContext** For the sake of security, which is what encrypting sensitive data is all about, the NTFS driver invokes the EFS callback function *EfsFreeContext* when the context data buffer is no longer required.

The Encryption Process

Before EFS encryption can be used in Windows, the EFS device driver must be installed. When the EFS driver initializes, it notifies the NTFS driver of its existence, and it registers seven related functions at that time. In the registration of these functions, the EFS driver seems to be telling the NTFS driver, "Here is a list of tasks I can do for you." (See the sidebar for the list of the EFS callback functions.)

When the NTFS driver receives a request for EFS, it looks into the table of EFS callback functions and invokes the function that the EFS driver must execute. The EFS driver will not communicate directly with the LSASS, which runs in unprotected user mode. The EFS driver sends a request to encrypt or decrypt a file to the LSASS, but an additional driver intercepts this request in kernel mode. The driver used to send the actual LPC message to the LSASS, KsecDD, resides in kernel mode. The Local Security Authority Server, which is part of the LSASS, listens for the LPCs. When the LSASRV receives a call from the File Encryption Client DLL (FEClient) to encrypt a file, it invokes the internal function *EfsRpcEncryptFileSrv*.

EfsRpcEncryptFileSrv handles the following tasks in the early stages of a file encryption request:

1. Impersonates the user making the encryption request
2. Creates a log file that LSASRV uses to keep a record of the encryption process from start to finish
3. Loads the impersonated user's profile into the Registry
4. Makes a call to the internal function *EncryptFileSrv*

You might be wondering about the first step—impersonating a user. Impersonation occurs for a reason. The LSASS has always used the System account by default. If this account were used for the encryption process, the System's private key would be needed to decrypt the file. EFS's objective is to encrypt the file and then require a unique private key belonging to the user for any future use. By impersonating the user, the proper private key is used to manipulate the file.

The log file that is created when an encrypt file request is received is used to record the events in the encrypting process. The log file is on the same drive as the encrypted file in the System Volume Information subdirectory. The name of the log file is EFS0.log. If an EFS0.log file already exists, the name of the new log file is generated by incrementing the numeric value by one digit.

This need exists despite the fact that a user's profile has already been loaded into the Registry because logging on the system is mandatory. In most circumstances, the profile would already be loaded, but software engineers cannot leave anything to chance, especially when dealing with security issues. If the user executed the *Run As* command included in the Windows 2000 and XP/.NET operating systems, which allows a logged-on user to use a different account (such as an administrator's account) to perform tasks, the loaded profile would be the result of logging on the system, not the profile of the user making the encryption request.

When control is passed to the *EncryptFileSrv* function, an entirely new list of tasks must be performed. *EncryptFileSrv* is in user mode, and the *EncryptFileSrv* function takes on the remaining tasks in the encryption process. Specifically, the *EncryptFileSrv* function is responsible for the following tasks:

1. Queries the NTFS driver about the data stream being used in the file
2. Calls the *GenerateFEK* function
3. Constructs the EFS information that is stored with the encrypted file
4. Creates a backup file
5. Initializes the log file
6. Sends an encrypted command to the NTFS driver to encrypt the file

In order for the *EncryptFileSrv* function to generate the FEK, a function called *GenerateFek* is used. *GenerateFek* initiates a session with the Microsoft Base Cryptographic Provider and requests to use the RSA encryption algorithm. When *GenerateFek* has established the session, it calls another function to have the provider generate the FEK. After the FEK is created, the session with the Microsoft Base Cryptographic Provider is closed, and control is returned to the internal *EncryptFileSrv* function.

EncryptFileSrv uses the FEK and the user's key pair to create the EFS file information. At this point in the encryption process, a key pair is created if the user does not have one. The system can easily identify a user's lack of a key pair by the absence of the *CertificateHash* value found in the Registry for the current user.

After the EFS file information is built, a backup file named EFS0.tmp is created for the original plaintext file. The security descriptor for this backup file is set up so that only the system account will have access to the file.

EncryptFileSrv now sends an encrypted control command to the NTFS driver to add the recently constructed EFS file information to the original file. The NTFS driver understands an encrypted command in this way: At boot time, EFS receives from the LSASS a session key that is used to decrypt any control command received from user mode. When the NTFS driver receives the encrypted control command, the driver makes a request to the EFS callback function, *EfsFileControl*. The EFS driver applies the session key to decrypt the control command and adds the EFS file information to the original file. The EFS driver also creates the *$EFS NTFS* metadata attribute. This attribute was added to the Windows 2000 operating system, and it contains the EFS file information.

After the EFS file information is added to the file, the activity is once again handed back to the *EncryptFileSrv* internal function, and then *EncryptFileSrv* performs these tasks:

1. Records in the log file that the backup file was created
2. Sends another encrypted control command to the NTFS driver to encrypt the file at this time

When the NTFS receives the encrypted control command, it makes a request to the EFS callback function *EfsWrite*. *EfsWrite* uses the unencrypted FEK to do secret key encryption of the file one sector at a time. The data is encrypted before the NTFS driver writes the data to disk. In the United States, EFS uses a 56-bit standard DESX encryption key.

When the file is completely written to disk in ciphertext form, *EncryptFileSrv* is handed control once again. The EncryptFileSrv function completes the encryption process by doing these tasks:

1. Records in the log file that the encryption process was successfully completed without errors
2. Deletes the backup copy of the original file
3. Deletes the log file
4. Passes control back to the user

These concluding tasks draw together the built-in, fault-tolerant side of the encryption process. A backup copy of the original file is always available until the encryption process is completed successfully. If a system crash or other fatal error occurs, the log file indicates where the encryption process stopped, and the original copy of the file can be used to redo the entire process.

The EFS File Information

After the FEK has been created, the EFS file information can be constructed. The LSASRV function named *EncryptFileSrv* controls the creation of the EFS file information that is stored with the file. The user's key pair is needed to supply the necessary information in the encrypted file's header. The function CryptAPI is called to get a handle to the needed key pair. If the user does not have a key pair and if this is the first file to be encrypted, a key pair must be created. The function *GenerateUserKey* is used to create the key pair and returns the signed certificate for the pair.

The generation of the key pair will happen on a domain controller or on the local machine as determined by the computer's environment. When the signed certificate is received, it is stored in the Registry in the subkey HKEY_CURRENT_USER\Software\Microsoft\WindowsNT\CurrentVersion\EFS\CurrentKeys\CertificateHash.

Now that *EncryptFileSrv* has the user's key pair, a function is used to obtain information about the provider that was used to generate the key pair. The user information that is needed at this point is the provider's name and the container used to store the key pair, which in fact is nothing more than a file specification.

An example of a container is as follows:

```
D:\Documents and Settings\Administrator\Application Data\Microsoft\
    SystemCertificates\My\Certificates\1612DAFAD20E037F2DBACD4113FC7
    55BC23B6711
```

EFS now uses the function *CryptAcquireContext* to set up a cryptographic session with the provider, using the provider's name, the container's name, and the fact that it desires to use the RSA encryption service of the Windows operating system. The provider's name must be identified at this point because the operating system allows software vendors to write their own providers and implement them if they want to. RSA is the public key encryption algorithm that was written by Rivest, Shamir, and Adleman. The provider creates 128 bits of random data that will become the file's FEK, and then a function is called to close the session with the Microsoft Base Cryptographic Provider.

Now that *EncryptFileSrv* has a FEK, the EFS file information can be constructed and stored with the file. The function *GetCurrentKey* is used to read the Registry information and get a handle to the user's public key. A Local Security Authority Server function uses the public key to store the EFS information with the file. Figure 5.25 identifies the components that make up the EFS file information.

The data decryption field (DDF) contains entries for each user who has access to the encrypted file. Each individual entry is referred to as a *DDF key entry*. The components of the DDF key entry provide information to represent a user's public key. The user's security identifier (SID) is a component of the key entry. Also included in the key entry is the provider name and container name, the public/private key pair certificate hash, and the encrypted FEK. Any collection of multiple key entries in the EFS file information is called a *key ring*.

Figure 5.25 EFS File Information

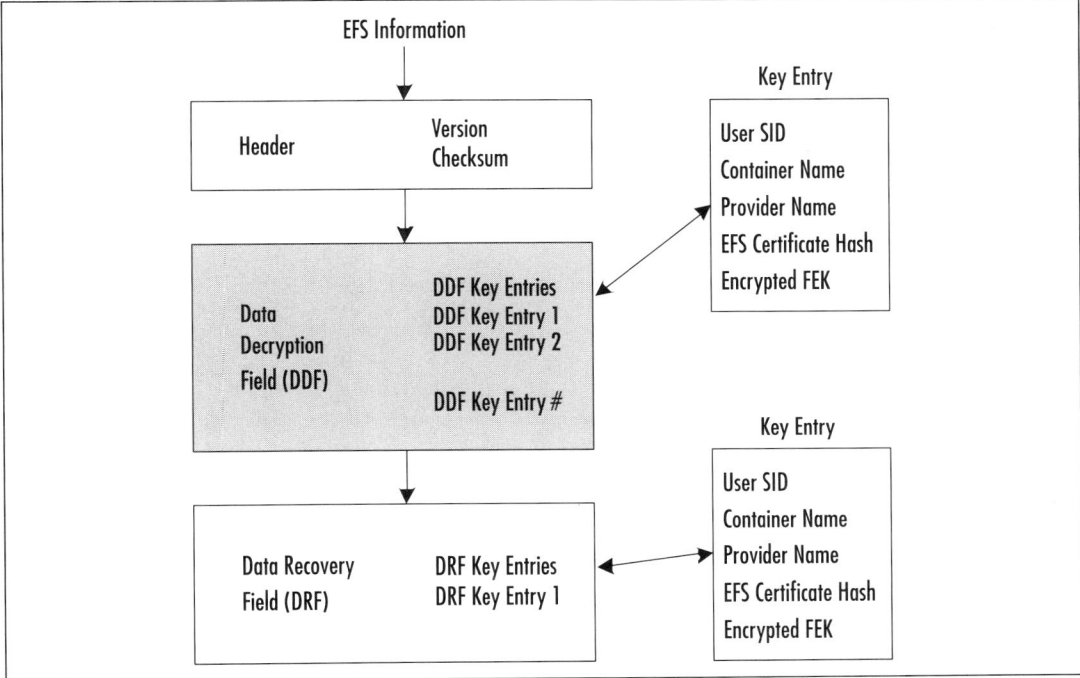

The EFS file information component of the Encrypting File System is not yet completed. An entry needs to be created that will provide recovery if the user's private key somehow becomes corrupted. The EFS creates another key ring that contains recovery key entries. All information tied to the recovery process is in the file's c (DRF). The information in the DRF entries uses the same format as the DDF entries. The number of entries created here is determined by the recovery agents previously defined using the Recovery Agent Wizard.

That means the Local Security Authority Server will have to read the recovery policy at boot time or when it receives notification of policy changes so that the correct DRF entries can be created. The EFS will use the same provider (typically the Microsoft Base Cryptographic Provider 1.0) to create a DRF entry key for each recovery agent.

The EFS adds recovery agent entries to the DRF section of the EFS file information for each recovery key pair on the system. The system administrator can create any number of recovery agents by assigning their accounts access to an EFS recovery key pair. The number of recovery agents should be kept to a minimum for security reasons.

The final step in building all this EFS information is to calculate a checksum value for the DDF and DRF. EFS stores the checksum value with the other header information. This checksum is tied to the decryption process. In order to guarantee that the EFS file information has not been changed, the checksum is used for verification during the decryption process.

The information saved with the encrypted file as the EFS file information must be current; otherwise, users who are issued new certificates will be unable to access their protected, encrypted files. To compensate, when the key field that can successfully decrypt the FEK is located, a function is used to compare the SID, provider name, container name, and certificate hash value to the properties of the user's current EFS cryptographic key pair. If any of the information in the key field does not match the current Registry values, the key field is updated in the EFS file information. If the key field needs to be updated, a new key field is created containing the new matching information, and then the old key field is deleted.

The Decryption Process

When a user accesses an encrypted file, the decryption process begins. Once again, this lengthy process is transparent to the user. The following discussion is highly technical and discusses what goes on "under the hood" when a file or folder is decrypted. From the user's point of view, if he or she has authority to access the encrypted file, the file is automatically decrypted and displayed as plaintext when the user opens it. (If an unauthorized user attempts to open it, he or she will receive an "Access denied" message.)

As is the case when any file on an NTFS volume is accessed, the NTFS driver looks at the file's attributes. If the file is indeed encrypted, the NTFS driver invokes the EFS callback function, *EfsOpenFile*, which EFS registered at the time it initialized. The task of reading the EFS attribute is now handed over to the EFS driver. The EFS callback function, *EfsOpenFile*, then performs the following tasks:

1. Opens the Encrypting File System attribute
2. Calls the NTFS function *NtOfsQueryLength* to determine the attribute's length
3. Allocates the appropriate amount of buffer space based on the length
4. Copies the EFS attribute to the buffer

If the EFS attribute fails to open for any reason, the user receives an error message. If the EFS attribute successfully opens, the NTFS driver again invokes a registered EFS callback function, this time named *EfsFilePostCreate*.

If all has gone smoothly, *EfsFilePostCreate's* job is to make sure that the user requesting to open the file has access to the file's encrypted data. In order for the user to have access to an encrypted file's data, the user needs a private key to decrypt the FEK, which in turn is used to decrypt the file itself.

The actual decryption of the FEK is handled by the Local Security Authority service, which resides in user mode. To perform the FEK decryption, the *EfsFilePostCreate* sends an LPC message to the LSASRV by way of KsecDD. The Microsoft Base Cryptographic Provider is used to encrypt and decrypt. This cryptographic provider functions in user mode and is attached to the LSASS.

Much as is the case with the encryption process, impersonation must occur in the LSASS process when the user opens the file, because the LSASS executes using the System account. This impersonation must be set up before the KsecDD sends the LPC message to LSASRV and is handled by the *EfsFilePostCreate* EFS callback function.

When the LSASRV receives the LPC message from KsecDD, a function call is used to load the user's profile into the Registry if it is not already there. A second function call named *DecryptFek* is called to perform the actual file decryption.

This *DecryptFek* has some additional tasks to complete before it actually decrypts the file. The *DecryptFek* must use the EFS certificate hash, stored as a component of the key entry, to identify the private key to be used. *DecryptFek* uses the user's private key to try to decrypt the ciphered FEK in each key entry in both the DDF and the DRF of the EFS file information.

When every DDF and DRF entry has been tried with the result that the entry's FEK cannot be decrypted, the user is denied access to the file, but if a private key can decrypt the FEK, a cryptographic session with the Microsoft Base Cryptographic Provider is established. Similarly to the encryption process, in establishing a session with the Microsoft Base Cryptographic Provider, the container name and the provider name must be known, but this time the information is indicated by the key fields of the EFS file information.

After the session with the provider is created, the FEK decryption is completed via the user's private key. As an added security step, the hashing of the EFS attribute and the decrypted FEK take place and are compared with the checksum value located in the header information. Any different values seen here indicate that the file has been compromised in some way, and an error results. If the file isn't compromised in any way, Windows establishes another session with the Microsoft Base Cryptographic Provider. This session uses the plaintext FEK and the RSA algorithm to completely decrypt the file.

Troubleshooting EFS

Even though EFS is almost foolproof, you could encounter trouble with it from time to time. Table 5.5 outlines some of the more common problems and their corrective actions.

EXAM WARNING

These troubleshooting issues are all likely exam questions. The most important point to remember when trying to troubleshoot EFS issues is to determine what has changed and what has not changed. Remember the finer points of working with EFS, such as delegating remote servers for EFS encryption and the effects of encrypting a document with a different user account than you are trying to decrypt it with. Some of the EFS questions can be quite tricky if you do not approach them carefully and methodically.

Table 5.5 Troubleshooting EFS

Problem	Corrective Action
I cannot add multiple users to an encrypted document.	This feature is only supported in Windows XP Professional and Windows .NET Server, not in Windows 2000.
I cannot add multiple users to an encrypted folder.	You must add additional users to individual files themselves, not to folders. Note that this feature only works in Windows XP Professional and Windows .NET Server, not in Windows 2000.
I've lost my private keys and I need to decrypt some important documents.	The EFS Recovery Agent will have to decrypt these files for you. The best way is to recover the files from backup onto a decryption workstation, remove the encryption bit, and then copy them back to their original location. You can then re-encrypt the files with your new certificate and keys.
I want to create a new EFS Recovery Agent, but I cannot. I keep getting an error message at the end of the process.	The most likely reason for this error message is either that you have no CA in place or the CA cannot be contacted to complete the process. Ensure that you have a functioning CA installed and configured on your network and that it has basic network connectivity with the computer from which you are performing your request.
I try to encrypt files, but I cannot.	Any number of things could be the cause of this issue. Check to see that you have proper NTFS permissions for the file, that you have an EFS

Continued

Table 5.5 Troubleshooting EFS

Problem	Corrective Action
	Recovery Agent Policy in place, that the file is not NTFS compressed, and that the volume the file is located on is NTFS formatted.
I cannot open a file that I had previously encrypted.	Most likely, the certificate that you used to encrypt the file has expired. If it cannot be located (they can be deleted), you will have to initiate an EFS Recovery procedure to decrypt the file again.
I can't tell if my files are encrypted or not.	The easiest way to get a detailed listing of file encryption status is to use the *cipher* command from the command line. Execute it from the directory where your files are located, and it will report back the encryption status of each file.
I cannot decrypt files on my portable computer. I just encrypted them last week. We have a Windows 2000 Active Directory network.	It is possible that the files were encrypted using a local user account instead of a domain user account. Attempt to decrypt them using a local user account. You can then later re-encrypt them using your domain user account.
My antivirus program complains that there are several files on the volume that it cannot read.	This is a common occurrence where multiple users have encrypted files on a particular volume. The virus-scanning program is only able to scan the files that have been encrypted by you.
I am trying to encrypt a file on the file server and get an error message saying the server is not trusted.	Remote file servers that you will enable EFS encryption on must be trusted for delegation. This is done from the server properties in Active Directory Users and Computers.

Summary of Exam Objectives

In Windows 2000, Microsoft provided users with the ability to encrypt files that contain sensitive information via a feature called the Encrypting File System. In Windows XP/.NET, improvements were made to EFS that added functionality. With EFS, encryption can be set both at the directory level and the file level. This new security feature is efficient in that the encryption/decryption process is totally transparent to users after the files are marked for encryption.

Basic file encryption is accomplished using two methods: secret key and public key. Secret key encryption uses the same key for encrypting and decrypting data (and thus is considered less secure than public key encryption). The secret key algorithm is relatively fast and therefore is appropriate for encrypting large amounts of data. Public key cryptography uses a key pair.

The public key is used to encrypt a file, and the private key is used to decrypt the file. This method of encryption provides more security because only a private key (which is never shared with anyone) can unscramble the ciphertext into plaintext. Slower performance is the price you pay for this higher level of security. Because the process is slow, public key cryptography should only be used on small amounts of data.

Windows EFS uses both methods of encryption. A file is encrypted using a secret key called the FEK, with the DESX (or in Windows XP, 3DES) algorithm. To further protect the FEK from unauthorized access, the FEK is then encrypted by the owner's public key.

When it comes to the user actually working with sensitive data, no additional configuration steps are needed. When a file or directory is marked for encryption, the whole encrypting/decrypting process is transparent to users. A user can identify for the Windows 2000 operating system the files that are to be encrypted through either the Windows Explorer interface or a command-line utility called the Cipher Utility.

File encryption does not modify the normal file operations of renaming or moving. When you move an encrypted file on the same partition, the pointer in the directory is changed, but nothing in the encryption fields is modified. A rename operation on an encrypted file changes only the filename, once again modifying no field tied to the encryption process. Encrypted files can be copied or moved only by those with authorization to access the files.

The new Cipher Utility allows users to encrypt and decrypt files or directories at the command prompt. The included switches for this utility allow users to indicate whether a requested operation should be performed on all files and subdirectories and whether the operation should continue in the event an error has occurred and to force encryption of already encrypted files.

The EfsRecvr Utility can be used to recover an encrypted file if the owner's private key is corrupted or lost. The EfsRecvr utility has switches that are similar to the Cipher Utility in that the recovery agent can indicate how much of the directory structure is to be recovered and whether the process should continue, even if an error occurs.

EFS follows the Windows NT/2000/XP/.NET operating system architectural model. Some of the encryption activity is handled in protected mode, known as *kernel mode*, whereas other tasks are performed in user mode. Windows 2000 added the EFS driver in kernel mode, which, at initialization time, registers seven EFS callout functions with the NTFS driver. When the NTFS driver needs to do any EFS operation, the NTFS makes a call to one of the appropriate callout functions. The other component employed in kernel mode is known as the *KsecDD driver*. The role of the KsecDD driver in the encryption process is to send the LPC messages from the EFS driver to the Local Security Authority Subsystem, or LSASS.

Windows 2000 also added to the LSASS, which runs in user mode, a series of internal functions for encryption/decryption operations. In the encryption process, the internal function *EncryptFileSrv* plays a major role. Also located in user mode is a cryptographic provider, the Microsoft Base Cryptographic Provider. One major responsibility of this cryptographic provider is to provide the RSA encryption operation after a session has been established.

The EFS file information is created by the *EncryptFileSrv* function call. The information includes a checksum, the data decryption field (DDF), and the data recovery field (DRF). The checksum is used at decryption time to verify the integrity of the EFS file Information. The DDF is a list of owner key entries, and the DRF is a list of recovery agents' key entries. This EFS file information is used with every occurrence of decryption.

The addition of file encryption to Windows provides added security for sensitive data stored on the hard disk and makes it unnecessary for users to seek third-party solutions when they need to ensure the highest level of protection for their data.

Exam Objectives Fast Track

The Role of EFS in a Network Security Plan

☑ A good network security plan is multilayered and includes perimeter control, internal security, and object-specific security.

☑ File encryption, such as that afforded by EFS, provides security for specific, valuable/sensitive objects (files or folders).

Using the Encrypting File System

- ☑ An important part of security planning is determining the assets that most need protection. You should assess your data to determine which files and folders should be encrypted.

Using the Encrypting File System

- ☑ EFS uses both public key encryption and secret key encryption.
- ☑ An encrypted file can be read by anyone with a private key that can decrypt the File Encryption Key (FEK) used to encrypt the file.
- ☑ The default recovery agent in a workgroup environment is the local administrator. The default recovery agent in a domain environment is the domain administrator.

User Operations

- ☑ The user operations that use file encryption are encrypting a file, accessing an encrypted file, copying an encrypted file, moving an encrypted file, renaming an encrypted file, decrypting a file, encrypting a directory, and recovery operations.
- ☑ The only requirement for EFS is an NTFS partition. Accessing an encrypted file requires no special action by the user.
- ☑ Renaming an encrypted file changes the file's name but does not change the encryption attribute.
- ☑ When an encrypted file is moved on the same NTFS partition, it retains its encrypted status. When an encrypted file is moved to a different NTFS partition, the file is first decrypted and then encrypted.
- ☑ Windows 2000 allows users to use file encryption from the command prompt using the Cipher Utility.
- ☑ EFS allows encryption to be set at directory and file levels.

EFS Architecture and Troubleshooting

- ☑ Windows 2000 contains both a user mode and a kernel mode. EFS activity occurs in each of these modes.
- ☑ In Windows 2000, the Local Security Authority Subsystem performs additional functions in order for EFS to work properly. The functions are grouped as EFS functions.

- ☑ The new EFS components include the EFS driver, EFS callouts, KsecDD, EFS services, and the cryptographic provider.
- ☑ Users who cannot decrypt files can have their files recovered by the data recovery agent.
- ☑ Files encrypted while logged in with a local computer account cannot be accessed by a domain user account (and vice versa). This is a common problem for portable computer EFS users.
- ☑ Windows XP and Windows .NET Server add the functionality of having multiple EFS users on a single document. Windows 2000 does not support this functionality.

Exam Objectives Frequently Asked Questions

The following Frequently Asked Questions, answered by the authors of this book, are designed to both measure your understanding of the Exam Objectives presented in this chapter, and to assist you with real-life implementation of these concepts.

Q: Do encrypted files have be stored on the local hard drive, which would result in users' having to be responsible for backing up their hard drives daily?

A: EFS is not limited in design to storage only on the local hard drive. The encrypted file can be stored on any file server located on the network. EFS is responsible for file encryption and is not assigned the additional task of securing packets on the network. The functionality of packet security on the network is part of Secure Sockets Layer (SSL). You might need to configure a remote server to be trusted for delegation.

Q: Our corporation is an international company. Can I use the 128-bit encryption at some locations and not at others without having encryption problems?

A: By default, EFS provides standard 56-bit encryption to its U.S. customers. For security reasons, customers can obtain the 128-bit encryption by ordering the Enhanced CryptoPAK from Microsoft. The files encrypted with the Enhanced CryptoPAK cannot be decrypted, accessed, or recovered on a system that supports 56-bit encryption only.

Q: How would you summarize the basic steps that occur in Windows 2000 when a file is encrypted?

A: The basic steps are:

1. When a user executes an encryption request, the NTFS driver makes a request to the appropriate EFS callout function.
2. The requester's user profile is loaded into the Registry if it is not already there.
3. A log file is created that records events as they occur during the encryption process.
4. EFS identifies the user's key pair and then uses the public key to create an entry for the user in the data decryption field.
5. Entries are created in the data recovery field for each recovery agent.
6. A backup file is created and used to guarantee a fault-tolerant EFS.
7. All entries in the DDF and DRF are added to the file's header.
8. Encryption of the file occurs.
9. The log file and the backup file are deleted at the end of the encryption process.
10. The requester's profile is unloaded from the Registry if needed.

Q: How much training is needed for users of sensitive data that requires encryption?

A: The Windows Encrypting File System is transparent to users after a file or directory is marked for encryption. Setting the encryption attribute through the graphical interface is a simple matter of checking or unchecking a check box. Minimum training might be needed to introduce the Windows Explorer interface and the new switches for the *copy* command and to introduce the Cipher Utility.

Q: What happens to data if a system crashes during the encryption process?

A: EFS is designed to be fault-tolerant. Throughout the entire encryption process, a log file keeps track of certain operations as they are completed. If a system crashes before a file is completely encrypted, the Local Security Authority service looks for log files at boot time. If the LSASRV locates any Encryption log file, the contents are read. Usually, the LSASRV copies the backup file over the original semi-encrypted file and then deletes the backup and log files. If the LSASRV finds that the original file has not been modified, it deletes the backup and log files.

Q: When does encryption actually occur when reading or writing to an encrypted file?

A: The NTFS driver calls the EFS callback function *EfsRead*, when an encrypted file needs to be read. The data is decrypted as the NTFS driver reads it from the hard drive and before it is placed in the file system cache. When an application writes to an encrypted file, the data in the file system cache is in plaintext. When the application or the Cache Manager flushes the data to disk, the NTFS driver calls the EFS callback function, *EfsWrite*, to encrypt the data.

Q: Can I use compression and encryption at the same time on a file?

A: No. Compression and encryption are incompatible. The Windows graphical interface clearly shows that compression and encryption cannot both be enabled at the same time on a file. The interface has check boxes for the compression and encryption attributes. Selecting one check box deselects the other check box.

Q: Can I store an encrypted file in an unencrypted directory?

A: A user who is trying to mark a file for encryption in a directory that is not marked for encryption receives a message stating, "You have chosen to encrypt a file that is not in an encrypted directory. The file can become decrypted when it is modified. Because files saved in encrypted directories are encrypted by default it is recommended that you encrypt the file and the parent folder." The user can then choose whether to encrypt the file and parent folder or to encrypt the file only.

Self Test

A Quick Answer Key follows the Self Test questions. For complete questions, answers, and epxlanations to the Self Test questions in this chapter as well as the other chapters in this book, see the Self Test Appendix.

The Role of EFS in a Network Security Plan

1. Jon uses EFS to encrypt his files on the network file server. By using EFS, has Jon protected his files at all times?

   A. No, because the files are decrypted on the file server and then sent in plaintext across the network.

   B. Yes, because the files are sent in ciphertext across the network and decrypted on his local computer.

   C. Yes, because EFS also provides end-to-end security for data.

   D. No, because EFS cannot be used on network file servers, only on a local computer.

2. Andrea is attempting to encrypt a folder on her Windows 2000 Professional computer. When she encrypts the folder, she notices that it is no longer NTFS compressed. Why is this so?

   A. Andrea is not logged in with a domain account. Domain accounts are required to implement both encryption and compression at the same time.

   B. Andrea is not a member of the Administrators group. Only Administrators can implement both encryption and compression at the same time.

   C. EFS encryption and NTFS compression are mutually exclusive. You cannot implement both encryption and compression at the same time.

   D. Extra users have been added to the files contained in the folder. You must not have extra users added to a file in order to apply both encryption and compression to it.

3. Catherine is the senior member of the accounting department in your company. She has several database files that need to be protected from access by other members of her department who have NTFS permissions allowing them read and write access to the network share where the database files are located. What is the

easiest thing you can do to help Catherine secure her database files without adding to your administrative workload or changing any user's NTFS permissions? (Choose all that apply.)

A. Instruct Catherine to create a new folder and place her database documents inside it.

B. Create a batch file for Catherine that uses the *cipher* command to encrypt her files for her in their current folder.

C. Instruct Catherine to configure EFS encryption on the folder itself from Windows Explorer.

D. Remove all the other users in Catherine's department from the OU they are located in and place them in a new OU with different effective NTFS permissions.

Using the Encrypting File System

4. Chris wants to use EFS encryption on some of her files that are stored on the network file server. The file server is running Windows NT 4.0 SP6. Will she be able to use EFS encryption? Why or why not?

   A. Yes. SP6 upgrades NTFS v4 to NTFS v5, which is the version used by Windows 2000.

   B. No. EFS encryption cannot be used on a network file server, only on a local computer.

   C. No. EFS encryption can only be used in Windows 2000, Windows XP, and Windows .NET, not in Windows NT 4.0 or any other Windows product.

   D. Yes. As long as her computer is using Windows 2000, it makes no difference what operating system the file server is running.

5. What is the result of applying a public key to an unencrypted file called?

   A. Plaintext

   B. Encoded

   C. Ciphertext

   D. Signed

6. Hannah has several critical payroll files on which she would like to increase security by encrypting them with EFS encryption. The files are named payroll1.pay, payroll2.pay, and payroll3.pay and are located in the Payroll folder on her computer. What does she need to encrypt to ensure maximum security is obtained for these files and the data they contain?

   A. Hannah needs to implement EFS encryption on the payroll1.pay file, the payroll2.pay file, and the Payroll folder.

   B. Hannah needs to implement EFS encryption on the Payroll folder only.

   C. Hannah needs to implement EFS encryption on the payroll1.pay, payroll2.pay, and payroll3.pay files only.

   D. Hannah need to implement EFS encryption on the root of the volume on which the files are stored.

User Operations

7. Austin is preparing to copy several hundred EFS encrypted files from one Windows 2000 NTFS folder to another Windows 2000 NTFS folder. All the files are EFS encrypted. The source folder is EFS encrypted. The destination folder is not EFS encrypted. What will be the result of his action to copy these files?

   A. EFS encrypted files cannot be copied, thus nothing will happen. He will need to decrypt them before copying.

   B. The files will become decrypted because the destination folder is not encrypted.

   C. He will be prompted to choose whether or not each file should remain encrypted after the files have been copied to the destination folder.

   D. The files will remain encrypted because the files themselves are encrypted.

8. Chan has identified several folders on several of his Windows 2000 file servers that he would like to encrypt using his EFS certificate. Rather than perform the encryption process manually through Windows Explorer, he wants to use the cipher command. He plans to use the cipher command in a script and does not want it to stop running if an error is encountered during the process. What command should be used on these folders to achieve this result?

   A. *cipher /e /d /s* directory

   B. *cipher /e /i /s* directory

   C. *cipher /d /i /s* directory

   D. *cipher /e /f /s* directory

9. On a local computer, who is the default data recovery agent?

   A. There is no default data recovery agent on a local computer.

   B. The first user added to the Administrators group after installation is complete.

   C. The first user to log into the computer after installation is complete.

   D. The built-in administrative account.

10. In a Windows 2000 Active Directory domain, who is the default data recovery agent?

    A. The built-in administrative account on each computer.

    B. The built-in domain administrative account.

    C. The first user to be added to the Administrators group after creating the domain.

    D. The user who installs the first Enterprise Root CA in the domain.

11. You want to create a new data EFS data recovery agent for your Windows 2000 Active Directory domain. From where will you perform this task?

    A. The Certificate Authority console.

    B. The Local Computer Security console on the first domain controller.

    C. The System applet on the Root CA.

    D. The Group Policy object that is applied to the root domain.

12. What is the effect of running the *cipher* command from a directory without specifying any switches?

    A. It will encrypt all files and folders in the directory except for those that are already encrypted.

    B. It will decrypt all files and folders in the directory that are currently encrypted.

    C. It will prompt you for action (encryption or decryption) for every file and folder located in that directory.

    D. It will provide an output showing the encryption status of every file and folder located in that directory.

EFS Architecture and Troubleshooting

13. You are the data recovery agent for your Windows 2000 Active Directory domain. Pat informs you that she can no longer access files that she had previously encrypted. You discover that her EFS certificate has expired and issue her a new one. She still cannot access the files. What do you need to in order for her to be able to access these files? (Choose all that apply.)

    A. Use Windows Explorer to decrypt the files for Pat.

    B. Delete Pat's Windows user account and recreate it for her.

    C. Place the files in the location where Pat had saved them originally.

    D. Restore the files to a recovery computer that has the recovery certificates installed.

14. You are the data recovery agent for your Windows 2000 Active Directory domain. Jon informs you that he can no longer access files that he had previously encrypted. You discover that Jon's EFS certificate has expired, so you issue him a new one. Jon still cannot access the files. What do you need to do in order for Jon to be able to access these files? (Choose all that apply.)

    A. Export your recovery certificate.

    B. Restore the encrypted files from a backup tape.

    C. Issue Jon an EFS Recovery Agent certificate.

    D. Import your recovery certificate onto the computer that contains Jon's encrypted files.

15. Andrew is one of your traveling salespeople. Andrew has a Windows 2000 portable computer on which he uses EFS encryption. While Andrew was traveling last week, he encrypted several files on his computer. This week when he placed his portable computer in the port replicator and logged into the corporate network, he reports to you that he cannot access these files any longer, although they are still on his computer. What is the most likely reason for this problem?

A. His EFS certificate expired since last week.

B. He encrypted the files using his local computer user account.

C. He encrypted the files using his cached domain user account.

D. His hard drive is not NTFS formatted.

Self Test Quick Answer Key

For complete questions, answers, and epxlanations to the Self Test questions in this chapter as well as the other chapters in this book, see the Self Test Appendix.

1. **A**
2. **C**
3. **A, C**
4. **C**
5. **C**
6. **B**
7. **D**
8. **B**
9. **D**
10. **B**
11. **D**
12. **D**
13. **A, C, D**
14. **A, D**
15. **B**

MCSE/MCSA 70-214 Part IV

Implementing, Managing, and Troubleshooting Secure Communication Channels

Chapter 6

MCSE/MCSA 70-214

Configuring and Troubleshooting Windows IP Security

Exam Objectives in this Chapter:

- **3.1** Configure IPSec to secure communication between networks and hosts. Hosts include domain controllers, Internet Web servers, databases, e-mail servers, and client computers.
- **3.1.1** Configure IPSec authentication.
- **3.1.2** Configure appropriate encryption levels.
- **3.1.3** Configure the appropriate IPSec protocol. Protocols include AH and ESP.
- **3.2** Troubleshoot IPSec. Typical issues include IPSec rule configurations, firewall configurations, routers, and authentication.

☑ Summary of Exam Objectives
☑ Exam Objectives Fast Track
☑ Exam Objectives Frequently Asked Questions
☑ Self Test
☑ Self Test Quick Answer Key

Introduction

Chapter 5 discussed how encryption (in the form of the Encrypting File System [EFS]) can be used to protect data stored on disk. Equally important to today's network administrator is the protection of sensitive data as it travels across a network. In the early days of networking, local area networks (LANs) were lone entities. These isolated networks typically ran NETBIOS Extended User Interface (NetBEUI) in small workgroups of fewer than 200 computers and were not connected to any other networks. The major security concerns in this isolated environment typically revolved around employees located at the site. Security efforts focused on local access controls, such as locking down disk drives on employee workstations and checking briefcases and handbags for printed materials. Extremely sensitive data was encrypted onto disk.

Today's networks are very different from the isolated NetBEUI networks of yesteryear. Most likely, your network is connected to other networks, including the global Internet, by way of dedicated leased lines or your organizational remote access server (RAS). Some workstations on your LAN might even have their own link to the outside via a modem and phone line.

Each of these points of access represents an ever-increasing security risk. In the "old" days, electronic documents had to be copied to a disk or printed in order to leave the company's premises; now, transporting data is as easy as sending an e-mail attachment over the Internet. Your organization's prized database can easily be posted to an electronic newsgroup. Hackers can penetrate the network and gain usernames and passwords that allow them to bypass normal access controls. Innocent experimentation by fledgling systems engineers and power users can corrupt or destroy data just as effectively as the actions of the most malignant hackers.

Effective network security standards are the sum total of a well-planned and carefully implemented security infrastructure. These measures include hardware security, file and folder access controls, strong passwords, smart cards, social security, physical sequestration of servers, file encryption, and protection of data as it moves across the wire within the organizational intranet and as it moves outside the organization.

This chapter focuses on protecting the integrity and confidentiality of information while it is in transit across a network. First, we look at some of the common security risks incurred as data moves across the wires. Next, we discuss the basics of cryptography and how these basic tasks function within the framework of Microsoft's implementation of the industry-standard Internet Protocol Security (IPSec). Finally, we cover the specifics of implementing IPSec in your network.

The Need for Network Security

Today, the vast majority of networks are connected to the Internet, allowing users to take advantage of fast and efficient world wide e-mail communication, newsgroups, file transfer, and the tremendous research capabilities offered by the World Wide Web (WWW). Unfortunately, this connectivity makes the network vulnerable to all the "bad guys" lurking out there, looking to break into systems for fun or profit. Who they are and why they do it is beyond the scope of this book. In this chapter, we confine our discussion to what the "bad guys" do and how you can defend your network against them.

Hackers, crackers, and network attackers (including "script kiddies" who have little technical expertise) can use a number of methods to circumvent network security and gain access to information, including:

- Snooping
- Spoofing
- Password compromise
- Denial-of-Service (DoS) attack
- Man-in-the-Middle (MITM) attack
- Application-directed attack
- Compromised Key attack

Test Day Tip

As the network administrator or security administrator you must become intimately familiar with the various types of attacks your network is subject to, but you do not have to memorize every detail of them for this particular exam. What you do need to know for this exam are the basics of how each attack works and how IPSec can be used as part of a multilayered security solution to help prevent them.

Snooping

Most data sent over a network is transmitted in cleartext. An individual with a network sniffer such as the Network Monitor program that comes with Systems Management Server or a third-party program such as Sniffer Pro, can easily read cleartext messages as they traverse a network.

This is also true of sensitive data, such as user account passwords. Some server applications that maintain their own username and password lists allow for this type of critical logon information to cross the network in cleartext format. A network snooper, using easily accessible sniffing programs, can plug into an available port in a hub or switch and access the information. The person using the snooping program can now use the stolen credentials to access the network at any time, posing as an authorized user. Other information that can be intercepted includes credit card numbers, Social Security numbers, contents of personal e-mail messages, and proprietary organizational secrets.

Spoofing

The source and destination Internet Protocol (IP) addresses are prerequisites for establishing sessions between computers on a Transmission Control Protocol/Internet Protocol (TCP/IP)-based network. The act of IP *spoofing* involves assuming the identity of a legitimate trusted host computer on a network in order to gain access to computers on the internal network. This is done by forging someone else's source IP address. Another term for spoofing is *impersonation*, because the intruder impersonates a computer with a legitimate IP address. A common spoofing-based attack is the TCP/IP sequence number attack. Further, some software tools are available that allow people without technical skills to easily spoof addresses.

The TCP/IP Sequence Number Attack

TCP is responsible for the reliability of communications on a TCP/IP-based network. This responsibility includes acknowledgment of information sent to a destination host. To track bytes sent over a network, each segment is given a sequence number. A sophisticated attacker can establish the sequencing pattern between two computers because the sequence pattern is not random.

First, the attacker must gain access to the network. Then, they must connect to a server and analyze the sequence pattern between the server and a legitimate host with which it is communicating at the time. The TCP/IP sequence number attacker then attempts to connect to the server by spoofing (falsely assuming) a legitimate host's IP address. To prevent the legitimate host from responding, the spoofer starts a DoS attack on the legitimate host.

Because the legitimate host cannot respond, the spoofer waits for the server to send its reply and then responds with the correct sequence number. The server then believes that the spoofing computer is the legitimate host, and the spoofer can begin data transfer.

Spoofing Tools

Hackers are all too willing to share their knowledge with others. Many hackers will not only teach hacker "wannabes" how to perform various attacks, but they will even create software tools to perform these tasks so that people with little or no technical expertise can use the same techniques. Those who run these scripts instead of performing the steps manually themselves are known as "script kiddies."

IP spoofing utilities are commonly found on hacker sites. Additionally, many distributed attack tools (those used to launch distributed DoS attacks) use source IP address spoofing to hide the origin of an attack. Tools such as Mendax (for Linux), Spoofit, and detailed spoofing guides can be downloaded from the Web or exchanged in hacker newsgroups. Some of these are marketed as legitimate systems administration tools designed to test a network's vulnerability to spoofing, but they can also be used for nefarious purposes.

Password Compromise

Users who gain illegitimate access to network passwords can access resources they would not otherwise be able to use. An attacker can gain knowledge of passwords in a number of ways, including:

- **Social Engineering** The attacker contacts an individual who has access rights to the information of interest. Often using an assumed identity, the attacker makes a request for a password from the individual, using a persuasive story and/or a charming personality to con the victim into revealing the password. Many infamous hackers, such as Kevin Mitnick, have used social engineering to aid in their hacking efforts.

- **Sniffing** Many network applications (for example, Post Office Protocol [POP] and File Transfer Protocol [FTP]) allow a username and password to cross a network in cleartext. The attacker can use a network sniffer application (also called a *network monitor* or *protocol analyzer*) to intercept the information and look at the data inside the packet.

- **Cracking** A cracker uses a number of techniques to gain illegal access to passwords. Examples of cracking techniques include dictionary attacks and brute-force attacks. Crackers also rely on the tendency of many users to select easily guessed passwords, such as Social Security numbers, a spouse's name, or other information that can be obtained through a little investigative research.

If an administrator's password is compromised, the attacker has access to all network resources that are protected with access controls. The intruder also has access to the entire user account database and can use this information to access all files and folders, change routing information, and alter information without the knowledge of users who depend on the information.

Damage & Defense...

The Importance of Password Policies

A good password policy is the first line of defense in protecting a network from intruders. Careless password practices (choosing common passwords, such as "God" or "love" or a user's spouse's name; choosing short, all-alpha, one-case passwords; writing passwords down; or sending passwords across the network in plaintext) are like leaving your car doors unlocked with the key in the ignition. Although some intruders might be targeting a specific system, many others are just "browsing" for a network that is easy to break into. Lack of a good password policy is an open invitation.

Best practices for password creation require that you address the following:

- Password length and complexity
- Who creates the password
- Forced changing of passwords

A few rules of thumb for creating good password policies include:

- Passwords should have a minimum of eight characters.
- Passwords should not be "dictionary" words.
- Passwords should consist of a mixture of alpha, numeric, and symbol characters.
- Passwords should be created by their users.
- Passwords should be easy for users to remember.
- Passwords should never be written down.
- Passwords should be changed on a regular basis.
- Passwords should be changed anytime compromise is suspected.
- Password change policies should prevent users from making only slight changes when creating new passwords.

In a high security environment, you might need to go beyond the use of just passwords (something you probably already know) in authenticating users to access the network. A multifaceted authentication scheme also requires that users provide something they *have* (such as smart cards or tokens) and/or something they *are*, that is, biometric identifiers, such a fingerprints or retinal scans.

DoS Attacks

A common type of network attack is the *DoS* attack. Rather than actually breaking into a network to access its data, this type of attacker attempts to overload a network or server to cause a shutdown, thereby denying network services to legitimate users. A DoS can be created in a number of ways. All DoS attack techniques have the ability to disrupt normal computer or operating system functioning on a targeted machine. These attacks can flood a network with useless packets, corrupt or exhaust memory resources, or exploit a weakness in a network application. DoS attacks include:

- TCP SYN attacks
- SMURF attacks
- Teardrop attacks
- Ping-of-Death attacks

TCP SYN Attacks

When computers on a TCP/IP-based network establish a session, they go through a three-way handshake process as follows:

1. The originating client sends a packet with the SYN flag set to **On**. This host includes a sequence number in the packet. The server uses this sequence number in the next step.

2. The server returns a packet to the originating host with its SYN flag set to **On**. This packet has a sequence number that is incremented by 1 over the number that was sent by the requesting computer.

3. The client responds to the request with a packet that acknowledges the server's sequence number by incrementing the sequence number by 1.

Whenever a host requests a session with a server, the pair goes through the three-way handshake process. The attacker can take advantage of this process by initiating multiple session requests that originate from bogus-source IP addresses. The server keeps each open request in a queue while it waits for Step 3 to occur. Entries into the queue are typically emptied every 60 seconds. If the attacker is able to keep the queue filled, legitimate connection requests will be denied, so service is denied to legitimate users of e-mail, Web, FTP, and other IP-related services.

SMURF Attacks

A *SMURF attack* attempts to disable a network by flooding it with Internet Control Message Protocol (ICMP) echo requests and echo replies. In a SMURF attack, the attacker spoofs a source IP address and then issues an ICMP echo request to a broadcast address. This action causes all the machines on a segment to reply to the bogus request. If the attacker can maintain this attack for an extended period of time, no useful information can be passed though the network due to the flood of ICMP echo request and reply messages traversing the wire.

Teardrop Attacks

A *Teardrop* attack is executed using a program such as teardrop.c, that causes fragmentation similar to that seen in a Ping-of-Death attack (described next). A teardrop attack takes advantage of a weakness in the reassembly process and can cause a system to hang or crash.

Ping-of-Death Attacks

The *Ping-of-Death* attack exploits features of the ICMP and the maximum transfer unit (MTU) sizes of various network architectures. The PING command issues an ICMP echo request and is returned an ICMP echo reply by the destination host. The ICMP echo request message is encapsulated in an IP packet that is limited by 65,535 octets. The MTU defines the maximum size of a unit for a defined network architecture, which varies with the media type.

If the size of a packet is larger than the MTU, the packet is fragmented and then reassembled at its destination. It is possible to send a packet with more than the legal number of octets. When packets are fragmented, an offset value is included with the packet. This offset value is used to reassemble fragments at their destination. The attacker could include with the last fragment a legal offset and a larger packet size. This will exceed the legal number of octets in the data portion of the ICMP echo request. When reassembly is attempted, the destination computer could respond by rebooting or crashing.

MITM Attacks

A MITM attack occurs when two parties believe that they are communicating only with each other, but in fact there is an intermediary silently listening in on the conversation. The man in the middle can intercede in the conversation by impersonating the identity of either the sender or the receiver. During the attacker's intercession, they can alter or destroy messages during transit.

Using a network sniffer, an attacker can record and save messages for later use, allowing the attacker to issue a subsequent replay attack. The man in the middle, having recorded aspects of a conversation, can replay this information to get around network authentication mechanisms in the future. This is known as a *replay* attack.

Application-directed Attacks

Application-directed attacks seek to take advantage of weaknesses inherent in certain network applications. By exploiting weaknesses in network applications, an intruder can:

- Corrupt or alter important operating system files
- Change the content of data files
- Cause a network application or an entire operating system to operate abnormally or even crash
- Disrupt normal security and access controls maintained by the application or operating system
- Plant a program or programs that can return information to the attacker; Back Orifice is an example of such an application

Numerous types of application-directed attacks exist. Web servers are often the targets of such attacks. One example is the Code Red worm that caused considerable damage to numerous systems a few years ago. This worm exploits vulnerabilities in the Internet Information Services (IIS) running on Windows NT 4 and Windows 2000 systems. It can deface Web sites running on a server. It can also install DoS tools. After affecting a system, the worm attempts to propagate itself to other unprotected IIS servers. Variants of the Code Red worm have been created as well, each with its own symptoms. Microsoft creates security patches to protect against known application vulnerabilities such as Code Red. Always check the http://microsoft.com/security site for information about the latest attacks and their patches.

These application-level attacks provide the most fertile ground for would-be intruders. Many network applications have not completed the degree of security assessment and testing that is required to optimize their immunity to attacks aimed against them.

Compromised Key Attacks

A *key* is a number, or *cipher*, that can be used in combination with an encryption *algorithm* to either verify the integrity of a communication or encrypt the contents of a communication. Various types of keys are available. One type is known as a *secret key*. A sending computer encrypts the contents of a message using a secret key, and the receiving computer decrypts the message with the same secret key. Using this *shared secret*, two computers can communicate in private.

Another type of secret key is the *private key*. The secret private key can be used to confirm a sender's identity. This process is known as *signing a message*. A recipient who receives a message signed by someone's private key can be confident that the person who claims to have sent the message is indeed that person. The private key is part of a *key pair*, two mathematically related keys. The other part of the pair is a *public key*. The private key is kept secret, and the public key is published to the world. If the public key belonging to a certain person can be used to decrypt their messages, that affords assurance that the message was encrypted with the related private key, which is known only to the person. As discussed in Chapter 9, key pairs can also be used in the opposite way: A message can be encrypted by a sender using the recipient's public key, and only the person who holds the associated private key can decrypt the message, providing confidentiality for the data.

An attacker who somehow gains access to secret or private keys can decrypt messages intended for someone else or communicate with an assumed identity using someone else's private key. When secret or private keys no longer remain secret and private, they are said to be *compromised*. After keys are compromised they can no longer be used to secure identities and information. Detecting whether a key has been compromised is difficult. Often, the compromise of a key is discovered only after some vital piece of information is found to no longer be secret, as in cases of corporate espionage.

IP Security Overview

IPSec defines a network security architecture that allows secure network transmissions for an enterprise while introducing a minimum of overhead. IPSec allows you to secure packets at the network layer. By performing services at the network layer, IPSec secures information in a manner that is transparent to users and to the protocols that lie above the transport layer. IPSec provides layer 3 protection.

The IPSec architecture exercises an end-to-end security model. Only the endpoints of a communication need to be IPSec-aware. Computers and devices that serve as intermediaries of message transfer do not need to be IPSec-enabled. This allows a network administrator to implement IPSec for end-to-end security over diverse network infrastructures, including the Internet. Network connectivity devices such as bridges, switches, and routers can be oblivious to IPSec without compromising its efficacy. This end-to-end capability can be extended to various communication scenarios, including:

- Client-to-client
- Gateway-to-gateway

When IPSec is used to protect communications between two clients—for example, on the same LAN—the machines can utilize IPSec in *transport mode*. In transport mode, both clients must use TCP/IP as their network protocol. In this example, the endpoints of the secure communication are the source machine and the destination host.

In contrast, with a gateway-to-gateway solution, information traversing a transit network (such as the Internet), is protected by IPSec. Packets are protected as they leave the exit gateway and then decrypted or authenticated at the destination network's gateway. In this scenario, the host and destination computers do not have to employ IPSec and can use any LAN protocol supported by IPSec (such as Internetwork Packet Exchange/Sequenced Packet Exchange [IPX/SPX], AppleTalk, NetBEUI, or TCP/IP).

When gateways represent the endpoints of secure communication, IPSec works in *tunnel mode*. In tunnel mode, a tunnel is created between the gateways, and client-to-client communications are encapsulated in the tunnel protocol headers. You can create tunnels using IPSec as the tunneling protocol, or you can combine IPSec with Layer 2 Tunneling Protocol (L2TP). In the latter case, L2TP rather than IPSec creates the tunnel, and IPSec provides the encryption.

Exam Warning

You must know the differences in the transport mode and tunnel mode implementations of IPSec.

Overview of IPSec Cryptographic Services

IPSec ensures security of communications by employing a variety of cryptographic techniques. *Cryptography* encompasses *encryption,* which is the making and deciphering of hidden or scrambled messages in such a manner that if the message or communication is intercepted, the thief cannot easily ascertain the contents of the message.

A good security system has several component features. The IPSec security architecture is designed to provide the following:

- Message integrity
- Message authentication
- Confidentiality

Exam Warning

Ensure that you are familiar not only with the benefits that IPSec provides, but also with how it works to provide them for you.

Message Integrity

The term *integrity* refers to the assurance that the message received is identical to the message that was sent. Integrity is violated if a communication is somehow altered between the sending and receiving computers. Message integrity can be assured via the creation of *digital signatures*. A digital signature is like an electronic fingerprint. This fingerprint is a representation of a document's content. If an intruder were to capture the message in transit and change its contents, they would leave on the message a fingerprint that is different from the original fingerprint. The destination machine would detect that other hands had touched the document and therefore would consider the document's content invalid. *Hash functions* can be used to create the original fingerprint.

Hashing Messages

A message can be hashed by running it through a hashing algorithm. A key (a variable called a *hash value*) is used together with the hashing algorithm to create a hash so that only computers that know the key can create the same hash output of a message. The hashed output is always the same length; the algorithm creates fixed-length outputs from variable-length messages. This hashed output is often referred to as a *message digest* or a *hash signature*. You cannot reverse-engineer a digest to get the original message. Each packet must have a different hashed result.

For example, if I send you a message that states, "Cash the check," I will hash the message using a secret key that only you and I know about. After sending "Cash the check" through the hash algorithm using the secret key, we get a message digest of 12345.

Now I will send you the message, together with the message digest. In order to make sure that the original message was "Cash the check," you will send the contents of the message through the same hash algorithm and check the result. If you get 12345, it matches the digest sent to you. You know that indeed "Cash the check" was the original content of the message.

If a man in the middle had intercepted the message, they might have changed the content of the message to state "Don't cash the check." When you received the message, it would read "Don't cash the check." You would then run "Don't cash the check" though the hash algorithm, and the result would be 12389. This result does not match the message digest included with the message. Therefore, you know that the integrity of the message has been violated and should not be considered valid.

These message digests are also known as hash message authentication codes (HMACs). To derive an HMAC, Microsoft's implementation of IPSec uses one of two algorithms:

- **Message Digest 5 (MD5)** This algorithm was developed by Ron Rivest of MIT and is defined in RFC 1321. MD5 processes each message in blocks of 512 bits. The message digest ends up being 128 bits.

- **Secure Hash Algorithm (SHA1)** This algorithm also processes messages in blocks of 512 bits. However, the resulting message digest is 160 bits long. This confers a greater degree of security but is a bit more processor intensive and is therefore slower than MD5.

A shared secret key is required to make the hash method work. To ensure the validity of the secret key, you must utilize other technologies, such as a public key infrastructure, which can also take advantage of asymmetric key exchange to provide a higher degree of assurance.

Message Authentication

Authentication is concerned with establishing the identity of a sender or recipient. Integrity concerns itself with making sure that the message has not changed during transit. Authentication focuses on confirming the identities of the conversation participants. It would be of little value to receive a message of uncompromised integrity from an imposter.

IPSec uses three methods to carry out message authentication:

- Preshared key authentication
- Kerberos authentication
- Public key certificate-based digital signatures

Preshared Key Authentication

Preshared key authentication schemes depend on both members of the communication having preselected a secret key that will be used to identify them to each other. Data leaving the sending computer is encrypted with this agreed-upon key and decrypted on the other end using the same key.

Both members of the communication assume that if the other side has access to this preselected key, both members are who they claim they are. This type of authentication is accomplished in the following way:

1. The sending computer can hash a piece of data (called a *challenge*) using the shared key and forward this hashed data to the destination computer.

2. The destination computer receives the challenge and performs a hash using the same secret key. It then sends this hashed data back to the first sending computer.

3. If the hashed results are identical, the computers share the same secret key and are thus authenticated.

Even though preshared keys are effective in authenticating that each member has access to the same shared secret, this solution is not easily scalable. The shared secret must be manually keyed into the IPSec policy, which is not an issue if the same policy applies to the entire domain tree, but can become cumbersome when subdomains, organizational units, and individual machines require varying IPSec policies.

Kerberos Authentication

The *Kerberos authentication* method is also based on the shared secret principle. In this case, the shared secret is a hash of the user's password. For more information about the Kerberos authentication protocol, see the Chapter 8.

Public Key Certificate-Based Digital Signatures

As mentioned earlier in this chapter, a *message digest* is a hash of a message's contents. The combination of a key and a hash algorithm is used to create a message digest. A *digital signature* is an encrypted message digest. A message is authenticated when the digest is first decrypted, and then the decrypted hash must match the hash derived at the destination host.

The sending computer uses its private key to complete this process. Public key-based authentication is based on the principle that each computer has a public and private key pair created for it in advance. The public key is freely available to anyone who wants it; the private key is available only to the computer that owns it. For a public key infrastructure to work, the private key must be kept private. If a private key is compromised, all messages from that computer should be considered suspect and possibly originating from an imposter. A viable public key infrastructure includes these elements:

- Private keys that are kept absolutely secret
- Public keys that are freely available to anyone
- A trusted third party to confirm the authenticity of the public key (to ensure that the public key does indeed belong to the party who claims it)

The trusted third party is known as a certification authority (CA). The CA is required to digitally sign each party's public key to prevent attackers from providing a public key that they claim is that of another person but is in fact not the public key of the person they are impersonating.

A CA will digitally sign each user's public key. In this way, if someone sends you their public key, you can be sure that it is theirs, because a trusted third party has confirmed their identity and signed their public key. Here are two scenarios that illustrate the need for digital certificates and digital signatures: In the first scenario, say your boss wants to authenticate your identity using your public key. One way she can do this is by sending you a challenge message, which you encrypt with your private key. You then send it back to her after you have encrypted it. She can then use your public key to decrypt the message. If the message that she decrypts is the same as the message that she sent you, she can confirm that indeed it was you with whom she was communicating.

The problem is that she received your public key from you, yourself. How does she know that you, and not someone impersonating you, sent her your public key? You can solve this problem by having a mutually trusted third party digitally sign your public key. Both you and your boss trust that the third party has verified the identity of anyone for whom the third party signs its public key.

> ### Notes from the Underground…
>
> ### Nothing in Life Is Perfect
> No security method is foolproof, and this includes the use of certification authorities to verify identity. In early 2001, someone tricked VeriSign into believing that they were a legitimate Microsoft employee and received two digital certificates from VeriSign that were to be used for code signing (see www.microsoft.com/technet/security/bulletin/ms01-017.asp). What is even more interesting (or scary depending on how you look at it) is that this security failure went unnoticed for a month before VeriSign caught onto the problem and revoked the digital certificates.
>
> So, if one of the pioneers in the digital certificate game can be tricked by some slick social engineering into giving out two high-level digital certificates, what are the odds that the same thing might not happen to you on your network? No matter how secure you think you are or how many layers deep your defensive posture is, always remember that an attacker may be one step ahead of you. Eventually every system can and will be penetrated if someone tries hard enough and has the capabilities to pull off the attack. This is why defense in depth is such a critical concept. The more layers of defense you have in your network, the better your odds are of keeping an attacker out, or at worst, detecting and tracking an attacker should they penetrate your defenses. Never stop thinking you have done enough to protect your network because nothing in life is perfect.

In the second scenario, say you want to be sure that your boss is who she says she is. You do not have her public key at this point, so you ask her to send it to you. She sends you her signed certificate (the certificate is essentially her public key signed by the trusted third party). You already have the public key of the trusted third party. You use the third party's public key to verify the signature on the certificate. You know that this verified key is her public key, which she sent you. You can now send a challenge to confirm that you are indeed communicating with your boss and not an imposter. Additionally, you can check the most recently published CRL to ensure that the certificate being presented is still valid and has not been revoked.

Public key authentication is used by IPSec when non-Kerberos-enabled clients need to be authenticated and no preshared key has been established. Public key authentication must also be used when using L2TP tunneling and IPSec. Preshared keys can be used between a Windows 2000 RAS and a third-party firewall product when the two are acting as gateways for a corporate wide area network (WAN).

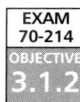

Confidentiality

Neither integrity nor authentication is concerned with protecting the privacy of information. Confidentiality is a matter of keeping private information private. To ensure confidentiality of IPSec communications, data must be encrypted using an encryption algorithm.

Data Encryption Standard

The encryption algorithm most commonly used with Microsoft's implementation of IPSec is the Data Encryption Standard (DES) algorithm. DES has long been the U.S. government standard for encryption. The DES algorithm is an example of a *symmetric encryption* algorithm. A symmetric encryption algorithm has each side of a communication employ the same secret key for encryption and decryption. This is in contrast to a public key infrastructure, in which two different keys are used. The public key approach is referred to as *asymmetric encryption*.

DES works on 64-bit blocks of data. The DES algorithm converts 64 input bits from the original data into 64 encrypted output bits. DES starts with 64-bit keys, but only 56 bits are actually used in the encryption process. The remaining 8 bits are used for parity.

A stronger version of DES is also available for use in Windows 2000/XP IPSec. This version is called *3DES*, or *Triple DES*. Triple DES processes each block three times, which increases the degree of complexity over that of DES.

NOTE

Although not used for IPSec at this time, the Advanced Encryption Standard (AES) is the new standard for encryption implemented by the U.S. government. The U.S. government encryption standard is known as the Federal Information Processing Standard (FIPS). AES uses the Rijndael symmetric encryption algorithm. Effective May 26, 2002, AES became an official government standard.

Cipher Block Chaining

Because the blocks of data are encrypted in 64-bit chunks, there must be a way to chain these blocks together. The chaining algorithm defines how the unencrypted text, the secret key, and the encrypted text (also known as *ciphertext*) will be combined to send to the destination host. These chaining algorithms also solve another problem. If the same data is sent twice, both blocks would look the same. This knowledge could be used by a cryptanalyst in trying to figure out the content of a message.

To prevent each block from looking the same, DES can be combined with cipher block chaining (CBC). This DES-CBC algorithm makes each ciphertext message appear different by using a different initialization vector (IV), which is a random block of encrypted data that begins each chain. In this fashion, each message's ciphertext can be made to appear different, even if the exact same message is sent a hundred times.

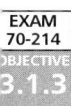

EXAM WARNING

Be sure that you are familiar with the various methods utilized in IPSec for integrity, authentication, and confidentiality. Expect to be tested on them and their various combinations on this exam.

IPSec Security Services

IPSec engages the following two protocols to implement security on an IP network:

- Authentication header (AH)
- Encapsulating Security Payload (ESP)

TEST DAY TIP

Ensure that you know and understand the differences between the AH and ESP protocols that make up IPSec. Be aware of how each is used to make secure communications possible in both transport and tunnel modes of operation.

The AH

The AH ensures data integrity and authentication, and can be used to prevent replay attacks. The AH does not encrypt data and therefore provides no confidentiality. When the AH protocol is applied in transport mode, the AH is inserted between the original IP header and the TCP header, as shown in Figure 6.1. The entire datagram is authenticated using AH.

Figure 6.1 The Datagram after Applying the Authentication Header in Transport Mode

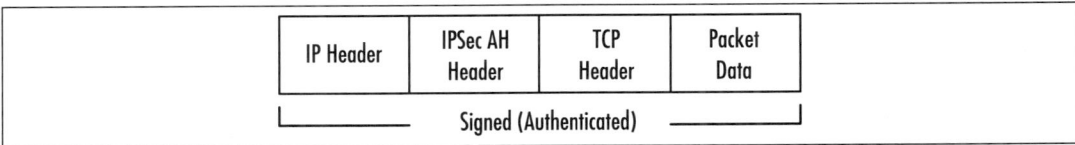

ESP

The ESP protocol can provide authentication, integrity, and confidentiality to an IP datagram. Authentication services are available with ESP, but the original IP header prior to application of the ESP header is not authenticated. The ESP header, in transport mode, is placed between the original header and the TCP header, as shown in Figure 6.2. Only the TCP header, data, and ESP trailer are encrypted. If authentication of the original IP header is required, AH and ESP may be combined and used together.

Figure 6.2 The Datagram after Applying the Encapsulating Security Payload Header in Transport Mode

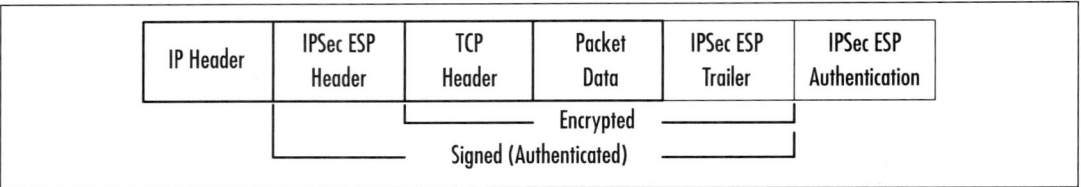

Figures 6.1 and 6.2 demonstrate packet configurations when AH or ESP is used in transport mode. Transport mode is used when point-to-point communications are taking place between source and destination computers. AH and ESP can be applied at a gateway machine connecting the LAN to a remote network. In this case, tunnel mode is used.

In tunnel mode, an additional IP header is added that denotes the destination tunnel endpoint. This tunnel header encapsulates the original IP header, which contains the IP address of the destination computer. Figure 6.3 shows a packet constructed for tunnel mode.

Figure 6.3 A Datagram with ESP Header in Tunnel Mode

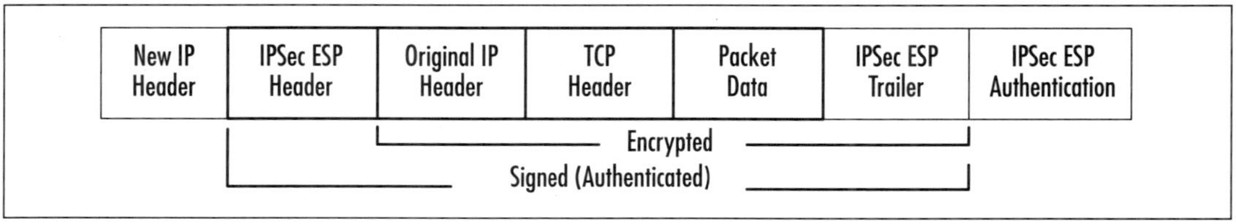

Security Associations and IPSec Key Management Procedures

Two concepts you need to understand when looking at how IPSec works are *security associations* and *key management*. In the following sections, we look at both of these concepts.

Security Associations

When two computers establish a connection using IPSec, they must come to an agreement regarding which algorithms and protocols they will use. A single security association (SA) is established for each link a computer maintains with another computer via IPSec. A security association consists of several parts: a destination address, a security protocol, and a security parameters index (SPI), which is a unique identifier. If a file server has several simultaneous sessions with multiple clients, a number of SAs will be defined, one for each connection via IPSec.

Each security association has associated with it these parameters:

- Encryption algorithm (DES or 3DES)
- Session key (via Internet Key Exchange [IKE])
- Authentication algorithm (SHA1 or MD5)

A security parameters index (SPI) tracks each SA. The SPI is a value that uniquely identifies each SA as separate and distinct from any other IPSec connections current on a particular machine. The index itself is derived from the destination host's IP address and a randomly assigned number. When a computer communicates with another computer via IPSec, it checks its database for an applicable SA. It then applies the appropriate algorithms, protocols, and keys and inserts the SPI into the IPSec header.

An SA is established for outgoing and incoming messages, which means at least two security associations are necessary for each IPSec connection. In addition, a single SA can be applied to either AH or ESP, but not both. If both are used, two more security associations are created—one SA for inbound and one SA for outbound communications.

IPSec Key Management

Keys must be exchanged between computers in order to ensure authenticity, integrity, and confidentiality. Key management defines the following:

- Procedure used to determine how keys are formed
- Strength of keys
- How often keys are changed
- When keys expire

The establishment of a shared secret key is critical to secure communications. A shared secret can be manually established using the prearranged key method, but this technique does not scale well due to its inherent lack of flexibility.

Automated key management is the preferred method of key exchange. Automated key management uses a combination of the Internet Security Association Key Management Protocol and the Oakley Protocol (ISAKMP/Oakley Protocol). This combination of protocols is often referred to collectively as the IKE. The IKE is responsible for exchanging key material (groups of numbers that will form the basis of new keys), session keys, SA negotiations, and authentication of peers participating in an IPSec interaction.

IKE takes place across two phases: Phase 1, in which the two computers agree on mechanisms to establish a secure, authenticated channel; and Phase 2, in which SAs are negotiated for security protocols, using AH, ESP, or both.

The first phase establishes what is called the ISAKMP security association (ISAKMP SA), and the second phase establishes the IPSec SA.

Phase 1: Establishing the ISAKMP SA

The following processes take place during the ISAKMP SA phase:

1. The computers establish a common encryption algorithm, either DES or 3DES.
2. A common hash algorithm, either MD5 or SHA1, is agreed upon.
3. An authentication method is established. Depending on policy, this method can be Kerberos, public key encryption, or a prearranged shared secret.
4. A Diffie-Hellman group is agreed upon in order to allow the Oakley Protocol to manage the key exchange process. Diffie-Hellman provides a mechanism for two parties to agree on a shared master key, which is used immediately or can provide keying material for subsequent session key generation. Oakley Protocol determines key refresh and regeneration parameters.

Phase 2: Establishing the IPSec SA

After a secure channel is established by the creation of the ISAKMP SA, the IPSec SAs are established. The process is similar, except that a separate IPSec SA is created for each protocol (AH or ESP) and for each direction of transmission (inbound and outbound). Each IPSec SA must establish its own encryption algorithm, hash algorithm, and authentication method.

One important difference is that each IPSec SA uses a different shared key than that negotiated during the ISAKMP SA. Depending on how the policy is configured, the IPSec SA repeats the Diffie-Hellman exchange or reuses key material derived from the original ISAKMP SA. All data transferred between the two computers takes place in the context of the IPSec SA.

Exam Warning

You should have a solid understanding of how the ISAKMP/Oakley Protocol SA process is conducted and carried out. Make sure you understand what is accomplished during each phase of the SA process.

IP Security Management Tools

There are a number of utilities you may need when configuring and monitoring IPSec. Although we are only going to examine the tools available on a local machine here, you can apply the same strategies to domain-based configuration via Site, Domain, and Organizational Unit (OU) Group Policy as required. Although local Group Policy is (as its name suggests) local, it is possible to configure and control these settings centrally using security templates (refer back to Chapter 1 for a review of security templates). You can also export and import IP security policies between computers.

If using certificates for IPSec authentication, you will also need the CA Microsoft Management Console (MMC) snap-in covered in Chapter 4 to issue certificates. Otherwise you will predominately use the following tools:

- IP Security Policies on local machine
- IP Security Monitor
- IPSec Policy Agent Service
- TCP/IP Advanced Options
- Certificates Snap-in (to confirm valid computer certificates if using these for authentication)
- Security Log

IP Security Policies on Local Machine

We first saw the computer's Local Security Settings in Chapter 1 when looking at configuring and securing Windows 2000 computers. You can either access the IP Security Policies by loading Local Security Policy under Administrative Tools, or use the Local Group Policy Editor (**gpedit.msc**) and navigate down the tree.

The **IP Security Policies on Local Machine** will be the utility you use most to configure what policies you want, how they are configured, and whether they should be in use. By default no IPSec policy is active on a Windows 2000 computer—a policy has to be specifically assigned. As shown in Figure 6.4, you will see three preconfigured built-in policies that will be covered later.

Figure 6.4 IPSec Policies Snap-in and Tasks

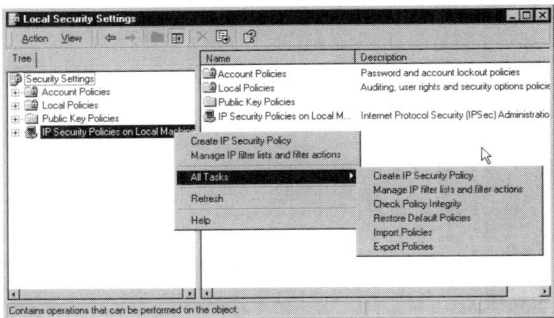

Right-clicking on **IP Security Policies | All Tasks** allows you to create a new policy, manage filter lists and actions (covered later), check a policy's integrity, restore the default policies, and import/export policies. The last two options allow you to both backup and restore known, working policies. But perhaps more usefully, they also provide the means of quickly transferring IPSec policies between computers.

IP Security Monitor

This is a rather strange Windows 2000 utility, somewhat lacking in elegance and cohesion when compared with the standard utilities. There is some important information missing from this utility (which will be covered later), but it does provide a basic graphical display of what is happening on a computer with regard to IPSec traffic.

The IP Security Monitor can be used to monitor IPSec status and test IPSec policies. In Windows 2000, the monitor can be started by typing **ipsecmon.exe** *computer_name* at the command line. With no computer name specified, it will default to loading on the local computer. When monitoring a remote computer, the following will be displayed on the title bar, for example: "IP Security Monitor on W2KSRV005." A locally monitored computer will simply have "IP Security Monitor" on the title bar.

The first thing the IPSec Monitor will tell you is whether IPSec is currently enabled on the selected computer (bottom right hand corner). If it is and a computer is currently connected using one of your policies that results in transmitting data from the computer, this will be displayed in the active window with limited details such as the security protocols in use, the source and destination computer, and so on. If it is using one of the built-in policies, the policy name will be displayed in readable form. However, any new policies created will be displayed rather unhelpfully as a hex string identifier. A later section of this chapter shows how to tie this back to the actual policy in use.

The example shown in Figure 6.5 shows the IPSec Monitor, with IPSec enabled on the computer, but no traffic having traversed the network yet. Over time, all of the counters will allow you to track the status of IPSec secured and unsecured communications on your network. You can use the IPSec monitor to view statistics regarding the following:

- Active security associations with other computers (for a log of SAs not currently active, see the Security Log in Event Viewer; SAs are shown as Netlogon events)
- Number of bytes of data sent using ESP for confidentiality
- Number of bytes of data received that were sent using ESP
- Number of bytes sent with authentication
- Number of packets with invalid security parameters index
- Number of packets that could not be decrypted
- Number of packets that could not be authenticated
- Number of keys sent by ISAKMP to the IPSec driver
- Number of SAs established during the first phase of ISAKMP
- Number of SAs established during the second phase of ISAKMP
- Number of ISAKMP negotiations in which cleartext data transfer was negotiated (known as *soft associations*)
- Number of failed authentications

Figure 6.5 The IPSec Monitor

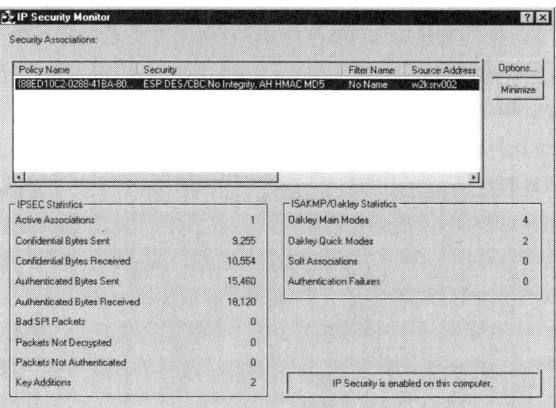

TEST DAY TIP

Become familiar with the information that is made available in the IPSec Monitor. It will prove useful in managing and troubleshooting IPSec policies on your network and on this exam.

For comparison, the IPSec Monitor in Windows XP and .NET has been turned into a modular MMC snap-in. To access it, you will need to create a custom MMC console and add the snap-in as you would any other snap-in. The Windows XP IPSec Monitor is shown in Figure 6.6.

Figure 6.6 The Windows XP IPSec Monitor Console

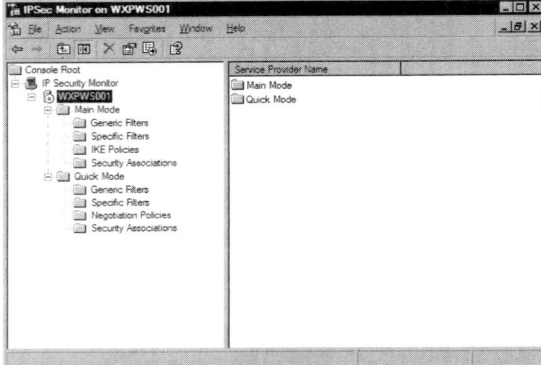

IPSec Policy Agent Service

A Windows 2000 computer will automatically have installed and started the IPSec Policy Agent, which is responsible for retrieving the assigned IP Security Policy (if one is assigned) from the registry and passing the information within the policy to the IPSec driver.

The policy is retrieved at system boot up and checked at regular intervals for any changes (modifications). By default, the IPSec policy is checked every three hours, but this can be changed under the policy's **General** tab. This setting is more relevant if you are running within an Active Directory and are centrally changing IP Security policies across the network or if you want to ensure that any locally changed policies cannot stay in place for a prolonged period of time.

When modifying or changing IPSec values locally, it is recommended that you use the Check Policy Integrity option seen in Figure 6.4 to ensure that the new values have been committed to the registry. However, it is often safer to actually stop and restart the IPSec Policy Agent to ensure the "slate is clean." Although this can be done using the Services snap-in, it is much easier to call up a command prompt and type:

```
Net stop policyagent
Net start policyagent
```

Alternatively, you can disable and then re-enable the network interface in a computer to get IPSec policy changes to take. In some, IPSec does not react well to changes in policy, even after stopping/restarting the policy agent or disabling and re-enabling the network adapter. It can sometimes take a while to renegotiate security options and settle down, but once going it is very stable and quick. When changing and testing different parameters, be prepared to be patient!

TCP/IP Advanced Options

This provides limited access to the IP Security Policies by selecting the **Advanced** button on your adapter's TCP/IP Properties, and then selecting **Options | IP security | Properties**.

As shown in Figure 6.7, you can see whether IPSec is currently enabled and toggle between using IPSec and not using it. The dropdown list box ("Use this IP security policy:") displays all of the available policies with their description displayed directly below.

Figure 6.7 Changing IP Security Policies through TCP/IP Properties

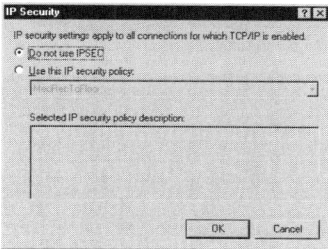

NOTE

The option to select an IPSec policy from the Advanced TCP/IP Properties page only exists in Windows 2000. In Windows XP and .NET Server, this has been removed in favor of configuration via the Group Policy Editor.

Certificates Snap-In

This is only used if you are using certificates for authentication. You have to load the Certificates Snap-in into a new MMC or add it to an existing MMC if not already done. When adding the snap-in, you will have the choice of selecting certificates for the local machine, current user, or services. It is important to remember that IP Security uses computer certificates, not user certificates, so be sure to choose the computer account option. Remember that security is in effect even when no one is logged on to the computer and that it is provided at the network layer, which is why the certificate has to be a computer certificate rather than service or user.

When deploying IP Security with certificates there are two different folders of interest within the Certificates Snap-in. The first is the CA certificate, which must be listed under **Trusted Root Certification Authorities | Certificates**. The second is the computer's certificate which must be listed under **Personal | Certificates**. If you do not have these certificates and you plan on using certificate-based authentication in IPSec, you should get them as detailed in Chapter 4.

Security Log

To record IPSec-related information in the Security Log, you must first enable Auditing through **Security Settings | Local Policies | Audit Policy**. We covered group policies in Chapter 1 and will be covering auditing in Chapter 10 if you need more information on how to do this, but essentially you can request auditing for things like account logon events and object access among other things. For IPSec it is a good idea to request both Success and Failure audits so that you are as equally aware of when IPSec is failing as you are confirming that it is working, and with what security parameters.

When auditing is enabled and an IPSec policy is active, this will record various events such as whether a secure connection was established successfully and what security parameters were in place (for example, details on the certificate used for authentication, whether encrypting, and so on). Equally, when negotiations fail, the reason for this will be recorded. For example, "IKE security association negotiation failed" with a Failure Reason such as "No response from peer." To understand fully the recorded information in the audit logs, you need a good understanding of the IPSec security protocols, acronyms, and workings, which were covered previously in this chapter.

Netdiag

NetDiag.exe is one of the Windows 2000 Support Tools that ships with Windows 2000. More information on its many uses can be found within the following MSKB Q article: http://support.microsoft.com/default.aspx?scid=KB;EN-US;321708&.

However, specifically for IPSec, NetDiag.exe can read and display all details of a current IPSec policy—this is where you can match a custom policy name to the long hex string displayed in IP Security Monitor. Unlike IP Security Monitor, it can display a more accurate reading of your IPSec statistics.

Type **netdiag /test:ipsec /v** for full statistical details of your current IPSec policy, including the name of your custom policy. There is an awful lot of information here, so either scroll through it or redirect the output to a text file. If you type **netdiag /test:ipsec /debug** you will see configuration information on the policy in use. Be aware that this will include your password in readable format, if using passwords rather than certificates. Fortunately, from a security point of view, it can only be run locally, and users without proper administrative credentials will not be able to see any sensitive information. They will see information that displays "IPSec policy service is active, but test failed to get current policy information" with a later "Access is denied."

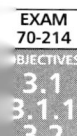

Deploying and Troubleshooting Windows IP Security

Planning takes on special importance when designing a security infrastructure that includes implementation of IPSec within an organization. After the planning phase comes the implementation phase. The Windows graphical interface makes it easy to develop an IPSec policy for any organization. IPSec policy, filters, and filter actions and interoperability with down-level clients and other operating systems are vital parts of implementation.

Evaluating Information

The first step in deploying Windows IP Security is to identify the technology assets. A company can break down their investment in information technology (IT) resources by enumerating their software, hardware, intellectual property (data), and human assets. What would it cost the organization if those assets were lost or destroyed? What expenditures in time and money would the organization incur if these assets were to fall into the hands of unscrupulous individuals?

Developing a security plan starts with the awareness that security represents a balance. Total security means that no one has access to anything. All assets would be protected at the cost of no one being able to use them. On the opposite end of the spectrum is total openness; no security controls are placed on assets or resources. In that scenario, no one has difficulty obtaining the information or resources they need but your assets have essentially become public domain.

To implement an effective security policy, accessibility and security must be balanced. The more secure the resource, the more difficult it is to access, even for those who are allowed access. Keep this point in mind when developing a security plan. Use Table 6.1 as an sample way to categorize your assets.

Table 6.1 Categorizing Corporate Assets

Type of Asset	Examples
Software	Word processor, spreadsheet, database, operating systems, accounting, inventory, human resource, utilities, diagnostic programs, drivers, communication programs, and enterprise integration systems
Hardware	Workstations, servers, RAM, hard disks, monitors, network interface cards, hubs, switches, bridges, routers, storage area networks, tape devices, modems, ISDN terminal adapters, and printers
Intellectual property (data)	Customer databases, human resource databases, payroll records, research and development databases and files, project development files, sales information, marketing information, backup tapes, offline storage facilities, floppy disks, removable hard disks, audit logs, information crossing the wire, documentation, and help databases
Human	Executives, administrators, developers, marketing staff, sales staff, clerical staff, help desk staff, and hardware technicians

Evaluating the "Enemy"

The "enemies" of a security plan are all those who seek to access a resource to which they have no explicit right. Most administrators envision the "black-hat hacker" as the foremost enemy of their information store. This image is not entirely accurate. More likely dangers are:

- Power users who are interested in "experimenting" to discover what can be done over a network

- Casual users who stumble upon information that was not secured properly

- Authorized users who access documents or files that have poorly designed access control, leading to misinformation situations that can create havoc in an organization

- Disgruntled employee seeking revenge on a current or former employer

- Greed-driven individuals who sell legitimate access controls to others for a profit

- Competitors who hire agents to carry out corporate espionage to access proprietary secrets

A common thread is that many of the risks emanate from within an organization. Although shoring up portals to the Internet and other external networks is important, the security analyst's concern and effort must also be aimed at breaches from within.

Keep in mind that someone within an organization can easily plug a notebook computer into an available port at a hub or switch and run sniffing software. These insiders listening on the wire should be of just as much concern as outside intruders.

Determining Required Security Levels

As mentioned, a mainstay approach to assessing security levels is to consider what the cost would be if resources were lost, altered, or stolen. Consider how important various resources are to an organization in the short, intermediate, and long term. How much time and money will it cost to return to normal operations if an organization's assets are compromised?

Security-level assessment can be accomplished by assigning an impact level to each item in the list of secure objects. Objects that do not appear to be the focus of security concerns should not be considered to have no impact on the security plan, because unsecured objects can create a backdoor access route to secured objects.

Assets should be rated as high, medium, or low in terms of their impact on the organization should they be compromised. Table 6.2 provides some examples of how to categorize security requirements for various types of information.

Table 6.2 Categorizing Impact Levels for Various Data Types

Type of Information	Impact Level
Corporate accounting data	High
Research data	High
Proprietary or patented information	High
Marketing information	Medium
Human resource information	Medium
Prospects database	Low
Parking permit database	Low

The security-level assessment is not the sole province of the security analyst. It is important to meet with all department managers to assess their views and level of understanding of security issues. Polling non-managerial employees is also important in making a security assessment, because employees are often the first ones to be encumbered when they try to access needed information that has been secured.

Building Security Policies with Customized IPSec Consoles

IPSec configuration and deployment in a Windows 2000 or .NET network are intimately intertwined with Active Directory and Group Policy. A policy must be created to deploy IPSec in an organization. A policy can be applied to a forest, a tree, a domain, an OU, or a single computer.

Within the Group Policy console, the administrator can choose from built-in policies or create custom policies to meet their specialized needs. These policies are configured by creating a MMC and then using the appropriate MMC plug-in. Exercise 6.01 walks through building an IPSec MMC console. A custom IPSec console can also be designed that is used to configure IPSec policy and monitor significant IPSec-related events.

EXERCISE 6.01

BUILDING AN IPSEC MMC CONSOLE

1. Create a new console by starting the **Run** command and typing **mmc**. Click **OK** to open an empty console.

2. Click the **Console** menu, and then click **Add/Remove Snap in**. Click **Add**, select **Computer Management**, and click **Add**. A dialog box appears that asks which computer the snap-in will manage. Select **Local Computer** (the computer on which the console is running). Then click **Finish**.

3. Scroll through the list of available snap-ins, select **Group Policy**, and then click **Add**. At this point a wizard appears and queries you on what Group Policy object you want to manage. In this case, confirm that the text box states **Local Computer**, and click **Finish**. If you want to define a policy for another Group Policy object, click **Browse** and select from the list.

4. Scroll through the list of Group Policy objects again, this time looking for Certificates. Select **Certificates** and click **Add**. A dialog box appears, asking you for what account you want the snap-in to always manage certificates (see Figure 6.8). Select **Computer Account**, click **Next**, and then select **Local Computer** for the computer that you want the snap-in to manage. Then click **Finish**.

5. Click **Close** in the **Add Standalone Snap-in** dialog box and then click **OK** in the **Add/Remove Snap-in** dialog box. Expand the first level of each of the snap-ins (see Figure 6.9).

Figure 6.8 Adding the Certificate Management Snap-in for the Local Computer

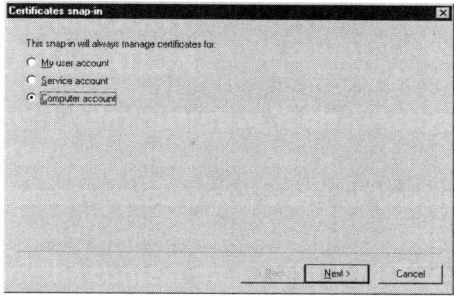

Figure 6.9 The Custom IPSec Security Management Console

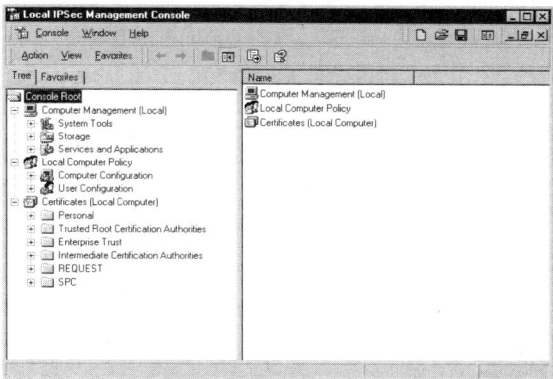

From this custom IPSec Management Console, IPSec policies are configured and monitored. In this example, IPSec policy is managed for the local machine only. This might be appropriate if configuring IPSec policy for a file or application server. If you want to manage policy for an entire domain or OU, you would select the appropriate policy when selecting the Group Policy snap-in configuration.

Flexible Security Policies

Now that the console is configured, you can begin building your IPSec security policy. Because IPSec policies are implemented via Group Policy, there is a great deal of flexibility in the places where they are implemented. You can choose from three built-in IPSec policies or create your own custom policies.

To begin, you need to navigate in the console to where the IP security policies are located. Expand the **Local Computer** policy; expand the **Computer Configuration** object; expand the **Windows Settings** object; then click **IP Security Policies on Local Machine**. In the right pane, you will see listed the three built-in IPSec Policies:

- Client (Respond Only)
- Secure Server (Require Security)
- Server (Request Security)

Your screen should look like the one shown in Figure 6.10.

Figure 6.10 The Three Built-in IPSec Policies

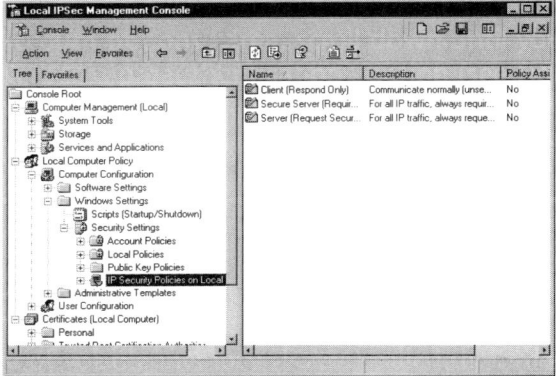

- **Client (Respond Only)** The Client (Respond Only) policy is used when you require secure IPSec connections only when another computer requests them. For example, if you are using a machine as a workstation that wants to connect to a file server and the file server requires IPSec security. The workstation with the built-in Client policy enabled will negotiate an IPSec security association. However, this client never requires IPSec security itself; it only uses IPSec to secure communications when requested to do so by another computer.

- **Secure Server (Require Security)** The Secure Server (Require Security) policy is used when all communications with a particular server need to be secured. Examples include file servers with highly sensitive information and security gateways at either end of an L2TP/IPSec tunnel. The server with the Secure Server policy always requests a secure channel. Most importantly, connections are denied to computers not able to respond to the request. Thus, a non-IPSec-aware computer will be unable to connect.

- **Server (Request Security)** The Server (Request Security) policy is used when you want to request IPSec security for all connections. This policy might be used for a file server that must serve both IPSec-aware clients (such as Windows 2000/XP) and non-IPSec-aware clients (such as Windows 9.x and NT). If a connection is established with an IPSec-aware computer, IPSec will be used to secure the session. With non-IPSec-aware computers, unsecured sessions are established. This scheme allows greater flexibility during the transition from mixed Windows networks to native Windows 2000 networks.

Test Day Tip

You should take the time to become familiar with the functions and purposes of each of the three built-in IPSec policies, both for this exam and for use in your organization.

Security policies are bidirectional. If a secure server attempts to connect to non-IPSec-aware network servers (such as Domain Name System [DNS], Windows Internet Naming Service [WINS], or Dynamic Host Configuration Protocol [DHCP] servers) the connection will fail. It is imperative that all scenarios be tested in a lab that simulates the production network before implementing IPSec policies on a live network. During the testing phase, the event logs must be assiduously checked to ascertain what services fail due to IPSec policies.

Head of the Class…

IPSec Finer Points

Implementing IPSec security affords a large measure of comfort in knowing that traffic as it traverses the wire is safe from interception and manipulation. However, IPSec can significantly impact network service interoperability.

Network servers that run the DHCP, WINS, or DNS services are a point of concern. This is particularly problematic when you run the Secure Server policy on a machine providing one of these services. Should you need to do so, be aware that negotiation will fail on non-IPSec-enabled computers. The result of the failed negotiation is that those clients will not be able to use that network service.

A special case is when you use DNS names in the IP filter list, and the DNS server you are using is not IPSec aware. The unaware DNS server will not be able to successfully negotiate secure communication, and therefore name resolution attempts will fail, with cascading results. To solve this problem, create a new filter list and rule to exempt traffic from the DNS from IPSec negotiation.

When you set the rule, use the **Permit** option to allow traffic to flow unimpeded. The filter should be for computer-to-computer IP addresses (not network IDs) and for the port number.

Rules

An IPSec policy has three main components: IP security rules, IP filter lists, and IP filter actions. Double-click the **Server Policy** to see the **Server (Request Security) Properties** dialog box, as shown in Figure 6.11.

Figure 6.11 The Server (Request Security) Properties Dialog Box

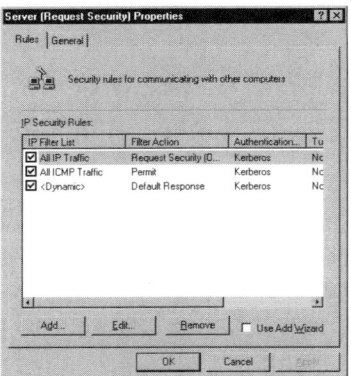

Rules are applied to computers that match criteria specified in a filter list. An IP filter list contains source and destination IP addresses. These can be individual host IP addresses or network IDs. When a communication is identified as a participant included in an IP filter list, a particular filter action that is specific for that connection is applied.

The All IP Traffic filter list includes all computers that communicate with the server via TCP/IP. Any instructions in the filter action associated with All IP Traffic are applied.

First, double-click the **All IP Traffic** filter list. This opens the **Edit Rule Properties** dialog box for the All IP Traffic filter. You should see a tabbed dialog box consisting of five tabs, as shown in Figure 6.12.

Figure 6.12 The All IP Traffic Edit Rule Properties Dialog Box

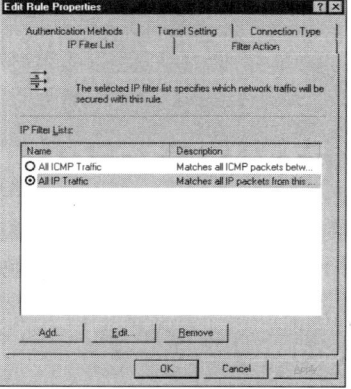

An option button for the IP filter list is selected and a description is included that explains the purpose of the list. Double-click the **All IP Traffic** filter list option to see the details of the All IP Traffic filter. The name, description, and details of the filter are displayed (see Figure 6.13).

Figure 6.13 The IP Filter List Dialog Box

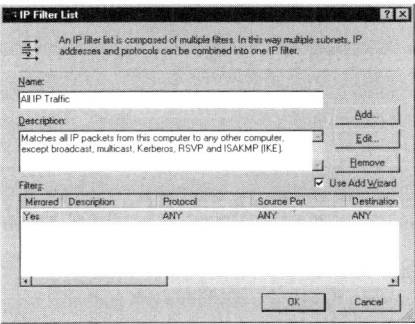

To see more details regarding the addressing, protocol, and description of the filter, click **Edit**. Then, click **Cancel** twice to return to the **Edit Rules Properties** dialog box.

Filter Actions

Filter actions define the type of security and the methods by which security is established. The primary methods are "Permit," "Block," and "Negotiate security." The Permit option blocks negotiation for IP security. This action is appropriate if you never want to secure traffic to which a rule applies. The Block action blocks all traffic from computers specified in the IP filter list. The Negotiate security action allows the computer to use a list of security methods to determine security levels for the communication. The list appears in descending order of preference. If the Negotiate security action is selected, both computers must be able to come to an agreement regarding the security parameters included in the list. The entries are processed sequentially in order of preference. The first common security method is enacted.

Click the **Filter Action** tab, and click **Request Security (Optional)** to view the options, as shown in Figure 6.14.

Checking the **Accept unsecured communication, but always respond using IPSec** check box allows unsecured communication initiated by another computer but requires the computers to which this policy applies to always use secure communication when replying or initiating. This is essentially the definition of the secure policy.

The **Allow unsecured communication with non IPSec-aware computer** option allows unsecured communication to or from another computer. This is appropriate if the computers listed in the IP filter lists are not IPSec enabled. However, if negotiations for security fail, this option disables IPSec for all communications to which this rule applies.

Figure 6.14 The Request Security (Optional) Properties Dialog Box

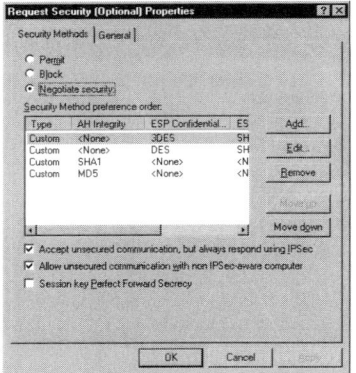

Perhaps the most important of these options is the **Session key Perfect Forward Secrecy** option. When you select this option, you ensure that session keys or keying material are not reused, and new Diffie-Hellman exchanges will take place after the session key lifetimes have expired.

Click **Cancel** to return to the **Edit Rule Properties** dialog box. Click the **Authentication Methods** tab. Here, you can select your preferred authentication method. Kerberos is the default authentication method. Other methods can be included in the list, and each will be processed in descending order. Click **Add** to include additional authentication methods, as shown in Figure 6.15.

Figure 6.15 The Authentication Methods Configuration Tab

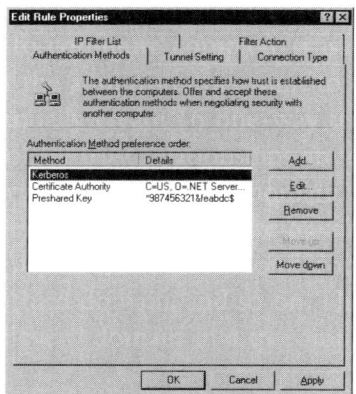

NOTE

Remember that if you are configuring a preshared key that both ends of the connection must have the same key configured.

Click the **Tunnel Setting** tab if the endpoint for the filter is a tunnel endpoint. Click the **Connection Type** tab to apply the rule to all network connections, LAN, or remote access, as shown in Figure 6.16.

Figure 6.16 The Connection Type Tab

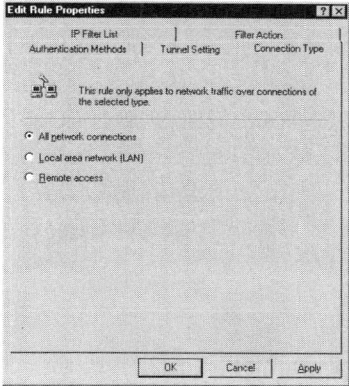

NOTE

You cannot delete the built-in policies, although you can edit them. However, it is recommended that you leave the built-in policies as they are and create new policies for custom requirements.

Flexible Negotiation Policies

Security method negotiation is required to establish an IPSec connection. You can use the default security policies, or you can create custom policies using a wizard-based approach. To add a new filter action that will be used to create a new security policy, click **Add** after selecting the **Filter Action** tab. When the wizard has completed, you can edit the security negotiation method.

When you double-click the **Request Security (Optional)** filter action, you will see the **Request Security (Optional) Properties** dialog box. If you select the **Negotiate security** option and then click **Add**, you can add a new security method, as shown in Figure 6.17.

Figure 6.17 The New Security Method Dialog Box

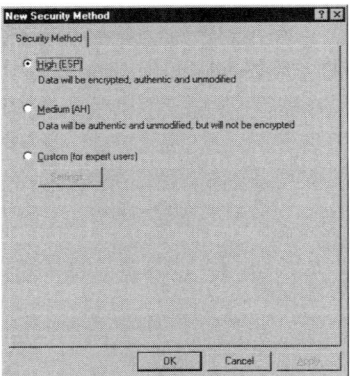

You can fine-tune your security negotiation method by selecting the **Custom (for expert users)** option and then clicking **Settings**. After doing so, you will see the **Custom Security Method Settings** dialog box, as shown in Figure 6.18.

Figure 6.18 The Custom Security Method Settings Dialog Box

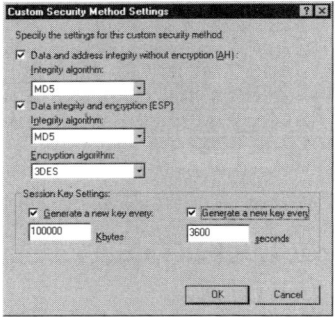

Here, you can configure whether you want to use AH, ESP, or both. For each option, you can select the integrity algorithm, the encryption algorithm, or both. All algorithms supported by the operating system are included. Session key lifetimes can be customized by entering new key generation intervals, based on the amount of data transferred (in kilobytes) or time span (in seconds).

Filters

Rules are applied to source and destination computers or networks based on their IP addresses. Filters specify the source and destination addresses of the IP traffic as well as the protocols that will be affected by the filter. To create a new filter, you can avail yourself of the Filter Wizard. To do this, return to the **Edit Rule Properties** dialog

Configuring and Troubleshooting Windows IP Security • Chapter 6

box, click the **IP Filter List** tab, and then click **Add**. This brings up the **IP Filter List** dialog box, where you enter the **Name** of the new filter and a **description** of the filter. Click **Add** to start the wizard.

When the wizard starts, you see the **Welcome** dialog box. Click the **Next** button. As shown in Figure 6.19, you choose the source address of the wizard. Your options appear after you click the down arrow on the list box. Note that you can identify the source by individual IP address, all IP addresses, DNS name, or subnet. Click **Next** to continue.

Figure 6.19 Specifying a Source IP Address for a New Filter

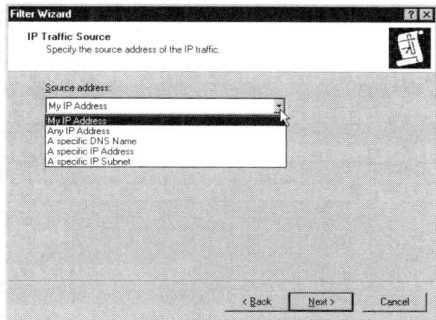

The next dialog box asks for the destination IP address. You are afforded the same options as when you designated the source. Click **Next** to continue with the wizard. At this point, you can select the protocols that will be included in the filter. All protocols are included by default, but you can select from a list of protocols or define your own by selecting **Other** and entering a protocol number. The IP Protocol Type dialog box is shown in Figure 6.20.

Figure 6.20 Selecting a Protocol Included in the New Filter

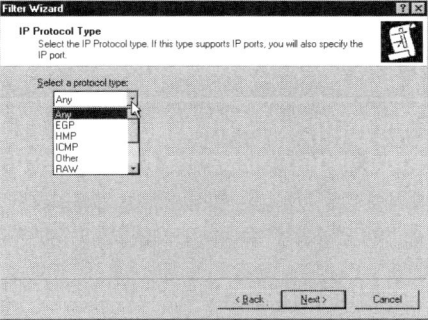

Click **Next | Finish**. Your new filter will appear in the IP filter lists included in the **IP Filter List** tab of the **Edit Rule Properties** dialog box.

Creating a Security Policy

To illustrate the process of creating a security policy, consider the following scenario: You are the network administrator for a large hospital. The network is subdivided into multiple subnets. The medical records department contains a large amount of data that must be kept secure. The hospital would incur significant legal liability if security were breached. Computers within the medical records department are closely monitored, and therefore the overhead of confidentiality is not required, but authentication and integrity should be applied to intradepartmental communications.

The medical records department must regularly send information to the hospital floor. The network infrastructure is more open to attack between the well-guarded medical records department and the less secure, open hospital environment. All computers within the medical records department are located in network ID 192.168.1.0, and all floor computers that access medical records database information are located on network ID 192.168.2.0. The default Class C subnet mask is used.

In order to implement your new security policy, you need to:

1. Create a security policy for the hospital's domain. In this way, all computers in the domain will inherit the IPSec policy.

2. Computers in the medical records department need to communicate with two sets of computers—machines within their own department and machines on the hospital floor. Characterizing these machines by subnet, you could say that machines on subnet 192.168.2.0 need to communicate with machines on 192.168.1.0, and machines on 192.168.1.0 need to communicate with machines on 192.168.2.0. When selecting the protocols, you select **All** so that all IP traffic is filtered. Therefore, you need to create two filters so that you can assign different filter actions to each filter.

3. Now you need to create two filter actions (negotiation policy); the first filter action will be applied to intradepartmental communications, in which only authentication and integrity are important, and the second filter action will be applied to extra-departmental communication, where authenticity, integrity, and confidentiality are required. The first filter action might use AH, which provides for authenticity and integrity. The second filter action might use a combination of AH and ESP, to provide the highest level of authentication and integrity while also providing confidentiality.

By implementing these combinations of filters and filter rules, you can effectively secure traffic in a customized fashion. You can easily implement this solution by invoking the Security Rule Wizard after you create the new security policy.

Making the Rule

The rule you make will create a filter for all communications emanating from 192.168.1.0 that are directed to 192.168.2.0. After the filter is created, you create a filter action. In this case, you need to ensure secure communications, because you are communicating with the unsecured hospital floor. You need to ensure integrity, authentication, and confidentiality. Perform Exercise 6.02 to accomplish these goals.

EXERCISE 6.02

CREATING A NEW IPSEC POLICY

1. Click **Start | Programs | Administrative Tools | Active Directory Users and Computers**. After the Active Directory Users and Computers console is open, right-click the domain name, then click **Properties**. In the Domain Properties window, click the **Group Policy** tab.

2. Select Default Domain Policy and click Edit.

3. This opens the Group Policy Editor. Expand Computer Configuration, expand Windows Settings, expand Security Settings, and then right-click IP Security Policies on Active Directory. Click Create IP Security Policy.

4. A wizard starts, welcoming you. Click Next.

5. You now need to enter the name of the policy, as shown in Figure 6.21. Name it MedRecToFloor then click Next.

Figure 6.21 Entering an IP Security Policy Name

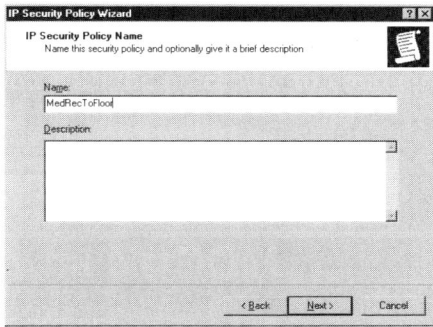

6. You will see the window shown in Figure 6.22. Remove the check mark in the **Activate the default response rule** check box. Click **Next**.

7. Now you are at the end of the wizard. Leave the check in the **Edit Properties** box, and click **Finish** (see Figure 6.23).

Figure 6.22 Handling Requests for Secure Communication

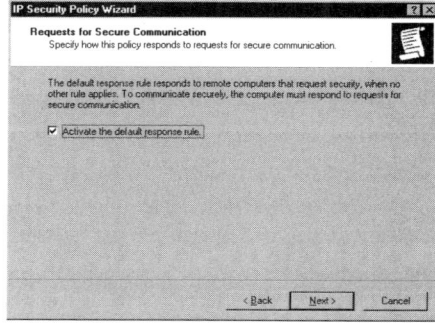

Figure 6.23 Completing the IP Security Policy Wizard

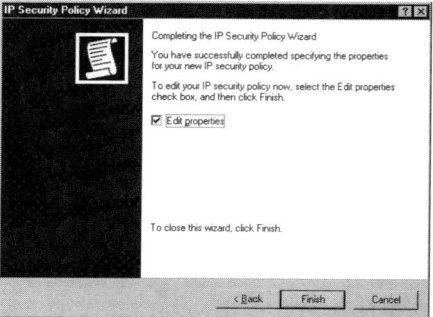

8. At this point, you have no IP filter lists. Use the Add Wizard to create a new filter list and filter action. Together, they create a filter rule. Make sure that there is a check in the **Use Add Wizard** check box and click **Add**, as shown in Figure 6.24.

Figure 6.24 The MedRecToFloor IPSec Policy Properties

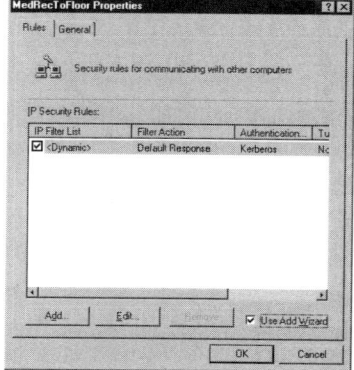

9. The Security Rule Wizard opens. The first dialog box is a welcome box. Click **Next**.
10. The next dialog box (see Figure 6.25) asks whether the rule applies to a tunnel endpoint. In this case, it does not, so select **This rule does not specify a tunnel**. Click **Next**.

Figure 6.25 Selecting a Tunnel Endpoint

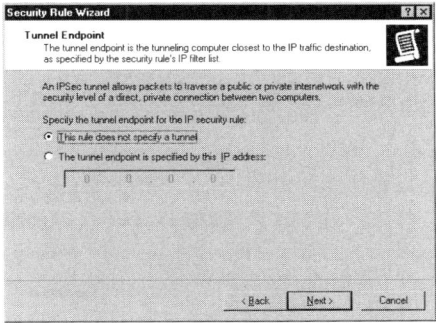

11. The wizard now asks what network connections this rule should apply to, as shown in Figure 6.26. Select **All network connections**, then click **Next**.

Figure 6.26 Choosing the Network Type

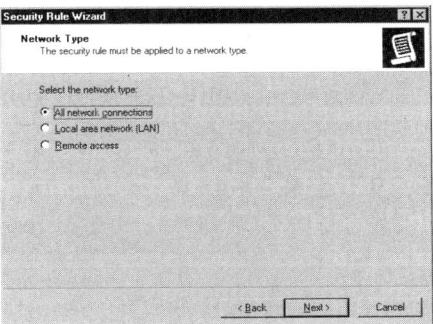

12. Now decide what default authentication protocol should be used. Select **Windows 2000 default (Kerberos V5 protocol)**, as shown in Figure 6.27. Then click **Next**.
13. Create the IP filter list by adding a filter for all traffic sent from 192.168.1.0 with the destination of 192.168.2.0. Click **Add**, as shown in Figure 6.28.

Figure 6.27 Select an Authentication Protocol

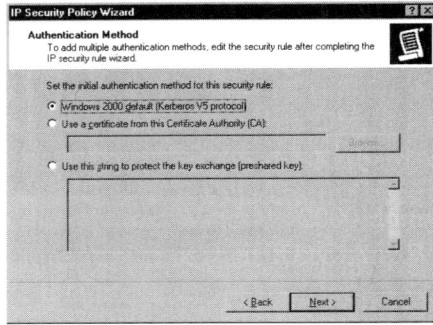

Figure 6.28 Adding a New Filter List

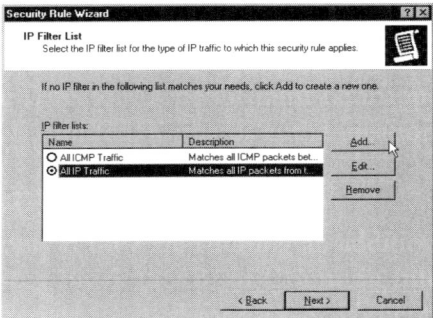

14. You now see the **IP Filter List** dialog box. Type **Secure from MedRec to Floor**, and make sure the **Use Add Wizard** check box is filled, as shown in Figure 6.29. Then click **Add**.

Figure 6.29 The IP Filter List

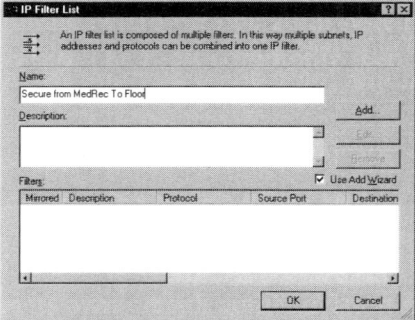

15. The IP Filter Wizard appears. Click **Next** to move past the Welcome dialog box. Now you are at the IP Traffic Source dialog box shown in Figure

6.30. Click the **down arrow** under Source address and select **A specific IP Subnet**. Type **192.168.1.0** and a subnet mask of **255.255.255.0**. Then click **Next**.

Figure 6.30 Choosing the IP Traffic Source

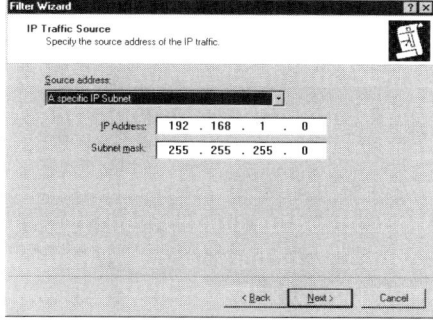

16. Now enter the IP traffic destination shown in Figure 6.31. Under the Destination address, click the **down arrow** and select **A specific IP Subnet**. Then type the destination subnet **192.168.2.0** with a subnet mask of **255.255.255.0**. Click **Next**.

Figure 6.31 Choosing the IP Traffic Destination

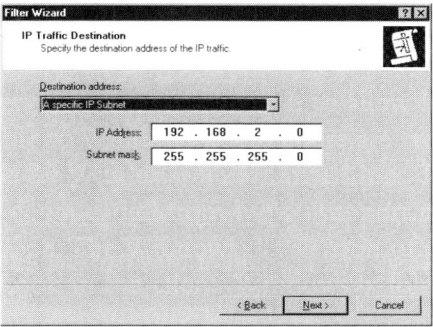

17. You want all the protocols to be included in the filter, so select **Any** (see Figure 6.32) for the protocol type, click **Next**, and then click **Finish** to complete the wizard.

18. This takes you back to the **IP Filter List** dialog box. Click **Edit** (see Figure 6.33). **Mirrored** should be checked. Match packets with the exact opposite source and destination addresses to ensure that machines from the destination subnet are also included in the incoming filter. Click **OK** to close the dialog box, and then click **Close**.

Figure 6.32 Choosing the IP Protocol Type

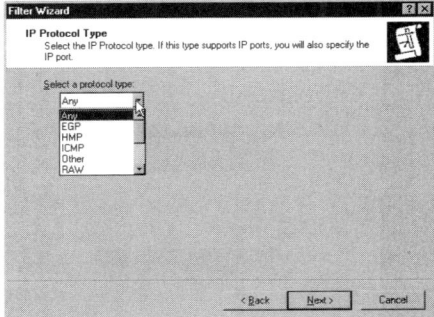

Figure 6.33 The Filter Properties Dialog Box

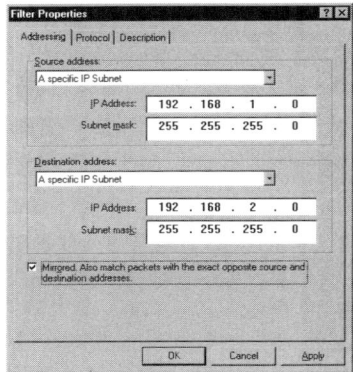

19. You are now back to the IP Filter List dialog box in the Security Rule Wizard. Select the **Secure from MedRec to Floor** filter list (see Figure 6.34) and click **Next**.

Figure 6.34 Selecting the MedRec to Floor Filter List

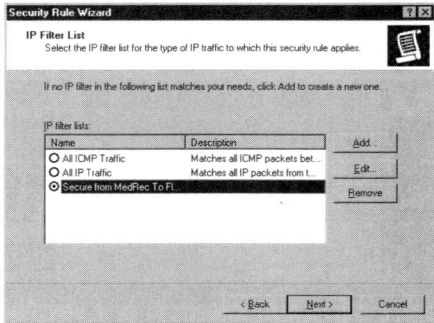

20. At this point, configure a filter action. Select the **Require Security** option. Make sure there is a check mark in the **Use Add Wizard** check box, and then click **Add** (see Figure 6.35).

Figure 6.35 The Filter Action Dialog Box of the Security Rule Wizard

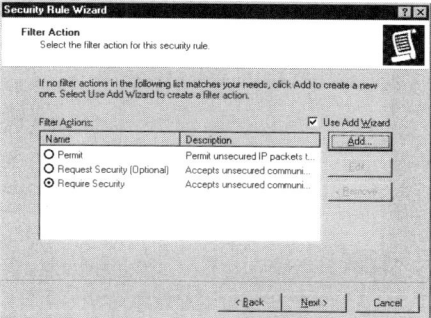

21. The IP Security Filter Action Wizard starts. Click **Next** to move past the Welcome dialog box. Here (see Figure 6.36) you are asked for a name; enter **SecureMedRec**, and click **Next**.

Figure 6.36 Naming the Filter Action

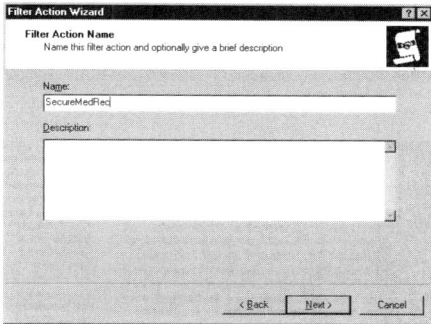

22. The **Filter Action General Options** dialog box shown in Figure 6.37 asks for a filter action behavior. Select **Negotiate security** and click **Next**.
23. You receive a dialog box that asks whether you want to support communications with computers that do not support IPSec. Select the **Do not communicate with computers that do not support IPSec** option (see Figure 6.38) and click **Next**.

Figure 6.37 Setting the Filter Action Behavior

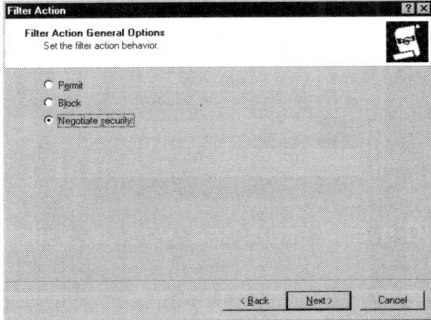

Figure 6.38 Preventing Communication with Non-IPSec Computers

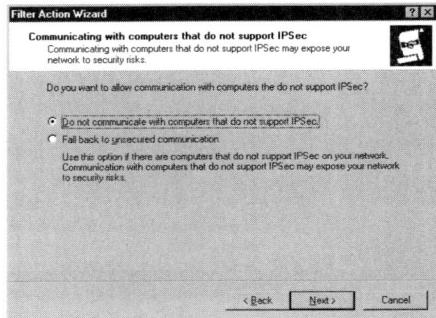

24. Now select the security method for IP traffic. To ensure confidentiality, authentication, and integrity, select **Custom** (see Figure 6.39) and then click **Settings** (see Figure 6.40).

Figure 6.39 Setting IP Traffic Security

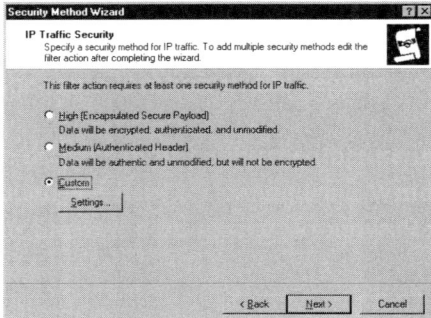

Figure 6.40 The Custom Security Method Settings

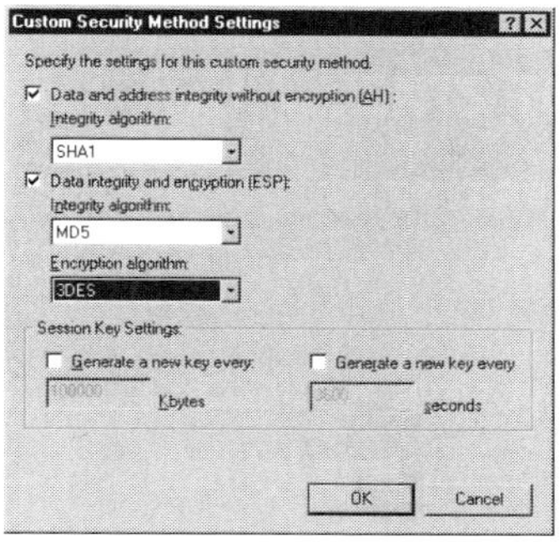

25. Select the **Data** and **address integrity without encryption (AH)** check box and then click the **down arrow** and select **SHA1**. Make sure that there is a check mark in the **Data integrity and encryption (ESP)** check box, and select **MD5** and **3DES**. Do not set the session key settings; you will select Perfect Forward Secrecy later. Click **OK**, then click **Next**.
26. The final dialog box appears. Ensure that a check mark is in the **Edit** box, and then click **Finish**.
27. You are brought to the **New Filter Action Properties** dialog box. Check **Session key Perfect Forward Secrecy** (see Figure 6.41). Click **OK** to return to the Security Rule Wizard, then click **Next**.

Figure 6.41 Enabling Perfect Forward Secrecy

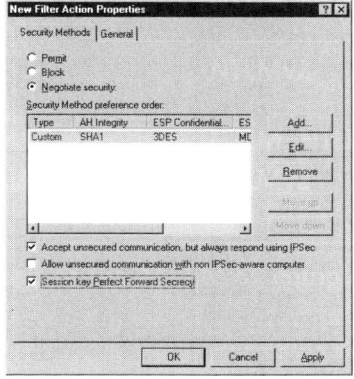

28. This is the last dialog box for the Security Rule Wizard. Click **Finish | OK** to close the **New Rule Properties** dialog box.
29. You are returned to the **MedRecToFloor Properties** box. Click the **General** tab (see Figure 6.42). You can configure how often the Policy Agent checks for policy changes here. Click **Advanced** to control the IKE process.

Figure 6.42 The General Tab for the IPSec Policy Properties

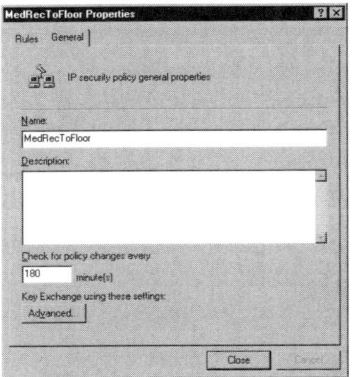

30. Here, you control the security of the IKE process (see Figure 6.43).

Figure 6.43 The Key Exchange Setting

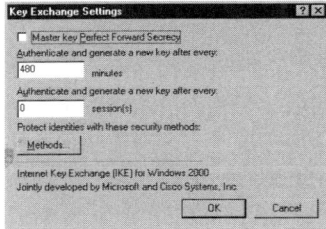

31. Click **Methods** to configure the security methods that are used to protect identities during the key exchange process (see Figure 6.44).

Figure 6.44 The Key Exchange Methods

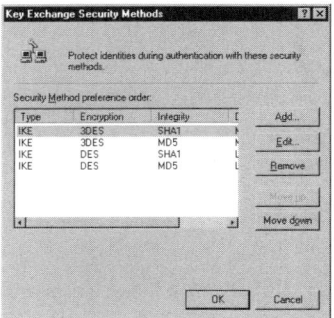

32. Click **OK | OK | Close**. Your new security policy appears in the console.

As can be seen, what looks easy on paper can be somewhat daunting when you actually apply the principles! With the rule you created, all traffic leaving 192.168.1.0 to 192.168.2.0 will be secured according to the filter rule you set up. Because it is mirrored, the same rule applies in the other direction.

Compatibility Notes

To fully engage the capabilities of the IPSec security architecture, the entire enterprise must use IPSec-aware devices. The only currently released Microsoft operating systems that are IPSec-aware at this point are Windows 2000 and XP. Windows .NET will also be IPSec-aware. Communications to or from any other version of Windows cannot be secured via IPSec.

NOTE

Microsoft released an L2TP/IPSec client for Windows 98, ME, and NT 4, which will allow the use of IPSec encryption in an L2TP virtual private network (VPN), but these operating systems do not support use of IPSec alone to secure network communications. The L2TP/IPSec VPN client can be downloaded from the Microsoft Web site at www.microsoft.com/windows2000/server/evaluation/news/bulletins/l2tpclient.asp.

Troubleshooting IP Security

IPSec can be a very complicated mechanism to get configured and working properly on a network. Many problems can occur, but more often than not they are related to simple design and implementation mistakes that can be prevented or easily corrected.

Before getting to deep into troubleshooting some of the more common problems, there are two bits of information that you must keep in mind at all times if IPSec is to be used successfully in your network.

- IPSec cannot be used with Network Address Translation (NAT) which involves changing the IP and/or TCP/User Datagram Protocol (UDP) headers, which then invalidates the packet integrity. Make sure you do not send client IPSec packets to a NAT server. Consider using Point-to-Point Tunneling Protocol (PPTP) instead, which is NAT friendly but has the disadvantage of only securing data between client and VPN server rather than offering end-to-end security.

- Routers and or firewalls may need to be configured to properly accommodate IPSec traffic. In particular:

- **Protocol ID 50 and 51** For ESP and AH traffic
- **UDP port 500** For IPSec negotiation traffic

Table 6.3 outlines some of the more common problems and their solutions when dealing with IPSec.

Table 6.3 Troubleshooting IPSec

Problem	Corrective Action
I am not able to establish an IPSec or any other connection with a server.	Test for basic network connectivity between the two computers using the PING command. In many cases, basic network connectivity issues will end up being the root cause of a communications failure. Ensure also that all required network services (DNS, DHCP, and so forth) are functioning properly. Additionally, check to ensure that both computers are part of the same domain, that is, check that the client is not in a workgroup and the server is in the domain. Removal of clients from the domain will cause IPSec communication to fail.
IPSec communications are not occurring as expected after configuring a new IPSec Policy.	Check to ensure the desired policy is actually in place by using the TCP/IP Advanced Properties window, the IPSec Monitor, or the Group Policy Editor. If the wrong (or no) policy is assigned, assign the correct policy and check for secured communications per the configured and assigned policy.
No hard SAs are being created between IPSec computers.	Soft SAs may be in place, which will prevent hard SAs from being formed. You will need to stop all traffic between the two computers for a long enough time so that the SA can time out—usually about 5 to 10 minutes. After the soft SA has timed out, you should restart the IPSec Policy Agent on both computers and see that a hard SA is formed. If not, then you should check to ensure that unsecured communications are not allowed.
I have configured IPSec to use digital certificates and now SA negotiations are failing.	Either the correct certificates are not installed on the computers attempting to make the SA or an incorrect CA is specified in the policy properties. Ensure that you have the correct certificates installed. Also check to see that you have the correct CA specified in the policy configuration.

Continued

Table 6.3 Troubleshooting IPSec

Problem	Corrective Action
Some of my computers are unable to establish a communications session with other computers.	Check to ensure that all computers are using the same policy settings. Secure computers that are not configured to allow unsecured communications will not allow connections from unsecured computers. Also check to ensure that if different policies are being used, all settings are configured correctly to allow the traffic between the computers.
I am not able to establish an IPSec connection through my firewall or router.	Check to ensure that the required ports are open on all firewalls and routers between the computers to establish IPSec communications. Ensure also that no NAT devices sit between the two computers, as NAT is incompatible with IPSec. Use MPPE if the NAT device cannot be removed.

Additional troubleshooting tips can be found in the Microsoft Knowledge Base, article Q259335, located at http://support.microsoft.com/default.aspx?scid=kb;en-us;259335.

Summary of Exam Objectives

Windows 2000 and its successors provide administrators with a new tool in their defense against security violations. IPSec allows administrators to secure information as it crosses a network. IPSec secures data at the network layer and carries out its activity transparently in the background. Users and applications do not need to be aware of IPSec. IPSec's implementation at the network layer gives it an advantage over security protocols, such as Secure Sockets Layer (SSL), for which applications must be specifically written to support.

Hallmarks of secure communications ensure authentication, integrity, and confidentiality. Authentication assures a receiver that a message was indeed sent by the individual who claims to have sent it. Data integrity ensures that message content has not been altered during transit. Confidentiality ensures that others cannot read data during transit. Combining all three provides solid end-to-end security between any two communicating hosts.

To meet the goals of authentication, integrity, and confidentiality, algorithms are used to represent the original data in a different fashion. Authentication methods available include Kerberos, public key certificates, and preshared keys. Integrity algorithms used by Windows 2000 IPSec include MD5 and SHA1. Confidentiality is ensured by scrambling messages using either DES or 3DES.

Algorithms must work with keys to carry out their functions. Computers must have access to the same shared secret key when they perform forward and reverse operations using these algorithms. IPSec implements IKE, which is a combination of ISAKMP and the Oakley protocols. Key management techniques ensure that intruders cannot compromise security by accessing a single key.

IPSec uses two protocols that add their own headers to IP datagrams. The authentication header provides authentication and integrity but not confidentiality. The Encapsulating Security Payload provides authentication, integrity, and confidentiality. The two protocols can be combined to provide a higher degree of security.

Each IPSec connection a computer establishes has its own security association. The two types of SA are ISAKMP and IPSec. The ISAKMP SA provides a secure channel for the exchange of keying information to provide a master key, and the IPSec SA defines parameters for each secure IPSec channel between computers. A separate IPSec SA is created for both inbound and outbound connections. Each IPSec SA is individualized by assigning it a security parameters index.

Planning security requirements involves taking an inventory of all hardware, software, intellectual property (data), and human resources. After the inventory, it is important to assess the cost to the organization if any of the assets are lost or compromised.

Assign each asset an impact value, and focus security concerns on the basis of the value assigned. Also, keep in mind that an enemy is most likely to be inside an organization.

Network security enabled by IPSec is policy driven. Policies are integrated into Active Directory on domain machines, or implemented as local machine policies. Each IPSec-aware computer uses a policy agent, which checks for IPSec policy during startup and periodically afterward.

IPSec policies are implemented as a series of rules. These rules include IPSec filter lists and IPSec filter actions. If a computer seeks to establish a session with a computer whose IP addressing information matches a number in one of the filter lists, a filter action affiliated with that list is triggered. The creations of IPSec policies, filter lists, and filter rules can be easily accomplished via wizard-driven interfaces. You can create your own policies or use one of the three built-in policies. The built-in policies are the Client, Server, and Secure Server IPSec policies.

Compatibility issues must be taken into account when enabling IPSec in an organization. Windows 2000 and XP/.NET are the only Microsoft operating systems that are IPSec aware. Connection failures will result if a computer configured with the Secure Server policy interacts with non-IPSec-aware machines.

The future of IPSec looks bright. The next generation of the IP—IPv6—has built-in support for IPSec. See RFCs 2411 and 2401 for descriptions and specifications for IPSec as an Internet standard.

Exam Objectives Fast Track

The Need For Network Security

- ☑ Snooping involves sniffing a cable and looking for information being sent across the wire in an attempt to gain someone's username and password.

- ☑ Spoofing involves impersonating another user or computer in an attempt to gain information with the stolen identity.

- ☑ Passwords can be compromised via one of the many password-cracking utilities on the market, by sniffing the cable (snooping), or by using social engineering to trick users into giving their passwords.

- ☑ DoS disrupts the services running on a computer in an attempt to make the server unavailable to legitimate requests.

- ☑ In a MITM attack, an intruder sits between a client and a server and watches the communications from both parties.

- ☑ Application-directed attacks try to exploit known vulnerabilities in applications.

- ☑ Compromised Key attacks are geared toward obtaining a user's private key. After the intruder has the user's private key, the intruder can use it to impersonate the user.

IP Security Overview

- ☑ IPSec provides security at the network layer. This makes IPSec completely transparent to the applications running on the computer.

- ☑ IPSec provides integrity, authentication, and confidentiality.

- ☑ IPSec has two modes—tunnel mode and transport mode. Transport mode uses TCP/IP to send IPSec-encrypted information directly between two clients. The clients send unencrypted information to a tunnel endpoint. The tunnel endpoints use TCP/IP and IPSec to encrypt the client information.

- ☑ IPSec uses two protocols—authentication header and Encrypted Security Payload. AH provides data integrity and authentication but not confidentiality. ESP can provide authentication, integrity, and confidentiality but does not encrypt the entire packet.

- ☑ IPSec uses a security association between two computers to determine the algorithms and protocols to be used by each computer.

IP Security Management Tools

- ☑ There are several tools available within Windows 2000 that allow you to configure and monitor all aspects of IPSec implementation and usage on your network. They are:
    - IP Security Policies
    - IP Security Monitor
    - IPSec Policy Agent Service
    - TCP/IP Advanced Options
    - Certificates Snap-in
    - Security Log

Deploying and Troubleshooting Windows IP Security

- ☑ IPSec is managed through a custom MMC console containing the IPSec Security Policy snap-in.
- ☑ An IPSec policy has three main components—IP security rules, IP filter lists, and IP filter actions.
- ☑ IP security rules apply to computers that match criteria in the filter list.
- ☑ An IP filter list contains source and destination IP addresses.
- ☑ IP filter actions determine the level of security (authentication and encryption) and the method by which security is negotiated.

Exam Objectives Frequently Asked Questions

The following Frequently Asked Questions, answered by the authors of this book, are designed to both measure your understanding of the Exam Objectives presented in this chapter, and to assist you with real-life implementation of these concepts.

Q: What happens if a computer attempts to connect to another computer with the Secure Server IPSec policy and it fails to authenticate?

A: The server will not accept connections from that host for at least one minute and as long as five minutes. This is something to be aware of when troubleshooting connectivity problems with IPSec-enabled machines.

Q: Can I use Kerberos authentication for my users who are using an L2TP/IPSec tunnel to dial into intranet servers?

A: VPN connections in Windows 2000 are designed to use certificate-based public key authentication, although there is a Registry hack that allows you to use preshared keys for testing purposes. In Windows XP, the interface provides an IPSec settings option that lets you use a preshared key for authentication.

Q: Our internal network uses NAT rather than public IP addresses. Can I use L2TP/IPSec tunnels to allow remote access VPN clients to access my internal resources?

A: No. Because of incompatibilities between NAT and IPSec, you cannot use both at the same time. L2TP over IPSec traffic is not translatable by a NAT because the UDP port number is encrypted.

Q: What is Perfect Forward Secrecy?

A: Perfect Forward Secrecy ensures that a key used to protect a transmission, in whichever phase, cannot be used to generate any additional keys. If the key used was derived from specific keying material, that material cannot be used to generate any other keys. This provides a high level of protection. If an intruder is able to access data and obtain a key, that key will not be valid on other packets, making the cracking process very difficult.

Self Test

A Quick Answer Key follows the Self Test questions. For complete questions, answers, and epxlanations to the Self Test questions in this chapter as well as the other chapters in this book, see the Self Test Appendix.

The Need For Network Security

1. Your network currently does not use IPSec to protect internal communications. An attacker could perform what sort of attack on your network to capture valuable information, such as user names and passwords?

    A. Snooping

    B. Spoofing

    C. DoS

    D. MITM

2. You have detected an unauthorized computer capturing all traffic between two servers on your network. You suspect that this computer has changed some or all of the transmissions that have been sent from both servers. What type of attack are you most likely experiencing?

    A. Snooping

    B. Spoofing

    C. DoS

    D. MITM

IP Security Overview

3. IPSec operates at what layer of the seven-layer open system interconnection (OSI) Model?

    A. Layer 2

    B. Layer 3

    C. Layer 6

    D. Layer 7

4. Jon is interested in deploying IPSec on his network. What benefits can Jon expect to gain by doing so? (Choose all that apply.)

    A. Integrity of traffic on his network

    B. Confidentiality of traffic on his network

    C. Authentication of traffic on his network

    D. Impersonation of traffic on his network

5. In regards to IPSec, the AH does what for you?

    A. Ensures data integrity and authentication.

    B. Prevents capture of packets.

    C. Provides confidentiality.

    D. Encrypts the packets.

6. What is added to a standard IP datagram when the AH is used?

   A. Encryption to protect the contents of the packet.

   B. An AH header that provides authentication, anti-replay, and integrity for the entire packet.

   C. An AH header that provides assurance of delivery.

   D. An AH header and AH trailer that provides a checksum of the packet.

7. Andrea is configuring a new IPSec policy for her network. What methods does she have to choose from as far as authentication? (Choose all that apply.)

   A. Digital certificate

   B. SNMP string

   C. Shared secret

   D. Kerberos

8. During the process of starting an IPSec communication between two computers, how many SAs are created?

   A. One

   B. Two

   C. Three

   D. Depends on the IPSec policy requirements

9. Chris wants to use IPSec to secure communications between her main office and a remote office over the Internet. What is this called?

   A. Transport mode

   B. Internet mode

   C. Tunnel mode

   D. Transfer mode

10. You are interviewing a new candidate for the position of assistant network administrator. Bruno, the candidate, is in the process of answering the question "What does message integrity mean?" Which of the following answers should Bruno give you?

   A. The assurance that the message received is identical to the message that was sent.

   B. The assurance that the identity of a sender or recipient is verified.

   C. The assurance that the message is protected from prying eyes and is kept private.

   D. The assurance that the receiving user is authorized to receive the message.

IP Security Management Tools

11. You have recently configured and deployed an IPSec solution on your network between all computers in the Finance department. What can you use to verify that IPSec is in fact being used by these computers to secure their communications?

    A. IP Security Policies in the Group Policy Editor

    B. IP Security Monitor

    C. Certificates Snap-in

    D. IP Security Policy Agent

12. You have configured several different IPSec policies for your organization, one for each department within the organization. From where can a configured IPSec policy be selected for use on a computer? (Choose all correct answers.)

    A. IP Security Policies within Group Policy

    B. IP Security Monitor

    C. TCP/IP Advanced Properties

    D. Certificates Snap-in

Deploying and Troubleshooting Windows IP Security

13. Catherine is interested in deploying IPSec on her network to increase network security. She currently uses a NAT device to translate one Public IP address for her 25 internal clients (Windows 2000 Professional and Windows 98) using DHCP. What concerns should Catherine have in this situation? (Choose all that apply.)

    A. No concerns; IPSec is an ideal solution for any size network.

    B. IPSec is not compatible with DHCP; she will need to manually assign the client computer IP addresses.

    C. IPSec is not compatible with NAT devices; she will not be able to create IPSec connections outside of her network.

    D. IPSec is not supported with legacy operating systems such as Windows 98; these computers will not be able to make secure connections or communicate with other computers that require secure communications.

14. You are creating a new IPSec policy for your network. You have several highly sensitive servers that you do not want to allow any unsecured connections to. You have a mix of Windows 2000 Professional and Windows NT 4.0 client computers. You need all of your client computers to be able to connect securely to these servers. What do you need to do? (Choose all that apply.)

    A. Upgrade the Windows NT 4.0 computers to Windows 2000.

    B. Designate that the Windows NT 4.0 computers are to be trusted for delegation.

    C. Ensure that the servers have their archive bit set to false.

    D. Ensure that the "Do not communicate with computers that do not support IPSec" option is selected when you make your new IPSec policy.

15. Hannah wants to customize the IPSec hash algorithm that is in use in her organization's IPSec policy. What are her choices? (Choose all that apply.)

    A. SHA1

    B. WEP

    C. AES

    D. MD5

Self Test Quick Answer Key

For complete questions, answers, and epxlanations to the Self Test questions in this chapter as well as the other chapters in this book, see the Self Test Appendix.

1. **A**
2. **D**
3. **B**
4. **A, B, C**
5. **A**
6. **B**
7. **A, C, D**
8. **C**
9. **C**
10. **A**
11. **B**
12. **A, C**
13. **C, D**
14. **A, D**
15. **A, D**

Chapter 7

MCSE/MCSA 70-214

Implementing Secure Wireless Networks

Exam Objectives in this Chapter:

3.3 Implement security for wireless networks.

3.3.1 Configure public and private wireless LANs.

3.3.2 Configure wireless encryption levels. Levels include WEP and 802.1x.

3.3.3 Configure wireless network connection settings on client computers. Client-computer operating systems include Windows 2000 Professional, Windows XP Professional, and Windows CE 3.0.

- ☑ Summary of Exam Objectives
- ☑ Exam Objectives Fast Track
- ☑ Exam Objectives Frequently Asked Questions
- ☑ Self Test
- ☑ Self Test Quick Answer Key

Introduction to the Wireless LAN

Wireless local area networking (WLAN) is not exactly a new technology, but it has gained rapid acceptance in the past two years and is in wide use now with new deployments being set up every day. In the next sections we look at both the good and the bad of wireless networking. With any technology this young, it should come as no surprise that it has distinct problems—primarily in securing wireless networks. In addition to discussing these problems, we look at an example of the basic architecture and operation of the most typical wireless networking technology you will likely see in your organization: IEEE 802.11b WLAN technology.

Benefits of the Wireless LAN

Wireless networking provides a new era of data connectivity unmatched by cabled networks. Increases in the speed of deployment, access to data, and scalability mean that the needs of specific user communities can be addressed in ways that were unavailable to network architects a few years ago.

New streams of end-user applications and services are being developed to provide businesses and consumers alike with advanced data access and manipulation. The main benefits of wireless integration fall primarily into two major categories:

- Convenience
- Productivity

Test Day Tip

Microsoft gives almost no WLAN security objectives for this exam. In order to better prepare you, this chapter provides a wealth of background information about IEEE 802.11b WLAN information. If you do not want to learn about WLAN technologies and issues, you can skip directly to the "Configuring Windows Client Computers for Wireless LAN Security" section later in this chapter to get the basic information you need for this exam objective. If you are new to WLANs or want to build your knowledge a bit, you should read this entire chapter.

Convenience

First and foremost in the minds of IT professionals, business leaders, and consumers when they discuss wireless networking is the aspect of convenience. This basic benefit outweighs all other benefits combined in terms of user interest in wireless and is predominantly the main reason for their deployments. Convenience can be broken into three areas of interest:

- Flexibility
- Roaming
- Mobility

Flexibility

Wireless technologies provide the greatest flexibility of design, integration, and deployment of any networking solution available. With only transceivers to install in the local station and a wireless hub or Access Point (AP) to be configured for local access, it is simple to retrofit wireless networking within existing structures or create access services that traditional networking infrastructures are not capable of addressing.

TEST DAY TIP

The Wireless Access Point (WAP) should not be confused with Wireless Application Protocol (WAP) commonly used in the wireless telephone industry. Some people attempt to call Access Points *WAPs*, but this is incorrect. For the sake of clarity, we always refer to them as access points, or APs.

An Access Point is defined as a Layer 2 network device that serves as an interface between the wireless network and the wired network. APs are the wireless networking equivalent of a standard Ethernet hub in that they allow multiple clients using the same network technology to access the core network.

With traditional networking infrastructures, a physical path is needed between the core network components (the servers, Internet connection, and so on) and each of the network users. This means that a wired connection needs to be created from one end of the network to the other for users to communicate with each other and with network resources.

Wired network connections are generally static in location, in that the access is provided from a specified point that cannot easily be moved from one physical location to another. This also implies that if an existing access drop is in use, other users must wait their turn to gain access to the network if the next closest available drop is not conveniently located.

Existing environments might not always be friendly to new installations. Many older buildings, houses, and apartments do not provide facilities for installing new cabling. In these environments, building contractors and engineers might need to get involved to devise ways of running new cabling systems. When existing cable-run facilities are available, they do not always offer the optimum path between existing LAN resources and new users. Security concerns also need to be addressed if a common wiring closet or riser is to be shared with other tenants. For these reasons, the cost involved in installing new cabling can be prohibitive in terms of time, materials, or installation costs.

Another factor involving the installation of new cabling is loss of revenue due to the unavailability of facilities during the installation itself. Hotel chains, convention centers, and airports stand to lose revenues during a cable installation project if a section of the building needs to be closed off to customer access for safety reasons. Intangible costs need to be explored as well when you're investigating the installation of new cable runs. These costs include customer dissatisfaction and loss of customer goodwill during and after the retrofit project itself.

With wireless networking, all that is required to create a new network connection is radio wave access between end nodes (users) and a wireless AP within close enough proximity to users. Radio waves can travel through walls, floors, and windows. This physical property of the transmission medium gives network architects the flexibility to design networks and install wireless APs where they're most needed. This means that a wireless AP, when properly placed, can be used to support multiple user environments at the same time.

An example of this flexibility in a WLAN configuration consists of locating a wireless AP on the inside part of an eastern-facing exterior wall on the second floor of an office building. This one wireless AP could simultaneously service the needs of a group of users on the eastern corner of the first floor, the second floor, and the third floor, along with users on the terrace located outside the first-floor eastern corner. In this configuration, access is provided to users located on different floors inside and outside the building with a minimal commitment in terms of equipment and resources.

Another example of a WLAN configuration consists of providing networking access within a large public area such as a library. In this scenario, properly placed APs could provide network coverage of the entire floor area without impacting the day-to-day use of the facilities. In addition, the APs could be located in an area of the library that has restricted access and is physically secure from daily activities.

Roaming

A *wireless network access zone* is an area of wireless network coverage. Compared with the situation in traditional wire-based networks, a wireless user is not required to be located at a specific spot to gain access to the network. A user can gain access to the wireless network provided he or she is within the area of wireless coverage where the radio signal transmissions to and from the AP are of enough strength to support communications and they are granted access by the wireless AP.

For a more flexible and robust solution, you can organize multiple APs to overlap coverage in a single area, thus allowing users to roams seamlessly between APs without a loss of connection. With the always-on connectivity provided by wireless LANs, a roaming user is one that has the capability to:

- Physically roam from one location to another within the wireless access zone
- Logically roam a session from one wireless AP to another

When discussing physical roaming, we include both a user's movement within a single AP's wireless network access zone or within the combined network access zones for all the APs that are part of this network.

When discussing logical roaming, we refer to the *transference* of a networking session from one wireless AP to another, without the need for any user interaction during the session reassociation process. When a user moves from one wireless AP's area of coverage to another AP's area of coverage, the user's transmission signal strength is assessed. As the signal reaches a threshold, the user credentials are carried over from the old "home base" AP to the new "home base" AP using a session token or other transparent authentication scheme.

This combination of physical and logical roaming allows users to keep data sessions active as they move freely around the area of coverage. This is of great benefit to users who require maintaining a data session with networked resources as they move about a building or facility.

For example, imagine the job of an internal technical service agent. In their day-to-day activities, these agents could be called on to service end stations where access to technical troubleshooting databases, call tickets, and other support resources are required. By having access to these services over the wireless network, technicians can move from one call ticket to another without being forced to reconnect to the wireline network as they move about. Another benefit to maintaining an always-on session is that the technicians could provide live updates to the ticketing databases or order replacement supplies at the time of service.

Next, let's take a look at a senior manager who is attending a status meeting in a conference room where a limited number of data ports will be available to access e-mail, databases, and other information stores. If this manager had access to wireless networking capabilities on her laptop, she could maintain a connection to the same services she has available at her local desktop. Real-time reports with up-to-the-minute metrics on business activities and critical information flows could be more efficient and timely, enhancing the manager's job performance as well as the company's success.

As can be noted in the previous examples, any networking solution using traditional wireline media would hit a major limitation when exposed to the same requirements of access coverage. The costs in cabling materials alone would preclude any such contemplation.

Mobility

The last concept dealing with convenience is that of mobility. This benefit alone is often the biggest factor in making organizations decide to go for a wireless-based networking solution.

In traditional wireline networking environments, once a cabling infrastructure is set in place, rarely does it move with a tenant when that tenant leaves for a new facility or area of a building. Cabling installations are considered part of the cost of the move and are essentially tossed out with each departing tenant.

With a wireless networking environment, wireless APs can be unplugged from the electrical outlet and redeployed in the new facility. Very few cables, if any, are left behind as a "going-away present" to the building owner. This allows the network architects to reuse networking equipment as required to address the networking realities of each environment.

For example, it is possible to move part or all of a network from one functional area to another or from one building to another. Doing so facilitates the job of IT managers, who are constantly faced with network resource rationalizations and optimizations such as decommissioning access ports or moving equipment and personnel from one area to another.

Productivity

The net result of the increased level of flexibility, mobility, and convenience provided through wireless networking is increased productivity. Networked resources can become accessible from any location, thus providing the ability to design and integrate environments where users and services can be collocated where best suited. Time can be spent working with data instead of traveling to the data store. Wireless networking can provide opportunities for higher level of service and productivity unmatched through cabled networking.

Wireless LAN Concepts

This section covers most wireless technology in use today for wireless networking: WLAN networks based on the IEEE 802.11 specification. IEE 802.11 is not the only wireless networking technology available, but it is certainly the most popular and must be understood in order to gain a solid background for working with wireless networking in Windows 2000 and XP.

The process of connecting to a wireless network is often transparent to users and, from their perspective, is no different from connecting to a copper- or fiber-based

Ethernet network, with the exception that no wires are involved. With Windows XP, which boasts automatic configuration and seamless roaming from one wireless network to another through its Wireless Zero Configuration service, the ease with which users can connect to wireless networks further belies the complexity of the technology involved and differences between the two kinds of networks.

Furthermore, because the experience of using a wireless network is identical to that of using an Ethernet network, there is a tendency to treat both kinds of networks as though they were the same. However, they are quite different from one another, and an understanding of those differences is critical to providing an informed and effective implementation of a secure wireless network.

Communication in a Wireless Network

Wireless networks, like their wired counterparts, rely on the manipulation of electrical charge to enable communication between devices. Changes or oscillations in signal strength from 0 to some maximum value (*amplitude*) and the rate of those oscillations (*frequency*) allow the encoding and decoding of information.

When two devices understand the method(s) used to encode and decode information contained in the changes to the electrical properties of the communications medium, they can communicate with each other. A network adapter is able to decode the changes in the electrical current it senses on the wire and convert them to meaningful information (bits) that it can subsequently send to higher levels for processing. Likewise, a network adaptor can encode information (bits) by manipulating the properties of the electrical current for transmission on the communications medium (the cable, in the case of wired networks).

Radio Frequency Communications

The obvious and primary difference between wired and wireless networks is that wireless networks use radio waves to transmit their data across an intermediate medium, instead of pushing electrons through a wired connection. Radio waves are created by applying *alternating current (AC)* to an antenna to produce an *electromagnetic (EM)* field. The resulting *radio frequency (RF)* field is used by devices for broadcast and reception.

In the case of wireless networks, the medium for communications is the EM *field*, the region of space that is influenced by the electromagnetic radiation. (Unlike audio waves, radio waves do not require a medium such as air or water to propagate.) As with wired networks, amplitude decreases with distance, resulting in the degradation of signal strength and the ability to communicate. However, the EM field is also dispersed according to the properties of the transmitting antenna, not tightly bounded as is the case with communication on a wire. The area over which the radio waves propagate from an electromagnetic source is known as the *Fresnel zone*.

Like the waves created by throwing a rock into a pool of water, radio waves are affected by the presence of obstructions and can be reflected, refracted, diffracted, or scattered, depending on the properties of the obstruction and its interaction with the radio waves. Reflected radio waves can be a source of interference on wireless networks. The interference created by bounced radio waves is called *multipath interference*.

When radio waves are reflected, additional wave fronts are created. These different wave fronts can arrive at the receiver at different times and be in phase or out of phase with the main signal. When the peak of a wave is added to another wave (in phase), the wave is amplified. When the peak of a wave meets a trough (out of phase), the wave is effectively cancelled.

Multipath interference can be the source of problems that are very difficult to troubleshoot. In planning for a wireless network, administrators should consider the presence of common sources of multipath interference. These include metal doors, metal roofs, water, metal vertical blinds, and any other source that is highly reflective of radio waves. Antennas could help compensate for the effects of multipath interference, but these have to be carefully chosen. In fact, many wireless APs have two antennas for precisely this purpose. However, a single omnidirectional antenna might be of no use at all in curbing this kind of interference.

Another source of signal loss is the presence of obstacles. Whereas radio waves can travel through physical objects, they will be degraded according to the properties of the object they travel through. A window, for example, is fairly transparent to radio waves, but it could reduce the effective range of a wireless network between 50 and 70 percent, depending on the presence and nature of coatings on the glass. A solid core wall can reduce the effective range of a wireless network up to 90 percent or greater.

EM fields are also prone to interference and signal degradation by the presence of other EM fields. In particular, 802.11 wireless networks are prone to interference produced by cordless phones, microwave ovens, and a wide range of devices that use the same unlicensed Industrial, Scientific, and Medical (ISM) or Unlicensed National Information Infrastructure (UNII) bands.

To mitigate the effects of interference from these devices and other sources of electromagnetic interference, RF-based wireless networks employ *spread-spectrum technologies*. Spread-spectrum provides a way to "share" bandwidth with other devices that are operating in the same frequency range. Rather than operating on a single, dedicated frequency such as is the case with radio and television broadcasts, wireless networks use a "spectrum" of frequencies for communication.

Spread-Spectrum Technology

First conceived of by Hollywood actress Hedy Lamarr and composer George Antheil in 1940 as a method to secure military communications from jamming and eavesdropping during WWII, spread-spectrum defines methods for wireless devices to simultaneously use a number of narrowband frequencies over a range of frequencies for communication.

The narrowband frequencies used between devices change according to a random-appearing but defined pattern, allowing the use of individual frequencies to contain parts of the transmission. Someone listening to a transmission using spread-spectrum would hear only noise, unless their device "understood" in advance what frequencies were used for the transmission and could synchronize with them.

Two methods to synchronize wireless devices are:

- Frequency-hopping spread-spectrum (FHSS)
- Direct-sequence spread-spectrum (DSSS).

Frequency-Hopping Spread-Spectrum

As the name implies, FHSS works by quickly moving from one frequency to another according to a pseudo-random pattern. The frequency range used by the frequency hop is relatively large (83.5 MHz), providing excellent protection from interference. The amount of time spent on any given frequency is known as *dwell time*; the amount of time it takes to move from one frequency to another is known as *hop time*. FHSS devices begin their transmission on one frequency and move to other frequencies according to the predefined pseudo-random sequence and then repeat the sequence after reaching the final frequency in the pattern. Hop time is usually very short (200 to 300 μs) and not significant relative to the dwell time (100 to 200 ms).

The frequency-hopping sequence creates the channel, allowing multiple channels to coexist in the same frequency range without interfering with one another. As many as 79 FCC-compliant FHSS devices using the 2.4 GHz ISM band may be colocated with each other. However, the expense of implementing such a large number of systems limits the practical number of colocated devices to well below this number. FHSS is less subject to EM interference than DSSS but usually operates at lower rates of data transmission (typically 1.6 Mbps but possibly as high as 10 Mbps) than networks that use DSSS.

Direct-Sequence Spread-Spectrum

DSSS works somewhat differently from FHSS. With DSSS, the data is divided and simultaneously transmitted on as many frequencies as possible within a particular frequency band (the channel). DSSS adds redundant bits of data known as *chips* to the data to represent binary 0s or 1s. The ratio of chips to data is known as the *spreading ratio*: The higher the ratio, the more immune to interference the signal because if part of the transmission is corrupted, the data can still be recovered from the remaining part of the chipping code. This method provides greater rates of transmission than FHSS, which uses a limited number of frequencies but fewer channels in a given frequency range. In addition, it also protects against data loss through the redundant, simultaneous transmission of data.

However, because DSSS floods the channel it is using, it is also more vulnerable to interference from EM devices operating in the same range. In the 2.4 GHz to 2.4835 GHz frequency range employed by 802.11b, DSSS transmissions can be broadcast in any one of 14 22-MHz-wide channels. The number of center-channel frequencies used by 802.11 DSSS devices depends on the country. For example, North America allows 11 channels operating in the 2.4 GHz to 2.4835 GHz range, Europe allows 13, and Japan allows 1. Because each channel is 22 MHz wide, channels may overlap each other. With the 11 available channels available in North America, only a maximum of three channels (1, 6, and 11) may be used concurrently without the use of overlapping frequencies.

Wireless Network Architecture

The seven-layer Open Systems Interconnect (OSI) networking model defines the framework for implementing network protocols. Wireless networks operate at the physical and data link layers of the OSI model. The physical layer is concerned with the physical connections between devices, such as how the medium and low bits (0s and 1s) are encoded and decoded. Both FHSS and DSSS, for example, are implemented at the physical layer. The data link layer is divided into two sublayers, the media access control (MAC) and logical link control (LLC) layers.

The MAC layer is responsible for such things as:

- Framing data
- Synchronization
- Collision detection and avoidance

The Ethernet 802.3 standard, which defines the Carrier Sense Multiple Access with Collision Detection (CSMA/CD) method for protecting against data loss as result of data collisions on the cable, is defined at this layer.

TEST DAY TIP

Wireless network security in Windows will be tested on the exam. This whole section on the explanation of wireless, how it works, and what you can do with it is strictly background information to further your understanding of the technology and your education. Exam questions will not be based on FHSS and DSSS technologies, so if this information seems overly technical, don't panic!

As a security administrator, it is important, however, that you know this information, and that's the reason it's here. It serves you no good to pass an exam and not understand the underlying technology. It is our mission to teach you and help you make the transition from the exam to the real world of security analysts who know all the underpinnings of, for example, wireless technologies, so that when you walk into your next position—or stay in the one you have now—you will become a powerhouse of security-related information.

CSMA/CD and CSMA/CA

In contrast to Ethernet 802.3 networks, wireless networks defined by the 802.11 standard do not use CSMA/CD as a method to protect against data loss resulting from collisions. Instead, 802.11 networks use a method known as Carrier Sense Multiple Access with Collision Avoidance (CSMA/CA). CSMA/CD works by detecting whether a collision has occurred on the network and then retransmitting the data in the event of such an occurrence. However, this method is not practical for wireless networks because CSMA/CD relies on the fact that every workstation can hear all the other workstations on the cable segment to determine if there is a collision.

In a wireless network, usually only the AP can hear every workstation that is communicating with it. (For example, both workstation A and B might be able to communicate with the same AP, but they might be too far apart from each other to hear their respective transmissions.) Additionally, wireless networks do not use full-duplex communication, which is another way to protect data against corruption and loss as a result of collisions.

CSMA/CA solves the problem of potential collisions on the wireless network by taking a more active approach than CSMA/CD, which kicks in only after a collision has been detected. Using CSMA/CA, a wireless workstation first tries to detect if any other device is communicating on the network. If it senses it is clear to send, it initiates communication. The receiving device sends an acknowledgment (ACK) packet to the transmitting device, indicating successful reception. If the transmitting device does not receive an ACK, it assumes a collision has occurred and retransmits the data. However, it should be noted that many collisions can occur and that these collisions can be used to compromise the confidentiality of Wired Equivalent Privacy (WEP) encrypted data—a discussion that we have later in this chapter.

CSMA/CA is only one way in which wireless networks differ from wired networks in their implementation at the MAC layer. For example, the IEEE standard for 802.11 at the MAC layer defines additional functionality, such as Virtual Collision Detection (VCD), roaming, power saving, asynchronous data transfer, and encryption.

The fact that wireless encryption using the WEP protocol is defined at the MAC layer is particularly noteworthy and has significant consequences for the security of wireless networks. This means data at the higher levels of the OSI model, in particular TCP/IP data, is also encrypted. Because many of the TCP/IP communications that occur between hosts contain a large amount of frequently repeating and well-known patterns, WEP is more prone to cracking than it would be if implemented in a different fashion, although it does include safeguards against this kind of attack. Later in this chapter we explore in more detail the particular weaknesses of WEP.

Exam Warning

Make sure that you completely understand WEP and its vulnerabilities. WEP is discussed in more detail later in this chapter. You will likely be faced with an exam question in which you need to implement WEP.

IEEE 802.11 Wireless Local Area Networks

WLANs are covered by the IEEE 802.11 standards. The purpose of these standards is to provide a wireless equivalent to IEEE 802.3 Ethernet-based networks. The IEEE 802.3 standard defines a method for dealing with collisions (CSMA/CD), speeds of operation (10 Mbps, 100 Mbps, and faster), and cabling types (Category 5 twisted pair and fiber). The standard ensures the interoperability of various devices, despite different speeds and cabling types.

As with the 802.3 standard, the 802.11 standard defines methods for dealing with collisions and speeds of operation. However, because of the differences in the media (air as opposed to wires), the devices used, the potential mobility of users connected to the network, and the possible wireless network topologies, the 802.11 standards differ significantly from the 802.3 standard.

In addition to providing a solution to the problems created by collisions that occur on a wireless network, the 802.11 standard must deal with other issues specific to the nature of wireless devices and wireless communications in general. For example, wireless devices need to be able to locate other wireless devices, such as APs, and be able to communicate with them. Wireless users are, more often than not, mobile and therefore should be able to move seamlessly from one wireless zone to another as required. Many wireless-enabled devices, such as laptops and handheld computers, use battery power and should be able to conserve power when they are not actively communicating with the network. Wireless communication over the air needs to be secure to mitigate both passive and active attacks.

The original 802.11 standard was developed in 1989 and defines the operation of wireless networks operating in the 2.4 GHz range using either DSSS or FHSS at the physical layer of the OSI model. The standard also defines the use of infrared for wireless communication. The intent of the standard is to provide a wireless equivalent for standards, such as 802.3, that are used for wired networks. DSSS devices that follow the 802.11 standard communicate at speeds of 1 Mbps and 2 Mbps and generally have a range of around 300 feet. Because of the need for higher rates of data transmission and the need to provide more functionality at the MAC layer, other standards were developed by the 802.11 Task Groups (or in some cases, the 802.11 standards were developed from technologies that preceded them).

The IEEE 802.11 standard provides for all the necessary definitions and constructs for wireless networks. Everything from the physical transmission specifications to the authentication negotiation is defined by the standard. Wireless traffic, like its wired counterpart, consists of frames transmitted from one station to another. The primary feature that sets wireless networks apart from wired networks is that at least one end of the communication pair is either a wireless client or a wireless access point.

IEEE 802.11b

The most common standard in use today for wireless networks, the 802.11b standard defines DSSS networks that use the 2.4 GHz ISM band and communicate at speeds of 1, 2, 5.5, and 11 Mbps. The 802.11b standard defines the operation of *only* DSSS devices and is backward compatible with 802.11 DSSS devices. The standard is also concerned only with the physical and MAC layers. Layer 3 and higher protocols are considered payload.

Three frame types are used by 802.11b networks: control, management, and data. Each frame has a distinct function on the wireless network and is put together differently. One thing all 802.11b frames share is the maximum size of 2346 bytes, although they are often fragmented at 1518 bytes as they traverse an AP to communicate with Ethernet networks.

In general, the frame type provides methods for wireless devices to discover, associate (or disassociate), and authenticate with one another; to shift data rates as signals become stronger or weaker; to conserve power by going into sleep mode; to handle collisions and fragmentation; and to enable encryption through WEP. With regard to WEP, we should note that the standard defines the use of only 64-bit (also sometimes referred to as 40-bit, to add to the confusion) encryption, which can cause issues of interoperability between devices from different vendors that use 128-bit or higher encryption.

IEEE 802.11a

In spite of its nomenclature, 802.11a is a more recent standard than 802.11b. The standard defines wireless networks that use the 5 GHz UNII bands. The 802.11a standard supports much higher rates of data transmission than 802.11b. These rates are 6, 9, 12, 16, 18, 24, 36, 48, and 54 Mbps, although higher rates are possible using proprietary technology and a technique known as *rate doubling*.

Unlike 802.11b, 802.11a does not use spread-spectrum and Distributed Quadrature Phase Shift Keying (DQPSK) as a modulation technique at the physical layer; instead, it uses a modulation technique known as Orthogonal Frequency Division Multiplexing (OFDM).

To be 802.11a compliant, devices are only required to support data rates of at least 6, 12, and 24 Mbps; the standard does not require the use of other data rates. Although identical to 802.11b at the MAC layer, 802.11a is *not* backward compatible with 802.11b due to its use of a different frequency band and the use of OFDM at the physical layer, although some vendors are providing solutions to bridge the two standards at the AP.

However, both 802.11a and 802.11b devices can be easily colocated because their frequencies do not interfere with each other, providing a technically easy, but relatively expensive, migration to a pure 802.11a network. At the time of this writing, 802.11a-compliant devices are becoming more common, and their prices are falling quickly. However, even if the prices for 802.11b and 802.11a devices were identical, 802.11a would require more APs and be more expensive than an 802.11b network to achieve the highest possible rates of data transmission because the higher-frequency 5GHz waves attenuate more quickly over distance.

NOTE

If all these wireless networking terms have got your head in a spin, a visit to the 80211-planet Web site might be the cure. See the 802.11b glossary at http://80211-planet.webopedia.com.

IEEE 802.11g

In order to provide both higher data rates (up to 54 Mbps) in the ISM 2.4 GHz bands and backward compatibility with 802.11b, the IEEE 802.11g Task Group members, along with wireless vendors, are working on the specifications of the 802.11g standard. Although 802.11g has been approved as a standard, the specifications for the standard are still in draft form at the time of this writing and are due for completion in late 2002.

To achieve the higher rates of transmission, 802.11g devices use OFDM, in contrast to DQPSK, which is used by 802.11b devices as a modulation technique. However, 802.11g devices are able to automatically switch to DQPSK to communicate with 802.11b devices. At the time of this writing, no 802.11g devices are on the market, although Cisco has announced that its 802.11g-compliant Aironet 1200 will be available in 2003. The 802.11g standard appears to have advantages over 802.11a in terms of providing backward compatibility with 802.11b; however, migrating to and coexistence with 802.11b might still prove problematic due to interference in the widely used 2.4 GHz band. For this reason, it is unclear whether 802.11g will be a popular alternative to 802.11a to achieve higher rates of transmission on wireless networks.

802.11 Communication Modes

The 802.11 standard provides for two modes for wireless clients to communicate: ad hoc and infrastructure. The ad hoc mode is geared toward a network of stations within communication range of each other. Ad hoc networks are created spontaneously between the network participants. In infrastructure mode, APs provide for a more permanent structure for the network. An *infrastructure* consists of one or more APs as well as a distribution system (such as a wired network) behind the APs, which tie the wireless network to the wired network. Figures 7.1 and 7.2 diagram an ad hoc network and an infrastructure network, respectively.

Figure 7.1 An Ad Hoc Network Configuration

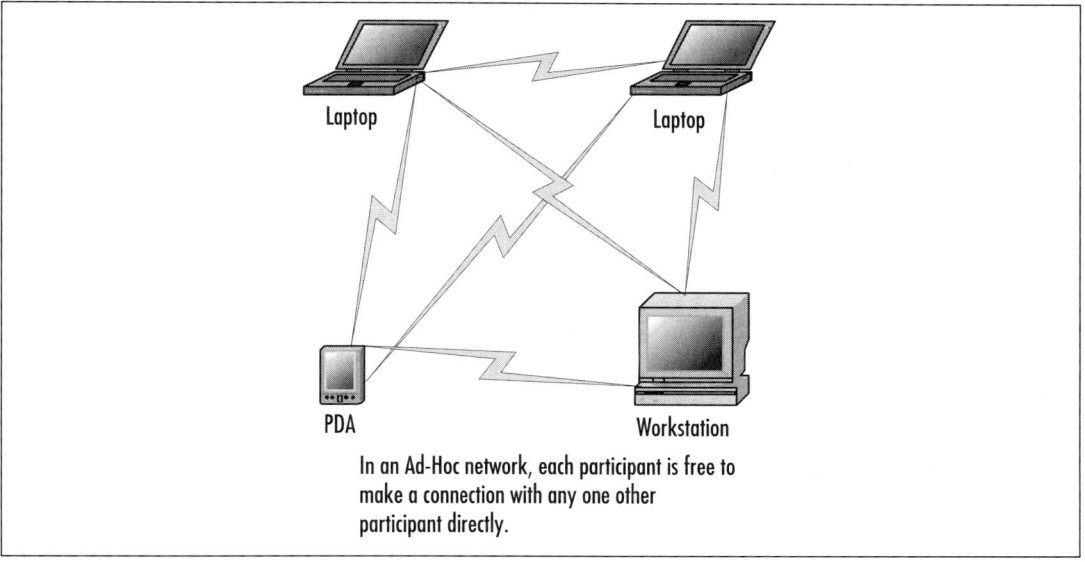

Figure 7.2 Infrastructure Network Configuration

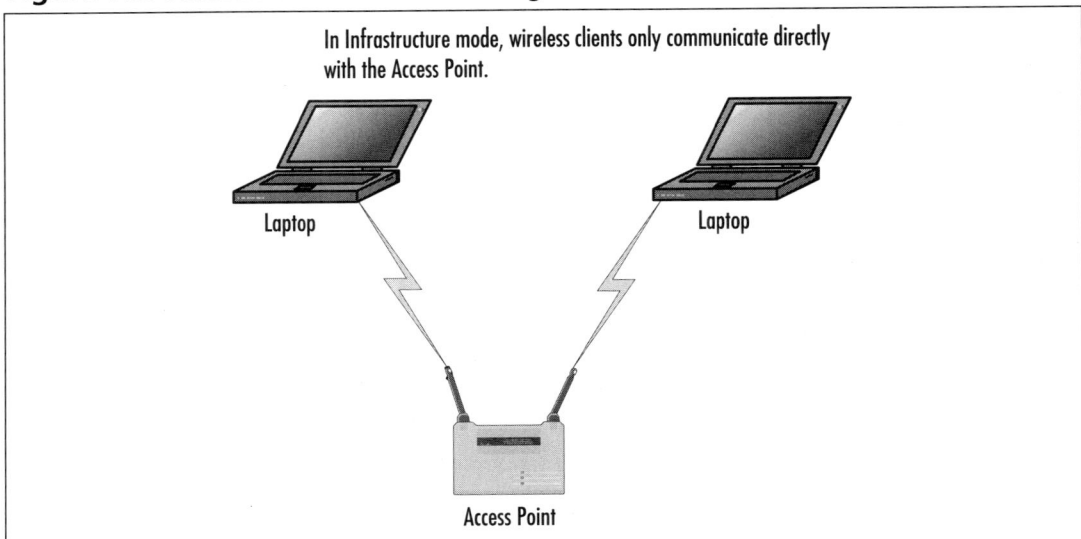

To distinguish different wireless networks from one another, the 802.11 standard defines the Service Set Identifier (SSID). The SSID can be considered the identity element that "glues" together various components of a wireless LAN. Traffic from wireless clients that use one SSID can be distinguished from other wireless traffic using a different SSID. Using the SSID, an AP can determine which traffic is meant for it and which is meant for other wireless networks.

802.11 traffic can be subdivided into three parts:

- Control frames
- Management frames
- Data frames

Control frames include such information as request to send (RTS), clear to send (CTS), and ACK messages. Management frames include beacon frames, probe request/response, authentication frames, and association frames. Data frames are, as the name implies, 802.11 frames that carry data. That data is typically considered network traffic, such as IP encapsulated frames.

Wired Equivalent Privacy

The IEEE 802.11 standard covers the communication between WLAN components. RF poses challenges to privacy in that it travels through and around physical objects. Due to the nature of 802.11 WLANs, the IEEE working group implemented a mechanism to protect the privacy of individual transmissions. The intent was to mirror the privacy found on the WLAN, and the mechanism became known as the Wired Equivalent Privacy protocol, or WEP.

Because WEP utilizes a cryptographic security countermeasure for the fulfillment of its stated goal of privacy, it has the added benefit of becoming an authentication mechanism. This benefit is realized through shared key authentication that allows the encryption and decryption of wireless transmissions. Up to four keys can be defined on an AP or a client. These keys can be rotated to add complexity for a higher-security standard in the WLAN policy.

WEP was never intended to be the absolute authority in wireless security. The IEEE 802.11 standard states that WEP provides for protection from "casual eavesdropping." Instead, the driving force behind WEP is privacy. In cases that require high degrees of security, other mechanisms should be utilized, such as authentication, access control, password protection, and virtual private networks.

Despite its flaws, WEP still offers some level of security, provided that all its features are used properly. This means taking great care in key management, avoiding default options, and ensuring that adequate encryption is enabled at every opportunity.

Proposed improvements in the standard should overcome many of the limitations of the original security options and should make WEP more appealing as a security solution. Additionally, as WLAN technology gains popularity and users clamor for functionality, both the standards committees and the hardware vendors will offer improvements. It is critically important to keep abreast of vendor-related software fixes and changes that improve the overall security posture of a wireless LAN.

With data security enabled in a closed network, the settings on the client for the SSID and the encryption keys have to match the AP when attempting to associate with the network, or the network will fail. The next few sections discuss WEP in its relation to the functionality of the 802.11 standard, including a standard definition of WEP, the privacy created, and the authentication.

WEP provides some security and privacy in transmissions to prevent curious or casual browsers from viewing the contents of the transmissions held between the AP and the clients. In order to gain access, an intruder must be more sophisticated and needs to have specific intent to gain access. Some of the other benefits of implementing WEP include the following:

- All messages have a CRC-32 checksum calculated that provides some degree of integrity.

- Privacy is maintained via the RC4 encryption. Without possession of the secret key, the message cannot be easily decrypted.

- WEP is extremely easy to implement. All that is required is to set the encryption key on the APs and on each client.

- WEP provides a very basic level of security for WLAN applications.

- WEP keys are user definable and unlimited. WEP keys can, and should, be changed often.

Creating Privacy with WEP

WEP provides for several implementations: no encryption, 64-bit encryption, and 128-bit encryption. Clearly, no encryption means no privacy. When WEP is set to no encryption, transmissions are sent in cleartext, and they can be viewed by any wireless sniffing application that has access to the RF signal propagated in the WLAN (unless some other encryption mechanism, such as IPSec, is used). In the case of the 64- and 128-bit varieties (just as with password length), the greater the number of characters (bits), the stronger the encryption. The initial configuration of the AP includes the setup of the shared key. This shared key can be in the form of either alphanumeric or hexadecimal strings and must be matched on the client.

WEP uses the RC4 encryption algorithm, a stream cipher developed by Ron Rivest of RSA Security (rsasecurity.com). Both the sender and receiver use the stream cipher to create identical pseudorandom strings from a known shared key. The process entails having the sender logically XOR the plaintext transmission with the stream cipher to produce the ciphertext. The receiver takes the shared key and identical stream and reverses the process to gain the plaintext transmission.

NOTE

XOR, or exclusive OR, is a Boolean logic operator that returns a value of TRUE only if one of its operands is true, as opposed to an inclusive OR, which returns a value of TRUE if either of its operands are true.

The Boolean logic involved in the WEP process can become extremely complex and is not something that most wireless network users, administrators included, will ever get into. The discussion is presented here only for the sake of briefly explaining how WEP functions, which helps to understand how it can be cracked with the right tools and the right amount of time. The steps in the process are as follows:

1. The plaintext message is run through an integrity check algorithm (the 802.11 standard specifies the use of CRC-32) to produce an integrity check value (ICV).

2. The ICV is appended to the end of the original plaintext message.

3. A "random" 24-bit initialization vector (IV) is generated and *prepended to* (added to the beginning of) the secret key which is then input to the RC4 Key Scheduling Algorithm (KSA) to generate a seed value for the WEP pseudo-random number generator (PRNG).

4. The WEP PRNG outputs the encrypting cipher stream.

5. This cipher stream is then XORed with the plaintext/ICV message to produce the WEP ciphertext.

6. The ciphertext is then prepended with the IV (in plaintext), encapsulated, and transmitted.

A new IV is used for each frame to prevent the key's reuse weakening the encryption. This means that for each string generated, a different value is used for the RC4 key. Although this is a secure policy in itself, its implementation in WEP is flawed because of the nature of the 24-bit space. The space is so small with respect to the potential set of IVs that in a short period of time, all keys are reused. When this happens, two different messages are encrypted with the same IV and key, and the two messages can be XORed with each other using specially crafted WEP cracking tools to cancel out the key stream, allowing an attacker who knows the contents of one message to easily figure out the contents of the other. Unfortunately, this weakness is the same for both the 40- and 128-bit encryption levels because both use the 24-bit IV.

To protect against some rudimentary attacks that insert known text into the stream to attempt to reveal the key stream, WEP incorporates a checksum in each frame. Any frame not found to be valid through the checksum is discarded.

Authentication

There are two authentication methods in the 802.11 standard:

- Open authentication
- Shared-key authentication

Open authentication is most precisely described as device-oriented authentication and can be considered a null authentication; all requests are granted. Without WEP, open authentication leaves the WLAN wide open to any client who knows the SSID. With WEP enabled, the WEP secret key becomes the indirect authenticator.

The *shared-key authentication* process shown in Figure 7.3 is a four-step process that begins when the AP receives the validated request for association. After the AP receives the request, a series of management frames is transmitted between the stations to produce the authentication. This includes the use of the cryptographic mechanisms employed by WEP as a validation. The four steps break down in the following manner:

1. The requestor (the client) sends a request for association.
2. The authenticator (the AP) receives the request and responds by producing a random challenge text and transmitting it back to the requestor.
3. The requestor receives the transmission, encrypts the challenge with the secret key, and transmits the encrypted challenge back to the authenticator.
4. The authenticator decrypts the challenge text and compares the values against the original. If they match, the requestor is authenticated. On the other hand, if the requestor doesn't have the shared key, the cipher stream cannot be reproduced. Therefore, the plaintext cannot be discovered, and theoretically, the transmission is secured.

Figure 7.3 Shared-Key Authentication

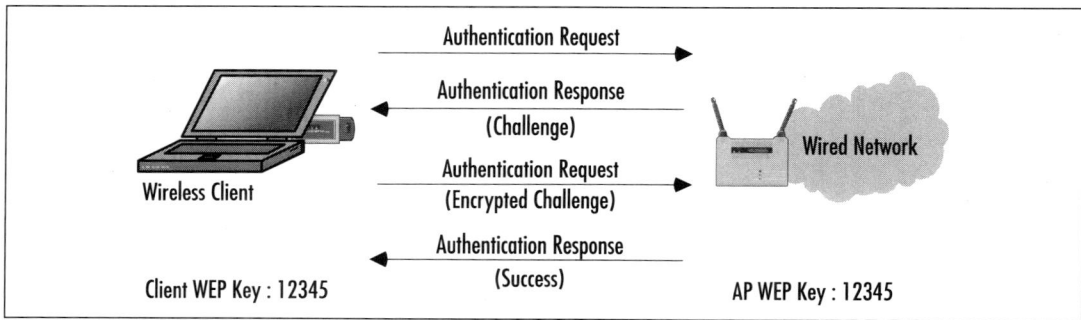

One of the greatest weaknesses in shared-key authentication is the fact that it provides an attacker with enough information to try to crack the WEP secret key. The challenge, which is sent from authenticator to requestor, is sent in the clear. The requesting client then transmits the same challenge, encrypted using the WEP secret key, back to the authenticator. An attacker who captures both of these packets has two pieces to a three-piece puzzle: the cleartext challenge and the encrypted ciphertext of that challenge. The algorithm, RC4, is also known. All that is missing is the secret key.

To determine the key, the attacker simply tries a brute-force search of the potential key space using a dictionary attack. At each step, the attacker tries to decrypt the encrypted challenge with a dictionary word as the secret key. The result is then compared against the authenticator's challenge. If the two match, the attacker has determined the secret key. In cryptography, this attack is called a *known-plaintext attack* and is the primary reason that shared-key authentication is considered slightly weaker than open authentication.

802.1x Authentication

The current IEEE 802.11b standard is severely limited because it is available only for the current open and shared key authentication scheme, which is nonextensible. To address the weaknesses in the authentication mechanisms we've discussed, several vendors (including Cisco and Microsoft) adopted the IEEE 802.1x authentication mechanism for wireless networks.

The IEEE 802.1x standard was created for the purpose of providing a security framework for port-based access control that resides in the upper layers of the protocol stack. The most common method for port-based access control is to enable new authentication and key management methods without changing current network devices. The benefits that are the end result of this work include the following:

- There is a significant decrease in hardware cost and complexity.
- There are more options, allowing administrators to pick and choose their security solutions.
- The "latest and greatest" security technology can be installed and it should still work with the existing infrastructure.
- You can respond quickly to security issues as they arise.

Exam Warning

The 802.1x standard typically is relevant to wireless networks due to the fact that it is quickly becoming the standard method of securely authenticating on a wireless network. However, do not confuse 802.1x with 802.11x.

When a client device connects to a port on an 802.1x capable AP, the AP port can determine the authenticity of the devices. Before discussing the workings of the 802.1x standard, we must define some terminology. In the context of 802.1x, the following terms have these meanings:

- **Port** A port is a single point of connection to the network.
- **Port access entity (PAE)** The PAE controls the algorithms and protocols that are associated with the authentication mechanisms for a port.
- **Authenticator PAE** The authenticator PAE enforces authentication before it will allow access to resources located off that port.
- **Supplicant PAE** The supplicant PAE tries to access the services that are allowed by the authenticator.

- **Authentication server** The authentication server is used to verify the supplicant PAE. It decides whether or not the supplicant is authorized to access the authenticator.

- **Extensible Authentication Protocol Over LAN (EAPOL)** The 802.1x standard defines a standard for encapsulating Extensible Authentication Protocol (EAP) messages so that they can be handled directly by a LAN MAC service. 802.1x tries to make authentication more encompassing rather than enforcing specific mechanisms on the devices. For this reason, 802.11x uses EAP to receive authentication information.

- **Extensible Authentication Protocol Over Wireless (EAPOW)** When EAPOL messages are encapsulated over 802.11 wireless frames, they are known as EAPOW.

Head of the Class…

So What Are 802.1x and 802.11x, Exactly?

Wireless technology provides convenience and mobility, but it also poses massive security challenges for network administrators, engineers, and security administrators. Security for 802.11 networks can be broken into three distinct components:

- The authentication mechanism
- The authentication algorithm
- Data frame encryption

Current authentication in the 802.11 IEEE standard is focused more on wireless LAN connectivity than on verifying user or station identity. Since wireless can potentially scale so high in terms of the number of possible users, you might want to consider a way to centralize user authentication, and this is where the IEEE 802.1x standard comes into play.

The 802.1x works in a similar fashion both for EAPOL and EAPOW. As shown in Figure 7.4, the EAP supplicant (in this case, the wireless client) communicates with the AP over an "uncontrolled port." The AP sends an EAP-request/identity to the supplicant as well as a Remote Access Dial-In User Service (RADIUS)-access-request to the RADIUS access server. The supplicant responds with an identity packet, and the RADIUS server sends a challenge based on the identity packets sent from the supplicant. The supplicant provides its credentials in the EAP-response that the AP forwards to the RADIUS server. If the response is valid and the credentials are validated, the RADIUS server sends a RADIUS-access-accept to the AP, which then allows the supplicant to communicate over a "controlled" port. This is communicated by the AP to the supplicant in the EAP-success packet.

Figure 7.4 EAPOL Traffic Flow

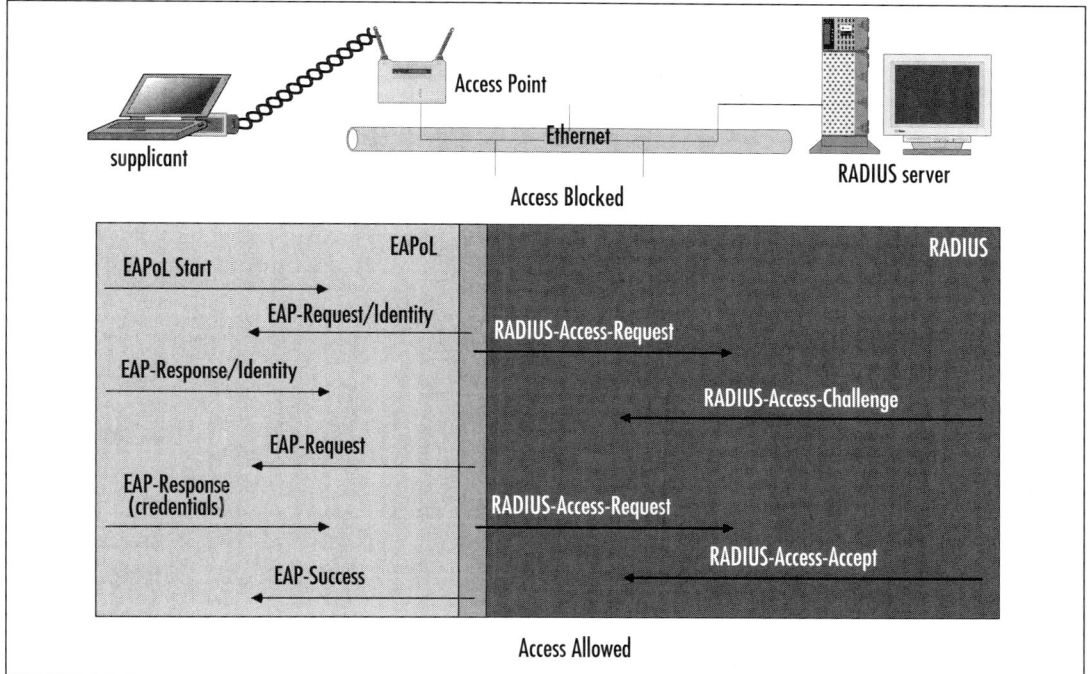

User Identification and Strong Authentication

With the addition of the 802.1x standard, clients are identified by usernames, not by the MAC addresses of the devices. This design not only enhances security, it also streamlines the process for authentication, authorization, and accountability for the network. The 802.1x standard was designed so that it could support extended forms of authentication, using password methods (such as one-time passwords, or GSS_API mechanisms such as Kerberos) and nonpassword methods (such as biometrics, Internet Key Exchange [IKE], and smartcards).

Dynamic Key Derivation

The 802.1x standard allows for the creation of per-user session keys. With 802.1x, WEP keys do not need to be kept at the client device or AP. These WEP keys will be dynamically created at the client for every session, thus making it more secure. The Global key, like a broadcast WEP key, can be encrypted using a unicast session key and then sent from the AP to the client in a much more secure manner.

Mutual Authentication

The 802.1x standard and EAP provide for a mutual authentication capability. This capability makes the clients and the authentication servers mutually authenticating end points and assists in the mitigation of attacks from man-in-the-middle types of devices. Any of the following EAP methods provides for mutual authentication:

- **TLS** This requires that the server supply a certificate and establish that it has possession of the private key.
- **IKE** This requires that the server show possession of a preshared key or private key. (This can be considered certificate authentication.)
- **GSS_API (Kerberos)** This requires that the server can demonstrate knowledge of the session key.

Per-Packet Authentication

EAP can support per-packet authentication and integrity protection, but this authentication and integrity protection are not extended to all types of EAP messages. For example, negative acknowledgment (NAK) and notification messages are not able to use per-packet authentication and integrity. Per-packet authentication and integrity protection work for the following (packet is encrypted unless otherwise noted):

- TLS and IKE derived session key
- TLS ciphersuite negotiations (not encrypted)
- IKE ciphersuite negotiations
- Kerberos tickets
- Success and failure messages that use a derived session key (through WEP)

Damage & Defense...

Preventing Dictionary Attacks Using EAP

EAP can be employed in your wireless network to add security by preventing offline dictionary attacks against network passwords. When choosing an EAP type, consider the use of EAP-TLS. EAP-TLS is a PKI based authentication method that uses digital certificates for user verification and provides for mutual authentication without the need for username and password entry, thereby mitigating the possibility of a dictionary attack. EAP-MD5 is not recommended for securing wireless connections because it relies on a standard challenge/response authentication method using a username and password combination, which opens you up to dictionary attacks which are precisely what you are attempting to prevent.

Test Day Tip

You might find it helpful to write out a table showing the various authentication methods used in 802.11 networks (such as open authentication, shared-key authentication, and 802.1x authentication) with the various properties that each of these authentication methods require. This table will help keep them straight in your mind when you take the test.

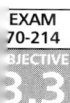

Wireless LAN Security Issues

In general, attacks on wireless networks fall into four basic categories: passive attacks, active attacks, man-in-the-middle attacks, and jamming attacks. After we have examined each of these attack types, we will spend some time examining the problems associated with the current wireless security solutions.

Passive Attacks on Wireless Networks

A *passive attack* occurs when someone listens to or eavesdrops on network traffic. Armed with a wireless network adapter that supports promiscuous mode, the eavesdropper can capture network traffic for analysis using easily available tools, such as Network Monitor in Microsoft products, TCPDump in Linux-based products, or AirSnort (developed for Linux, but Windows drivers can be written for it).

A passive attack on a wireless network might not be malicious in nature. In fact, many in the war-driving community claim their war-driving activities are benign or "educational" in nature. (*War driving* is the act of searching for wireless networks—via car, by foot, or by other vehicle—by means of a roaming wireless client.) Wireless communication takes place on unlicensed public frequencies, which anyone can use. This makes it more difficult to protect a wireless network from passive attacks. However, by its very definition, a *passive* attack can not be an attack at all. The supposed "passive attacker" is merely a bystander. The relative "passivity" of the interaction completely changes when there is criminal intent to either capture or change data on a network the user is not explicitly authorized to access.

Passive attacks are, by their very nature, difficult to detect. If an administrator is using the same DHCP scope and subnet to serve clients on the wireless network (this is not recommended), he or she might notice that an unfamiliar MAC address has acquired an IP address from this scope in the DHCP server logs. Then again, he or she might not notice this. See the "Using a Separate Subnet for Wireless Networks" section later in this chapter for a solution to the DHCP problem. Perhaps the administrator notices a suspicious-looking car sporting an antenna protruding from one of its windows. If the car is parked on private property, the driver could be asked to move or possibly charged with trespassing. However, the legal response might be severely limited, depending on the laws in your jurisdiction. Circumstances under which the war driver is susceptible to being charged with a data-related crime depends entirely on the country or state in which the activity takes place.

Passive attacks on wireless networks are extremely common, almost to the point of being ubiquitous. Detecting and reporting on wireless networks has become a popular hobby for many wireless war-driving enthusiasts. In fact, this activity is so popular that a new term, *war plugging*, has emerged to describe the behavior of people who actually want to advertise both the availability of an AP and the services they offer by configuring their SSIDs with text such as "Get_food_here!"

War Driving

Most war-driving enthusiasts use a popular freeware program called NetStumbler, available from www.netstumbler.com. The NetStumbler program works primarily with wireless network adapters that use the Hermes chipset due to its ability to detect multiple APs that are within range and WEP, among other features. (A list of supported adapters is available at the NetStumber Web site.) The most common card that uses the Hermes chipset for use with NetStumbler is the ORiNOCO gold card. Another advantage of the ORiNOCO card is that it supports the addition of an external antenna, which can extend the range of a wireless network by many orders of magnitude, depending on the antenna.

Head of the Class…

The Legal Status of War Driving and Responsibility of Wireless Network Owners and Operators

Standard disclaimer: The law is a living and dynamic entity. What might appear to be legal today could become illegal tomorrow, and vice versa. And what might be legal in one country or state could be illegal in another. Furthermore, the legal status of any particular activity is complicated by the fact that such status arises from a number of sources, such as statutes, regulations, and case law precedents. The following text summarizes some of the current popular thinking with regard to the legal status of war driving and related activities in the United States. However, you should not assume that the following in any way constitutes authoritative legal advice or is definitive with regard to the legal status of war driving.

If we define war driving as the relatively benign activity of configuring a wireless device to receive signals (interference) from other wireless devices and then moving around to detect those signals without the presence of an ulterior or malicious motive on the part of the war driver, the activity is most probably legal in most jurisdictions. (Whether or not it is ethical is a separate issue.) Most of this thinking is based on Part 15 of the Federal Communications

Continued

Commission (FCC) regulations, which can be found at www.access.gpo.gov/nara/cfr/waisidx_00/47cfr15_00.html. In the regulations, wireless devices fall under the definition of Class B devices. Class B devices must not cause harmful interference, and they must accept interference they receive, including interference that harms operations. (In Canada, the situation is identical, except that Class B devices are known as Category I devices. For more information on Canadian regulations regarding low-power radio devices, see the Industry Canada Web site at http://strategis.ic.gc.ca/SSG/sf01320e.html.) In other words, simply accepting a signal from another wireless device could be considered a kind of interference that the device must be able to perform.

So far, war driving appears legal from this point of view. However, this has been the case in the past only because little or no law has specifically addressed this situation, which involves computer-related transmission of data. On the other hand, cordless phones use the same ISM or UNII frequencies as wireless networks, but wiretap laws in place for quite a while make it illegal to intercept and receive signals from cordless phones without the consent of all the parties involved, unless the interception is conducted by a law enforcement agency in possession of valid warrant. (In Canada, the situation is a little different and is based on a reasonable expectation of privacy. Savvy dope peddlers in Canada know better than to use cordless phones to make their drug deals.)

No one to my knowledge has been charged with violating FCC regulations with regard to war driving and the passive reception of computer-related data over the ISM or UNII bands. However, in the wake of September 11, 2001, both the U.S. federal government and state governments have passed new criminal laws addressing breach of computer network security. Some of these laws are written in a way that makes illegal *any* access to network communications without authorization. Although many of the statutes have not yet been tested in court, it is safest to take the conservative path and avoid intentionally accessing any network that you don't have permission to access.

The issue gets a little more complicated when we consider the implications of associating with a wireless network. If the wireless network administrator has configured a DHCP server on the wireless network and allows any wireless station to authenticate and associate with the wireless network, any wireless user in the vicinity, not just war drivers, could find that the wireless station has automatically received IP address configuration and has associated with the wireless network, simply by being in close proximity to the network. That is, without any intent on his or her part, the person using a wireless-equipped computer is able to use the services of the wireless network, including access to the Internet. Assume that the person used this automatic configuration to gain access to the Internet through the wireless network. Technically, this could be considered theft of service in some jurisdictions, although the person has been, for all intents and purposes, welcomed onto the wireless network.

Continued

Regardless of this "welcome," however, if the laws in that jurisdiction prohibit all unauthorized access, the person may be charged. Most such statutes set the required culpable mental state at "intentional or knowing." Thus, if the person knows that he or she is accessing a network and does not have permission to do so, the elements of the offense have been satisfied.

Where war driving almost always crosses the line from a "semi-legal" to an illegal activity appears to be when the war driver collects and analyzes data with malicious intent and when the war driver causes undesirable interference with the operation of the network. Cracking WEP keys and other encryption on the network is almost universally illegal. In this case, it is presumed that malicious intent to steal data or services or interfere with operations could be established, since it requires a great deal of effort, time, and planning to break into an encrypted network.

From the point of view of the administrator of a wireless network, the onus to exercise due diligence to protect the wireless network falls squarely on him or her, just as it is the responsibility of corporate security personnel to ensure that tangible property belonging to the company is secured and safe from theft, regardless of laws that prohibit stealing. That is, it is up to the administrator to ensure that the network's data is not radiating freely into space in such a way that anyone can receive it and interpret it using only licensed wireless devices. This much is clear: Administrators who don't take care to protect their wireless networks put their companies at risk. This is true regardless of whether or not laws exist for the purpose of mitigating that risk.

For more information about legal aspects of war driving and other computer-related criminal offenses, see *Scene of the Cybercrime: Computer Forensics Handbook*, published by Syngress Publishing (ISBN 1-931836-65-5, 2002).

NOTE

War drivers often make their own Yagi-type (tubular or cylindrical) antenna. Instructions for doing so are easy to find on the Internet, and effective antennas have been made from such items as Pringles potato chip cans. Another type of antenna that can be easily homemade is the dipole, which is basically a piece of wire of a length that's a multiple of the wavelength, cut in the center and attached to a piece of cable that is connected to the wireless network interface card (NIC).

A disadvantage of the Hermes chipset is that it doesn't support promiscuous mode, so it cannot be used to sniff network traffic. For that purpose, you need a wireless network adapter that supports the PRISM2 chipset. The majority of wireless network adapters targeted for the consumer market use this chipset (for example, the Linksys WPC network adapters). Sophisticated war drivers arm themselves with both types of cards—one for discovering wireless networks and the other for capturing the traffic.

In spite of the fact that NetStumbler is free, it is a sophisticated and feature-rich product that is excellent for performing wireless site surveys, for legitimate purposes or otherwise. Not only can it provide detailed information on the wireless networks it detects, it can be used in combination with a global positioning system (GPS) to provide exact details on the latitude and longitude of the detected wireless networks. Figure 7.5 shows the interface of a typical NetStumbler session.

Figure 7.5 Discovering Wireless LANs Using NetStumbler

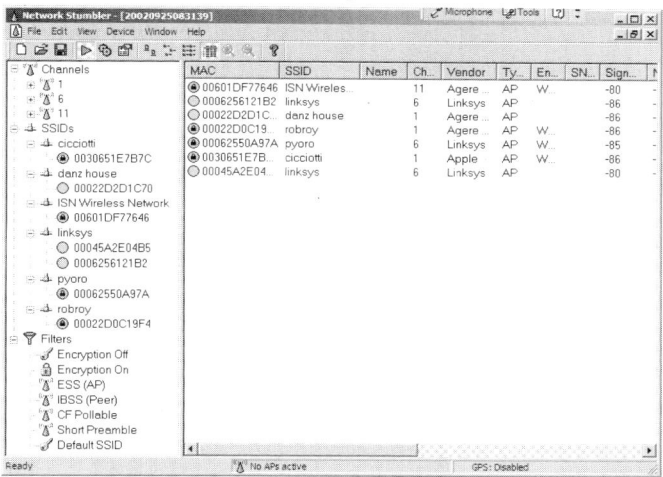

As you can see from Figure 7.5, NetStumbler displays information on the SSID, the channel, and the manufacturer of the wireless AP. A few things are particularly noteworthy about this session. The first is that a couple of APs are still configured with the default SSID supplied by the manufacturer, which should always be changed to a non-default value on setup and configuration. Another is that at least one network uses a SSID that could provide a clue about the entity that has implemented it; again, this is not a good practice when configuring SSIDs. Finally, we can see which of these networks have implemented WEP.

If the network administrator has been kind enough to provide a clue about the company in the SSID or is not encrypting traffic with WEP, the potential eavesdropper's job is made a great deal easier. Using a tool such as NetStumbler is only a preliminary step for the attacker. After discovering the SSID and other information, the attacker can connect to the wireless network to sniff and capture network traffic. This network traffic can reveal a plethora of information about the network and the company that uses it.

For example, looking at the network traffic, the attacker can determine what DNS servers are being used, the default homepages configured on browsers, network names, logon traffic, and so on. The attacker can use this information to determine if the network is of sufficient interest to proceed further with other attacks. Furthermore, if the network is using WEP, the attacker can, given enough time, capture a sufficient amount of traffic to crack the encryption.

NetStumbler works on networks that are configured as *open systems*. This means that the wireless network indicates it exists and will respond with the value of its SSID to other wireless devices when they send out a radio beacon with an "empty set" SSID. This does not mean that the wireless network can be easily compromised, *if* other security measures have been implemented.

To defend against the use of NetStumbler and other programs to easily detect a wireless network, administrators should configure the wireless network as a *closed system*. This means that the AP will not respond to "empty set" SSID beacons and will consequently be "invisible" to programs such as NetStumbler, which rely on this technique to discover wireless networks. However, it is still possible to capture the "raw" 802.11b frames and decode them through the use of programs such as Ethereal and Wild Packet's AiroPeek to determine this information. RF spectrum analyzers can be used to discover the presence of wireless networks. Notwithstanding this weakness of closed systems, you should choose wireless APs that support this feature.

Sniffing

Originally conceived as a legitimate network and traffic analysis tool, *sniffing* remains one of the most effective techniques in attacking a wireless network, whether it's to map the network as part of a target reconnaissance, to grab passwords, or to capture unencrypted data.

Sniffing is the electronic form of eavesdropping on the communications that computers transmit across networks. In early networks, the equipment that connected machines allowed every machine on the network to see the traffic of all others. These devices, repeaters and hubs, were very successful at getting machines connected, but they allowed an attacker easy access to all traffic on the network because the attacker only needed to connect to one point to see the entire network's traffic.

Wireless networks function very similarly to the original repeaters and hubs. Every communication across the wireless network is viewable to anyone who happens to be listening to the network. In fact, the person who is listening does not even need to be associated with the network in order to sniff!

The hacker has many tools available to attack and monitor a wireless network. A few of these tools are AiroPeek (www.wildpackets.com/products/airopeek) in Windows; Ethereal in Windows, UNIX, or Linux; and TCPDump or ngrep (http://ngrep.sourceforg.net) in a UNIX or Linux environment. These tools work well for sniffing both wired and wireless networks.

All these software packages function by putting your network card in what is called *promiscuous mode*. When the NIC is in this mode, every packet that goes past the interface is captured and displayed within the application window. If the attacker is able to acquire a WEP key, he or she can then utilize features within AiroPeek and Ethereal to decrypt either live or post-capture data.

Active Attacks on Wireless Networks

Once an attacker has gained sufficient information from the passive attack, the hacker can then launch an active attack against the network. There is a potentially large number of active attacks that a hacker can launch against a wireless network. For the most part, these attacks are identical to the kinds of active attacks that are encountered on wired networks. These include, but are not limited to, unauthorized access, spoofing, denial of service (DoS), and flooding attacks, as well as the introduction of *malware* (malicious software) and the theft of devices.

With the rise in popularity of wireless networks, new variations of traditional attacks specific to wireless networks have emerged, along with specific terms to describe them, such as *drive-by spamming,* in which a spammer sends out tens or hundreds of thousands of spam messages using a compromised wireless network.

Due to the nature of wireless networks and the weaknesses of WEP, unauthorized access and spoofing are the most common threats to wireless networks. *Spoofing* occurs when an attacker is able to use an unauthorized station to impersonate an authorized station on a wireless network. A common way to protect a wireless network against unauthorized access is to use MAC filtering to allow only clients that possess valid MAC addresses access to the wireless network. The list of allowable MAC addresses can be configured on the AP, or it can be configured on a RADIUS server with which the AP communicates.

However, regardless of the technique used to implement MAC filtering, it is a relatively easy matter to change the MAC address of a wireless device through software, to impersonate a valid station. In Windows, this is accomplished with a simple edit of the Registry, in UNIX through a root shell command. MAC addresses are sent in the clear on wireless networks, so it is also a relatively easy matter to discover authorized addresses.

WEP can be implemented to provide more protection against authentication spoofing through the use of shared-key authentication. However, as we discussed earlier, shared-key authentication creates an additional vulnerability. Because shared-key authentication makes visible both a plaintext challenge and the resulting ciphertext version of it, it is possible to use this information to spoof authentication to a closed network.

Once the attacker has authenticated and associated with the wireless network, he or she can then run port scans, use special tools to dump user lists and passwords, impersonate users, connect to shares, and, in general, create havoc on the network through DoS and flooding attacks. These DoS attacks can be traditional in nature, such as a *ping flood*, *SYN*, *fragment*, or *distributed DoS (DDoS)* attacks, or they can be specific to wireless networks through the placement and use of *rogue APs* to prevent wireless traffic from being forwarded properly (similar to the practice of router spoofing on wired networks).

Spoofing and Unauthorized Access

The combination of weaknesses in WEP and the nature of wireless transmission has highlighted the art of *spoofing*, or interception, as a real threat to wireless network security. Some well-publicized weaknesses in user authentication using WEP have made authentication spoofing just one of an equally well-tested number of exploits by attackers.

One definition of spoofing is an attacker's ability to trick the network equipment into thinking that the address from which a connection is coming is one of the valid and allowed machines from its network. Attackers can accomplish this trick in several ways, the easiest of which is to simply redefine the MAC address of the attacker's wireless or network card to a valid MAC address. This can be accomplished in Windows through a simple Registry edit. Several wireless providers also have an option to define the MAC address for each wireless connection from within the client manager application that is provided with the interface.

There are several reasons that an attacker would spoof. If the network allows only valid interfaces through MAC or IP address filtering, an attacker would need to determine a valid MAC or IP address to be able to communicate on the network. Once that is accomplished, the attacker could then reprogram his or her interface with that information, allowing the attacker to connect to the network by impersonating a valid machine.

IEEE 802.11 networks introduce a new form of spoofing: authentication spoofing. As described in a paper, *Intercepting Mobile Communications: The Insecurities of 802.11*, the authors Borisov, Goldberg, and Wagner identified a way to utilize weaknesses within WEP and the authentication process to spoof authentication into a closed network. The process of authentication, as defined by IEEE 802.11, is very simple. In a shared-key configuration, the AP sends out a 128-byte random string in a cleartext message to the workstation that is attempting to authenticate. The workstation then encrypts the message with the shared key and returns the encrypted message to the AP. If the message matches what the AP is expecting, the workstation is authenticated onto the network and access is allowed.

As described in the paper, if an attacker has knowledge of both the original plaintext and the ciphertext messages, it is possible to create a forged encrypted message. By sniffing the wireless network, an attacker is able to accumulate many authentication requests, each of which includes the original plaintext message and the returned ciphertext-encrypted reply. From this information, the attacker can easily identify the key stream used to encrypt the response message. The attacker can then use the key stream to forge an authentication message that the AP will accept as a proper authentication.

Notes from the Underground...

MAC Spoofing

For some time after it was introduced into production APs, administrators actually believed that MAC filtering was an effective solution on its own, without using WEP or any other solutions. Taking that train of thought one step further, many administrators actually believed it was more secure to use only MAC filtering for security on their wireless networks. As they found out shortly thereafter, nothing could be further from the truth. Let's look at two different scenarios in which MAC filtering is being used to get an idea of its rightful place in the wireless security arena.

The first scenario involves a small three-node wireless network that you have established in your house to allow your children's computers access to your cable modem connection as well as allowing you to work on your portable computer on the back deck—all without having to run CAT5 cable around the house to various locations. You have implemented MAC filtering but not WEP on your AP. Are you completely secure? Not at all. Are you secure enough? It depends on your interpretation of secure. Let's say now that you have implemented WEP as well on your small home network. Now are you secure? Yes. Why? The odds of someone parking themselves in your driveway or otherwise close enough to your house for a long enough period of time (several days in a small network, several hours in a large network) to capture enough traffic to crack your WEP key is unlikely. In this case, you have put together a fairly effective protective mechanism to keep casual war drivers and most script kiddies—not to mention your next-door neighbor who just wants to ride on your cable modem's bandwidth for a while—off your wireless network.

Now consider the scenario in which you are building a large enterprise wireless network for a hospital. Not only do you need to provide wireless access in a large portion of the hospital building itself, you also need to provide wireless network access to a small outpatient building 500 yards away from the main hospital building itself. Would you rely on only MAC filtering to ensure security in this case? Probably not. Just the same, you will probably be looking

Continued

> for a more robust and secure authentication and authorization mechanism than WEP, such as LEAP with a RADIUS server using TKIP to protect the network transmissions themselves.
>
> The moral of this discussion is, if you rely on simple protective measures to keep your wireless network secure, it will be just that much simpler for an attacker to break through your plan and gain access to your wired network. In short, use every possible means at your disposal to secure wireless networks without adding undue management traffic that causes the wireless network to be a nonviable solution. In addition, consider the use of wireless demilitarized zones (DMZs) and virtual LANs (VLANs) to further segregate wireless traffic from your protected and trusted network backbone.

The wireless hacker does not need many complex tools to succeed in spoofing a MAC address. In many cases, these changes either are features of the wireless manufacturers or can be easily changed through a Windows Registry modification or through Linux system utilities. Once a valid MAC address is identified, the attacker needs only to reconfigure his device to trick the AP into thinking he or she is a valid user.

The ability to forge authentication onto a wireless network is a complex process. No known "off the shelf" packages provide these services. Attackers need to either create their own tool or take the time to decrypt the secret key using AirSnort or WEPCrack.

If the attacker is using Windows 2000 and his network card supports reconfiguring the MAC address, there is another way to reconfigure this information. A card supporting this feature can be changed through the System Control Panel.

Once the attacker is utilizing a valid MAC address, he is able to access any resource available from the wireless network. If WEP is enabled, the attacker must either identify the WEP secret key or capture the key through malware or by stealing the user's notebook.

Denial of Service and Flooding Attacks

The nature of wireless transmission, especially via the use of spread-spectrum technology, makes a wireless network especially vulnerable to *denial of service (DoS)* attacks. The equipment needed to launch such an attack is freely available and very affordable. In fact, many homes and offices contain the equipment that is necessary to deny service to their wireless networks.

A denial of service occurs when an attacker has engaged most of the resources a host or network has available, rendering it unavailable to legitimate users. One of the original DoS attacks is known as a *ping flood*. A ping flood utilizes misconfigured equipment along with bad "features" within TCP/IP to cause a large number of hosts or devices to send an ICMP echo (ping) to a specified target. When the attack occurs, it tends to use a large portion of the resources of both the network connection and the host being attacked. This makes it very difficult for valid end users to access the host for normal business purposes.

In a wireless network, several items can cause a similar disruption of service. Probably the easiest method is through a conflict within the wireless spectrum, caused by different devices attempting to use the same frequency. Many new wireless telephones use the same frequency as 802.11 networks. Through either intentional or unintentional uses of another device that uses the 2.4 GHz frequency, a simple telephone call could prevent all wireless users from accessing the network.

Another possible attack occurs through a massive number of invalid (or valid) authentication requests, known as *flooding*. If the AP is tied up with thousands of spoofed authentication attempts, authorized users attempting to authenticate themselves would have major difficulties acquiring a valid session.

As demonstrated earlier, the attacker has many tools available to hijack network connections. If a hacker is able to spoof the machines of a wireless network into thinking that the attacker's machine is their default gateway, not only will the attacker be able to intercept all traffic destined for the wired network, but she would also be able to prevent any of the wireless network machines from accessing the wired network. To do this, the hacker needs only to spoof the AP and not forward connections to the end destination, preventing all wireless users from doing valid wireless activities.

Not much effort is needed to create a wireless DoS. In fact, many users create these situations with the equipment found within their homes or offices. In a small apartment building, you could find several APs as well as many wireless telephones, all of which transmit on the same frequency. These users could easily inadvertently create DoS attacks on their own networks as well as those of their neighbors.

A hacker who wants to launch a DoS attack against a network with a flood of authentication strings doesn't even need to be a well-skilled programmer in most cases. Many tools are available to create this type of attack, so even the most unskilled of Black Hats, the *script kiddie*, can launch this type of attack with little or no knowledge of how it works or why.

Many apartments and older office buildings are not wired for the high-tech networks in use today. To add to the problem, if many individuals are setting up their own wireless networks without coordinating the installations, many problems can occur that will be difficult to detect.

Only a limited number of frequencies are available to 802.11 networks. In fact, once the frequency is chosen, it does not change until it's manually reconfigured. Considering these problems, it is not hard to imagine the following situation occurring.

Say that a person purchases a wireless AP and several network cards for his home network. When he gets home to his apartment and configures his network, he is extremely happy with how well wireless networking actually works. Then suddenly none of the machines on the wireless network are able to communicate. After waiting on hold for 45 minutes to get through to the tech support phone line of the vendor who made the device, he finds that the network has magically started working again, so he hangs up.

Later that week, the same problem occurs, except that this time he decides to wait on hold when he calls tech support. While waiting, he goes onto his porch and begins discussing his frustration with his neighbor. During the conversation, his neighbor's kids come out and say that their wireless network is not working.

So they begin to do a few tests (while still waiting on hold, of course). First, the man's neighbor turns off his AP (which is usually off unless the kids are online, to "protect" their network). When this is done, the original person's wireless network starts working again. Then they turn on the neighbor's AP and his network stops working again.

At this point, a tech support rep finally answers and the caller describes what has happened. The tech support representative has seen this situation several times and informs the user that he will need to change the frequency used in the device to another channel. He explains that the neighbor's network is utilizing the same channel, causing the two networks to conflict. Once the caller changes the frequency, everything starts working properly.

Man-in-the-Middle Attacks on Wireless Networks

Placing a rogue access point within range of wireless stations is a wireless-specific variation of a man-in-the-middle attack. If the attacker knows the SSID the network uses (which, as we have seen, is easily discoverable) and the rogue AP has enough strength, wireless users have no way of knowing that they are connecting to an unauthorized AP.

Using a rogue AP, an attacker can gain valuable information about the wireless network, such as authentication requests, the secret key that is in use, and so on. Often, the attacker will set up a laptop with two wireless adapters, in which one card is used by the rogue AP and the other is used to forward requests through a wireless bridge to the legitimate AP. With a sufficiently strong antenna, the rogue AP does not have to be located in close proximity to the legitimate AP.

For example, the attacker can run the rogue AP from a car or van parked some distance away from the building. However, it is also common to set up hidden rogue APs (under desks, in closets, and so on) close to and within the same physical area as the legitimate AP. Because of their virtually undetectable nature, the only defense against rogue APs is vigilance through frequent site surveys (using tools such as AirMagnet, NetStumbler, and AiroPeek) and physical security.

Frequent site surveys also have the advantage of uncovering the unauthorized APs that company staff members might have set up in their own work areas, thereby compromising the entire network and completely undoing the hard work that went into securing the network in the first place. These unauthorized APs are usually set up with no malicious intent but rather for the convenience of the user, who might want to be able to connect to the network via his or her laptop in meeting rooms or break rooms or other areas that don't have wired outlets. Even if your company does not use or plan to use a wireless network, you should consider doing regular wireless site surveys to see if someone has violated your company security policy by placing an unauthorized AP on the network, regardless of that person's intent.

Network Hijacking and Modification

Numerous techniques are available for an attacker to "hijack" a wireless network or session. Unlike some attacks, network and security administrators might be unable to tell the difference between the hijacker and a legitimate "passenger."

Many tools are available to the network hijacker. These tools are based on basic implementation issues within almost every network device available today. As TCP/IP packets go through switches, routers, and APs, each device looks at the destination IP address and compares it with the IP addresses it knows to be local. If the address is not in the table, the device hands the packet off to its default gateway.

This table is used to coordinate the IP address with the MAC addresses that are known to be local to the device. In many situations, this list is a dynamic one that is built up from traffic that is passing through the device and through Address Resolution Protocol (ARP) notifications from new devices joining the network. There is no authentication or verification that the request the device received is valid. Thus a malicious user is able to send messages to routing devices and APs stating that his MAC address is associated with a known IP address. From then on, all traffic that goes through that router destined for the hijacked IP address will be handed off to the hacker's machine.

If the attacker spoofs as the default gateway or a specific host on the network, all machines trying to get to the network or the spoofed machine will connect to the attacker's machine instead of the gateway or host to which they intended to connect. If the attacker is clever, he will only use this information to identify passwords and other necessary information and route the rest of the traffic to the intended recipients. If he does this, the end users will have no idea that this "man in the middle" has intercepted their communications and compromised their passwords and information.

Another clever attack can be accomplished through the use of rogue APs. If the attacker is able to put together an AP with enough strength, the end users might not be able to tell which AP is the authorized one that they should be using. In fact, most will not even know that another AP is available. Using this technique, the attacker is able to receive authentication requests and information from the end workstation regarding the secret key and where users are attempting to connect.

These rogue APs can also be used to attempt to break into more tightly configured wireless APs. Utilizing tools such as AirSnort and WEPCrack requires a large amount of data to be able to decrypt the secret key. A hacker sitting in a car in front of your house or office is noticeable and thus will generally not have time to finish acquiring enough information to break the key. However, if the attacker installs a tiny, easily hidden machine in an inconspicuous location, this machine could sit there long enough to break the key and possibly act as an external AP into the wireless network it has hacked.

Attackers who want to spoof more than their MAC addresses have several tools available. Most of the tools available are for use in a UNIX environment and can be found through a simple search for *ARP spoof* at http://packetstormsecurity.com. With these tools, the hacker can easily trick all machines on the wireless network into thinking that the hacker's machine is another machine. Through simple sniffing on the network, an attacker can determine which machines are in high use by the workstations on the network. If the attacker then spoofs the address of one of these machines, the attacker might be able to intercept much of the legitimate traffic on the network.

AirSnort and WEPCrack are freely available. It would take additional resources to build a rogue AP, but these tools will run from any Linux machine.

Once an attacker has identified a network for attack and spoofed his MAC address to become a valid member of the network, the attacker can gain further information that is not available through simple sniffing. If the network being attacked is using SSH to access the hosts, just stealing a password might be easier than attempting to break into the host using an available exploit.

By simply ARP spoofing the connection with the AP to be that of the host from which the attacker wants to steal the passwords, the attacker can cause all wireless users who are attempting to SSH into the host to connect to the rogue machine instead. When these users attempt to sign on with their passwords, the attacker is then able to, first, receive their passwords and second, pass on the connection to the real end destination. If the attacker does not perform the second step, it increases the likelihood that the attack will be noticed because users will begin to complain that they are unable to connect to the host.

Jamming Attacks

The last type of attack is the *jamming attack*. This is a fairly simple attack to pull off and can be done using readily available, off-the-shelf RF testing tools (although they were not necessarily designed to perform this function). Whereas hackers who want to get information from your network would use other passive and active types of attacks to accomplish their goals, attackers who just want to disrupt your network communications or even shut down a wireless network can jam you without ever being seen. Jamming a wireless LAN is similar in many ways to targeting a network with a DoS attack. The difference is that in the case of the wireless network, the attack can be carried out by one person with an overpowering RF signal. This attack can be carried out using any number of products, but the easiest is with a high-power RF signal generator, readily available from various vendors.

The jamming attack is sometimes the most difficult type of attack to prevent against, since the attacker does not need to gain access to your network. The attacker can sit in your parking lot or even further away, depending on the power output of her jamming device. You might be able to readily determine the fact that you are being jammed, but you could find yourself hard pressed to solve the problem. Indications of a jamming attack include clients' sudden inability to connect to APs where there was not a problem previously.

The problem will be evident across all or most of your clients (the ones within the range of the RF jamming device) even though your APs are operating properly. Jamming attacks are sometimes used as the prelude to further attacks. One possible example includes jamming the wireless network, thereby forcing clients to lose their connections with authorized APs. During this time, one or more rogue APs can be made available operating at a higher power than the authorized APs. When the jamming attack is stopped, the clients will tend to associate back to the AP that is presenting the strongest signal. Now the attacker "owns" all the network clients attached to his rogue APs. The attack continues from there.

In some cases, RF jamming is not always intentional and could be the result of other, nonhostile sources such as a nearby communications tower or another wireless LAN that is operating in the same frequency range. Baby monitors, cordless telephones, microwave ovens, and many other consumer products can also be sources of interference.

You can take some comfort in knowing that although a jamming attack is easy and inexpensive to pull off, it is not the preferred means of attack. The only real victory with a jamming attack for most hackers is temporarily taking your wireless network offline.

Wireless LAN Security: It's Not Perfect

Wireless technologies are inherently more vulnerable to attack due to the nature of the network transmissions. Wireless network transmissions are not physically constrained within the confines of a building or its surroundings, thus an attacker has ready access to the information in the wireless networks. As wireless network technologies have emerged, they have become the focus of analysis by security researchers and hackers, who have realized that wireless networks can be insecure and often can be exploited as a gateway into the relatively secure wired networks beyond them.

WEP Vulnerabilities

Like any standard or protocol, WEP has some inherent disadvantages. The focus of security is to allow a balance of access and control while juggling the advantages and disadvantages of each implemented countermeasure for security gaps. Some of WEP's disadvantages include:

- The RC4 encryption algorithm is a known stream cipher. This means that it takes a finite key and attempts to make an infinite pseudo-random key stream in order to generate the encryption.

- Altering the secret must be done across the board. All APs and all clients must be changed at the same time.

- Used on its own, WEP does not provide adequate WLAN security.

- To be effective, WEP has to be implemented on every client as well as on every AP.

WEP is part of the 802.11 standard defined for wireless networks in 1999. WEP differs from many other kinds of encryption employed to secure network communication in that it is implemented at MAC sublayer of the data link layer (Layer 2) of the OSI model. Security can be implemented at many layers of the model. IPSec, for example, is implemented at the network layer (Layer 3) of the OSI model; PPTP creates a secure end-to-end tunnel using the network layer (GRE) and transport layer protocols to encapsulate and transport data; HTTP-S and SSH are application layer (Layer 7) protocols for encrypting data. Due to the complexity of the 802.11 MAC and the amount of processing power it requires, the 802.11 standard made 40-bit WEP an optional implementation.

Vulnerability to Plaintext Attacks

Right from the outset, knowledgeable people warned that because of the way WEP was implemented, it was vulnerable. In October 2000, Jesse Walker, a member of the 802.11 working group, published his now famous paper, *Unsafe at Any Key Size: An Analysis of WEP Encapsulation*. The paper points out a number of serious shortcomings of WEP and recommended that WEP be redesigned.

For example, WEP is vulnerable to *plaintext attacks* because it is implemented at the data link layer, meaning that it encrypts IP datagrams. Each encrypted frame on a wireless network, therefore, contains a high proportion of well-known TCP/IP information, which can be revealed fairly accurately through traffic analysis, even if the traffic is encrypted. If someone is able to compare the ciphertext (the WEP-encrypted data) with the plaintext equivalent (the raw TCP/IP data), he or she has a powerful clue for cracking the encryption used on the network. To uncover the keystream used to encrypt the data, all the hacker has to do is plug the two values, the plaintext and the ciphertext, into the RC4 algorithm WEP uses. There are a number of ways to speed up the process of acquiring both the plaintext and ciphertext versions: by sending spam into the network, by injecting traffic into the network, using social engineering to get a wireless user to send the hacker e-mail, and so on.

Vulnerability of RC4 Algorithm

As alluded to in the previous section, another vulnerability of WEP is that it uses a stream cipher called RC4, developed by RSA, to encrypt the data. In 1994, an anonymous user posted the RC4 algorithm to a cipherpunk mailing list; the algorithm was subsequently reposted to a number of Usenet newsgroups the next day with the title "RC4 Algorithm Revealed."

Until August 2001, it was thought that the underlying algorithm RC4 uses was well designed and robust, so even though the algorithm was no longer a trade secret, it was still thought to be an acceptable cipher to use. However, Scott Fluhrer, Itsik Mantin, and Adi Shamir published a paper, *Weaknesses in the Key Scheduling Algorithm of RC4*, that demonstrated that a number of keys used in RC4 were weak and vulnerable to compromise. The paper designed a theoretical attack that could take advantage of these weak keys. Because the algorithm for RC4 is no longer a secret and because a number of weak keys were used in RC4, it is possible to construct software that is designed to break RC4 encryption relatively quickly using the weak keys in RC4. Not surprisingly, a number of open-source tools have appeared that do precisely that. Two such popular tools for cracking WEP are AirSnort and WEPCrack.

Some vendors, such as Agere (which produces the ORiNOCO product line), responded to the weakness in key scheduling by making a modification to the key scheduling in their products to avoid the use of weak keys, making them resistant to attacks based on weak key scheduling. This feature is known as *WEPplus*. However, not all vendors have responded similarly.

Stream Cipher Vulnerability

WEP uses an RC4 stream cipher. A stream cipher differs from a block cipher such as DES or AES, which performs mathematical functions on blocks of data, in that the data or the message is treated as a stream of bits. To encrypt the data, the stream cipher performs an XOR of the plaintext data against a key stream to create the ciphertext stream. (An XOR is a mathematical function used with binary numbers. If the bits are the same, the result of the XOR is 0; if the bits are different, the result of the XOR is 1.)

If the key stream were always the same, it would be a relatively trivial matter to crack the encryption if the attacker had both the plaintext and the ciphertext versions of the message (a known plaintext attack). In order to create key streams that are statistically random, a key and a PRNG are used to create the key stream that is XORed against the plaintext message to generate the ciphertext.

A central problem with WEP is the potential for reuse of the IV. A well-known vulnerability of stream ciphers is the reuse of an IV and key to encrypt two different messages. When this occurs, the two ciphertext messages can be XORed with each other to cancel out the keystream, resulting in the XOR of the two original plaintexts. If the attacker knows the contents of one of these plaintext messages, he or she can then easily obtain the plaintext of the other message.

Although there are 2^{24} (16,777,216) possible combinations for the IV, this is in fact a relatively small number. On a busy wireless network, the entire range of possible combinations for the IV can be exhausted in a number of hours. (Remember, each frame or packet uses a different IV.) Once an attacker has collected enough frames that use duplicate IVs, he or she can use this information to derive the shared-secret key. In the absence of other solutions (which are usually proprietary) for automatic key management and out-of-band or encrypted dynamic key distribution, the shared-secret WEP keys have to be manually configured on the APs and wireless client workstations. In addition, because of the administrative burden of changing the shared-secret key, administrators often do not change the shared-secret key frequently enough.

To make matters worse, a hacker does not even need to wait until the 24-bit IV key space is exhausted to find duplicate IVs. (Remember, these are transmitted in the frame of the message.) In fact, it is almost certain that the attacker will encounter a duplicate IV in far fewer frames or discover a number of weak keys. The reason is that upon reinitialization, wireless PC cards will reset the IV to 0.

When the wireless client begins transmitting encrypted frames, it increments the IV by 1 for each subsequent frame. On a busy network, there are likely to be many instances of wireless PC cards being reinitialized, thereby making the reuse of the low-order IVs a common occurrence. Even if the IVs were randomized rather than being used in sequence, this would not be an adequate solution due to the *birthday paradox*. The birthday paradox predicts the counterintuitive fact that within a group as small as 23 people, there is a 50-percent chance that two people will share the same birthday.

It doesn't really matter whether the wireless network is using 64- or 128-bit encryption (in reality, these constitute 40- and 104-bit encryption, once the 24 bits for the IV are subtracted). Both use a 24-bit IV. Given the amount of traffic on a wireless network and the probability of IV collisions within a relatively short period of time, a 24-bit IV is far too short to provide any kind of meaningful protection against a determined attacker.

> **Head of the Class…**
>
> ### More Information on WEP
>
> Readers can consult many excellent resources freely available on the Internet to learn more about WEP and its weaknesses. Readers might want to start with Jesse Walker's famous white paper, entitled *Unsafe at Any Key Size: An Analysis of WEP Encapsulation,* which started the initial uproar about WEP's weaknesses. This paper can be found at http://grouper.ieee.org/groups/802/11/Documents/DocumentHolder/0-362.zip.
>
> Another excellent source of information is *Intercepting Mobile Communications: The Insecurity of 802.11*, by Nikita Borisov, Ian Goldberg, and David Wagner. This paper can be found at www.cs.berkeley.edu/~daw/papers/wep-mob01.pdf. *Your 802.11 Wireless Network Has No Clothes*, by William A. Arbaugh, Narendar Shankar, and Y.C. Justin Wan, covers similar ground as the previous two papers but also introduces important information on the problems with access control and authentication mechanisms associated with wireless networks. This paper can be found at www.cs.umd.edu/~waa/wireless.pdf.

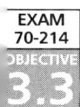

Should You Use WEP?

The existence of these vulnerabilities does not mean that you should not use WEP. One of the most serious problems with wireless security is not that WEP is insecure but that a high percentage of wireless networks discovered by war drivers are not using WEP at all. In fact, at a minimum, all wireless networks should be configured to use WEP. It is available for free with wireless devices. At the very least, WEP prevents casual war drivers from compromising your network and slows the knowledgeable and determined attackers. In the following section, we look at how to configure Windows wireless clients for WLAN security.

EXAM WARNING

This level of knowledge about WEP presented in this chapter is crucial to functioning in a wireless environment and should be something you know well if you plan to work in such an environment. However, for the exam, focus on WEP's basic definition and its basic weaknesses.

Security of 64-Bit Versus 128-Bit Keys

It might seem to a nontechnical person that something protected with a 128-bit encryption scheme would be twice as secure as something protected with a 64-bit encryption scheme. This, however, is not the case with WEP. Since the same IV vulnerability exists with both encryption levels, they can be compromised within similar time limits.

With 64-bit WEP, the network administrator specifies a 40-bit key—typically 10 hexadecimal digits (0–9, a–f, or A–F). A 24-bit IV is appended to this 40-bit key, and the RC4 key scheme is built from these 64-bits of data. This same process is followed in the 128-bit scheme. The administrator specifies a 104-bit key—this time 26 hexadecimal digits (0–9, a–f, or A–F). The 24-bit IV is added to the beginning of the key, and the RC4 key schedule is built.

Because the vulnerability stems from capturing predictably weak IVs, the size of the original key does not make a significant difference in the security of the encryption. This is due to the relatively small number of total IVs possible under the current WEP specification. Currently, there is a total of 2^{24} (16,777,216) possible IV keys. Because every frame or packet uses an IV, this number can be exhausted within hours on a busy network. If the WEP key was not changed within a strictly defined period of time, all possible IV combinations could be intercepted off a 802.11b connection, captured, and made available for cracking within a short period of time. This is a flaw in WEP's design and bears no correlation to whether the wireless client is using 64-bit WEP or 128-bit WEP.

IEEE 802.1x Vulnerabilities

The IEEE 802.1x standard is still relatively new in relation to the IEEE 802.11 standard, and the security research community is only recently beginning to seriously evaluate the security of this standard. One of the first groups to investigate the security of the 802.1x standard was the Maryland Information Systems Security Lab (MISSL) at the University of Maryland at College Park. This group, led by Dr. William Arbaugh, was the first to release a paper (www.missl.cs.umd.edu/Projects/wireless/ix.pdf) documenting flaws in the IEEE 802.1x standard. In this paper, the group noted that 802.1x is susceptible to several attacks, due to the following vulnerabilities:

- The lack of the requirement of strong mutual authentication. EAP-TLS does provide strong mutual authentication, but it is not required and can be overridden.
- The vulnerability of the EAP success message to a man-in-the-middle attack.
- The lack of integrity protection for 802.1x management frames.

These flaws provide avenues of attack against wireless networks. Although the networks are not as vulnerable as they would be without EAP and 802.1x, the "silver-bullet" fix designers had hoped for was not provided in the form of 802.1x.

Configuring Windows Client Computers for Wireless LAN Security

Wireless LAN security is provided through myriad solutions. Some of these mechanisms are internal to Windows itself; others are third-party solutions or part of the IEEE 802.11 standard. In this section, we focus primarily on using WEP and 802.1x-based security on Windows 2000 Professional and Windows XP Professional computers. Whatever security mechanism you decide to implement, you must ensure that you are diligent about getting it done right. There is rarely a second chance for security, especially when it comes to securing a wireless LAN.

Windows XP Professional

Windows XP has been hailed as the operating system of choice for wireless LAN users. Whatever your feelings are about this popularity, it is a fact that Windows XP brings to the mainstream excellent support for 802.11b wireless networks and 802.1x security. The only flaw in Windows XP's solution is that it takes the majority of control away from a user. Sometimes this can be a good thing, though. Configuring WEP and 802.1x security on a Windows XP Professional computer is outlined in Exercise 7.01.

EXERCISE 7.01

ENABLING WEP AND 802.1X SECURITY IN WINDOWS XP PROFESSIONAL

1. Click **Start | Settings | Control Panel | Network Connections**.
2. Double-click your wireless LAN connection.
3. Click the **Properties** button and switch to the **Wireless** tab, as shown in Figure 7.6.
4. To configure a new connection, click **Add**. Configure all required information, including the WEP key, as shown in Figure 7.7.
5. If your network uses a dynamic keying server, you need only select **The key is provided for me automatically** instead of specifying the WEP key specifics.
6. Click **OK** when you have entered all the required information.
7. To configure 802.1x security on the network connection, change to the **Authentication** tab, as shown in Figure 7.8.

Figure 7.6 The Wireless Tab

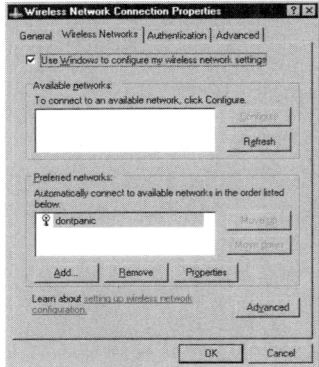

Figure 7.7 Configuring a New Connection

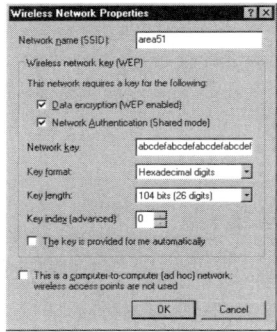

Figure 7.8 Configuring 802.1x Security

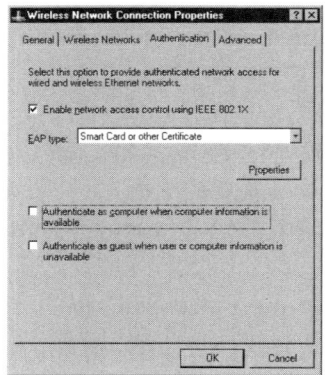

8. Select **Enable network access control using IEEE 802.1x**. Select your EAP type from the drop-down list. Most commonly, your EAP type will be **Smart Card or other Certificate**. By clicking **Properties** (see Figure 7.9) you can configure the certificate and CA to be used for this authentication.

Figure 7.9 Configuring the Certificate Properties

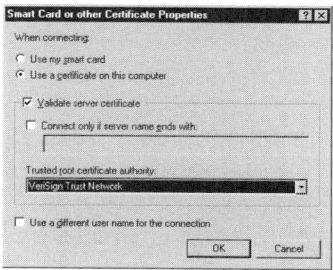

9. For increased security, ensure that the **Authenticate as computer when computer information is available** and **Authenticate as guest when user or computer information is unavailable** options are *not* selected. Click **OK** to accept the settings.

Windows 2000 Professional

Windows 2000 provides none of the built-in niceties for wireless networking that Windows XP provides. It also doesn't take control of your wireless network connection. All configuration and security are the user's job. Exercise 7.02 outlines the process to enable WEP for a wireless network connection in Windows 2000 Professional.

EXERCISE 7.02

ENABLING WEP IN WINDOWS 2000 PROFESSIONAL

1. Click **Start | Settings | Control Panel | Network Connections**.
2. Double-click your wireless LAN connection.
3. Click the **Properties** button. Notice that the **Wireless** and **Authentication** tabs do not show up in Windows 2000, as shown in Figure 7.10.

Figure 7.10 Windows 2000 Network Adapter Properties

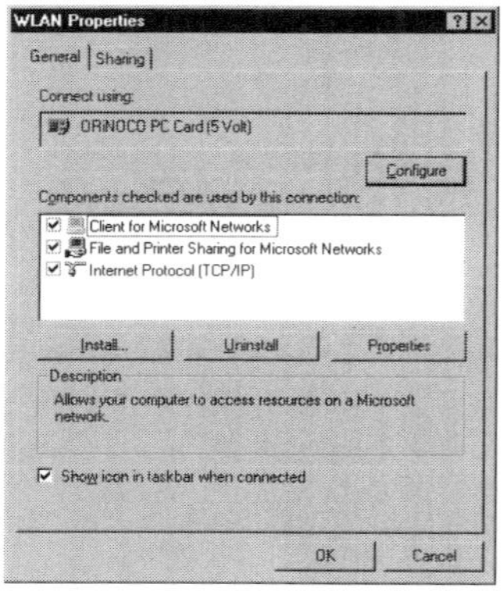

4. Close the network adapter **Properties** window.
5. Configure a wireless LAN connection profile using your WLAN network adapter client utility, such as the ORiNOCO Client Manager or the Cisco ACU. We use an ORiNOCO network adapter for this example.
6. Open the **Client Manager** and click **Actions | Add/Edit Configuration Profile**, as shown in Figure 7.11.

Figure 7.11 Configuring a New Profile

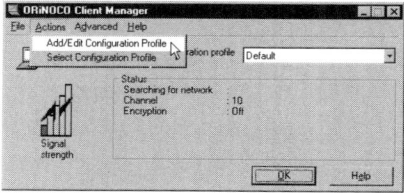

7. Click **Add** to start the process of creating a new profile.
8. Enter the **Profile Name** and **Network Type**, as shown in Figure 7.12, and click **Next**.

Figure 7.12 Specifying a New Profile

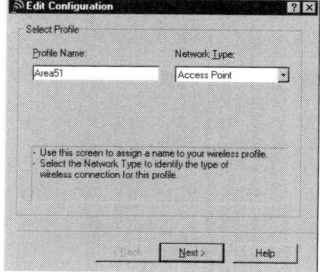

9. Enter the **Network Name** and click **Next**. This is the SSID of the network.
10. Select **Enable Data Security** and enter your WEP key or keys, as shown in Figure 7.13. Click **Next** to continue.

Figure 7.13 Configuring the WEP Properties

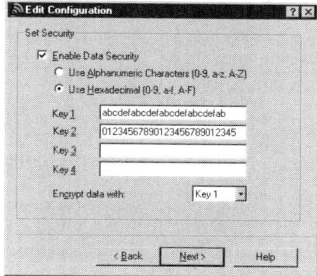

11. Configure the power management function you want and click **Next**.
12. Configure to renew the IP address of the network adapter upon connecting as desired and click **Next**.

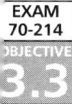

Additional Security Measures for Wireless LANs

Although 802.1x authentication provides good security through the use of dynamically generated WEP keys, security administrators might want to add more layers of security. Additional security for wireless networks can be introduced through the design of the network itself. As we stated previously, a wireless network should always be treated as an *untrusted* network. This fact has implications for the design and topology of the wireless network.

Test Day Tip

The extra security measures and best practices discussed over the next several pages are presented for your reference should you find yourself faced with the task of implementing a wireless network. Don't expect to be directly tested on any of this material during your exam.

Using a Separate Subnet for Wireless Networks

Many wireless networks are set up on the same subnets as the wired network. Furthermore, to make life easier for administrators and users alike, both wired and wireless clients are often configured as DHCP clients and receive IP address configurations from the same DHCP servers. There is an obvious security problem with this approach. This configuration makes it easy for hackers to acquire valid IP address configurations that are on the same subnet as the corporate networks, posing a significant threat to network security.

The solution is to place wireless access points on their own separate subnets, creating, in effect, a kind of DMZ for the wireless network. The wireless subnet could be separated from the wired network by either a router or a full-featured firewall, such as ISA Server. This approach has a number of advantages. When the wireless network is placed on a separate subnet, the router can be configured with filters to provide additional security for the wireless network. Furthermore, through the use of an extended subnet mask on the wireless network, the number of valid IP addresses can be limited to approximately the number of valid wireless clients. Finally, in the case of potential attack on the wireless network, you can quickly shut down the router and prevent any further access to the wired network until the threat has been removed.

If you have to support automatic roaming between wireless zones, you will still want to use DHCP on the wireless subnets. However, if you don't need to support automatic roaming, you might want to consider not using DHCP and manually configuring IP addresses on the wireless clients. This solution will not prevent a hacker from sniffing the air for valid IP addresses to use on the wireless subnet, but it will provide another barrier for entry and consume time. Additionally, if a hacker manually configures an IP address that is in use by another wireless client, the valid user will receive an IP address conflict message, providing a crude method for detecting unauthorized access attempts.

Using VPNs for Wireless Access to Wired Networks

In high-security networks, administrators might want to leverage the separate subnet by only allowing access to the wired network through a VPN configured on the router or firewall. In order for wireless users to gain access to the wired network, they would first have to successfully authenticate and associate with the AP and then create a VPN tunnel for access to the wired network.

Some vendors, such as Colubris, offer VPN solutions built into wireless devices. These devices can act as VPN-aware clients that will forward only VPN traffic from the wireless network to the wired network, or they can provide their own VPN server for wireless clients. However, it is not necessary to use a proprietary hardware-based solution. One solution is to use a freeware solution known as Dolphin from www.reefedge.com that will turn a PC into an appliance that will encrypt wireless traffic with IPSec.

NOTE

For more information on this technology, see www.colubris.com/en/support/whitepapers.

When a VPN is required for access to the corporate network from the wireless network subnet, all traffic between the two networks is encrypted within the VPN tunnel. If you are using static WEP, a VPN will ensure a higher degree of confidentiality for your traffic. Even if the WEP encryption is cracked, the hacker would then have to crack the VPN encryption to see the corporate traffic, which is a much more difficult task. If a wireless laptop is stolen and the theft unreported, the thief would have to know the laptop user's credentials to gain access to the VPN.

NOTE

It is important to ensure that the user doesn't configure the VPN connection to save the username and password. Although this makes it more convenient for the user, who doesn't have to type the account name and password each time he or she uses the VPN connection, it provides a thief with the credentials needed to access the VPN.

Of course, this kind of configuration is still vulnerable to attack. If, for example, the attacker has somehow acquired usernames and passwords (or the user has saved them in the VPN connection configuration), the hacker can still access the wired network through the VPN. Another consideration is the additional overhead of encryption used in the VPN tunnel. If you are also using WEP, the combined loss of bandwidth as a result of the encryption could easily be noticeable. Again, administrators will have to compare the benefits of implementing a VPN for wireless clients in a DMZ against the cost of deployment in terms of hardware, software, management, loss of bandwidth, and other factors.

Setting up this kind of configuration can be a relatively complex undertaking, depending on a number of factors. If, for example, you are using 802.1x authentication, you might have to ensure that 802.1x-related traffic can pass between the wireless and wired networks without a VPN tunnel. If you are using ISA Server to separate the networks, you would have to publish the RADIUS server on the corporate network to the wireless network. You can find information on setting up ISA Server for this kind of configuration throughout this book.

Temporal Key Integrity Protocol

As we noted earlier, the use of WEP, even in combination with 802.1x authentication and EAP-TLS, provides a much higher standard of security but does not mitigate all the potential threats to the confidentiality and integrity of the data. As an interim solution, until the IEEE 802.11i standard is implemented and finalized, many vendors are using or considering using a temporary solution called Temporal Key Integrity Protocol (TKIP) to enhance the security of wireless networks. The TKIP standard has been accepted by the Wi-Fi Alliance for inclusion in 802.11b Wi-Fi certified devices and is being called Wi-Fi Protected Access, or WPA. Cisco has been using TKIP for some time now in its Aironet line of products.

TKIP can be used with or as an alternative to 802.1x authentication. TKIP comprises a set of algorithms that enhance WEP. It provides more security than WEP through the use of key mixing, an extended IV, a message integrity check (MIC), and rekeying. A primary advantage of TKIP is that it can be implemented through firmware updates of current devices (another reason that you should only purchase devices capable of firmware updates). TKIP addresses the problem of static WEP keys by frequently changing the *temporal key* used for the encryption process every 10,000 packets.

Additionally, the use of TKIP addresses another vulnerability of static WEP: the use of the same shared key by all the wireless devices. TKIP ensures that each wireless station uses a different key for the encryption process. TKIP accomplishes this task by using a 128-bit *temporal key* that is shared between the wireless workstations and the AP. The temporal key is then combined with the MAC address of each of the wireless devices to provide the encryption key used for RC4 encryption on the wireless network by that device. This also adds another layer of encryption to reduce the vulnerability to attacks based on the fact that the IV is sent in the clear in standard WEP implementations.

Message Integrity Code

Another vulnerability of WEP is that it is a relatively easy matter for a knowledgeable and determined attacker to modify (flip) bits in an intercepted message, recalculate the appropriate CRC (also known as the *integrity check value*, or *ICV*), and then send the altered message to the AP. Because the CRC is spoofed, the AP will accept the altered message and reply to it, providing information that the attacker could use to crack the WEP encryption. This form of attack was described in a paper, *Intercepting Mobile Communications: The Insecurity of 802.11*, by Nikita Borisov, Ian Goldberg, and David Wagner.

MIC, which is also part of the TKIP algorithms, provides a much stronger mechanism for checking the message for evidence of tampering by adding a MIC value that is encrypted and sent with the message. When the message is received, the MIC value is decrypted and compared with the expected value. MIC is, in reality, a form of Message Authentication Code, often referred to as MAC, which is a standard cryptographic term. However, because the acronym *MAC* is already used quite frequently with regard to wireless networks in regard to the Media Access Control address, *MIC* is used to differentiate the two.

NOTE

To add to the confusion, MIC is variously referred to as *message integrity code* or *message integrity check*. As with TKIP, MIC is a technology originally developed by Cisco (which uses the term *check*) for use in its products and is not widely available at the time of this writing.

The IEEE 802.11i Standard

The negative response to WEP's weaknesses has been vociferous and strong. To address the criticisms leveled at WEP and to provide a stronger standards-based security mechanism that vendors can implement in their products, the IEEE 802.11i task group is working on the upcoming 802.11i standard.

Although the standard is not finalized, some things about its final form are fairly certain. The standard will combine into a single, coherent standard the best of the available technologies for securing wireless networks. The following are expected to be included in the standard:

- The 802.11i standard will require the use of 802.1*x* authentication based on EAP.

- The 802.11i standard will also likely require the use of TKIP and MIC.

- For new devices, the standard will also require the use of Advanced Encryption Standard (AES) as a replacement for the compromised RC4 algorithm.

AES provides much stronger encryption than RC4. However, because of the additional processing power required for AES encryption, the addition of a coprocessor in the hardware of wireless devices will likely be necessary. When this technology becomes available in the marketplace, replacing legacy wireless devices could result in a significant expenditure. As with all other security measures, administrators and managers will have to compare the costs of implementation against the threats the implementation will mitigate.

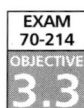

Implementing Wireless LAN Security: Common Best Practices

As we have seen from the previous discussion, wireless security is a large, complex topic. Administrators who want to implement wireless networks should exercise due care and due diligence by becoming as familiar as they can with operation and vulnerabilities of wireless networks and the available countermeasures for defending them. Installing a wireless network opens the current wired network to new threats. The security risks created by wireless networks can be mitigated, however, to provide an acceptably safe level of security in most situations.

In some cases, the security requirements are high enough that the wireless devices require proprietary security features. This might include, for example, the ability to use TKIP and MIC, which is currently only available on some Cisco wireless products but might become available on other products in the near future. In many cases, however, standards-based security mechanisms that are available on wireless products from a wide range of vendors are sufficient.

Even though many currently implemented wireless networks support a wide range of features that can potentially be enabled, the sad fact is that most administrators do not use them. The media is full of reports of the informal results of site surveys conducted by war drivers. These reports provide worrisome information—for example, that most wireless networks are not using WEP and that many wireless networks are using default SSIDs. Many of these networks are located in technology-rich areas such as Silicon Valley, where you would think people would know better, making the information a potential source of serious concern.

There is really no excuse for not minimizing the security threats created by wireless networks through the implementation of security features that are available on most wireless networks. The following is a summary of common best practices that could be employed now on many current or future wireless networks:

- Carefully review the available security features of wireless devices to see if they fulfill your security requirements. The 802.11 and Wi-Fi standards specify only a subset of features that are available on a wide range of devices. Over and above these standards, there is a great deal of divergence among supported features.

- At a minimum, wireless access points and adapters should support firmware updates, 128-bit WEP, MAC filtering, and the disabling of SSID broadcasts.

- Wireless vendors are continually addressing the security weaknesses of wireless networks. Check the wireless vendors' Web sites frequently for firmware updates and apply them to all wireless devices. You could leave your network exposed if you fail to update even one device with the most recent firmware.

- In medium- to high-security environments, wireless devices should support EAP-based 802.1x authentication and, possibly, TKIP. Another desirable feature is the ability to remotely administer the wireless AP over a secure, encrypted channel. Being able to use IPSec for communications between the AP and the RADIUS server is also desirable.

- Always use WEP. Although it is true that WEP can be cracked, doing so requires knowledge and time. Even 40-bit WEP is better than no WEP.

- Always rotate static WEP keys frequently. If this is too great an administrative burden, consider purchasing devices that support dynamic WEP keys.

- Always change the default administrative password you use to manage the AP. The default passwords for wireless APs are well known. If possible, use a password generator to create a difficult and sufficiently complex password.

- Change the default SSID of the AP. The default SSIDs for APs from different vendors are well known, such as tsunami and Linksys for Cisco and Linksys APs, respectively. A fairly inclusive listing of default SSIDs can be found at www.area51partners.com/files/SSID.txt.

- Do not put any kind of identifying information in the SSID, such as your company name, address, products, divisions, and so on. If you do so, you provide too much information to potential hackers and let them know whether your network is of sufficient interest to warrant further effort.

- If possible, disable SSID broadcasts. This will make your network invisible to site survey tools such as NetStumbler. However, disabling SSID broadcasts will cause an administrative burden if you are heavily dependent on Windows XP clients being able to automatically discover and associate with the wireless network.

- If using DHCP for your wireless clients, strongly consider the use of a separate DHCP scope and subnet for wireless clients. In this way you can lock wireless clients into a specific subnet. Wireless clients should always be treated as untrusted and placed in a controlled environment, such as DMZ, if possible.

- Do not use shared-key authentication. Although it can protect your network against specific types of DoS attacks, it allows other kinds of DoS attacks. Shared-key authentication exposes your WEP keys to compromise.

- Enable MAC filtering. It's true that MAC addresses can be easily spoofed, but your goal here is to slow potential attackers. If MAC filtering is too great an

- administrative headache, consider using port-based authentication available through 802.1*x*.

- Consider placing your wireless network in a wireless demilitarized zone (WDMZ), separated from the corporate network by a router or a firewall.

- In a WDMZ, restrict the number of hosts on the subnet through an extended subnet mask, and do not use DHCP.

- Learn how to use site survey tools such as NetStumbler and conduct frequent site surveys to detect the presence of rogue APs and vulnerabilities in your own network.

- Don't place the AP near windows. Try to place it in the center of the building so that interference will hamper the efforts of war drivers and others trying to detect your traffic. Ideally, your wireless signal would radiate only to the outside walls of the building, not beyond. Try to come as close to that ideal as possible.

- If possible, purchase an AP that allows you to reduce the size of the wireless zone (cell sizing) by changing the power output.

- Educate yourself as to the operation and security of wireless networks.

- Educate your users about safe computing practices, in the context of the use of both wired and wireless networks.

- Perform a risk analysis of your network.

- Develop relevant and comprehensive security policies, and implement them throughout your network.

Summary of Exam Objectives

Wireless LANs are attractive to many companies and home users because of the increased productivity that results from the convenience and flexibility of being able to connect to the network without the use of wires. WLANs are especially attractive when they can reduce the costs of having to install cabling to support users on the network. For these and other reasons, WLANs have become very popular in the past few years. However, WLAN technology has often been implemented poorly and without giving due consideration to the security of the network. For the most part, these poor implementations result from a lack of understanding of the nature of wireless networks and the measures that can be taken to secure them.

WLANs are inherently insecure due to their very nature—the fact that they radiate radio signals containing network traffic that can be viewed and potentially compromised by anyone within range of the signal. With the proper antennas, the range of WLANs is much greater than is commonly assumed. Many administrators wrongly believe that their networks are secure because the interference created by walls and other physical obstructions combined with the relative low power of wireless devices will contain the wireless signal sufficiently. Often, this is not the case.

You can deploy a number of types of wireless networks. These include 802.11b and 802.11a networks as well as several other types not discussed here. The most common type of WLAN in use today is based on the IEEE 802.11b standard.

The 802.11b standard defines the operation of WLANs in the 2.4 GHz to 2.4835 GHz unlicensed Industrial, Scientific, and Medical (ISM) band. 802.11b devices use direct sequence spread-spectrum (DSSS) to achieve transmission rates of up to 11 Mbps. All 802.11b devices are half-duplex devices, which means that a device cannot send and receive at the same time. In this, they are like hubs and therefore require mechanisms for contending with collisions when multiple stations are transmitting at the same time. To contend with collisions, wireless networks use Carrier Sense Multiple Access with Collision Avoidance (CSMA/CA).

The 802.11a and forthcoming 802.11g standards define the operation of wireless networks with higher transmission rates. 802.11a devices are not compatible with 802.11b because they use frequencies in the 5 GHz band. Furthermore, unlike 802.11b networks, they do not use DSSS. 802.11g uses the same ISM frequencies as 802.11b and is backward compatible with 802.11b devices.

The 802.11 standard defines the 40-bit Wired Equivalent Privacy (WEP) protocol as an optional component to protect wireless networks from eavesdropping. WEP is implemented in the MAC sub layer of the data link layer (Layer 2) of the OSI model.

WEP is insecure for a number of reasons. The first is that because it encrypts well-known and deterministic IP traffic in Layer 3, it is vulnerable to plaintext attacks. That is, it is relatively easy for an attacker to figure out the plaintext traffic (for example, a DHCP exchange) and compare that with the ciphertext, providing a powerful clue for cracking the encryption.

Another problem with WEP is that it uses a relatively short (24-bit) initialization vector (IV) to encrypt the traffic. Because each transmitted frame requires a new IV, it is possible to exhaust the entire IV key space in a few hours on a busy network, resulting in the reuse of IVs. This reuse is known as *IV collisions*. IV collisions can also be used to crack the encryption. Furthermore, IVs are sent in the clear with each frame, introducing another vulnerability.

The final stake in the heart of WEP is the fact that it uses RC4 as the encryption algorithm. The RC4 algorithm is well known; recently it was discovered that it uses a number of weak keys. AirSnort and WEPcrack are two well-known open-source tools that exploit the weak key vulnerability of WEP.

Although WEP is insecure, it does nonetheless potentially provide a good barrier, and its use will slow determined and knowledgeable attackers. For this reason, WEP should always be implemented. The security of WEP is also dependent on how it is implemented. Because the IV key space can be exhausted in a relatively short amount of time, static WEP keys should be changed on a frequent basis.

The best defense for a wireless network involves the use of multiple security mechanisms to provide multiple barriers that will slow attackers, making it easier for you to detect and respond to attacks. This strategy is known as *defense in depth*.

Securing a wireless network should begin with changing the default configurations of the wireless network devices. These configurations include the default administrative password and the default SSID on the access point.

The Service Set Identifier (SSID) is a kind of network name, analogous to an SNMP community name or a VLAN ID. In order for the wireless clients to authenticate and associate with an access point, they must use the same SSID as the one in use on the AP. The SSID should be changed to a unique value that contains no information that could potentially be used to identify the company or the kind of traffic on the network.

By default, SSIDs are broadcast in response to beacon probes and can be easily discovered by site survey tools such as NetStumbler and Windows XP. It is possible to turn off SSID on some APs. Disabling SSID broadcasts creates a "closed network." If possible, SSID broadcasts should be disabled, although this will interfere with Windows XP's ability to automatically discover wireless networks and associate with them. However, even if SSID broadcasts are turned off, it is still possible to sniff the network traffic and see the SSID in the frames.

Wireless clients can connect to access points using either open system or shared-key authentication. Shared-key authentication provides protection against some DoS attacks, but it creates a significant vulnerability for the WEP keys in use on the network and should not be used.

MAC filtering is another defensive tactic that can be employed to protect wireless networks from unwanted intrusion. Only the wireless stations that possess adapters that have valid MAC addresses are allowed to communicate with the access point. However, MAC addresses can be easily spoofed, and maintaining a list of valid MAC addresses could be impractical in a large environment.

A much better way of securing WLANs is to use 802.1x technology. 802.1x was originally developed to provide a method for port-based authentication on wired networks. However, it was found to have significant application in wireless networks. With 802.1x authentication, a supplicant (a wireless workstation) needs to be authenticated by an authenticator (usually a RADIUS server) before access is granted to the network itself. The authentication process takes place over a logical uncontrolled port that is used only for the authentication process. If the authentication process is successful, access is granted to the network on the logical controlled port.

802.1x relies on Extensible Authentication Protocol (EAP) to perform the authentication. The preferred EAP type for 802.1x is EAP-TLS. EAP-TLS provides the ability to use dynamic per-user, session-based WEP keys, eliminating some of the more significant vulnerabilities associated with WEP. However, to use EAP-TLS, you must deploy a Public Key Infrastructure (PKI) to issue digital X.509 certificates to the wireless clients and the RADIUS server.

Other methods that can be used to secure wireless networks include placing wireless APs on their own subnets in wireless DMZs (WDMZ). The WDMZ can be protected from the corporate network by a firewall or router. Access to the corporate network can be limited to VPN connections that use either PPTP or L2TP. New security measures continue to be developed for wireless networks. Future security measures include Temporal Key Integrity Protocol (TKIP) and Message Integrity Code (MIC).

Exam Objectives Fast Track

Introduction to the Wireless LAN

- ☑ Wireless Equivalent Privacy (WEP) is the security method used in IEEE 802.11 WLANs, and Wireless Transport Layer Security (WTLS) provides security in WAP networks.

- ☑ WEP provides for two key sizes: 40-bit and 104-bit secret keys. These keys are concatenated to a 24-bit initialization vector (IV) to provide either a 64- or 128-bit key for encryption.

- ☑ WEP uses the RC4 stream algorithm to encrypt its data.

- ☑ 802.11 networks use two types of authentication: open system authentication and shared-key authentication.

- ☑ There are two types of 802.11 network modes: ad hoc and infrastructure. Ad hoc 802.11 networks are peer-to-peer in design and can be implemented by two clients with wireless network cards. The infrastructure mode of 802.11 uses Access Points (APs) to provide wireless connectivity to a wired network beyond the AP.

- ☑ To protect against some rudimentary attacks that insert known text into the stream to attempt to reveal the key stream, WEP incorporates a checksum in each frame. Any frame not found to be valid through the checksum is discarded.

- ☑ Used on its own, WEP does not provide adequate WLAN security.

- ☑ To be effective, WEP must be implemented on every client as well as every AP.

- ☑ WEP keys are user definable and unlimited. They do not have to be predefined and can and should be changed often.

- ☑ Despite WEP's drawbacks, you should implement the strongest version of WEP available and keep abreast of the latest upgrades to the standards.

- ☑ The IEEE 802.1x specification uses the Extensible Authentication Protocol (EAP) to provide for client authentication.

Wireless LAN Security Issues

- ☑ Examining the common threats to both wired and wireless networks provides a solid understanding in the basics of security principles and allows the network administrator to fully assess the risks associated with using wireless and other technologies.

- ☑ Threats can come from simple design issues, where multiple devices utilize the same setup, or intentional denial of service attacks, which can result in the corruption or loss of data.

- ☑ Malicious users aren't the source of all threats. Threats can also be caused by a conflict of similar resources, such as 802.11b networks and cordless telephones.

- ☑ With wireless networks going beyond the border of the office or home, chances are greater that users' actions might be monitored by a third party.

- ☑ Electronic eavesdropping, or sniffing, is passive and undetectable to intrusion detection devices.

- ☑ Tools that can be used to sniff networks are available for Windows (such as Ethereal and AiroPeek) and UNIX (such as TCPDump and ngrep).

- ☑ Sniffing traffic allows attackers to identify additional resources that can be compromised.

- ☑ Even encrypted networks have been shown to disclose vital information in cleartext, such as the network name, that can be received by attackers sniffing a WLAN.

- ☑ Any authentication information that is broadcast can often be simply replayed to services requiring authentication (NT Domain, WEP authentication, and so on) to access resources.

- ☑ The use of virtual private networks (VPNs), Secure Sockets Layer (SSL), and Secure Shell (SSH) helps protect against wireless interception.

- ☑ Due to the design of TCP/IP, there is little that you can do to prevent MAC/IP address spoofing. Static definition of MAC address tables can prevent this type of attack. However, due to significant overhead in management, this prevention is rarely implemented.

- ☑ Wireless network authentication can be easily spoofed by simply replaying another node's authentication back to the AP when attempting to connect to the network.

- ☑ Many wireless equipment providers allow end users to redefine the MAC address for their cards through the configuration utilities that come with the equipment.

- ☑ External two-factor authentication such as Remote Access Dial-In User Service (RADIUS) or SecureID should be implemented to additionally restrict access requiring strong authentication to access the wireless resources.

- ☑ Due to the design of TCP/IP, some spoof attacks allow attackers to hijack, or take over, network connections established for other resources on the wireless network.

- ☑ If an attacker hijacks the AP, all traffic from the wireless network gets routed through the attacker, so the attacker can then identify passwords and other information that other users are attempting to use on valid network hosts.

- ☑ Many users are susceptible to man-in-the-middle attacks, often entering their authentication information even after receiving many notifications that SSL or other keys are not what they should be.

- ☑ Rogue APs can assist an attacker by allowing remote access from wired or wireless networks. These attacks are often overlooked as faults in a user's machine, allowing attackers to continue hijacking connections with little fear of being noticed.

- ☑ Many wireless networks that use the same frequency within a small space can easily cause network disruptions and even DoS for valid network users.

- ☑ If an attacker hijacks the AP and does not pass traffic on to the proper destination, all users will be unable to use the network.

- ☑ Flooding the wireless network with transmissions can prevent other devices from utilizing the resources, making the wireless network inaccessible to valid network users.

- ☑ Wireless attackers can utilize strong and directional antennas to attack the wireless network from a great distance.

- ☑ An attacker who has access to the wired network can flood the wireless AP with more traffic than it can handle, preventing wireless users from accessing the wired network.

- ☑ Many new wireless products utilize the same wireless frequencies as 802.11 networks. A simple cordless telephone can create a DoS situation for the network.

Configuring Windows Client Computers for Wireless LAN Security

- ☑ Windows XP provides support for 802.1x protection on wireless networking connections.

- ☑ Windows XP integrated wireless networking into the operating system to a high degree. Windows XP takes control of your network connection in most cases.

- ☑ Windows 2000 does not offer the high degree of integrated wireless networking that Windows XP does.

- ☑ Both Windows 2000 and Windows XP can support WEP 64 and WEP 128 as well as any third-party solutions on the market.

Exam Objectives Frequently Asked Questions

The following Frequently Asked Questions, answered by the authors of this book, are designed to both measure your understanding of the Exam Objectives presented in this chapter, and to assist you with real-life implementation of these concepts.

Q: Do I really need to understand the fundamentals of security in order to protect my network?

A: Yes. You might be able to utilize the configuration options available to you from your equipment provider without a full understanding of security fundamentals. However, without a solid background in how security is accomplished, you will never be able to protect your assets from the unknown threats to your network through misconfiguration, back doors provided by the vendor, or new exploits that have not been patched by your vendor.

Q: Is 128-bit WEP more secure than 64-bit WEP?

A: Yes, but only to a small degree. WEP vulnerability has more to do with the 24-bit initialization vector than the actual size of the WEP key.

Q: Where can I find more information on WEP vulnerabilities?

A: Besides being one of the sources that brought WEP vulnerabilities to light, www.isaac.cs.berkeley.edu has links to other Web sites that cover WEP insecurities.

Q: If I have enabled WEP, am I now protected?

A: No. Certain tools can break all WEP keys by simply monitoring the network traffic (generally requiring less than 24 hours to do so).

Q: How can I protect my wireless network from eavesdropping by unauthorized individuals?

A: Because wireless devices are half-duplex devices, you cannot wholly prevent your wireless traffic from being listened to by unauthorized individuals. The only defense against eavesdropping is to encrypt Layer 2 and higher traffic whenever possible.

Q: Are wireless networks secure?

A: By their very nature and by definition, wireless networks are not secure. They can, however, be made relatively safe from the point of view of security through administrative efforts to encrypt traffic, implement restrictive methods for authenticating and associating with wireless networks, and so on.

Q: My AP does not support the disabling of SSID broadcasts. Should I purchase a new one?

A: Disabling SSID broadcasts adds only one barrier for the potential hacker. Wireless networks can still be made relatively safe even if the AP does respond with its SSID to a beacon probe. Disabling SSID broadcasts is a desirable feature. However, before you go out and purchase new hardware, check to see if you can update the firmware of your AP. The AP vendor might have released a more recent firmware version that supports the disabling of SSID broadcasts. If your AP doesn't support firmware updates, consider replacing it with one that does.

Self Test

A Quick Answer Key follows the Self Test questions. For complete questions, answers, and epxlanations to the Self Test questions in this chapter as well as the other chapters in this book, see the Self Test Appendix.

Introduction to the Wireless LAN

1. Your supervisor has charged you with determining which 802.11 authentication method to use when deploying the new wireless network. Given your knowledge of the 802.11 specification, which of the following is the most secure 802.11 authentication method?

   A. Shared-key Authentication

   B. EAP-TLS

   C. EAP-MD5

   D. Open authentication

2. What are the two WEP key sizes available in 802.11 networks?

   A. 64-bit and 104-bit keys

   B. 24-bit and 64-bit keys

   C. 64-bit and 128-bit keys

   D. 24-bit and 104-bit keys

3. Which of the following is a weakness in WEP related to the initialization vector (IV)? (Choose all that apply.)

   A. The IV is a static value, which makes it relatively easy for an attacker to brute-force the WEP key from captured traffic.

   B. The IV is transmitted in plaintext and can be easily seen in captured traffic.

   C. The IV is only 24 bits in size, which makes it possible that two or more data frames will be transmitted with the same IV, thereby resulting in an IV collision that an attacker can use to determine information about the network.

   D. There is no weakness in WEP related to the IV.

4. Bill, the network administrator, wants to deploy a wireless network and use open authentication. His problem is that he also wants to make sure that the network is not accessible by anyone. How can he authenticate users without a shared-key authentication mechanism? (Choose the best answer.)

   A. Use MAC address filters to restrict which wireless network cards can associate to the network.

   B. Deploy a RADIUS server and require the use of EAP.

   C. Set a WEP key on the APs and use it as the indirect authenticator for users.

   D. Use IP filters to restrict access to the wireless network.

5. The 802.1x standard specifies a series of exchanges between the supplicant and the authentication server. Which of the following is not part of the 802.1x authentication exchange?

   A. Association request

   B. EAPoL start

   C. RADIUS-access-request

   D. EAP-success

6. 802.1x provides for mutual authentication of the supplicant and the authenticator. Which of the following 802.1x methods support mutual authentication?

   A. EAP-MD5

   B. EAP-PWD

   C. EAP-RC4

   D. EAP-TLS

Wireless LAN Security Issues

7. The 802.1x standard requires the use of an authentication server to allow access to the wireless LAN. You are deploying a wireless network and will use EAP-TLS as your authentication method. What is the most likely vulnerability in your network?

   A. Unauthorized users accessing the network by spoofing EAP-TLS messages.

   B. Denial of service attacks occurring because 802.11 management frames are not authenticated.

   C. Attackers cracking the encrypted traffic.

   D. None of the above.

8. The tool NetStumbler detects wireless networks based on what feature?

   A. SSID

   B. WEP key

   C. MAC address

   D. CRC-32 checksum

9. Some DoS attacks are unintentional. Your wireless network at home has been having sporadic problems. The wireless network is particularly susceptible in the afternoon and the evenings. This is most likely due to which of the following possible problems?

   A. The AP is flaky and needs to be replaced.

   B. Someone is flooding your AP with traffic in a DoS attack.

   C. The wireless network is misconfigured.

   D. Your cordless phone is using the same frequency as the wireless network, and whenever someone calls or receives a call, the phone jams the wireless network.

10. You suspect that someone is stealing data from your company due to the fact that your closest competitor routinely seems to get its products to market weeks before you on every product you introduce. You have conducted sweeps of your organization's campus looking for surreptitious users and user actions but have yet to locate anything out of the ordinary. What type of wireless network attack are you most likely being subjected to?

    A. Spoofing

    B. Jamming

    C. Sniffing

    D. Man in the Middle

11. Your wireless network does use WEP to authorize users. You do, however, use MAC filtering to ensure that only preauthorized clients can associate with your APs. On Monday morning, you reviewed the AP association table logs for the previous weekend and noticed that the MAC address assigned to the network adapter in your portable computer had associated with your APs several times over the weekend. Your portable computer spent the weekend on your dining room table and was not connected to your corporate wireless network during this period of time. What type of wireless network attack are you most likely being subjected to?

    A. Spoofing

    B. Jamming

    C. Sniffing

    D. Man in the middle

12. The major weakness of WEP has to do with the fact that there are only a limited number of what available?

    A. IVs

    B. Packets

    C. Frames

    D. Beacons

Configuring Windows Client Computers for Wireless LAN Security

13. In Windows 2000, how do you configure WEP protection for a wireless client?

    A. Open the network adapter Properties page and configure WEP from the Wireless Networks tab.

    B. Install the high-security encryption pack from Microsoft.

    C. Issue the computer a digital certificate from a Windows 2000 Certificate Authority.

    D. Use the utilities provided by the manufacturer of the network adapter.

14. In Windows XP, how do you configure WEP protection for a wireless client?

    A. Open the network adapter Properties page and configure WEP from the Wireless Networks tab.

    B. Install the high-security encryption pack from Microsoft.

    C. Issue the computer a digital certificate from a Windows 2000 Certificate Authority.

    D. Use the utilities provided by the manufacturer of the network adapter.

15. You are attempting to configure a client computer wireless network adapter in Windows XP. You have installed and launched the utility program that came with the adapter, but you cannot configure the settings from it. What is the source of your problem?

    A. You are not a member of the Network Configuration Operators group.

    B. You do not have the correct Windows Service Pack installed.

    C. You do not configure wireless network adapters in Windows XP through manufacturer's utilities.

    D. Your network administrator has disabled SSID broadcasting for the wireless network.

Self Test Quick Answer Key

For complete questions, answers, and epxlanations to the Self Test questions in this chapter as well as the other chapters in this book, see the Self Test Appendix.

1. **D**
2. **C**
3. **B, C**
4. **C**
5. **A**
6. **D**
7. **B**
8. **A**
9. **D**
10. **C**
11. **A**
12. **A**
13. **D**
14. **A**
15. **C**

MCSE/MCSA 70-214 Part V

Configuring, Managing, and Troubleshooting Authentication and Remote Access Security

Chapter 8

MCSE/MCSA 70-214

Configuring Secure Network and Internet Authentication Methods

Exam Objectives in this Chapter:

4.5 Deploy and manage SSL certificates. Considerations include renewing certificates and obtaining self-issued certificates versus public-issued certificates.

4.5.2 Install certificates for SSL.

4.6 Configure SSL to secure communication channels. Communication channels include client computer to Web server, Web server to SQL Server computer, client computer to Active Directory domain controller, and e-mail server to client computer.

4.1 Configure and troubleshoot authentication.

4.1.1 Configure authentication protocols to support mixed Windows client-computer environments.

4.1.2 Configure the interoperability of Kerberos authentication with UNIX computers.

4.1.3 Configure authentication for extranet scenarios.

4.1.4 Configure trust relationships.

4.1.5 Configure authentication for members of non-trusted domain authentication.

4.2 Configure and troubleshoot authentication for Web users. Authentication types include Basic, Integrated Windows, anonymous, digest, and client certificate mapping.

Introduction

Previous chapters of this book examined ways to keep networks and systems secure from a variety of threats by implementing security configurations aimed at protecting traffic on a network. This chapter examines the concept of authentication: ensuring that users and servers are who they claim to be.

When Windows NT 4.0 and Windows 95 still had a major share of corporate networks, security analyst's used NT LAN Manager (NTLM) for authentication and hoped it worked. Truth be told, there were not many other easily implemented or understood solutions. With Windows 2000, this no longer holds true. Windows 2000 provides fully integrated Kerberos authentication support natively in all Windows 2000 Active Directory organizations. Although NTLM and NTLMv2 can still be used, it is not necessary in a purely Windows 2000 network. Networks containing legacy clients such as Windows NT or Windows 9.x computers, however, are forced to utilize NTLMv2 for authenticating these clients.

Likewise, when it came time for authenticating users who were accessing Web sites, security analyst's often relied on anonymous authentication and basic authentication. Anonymous authentication simply directs all user access attempts at a Web site towards one specially configured domain user account that has limited permissions. Basic authentication provides more control such as what Web site users can and cannot do, but transmits credentials in encoded plaintext across the Internet. Windows 2000 provides fairly robust Web authentication methods including anonymous and basic authentication as well as more advanced methods such as digest authentication, integrated Windows authentication, and client certificate mapping. Each of these Web authentication methods are described in detail in this chapter, discussing the strengths and weaknesses of each as well as how to configure and implement them.

The last item examined in this chapter is the concept of Kerberos trusts and how they are implemented between domains in Windows 2000. You will see that Kerberos provides a more secure and robust solution for creating trusts between domains with its default of two-way transitive trusts. Thanks to this feature, it is easier than ever before to share resources between domains.

Network Authentication in Windows 2000

Although Windows 2000 provides support for several authentication methods, only NTLM and Kerberos authenticate network users. Other methods authenticate dial-in users and users who access the network over the Internet, such as those accessing a Web or File Transfer Protocol (FTP) site.

The two supported network authentication methods in Windows 2000 are:

- **NTLM** Windows NTLM was the default network authentication protocol in Windows NT 4.0 and can be used, by default, by all legacy Windows clients. While support for NTLM is provided in Windows 2000 to enable authentication for legacy clients, it is not the recommended authentication protocol.

- **Kerberos v5** The Kerberos protocol was created in the late 1980s by a team of engineers at the Massachusetts Institute of Technology (MIT) and is widely accepted as the de facto standard for network authentication. Kerberos was originally designed for use on UNIX networks, but Microsoft included support for it in Windows 2000, following the specifications outlined in RFC 1510. Kerberos is the recommended network authentication protocol in pure Windows 2000 environments, due to its superior features as compared to NTLM.

By default, Kerberos is used for all network authentications in Windows 2000, except in the following situations:

- Windows 3.*x*, Windows 9.*x*, and Windows NT computers use NTLM for network authentication in Windows 2000 domains
- Windows 2000 computers use NTLM when authenticating to Windows NT 4.0 servers
- Windows 2000 computers use NTLM when accessing resources in Windows NT 4.0 domains
- Logging in locally to a Windows 2000 computer, where authentication is performed against the local Security Accounts Manager (SAM) instead of the Active Directory database

NTLM

NTLM is the mainstay of Windows NT and was once considered a relatively powerful protocol. However, NTLM suffers compared to Kerberos for several reasons:

- Authentication with NTLM is slower.
- NTLM performs one-way authentication only, which allows server spoofing.
- NTLM trusts are one-way and non-transitive and thus harder to manage.
- NTLM is proprietary and incompatible with non-Microsoft networks.

However, NTLM is necessary for establishing trusts with NT domains and for authenticating down-level NT clients. LAN Manager (LM) is used for authenticating Windows 3.*x* and Windows 9.*x* clients. By default, Windows 2000 is installed in mixed mode, meaning it can use any combination of Windows NT 4.0 and Windows 2000 domain controllers. After upgrading all of their computers (domain controllers and clients) to Windows 2000, security analyst's can disable LM and NTLM authentication, thereby increasing their overall authentication security.

NOTE

Windows 95, Windows 98, and Windows NT 4.0 clients running the directory services client (dsclient.exe) can use NTLMv2 for authentication. The Windows 9.x directory services client is located in the clients\win9x folder on the Windows 2000 Server CD-ROM. The Windows NT 4.0 directory services client can be downloaded from http://support.microsoft.com/default.aspx?scid=KB;en-us;288358. Microsoft has not produced a version of the dsclient specifically for Windows Me and does not support using the dsclient on Windows Me.

Kerberos

Kerberos is the default network authentication method in Windows 2000 because it is more secure, flexible, and efficient than NTLM. Using Kerberos instead of NTLM provides the following benefits to networks:

- **Increased Efficiency** When using NTLM for network authentication, each network resource must contact a domain controller to authenticate each client. When Kerberos is used, the network resource no longer needs to contact the domain controller because the client presents all of the identifying information required when resource access is requested. Additionally, clients receive identification of a network resource the first time they access it during a logon session, and store the information for the rest of that logon session.

- **Mutual Authentication** NTLM allows clients to be identified by the network resources they are attempting to access, however, it does not provide for identification of the network resource by the client. Additionally, NTLM does not provide a means for one network resource to verify the identity of another network resource. NTLM assumes that all servers are legitimate and authorized, thus providing a large security gap for an attacker to take advantage of. In contrast, Kerberos assumes all communications occur over an untrusted network, thus ensuring that both sides of a connection are authenticated to the other.

- **Delegation of Authentication** Kerberos includes a proxy mechanism that allows it to act as the client when attempting to connect to back-end server in a multitiered server arrangement. There is no provision for this in NTLM.

- **Simplified Trusts** In NTLM, an administrator has to manually configure a complex series of one-way non-transitive trusts between Windows NT domains within an organization. Kerberos simplifies this task by automatically creating two-way transitive trusts between root domains in a forest and between a parent and child domain. With this arrangement, the security credentials of any security authority (the Key Distribution Center [KDC]) in any location in the domain are accepted throughout the rest of the domain automatically. In cases where more than one domain exists, the same holds true for the entire forest.

- **Compatibility** Many operating systems rely on Kerberos v5 for network authentication. Compatibility is assured as long as the connecting operating systems are fully Kerberos v5-compliant (Windows 2000 is). NTLM is not compatible with any non-Windows operating system.

Kerberos Overview

As mentioned previously, one of the strengths of the Kerberos protocol is that it provides mutual authentication—that is, it provides authentication of a client's identity to a server or network resource and also provides authentication of the server's or network resources' identity back to the client. This makes it extremely difficult for unauthorized users or rogue servers to be placed on the network and to gain access to resources. The mutual authentication is performed before the network connection is even established. Kerberos assumes that this initial mutual authentication is taking place across an open untrusted network, such as the Internet, where the packets are subject to capture and possible modification. Kerberos takes steps to prevent attacks such as these from successfully bypassing its security mechanisms (discussed later in this chapter).

Test Day Tip

The material that follows in this section may or may not be on the exam, but it provides a critical foundation for understanding how Kerberos operates and how it is managed. It is necessary to cover this background information before examining the Kerberos implementation in Windows 2000. It is also good knowledge to have as an administrator dealing with Kerberos authentication in a Windows 2000 network.

The Kerberos protocol provides two services to a network:

- **Authentication Service (AS)** The AS of the KDC is responsible for authenticating users and issuing them their Ticket-Granting Ticket (TGT).

- **Ticket Granting Service (TGS)** The TGS is responsible for issuing individual session tickets that allow for network resource access by user based on their TGT.

We will examine how these two services are used in the following sections.

Kerberos Concepts

Kerberos relies extensively on the *shared key* concept. In shared key encryption, the encryption is symmetric meaning the same key can be used to both encrypt and decrypt the data being transmitted. Each side of the communication can verify the identity of the other due to the other having the secret key. This approach to validating traffic is much more secure than sharing a password.

Consider the following example: Two users want to communicate over the network. It is required that the receiving user be assured of the sender's identity. How can the sender prove their identity to the recipient? One possible method would be for them to send a shared secret in the message, thus proving that they know something only the two users know. The message containing the shared secret proves to the recipient that the sender is who they claim to be. Identity has been assured and communications can begin. There is, however, a flaw in this method. The sending of a shared secret in a message brings up the possibility of data capture and modification. Someone capturing packets between the two users could capture the shared secret and be able to impersonate one or both users. Clearly a better solution is required.

The trick here is to prove identity without revealing the shared secret in the process. Simply exchanging the shared secret cannot do this, so the solution is using the Kerberos protocol. Rather than sharing a secret in Kerberos, users can share a cryptographic key (see Chapter 4) and use it to safely verify each other's identity. Now, instead of sending a shared secret over the network, one user can encrypt a piece of data and send it to the other. If the receiving user successfully decrypts the data, it is assumed to be authentic and verifies the senders' identity. Remember that Kerberos makes use of a symmetric encryption key meaning that the same key is used both for encryption and decryption.

The Authenticator

As seen in the previous example, a user attempting to prove their authentication to another user or computer presented a piece of encrypted data. By presenting this data, which was encrypted with the shared encryption key, they proved that they know the shared secret. However, what is to prevent an attacker from capturing these packets and using them for their own purposes? The *authenticator* provides this protection. The authenticator also provides for mutual authentication, which is one of the foundations of the Kerberos protocol.

An authenticator is a piece of unique information encrypted using the shared encryption key. Each authenticator must be different than the previously issued authenticators, otherwise an attacker could simply replay back a captured authenticator and use it to gain access to resources they would otherwise be denied. To this end, each authenticator is time-stamped with the time on the sender's computer. Upon receipt of the authenticator, the receiver decrypts it and knows by examining the data contained within if the decryption was successful. If the decryption was successful, the receiver knows that the user who sent the authenticator has the correct shared encryption key. Since only authorized users have access to this key, the recipient safely assumes that the sender is who they claim to be.

To prove to the sender that the authorized recipient received the message, the recipient can initiate the process in reverse. The recipient extracts a small portion of the original message, encrypts it into a new authenticator, and sends it back to the sender. By decrypting and comparing the contents of this second authenticator to the data contained in the first authenticator, the sender can verify the recipient's identity. Again, only the authorized recipient would be able to successfully decrypt the original authenticator, so they must have the correct shared key. Mutual authentication has been assured.

The last issue that must be addressed is how to prevent replay attacks from occurring—wherein an attacker captures an authenticator and replays it later to trick the recipient into believing they are an authorized user. This protection is provided by time synchronization. After the original authenticator has been decrypted and the data extracted, the recipient examines the time stamp in the authenticator and compares it to the time on his own system. The times should match closely; within five minutes or less. If they match, the recipient can assume that the authenticator is valid. If the times are too far apart, the authenticator is rejected and no access is granted to the sender. However, one last check must be performed to further ensure that the time stamp is truly indicative of a valid authenticator. The recipient compares the time stamp in the offered authenticator to those contained in his memory. If the time stamp on the currently offered authenticator is the same as or earlier than any previously offered authenticator, the authenticator is invalid and is rejected. Through this time stamp comparison process, Kerberos prevents replay attacks from successfully gaining access for an attacker.

The time stamp plays another important role in mutual authentication. The authenticator that is sent back to the sender by recipient contains only the time stamp that was contained in the original authenticator. By providing only this one piece of information that is unique to the sending computer, the sender can be assured completely that the recipient has successfully received and decrypted the message. If the entire authenticator contents were sent back to the sender, the sender would not be able to tell the difference between a valid authenticator from the recipient or an attacker who just copied back the entire authenticator. This conclusively proves to the sender that the recipient is who they say they are.

> **Damage & Defense...**
>
> **No Replay Here**
>
> When Kerberos v4 was released to the public it was almost the same as the v5 release, but with two notable changes. One change was the addition of the cache on the KDC that keeps track of authenticators sent to it, as shown in Figure 8.1. It became apparent to the design team at MIT that just having the five-minute time skew rule between the client's system time and the KDC's system time was not going to provide protection against an attacker who would simply capture the authenticator as it traveled across the network and then immediately send it out to the KDC to launch a replay attack. The solution was to include a "replay cache" in v5 that keeps track of recently seen authenticators. Now if an attacker tried to capture an authenticator and replay it, it would be rejected because the legitimate authenticator would have already been received by the KDC and its time stamp recorded in the cache. The cache flushes automatically as time stamps exceed the configured time skew, which is typically five minutes.

Figure 8.1 provides a graphic illustration of the authenticator process.

The KDC

Kerberos provides the optimum solution for ensuring mutual authentication of both clients and servers on a network. But one problem remains that needs to be addressed: how to get the secret key to those users who should have it.

In cases where there are just a few clients who need access to a secret key, distributing is made easy by gathering everyone together at one time and in one location and then handing out the secret key at that time. Unfortunately, production networks do not work this way. Clients may want to access resources from anywhere on the network and those resources may not be anywhere near them. Another problem with this approach is that it is likely that clients will want to communicate with more than one server and a service may communicate with multiple clients. If the secret key is handed out manually, they would need to ensure that every client had every server's key and vice versa. As this is obviously not a good solution, they will need to implement an automatic trusted intermediary to store and disburse keys to both users and servers as required. Also, storing so many keys on each server and computer presents a large security risk that is better avoided.

Figure 8.1 The Authenticator Process

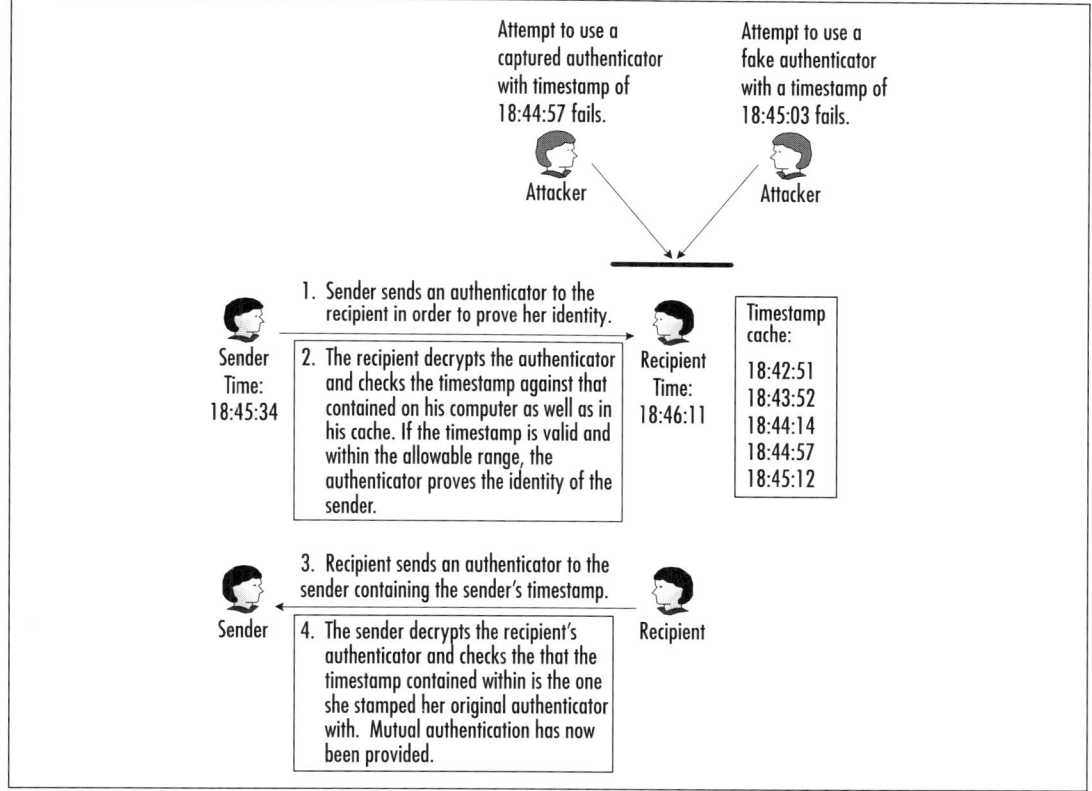

This problem is solved by the KDC, which forms the third part of the Kerberos system. In Greek mythology, there existed a fierce three-headed dog named Cerberus (Kerberos) that guarded the gates of the underworld. Like Cerberus, Kerberos uses three parts to guard access to networks: the client, the server, and a trusted intermediary—the KDC. The KDC sits between the client and the server, running as a service on a secure server on the network. It maintains the database of all account information for all security principals within its realm. A Kerberos realm is the equivalent of a Windows 2000 domain and is thus referred to as a domain for the remainder of this discussion. Included in the information the KDC stores about each security principal is a secret cryptographic key known only to the KDC and the security principal—be it a user, computer, or network service. This secret key, which is typically derived from a client's logon password, is used in exchanges between the KDC and the client and is referred to as the *long-term key*.

When a client requests access to a network resource, the KDC receives the request and creates a short-term key called the *session key*. This session key is used when the client and the server authenticate each other. The server's copy of the session key is encrypted in its long-term key and the client's copy of the session key is encrypted in its long-term key. This, however, still does not provide an efficient method for network clients to communicate with network servers and services. Key management would be a task that consumed massive amounts of resources from the KDC and a server would need to maintain a copy of every client's session key in memory while it waited for them to request access. Also, network traffic could cause a client's request for service to reach the intended server before the message from the KDC, thus causing the server to wait for a reply until the KDC's message has been received. This would force the server to commit more memory to holding the session state data. Fortunately, all of these problems are avoided by using *session tickets*.

The Session Ticket (ST)

When a client requests access to a service, this request is first sent to the KDC. Using the session ticket, however, results in both copies of the session key being sent back to the client. The client's copy of the session key is sent back to the client encrypted with the secret key that both the KDC and the client share (remember this is based on the client's network password). The server's copy of the session key is used to create what is called a session ticket (ST) that also contains information about the client. The session ticket is encrypted with a secret key that the KDC shares with the server. The session ticket contains the server's session key and can then be used to gain access to the requested service or resource without the client ever learning the server's secret key. Figure 8.2 illustrates the first two steps of a client requesting access to a network server.

The KDC does not keep track of its messages to ensure that they have been properly received. While this may seem like a security problem, in reality it is not. Remember that only the authorized client can open the client's copy of the session key (knowledge of the client's secret key is required) and only the authorized server can open the session ticket (knowledge of the server's secret key is required). When the client receives the client's copy of the session key and the session ticket, it places them into a secure location which is located in a secure portion of volatile memory (RAM); not on the hard disk. This provides assurance that this information cannot be retrieved from the computer by an attacker.

When the client wants access to the server, it presents the server with both the session ticket and an authenticator, as previously discussed. Together, these two items prove the client's identity to the server. The server using its secret key decrypts the session ticket, and the session key is extracted. Using the extracted session key, the server decrypts the client's authenticator. If the authenticator is verified, the server is assured that a trusted authority—the KDC, has verified the identity of the client. The server can then use its copy of the session key to encrypt the time stamp from the client's authenticator and return it to the client as the server's authenticator, as discussed previously. The process of the client requesting access to the server continues is shown in Figure 8.3.

Figure 8.2 Client Requests Access to the Server

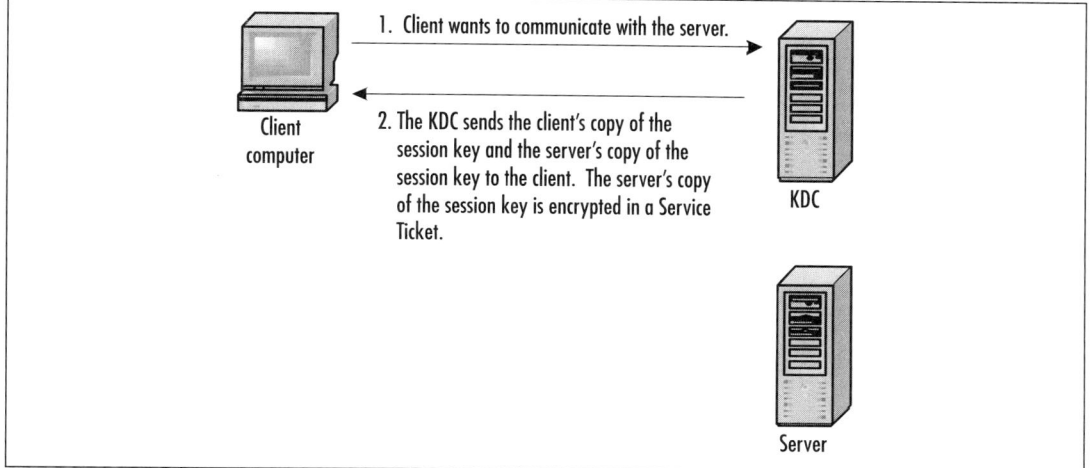

Figure 8.3 Client Sends the Session Ticket to the Server

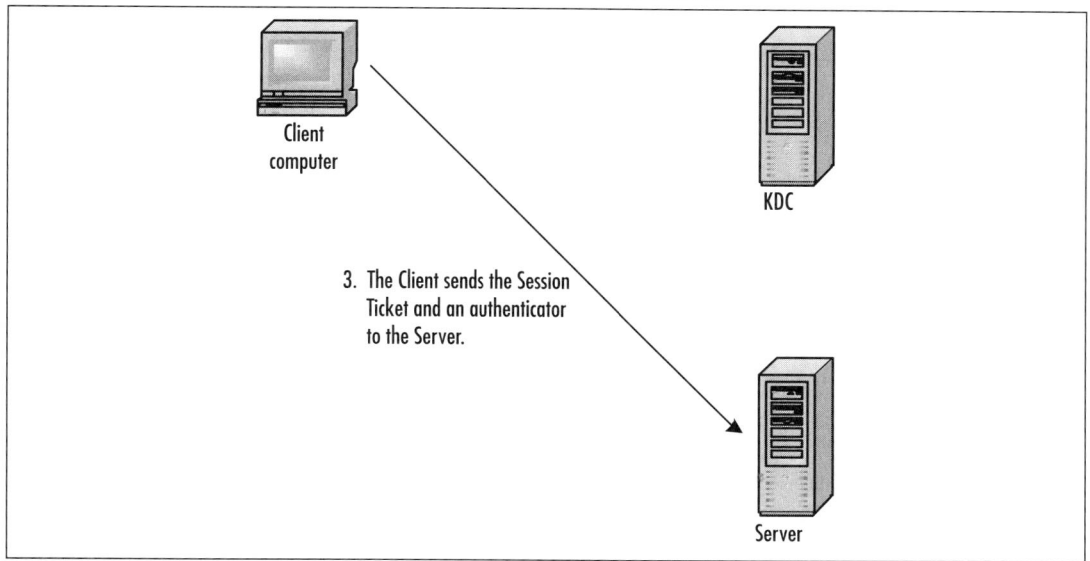

The server does not store a copy of the session ticket—it is the responsibility of the client to present this ticket to the server each and every time it wants to initiate a connection. The session ticket is decrypted each time using the server's secret key, which yields the session key. When the server no longer needs the session key, it is discarded, freeing up memory and resources on the server. Also, the client has no need to visit the KDC each time it needs to access the same server again, as it still has the session ticket in its volatile memory. Session tickets can be used and reused until they have expired. The expiration time serves as a form of protection against session ticket theft, as they are only valid for the length of time specified (10 hours by default in Windows 2000). This is designed to last the length of a typically user session—a workday—and then be flushed from volatile memory, destroying all session tickets and session keys at logoff or workstation shutdown.

The TGT

As discussed previously, a hash of the client's network password is used to create the long-term key. When a user logs into the network, the Kerberos client service on their workstation passes it through a one-way hashing algorithm to derive the secret cryptographic key. The resulting hash becomes the long-term key.

NOTE

By default, all implementations of the Kerberos protocol are required to support the Data Encryption Standard (DES)/CBC/Message Digest 5 (MD5) hash, although other algorithms may be added as desired.

After the workstation Kerberos client has performed the hash, it requests that the Kerberos service on the KDC compare the results to those that are stored in the user's account properties. If the hashes match, the user is authenticated by the KDC. The Kerberos client on the user's workstation then requests a session ticket and session key from the KDC that can be used for all future transactions involving the KDC during this particular login session. In response, the KDC provides the client with a special session ticket called the ticket-granting ticket (TGT).

Although it may seem like extra work, the creation and use of the TGT saves the KDC a small amount of time and resources every time a client requests access to a service or server that they do not already have an existing session ticket for. This savings comes as a result of the client not having to authenticate to the KDC each time—it simply presents its request for a new session ticket by sending the TGT and an authenticator to the KDC. The KDC replies with a new session key and session ticket for the newly requested access. The TGT can continue to be used and reused in this fashion just like a ST until the TGT expires, which is 10 hours by default in Windows 2000. At client logoff or workstation shutdown, the TGT, all STs, and all session keys are flushed from volatile memory.

The complete Kerberos process, from client logon to resource access is illustrated in Figure 8.4.

Figure 8.4 The Kerberos AS and TGS Processes

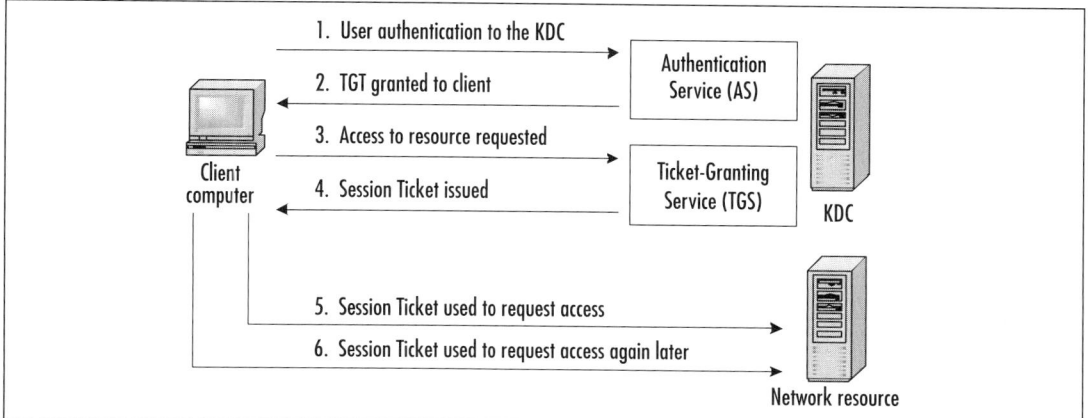

Kerberos Authentication across Domain Boundaries

Up to this point we have examined the operations of the Kerberos protocol contained on one domain. What happens when the resource the client has requested access to actually resides on another domain? Kerberos supports this situation through the use of a *referral ticket*. One additional thing must exist for cross-domain authentication to occur: the domains must share an inter-domain key. Once a trust has been established between domains (the sharing of this inter-domain key), the TGS of domain 1's KDC is registered as a security principal in domain 2 and vice versa. As a result of this, the TGS in each domain can now treat the TGS in the other domain as just another network service that it can issue session tickets for. Figure 8.5 illustrates the process of cross-domain authentication where a client in domain 1 requests access to a network resource in domain 2.

EXAM WARNING

Do not let the term's realm or domain throw you. They mean the same thing in Windows 2000, although to be absolutely correct, realm is the correct term to use when discussing an implementation of Kerberos outside of Windows 2000.

Figure 8.5 Cross-realm Authentication

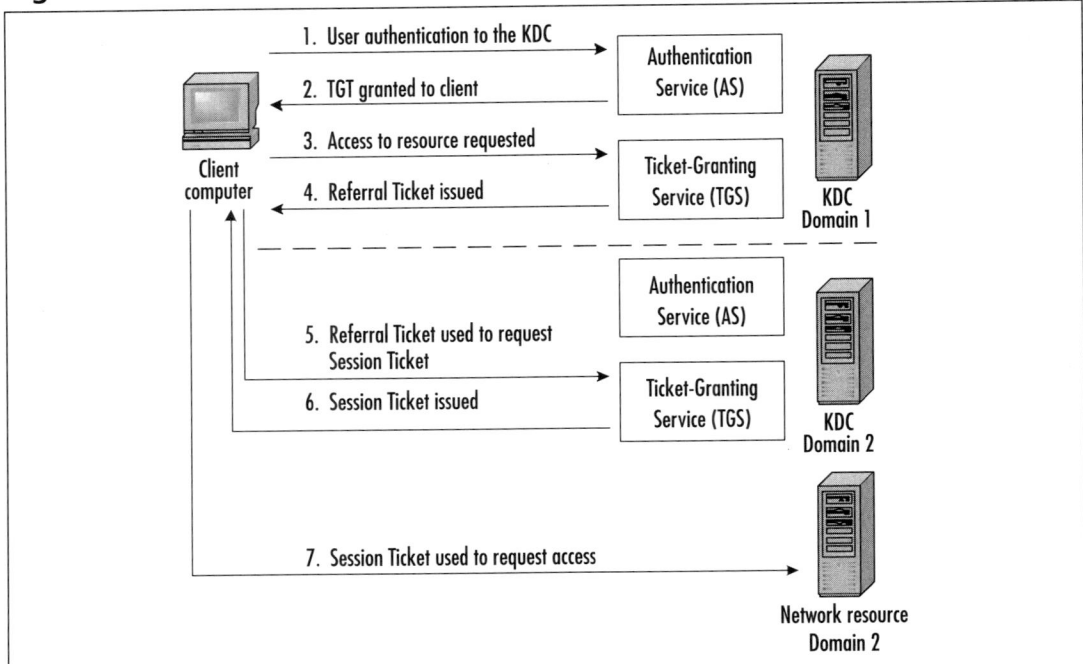

Delegation of Authentication

In the example domains discussed so far, the client is authenticated to directly access resources. But what happens when a multitiered arrangement exists where a client connects to a front-end server that must actually connect to a back-end server to process the access request and supply the requested information? The front-end server must have a ticket to access the back-end server. This ticket must limit the front-end server's access on the back-end server to what the client is authorized to do, not what the front-end server is authorized to do. In cases like this, some form of *delegation of authentication* must occur.

Delegation is fairly simple in concept: the client delegates authentication to a server by telling the KDC that the server is now authorized to represent the client. Thus, the front-end server can now represent the client in obtaining the session ticket for the back-end server. The client accesses the requested resource as if nothing special happened. There are two forms of delegation in Kerberos:

- **Proxy Tickets** The client obtains a ticket for the back-end server and then presents it to the front-end server. The front-end server then presents this ticket to the back-end server. This method is difficult to use because the client must know the name of the back-end server ahead of time.

- **Forwarded Tickets** In this method, the client issues the front-end server a TGT that it can then use to request tickets for the client as requested.

Proxy Tickets

The client obtains a proxy ticket by presenting a TGT to the TGS on the KDC, asking it for a ticket to the back-end server. In this request is a flag signaling that the client desires to receive a proxy ticket and includes the name of the front-end server who will be representing the client. If Kerberos policy permits proxy tickets, the KDC creates the ticket for the back-end server, marks it as a proxy ticket by using the PROXY flag, and sends it back to the client. The client sends the proxy ticket to the front-end server, which then uses the ticket to access the back-end server in the client's name. The client can now gain access to the back-end server. Figure 8.6 illustrates the proxy ticket process.

Figure 8.6 Using Proxy Tickets

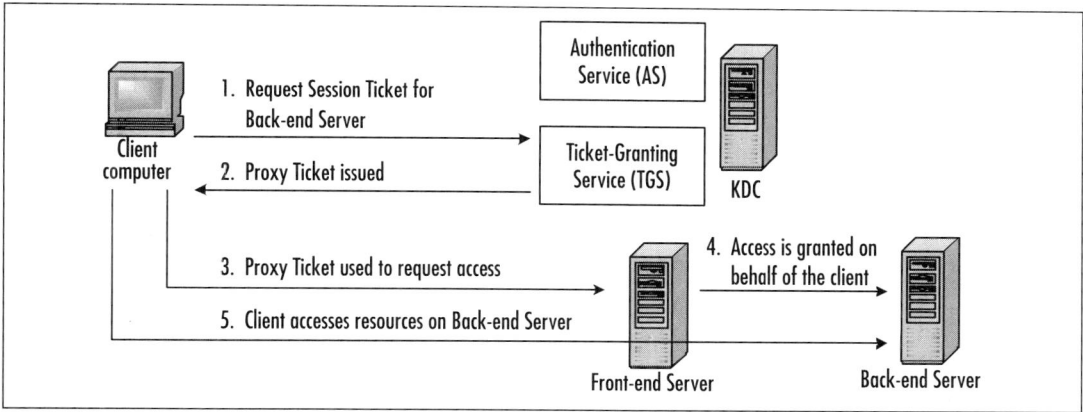

Forwarded Tickets

If the client wants to delegate the task of obtaining the ticket to access the back-end server to the front-end server, it must request a forwardable TGT from the KDC. This done by sending a request to the KDC indicating the name of the front-end server that will be acting as the proxy for the client. If Kerberos policy permits proxy tickets, the KDC creates a TGT for the front-end server to use in the client's name by marking it with the FORWARDABLE flag, and sends it back to the client. The client then forwards this TGT to the front-end server. Now when the front-end server requests a ticket on behalf of the client for the back-end server, it presents the client's forwardable TGT to the KDC. The KDC makes note of the FORWARDABLE flag in the TGT, flags the session ticket with the FORWARDABLE flag, and sends it back to the front-end server. The client can now gain access to the back-end server. Figure 8.7 illustrates the forwarded ticket process.

Figure 8.7 Using Forwarded Tickets

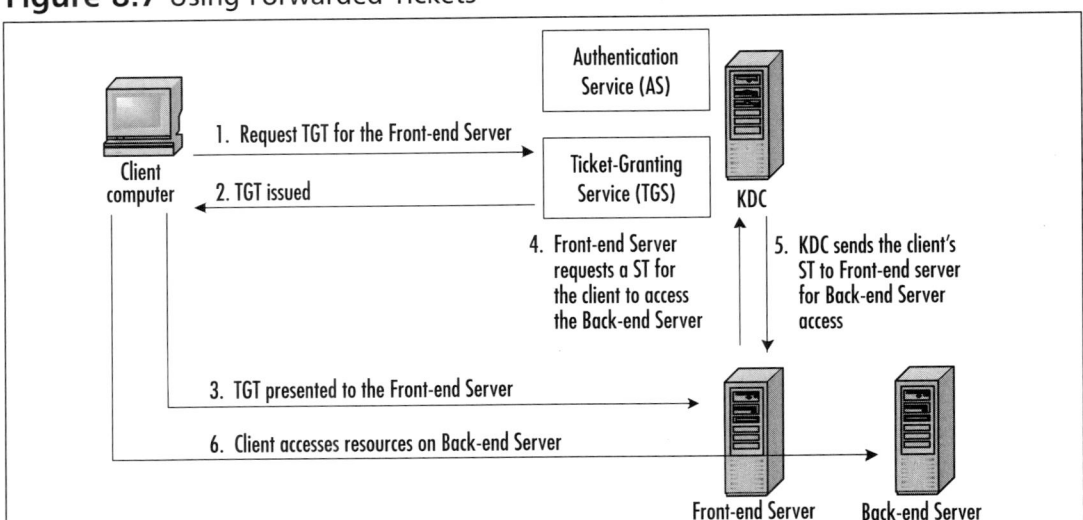

> **NOTE**
>
> For a look at the Kerberos protocol's creation, see *Designing an Authentication System: a Dialogue in Four Scenes* at http://web.mit.edu/kerberos/www/dialogue.html. The Kerberos main page at MIT can be found at http://web.mit.edu/kerberos/www/.

Kerberos in Windows 2000

The Kerberos implementation in Windows 2000 is called *Microsoft Kerberos* because Microsoft added its own extensions. This is not to say that Microsoft Kerberos is not Kerberos v5 compatible—it is—Microsoft has just modified it in the Windows 2000 implementation. Kerberos in Windows 2000 is fully Kerberos v5-compatible and can exist and interoperate with any other Kerberos v5 realm.

The implementation of Kerberos in Windows 2000 makes use of the same processes and entities as detailed previously in the general discussion of Kerberos and provides the same two services:

- **AS** The AS of the KDC is responsible for authenticating users and issuing them their TGT.
- **TGS** The TGS is responsible for issuing individual session tickets that allow for network resource access by the user based on the user's TGT.

The KDC and Account Database

The KDC is located on every Windows 2000 domain controller and runs as a domain service, as shown in Figure 8.8. The KDC uses the Active Directory database as its account database. Additionally, some information about users is retrieved from the Global Catalog server. Both the KDC and Active Directory services are started automatically at server startup by the domain controller's Local Security Authority (LSA). Furthermore, both of these services run in the process space of the LSA, preventing them from being stopped while the domain controller is in operation. Just as any domain controller in the domain can perform its designated function in Windows 2000, any Windows 2000 KDC in the domain can perform its designated function.

Figure 8.8 The Kerberos KDC Service

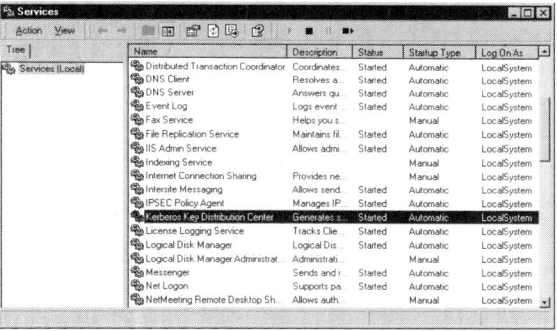

Every Kerberos KDC has its own principal name. The name used in Windows 2000 is *krbtgt*, which follows the guideline given in RFC 1510. When a Windows 2000 domain is created, a user account named krbtgt is created for the KDC principal, as shown in Figure 8.9. This account is a built-in account, so it cannot be deleted, renamed, or enabled for normal user use. Even though it appears that the account is disabled, in reality it is being used by the KDC. An administrator who attempts to enable the account receives the dialog box shown in Figure 8.10.

Figure 8.9 The krbtgt Account

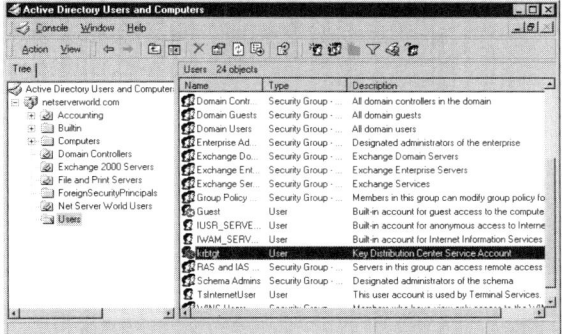

Figure 8.10 Attempting to Enable the krbtgt Account

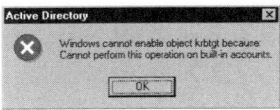

> ### Notes from the Underground...
>
> ### Safe Kerberos
>
> One of the more common actions an attacker who has compromised a system will carry out is to stop and start services of their choosing. Additionally, an attacker may install a rootkit into a system that modifies system files to mask their activities. Kerberos in Windows 2000 is not susceptible to this sort of attack due to the fact that it runs in the protected process space of the LSA. Kerberos cannot be stopped on a KDC without shutting down the entire server. This keeps the Kerberos service on the KDC safe from being compromised.
>
> Also, all sensitive Kerberos information that a client has, such as session tickets, session keys, and their TGT are kept in a non-paged section of volatile memory (RAM). This ensures that under no circumstances will any piece of Kerberos information related to that logon session ever be placed on a permanent storage medium, such as the hard disk of the client's computer. When the client logs off at the conclusion of their session, this section of volatile memory is flushed, taking with it all Kerberos-related information.

Windows 2000 automatically generates the password for the account, which the system changes automatically on a regular basis. The key used by the krbtgt account is based on its password, just like a normal user's long-term key. The long-term key of krbtgt is used to encrypt and decrypt the TGTs it gives out. The krbtgt account is used by all KDC's in a domain.

For example, a Windows 2000 domain could have five domain controllers, each of which has its own functioning KDC, but each KDC uses the krbtgt account. This allows each KDC to encrypt and decrypt TGTs using the same long-term key. A client knows which KDC to communicate with because the client computer queries the Domain Name System (DNS) for a domain controller—typically the one that is closest to it in regards to network topology. After the client locates a domain controller, it can begin the process of becoming authenticated and get a TGT.

EXAM WARNING

Make sure you understand how Microsoft implements the KDC in Windows 2000 and the specific domain user account created to act as the security principal for the KDC in Windows 2000.

Kerberos Policy

Policy for Kerberos in Windows 2000 is set at the domain level. Kerberos policy is stored within Active Directory, and only members of the Domain Admins group are allowed to change the policy. Figure 8.11 shows the options available in the Kerberos policy for the domain.

Figure 8.11 The Kerberos Policy Options

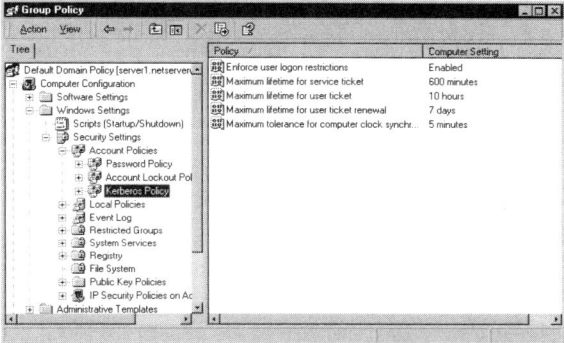

The settings included in the Kerberos policy are:

- **Enforce User Logon Restrictions** When enabled, this is used to validate every request for session tickets by making sure that the client has the correct user rights for logging onto the destination server. This is enabled by default. This setting can be disabled to speed up access to the network service or resource, but this will result in a less secure setting.

- **Maximum Lifetime for Service Ticket** The service ticket is the Microsoft name for a session ticket. This setting is used to configure how long a service ticket is valid for once it is issued. This is typically set for the same length as the user ticket lifetime, but does not have to be. The maximum setting for the lifetime of the service ticket cannot be more than the time specified in the maximum user ticket lifetime or less than 10 minutes. It can also be set to not expire by configuring a setting of 0 (zero) minutes. The default setting is 600 minutes (10 hours) and all settings are made in minutes.

- **Maximum Lifetime for User Ticket** The user ticker is the Microsoft name for the TGT. This setting is used to configure how long the user ticket is valid for. Typically this is set to the expected amount of time that a user is logged in during a work day, but can be set to a shorter time for increased security or longer if desired. The default setting is 10 hours and can be set to never expire by configuring a value of 0 (zero) hours.

- **Maximum Lifetime for User Ticket Removal** This setting controls how long a continuously renewed TGT is valid for before being removed from service. This is configured in days, with the default being seven days.

- **Maximum Tolerance for Computer Clock Synchronization** This setting determines the maximum difference in time allowed between a sender and a recipient in order to prevent the replay of authenticators. This setting is configured in minutes and is set for five minutes by default. If a network's time synchronization is really good, this number may be trimmed down even lower. Conversely, poor time synchronization may require an increase in this setting. This, however, can lead to security vulnerabilities in the Kerberos implementation.

EXAM WARNING

Pay careful attention to the wording of exam questions when dealing with Kerberos policy options. Do not mistake service tickets (session tickets) for user tickets (TGTs).

It is easy to change an attribute by double-clicking the attribute and changing the setting, as shown in Figure 8.12.

Figure 8.12 Changing the Maximum Lifetime for a User Ticket Renewal

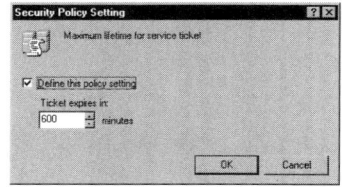

Delegation of Authentication

As discussed earlier, Kerberos supports two methods of delegation: proxy tickets and forwardable tickets. Several conditions must be met in Windows 2000 to allow delegation by way of forwardable tickets to occur:

- The client's Active Directory account must be enabled for delegation
- The service's Active Directory account must be enabled for delegation
- The client computer must be running Windows 2000 in a Windows 2000 Active Directory domain

- The computer that the service runs on must be running Windows 2000 in a Windows 2000 Active Directory domain

To enable the client's user account for delegation, complete the steps outlined in Exercise 8.01.

EXERCISE 8.01

CONFIGURING A CLIENT FOR KERBEROS DELEGATION

1. Click **Start | Programs | Administrative Tools | Active Directory Users and Computers**.
2. Locate the user account you want to enable delegation for and right-click on it.
3. Select **Properties** from the context menu and switch to the **Account** tab.
4. In the "Account options" area, scroll down until you see the "Account is sensitive and cannot be delegated" option. Ensure that this option is deselected, as shown in Figure 8.13.

Figure 8.13 Configuring a User for Delegation

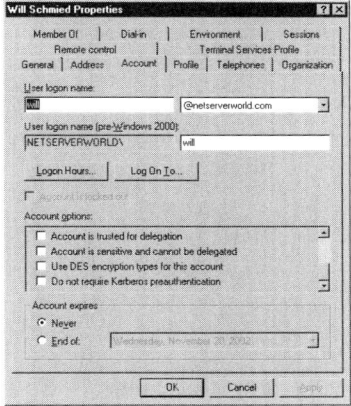

5. Click **OK** to accept any changes.

The process to configure the service for delegation is accomplished one of two ways, depending on the context in which that service is running—either under the host computer's local system account or under its own specific domain user account. Exercise 8.02 presents the process to configure delegation for a service that runs in the context of the host computer's local system account. Exercise 8.3 presents the process to configure delegation for a service that runs in the context of its own specific domain user account.

EXERCISE 8.02

CONFIGURING A LOCAL HOST SERVICE FOR KERBEROS DELEGATION

1. Click **Start** | **Programs** | **Administrative Tools** | **Active Directory Users and Computers**.
2. Locate the computer account you want to enable delegation for and right-click it.
3. Select **Properties** from the context menu and switch to the **General** tab.
4. Place a check mark in the **Trust computer for delegation** check box, as shown in Figure 8.14.

Figure 8.14 Configuring a Computer for Delegation

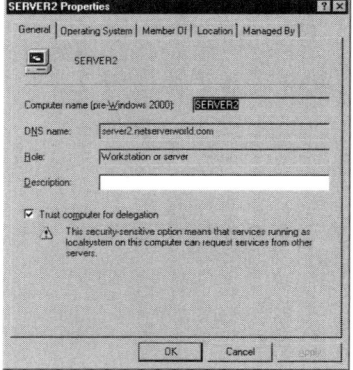

5. Click **OK** to accept any changes.

Exercise 8.03 details the process to configure a service's domain user account for delegation.

EXERCISE 8.03

CONFIGURING A DOMAIN ACCOUNT SERVICE FOR KERBEROS DELEGATION

1. Click **Start | Programs | Administrative Tools | Active Directory Users and Computers**.
2. Locate the service's domain account you want to enable delegation for and right-click it.
3. Select **Properties** from the context menu and switch to the **Account** tab.
4. In the "Account options" area, scroll down until you see the "Account is trusted for delegation" option. Ensure that this option is selected (refer to Figure 8.13).
5. Click **OK** to accept any changes.

EXAM WARNING

Do not confuse the different actions that must be taken to ensure delegation can take place on the network. By default, clients are already enabled for delegation due to the fact the "Account is sensitive and cannot be delegated" option is unchecked by default. Services running in the context of the local system account must have the computer trusted for delegation; services running in the context of their own domain user account need to have that domain user account trusted for delegation.

Preauthentication

Preauthentication is a Windows 2000 add-on to Kerberos that makes offline password guessing attacks very difficult. By default, the Windows 2000 KDC requires preauthentication of all client's accounts; however, this can be disabled if interoperability with another vendor's implementation of Kerberos is required. Exercise 8.04 details the process to disable preauthentication for a user's account.

> ### EXERCISE 8.04
>
> #### CONFIGURING KERBEROS PREAUTHENTICATION
>
> 1. Click **Start | Programs | Administrative Tools | Active Directory Users and Computers**.
> 2. Locate the user account you want to enable delegation for and right-click it.
> 3. Select **Properties** from the context menu and switch to the **Account** tab.
> 4. In the "Account options" area, scroll down until you see the "Do not require Kerberos preauthentication" option (see Figure 8.13). Ensure that this option is deselected.
> 5. Click **OK** to accept any changes.

Credentials Cache

The client uses an area of volatile memory (RAM) called the *credentials cache* to store its TGTs, STs, and session keys. This area of memory is protected by the LSA and is **never** placed in the page file or any other location on the hard disk. When the client logs off the network the cache is flushed from volatile memory, thus preventing an attacker from capturing any information that could be used to defeat the security Kerberos provides. When the user logs off the system, everything in the area of memory used for the credentials cache is flushed.

DNS Name Resolution

Microsoft Kerberos depends on the DNS to find an available KDC to send the initial authentication request. All Windows 2000 domain controllers are KDCs, and the KDC is registered as *_kerberos._udp.nameofDNSdomain* in the DNS service location record (also called the SRV record). Clients can query for this SRV record to locate the Information Protocol (IP) address for computers running the KDC service. A client that cannot find the SRV record can query for a host record (an "A" record) using the domain name.

If a Windows 2000 computer is a member of a different Kerberos realm (a UNIX realm and not a Windows 2000 domain), it cannot look for the SRV record. In this case, the name of the KDC server is stored in the Windows 2000 computer's registry. When the computer needs to locate the KDC, the Microsoft Kerberos Security Support Provider (SSP) locates the domain name for the KDC server from the registry and then uses DNS to find the IP address for the system. The following registry key can be edited to add the Kerberos domain name to the computer (see Figure 8.15):

`HKEY_LOCAL_MACHINE\System\CurrentControlSet\Control\LSA\Kerberos\Domains`

Figure 8.15 Manually Configuring a Kerberos Domain Name

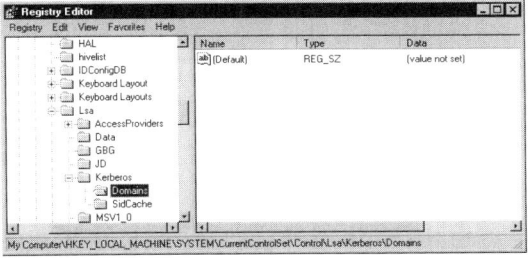

TEST DAY TIP

SRVs map a service to the hostname of a computer that offers that service. Host records (A records) map a hostname to an IP address. Windows 2000 DNS servers and Windows NT 4.0 DNS servers running Service Pack 4 or higher support SRVs. If using a BIND DNS server, it must be at least version 4.9.6 to support SRVs.

Authorization Data

The purpose of Kerberos is to verify that security principals are who they say they are, not to control access to resources. As such, Microsoft Kerberos tickets contain additional items that are not in other Kerberos implementations' tickets. Windows 2000 uses security identifiers (SIDs), just as in previous versions of Windows NT. SIDs are used to represent user accounts and groups. The SID for a user, along with any SIDs for the groups to which the user belongs, is included in tickets the client uses and is known as the Privilege Attribute Certificate (PAC). The PAC is not the same thing as a public key certificate. The user's name, also known as User Principal Name (UPN), is added to the ticket as UPN:name@domain. For example, UPN:stace@sdc.biloxi.ms.us is placed in a ticket to identify the user Stace.

KDC and Authorization Data

The Authorization Data field in a Microsoft Kerberos ticket contains a list of SIDs for the user, including group SIDs. The KDC retrieves this information from Active Directory and places it in the TGT given to the client. When the client requests a session ticket (or a service ticket, in Microsoft parlance), the KDC copies the data from the Authorization Data field of the TGT into the session ticket. The KDC signs the authorization data before the data is stored in the session ticket so that the LSA can detect whether the data has been modified. The LSA checks each session ticket to ensure that the signature is valid.

Services and Authorization Data

An access token is created after the credentials in a session ticket have been verified by the network server the service resides on. The PAC is extracted from the session ticket and used to construct an impersonation token that is used to access the service on the server. The impersonation token is presented to the service, and as long as the information in the PAC matches the data contained in the Access Control List (ACL) for the service, access is granted.

In Microsoft Kerberos, a session ticket is also required for access to services on local systems. The same process takes place for access to local resources; the LSA builds a local access token from the PAC contained in the session ticket.

UDP and TCP Ports

When a client sends Kerberos messages to the KDC, it defaults to using User Datagram Protocol (UDP) port 88, as long as certain criteria are met. On an Ethernet network, the maximum transmission unit (MTU) that can be carried is 1500 bytes. If the Kerberos message is smaller than 1472 bytes, Microsoft Kerberos uses UDP as the transport mechanism. If the message is between 1473 bytes and 2000 bytes, IP fragments the frame over UDP on port 88. If the Kerberos message is over 2000 bytes, it is sent by the Transmission Control Protocol (TCP) on port 88. RFC 1510 states that UDP port 88 should be used for all Kerberos messages, but since Microsoft Kerberos messages could very well be more than 2000 bytes because user and group SIDs are included, Microsoft also uses TCP port 88. A draft revision to RFC 1510 has been submitted to the Internet Engineering Task Force (IETF) proposing the use of TCP port 88, but this revision has not been included in the formal RFC yet. This modification will not have an affect on the interoperability with other Kerberos realms, as these extra pieces of information only pertain to the Windows 2000 Kerberos implementation.

Configuring Kerberos Trusts

When the first Windows 2000 Server computer in a network is promoted to domain controller, it creates the root domain for the organization. Since this domain is the first one created in the forest, it becomes the root for the forest and the root for its tree. It will have a DNS name, such as *mycompany.com*. When additional domains are created in the company's network (by promoting other Windows 2000 servers to domain controllers and designating them as domain controllers for the new domains), there are three options:

- They can be created as children of the forest root domain
- They can be created as root domains for new trees in the existing forest
- They can be created as root domains for a new forest

What are the components that make up the enterprise? Active Directory is made up of the following main components:

- **Forest** A logical grouping of trees; defines an organization
- **Tree** A logical grouping of domains
- **Domain** A security boundary and unit of replication for Active Directory
- **Organizational Units (OUs) (and Containers)** Hold objects and provide logical separation for the domain
- **Leaf Objects** Examples are users, machines, printers, and groups

OUs and leaf objects have nothing to do with trust relationships, therefore they will not be discussed any further. This section focuses on forests, domains, and trees and how they fit together.

Domains are the main boundary for Active Directory. Account policies are applied at the domain level. Users log into a domain; they do not log in to a tree or a forest. Every domain has its own set of objects (users, groups, machines, and so on). Every domain also has its own administrators. Domains are installed into trees.

A tree is a grouping of domains that share a contiguous namespace. What does this mean? There is something in common about all the domain names in a tree. Each child domain shares the naming context of its parent. The first domain created in a tree is called the tree root. Trees are created inside the forest.

A forest is a collection of trees (and domains). All domains within a forest share a common *schema* and *global catalog*. If there are two different schemas, there must be two separate forests. The first domain created in the forest is called the forest root. The entire forest is named after the forest root. Forestwide settings are set at the forest root domain only.

Let's apply these concepts to organization illustrated in Figure 8.16. There are two trees: mycompany.com and yourcompany.com. Mycompany.com was created before yourcompany.com, which makes mycompany.com the forest root. Both trees have sub-domains. There are four subdomains in all:

- Sales.mycompany.com
- Sales.yourcompany.com
- Accounting.yourcompany.com
- Payroll.accounting.yourcompany.com

Figure 8.16 The Relationships of Domains within a Tree and Trees within a Forest

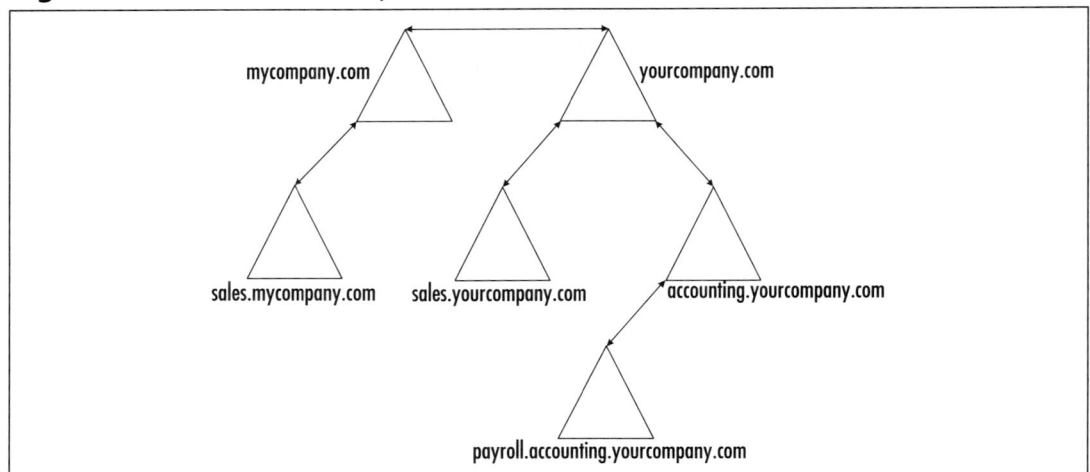

Notice how each of the subdomains has the name of its parent. The payroll domain is a subdomain of a subdomain. It shares both its parents' names. All these domains and trees are said to be in the mycompany.com forest.

The Great Link: Kerberos Trusts between Domains

In Windows NT networks, every domain was an island. In order for users in one domain to access resources in another, administrators of the two domains had to set up an explicit trust relationship, as discussed earlier in this chapter. Moreover, these trusts were one way. If the administrators wanted a reciprocal relationship, two separate trusts had to be created because these trusts were based on the NTLM security protocol, which does not provide for mutual authentication. Figure 8.17 gives an example of using Windows NT 4.0 trusts to configure complete trusts (all domains trust each other) between six domains. If the administrators want to configure all six domains to trust each other, they must manually create 16 one-way trusts.

With the Kerberos protocol, all trust relationships are two-way, and implicit, automatic trusts exist between every parent and child domain. It is not necessary for administrators to create these trusts. Finally, these trusts are *transitive*, which means that if the first domain trusts the second domain, and the second domain trusts the third domain, the first domain will trust the third domain, and so on. This transitive state comes about by using the Kerberos referral; every domain in a tree implicitly trusts every other domain in that tree.

One final benefit Is that the root domains in a forest of domain trees also have an implicit two-way transitive trust relationship with each other. By traversing the trees, every domain in the forest trusts every other domain. As long as a user's account has the appropriate permissions, the user has access to resources anywhere on the network, without worrying about the domain in which those resources reside.

Figure 8.17 Trust Relationships in Windows NT 4.0

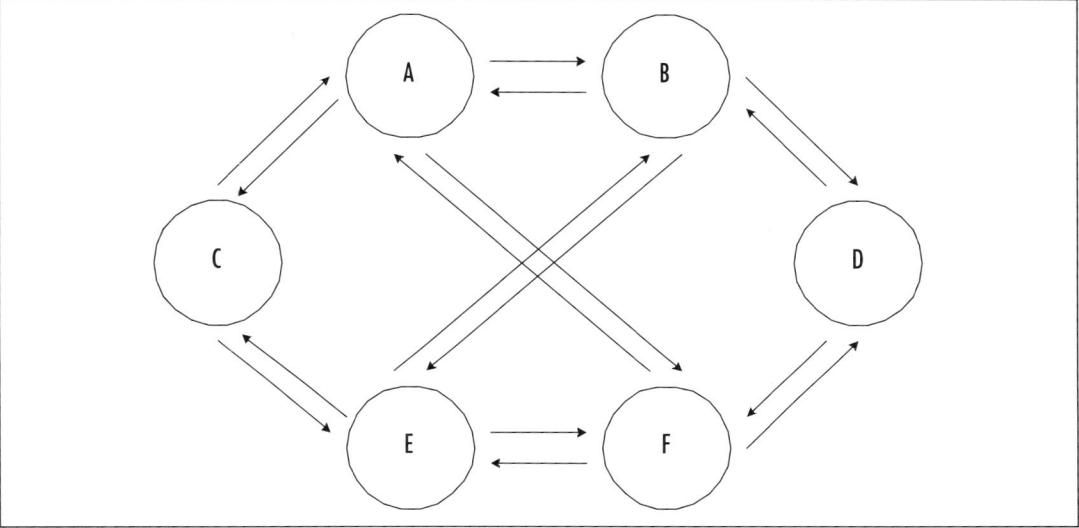

For practical purposes, a user in the payroll.accounting.yourcompany.com domain who needs to access a file or printer in the sales.mycompany.com domain can do so (provided that the user's account has the appropriate permissions). The user's domain, payroll.accounting.yourcompany.com, trusts its parent, accounting.yourcompany.com, which in turn trusts its own parent, yourcompany.com. Since yourcompany.com is an internal root domain in the same forest as mycompany.com, those two domains have an implicit two-way transitive trust; thus mycompany.com trusts sales.mycompany.com. This referral process is described as *walking the tree*. In Windows 2000, only five implicit trusts are needed to accomplish the same thing that Windows NT 4.0 needed 16 explicit trusts for . The best part is that all of the trusts are set up automatically in Windows 2000.

The Kerberos trusts apply only to Windows 2000 domains. If the network includes Windows NT 4.0 domains, they must still use the old NTLM one-way explicit trusts to share resources to or from the Windows 2000 domains.

Taking a Shortcut

Walking the tree requires many referrals, which is why *shortcut trusts* are useful. Shortcut trusts are two-way transitive trusts that allow administrators to shorten the path in a complex forest. These trusts must be explicitly designed by administrators to create a direct trust relationship between Windows 2000 domains in the same forest. A shortcut trust is used to optimize performance and shorten the trust path that Windows 2000 security must take for authentication purposes. The most effective use of shortcut trusts is between two domain trees in a forest.

Shortcut trusts are one of the two types of explicit domain trusts that can be established in Windows 2000; the other is the external trust used to establish a trust relationship with domains that are not part of the forest. The external trust is one-way and non-transitive, as in Windows NT 4.0 domain models. However, as with Windows NT, two one-way trusts can be established if a two-way relationship is desired. Figure 8.18 demonstrates both shortcut trusts and external trusts.

Figure 8.18 Connecting to an External Domain

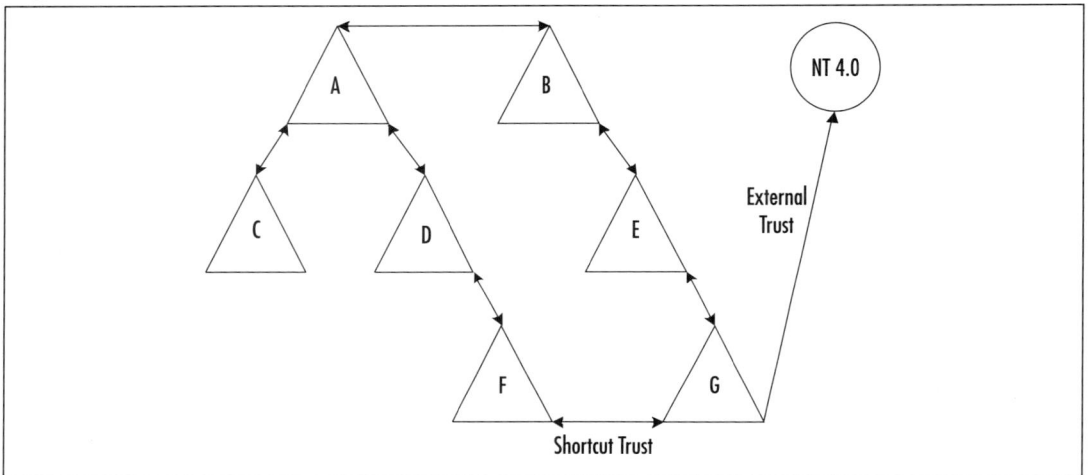

To keep things simple, the domains in Figure 8.14 are named A, B, C, D, E, F, G, and NT 4.0. Users within the forest (domains A through G) can access resources (if permissions allow it) at any of the domains within the forest. Users in domains F and G can share resources directly with each other without having to be referred up and down the tree. Lastly, users in the NT 4.0 domain can access resources in the G domain, but not vice versa.

Active Directory automatically creates the parent/child and tree root trusts for you. You must manually create all shortcut (domain F and domain G) and external trusts (domain G and domain NT 4.0). Trusts can be created from the command prompt using Netdom or from the graphical user interface (GUI) using Active Directory domains and trusts.

The Netdom command has the following syntax when working with Active Directory trusts (Netdom actually has a much more advanced syntax and can be used for a variety of Active Directory tasks):

```
netdom trust trusting_domain_name /Domain:trusted_domain_name
```

```
[/UserD:user] [/PasswordD:[password | *]] [/UserO:user]
[/PasswordO:[password | *]] [/Verify] [/Reset]
[/PasswordT:new_realm_trust_password] [/Add] [/Remove]
[/Realm] [/Twoway] [/Kerberos] [/Transitive[:{yes | no}]]
[/OneSide:{trusted | trusting}] [/Force]
```

Table 8.1 explains the syntax for using Netdom to create trusts.

Table 8.1 Netdom Syntax

Switch	Description
/Domain	Specifies the name of the trusted domain.
/UserD	Account used to make the connection to the trusted domain.
/PasswordD	Password of the user account specified by /UserD.
/UserO	User account for making the connection to the trusting domain.
/PasswordO	Password of the user account specified by /UserO.
/Verify	Verifies the trust.
/Reset	Resets the trust passwords.
/PasswordT	New trust password.
/Add	Specifies the trust to add.
/Remove	Specifies the trust to remove.
/Realm	Specifies a Kerberos realm if creating a Windows 2000 to Kerberos realm trust.
/Twoway	Specifies a bidirectional trust.
/Transitive	Creates a transitive trust.
/OneSide	Indicates that the trust should be created on only one domain.
/Force	Forces the requested operation.

TEST DAY TIP

You may find it helpful to memorize the functions of the Netdom prior to the exam and then write them down on scrap paper once you get into the testing center.

Exercise 8.05 goes through using Active Directory domains and trusts to create a new two-way trust. Exercise 8.06 goes through using Netdom to create a new two-way transitive trust.

EXERCISE 8.05

CONFIGURING TRUSTS WITH ACTIVE DIRECTORY DOMAINS AND TRUSTS

1. Click **Start | Programs | Administrative Tools | Active Directory Domains and Trusts**.

2. Within Active Directory Domains and Trusts (shown in Figure 8.19), right-click your **domain name** and choose **Properties**. You will see the window shown in Figure 8.20.

Figure 8.19 Active Directory Domains and Trusts

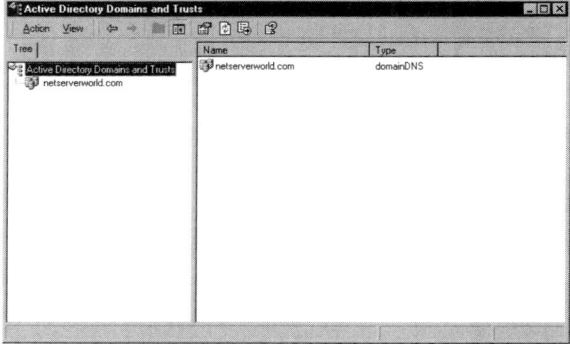

Figure 8.20 The Trusts Tab of the Domain Properties Window

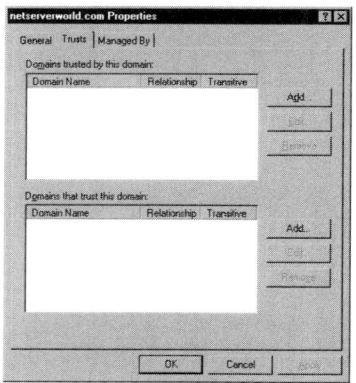

3. There are two sections in the Trusts tab of your domain's properties. You add the trusted domains to the top section and the trusting domains to the bottom section. Click the **Add** button in the "Domains trusted by this domain" section. You will see the window shown in Figure 8.21.

Figure 8.21 The Add Trusted Domain Window

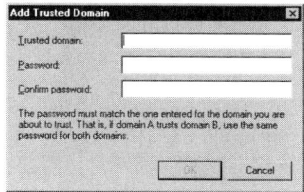

4. Type the **name of the trusted domain** and the **trust password twice**. When you are finished, click **OK** to return to the **Trusts** tab.
5. Click the **Add** button in the "Domains that trust this domain" section. You will see the window shown in Figure 8.22.

Figure 8.22 The Add Trusting Domain Window

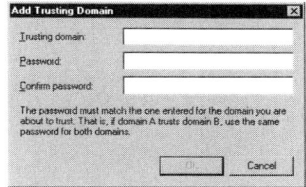

6. Type the **name of the trusting domain** and the **trust password twice**. When you are finished, click **OK** to return to the **Trusts** tab.
7. Click **OK** on the **Trusts** tab to save your changes, and close the Trusts window.

Exercise 8.06 will present you with the procedure to configure a new two-way transitive trust from the command line.

EXERCISE 8.06

CONFIGURING TRUSTS WITH NETDOM

1. Open a command prompt.
2. Enter the following command to create a two-way transitive trust. If the domain is Windows 2000, use the full DNS name; if it is Windows NT 4.0, use the domain name.

```
netdom trust trusting_domain /domain:trusted_domain
/userD:trusted_domain_admin_account
```

```
/passwordD:trusted_domain_admin_password
/userO:trusting_domain_admin_account
/passwordO:trusting_domain_admin_password
/ADD /Twoway /Trans:yes
```

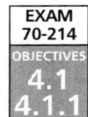

Configuring User Authentication

Very few companies run Windows 2000 as their only operating system. Most companies run a mixed environment of Windows 2000 Server and Windows NT 4.0 Server on their servers and a mixture of Windows 95, Windows 98, Windows NT 4.0 Workstation, and Windows 2000 Professional on their desktops. It is not uncommon for companies to run UNIX servers as well. More and more, administrators may also find themselves having to provide authentication means for users who are external to their network.

From a security standpoint, it is important to know how older operating systems work in the areas of authentication and file security. Security concerns have changed a great deal since the introduction of Windows 95, thus special attention must be paid to local security and authentication security. The best security is achieved when Windows 2000 is run exclusively. Running other systems, especially Windows 95 and Windows 98, weakens network security every time a client logs in. This section covers how to make Windows 95, Windows 98, and Windows NT 4.0 more secure when they authenticate to a Windows 2000 domain. It also examines how to authenticate external users to a domain and how to enable authentication for UNIX servers and legacy Microsoft clients.

Authentication for External Users

External users can easily be authenticated against an Active Directory domain once trust has been established a between your domain and the external domain. Once this trust has been established, security principals from the trusted external domain are automatically represented by a Foreign Security Principal object, which can then become a member of domain local groups. As these objects are automatically created by Active Directory, the administrator does not need to perform any manual modifications of them other than assigning Group membership. To view these foreign security principals, administrators need to enable Advanced Features within Active Directory Users and Computers (see Figure 8.23).

If there are no trusts established, the administrator can still authenticate external users via Internet Information Server (IIS) using Secure Sockets Layer (SSL), discussed later in this chapter.

Figure 8.23 Enabling Advanced Features

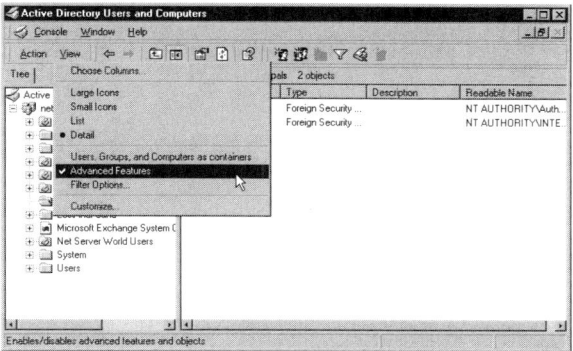

Configuring Interoperability with UNIX Servers

The type of authentication used by UNIX clients depends on the applications being used. UNIX clients can authenticate using any of the following methods:

- Cleartext authentication
- Certificate-based authentication
- Kerberos v5 protocol
- NTLM protocol

Using Cleartext Authentication

When UNIX clients use standard applications from the Transmission Control Protocol (TCP)/IP protocol suite, they can authenticate to Active Directory using cleartext authentication. These applications include the FTP, the Trivial File Transfer Protocol (TFTP), the Hypertext Transfer Protocol (HTTP), and Telnet. Unfortunately, cleartext authentication provides no security. Someone could read the packets on the cable and compromise the username and password.

If using cleartext authentication, the administrator should encrypt the communications with the server. They could use Secure Internet Protocol (IPSec) or SSL to encrypt authentication information. SSL is an application layer encryption method; IPSec is a network layer encryption method. In other words, applications must be SSL aware in order to use SSL. IPSec-encrypted packets appear as normal IP packets to applications, so no special support is needed (other than TCP/IP support).

Using Certificate-based Authentication

UNIX clients that are accessing Web sites can use certificate-based authentication. If accessing an SSL- or Transport Layer Security (TLS)-encrypted Web site, they would need a certificate that is trusted by that Web site. This requires both the client and the server to either have the same certificate authority or for their certificate authorities to trust each other. If this is not the case, client authentication fails.

Using the Kerberos v5 Protocol

There are two possible ways that UNIX clients can use Kerberos for authentication:

- They can authenticate directly to a Windows 2000 domain controller. They would view this domain controller as their KDC. Any Windows 2000 domain controller can fulfill the role of KDC.
- They can manually configure a trust relationship between the Windows 2000 domain and the UNIX realm (recall that a realm in UNIX is similar to a domain in Windows).

No matter which method is chosen, the UNIX client must have an account in Active Directory and the Active Directory account must be mapped to the UNIX account. If either of these steps is omitted, Kerberos authentication will not work.

Using NTLM Authentication

UNIX clients can use NTLM only if they are running an additional product that allows them to use Server Message Block (SMB) or Common Internet File System (CIFS). Two such products are Samba and LM for UNIX. If clients are using Samba, they must be running at least version 2.0.6. Any earlier version will result in cleartext authentication.

Configuring Interoperability with Legacy Windows Clients

Microsoft considers all clients running Microsoft operating systems earlier than Windows 2000 to be *down-level clients*. The most commonly seen legacy (down-level) clients in a network are:

- Windows 95
- Windows 98
- Windows NT 4.0

Each version of Windows has its own default authentication method. Whenever one of these clients authenticates to a Windows 2000 server, it attempts to use its default authentication method. These methods are:

- **LM** This is the default for Windows 95 and Windows 98

- **NTLM** This is the default for Windows NT 4.0
- **NTLMv2** Windows 95, 98, and NT 4.0 can be configured to use NTLMv2
- **Kerberos** This method is used by Windows 2000 clients only

Defining LM and NLM Authentication

LM and NTLM are forms of challenge/response authentication. LM is the weakest form of challenge/response authentication. LM is maintained in Windows 2000 for backward compatibility with Windows 3.*x* and Windows 9.*x*. It allows Windows 2000 machines to connect to shares on down-level clients. It also allows legacy clients to access a Windows 2000 machine with their default authentication method.

NTLM, the default authentication protocol used in Windows NT 4.0, can be used when computers running Windows 3.*x*, Windows 9.*x*, or Windows NT 4.0 authenticate to a Windows 2000 computer. Windows 2000 still supports NTLM for backward compatibility with these down-level clients.

At times, Windows 2000 uses NTLM to access resources. For instance, if computers are standalone servers or members of a workgroup rather than a domain, NTLM is used as the authentication method. When a Windows 2000 server authenticates to a Windows NT 4.0 server, NTLM is used. There are two versions of NTLM: NTLM version 1 and version 2.

Using the Directory Services Client

The purpose of the directory services client (dsclient) is to allow legacy clients to use some of the new features available to Windows 2000. There are two clients: one for Windows 9.*x* machines and one for Windows NT 4.0 machines. The Windows NT 4.0 directory services client can be downloaded from http://support.microsoft.com/default.aspx?scid=KB;en-us;288358. The Windows 9.*x* version of the client ships on the Windows 2000 Setup CD. Look in the client\Windows9x folder. The name of the setup executable is dsclient.exe.

Some of the features provided by installing the dsclient are:

- **NTLMv2** Legacy clients now use NTLMv2 rather than the weaker NTLM, when authenticating in Windows 2000 domains.
- **Site Awareness** This allows client computers to perform queries against DNS to locate the closest domain controller.
- **Active Directory Searching** This allows client computers to search Active Directory for a limited number of objects, including printers and users from the Search command on the Start menu.

- **Easier Password Changes** The client no longer has to locate and connect to the PDC emulator to change a password. Password changes can be done by connecting to any domain controller.

- **Dfs Capability** Clients are now capable of using Distributed file Share (Dfs) shares in Active Directory.

Some of the best features in Windows 2000 will still not be available to legacy clients after installing the dsclient. They include:

- **Kerberos** Only Windows 2000 clients can use Kerberos for network authentication.

- **Group Policy and Intellimirror** Only Windows 2000 clients can take advantage of the simplified and powerful management features offered by Group Policy and Intellimirror. The closest thing for legacy clients is the continued usage of system policies.

- **IPSec and Layer 2 Tunneling Process (L2TP)** There is no native support for IPSec or L2TP in legacy clients provided by the dsclient.

- **User Principal Name (UPN) Authentication** Legacy clients cannot authenticate using their UPN (user@domain.com).

Deploying NTLM Version 2

Installing the dsclient to get NTLMv2 support is perhaps the most important reason to install it on the legacy clients. By default, Windows 2000 allows clients to use their default authentication protocols (LM for Windows 9.x and NTLM for Windows NT 4.0). There are two steps to requiring NTLMv2 for use. Step one is configuring the domain controllers to require NTLMv2 and is outlined in Exercise 8.07. Step two involves configuring the clients to use NTLMv2 and is the subject of Exercises 8.08 and 8.09.

EXERCISE 8.07

CONFIGURING THE SERVERS TO REQUIRE NTLMv2

1. Open **Active Directory Users and Computers** from the Administrative Tools menu (Start | Programs | Administrative Tools | Active Directory Users and Computers).

2. Right-click the **Domain Controllers Organization Unit** and choose **Properties**. You will see the Domain Controllers Properties window shown in Figure 8.24.

Figure 8.24 The Domain Controllers Properties Window

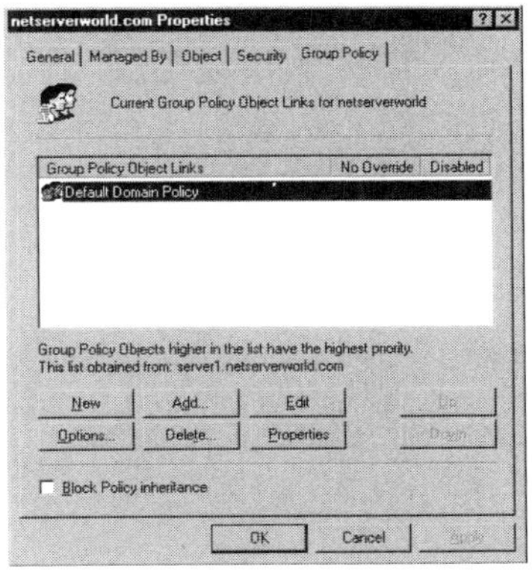

3. In the Domain Controllers Properties window, click the **Group Policy** tab.
4. Use your pointer to select the **Default Domain Controllers Policy**, and then click **Edit**.
5. Once in the Group Policy window, navigate to **Computer Configuration | Windows Settings | Security Settings | Local Policies | Security Options** (see Figure 8.25)

Figure 8.25 The Group Policy Editor Window

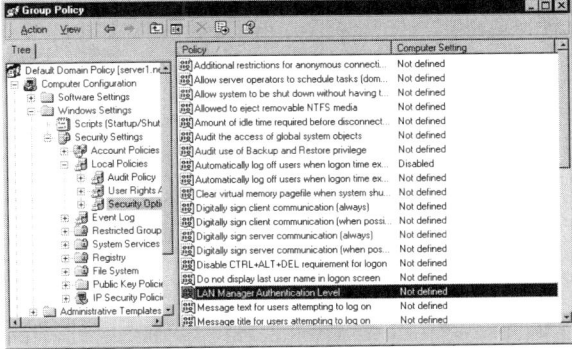

6. In the details pane (the right side), double-click **LAN Manager Authentication Level**. This will give you the Security Policy Setting window shown in Figure 8.26.
7. Choose the desired setting from the Security Policy Setting Window and click **OK**.

Figure 8.26 The Security Policy Setting Window

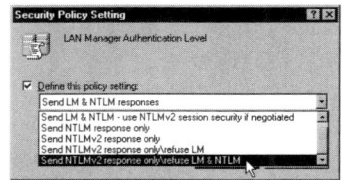

8. Close the Group Policy window and close Active Directory and Computers.

Each domain controller has six possible settings for its LM authentication level:

- Send LM & NTLM responses
- Send LM & NTLM – use NTLMv2 session security if negotiated
- Send NTLM response only
- Send NTLMv2 response only
- Send NTLMv2 response only\refuse LM
- Send NTLMv2 response only\refuse LM & NTLM

As long as the directory service client is installed on all the legacy clients, it is all right to refuse LM authentication. Administrators should be cautious with this setting, however. If it is enabled it and they still have Win9.x clients without the dsclient installed and configured, those clients will not be able to authenticate to the domain.

Making Clients Use NTLMv2

Configuring legacy clients to use NTLMv2 as their preferred authentication method is not as easy as configuring the server. To enable the clients, administrators must edit the registry. Luckily, it is edited in the same location in the registry as Windows 9.x and Windows NT.

For Windows 9.x clients, the dsclient must be installed before making changes to the registry. Exercise 8.08 walks through the steps for configuring Windows NT 4.0 to use NTLMv2. Exercise 8.09 walks us through configuring Windows 9.x to use NTLMv2.

EXERCISE 8.08

CONFIGURING WINDOWS NT 4.0 CLIENTS TO USE NTLMv2

1. Open a registry editor, such as **regedit** or **regedt32**.
2. Navigate to **HKEY_LOCAL_MACHINE\SYSTEM\CurrentControlSet\Control\Lsa**.
3. Add the following value (if the value is already present, verify it):
   - Value Name: **LMCompatibilityLevel**
   - Data Type: **REG_DWORD**
   - Value: **3** (possible values are 0 through 5)

Table 8.2 defines the possible values for this key.

Table 8.2 LM Compatibility Levels

Value	Description	Clients Use	Server Supports
0	Never use NTLMv2 session security. Always use LM or NTLM.	LM or NTLM	LM, NTLM, NTLMv2
1	Only use NTLMv2 session security if negotiated.	LM, NTLM, NTLMv2	LM, NTLM, NTLMv2
2	Use NTLM only.	NTLM, NTLMv2	LM, NTLM, NTLMv2
3	Use NTLMv2 only.	NTLMv2	LM, NTLM, NTLMv2
4	Domain controllers deny LM responses.	NTLM, NTLMv2	NTLM, NTLMv2
5	Domain controllers deny LM and NTLM responses.	NTLMv2	NTLMv2

To configure Windows 9.x clients to use NTLMv2, complete the steps outlined in Exercise 8.09.

EXERCISE 8.09

CONFIGURING WINDOWS 9.x CLIENTS TO USE NTLMv2

1. Install Internet Explorer 4.x or higher if it is not already installed. Microsoft recommends upgrading to 128-bit support if your local import and export laws allow it. For Windows 95 clients, you need to have the active desktop feature turned on before you go to Step 2.
2. Install the directory services client. It can be found on the Windows 2000 CD at **client\Windows9x\dsclient.exe**.
3. Open a registry editor, such as **regedit** or **regedt32**.
4. Navigate to HKEY_LOCAL_MACHINE\SYSTEM\CurrentControlSet\Control\Lsa.
5. Add the following value (if the value is already present, verify it):
   - Value Name: LMCompatibilityLevel
   - Data Type: REG_DWORD
   - Value: 3 (Possible values are 0 through 5)
6. Again, refer to Table 8.2 for the possible values for this key.

Head of the Class…

Verifying Your Encryption Level

Depending on export laws, if you intend to export, install, or configure a PC outside the United States or Canada, you need to make sure that you are only running 56-bit encryption. Use the following steps to verify the encryption level on your PC:

1. Navigate to **%windir%\system** (system32 for NT 4.0 clients).
2. Right-click the **secur32.dll** file.
3. Go to **Properties** and click the **Version** tab.
4. The description tells which version you are running:
   - A description of Microsoft Win32 Security Services (Export Version) means that you are running 56-bit encryption.
   - A description of Microsoft Win32 Security Services (U.S. and Canada Only) means that you are running 128-bit encryption.

Configuring Web Authentication

Web authentication is the process of validating a user's credentials. A user cannot access a Windows 2000 Server unless the user has been authenticated and authorized. Since IIS 5.0 runs on Windows 2000, users also cannot access IIS without being authorized first. IIS supports the following types of authentication:

- Anonymous
- Basic
- Digest
- Integrated windows
- Client certificate mapping

Using Anonymous Authentication

Anonymous authentication is the most commonly used method on the Internet. It is used for public Web sites that are not concerned with user-level authentication. Using anonymous access, companies do not have to maintain user accounts for everyone who will be accessing their sites. Anonymous access works with browsers other than Internet Explorer.

IIS runs all HTTP and FTP requests in the security context of a Windows 2000 user account. Windows 2000 requires a logon. This means that for someone to log on or access files on a server, they must have a user account. For anonymous Web access to work, a Windows 2000 user account must exist. This account is used anytime someone connects to a server anonymously. IIS 5.0 creates a user account for this purpose when it is installed. The account is named IUSR_*computername*. Computername is a variable that is replaced with your computer's name. This user account is a member of the Everyone group and the Guest group. It also has permission to log on locally to the Web server.

Using Basic Authentication

Basic authentication is used by almost every Web browser to pass usernames and passwords back to the server. It is widely supported in both Web browsers and Web servers. Basic authentication has several benefits, including:

- It works through firewalls and proxy servers.
- It is compatible with lower versions of Internet Explorer.
- It allows users to access resources that are not located on the IIS server.
- It allows the use of NTFS permissions on a user-by-user basis to restrict access. Unlike anonymous access, each user has a unique username and password.

Basic authentication also has some drawbacks such as:

- Information is sent over the network as cleartext. The information is encoded with base64 encoding (see RFC 1521 for more information), but is sent in an unencrypted format. Someone could easily use a tool such as Network Monitor to view the information as it travels across the cable, and then use a base64 decoder to read it.
- By default, users must have the "Log on Locally" permission to use basic authentication.

For Web requests, basic authentication can be made more secure by using SSL to encrypt the session. SSL is a secure communication protocol invented by Netscape that is used to encrypt communication between two computers. SSL is processor-intensive and degrades the performance of a system. SSL must be used during the entire session because the browser sends the username and password to the server every time the user makes a request. If SSL is being used only for the initial logon, as soon as the user requests a different file, their username and password will be sent over the network as cleartext once again. Only use SSL on Web sites containing sensitive data.

Users authenticating with basic authentication must provide a valid username and password. The user account can be a local account or a domain account. By default, the IIS server looks locally or in its local domain for the user account. If the user account is in another domain, the user must specify the domain name during logon. The syntax for this is domain name\username, where domain name is the name of the user's domain. For example, if someone logs in as the user Bob in the Syngress domain, they would enter **Syngress\Bob** in the username field.

NOTE
If your Web server is also a domain controller, there are no local accounts.

Using Digest Authentication

Digest authentication has many similarities to basic authentication, but also addresses many of the problems with basic authentication. Digest authentication does not send usernames or passwords over the network. It is more secure than basic authentication, but requires more planning to make it work.

Some of the similarities with basic authentication are:

- Users must have the "Log on Locally" permission.
- Both methods work through firewalls and proxy servers.

Like all authentication methods, digest authentication has some drawbacks including:

- Users can only access resources on the IIS server. Their credentials cannot be passed to another computer.
- The IIS server must be a member of a domain.
- All user accounts must store passwords using reversible encryption.
- Digest authentication works only with Internet Explorer version 5.0 or higher.

Digest authentication is secure due to the way it passes authentication information over the network. Usernames and passwords are never sent. Instead, IIS uses a message digest (also called a hash) to verify the user's credentials. A hash works by applying a one-way mathematical formula to data. The data used here is the user's username and password. Because the hash is one-way, it cannot be reversed to recover a user's information.

For digest authentication to work, all user accounts must be stored using reversible encryption. When an IIS server receives a digest authentication request, it receives a hash value. IIS sends the hash value to Active Directory to verify that the user's information is correct. Active Directory must run the same hashing formula against the user's information. If the hash value that Active Directory receives matches the hash it received from the IIS, the user's information is correct. If Active Directory reaches a different value, the user's information is considered incorrect. Active Directory can only run the hashing formula against the user's information if it has a plaintext copy of the password. Choosing the "Store Passwords Using Reversible Encryption" option on a user account (see Figure 8.27) stores a plaintext copy of the password in Active Directory. After enabling this setting for a user account, the user's password must be changed to create the plaintext copy.

Figure 8.27 User Account Properties

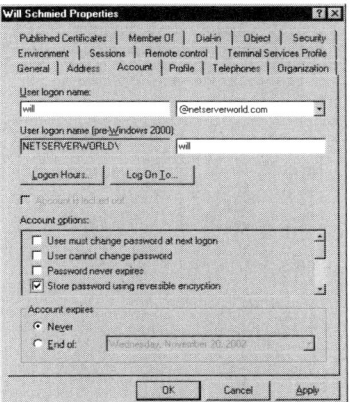

Using Integrated Windows Authentication

Integrated Windows Authentication (IWA) is secure because usernames and passwords are not transmitted across the network. IWA is convenient because if a user is already logged on to the domain and has the correct permissions for the site, they are not prompted for their username and password. Instead, IIS attempts to use the user's cached credentials for authentication. The cached credentials are hashed and sent to the IIS server for authentication. If the cached credentials do not have the correct permissions, the user is prompted to enter a different username and password.

IWA uses either NTLM or Kerberos for authentication. The Web browser and the IIS server negotiate which type to use. Both Kerberos and NTLM have their own advantages and disadvantages. Kerberos is less likely to be compromised because it is more secure than NTLM. Unlike NTLM, which authenticates only the client, Kerberos authenticates both the client and the server, which helps prevent spoofing. Kerberos allows users to access remote network resources not located on the IIS server, while NTLM restricts users to the information located on the IIS server.

Kerberos is the preferred authentication method. Following are the requirements for Kerberos to be used instead of NTLM:

- The client machine must be in either the same domain as the IIS server or in a trusted domain.
- The client machine must be running Windows 2000.
- The client must be using Internet Explorer version 5.0 or higher.

IWA has a few limitations including :

- It works only with Internet Explorer version 2.0 or higher (for NTLM authentication).
- While NTLM can generally get past firewalls, it is usually stopped by proxy servers.
- Kerberos can get past the proxy server, but is usually stopped by the firewall.

Using Client Certificate Mapping

Client certificate mapping is the process of mapping a certificate to a user account. There are two types of certificate mappings, both of which require the use of SSL:

- One-to-one mapping
- Many-to-one mapping

Before discussing the differences between these types of mapping, it is important to understand why mapping is beneficial. Normally, if an administrator wants to give a user access to a site, they create a user account. (assuming they are not allowing anonymous access.) They would give the user the username and password and let them use one of the three authentication methods previously discussed—basic, digest, or Windows Integrated. This is done because the operating system requires the use of user accounts for controlling access. To provide better security and reduce the administrative workload, the administrator can give users a certificate (see Chapter 4). Certificates are used to verify a user's identity. Using a certificate is more efficient than using a user account because certificates can be examined without having to connect to a database. It is also safer to distribute certificates than user accounts because it is much easier to guess or crack someone's password than it is to forge a certificate.

Where does mapping fit into the picture? If certificates are more secure and easier to distribute than user accounts, but the operating system requires a user account to control access, what should be done? A mapping between the user account and the certificate can be created. When a user presents the certificate to the operating system, they are given whatever rights are assigned to the mapped account. The end result is identical to the user logging on with a username and password. This solution provides the best of both worlds because they do not have to distribute usernames and passwords to all users, but can still employ user accounts to secure resources.

One-to-One Certificate Mapping

As the name indicates, one-to-one mappings map one user account to one certificate. The user presents his certificate, and the IIS compares the certificate to the certificate that it contains for the user. If the certificates match, the user is authenticated with their mapped account. For this system to work, the server must contain a copy of all client certificates. Generally, one-to-one mappings are used in small environments. One of the reasons mapping is used is to make networks easier to administer. If one-to-one mapping is used in a large environment, a large database is created because every certificate is mapped to a unique account.

Many-to-One Certificate Mapping

Many-to-one mappings map many certificates to one user account. Many-to-one mappings are processed differently than one-to-one mappings. Since there is no one-to-one association between user accounts and certificates, the server does not have to maintain a copy of individual user certificates. Instead, it uses rules to verify a client. Rules are configured to look for certain items in a client's certificate. If those items are correct, the user is mapped to the shared user account. For example, a rule can be set up to check which certificate authority (CA) issued the certificate. If a company's CA issued the certificate, the mapping would be allowed. If the certificate was issued by another CA, the user would be denied access.

> **TEST DAY TIP**
>
> It will be useful if you write down the various methods of Web authentication on your scrap paper before beginning the exam. Be sure to write down the pluses and minuses of each method and any special considerations that must be taken into account when working with each method.

Combining Authentication Methods

Table 8.3 summarizes the different authentication methods supported in IIS 5.0. Now it is important to learn how the IIS handles authentication when multiple protocols are allowed. Internet browsers always attempt to use client mappings first, followed by anonymous authentication. If anonymous authentication access fails, it is then the responsibility of the Web server to send a list of alternate authentication methods that are supported. The browser attempts to use the alternate authentication methods that it supports in the following order:

- Integrated Windows authentication (Kerberos-based)
- Integrated Windows authentication (NTLM-based)
- Digest authentication
- Basic authentication

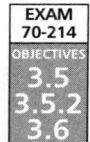

Configuring Web Site Authentication

Before certificates can be used on a Web server for authentication, there are two server certificates that must be available. The first is for the CA itself, and the second is for the Web server. There must be two different certificates for these two different functions, even if both reside on the same server. It is assumed that a Windows 2000 CA is already in place (see Chapter 4 for how to configure a CA). To obtain a server certificate for an IIS server, complete the procedure outlined in Exercise 8.10

Table 8.3 Summary of the Authentication Methods Supported in IIS 5.0

	Anonymous (Password Controlled by IIS)	Anonymous (Password Controlled by AD)	Basic	Digest	Integrated Windows (Kerberos)	Integrated Windows (NTLM)	Certificate Mapping (IIS)	Certificate Mapping (AD)
Works through firewalls	Yes	Yes	Yes	Yes	No*	Yes*	Yes	Yes
Works through proxy servers	Yes	Yes	Yes	Yes	Yes*	No*	Yes	Yes
Compatible with lower versions of Internet Explorer (2.0 and lower)	Yes	Yes	Yes	No	No	Yes	Yes	Yes
Allows users to access remote resources	No	Yes	Yes	No	Yes	No	Yes	No
Compatible with browsers other than Internet Explorer	Yes	Yes	Yes	Varies	No	No	Varies	Varies
Requires Internet Explorer 5.0 or higher	No	No	No	Yes	Yes	No	No	No

Refer back to the discussion on IWA concerning passing through firewalls and proxy servers.

EXERCISE 8.10

REQUESTING A SERVER CERTIFICATE FOR THE IIS SERVER

1. Open the **Internet Services Manager** from the Administrative Tools folder.
2. Select your Web site, right-click, and select **Properties** from the context menu (see Figure 8.28).

Figure 8.28 Opening the Web Site Properties

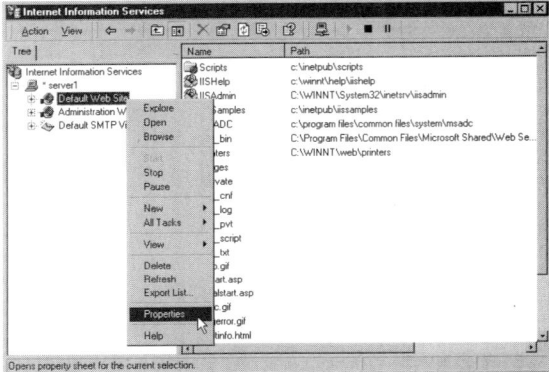

3. Switch to the **Directory Security** tab (see Figure 8.29) and click **Server Certificate** to start the Web Server Certificate Wizard.

Figure 8.29 Configuring Web Site Security

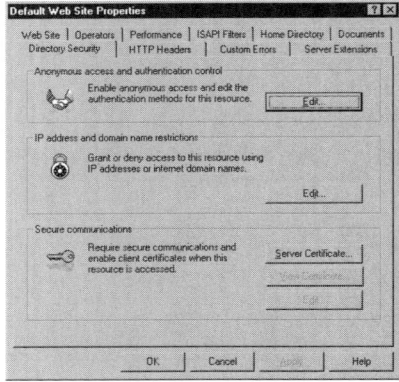

4. Dismiss the opening page of the Wizard.
5. Select **Create a new certificate** and click **Next**.

6. If you already have an online CA configured, you should select **Send the request immediately to an online certification authority** and then click **Next** to continue.

7. Configure the certificate name and key length as shown in Figure 8.30, and click **Next** to continue.

   Figure 8.30 Configuring the Certificate Name and Key Length

   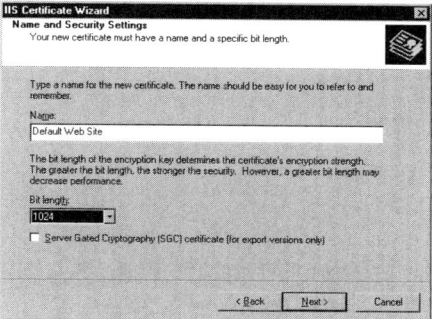

8. Enter or select the organization name and OU as shown in Figure 8.31, and click **Next** to continue.

   Figure 8.31 Selecting the Organization Name and OU Information

   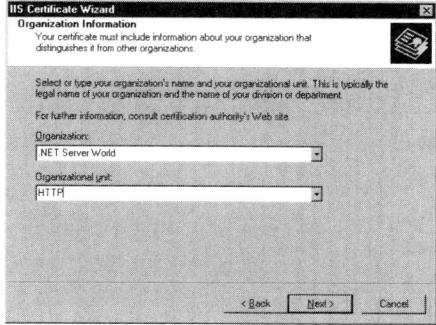

9. Enter the IIS server's common name—the FQDN if on the Internet or the NetBIOS name if on an Intranet—and click **Next** to continue. This name is extremely critical and must be configured *exactly* the same as the name that users will use to connect to the site.

10. Enter the required geographical information and click **Next** to continue.

11. Select a CA to issue the certificate and click **Next**.

12. Click **Next** after you have reviewed the configuration to start the issuance process.

13. Click **Finish** when you are done. You now have a server certificate for your IIS server. The View Certificate and Edit buttons previously grayed out in Figure 8.29 are now available for configuring.

In Exercise 8.11 you will configure various Web site authentication methods that do not use SSL. Exercise 8.12 will examine configuring Web site authentication using SSL based methods.

EXERCISE 8.11

CONFIGURING ANONYMOUS, BASIC, DIGEST, AND INTEGRATED WINDOWS WEB SITE AUTHENTICATION

1. Open the **Internet Services Manager** from the Administrative Tools folder.
2. Select your Web site, right-click, and select **Properties** from the context menu.
3. Click the **Directory Security** tab.
4. Click **Edit** in the "Anonymous Access and Authentication Control" section of the **Directory Security** tab, as shown in Figure 8.32.

Figure 8.32 The Directory Security Tab of a Web Site's Properties

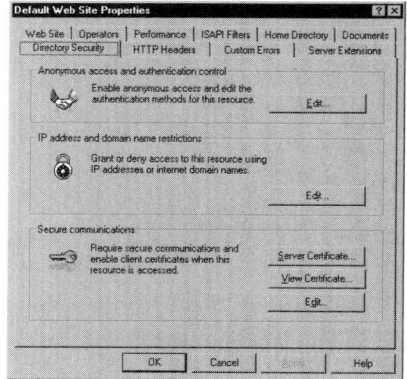

5. Choose the authentication methods that you want to allow (see Figure 8.33). Anonymous access is enabled by default.
6. You can change the account that the IIS uses for anonymous access by clicking the **Edit** button. Figure 8.34 shows the configuration window with the default anonymous access account.

Figure 8.33 Choosing Authentication Methods

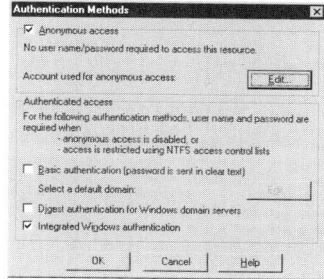

Figure 8.34 Changing the Account Used for Anonymous Access

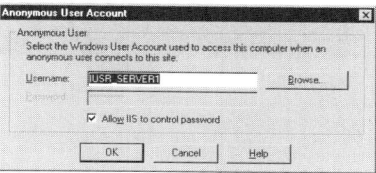

7. If you enable basic authentication, you will receive the warning dialog shown in Figure 8.35. As the warning states, this is not a big problem if you require SSL connections (Exercise 8.10).

Figure 8.35 The Cleartext Warning Dialog

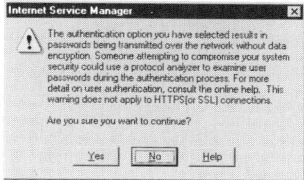

8. If your authentication domain is different from the domain the IIS server is located in, you will need to configure authentication domain as shown in Figure 8.36. If it is the same domain, you can safely leave this box blank, which forces the default behavior of the authenticating users to the domain the IIS server is located in.

Figure 8.36 Configuring the Basic Authentication Default Domain

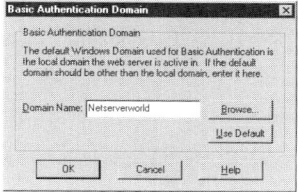

9. If you configure digest authentication, you will receive the warning dialog shown in Figure 8.37. You will need to ensure that you have configured user accounts for Store Passwords Using Reversible Encryption, as shown in Figure 8.27.

Figure 8.37 The Digest Authentication Warning Dialog Box

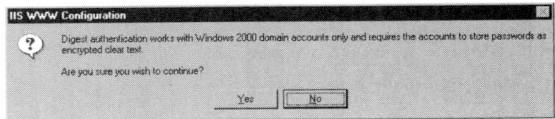

10. Click **OK** to accept your changes when you are done.

Head of the Class...

Allow IIS to Control Password

When an account is authenticated by the IIS, it is made a member of the Network group. When Windows authenticates a user, they are made a member of the Interactive group. To enable Windows to do the authentication, uncheck the **Allow IIS to Control Password** box. The Network group consists of users who are given access to resources over the network. The Interactive group consists of users who log on locally.

What does this mean? The "Allow IIS to Control Password" option controls whether users can access network resources or if they are limited to the IIS server only. If the IIS authenticates the anonymous account, the user can only access resources on the IIS server. The network group does not have rights to remote resources. If Windows authenticates the anonymous account, the user can access other network resources. The Interactive group is given the "Log on Locally" permission that can be forwarded to other servers for authentication.

EXERCISE 8.12

CONFIGURING WEB AUTHENTICATION USING SSL

1. Open the **Internet Services Manager** from the Administrative Tools folder.
2. Select your Web site, right-click, and select **Properties** from the context menu.

3. Click the **Directory Security** tab.
4. Click **Edit** in the "Secure Communications" section of the **Directory Security** tab, as shown in Figure 8.32. The window shown in Figure 8.38 will open.

Figure 8.38 Configuring SSL Properties

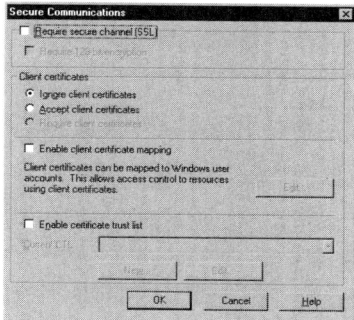

5. Configure your secure communication settings as desires.

   - Select the **Require secure channel (SSL)** check box to configure SSL)-encrypted communication for visitors using a Web browser that supports secure communications—URLs starting with *https://*.

   - Select the **Require 128-bit encryption** check box to require a 128-bit encrypted communication link for a Web browser to connect with this Web site. This setting is only available once you have selected the **Require secure channel (SSL)** option.

   - Selecting **the Ignore client certificates** option allows users to have access without being prompted to present a client certificate. This is not a recommended setting as it degrades overall security.

   - Selecting the **Accept client certificates** option allows users with client certificates access, but does not require the certificate. A user that has a valid certificate can use certificate mapping; a user without a valid certificate must use one of the previously discussed authentication methods.

   - Selecting the **Require client certificates** will allow only users with a valid client certificate to connect to the Web site. Users without a valid client certificate will be denied access. This setting is only available once you have selected the **Require secure channel (SSL)** option.

6. If you want to use certificate mapping, select the **Enable client certificate mapping** check box and then click **Edit** to configure the mappings, as previously described.

7. To create or edit approved certificate trust lists (CTL) for the Web site, enable this option and click **New** or **Edit** to configure it. A CTL is a list of approved CAs for a particular Web site.

8. Click **OK** to close out the Secure Communications dialog.

9. Remember that SSL uses port 443 by default, so make sure you have not blocked this at your firewall.

TEST DAY TIP

If you set the Require 128-bit encryption option and clients attempt to connect with a valid certificate but with a browser that cannot support 128-bit encryption, they will not be able to connect. Also note that this option is available even if your IIS 5.0 computer does not support 128-bit itself. Select this option with care!

Troubleshooting Web Authentication

Any number of issues may occur that will prevent successful Web authentication from occurring. The most common, however, are easily checked and can be prevented with careful planning and execution when it comes time to configure authentication for Web users.

Putting aside any issues that may arise due to network communications problems (which can be many and varied), the most common problems experienced with Web authentication are summarized in Table 8.4.

Table 8.4 Troubleshooting Common Web Authentication Problems

Problem	Possible Cause and Solution
The user is attempting to connect to an incorrect port number.	This can happen if a custom (non-standard port) is configured for a Web server—such as in the case where SSL is enabled and the port is changed to something other than 443. Either the port the server is operating on must be changed to the standard port (best option) or clients must be instructed to access the correct port by appending it onto the URL, such as *https://www.myverysecuresite.com:4563*

Continued

Table 8.4 Troubleshooting Common Web Authentication Problems

Problem	Possible Cause and Solution
Anonymous users cannot access the Web site.	The Web site is probably not configured for anonymous access. If anonymous access is desired, it must be re-enabled from the Web site **Properties** page, **Directory Security** tab. (See Exercise 8.11).
Anonymous users cannot access the Web site.	The anonymous user account either does not exist or is configured incorrectly. The built-in local user account for IIS anonymous access should be used. It is important to ensure that the permissions have not been changed such that this account has the right to log on locally.
Digest authentication users cannot access the Web site.	The user most likely does not have a valid, active Windows 2000 user account in an Active Directory domain. If the Web site is configured to use digest authentication or integrated Windows authentication only (that is, no Basic authentication or certificate mapping), then the user must have a valid, active Windows 2000 user account. Additionally, for digest authentication, the user's account must be in a Windows 2000 Active Directory domain.
Integrated Windows authentication users cannot access the Web site.	The user most likely does not have a valid, active Windows 2000 user account. If the Web site is configured to use digest authentication or integrated Windows authentication only (that is, no basic authentication or certificate mapping), then the user must have a valid, active Windows 2000 user account
SSL users cannot access the Web site.	The user may be attempting to access the wrong port or may not have the required credentials. It is important to ensure that clients are accessing the correct port (443 for HTTP, although SSL can be used for other traffic, such as POP and IMAP). It is also important to ensure that the client has the required credentials and digital certificates to allow for SSL communications.

Summary of Exam Objectives

Windows 2000 supports several authentication protocols, including Windows NTLM, Kerberos v5, Distributed Password Authentication, Extensible Authentication Protocol, and Secure Channel. The two protocols used for network authentication, for logging on locally or as an interactive user, are NTLM and Kerberos v5. Kerberos is the default authentication protocol used in Windows 2000; NTLM is provided for backward compatibility and is used to authenticate Windows 2000 member and standalone servers.

Kerberos provides several advantages over NTLM, which was the authentication protocol of choice in previous versions of Windows NT. One of the advantages Kerberos provides is mutual authentication wherein the client can also verify the server's identity. Another advantage is that Windows 2000 Kerberos domains can communicate with Kerberos realms of other implementations of Kerberos. This cannot be accomplished with NTLM, which is proprietary to Microsoft operating systems.

Kerberos is made up of several components, including the KDC, session tickets, and TGTs. The KDC comprises two services: the AS and the TGS. Three subprotocols Kerberos uses are the AS Exchange, the TGS Exchange, and the Client/Server Exchange.

Microsoft implements its own flavor of Kerberos in Windows 2000. Microsoft Kerberos adds extensions to the Kerberos standard to meet specific requirements necessary for Windows 2000, such as the ability to use public key certificates instead of the normal shared key to log on to Windows 2000 domains. Microsoft implements the KDC as a service in Windows 2000, and the service is automatically installed on all domain controllers. Microsoft Kerberos stores the PAC in tickets. The PAC consists of the user's SID as well as group SIDs for the groups of which the user is a member. The PAC is extracted after the server authenticates the user's identity. The server then uses the PAC to create an impersonation token for access to the service the client has requested to use.

Trusts between Windows 2000 domains within a forest are automatic, two-way and transitive. This is a vast improvement over Windows NT 4.0 trusts. which had to be created manually and were only one-way. Two types of manual trusts can be created if needed: shortcut trusts (used to directly connect two trusting child domains or root-level domains to make searches and other directory services features faster) and external trusts (used to connect to Windows NT 4.0 domains and external Kerberos realms). Trusts can be created manually with the Netdom command or from the Active Directory domains and trusts console.

Exam Objectives Fast Track

Network Authentication in Windows 2000

- ☑ Windows 2000 supports five methods of authenticating user identity:
    - Windows NTLM
    - Kerberos v5
    - Distributed Password Authentication (DPA)
    - Extensible Authentication Protocol (EAP)
    - Secure Channel (Schannel)

- ☑ Windows 2000 uses only NTLM and Kerberos for network authentication. DPA, EAP, and Schannel are for authentication over dial-up connections or the Internet.

- ☑ Windows NT 4.0 uses Windows NTLM as the default network authentication protocol. For that reason, NTLM is still available in Windows 2000 to maintain backward compatibility with previous versions of Microsoft operating systems. It is also used to authenticate logons to Windows 2000 standalone computers.

- ☑ Kerberos is the default network authentication for Windows 2000. Kerberos is a widely used authentication protocol based on an open standard. All Windows 2000 computers use Kerberos v5 in the network environment, except in these situations:
    - Windows 2000 computers use NTLM when they authenticate to Windows NT 4.0 servers
    - Windows 2000 computers use NTLM when they access resources in Windows NT 4.0 domains
    - Windows 2000 domain controllers use NTLM when authenticating Windows NT 4.0 clients
    - Logging in locally to a Windows 2000 domain controller

- ☑ NTLM suffers in comparison to Kerberos for several reasons:
    - Authentication with NTLM is slower than with Kerberos
    - NTLM performs one-way authentication only, which allows server spoofing

- NTLM trusts are one-way and non-transitive and thus harder to manage
- NTLM is proprietary and not compatible with non-Microsoft networks

Kerberos Overview

- ☑ Kerberos operates on the assumption that the initial transactions between clients and servers are done on an unsecured network.
- ☑ Kerberos depends on shared secrets to perform its authentication.
- ☑ An authenticator is unique information encrypted in the shared secret.
- ☑ The KDC, the trusted authority used in Kerberos, maintains a database with all account information for principals in the Kerberos realm. A principal is a uniquely named entity that participates in network communication; a realm is an organization that has a Kerberos server.
- ☑ Another key used with the KDC is the session key, which the KDC issues when one principal wants to communicate with another principal. For example, if a client wants to communicate with a server, the client sends the request to the KDC, and the KDC in turn issues a session key so that the client and server can authenticate with each other. Each portion of the session key is encrypted in the respective portion of the long-term key for both the client and server.

Kerberos in Windows 2000

- ☑ The KDC service runs on every Windows 2000 domain controller. This eliminates a single point of failure for the KDC service (unless, of course, you only have one domain controller).
- ☑ Policy for Kerberos in Windows 2000 is set at the domain level through the Default Domain Policy group policy object.
- ☑ Unlike standard Kerberos, which supports two methods of delegation (proxiable tickets and forwardable tickets), Microsoft Kerberos supports forwardable tickets only.
- ☑ Kerberos verifies user's identities, but does not authorize which resources they can use.
- ☑ The authorization data field in a Microsoft Kerberos ticket contains a list of user SIDs and group SIDs for the user.
- ☑ An access token is created after the credentials in a session ticket have been verified. This information is used to construct an impersonation token for

Configuring Kerberos Trusts

- ☑ In order for users in one Windows NT domain to access resources in another, administrators of the two domains had to set up an explicit trust relationship. These trusts were one-way; if the administrators wanted a reciprocal relationship, two separate trusts had to be created because these trusts were based on the NTLM security protocol, which does not include mutual authentication.

- ☑ In Windows 2000 networks, with the Kerberos protocol, all trust relationships are two-way, transitive and an implicit, automatic trust exists between every parent and child domain; it is not necessary for administrators to create these trusts. This transitive state comes about through the use of the Kerberos referral; as a result, every domain in a tree implicitly trusts every other domain in that tree.

- ☑ Shortcut trusts are two-way transitive trusts that allow you to shorten the path in a complex forest. These trusts must be explicitly created by the administrator's to create a direct trust relationship between Windows 2000 domains in the same forest. A shortcut trust is used to optimize performance and shorten the trust path that Windows 2000 security must take for authentication purposes. The most effective use of shortcut trusts is between two domain trees in a forest.

- ☑ Shortcut trusts are one of the two types of explicit domain trusts that can be established in Windows 2000; the other is the external trust used to establish a trust relationship with domains that are not part of the forest. The external trust is one-way and non-transitive, as in NT 4.0 domain models. However, as with NT, two one-way trusts can be established if a two-way relationship is desired.

- ☑ Active Directory automatically creates the parent/child and tree root trusts. You must manually create all shortcut and external trusts.

- ☑ Trusts can be created from the command prompt using Netdom or from the GUI using Active Directory domains and trusts.

Configuring User Authentication

- ☑ LM authentication is the least secure Windows 2000 authentication model. It is the default for Windows 95 and Windows 98 clients.

- ☑ NTLM version 1 is the default authentication method for Windows NT 4.0. It is more secure than LM but less secure than Kerberos. Kerberos is the default authentication method for Windows 2000. It does not authenticate the server; it authenticates only the client.
- ☑ NTLM version 2 is more secure than NTLM version 1 or LM. Windows 9.x and Windows NT 4.0 clients can be configured to use NTLMv2. We have to make a registry change to both platforms in order for them to use NTLMv2. Windows 9.x clients also need the directory services clients installed, whereas NT 4.0 clients must have SP 4 or above installed.
- ☑ NTLM authentication is slower than Kerberos authentication.
- ☑ NTLM performs one-way authentication. Kerberos provides mutual (two-way) authentication.
- ☑ NTLM trusts are one-way and nontransitive. Kerberos trusts are two-way and transitive.
- ☑ NTLM is proprietary and not compatible with non-Microsoft networks.
- ☑ Kerberos is a private key encryption protocol.
- ☑ Windows 2000 domain controllers run the Kerberos server service, which allows Kerberos passwords and identities to be stored in Active Directory.

Configuring Web Authentication

- ☑ Web authentication can be provided by many mechanisms, including:
  - Anonymous authentication
  - Digest authentication
  - Integrated Windows authentication
  - Certificate mapping
  - SSL
- ☑ SSL and TLS are public key-based security protocols. If supported by your Web browser and server, SSL and TLS provides mutual authentication, message integrity, and confidentiality.
- ☑ Most Web authentication problems can be traced to incorrectly (or missing) configured user accounts or lack of required client credentials.

Exam Objectives Frequently Asked Questions

The following Frequently Asked Questions, answered by the authors of this book, are designed to both measure your understanding of the Exam Objectives presented in this chapter, and to assist you with real-life implementation of these concepts.

Q: What do you consider the main benefit of using Kerberos authentication?

A: Kerberos provides mutual authentication for the server and the client. This makes network communication more secure than the one-way authentication (NTLM) of the past.

Q: Do I need to manually create the Kerberos settings for my Windows 2000 domain?

A: Windows 2000 Server ships with a default domain policy that includes reasonable settings for the Kerberos policy. The only reason to change from the default settings is if your organization's requirements differ from the default value settings.

Q: Can my Windows 9.x clients authenticate using Kerberos?

A: No, Microsoft is not releasing a Kerberos add-on for Windows 9.x. Windows 9.x clients can only authenticate using the NTLM authentication protocol. To enhance the security of Windows 2000 domains, Microsoft recommends that you upgrade all clients to Windows 2000 so that the more secure Kerberos authentication protocol is utilized by all systems in the domain.

Q: How does a server know that a user is authorized access to a service, even though it has authenticated the user's identity?

A: Microsoft Kerberos includes a PAC in every ticket. The PAC includes the user's SID and the SIDs for all groups of which the user is a member. The server compares this data with the data for the ACL on the service to determine if access is allowed or denied. If access is allowed, the server also determines the level of access based on information in the ACL.

Q: How does a Windows 2000 client find a Microsoft KDC?

A: It uses DNS to locate KDCs in the domain.

Q: I have one server that is both my domain controller and my DNS server. Everything seems to be running fine, but I cannot log on from any of my clients using Kerberos. All of my clients are running Windows 2000. What could be the problem?

A: Clients use DNS SRVs to find KDC servers on the network. DNS can be running fine, but if the SRVs do not exist, the clients cannot find the domain controllers. When domain controllers start the netlogon service when booting, they automatically go to their configured DNS server and register all the needed SRV records. If the DNS dynamic updates feature is turned off, this process must be done manually. Make sure dynamic updates are turned on for your DNS zone, or you could also create all the SRV records manually (but this practice is not recommended). To enable dynamic updates, open the **DNS Management** console. Expand your server. Expand **Forward Lookup Zones**. Right-click the zone that you want to enable for dynamic updates, and go to **Properties**. Choose **Yes** from the drop-down arrow next to allow dynamic updates.

Q: Why are TGTs necessary?

A: To prove to the KDC that the clients requesting a session ticket are really who they say they are. The KDC issues the TGT to the client when it first logs on to the domain.

Q: How can Windows 2000 be configured to use forwardable tickets?

A: By default, members of the Domain Admins group can forward tickets. For other users, the option has to be configured individually.

Self Test

A Quick Answer Key follows the Self Test questions. For complete questions, answers, and epxlanations to the Self Test questions in this chapter as well as the other chapters in this book, see the Self Test Appendix.

Network Authentication in Windows 2000

1. You are the administrator of a mixed-mode Windows NT 4.0 domain. You have Windows 2000 and Windows NT 4.0 servers as well as Windows 2000 Professional, Windows NT Workstation, and Windows 95 client computers. What is the best network authentication method that you can reasonably hope for in your network?

    A. NTLM

    B. Kerberos

    C. Challenge-Handshake Authentication Protocol (CHAP)

    D. NTLMv2

2. You are the administrator of a Windows 2000 Active Directory domain. Your clients consist of Windows 2000 Professional, Windows NT 4.0, Windows 95, and Windows 3.11 clients. What form of network authentication will your Windows 2000 Professional clients use in this situation?

    A. NTLM

    B. Kerberos

    C. CHAP

    D. NTLMv2

Kerberos Overview

3. Kerberos provides two services to the network. What are the services that are provided to the network? (Choose two that apply.)

    A. TGS—issues individual session tickets that can be used to gain access to network resources.

    B. STS—issues individual session tickets that can be used to gain access to network resources.

    C. AS—authenticates users in the KDC's database and issues them a TGT.

    D. AS—authorizes users in the KDC's database and issues them a TGT.

4. When using forwarded tickets, who acquires the session ticket for a client to access a back-end resource?

    A. The client

    B. The front-end server

    C. The back-end server

    D. The KDC

Kerberos in Windows 2000

5. The Kerberos protocol in Windows 2000 runs as a service on all domain controllers, thus all domain controllers are KDCs. What does the KDC use as its account database in Windows 2000?

    A. Active Directory

    B. Security Accounts Manager

    C. LSA

    D. HOSTS

6. You have several services that run in a front-end/back-end configuration on your network. All of your computers run Windows 2000 Server or Windows 2000 Professional. The back-end services run in the context of the local system account on the back-end servers. What do you need to do to enable forwarded authentication to occur so that your clients can authenticate to the services running on the back-end server? (Choose all that apply.)

A. Select the **Account is trusted for delegation** check box on the client's domain user account properties page.

B. Deselect the **Account is sensitive and cannot be delegated** check box on the client's domain user account properties page.

C. Select the **Trust computer for delegation** check box on the back-end server's domain computer account properties page.

D. Select the **Account is trusted for delegation** check box on the domain user account properties page that the services run under.

7. In Windows 2000, what type of DNS record does a client use to locate a KDC?

   A. PTR
   B. A
   C. SRV
   D. MX

Configuring Kerberos Trusts

8. Hannah needs to configure a new external trust to a Windows NT 4.0 domain. How can she perform this task? (Choose all that apply.)

   A. She can configure the trust by using the Netdom command.
   B. She can configure the trust by using the Active Directory users and computers console.
   C. She can configure the trust by using the Netsh command.
   D. She can configure the trust by using the Active Directory domains and trusts console.

9. What type of trust does Kerberos create between domains in Windows 2000?

   A. One-way non-transitive manual
   B. Two-way non-transitive automatic
   C. Two-way transitive automatic
   D. Two-way transitive manual

Configuring User Authentication

10. Christopher is the network administrator of his company's Windows 2000 network, which consists of Windows 2000 Servers, Windows 2000 Professional clients, and Windows 98 clients. Christopher wants to ensure that only secure NTLM authentication occurs between his servers and clients. What must be done to make the Windows 2000 computers use NTLMv2 only?

    A. Christopher will need to install the DSClient on his Windows 2000 computers to enable NTLMv2.

    B. Christopher will need to install a security certificate on each of the Windows 2000 computers to enable NTLMv2.

    C. Christopher cannot use NTLMv2 on his Windows 2000 computers without installing at least one Windows .NET Server Domain Controller on the network with the high-encryption update.

    D. Christopher can require NTLMv2 via group policy and apply this to the entire domain.

11. Christopher is the network administrator of his company's Windows 2000 network, which consists of Windows 2000 Servers, Windows 2000 Professional clients, and Windows 98 clients. Christopher wants to ensure that only secure NTLM authentication occurs between his servers and clients. What must be done to make the Windows 98 computers use NTLMv2 only?

    A. Christopher will need to install the DSClient on his Windows 98 computers to enable NTLMv2.

    B. Christopher will need to install a security certificate on each of the Windows 98 computers to enable NTLMv2.

    C. Christopher will need to enable the NTLMv2 setting for the OU that contains his Windows 98 computers.

    D. Christopher will need to install a Windows 2000-based Remote Authentication Dial-In User Service (RADIUS) server on his network to allow him to use NTLMv2.

Configuring Web Authentication

12. You have configured digest authentication for your Web servers. Jon, one of your user's who needs to authenticate to the Web servers, cannot do so. You have

checked Jon's user account properties and found that the "Store Passwords Using Reversible Encryption" option has been checked but Jon still cannot authenticate. What is the most likely reason for his troubles?

A. Jon's user account is disabled. You should enable it from Active Directory users and computers.

B. Jon did not change his password after the "Store Passwords Using Reversible Encryption" option was enabled for his account.

C. Jon changed his password after the "Store Passwords Using Reversible Encryption" option was enabled for his account, which disabled this setting.

D. Jon's computer that he is attempting to make the connection with does not have the 128-bit high encryption patch applied.

13. Andrew is the network administrator for a small Windows 2000 Active Directory domain. He has configured Integrated Windows authentication for users attempting to authenticate to the Web server. Andrew's network is protected from the Internet by a Cisco PIX firewall. Users attempting to authenticate using Integrated Windows authentication complain that they cannot authenticate. What is the most likely cause of the troubles?

    A. Andrew has not configured the user's account properties with the "Store Passwords Using Reversible Encryption" option.

    B. Integrated Windows authentication fails when access is through a firewall due to the fact that the firewall places its IP address in the hash, thus rendering the authentication request invalid.

    C. Andrew has not configured for Integrated Windows authentication in the group policy object that covers the IIS server's computer account.

    D. Andrew has not configured for Integrated Windows authentication in the group policy object that covers the user's accounts.

14. Catherine is the administrator of a Windows 2000 network. She has configured anonymous authentication for her Web servers. Users attempting to use anonymous authentication complain to her that they cannot access the site and instead receive a 401 error "Unauthorized: Logon failed" when they attempt to access the Web site. Catherine has checked her IIS servers and they show no unusual conditions. What is the most likely reason for this problem?

    A. The IIS server is hung. A restart of the server will clear the problem up.

    B. The anonymous account is either missing, misconfigured, or does not have the permissions required.

    C. The users do not have user accounts on the IIS server.

    D. The users are not using Internet Explorer 5.5 or later.

15. You have enabled SSL on your Web site but now users complain to you that they cannot establish secure connections on port 80. You know that port 80 is the standard HTTP port, not the secure HTTP port. What port should they be attempting to connect to?

    A. 8080

    B. 443

    C. 25

    D. 110

Self Test Quick Answer Key

For complete questions, answers, and epxlanations to the Self Test questions in this chapter as well as the other chapters in this book, see the Self Test Appendix.

1. **D**
2. **B**
3. **A, C**
4. **B**
5. **A**
6. **B, C**
7. **C**
8. **A, D**
9. **C**
10. **D**
11. **A**
12. **B**
13. **B**
14. **B**
15. **B**

Chapter 9

MCSE/MCSA 70-214

Configuring and Troubleshooting Remote Access and VPN Authentication

Exam Objectives in this Chapter:

4.3 Configure authentication for secure remote access. Authentication types include PAP, CHAP, MS-CHAP, MS-CHAP v2, EAP-MD5, EAP-TLS, and Multi-factor authentication with smart cars and EAP.

4.4 Configure and troubleshoot virtual private network (VPN) protocols. Considerations include Internet service provider (ISP), client-computer operation system, Network Address Translation (NAT) devices, Routing and Remote Access server, and firewall server.

4.5 Manage client-computer configuration for remote access security. Tools include remote access policy and Connection Manager Administration Kit.

- ☑ Summary of Exam Objectives
- ☑ Exam Objectives Fast Track
- ☑ Exam Objectives Frequently Asked Questions
- ☑ Self Test
- ☑ Self Test Quick Answer Key

Introduction

Much of this book has discussed the different ways to secure Windows 2000 systems, both from a server perspective and by securing network-connected users. In this chapter, we cut the cord—it's time to discuss how to provide secure connectivity to your remote users. Welcome to the world of the mobile employee, the driving force behind the need for secure remote access.

One of the largest security challenges facing network administrators and security professionals in today's business environment is the fact that every employee needs access to data. Mail, the corporate intranet, the sales database—all need to be accessed from virtually anywhere. Users are no longer tied to corporate networks, and in many companies it's more likely for an employee to connect to the Internet than it is for them to connect to the company's physical network. This situation has resulted in the blurring of the lines between what is considered the corporate network and the Internet, as well as a blurring of the obligations of IT departments in keeping companies' proprietary information secure. Gone are the days when building a strong perimeter with firewalls and screening routers is enough to ensure the integrity of your data. Now the chances are very good that part of your job will be to create breaches in that perimeter to provide access to the very information you need to protect. This increasing demand has driven some of the largest innovations in the Windows 2000 operating system.

Unlike many of its predecessors, Windows 2000 was architected with these new demands in mind. Microsoft recognized the challenges faced by the administrators of its operating systems and provided the tools and mechanisms to provide connectivity from beyond the LAN/WAN while still providing security as part of the core design. Microsoft has been much maligned over the security of its operating systems, but a properly configured Windows 2000 server can be used to deliver secure connectivity over the now commonplace dial-up and Internet-based connection methods used by today's companies.

The tools and services included with the Windows 2000 operating system not only provide a wide range of connectivity methods, they also give administrators a high degree of control and flexibility. These solutions range from the use of new authentication methods and secure dial-up procedures to the latest in strong encryption protocols and IP security.

The two services we discuss in the chapter are the Remote Access Service (RAS) and virtual private networks (VPNs), both of which are included as part of the Routing and Remote Access Service (RRAS) of the Windows 2000 operating system. Although on the surface these services might seem completely different types of remote access mechanism, they are very closely integrated in the RRAS and can be used in combination to provide secure, flexible remote access solutions for virtually every need.

To truly understand the use of these technologies, you must understand how to configure and maintain *remote access policies*. Remote access policies are the core of the Windows 2000 RRAS and provide incredibly granular and flexible configuration settings for both RAS and VPN connections. This granularity and flexibility unfortunately come at the expense of ease of use; remote access policies can be very complex, and you need an in-depth understanding of them if you are to successfully provide secure remote access to your users.

To ensure that you fully understand these services, we cover in detail how to configure authentication for secure remote access and how to configure and troubleshoot VPN protocols. From there we take a closer look at how remote access policies work. We finish the chapter with a discussion of configuring secure client connections to take advantage of remote access and VPN services. As you work your way through the chapter, it's important to remember that Microsoft has provided a solid, scalable, secure remote access solution for business requirements. While we discuss these services in context of the 70-214 exam, think about how you might use these services to solve real-world business problems. Not only will this perspective help you understand the information in the chapter, it will also serve you in good stead in your existing or future job. Remote access and security are critical components of many of the Windows 2000-related jobs today and will only become more critical as the environment and business challenges continue to evolve.

Before we jump into setting up our first RAS, we need to cover some of the theory behind remote access authentication in the Windows 2000 operating system. Let's start by discussing the remote access authentication protocols supported by Windows 2000.

Remote Access Authentication Methods

Before we discuss the remote access authentication methods available within the Windows 2000 RRAS, we should briefly discuss the underlying access protocol, the Point-to-Point Protocol.

Point-to-Point Protocol

Detailed in request for comment (RFC) 2484, *PPP LCP Internationalization Configuration Option,* dated January 1999, the Point-to-Point Protocol (PPP) provides a standard transport method for point-to-point links. (You can locate this and other RFCs at www.rfc-editor.org.) In the context of this book, the point-to-point links referred to are dial-up connections such as asynchronous modem connections or even Integrated Services Digital Network (ISDN) connections. In addition to a transport method, PPP also defines the authentication protocols that can be used to negotiate a connection prior to allowing network-layer protocols such as TCP/IP or IPX to be transmitted over the connection.

Test Day Tip

Know the authentication protocols as well as their strengths and weaknesses. Do not assume that the only protocols that will show up on the exam are the "strong" ones.

Password Authentication Protocol

Detailed in RFC 1334, *PPP Authentication Protocols,* dated August 1996, the Password Authentication Protocol (PAP) uses unencrypted (plaintext) passwords for authenticating users on a PPP link. PAP is generally considered an obsolete protocol due to the fact that it is the least secure PPP authentication protocol available. Although PAP does provide a simple method for establishing a PPP connection, about the only place you might encounter it would be if you needed to connect to a legacy, non-Windows server.

Challenge Handshake Authentication Protocol

Detailed in RFC1994, *PPP Challenge Handshake Authentication Protocol (CHAP),* dated August 1996, the Challenge Handshake Authentication Protocol (CHAP) provides a more secure PPP authentication mechanism than PAP by negotiating an encrypted authentication using Message Digest 5 (MD5). MD5 is an industry-standard hashing scheme that allows connection authentication without actually transmitting the password over the network. You will generally see CHAP used to allow Windows 2000 to securely connect to third-party PPP servers, leveraging the fact that CHAP is an industry-standard protocol.

Microsoft Challenge Handshake Authentication Protocol

Anything the industry can develop, Microsoft can improve on. The Microsoft Challenge Handshake Authentication Protocol (MS-CHAP) is an extension of the CHAP authentication protocol used to authenticate remote Windows workstations to Windows PPP servers. This extension increases the core CHAP protocol's capabilities by integrating the encryption and hashing algorithms used on Windows networks. MS-CHAP supports LAN Manager authentication as well as the ability to change passwords as part of the authentication process (similar to the capability available when you log into a Windows 2000 network locally). Like CHAP, MS-CHAP uses a challenge-response mechanism called *password hashing*, which keeps the password from being sent across the connection. Although Microsoft kept MS-CHAP as consistent with standard CHAP as possible, the MS-CHAP protocol is designed specifically for use on Windows computers.

> **Head of the Class…**
>
> ### Hash: Not Just for Breakfast Anymore
>
> Discussed in the context of authentication and encryption, a *hash* is, in its simplest form, a number generated from a string of text. In the context of authentication, a user's password is stored on the system as a *hash value*, created by applying a specific hashing algorithm to derive the value. When the user attempts to authenticate to the system, he or she enter a password, to which the system applies the same hashing algorithm. That value is then passed across the connection, where it is compared to the stored hash on the host system. If the hashes agree, the password is valid and the connection is established.
>
> For example, let's say Carol has a password of *Aardvark*. Let's also say that our hashing algorithm states that each letter is supposed to be converted to a number by dividing the numeric value of each letter in the alphabet by 5, then rounding down to the nearest whole number. If the result of the algorithm is less than 1, a 0 is put used instead of the fraction. Once the number is converted, all 0s are removed and the result is the hash. In our example, the initial conversion for *Aardvark* would be 00304032. Remove the zeros, and the hash becomes 3432. There is no easy way for a cracker to retrieve the password from that hash, and by comparing that number to the stored value you can verify the user's password without ever transmitting it across the network.

MS-CHAP v2

Windows 2000 shipped with a new version of the MS-CHAP known as Version 2 (MS-CHAP v2). The new version corrects several of the issues with the previous version, including removing the support for the notoriously weak LAN Manager authentication, adding the ability for two-way authentication (which allows the client to authenticate the PPP host to which it is connecting), and support for much stronger cryptographic keys for the authentication process.

TEST DAY TIP

In a pure Microsoft environment, MS-CHAP v2 is the most secure PPP authentication protocol and should be used whenever you are authenticating using a user ID and password.

Extensible Authentication Protocol

Detailed in RFC2284, *PPP Extensible Authentication Protocol (EAP)*, dated March 1998, the Extensible Authentication Protocol (EAP) is an extension of the PPP. EAP was developed in response to an increasing need for stronger authentication mechanisms for remote user access services such as RAS and VPN. As the number of mobile users increased and the technical sophistication of attackers also increased, user ID/password authentication was not secure enough for many organizations that had higher security needs. EAP provides a standard mechanism for support of *additional* authentication methods within PPP, such as token cards, one-time passwords, or public key authentication using smartcards or certificates. Unlike the user ID/password capabilities of the other PPP authentication protocols, EAP, in conjunction with external authenticators such as a smartcard or token card, is not vulnerable to brute-force or dictionary password attacks.

Windows 2000 leverages the EAP-MD5 CHAP and EAP-TLS authentication methods as part of its remote access and VPN services.

EAP-MD5 CHAP

EAP-MD5 CHAP is an EAP type that uses the same challenge handshake protocol as PPP-based CHAP, but the challenges and responses are sent as EAP messages. In other words, EAP MD5 allows for the use of external authentication utilizing external hosts while still allowing the use of a user ID and password.

An example of this use is using EAP in conjunction with an external Remote Authentication Dial-In User Service (RADIUS) server for storing the database of user accounts and passwords that could authenticate to a RAS server. The specifics of this use are detailed in RFC2869, *RADIUS Extensions,* dated June 2000. Windows 2000 Server operating systems include RADIUS authentication capabilities as part of the Internet Authentication Service (IAS).

It is important to note that although this form of EAP does add capabilities for PPP authentication, because the underlying authentication is still based on a user ID/password combination, this type of EAP is still vulnerable to a brute-force or dictionary password attack.

EAP-TLS

Detailed in RFC2716, *PPP EAP TLS Authentication Protocol,* dated October 1999, EAP-TLS is a *mutual authentication* method similar to MS-CHAPv2. This means that not only can the server authenticate the client as part of the authentication process, but the client can also verify the identity of the server. EAP-TLS is also the EAP type that is used in certificate-based or token-based security environments. As a result, EAP-TLS provides the most secure authentication method.

 **EXAM WARNING**

EAP-TLS is not supported on a Windows 2000 RRAS server running as a standalone server. In order to use EAP-TLS, the Windows 2000 RRAS server must be a member of a Windows 2000 mixed-mode or native-mode domain.

EAP and Smartcards/Certificates

If you want to use the strongest authentication available for Windows 2000, you will need to use a *smartcard*. A smartcard is like a credit card with an embedded computer chip that stores user data. In the case of Windows 2000 authentication, this data is an X.509 certificate that proves you are who you say you are. The card data is provided to the system via an external smartcard reader, connected to the authenticating computer. As we have discussed, in order to use a smartcard for remote access authentication, you must use EAP-TLS.

This topic is outside the scope of the exam, but if you want to use smartcards for remote access authentication, you need to take the following steps:

1. Purchase a smartcard and a smartcard reader for your remote computer. You need to be able to write your certificate data to the card for authentication.
2. Enable and configure remote access on your Windows 2000 RRAS server. (We do some exercises on this topic in the next sections of the chapter.)
3. Install a PKI computer certificate on your Windows 2000 RRAS server. This certificate is used to authenticate the identity of the remote access server. In order to do this, you need a certificate authority for issuing certificates.
4. Enable a smartcard logon process for the domain your Windows 2000 RRAS server is in.
5. Enable EAP and configure the smartcard service on your Windows 2000 RRAS server.
6. Enable smartcard authentication on the remote access client computer.

This is a very high-level process. If you determine you need to utilize smartcard authentication with your Windows 2000 RRAS server, refer to the Microsoft Windows 2000 documentation for specific instructions. This discussion is included here to provide an understanding of the complexity of utilizing smartcards for remote access authentication with the EAP TLS protocol.

Now let's take a look at actually configuring a Windows 2000 RAS for dial-in access.

Configuring a Remote Access Server

In the chapter introduction, we spent a little time discussing the challenges associated with the highly diverse and mobile user populations many companies are struggling to deal with today. From the CEO who travels frequently to an executive round table in Paris, the salesperson who needs to check pricing from a customer's office, or the systems engineer who needs to verify a router configuration and doesn't want to drive to the office at 3:00 A.M., employees have varied and legitimate needs for accessing the corporate network remotely. One service that Microsoft's Windows 2000 Server operating system provides that can help you deal with these challenges is the RRAS, which can be used to create an RAS.

> ### Head of the Class...
>
> ### RAS versus RRAS: What's the Difference?
>
> One of the more confusing terminologies associated with Windows 2000's remote access capabilities is RAS (Remote Access Server) and RRAS. This is particularly confusing because the predecessor to RRAS was RAS (Remote Access Services). RAS is also the generic industry terminology to identify any server that supports dial-in network access. In any discussions of Windows 2000's remote access capabilities, the term RAS should be interpreted as the dial-in portion of the RRAS suite of services. RRAS includes not only the dial-in capabilities of its predecessors but also the added VPN functionality discussed later in the chapter.

Why would you want to deploy an RAS server in 2003? Everyone is doing it with VPN these days, right? Wrong. Although there is a huge demand for VPN capabilities, there is still a large requirement for the older dial-in technology. RAS servers are used in many businesses for providing inexpensive access to the network, by companies that don't have Internet connections (although this list is growing smaller and smaller), in places where the overhead associated with supporting a VPN solution is not practical and in many cases as a backup access method in case there is an issue with the primary VPN service. It has been said by many industry insiders that the RAS server is dead, but it will be quite some time before you see it go the way of the card punch. RAS servers are a proven technology that is relatively inexpensive, highly reliable, and, with the Windows 2000 RRAS, very easy to configure. In fact, let's take a look at setting up a RAS server using the Windows 2000 RRAS.

Installing and Configuring the Remote Access Server

Before we get into Exercise 9.01 on setting up your Windows 2000 Server as a dial-in server, there is one thing that is very important to understand about enabling the RRAS so that you can set up the your RAS. Unlike previous incarnations of the Windows server operating system, in which the Remote Access Services were an option, the RRAS is an integral part of the Windows 2000 Server operating system and is installed as part of the installation of Windows 2000 Server. For that reason we will jump right into the topic of configuring the RAS.

EXERCISE 9.01

CONFIGURING THE ROUTING AND REMOTE ACCESS SERVICE FOR DIAL-IN ACCESS

1. Click **Start | Programs | Administrative Tools | Routing and Remote Access** to open the Routing and Remote Access console (see Figure 9.1).

   Figure 9.1 The Routing and Remote Access Console

   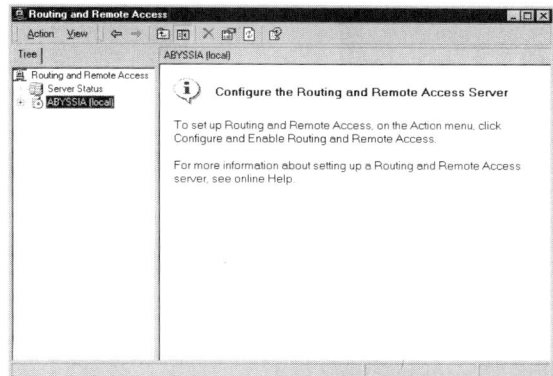

2. Within the Routing and Remote Access console, select **Configure and Enable Routing and Remote Access** from the **Action** menu (see Figure 9.2).

3. The Routing and Remote Access Server Setup wizard opens (see Figure 9.3). Select **Next** to continue the configuration process.

4. From the **Common Configurations** screen (see Figure 9.4), select **Remote access server** and select **Next** to continue.

Figure 9.2 The Action Menu of the Routing and Remote Access Console

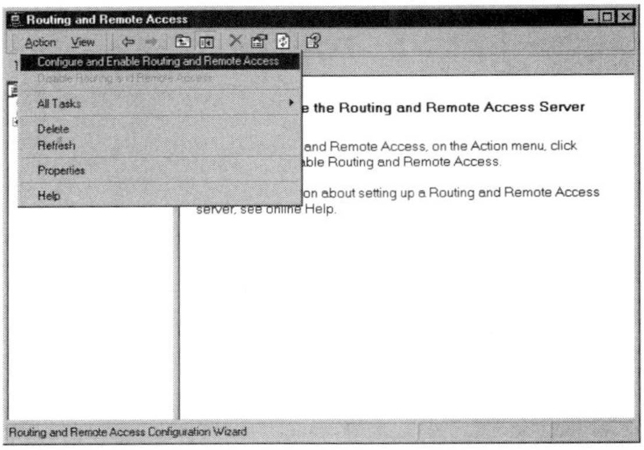

Figure 9.3 The Routing and Remote Access Server Setup Wizard

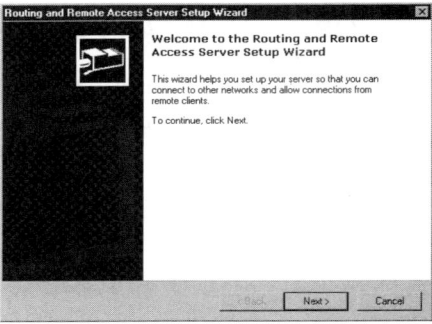

Figure 9.4 Common Configurations

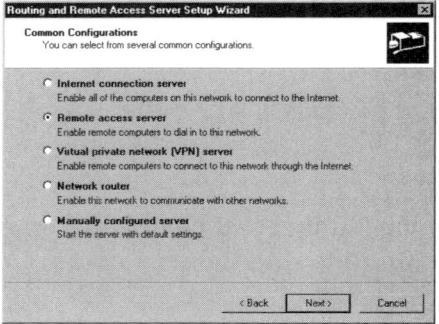

5. From the **Remote Client Protocols** screen (see Figure 9.5), ensure that TCP/IP is one of the listed protocols (it is included by default), and select **Next** to continue.

Figure 9.5 Remote Client Protocols

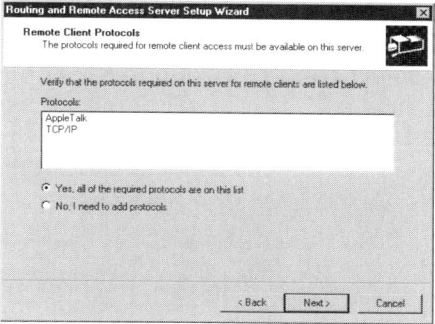

6. If the AppleTalk protocol is one of the protocols listed on your server, as it is in this exercise, the Macintosh Guest Authentication dialog box will be displayed (see Figure 9.6). This step is included in the exercise to remind you that selecting **Allow unauthenticated access for all remote clients** is a very bad idea unless you have no need for security on your network. You should always force username and password authentication for remote users. Select **Next** to proceed.

Figure 9.6 Macintosh Guest Authentication

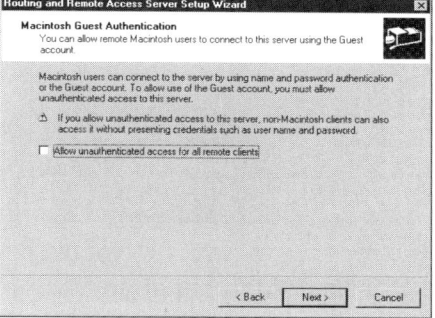

7. The IP Address Assignment screen (see Figure 9.7) is used to determine how IP addresses will be assigned to remote users. If you select the **Automatically** option, the server will request IP addresses from the network DHCP server in blocks of 10 addresses and hand them out to remote users. Select the **From a specified range of addresses** option, and select **Next** to continue.

8. The Address Range Assignment screen (see Figure 9.8) is used to assign a block of addresses to your RAS server. Select **New** to open the New Address Range screen (see Figure 9.9) and create a pool of addresses. You can use the addresses in the example or make up your own. If you

are working in a production environment, be sure to get your address assignments from the networking administrators. Select **OK** to add the address range to the list. Figure 9.10 shows the newly created address range. Select **Next** to continue the configuration process.

Figure 9.7 IP Address Assignment

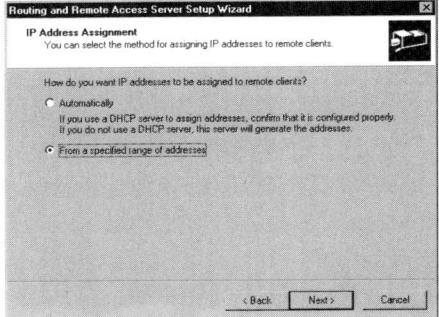

Figure 9.8 Address Range Assignment

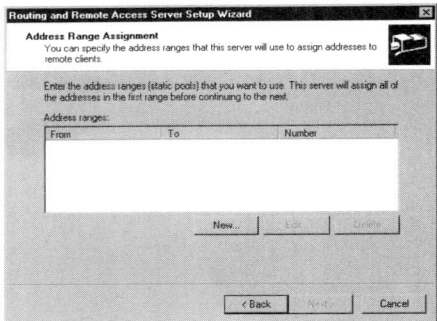

Figure 9.9 New Address Range

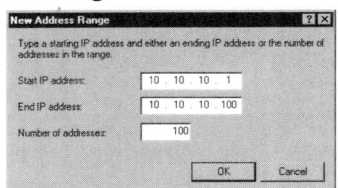

Figure 9.10 Address Range Assignment with the Newly Created Address Pool

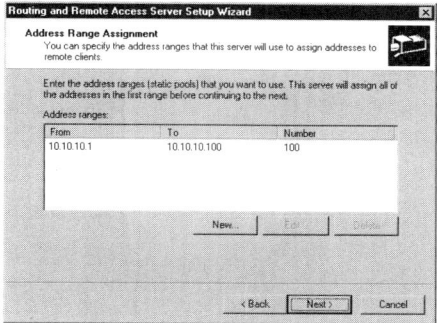

9. The Managing Multiple Remote Access Servers screen opens (see Figure 9.11). This option is used if you want to have multiple RAS servers authenticate against a central RADIUS authentication database. Select **No, I don't want to set up this server to use RADIUS now** and select **Next** to continue.

Figure 9.11 Managing Multiple Remote Access Servers

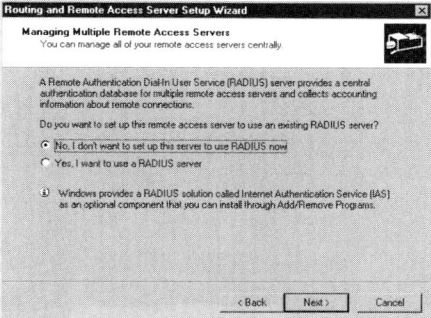

10. You are now at the last screen (see Figure 9.12) for configuring your RAS server. To complete the process, select **Finish**. You will see the Completing Initialization message shown in Figure 9.13 while the system completes the configuration of the service. Once this process completes, that message will close, and the RAS server is configured. If you select **Display Help about managing a remote access server when I close this wizard**, as is selected in the example, you will get the Routing and Remote Access help file (see Figure 9.14), which contains some excellent information on the specifics of the service.

Figure 9.12 Managing Multiple Remote Access Servers

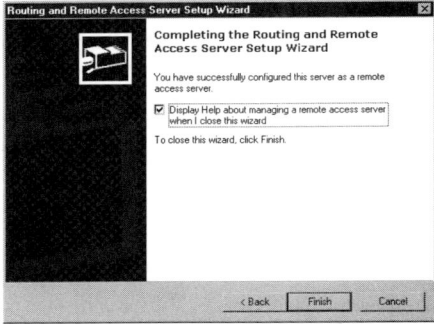

Figure 9.13 Initializing the Routing and Remote Access Service

Figure 9.14 Help Screens

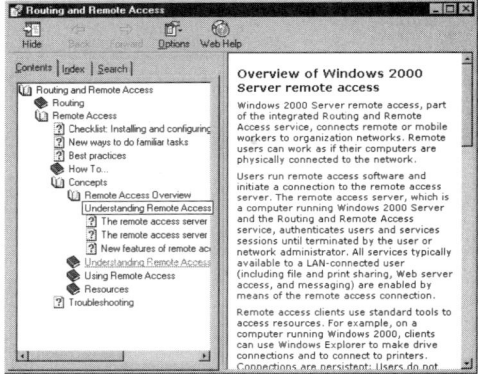

Notes from the Underground…

Identify Remote Users

You should always assign unique address ranges to your remote access users so that they can be easily distinguished from LAN users. Doing so not only allows you to easily segregate network access if some areas of your network need to be secured from remote users; it also allows a remote user to be easily identified in log files and on intrusion detection systems. If you configure your remote access server to distribute addresses automatically, you have no easy way of differentiating a remote user from a local user. The remote access server will pull a block of addresses from your DHCP server and will take the next 10 addresses available; these are addresses from the same IP scope from which your LAN users are getting their addresses.

An attacker would be able to take advantage of this configuration by masquerading as a local user and forcing you to spend extra time tracking them down. To identify an attacker in this scenario, you would need to go to the DHCP server and check the log for the name of the system that was using the address at the time of the attack, then go to the remote access server to determine which account or connection was assigned the address. To make matters worse, if the time synchronization between your servers is not accurate, you might have no way to track an IP address back to its true source. As is usually the case, the manual configuration option is the more secure option. It takes longer, but it gives you much better capabilities for tracking down IP addresses on the network.

Working with RAS Ports

Now that you have successfully configured your RAS server, we need to dig a little deeper into the underlying port configuration, where you can configure the authentication methods and other important security parameters related to dial-in access. Exercise 9.02 walks you through the configuration of the modem ports on your Windows 2000 RAS server.

NOTE

You need to have a modem or modems configured on your test system in order to complete Exercise 9.02.

EXERCISE 9.02

CONFIGURING ROUTING AND REMOTE ACCESS SERVICE MODEM PORTS

1. Click **Start | Programs | Administrative Tools | Routing and Remote Access** to open the Routing and Remote Access console (see Figure 9.15). This console now shows an active server and all the associated options.

   Figure 9.15 Routing and Remote Access Console Configured for Use

   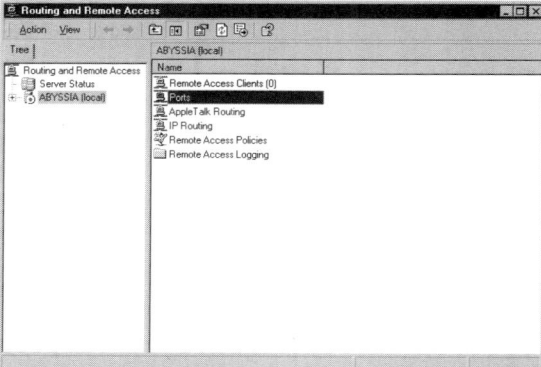

2. Within the Routing and Remote Access console, select **Ports** in the right-hand pane, and select **Properties** from the **Action** menu (see Figure 9.16).

   Figure 9.16 Opening the Port Properties

   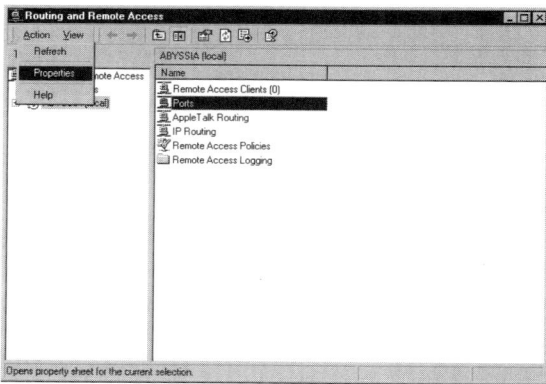

3. The Port Properties screen (see Figure 9.17) opens. This screen displays all the ports currently configured for use by the RRAS. Since we are working with modem ports for this exercise, select a modem port and select **Configure** to continue.

Figure 9.17 Port Properties

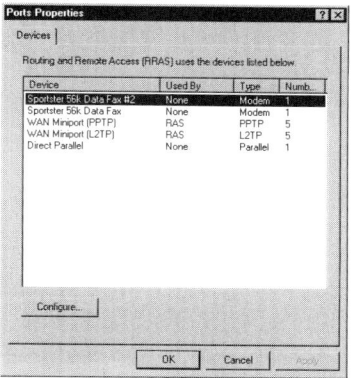

4. From the Configure Device screen (see Figure 9.18), select **Remote access connections (inbound only)**. This choice makes the port available for dial-in use. The other parameters on this screen would be used if the server were going to be used as a demand-dial router, which is out of scope for this exercise. Select **OK** to assign this port for use for remote access connections.

Figure 9.18 Configuring a Device Port for Inbound Remote Access Connections

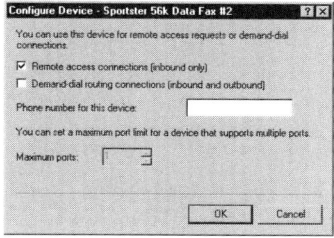

5. In Figure 9.19 you can see that the modem port you selected has been assigned to the RAS service. Select **OK** to return to the Routing and Remote Access console.

6. To check the status of the port, double-click the **Ports** icon in the Routing and Remote Access console. Each available port is displayed (see Figure 9.20). Double-click the name of the modem you configured in the first portion of this exercise.

7. The Port Status screen (see Figure 9.21) displays many useful statistics when a session is in progress, including how long the user has been connected, how much traffic has passed across the line, and the session

addressing information. Select **Close** to return to the Routing and Remote Access console to complete this exercise.

Figure 9.19 The Modem Port Has Been Assigned to RAS

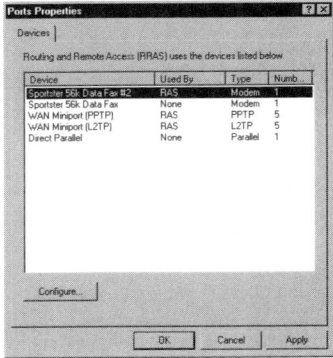

Figure 9.20 Configuring a Device Port for Inbound Remote Access Connections

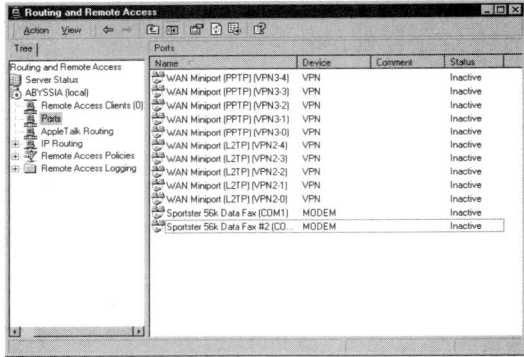

Figure 9.21 Checking the Port Status

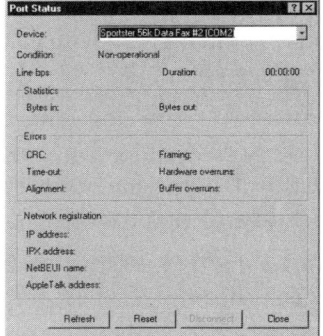

Head of the Class…

Why Do We Need to Worry About an RAS Server? No One Uses Them Anymore, Right?

It is a common misconception that in this age of high-speed broadband Internet access and VPNs, the RAS server has gone the way of the dinosaur. This is not true. The reason Microsoft insists on your understanding how to securely configure a RAS server under Windows 2000 is that although the RAS server's role has changed, it is still an important component of most corporate remote access environments. The usual complaint about RAS servers is that they are just too slow. Usually you hear this from the director who just got his cable modem installed. Furthermore, the rapidly approaching ubiquity of broadband Internet access solutions does make a compelling argument for shifting your remote access solutions away from modem-based RAS to an Internet-based VPN solution. But let's talk about reality for a moment. Why does an RAS server still make sense?

First, what are your plans for the day that your Internet router decides to stop routing? You can always spend thousands of dollars in load balancing, redundant Internet connections, and hot spare equipment, or you can put in a low-cost RAS server to accommodate your remote users until your Internet connection is back up and running.

Another good reason for a RAS solution is that you don't need firewalls and intrusion detection systems (IDS) in order to support modem-based remote access. Although it's true that most companies today have some level of security on the corporate Internet connection, what about the remote users? Are you ready to roll out firewalls and IDSs to all your remote users? One of the favorite tricks for bypassing a corporate firewall is to compromise one of the remote clients, load a Trojan horse remote control program on it, and then wait for remote users to establish a VPN connection to the internal network. Once your unsuspecting employee has carried the attacker across the network threshold, you have handed the attacker a high-speed open door to start attacking your internal systems.

A final reason that we keep discussing RAS servers whenever we talk about remote access is that they are still useful for low-bandwidth applications. Do you need a 6 Mbps Internet connection if what you want to do is Telnet to a router to check processor utilization? The answer is no. So in some environments you will see the legacy RAS servers being reutilized as network management devices, used by engineers for managing network environments remotely.

All that being said, there are many compelling reasons (which we discuss a little later in the chapter) for implementing a VPN solution for remote access. But don't plan on retiring your RAS server just yet—you might find it has not outlived its usefulness after all.

www.syngress.com

Configuring a Virtual Private Networking Server

We have covered the dial-up modem features of the Windows 2000 RRAS in some detail. Now we need to take a look at the other side of the coin: the VPN capabilities of the Windows 2000 RRAS server.

Let's begin this discussion with a brief introduction to VPNs. A VPN creates a logical private network across an existing public network infrastructure such as the Internet. This connection is called *virtual* because the logical connection is built independently of the underlying physical network. In other words, the VPN connection is not aware of the physical route the packets take across the network; it is only aware of the endpoints of the virtual connection.

The purpose of a VPN is to securely extend your private internal network to users and external networks. When a VPN is configured correctly, a user should be unable to differentiate a VPN connection from a LAN connection. More important, the user's applications cannot differentiate between the two types of connections, providing a seamless method for integrating remote users or locations into the private network.

You will encounter two common types of VPN:

- **Remote access VPN** A remote access VPN is typically used to allow remote users to securely connect to a private corporate network. This was one of the major drivers of the VPN technology—it allowed users to connect to the corporate network without requiring the extensive modem cards and lines needed for large RAS implementations.

- **Site-to-site VPN** Also known as a *network-to-network VPN*, a site-to-site VPN is typically used to replace expensive WAN links with lower-cost VPN connections, utilizing the Internet as the underlying public network. Widespread adoption of this type of connection has been delayed by factors such as Internet reliability, VPN reliability, and the dramatic reductions in WAN technologies such as Frame Relay or asynchronous transfer mode (ATM), but they are becoming more common now that the Internet's reliability is more accepted and the VPN technology has become more stable. One other driver for site-to-site VPNs is the growing requirement for companies to interconnect with business partners, vendors, and customers. Not only do VPNs provide a secure mechanism for these interconnections—they can be created much more quickly than installing a WAN connection, which typically takes from 45 to 60 days.

One other type of VPN connection that is less common but growing in popularity is the VPN connection across the private network. This type of connection is typically used in environments in which different sections of the internal network require different levels of security. A VPN might be required to access the research and development network within a company, to ensure secure connections between corporate offices that exchange sensitive data, or within the government to secure top-secret data files traversing the internal network. All three of these VPN types are easily supported with Windows 2000 RRAS servers.

Now that we have seen what a VPN is, let's take a look at how you configure your Windows 2000 server to function as a VPN server.

Installing and Configuring the VPN Server

In Exercise 9.03 we install our VPN server to allow remote users to access the local network via a VPN connection. Not only is this the most common configuration you will encounter, it is also the easiest to perform in a lab environment.

NOTE

If you initially configured the RRAS server to be an RAS server and not a VPN server, or if you want to configure it manually, it will still list VPN ports if you have more than one network card in your server. However, the number of these ports by default will be 10 (five PPTP ports and five L2TP ports). If you initially configured the RAS server to be a VPN server rather than an RAS server, the number of VPN ports will total 256 (128 PPTP and 128 L2TP ports), and it will still list your direct parallel port and any modems installed. You can observe this fact by comparing the ports shown in Figure 9.20 from Exercise 9.02 with the ports shown in Exercise 9.04. In Exercise 9.02, we examine the RAS ports, following the configuration of RRAS as an RAS server. In Exercise 9.04, we look at the VPN ports, following the configuration of RRAS as a VPN server.

NOTE

You will need two network cards installed in your server to complete Exercise 9.03. Windows 2000 needs to see an Internet interface and a local LAN interface in order to install a VPN connection.

EXERCISE 9.03

CONFIGURING THE ROUTING AND REMOTE ACCESS SERVICE FOR REMOTE USER VPN ACCESS

1. Click **Start | Programs | Administrative Tools | Routing and Remote Access** to open the Routing and Remote Access console. To reset the Routing and Remote Access configuration. select **Disable Routing and Remote Access** from the **Action** menu (see Figure 9.22). This action resets the Routing and Remote Access to its initial condition and allows us to set up the VPN server as a clean installation. In Figure 9.23 you can see the warning message you receive when you reset the configuration. Resetting should only be done in a test or lab environment; resetting configured servers is discouraged.

Figure 9.22 Resetting the Configuration

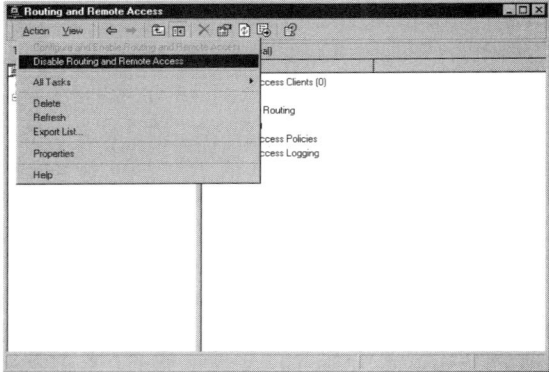

Figure 9.23 The Reset Warning Message

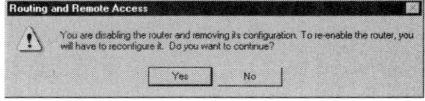

2. To begin the VPN server setup process, select **Configure and Enable Routing and Remote Access** from the **Action** menu to start the Routing and Remote Access Server Setup wizard. Select **Next** to open the Common Configurations screen.

3. From the Common Configurations menu (see Figure 9.24), select **Virtual private network (VPN) server** and select **Next** to continue.

Figure 9.24 Selecting VPN Server from the Common Configurations Menu

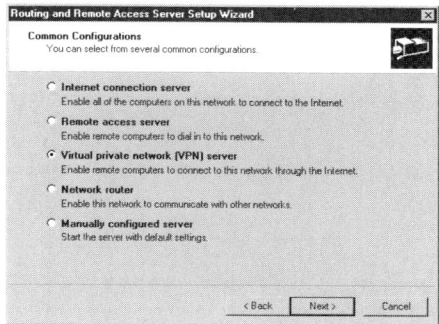

4. The Remote Client Protocols screen opens. Ensure that TCP/IP is one of the listed protocols (it is included by default), and select **Next** to continue. (We saw this screen and the next in Exercise 9.01; they do not change for the VPN setup.)

5. If the AppleTalk protocol is installed on your server, the Macintosh Guest Authentication screen opens. As in the dial-in RAS exercise, leave the **Allow unauthenticated access for all remote clients** unchecked and select **Next** to continue.

6. The Internet Connection screen opens (see Figure 9.25). In this screen you need to identify the Internet connection for your VPN server. Doing so allows the wizard to configure the public and private interfaces of the server correctly. Click **Next** to continue.

Figure 9.25 Selecting the Server's Internet Connection

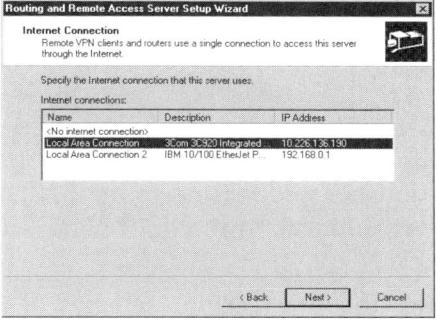

7. The IP Address Assignment screen (see Figure 9.26) is used to determine how IP addresses will be assigned to remote users. For this exercise, select **Automatically**, and then select **Next** to continue.

Figure 9.26 Selecting the Server's Internet Connection

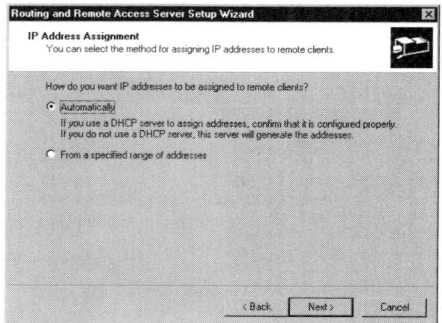

8. The Managing Multiple Remote Access Servers screen opens. Select **No, I don't want to set up this server to use RADIUS now** and select **Next** to continue.

9. You are now at the last screen (see Figure 9.27) for configuring your VPN server. To complete the process, select **Finish**. Note that the message in this screen states, "You have successfully configured a VPN server."

Figure 9.27 Completing the Installation

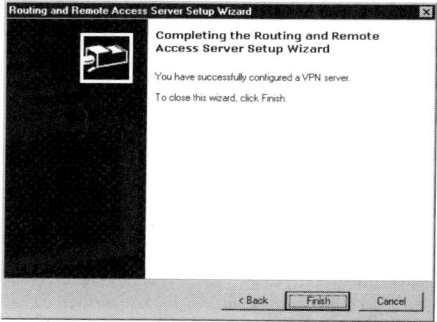

10. Before we end this exercise, we need to check some of the changes this installation has made to the server. From the main Routing and Remote Access Console screen (see Figure 9.28), expand the **IP Routing** section, and select **General**. In the right pane you will see the various network interfaces.

11. Right-click the interface you selected as your Internet interface and select **Properties** (see Figure 9.29). This action opens the Local Area Connection Properties screen (see Figure 9.30).

Figure 9.28 Checking the Changes Made to the Interfaces

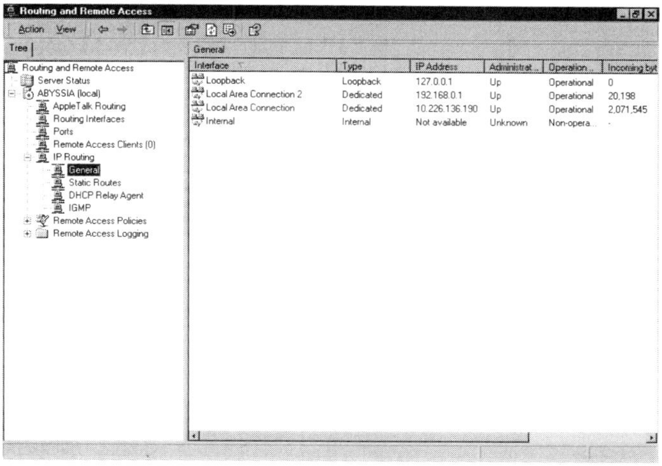

Figure 9.29 Selecting the Interface Properties

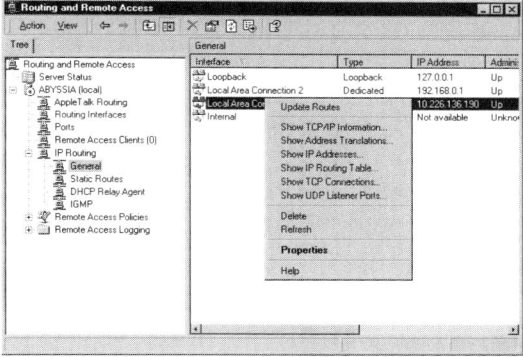

Figure 9.30 The General Tab of the Local Area Connection Properties Screen

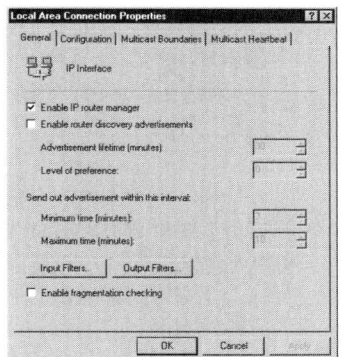

12. From the **General** tab of the Local Area Network Properties screen, select **Input Filters** (see Figure 9.31). These filters are applied by default during the VPN configuration process, and they are there to protect your Internet interface from unwanted traffic. Repeat this process for your other LAN interface(s) and note the lack of any filters. They are not installed by default on any interface that the wizard considers an internal (private) network interface.

    Figure 9.31 Input Filters

    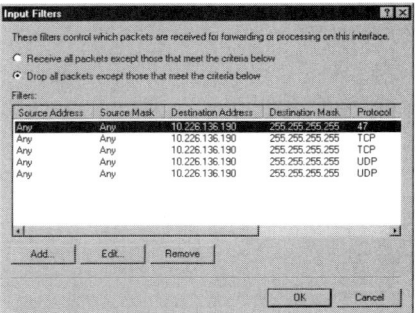

13. Click **OK** to return to the General tab and select **Output Filters** (see Figure 9.32). These filters are also applied by default during the VPN configuration process. Repeat this process for your other LAN interface(s) and note the lack of any filters. As with the input filters, the output filters are not installed by default on any interface that the wizard considers an internal (private) network interface.

    Figure 9.32 Output Filters

    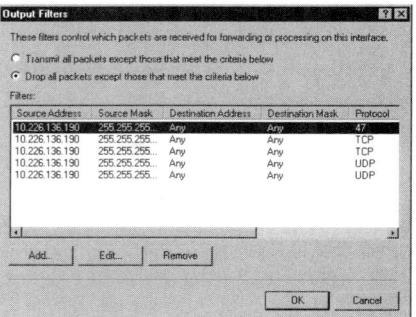

14. The final portion of this exercise involves looking at configuring the server properties. Click **OK** to return to the General tab, and click **OK** again to return to the Routing and Remote Access console. Select your server (in this exercise, the server name in the figures is *Abyssia*) and

select **Properties**. The <*server name*> (local) Properties screen opens (see Figure 9.33).

Figure 9.33 The Server Properties General Tab

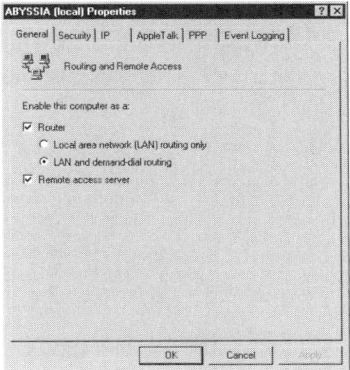

15. On the **General** tab of the Server Properties screen, you can enable your server to act as a router and/or as a remote access server. For this exercise, make sure the **Remote access server** is enabled.

16. On the **Security** tab of the Server Properties screen (see Figure 9.34), you can select the authentication provider (Windows authentication or RADIUS server) as well as the accounting provider (Windows accounting or RADIUS accounting.). Select the **Authentication Methods…** button to open the Authentication Methods screen (see Figure 9.35).

Figure 9.34 The Server Properties Security Tab

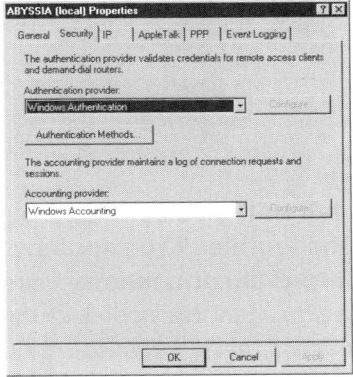

17. From the Authentication Methods screen shown in Figure 9.35, deselect any authentication methods except **Microsoft encrypted authentication version 2 (MS-CHAP v2)**. As we discussed earlier in the chapter,

this is the most secure of the user ID/password authentication protocols. If you are running older Windows clients (pre-Windows 2000), you might need to leave the MS-CHAP protocol enabled until you have time to update your clients.

Figure 9.35 The Authentication Methods Screen

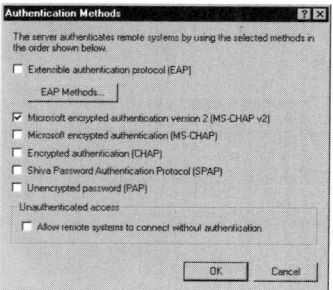

18. Select the **EAP Methods…** button to open the EAP Methods screen (see Figure 9.36). You can see that by default you have the MD5-Challenge and Smart Card or other Certificate options. Select **OK**, then select **OK** again to return to the Server Properties screen.

Figure 9.36 The Extensible Authentication Protocol Methods Dialog Box

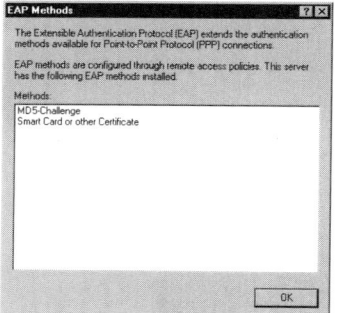

19. On the **IP** tab of the Server Properties screen (see Figure 9.37), make sure that the **Enable IP routing** and **Allow IP-based remote access and demand-dial connections** boxes are selected. From this tab you can also set the IP address distribution method (DHCP or Static Pool) and set which interface should be getting DHCP, DNS, and WINS addresses for remote clients. This will almost always be the port on the internal network, since the remote users will be trying to access systems and services on that network.

Figure 9.37 The Server Properties IP Tab

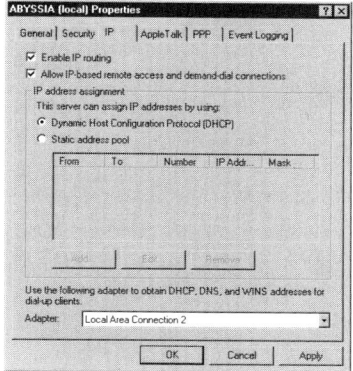

20. The **AppleTalk** tab allows you to enable or disable AppleTalk. Ensure that AppleTalk is enabled.
21. The **PPP** tab (see Figure 9.38) allows you to configure specific PPP settings, which we discuss later in the chapter.

Figure 9.38 The Server Properties PPP Tab

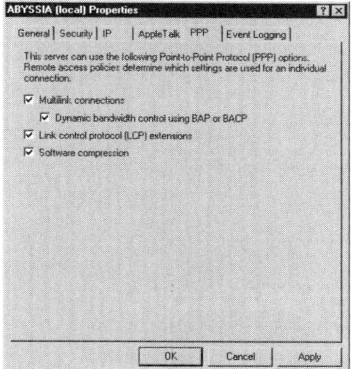

22. The **Event Logging** tab (see Figure 9.39) allows you to set the level of Event Logging your server maintains. For this exercise, leave **Log errors and warnings** selected. You will generally only use the **Log the maximum amount of information** setting if you are troubleshooting an issue or if you work in a very high-security environment. Generally the amount of data logged under that setting provides too much data; you never have time to review it, and you could lose important information related to events due to the amount of information you have to work through.

Figure 9.39 The Server Properties Event Logging Tab

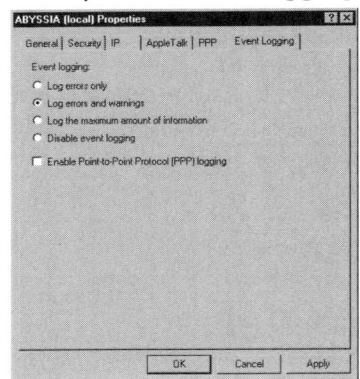

23. Click **OK** to return to the General tab, and click **OK** again to return to the Routing and Remote Access console. Close the console to complete this exercise.

Exam Warning

One of Microsoft's favorite exam topics is event logging and viewing. Be sure you understand where the logging is set and that the remote access events listed here can be viewed using the Event Viewer. They are logged to the Application Log.

Working with VPN Ports

We have discussed in some detail what a VPN is, and how to set one up. Now we need to look into the underlying architecture that Windows 2000 uses to support these VPN connections. As we saw in Exercise 9.03, configuring the Windows 2000 RRAS service installs two types of ports, L2TP and PPTP. PPTP and L2TP are two of the protocols that the Windows 2000 supports for creating VPN connections.

Point-to-Point Tunneling Protocol

Point-to-Point Tunneling Protocol (PPTP) is a proprietary VPN protocol originally developed by the PPTP Forum, a group of vendors that included Ascend Communications, Microsoft Corporation, 3Com, ECI Telematics, and U.S. Robotics. PPTP was designed as an extension of PPP to allow PPP to be tunneled through an IP network. One of the main differentiators between PPTP and IPSec is that PPTP supports the encapsulation of not only IP but IPX or NetBEUI as well. This feature is particularly useful in Windows or Novell environments that have not migrated to TCP/IP.

PPTP used Microsoft Point-to-Point Encryption (MPPE) to encrypt the link between the VPN client and the server and uses the Generic Routing Encapsulation (GRE) protocol to encapsulate the encrypted PPTP data in the PPP frame. This can be an IP datagram, an IPX datagram, or a NetBEUI frame.

One of the key benefits of PPTP is that because Microsoft helped develop it, it has been bundled with all current versions of Microsoft's operating systems. One of the issues with PPTP when it was introduced was whether the protocol was in fact secure enough for use as a VPN. Fortunately, the Windows 2000 implementation of PPTP includes the security updates needed to address issues related to earlier protocol versions. Another early issue with PPTP until it was more widely deployed was support for PPTP on Internet routers. To connect to your PPTP server, every router you traversed needed to be able to route PPTP. This is not an issue now, but in the late 1990s not all Internet service providers (ISPs) supported PPTP on their routers.

At one time PPTP was the most widely used VPN protocol, but the release of IPSec has had a significant impact on PPTP's use. Very popular with Microsoft shops and when Windows 2000 is being used as the VPN server, IPSec is enjoying increasing popularity.

For more details on PPTP, see RFC2637, *Point-to-Point Tunneling Protocol*, July 1999. It is important to note that this is an informational RFC and was never adopted as a standard. This is a key difference between PPTP and IPSec.

Layer 2 Tunneling Protocol

Layer 2 Tunneling Protocol (L2TP) is a combination of the best features of PPTP and the Layer 2 Forwarding (L2F) protocol, which was an early competing protocol for PPTP, developed by Cisco Systems. Like PPTP, L2TP was designed as an extension of PPP to allow PPP to be tunneled through an IP network. However, L2TP defines its own tunneling protocol, based on L2F. L2TP support was first included in a Microsoft server product with the release of Windows 2000 Server. Prior to Windows 2000, PPTP was the only supported protocol.

L2TP uses one of the IPSec protocols, Encapsulating Security Payload (ESP), for encryption. For this reason, L2TP under Windows 2000 is also known as L2TP/IPSec. The use of IPSec as the encryption mechanism allows L2TP/IPSec to utilize third-party encryption hardware to offload the encryption functions of the VPN connections from the VPN server. In addition, the standard implementation of L2TP/IPSec requires the use of machine PKI certificates. This ensures a more secure connection but at the cost of a more complex implementation; you must have access to a certificate authority (CA) in order to implement an L2TP/IPSec VPN connection.

> **Damage & Defense...**
>
> ### Considerations for L2TP Ports
> Despite offering a more secure form of connection for remote access clients, L2TP carries the expense of additional overheads in terms of configuration, maintenance, and processing. In addition, it is not widely supported by all clients. For example, Windows 2000 is the first Windows remote access client that can natively support L2TP/IPSec, so you might have to offer PPTP ports as well on your VPN server to ensure connectivity. However, if you are sure that only L2TP/IPSec clients will be using your VPN server, configuring only L2TP ports for remote access is a good security measure.

Internet Protocol Security

Internet Protocol Security (IPSec) is actually a set of protocols developed by the Internet Engineering Task Force (IETPF) to allow for the secure exchange of data via the Internet Protocol (IP). This was seen as a critical success factor for the next version of IP, known as IPv6, but it is also usable with IPv4, the version of IP used on the Internet today. As a result, IPSec is used by many vendors to deliver VPN services. One of the major limitations of IPSec is that the IETF guidelines do not allow IPSec to support the traversal of networks using Network Address Translation (NAT). Although many VPN manufacturers have implemented proprietary solutions to work around this limitation in the protocol, Microsoft has not. The Windows 2000 implementation of L2TP/IPSec does not support NAT.

Two encryption modes are supported by standard IPSec: Transport and Tunnel. Transport mode IPSec only encrypts the data portion of a packet. The packet's header information is left intact. For a more secure connection, using Tunnel mode IPSec encrypts not only the data portion of a packet but also the header.

The protocols used by IPSec include:

- **Internet Security Association and Key Management Protocol/Oakley (ISAKMP/Oakley)** This protocol is used to share a public key between sender and receiver of a secure connection. The ISAKMP/Oakley protocol allows the receiving system to retrieve a public key and then authenticate the sender using digital certificates.

- **Internet Key Exchange (IKE)** This protocol is used to authenticate the endpoints of an IPSec connection, negotiate the exchange of IPSec keys, and negotiate IPSec Security Associations (SAs). An SA is used by the IPSec endpoints to define how data will be encrypted and decrypted. IKE also uses the Diffie-Hellman public-key cryptography protocol to exchange the session keys used to create the initial secure connection.

- **Authentication Header (AH)** Authenticates the data packet and ensures the integrity of the data being sent. In order to ensure packet and data integrity, AH uses hashing algorithms to "sign" the packets. The algorithms AH uses include MD5 and Secure Hash Algorithm (SHA).
- **Encapsulating Security Payload (ESP)** This protocol encrypts the data contents of the packet.
- **IPSec** Can use a number of encryption algorithms, including Data Encryption Standard (DES), Triple DES (3DES), or 40-bit DES, a version that is almost never used due to the poor key strength.

There are a couple of important features of IPSec in the Windows 2000 operating system. First, a pure IPSec connection (in other words, not L2TP/IPSec) will not appear in the list of ports shown in the RRAS console. If you need to install and support a pure IPSec connection, you need to use the ipsecmon.exe tool.

Exam Warning

One of the key differences among the VPN protocol types is which protocol can traverse a firewall that is using NAT. Later in the chapter, we discuss the challenges of NAT in conjunction with VPNs; for the exam, be sure you know that the only protocol Windows 2000 supports that can traverse a firewall or network using NAT is PPTP. The IPSec protocol suite is not currently written to permit traversing a NAT environment, which impacts not only your IPSec connections but your L2TP/IPSec connections as well. IPSec and L2TP are unable to pass traffic across a NAT connection.

Now that we have discussed the types of VPN connections your Windows 2000 VPN server setup uses, let's take a look at how we can configure the VPN ports in Exercise 9.04.

EXERCISE 9.04

Configuring the PPTP and L2TP Ports for Inbound Access Only

1. Click **Start | Programs | Administrative Tools | Routing and Remote Access** to open the Routing and Remote Access console.

2. In the left pane of the Routing and Remote Access console, right-click **Ports** and select **Properties.** The Ports Properties screen (see Figure 9.40) opens.

Figure 9.40 Ports Properties: Configuring the WAN Miniport (PPTP) Ports

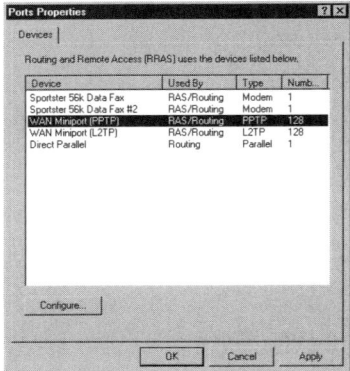

3. Select **WAN Miniport (PPTP)** and click the **Configure** button to open the Configure Device screen (see Figure 9.41).

Figure 9.41 The Configure Device – WAN Miniport PPTP Dialog Box

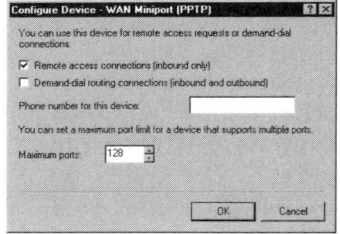

4. From this screen, make sure that the only option selected is **Remote access connections (inbound only)**. This will make your VPN server an inbound VPN server only and will prevent this server from making site-to-site VPN connections. On this screen, you can also modify the number of PPTP ports supported by this server. Click **OK** to close this screen and return to the Ports Properties screen.

5. Repeat the same steps for the WAN Miniport (L2TP) port. When you have completed the steps for the L2TP ports, click **Apply** to update the configuration, and click **OK** to close the Ports Properties screen.

Now that you know how to work with the configuration of your VPN ports, let's look at checking the status of one of those ports in Exercise 9.05.

EXERCISE 9.05

CHECKING THE STATUS OF A CONNECTED VPN PORT

1. From the Routing and Remote Access Console, select **Ports** in the left pane. The list of all configured ports appears.
2. Select a port to check, right-click it, and select **Status** from the menu. (Later in the chapter, you will learn how to check an active port. Once you've completed that exercise, you can review this exercise to see what an active port status looks like.)
3. Review the statistics. In the Figure 9.42, you can see that the user is logged on as Administrator and has been logged in for a little over 27 minutes. You can also review the packet statistics, errors, and network information. In this example, the only protocol in use is TCP/IP, so the only information available is the IP address. From this window you can also disconnect the user by selecting the **Disconnect** button.

Figure 9.42 The Port Status – WAN Miniport PPTP VPN Port Dialog Box

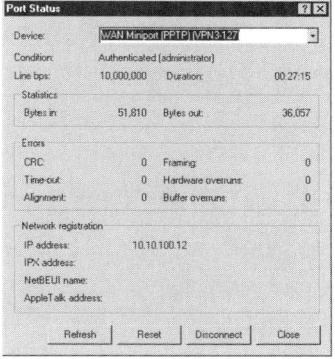

Configuring L2TP Ports

L2TP ports are new in Windows 2000, and together with IPSec and computer certificates they offer a more secure form of VPN connection than the legacy PPTP protocol. Because it is used with IPSec, L2TP can also offer end-to-end security from remote access client to the internal network resource if that system is also using IPSec. In comparison, PPTP offers only client to RAS server secure communication. Once the traffic passes the RAS server with PPTP, it is passed as unencrypted data.

In most instances, this level of security is not a requirement, especially since the overhead of setting up and maintaining this sort of configuration can be substantial. In addition, you need to be very IPSec-savvy in order to successfully integrate the Windows 2000 L2TP/IPSec connection with an internal server. The one bright spot in using L2TP/IPSec is that there is no need to configure specific IPSec policies to support this connection, because a default policy is created for you automatically on both the Windows 2000 server and the Windows 2000 remote access client. The real challenge in the configuration, as we have discussed before, is that by default, the L2TP/IPSec policy uses certificates rather than a preshared key or Kerberos for authentication. Therefore, your VPN server and remote access client must have a computer certificate for authentication that is issued by the same CA. In addition, IPSec requires computer certificates, not user certificates, for authentication.

Exam Warning

The successful creation of the default L2TP/IPSEc policy depends on the IPSec Policy Agent, which must be loaded in order for the policy to be created. Furthermore, stopping the IPSec Policy Agent will cause the L2TP/IPSec policy to be removed. If you must stop and restart the IPSec Policy Agent, be sure to also restart the RRAS server afterward. This is a critical step because this policy is hidden and these issues will not be obvious in the event you need to troubleshoot an issue with L2TP/IPSec connections.

Configuring Remote Access Policies

Now that we have discussed in detail all the components needed to access your Windows 2000 RRAS server via dial-up and VPN connections, we need to discuss the concept of remote access policies.

In the pre-Windows 2000 RAS service, dial-in permissions were either Grant or Deny. This made it very easy to configure permissions, but it lacked any flexibility of configuration. To make matters worse, you also needed to do configuration on a per-user basis. With the release of Windows 2000, Microsoft has given administrators a great deal of flexibility when it comes to granting remote access permissions. Under Windows 2000, authorization is granted based on the dial-in properties of a user account and the server's remote access policies.

But what is a remote access policy? *Remote access policies* are sets of conditions and connection settings that determine connection permissions. With a remote access policy, you can configure Grant or Deny permissions based on the time of day or day of the week (as illustrated in the next exercise) by Windows 2000 group, by protocol or VPN protocol, by connection type, and a number of other factors. You can also use the remote access profile portion of the policy to set idle timeouts, maximum session times, authentication protocols, encryption strengths, and several other connection parameters, which we discuss in detail later in the chapter.

TEST DAY TIP

Remember where the remote access policies are stored; they are stored locally. If you want a central policy, you have to use a central RADIUS solution for policy authentication.

EXAM WARNING

Remember, a remote access connection will only be authorized if the connection configuration matches a remote access policy. If the connection matches no remote access policies, the connection request will be denied—even if the dial-in properties of the user's account are set to grant access. If you are trying to deny access in a remote access policy, keep in mind that the policies are processed in order and do not stop being processed until the conditions for a connection are met or all the policies have been processed. One of hardest concepts in the new Windows 2000 remote access architecture is the concept of conflicting remote access permissions and policies.

The best way to get an understanding of remote access policies is to set one up. Let's do this in Exercise 9.06.

EXERCISE 9.06

CREATING A NEW REMOTE ACCESS POLICY TO RESTRICT REMOTE USER ACCESS TIMES

1. Open the Routing and Remote Access Service console and select **Remote Access Policies** from the left pane.

2. Right-click **Remote Access Policies** and select **New Remote Access Policy** from the menu. The Add Remote Access Policy screen opens (see Figure 9.43).

3. Enter a descriptive name in the **Policy friendly name** box, and select **Next** to continue. If you are in a complex environment in which there

are lots of remote access policies, you might even need a naming convention for these policies to keep them straight.

Figure 9.43 The Add Remote Access Policy Screen: Policy Name

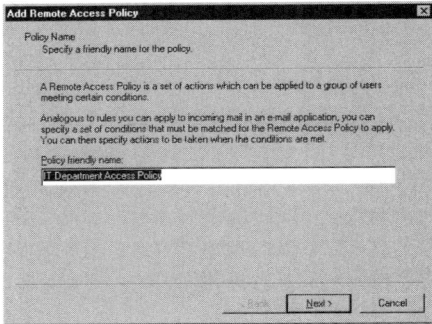

4. The Add Conditions screen opens (see Figure 9.44). From this screen you will add the conditions that need to be matched in order for this policy to take effect.

Figure 9.44 Add Remote Access Policy Conditions

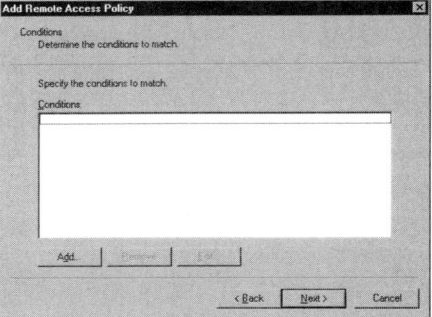

5. Click the **Add…** button to open the Select Attribute screen (see Figure 9.45). Since we are working on setting time restrictions for remote users, select **Day-and-Time Restrictions** from the list of conditions. On your own time, you should explore the rest of these conditions so you are familiar with them. Select the **Add…** button to add this attribute.

6. Because we are setting day and time restrictions, the **Time of day constraints** screen opens. It will initially be blank. Select the times from 6:00 A.M. until 8:00 P.M. for all days of the week. The result should look like Figure 9.46. Since this is one of the more common constraints you will implement, try setting other days and times to be sure you are comfortable with the results. Select **OK** to continue.

Figure 9.45 Selecting the Attribute(s)

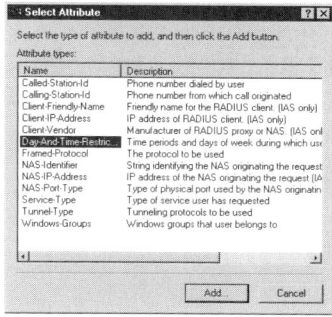

Figure 9.46 Time of Day Constraints

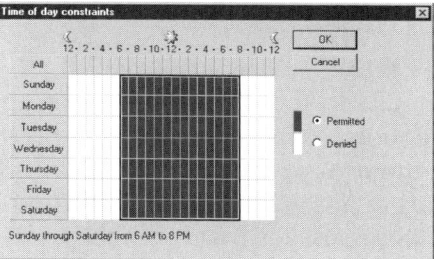

7. In Figure 9.47, the condition you configured should show up in the Conditions window. At this point you can add more conditions, but for this exercise, simply select **Next** to continue.

Figure 9.47 The New Access Policy Condition

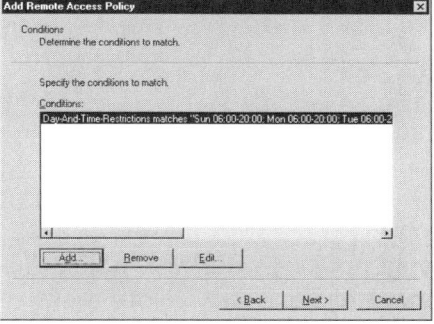

8. On the Permissions screen (see Figure 9.48), you can select whether to grant or deny access based on the condition(s) you just set. As you might guess, creating a policy can be a very intricate process. Be sure you understand exactly the results you need before you create a new

policy. In this case, select **Grant remote access permission**, and then click **Next** to continue.

Figure 9.48 Add Access Policy Conditions

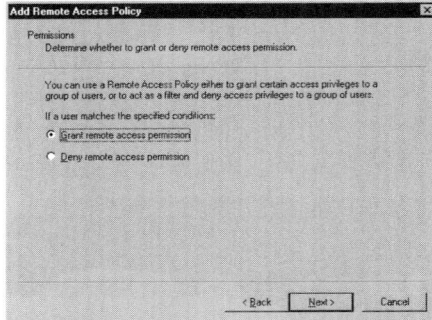

9. The User Profile screen (see Figure 9.49) is used to modify the profile associated with the policy. We discuss this topic later in the chapter. Pay attention to the Microsoft note on this screen; a profile can be used if the policy conditions are overridden at the user level. This feature adds additional complexity to troubleshooting in the event of remote access issues that are policy related. Select **Finish** to complete the creation of your new remote access policy.

Figure 9.49 Add Access Policy Conditions

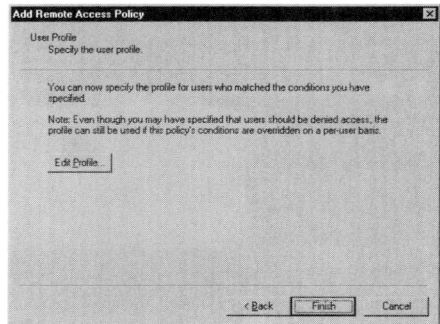

10. You should now see your new policy. (In Figure 9.50 it is called the IT Department Access Policy.) Note the Order column of this screen. Remote access policies are processed in the order in which they appear in this screen. If you want to make your new policy the first on the list, right-click it and select **Move Up** from the menu.

Figure 9.50 The New Remote Access Policy Has Been Entered

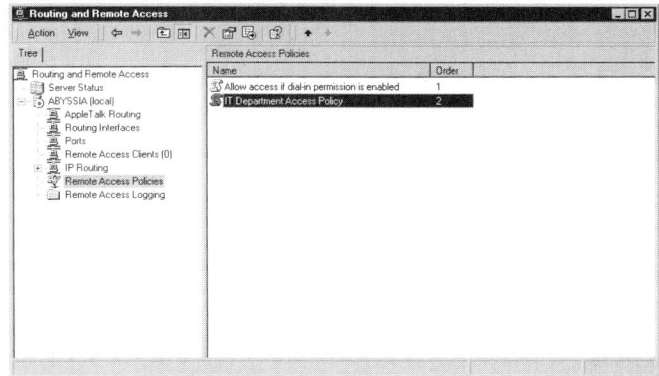

You have successfully created a new remote access policy. These policies can be used to configure the permissions for remote access connections. Now let's look at what you can do with the remote access profile that we passed over in this exercise. It is the final component you need to complete the configuration of your remote access policy.

Configuring Remote Access Profiles

Let's take a look at the various portions of the remote access profile. You can modify a remote access profile during the creation of a remote access policy, as we did in the last exercise, or you can review or modify a profile for an existing remote access policy by right-clicking the policy, selecting **Properties**, and then clicking the **Edit Profile** button. Five tabs are available in the configuration screen. Let's look at them one at a time.

Dial-in Constraints

The parameters that can be configured on the Dial-in Constraints screen (see Figure 9.51) include:

- **Disconnect if idle for** This setting allows you to set the number of minutes of inactivity a user has before the system disconnects the user. The more stringent your security requirements, the shorter this time should be, to prevent an attacker using an idle system to access your network.

- **Restrict maximum session to** This setting allows you to set the total number of minutes a session can last. From a security perspective, setting this option as short as possible is a good idea because it limits the amount of time a successful attacker can stay connected to your system. This risk needs to be balanced against the usability requirements of your end users; they might get annoyed if they keep getting bumped offline after 15 minutes while trying to synchronize their mail.

- **Restrict access to the following days and times** This setting allows you another place where you can limit the time during which the system will accept connections.

- **Restrict Dial-in to this number only** This setting is useful only if all your users connect from the same number or if you only have one user connecting using this remote access policy for authorization to this server (an administrator, for example) and you want that user to only connect from his or her home number.

- **Restrict Dial-in media** This is not a commonly used parameter, but you can use it to limit the media that can be used to connect to this system.

Figure 9.51 Remote Access Profile Dial-in Constraints

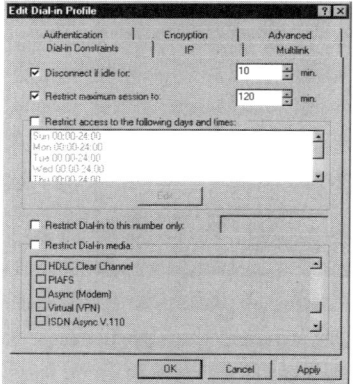

IP

The parameters that can be configured on the IP screen (Figure 9.52) include:

- **IP Address Assignment Policy** This setting defines how users being authorized by this policy will get their IP addresses. This is typically left at the default setting, but can be used to restrict how IP addresses are assigned.

- **IP Packet Filters** This setting allows you to set IP packet filters on the connection. For example, if this were being used only for getting Web access to your intranet server, you might set an inbound filter for port 80 (HTTP) to access only the intranet server.

Figure 9.52 Remote Access Profile IP

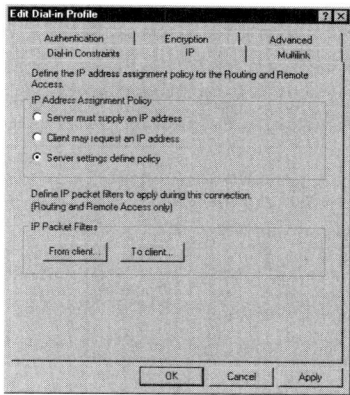

Multilink

The parameters that can be configured on the Multilink screen (see Figure 9.53) include:

- **Multilink** This setting allows you to permit or restrict the number of ports via which a single client can connect. Windows 2000 and later support the use of multiple connections to a single server, which are aggregated to provide additional bandwidth. Although this greatly improves performance, it can be a very resource-intensive solution for larger environments. Not only does it require multiple ports per user at the server end, it requires multiple modems and phone lines on the user's end.

- **Bandwidth Allocation Protocol (BAP)** BAP monitors the utilization on a multilink connection and dynamically reduces the number of connected lines if the user's utilization drops below a certain amount.

Figure 9.53 Remote Access Profile Multilink

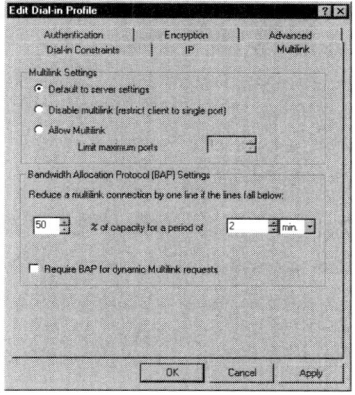

Test Day Tip

The only place that you can configure the Multilink or BAP settings is in the remote access profile. This is a commonly used setting for Windows 2000 RAS servers and is a ripe area for exam questions. Just remember, you edit the remote access policy, then open the remote access profile to get to these settings.

Authentication

The parameters that can be configured on the Authentication screen (see Figure 9.54) include:

- **Authentication methods** This section allows you to select the protocols that can be used to authenticate a user connecting via this remote access policy. Whenever possible, use MS-CHAPv2 or EAP; they provide the most secure authentication.

- **Unauthenticated access** Never enable this setting. It essentially allows clients to connect without authenticating first, and so it should never be used, since it bypasses all authentication security.

Figure 9.54 Remote Access Profile Authentication

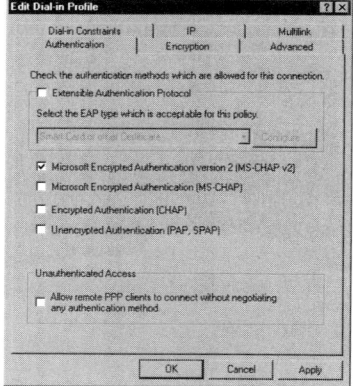

Encryption

The entire purpose of the Encryption screen (see Figure 9.55) is to select how strong the encryption used by this connection must be. If you are running an entirely Windows 2000 or later client population, you should only permit the strongest level of encryption. If you have older clients, you might need to permit weaker encryption levels.

Figure 9.55 Remote Access Profile Encryption

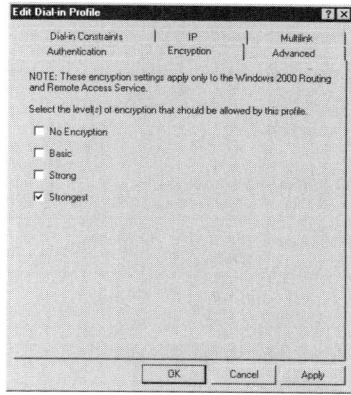

Advanced

The purpose of the Advanced screen (see Figure 9.56) is to specify additional connection attributes, typically related to RADIUS requirements for a connection. This screen is generally only used for very complex implementations involving centralized RADIUS servers for remote access policy storage.

Figure 9.56 Remote Access Profile Advanced

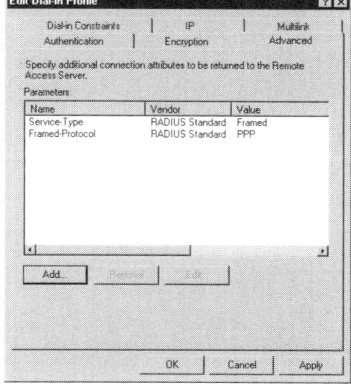

Remote Access Policy Administrative Models

The final remote access policy topic we need to cover is how remote access permissions are administered. Under the new Windows 2000 model, you might encounter three remote access and connection settings administration models:

- **Access by user** In this model, remote access permissions are determined by the remote access permission on the Dial-in tab of the user account, much as they were in the pre-Windows 2000 RAS environment. Remote access permissions are set on a per-user basis by setting the remote access permission to either Allow access or Deny access. The key to this model is the fact that the remote access permission setting on the remote access policy is effectively overridden by the user account permissions. The good news under this model is that you can still enforce the connection settings by modifying the remote access policy conditions and profile properties. The major drawback of this solution is that you are managing your remote access security on a user-by-user basis, which is not very efficient or effective. This model is typically used if you have Windows NT 4.0 RAS servers. It works on a standalone Windows 2000 RAS server, a Windows 2000 RAS server in either a native mode or mixed domain, or even a Windows 2000 RAS server that authenticates from a Windows NT 4.0 domain.

- **Access by policy in a Windows 2000 native-mode domain** In this model, the remote access permission on every user account is set to Control access through Remote Access Policy. This means that the remote access permissions are determined by the remote access permission setting on the remote access policy, which we just looked at configuring. This would be the other end of the spectrum from the access-by-user model, which ignores most of the profile settings. This is the most efficient model for managing your remote access security, but it is also the most complex, due to the overhead associated with creating and maintaining the remote access policies and profiles. This model can also be used with a standalone Windows 2000 RAS server, but it is not supported by either a Windows 2000 RAS server in a mixed mode (one or more Windows NT 4 domain controllers in a Windows 2000 domain) or a Windows NT 4 domain. For more information on mixed-mode versus native-mode domains, see Knowledgebase Article 186153 at support.microsoft.com/default.aspx?scid=KB;en-us;186153&.

- **Access by policy in a Windows 2000 mixed-mode domain** In this model, every user account's remote access permission is set to Allow access, the default remote access policy is deleted, and separate remote access policies are created for each type of connection that is allowed. As a result, you are still managing remote access through remote access policies, but it is not as efficient nor as simple as the previous two modes. In some ways, this model combines the worst of both models: there is the user dial-in access settings to contend with as well as the complexity of setting up your remote access policies and profiles. Furthermore, in this model you cannot combine policies, so you need a policy for each connection medium, further complicating things.

One benefit to this model is that it supports both a Windows 2000 RAS server in a mixed-mode domain or an NT 4 domain.

TEST DAY TIP

Be sure you remember what native-mode and mixed mode domains are and what administration models are available under each. Since this is a new capability under the Windows 2000 RRAS, it is a good place to look for an exam question or two; Windows NT 4.0 RAS only offered one administration model.

EXAM WARNING

Remember the Guest account. Depending on how you configure your remote access profiles, it is possible that your Guest account could be used for anonymous access. To prevent this scenario, make sure your Guest account doesn't have remote access permissions, is disabled, and has a strong password set on the account.

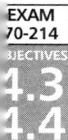

Configuring Network Clients for Secure Remote Access

Now that we have gone through all the steps for setting up your remote access server, we need to take a look at the other side of the equation: setting up a client to connect to the server. In Exercise 9.07, we look at setting up a Windows 2000 client to use a PPTP VPN connection to connect to a Windows 2000 server configured for remote access VPN connections.

EXERCISE 9.07

CONFIGURING WINDOWS 2000 FOR CONNECTING TO A PPTP SERVER

1. Right-click the **My Network Places** icon from the Desktop, and select **Properties**.
2. From the **Network and Dial-up Connections** window, select **Make New Connection**. The Network Connection wizard (see Figure 9.57) opens.

Figure 9.57 Creating a VPN Connection

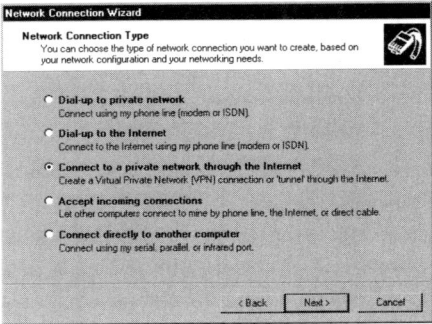

3. Select Connect to a private network through the Internet, and click Next to continue.

4. On the Public Network screen, you have the option to have the VPN connection make the initial public network connection for you. Select **Do not dial the initial connection**, and click **Next** to continue.

5. On the Destination Address screen (see Figure 9.58), enter the DNS name or IP address of the VPN server you need to connect to. Click **Next** to continue.

Figure 9.58 Entering the VPN Server DNS Name or IP Address

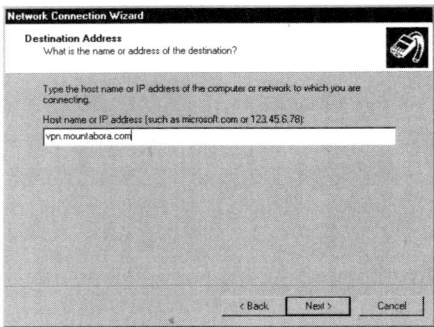

6. On the Connection Availability screen, select **For all users**, and click **Next** to continue.

7. The Completing the Network Connection wizard opens. Enter a descriptive name for the connection and select **Finish** to complete the configuration. You should see your new VPN connection in the Network and Dial-up Connections window.

8. To test your new connection, double-click the new entry. The Connect Virtual Private Connection screen (see Figure 9.59) opens. Enter the

user account and password for an account that is authorized to connect via remote access, and click **Connect** to open the connection. Under no circumstances should you ever select **Save Password** for a connection of this type. Not only is the storage of the password weak, but if your system is ever compromised, you give the attacker an open invitation to attack your internal network.

Figure 9.59 Creating a VPN Connection

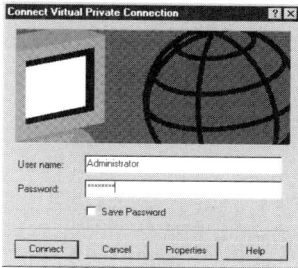

9. If your connection is successful, you will see the Connection Complete dialog box. If you do not successfully connect, see the "Troubleshooting Remote Access Problems" portion of this chapter to work out the reason the connection failed.

Once you have a connected VPN connection, you can double-click the entry in the Network and Dial-up Connections window. Doing so will open the Connection Status window, which can give you a snapshot of what is happening with the connection.

We have looked at how to set up a Windows 2000 VPN connection, but how would you do it for other operating systems? Let's get the easy one out of the way: For Windows XP, Microsoft's latest desktop operating system, you would do it in the exact same way. The two operating systems use the same installation wizard.

For Windows 98, ME, and Windows NT 4.0 operating systems, you can download the Microsoft L2TP/IPSec VPN Client from www.microsoft.com/windows2000/server/evaluation/news/bulletins/l2tpclient.asp.

To install the Microsoft L2TP/IPSec VPN Client, simply run the MSL2TP.EXE installer file on your computer. This installer provides a menu-driven install process for the Microsoft L2TP/IPSec VPN Client. It will also install the Microsoft IPSec VPN Configuration Utility and the Microsoft L2TP/IPSec VPN Client Help file. To access any of these applications, go to **Start | Programs | Microsoft IPSec VPN** and select the application you want to look at. You can remove the client using the Add or Remove Programs applet in the Control Panel.

Exam Warning

The latest version of the Microsoft L2TP/IPSec VPN Client includes support for proposed extensions to the IPSec protocol to support the ability for IPSec to traverse a NAT network. Microsoft plans to support these extensions in Windows .NET Server. However, within the context of this exam, NAT traversal is not supported by the L2TP/IPSec client.

If you install the Microsoft L2TP/IPSec VPN Client under Windows 98 or Windows Millennium Edition, you will find a Microsoft L2TP/IPSec VPN Adapter added to the list of installed network adapters and the Microsoft L2TP/IPSec VPN Adapter 1 added to the list of available devices for a dial-up network connection.

If you install the Microsoft L2TP/IPSec VPN Client under Windows NT Workstation 4.0, you will find the RASL2TPM added to the list of devices for remote access and the RASL2TPM (VPNx) added to the list of available devices for a phone-book entry in Dial-Up Networking.

Using the Connection Manager Administration Kit

This handy utility, the Connection Manager Administration Kit (CMAK), is very badly documented and undersold as an additional tool on a Windows 2000 Server. You no longer have to buy the Internet Explorer Administration Kit in order to be able to distribute fully configured remote access connections for users. These can be customized fully with your own company logos and icons, help desk telephone number prominently displayed, automatically downloading up-to-date phone book entries, launching key applications once the remote connection is established, and so on. Or users can use standard defaults, and you just supply the basic connection details required for the client's dialer program.

The Connection Manager Administration Kit wizard steps you through configuring a service profile, the set of files required to configure remote user's connection details bundled into a self-installing executable file that you distribute to users who need remote access. This service profile will work on any 32-bit Windows platform and requires, in all, about 1MB free hard disk space. Users must have the Connection Manager v1.2 software installed in order to use your configuration options, which can be included in the service profile. If they already have this software installed, the hard disk space required is greatly reduced (requires about 200KB).

The CMAK wizard steps you through the relevant stages of creating a customized connection utility (dialer) for your users. These steps can include adding a help desk telephone number, including your own customized bitmaps and icons, specifying programs to run automatically when connected, including a customized help file, and even adding the PPTP protocol for Windows 9*x* users. (However, this last capability must first be installed manually on NT4 machines.) The only stipulations are that users have a modem that is at least 9600 baud that and TCP/IP is installed prior to installation.

The last page of the wizard tells you where the self-extracting cabinet file is located so you can distribute it to users—for example, on CD or by allowing users to download from your FTP site. When users run the file, they'll have a choice of creating a Desktop shortcut for their connection or selecting it from their Network and Dial-Up Connections (or equivalent). When you distribute this file to remote users and partners, there will be far less chance of them not connecting to your remote access servers through a misconfigured connection, and it looks very professional because it's all pre-configured and can be branded with your own company image.

However, before using the CMAK, you must ensure that your RRAS and IAS work as designed by manually creating connections and testing your server setup. Once these connections are confirmed as working, you can use these details to define the connections for your users.

This section steps you through the following:

- Manually defining connections
- Using the CMAK
- How users install and use Connection Manager

Manually Creating the Connections

We assume that you successfully installed and configured the interfaces that will be used for your connections; in other words, your modem(s) on the RAS server and Internet connection and the modem on your remote access client.

Windows 2000 makes the process of defining dial-up connections for the client side incredibly easy with the Make New Connection option under Network and Dial-Up Connections. This tool loads the Network Connection wizard, which prompts you for the type of connection required. Choose **Dial-up to private network** to specify RAS connections or **Dial-up to the Internet** to specify an ISP connection.

For the RAS connection, you simply need to supply the telephone number of your RAS server's modem. The ISP connection probably will load the Internet Connection wizard; make sure that you select the last option, **I want to set up my Internet connection manually**, or **I want to connection through a local area network (LAN)**.

After you have created the connections, you can right-click them and select **Properties** to fine-tune their settings—for example, the redial attempt number and timeout value, whether to include the Windows logon domain in the credentials, authentication requirements, which protocols should be used, and so on. Note that under the

VPN connection you'll have **Automatic** selected under the Networking tab and **Type of VPN server I am calling**. This means that L2TP/IPSec will be tried first, and then PPTP. If you know users will not use L2TP/IPSec, you can change this setting to Point-to-Point Tunneling Protocol (PPTP) instead to ensure a faster connection.

Once you are happy that all connections are working satisfactorily, you are ready to use the CMAK to distribute these settings to users. If you prefer not to use the CMAK, you can supply information for users on how to create their own connections manually.

Creating a Static Phone Book

The simplest phone book you could create would be one connection—for example, the telephone number of your RAS server or, if you're specifying a VPN connection, you'll specify the telephone number of the ISP (the VPN server details will be added with the Connection Manager Administration Kit). When you have multiple RAS servers and multiple ISPs, you must decide whether to create one big phone book and let the user choose the appropriate connection or deploy multiple phone books with only the relevant connections.

The two files you'll need when specifying a static phone book are the .pbk file and a .pbr file. These files must be in the same directory, share the same base name, and have the same limitation as DOS-based naming formation (no spaces, maximum of eight letters).

The .pbr file refers to a region file that you create manually as a text file. The format of it is simple enough: The first line contains a number that is the number of regions you want to define—for example, if you had only one region (such as London), this would be the number 1. The remaining entries (one to a line) are the names of your regions. See the example for a three-region file:

```
3
London
Paris
New York
```

The format of the phone book is 11 fields, separated by commas and all filled. If a field has no value, it should contain the number 0. Although this file can be created manually by entering the information in a text file, we will discuss an easier way to create a phone book later in the section. The format of this file for each entry is the following:

```
Index,TAPICountryOrRegionID,StateOrPrvinceID,POPName,AreaCode,PhoneNumber,
    MinBaud,MaxBaud,Reserved,ServiceType,DUNEntry
```

For example, a single entry for the UK (44) uses our first regional number, where the point-of-presence name is Company (this is the text label for this phone number), the area code is 0208, the telephone number is 5441122, only modem access is allowed, and that has the connection name of Company RAS Server, as follows:

`1,44,1,Company,0208,5441122,0,0,0,41,Company RAS Server`

Save the file with the matching name and the .pbk extension, and you have created your first phone book.

Creating a Dynamic Phone Book

This involves creating a phone book with Phone Book Administrator, then transferring it to an FTP site so users can reference it via your Web service and download new or changed entries when they dial into your company. The Phone Book Administrator and Phone Book Service need to be installed directly from the Windows 2000 Server CD under **VALUEADD | MSFT | MGMT | PBA**. Run **pbainst.exe**, which installs the Phone Book Administrator (used to create the phone book entries) and Phone Book Service, which is an IIS5 extension that works with the FTP service so you can FTP connection entries and users can download phone book updates if necessary from your Web site, either automatically using FTP and a correctly configured profile or manually from the site.

You need to have your FTP virtual directory ready and configured to accept your phone book. The PBSData virtual directory is created when Connection Services is installed, but you'll need to enable write access to transfer the phone book and ensure that anonymous access is disabled. For security reasons, consider disabling the write permission between phone book transfers.

Exercise 9.08 walks you through the process of creating your phone book.

EXERCISE 9.08

CREATING A DYNAMIC PHONE BOOK

1. In the Phone Book Editor utility, click **File | New Phone Book** and specify the name you want to use (e.g., **Company**).
2. Make sure your new phone book entry is highlighted, and select **Tools | Regions Editor**.
3. Click **Add**, and change **New Region** to the name of the region you want to use (for example, **London**), press **Enter**, and click **OK**.
4. Click **Edit | Add POP** (*POP* stands for *point of presence*) and you'll see three tabs for Access Information, Settings, and Comments.
5. In the **Access Information** tab, fill in the details as appropriate. You'll notice that the **Region** list box contains the region you previously entered.

6. Now go into the **Settings** tab and specify the information you want to supply. The default POP settings are probably not appropriate for your needs, so you might want to remove the **Sign on** and **Multicast** options. The **Dial-Up Networking** entry is very important—this is the name users will see to identify their connection, so choose it with care.

7. Click **OK**. You should now see some of your phone book entries in the bottom pane.

8. Click **Tools | Publish Phone Book**.

9. Within the **Publish Phone Book** dialog box, click the **Options** button and define your IIS server details together with credentials (username/password) to use the FTP site.

10. Click **OK**. You should now see your server details appear on the bottom right of the Publish Phone Book dialog box.

11. Set a directory (or use the default) and click **Create**.

12. The **Post** button will now become available. Click **Post** and you'll be prompted to select your dial-up connection and connect.

Running the CMAK

The CMAK can be found in Administrative Tools and, like most Windows 2000 tools, utilizes a wizard to guide you through the process of creating a service profile. Exercise 9.09 shows you how to create a basic service profile, which creates a self-extracting file you could distribute to users.

EXERCISE 9.09

CREATING A BASIC SERVICE PROFILE

1. On the first page of the **CMAK** wizard, click **Next**.

2. On the **Service Profile Source** dialog box, click **Next** to create a new service profile.

3. The **Service and File Names** dialog box prompts for the name of a service profile (which will be displayed in the user's connection dialog box) and the name of the self-extracting distribution file. For simplicity, it's a good practice to use the same name for both. Type these names in and click **OK**.

4. On the **Merged Service Profiles** dialog box, click **Next**.

5. On the **Support Information** dialog box, type the text information you want displayed on the user's connection dialog box and click **Next**.

6. On the **Realm Name** dialog box, you can enter a realm. These are used in conjunction with RADIUS, usually to differentiate groups of users or companies. You would typically use this in conjunction with an ISP service. Click **Next** to continue.

7. On **Dial-Up Networking Entries**, click **Add** and manually type the name you supplied in the phone book. Click **OK**, and click **Next** to continue.

8. On the **VPN Support** dialog box, you can click **Next** and go to the **Next** screen if you're specifying a RAS connection.

9. On **Connect Actions**, unselect all three check boxes and click **Next** to continue.

10. On **Auto-Applications**, click **Next**.

11. On the **Logon Bitmap** dialog box, click **Next**.

12. On the **Phone Book Bitmap** dialog box, click **Next**.

13. On the **Phone Book** dialog box, browse for the static phone book (.pbk) you created. By default, this file would have saved in your My Documents folder. Select the .pbk file so that it's displayed, then click **Next**. If at this point you don't have a corresponding region file in the same directory, you'll be warned and not allowed to continue.

14. On the **Icons** dialog box, click **Next**.

15. On the **Status-Area-Icon** menu, click **Next**.

16. On the **Help File** dialog box, click **Next**.

17. On the **Connection Manager Software** dialog box, keep the default of selecting the **Connection Manager software**, and click **Next**.

18. On the **License Agreement** dialog box, click **Next**.

19. On the **Additional Files** dialog box, click **Next**.

20. On the Ready to Build the Service Profile screen, click **Next**.

21. You should now see the command prompt window showing the progress of your cabinet file. At the end you'll see the final page showing you that the Connection Manager Administration Kit Wizard has completed and the location and name of your self-extracting file.

You have now successfully used the Connection Manager to create a custom installation file for installing and configuring a remote access session.

Allowing Users to Use the Connection Manager

When users run the self-extracting service profile, they'll be asked whether the connection should be available for all users (a computerwide setting) or for only that user. They'll also be asked whether to add a shortcut for it on the Desktop.

When the program has installed, users will see a dialog box that displays the name of the service profile on the caption bar and the support information supplied when the service profile was created. Before they can connect, they'll need to go into Properties, where they'll see various tabbed options, depending on the options you chose with the CMAK.

The first time Connection Manager is loaded, users will need to load the phone book; you can't supply the phone book as a default. To make sure users load the phone book, select the top **Phone Book** button and select the access number. You'll notice on this dialog box that users could choose alternative service types (if you allowed them) and alternative countries or regions and access numbers.

The Internet Logon tab allows users to specify their company logon and password, which no doubt will be different from their ISP logon. The Options tab sets the number of redial attempts (defaults to 3) and the idle disconnection time (10 minutes), which can be between never and 24 hours. Once you configure any options that need to be set, they will remain set the next time Connection Manager is loaded. The user can then simply click **Connect**.

Troubleshooting Remote Access Problems

You've got your Windows 2000 RRAS server installed, configured, and supporting all your remote users as a RAS server and as a VPN server. The clients are installed, the phone books are configured, and all is right with the world—until something breaks. And unlike the LAN, when something breaks in a remote access environment, the number of possible problems multiplies exponentially. Is it a client configuration issue, a server problem, a problem with an ISP, or one of a dozen other common remote access problems? To make matters worse, because your users are now scattered around the country or even the world, troubleshooting their situation can be a real problem. You can't simply walk to a user's desk to see what's going on. You have to work with users remotely to determine the issue and resolution. For that reason, we spend the rest of the chapter looking at some of the common issues you could encounter while working with a Windows 2000 RRAS implementation. But before we get to the specifics, let's discuss troubleshooting as a general concept.

When many people start working in the IT industry, they generally use one of two troubleshooting methods when faced with their first major issue. They either panic, or they simply start trying solutions until the problem goes away. Neither of these courses of action is a recommended strategy for addressing issues. Whenever you run into an issue, you need to use a *structured approach* to troubleshooting. There are several benefits to this approach. First, if you have a plan, you generally won't panic. You'll know what to do. Second, a consistent approach allows you to correct issues more efficiently than merely trying things until the issue is corrected, which could waste a lot of time on blind alleys. Finally, if you use a consistent approach and document your results, you will be able correct an issue that recurs with a known solution. In fact, if your documentation is good, someone else will be able to apply your solution if a problem crops up again. This is very useful if you are on vacation; it's no fun getting paged on the beach in Maui because someone on your team doesn't know how you fixed the problem the last time.

To that end, one generic troubleshooting methodology is the following:

1. **Identify the symptoms** You can't fix a problem until you are sure what the problem is. Far too often, you will hear your coworkers make comments such as "The Internet is down" or "Mail is down." What exactly does that mean? "Internet down" might mean that people can get to Web sites but not FTP, or people can get to some Web sites but not others. Until you have specific symptoms, you cannot correct any issue.

2. **Determine the problem scope** How big is this problem? Is it one user, 100 users, or the entire company? Is it the secretary's cube, the entire floor, or the entire building? Not only will this information help you get a handle on the urgency of the issue, it also gives you valuable clues as to what the problem might be. If the north side of the floor is down, for example, you might look at the network infrastructure that supports that side of the building. In many cases, "The Internet is down" really means that your boss can't get to www.espn.com to see how his team did in the big game last night. That's still important, but you can probably finish your coffee before you run to his office.

3. **Look for changes** A remarkably high number of issues in a complex computing environment are related to changes. If it's a single user, did he or she install a "cool new game" that they received in an e-mail from a buddy? If you just lost access to the Internet, did anyone upgrade router code or install a new rule base on a firewall? Volumes have been written about how to control change in a network environment, but at a minimum you should have a shared calendar on your mail server where groups can post changes. The toughest part about troubleshooting a change-related issue is identifying what changed.

4. **Try the most likely solution** Fix it already! Once you have completed your information gathering, try the solution you think is the most likely to work.

5. **Is it fixed?** You've tried to fix it; did it work? If not, repeat Step 4 with the next most likely fix. Repeat this process until the problem is solved.

6. **Did you break anything else?** This is a critical step; changes to the environment, even if you are trying to fix something, can have unpredictable side effects. Look for them. The last thing you want to find out as you are headed home for the day is that the fix you put in for the sales department at lunch broke accounting's network. You could be in for a long night.

7. **Write it down** This is probably the most important part of the equation: Document your solution. In six months when you see the same problem, you don't want to rely on memory to come up with the solution. Make sure you have something in writing to refer to.

This is a very generic troubleshooting methodology that is only intended as a guideline. The real point is to make sure you have a formal, repeatable process that you can follow to resolve any problem you encounter. Use this list or come up with your own from scratch, as long as you have a process.

Now let's look at some common remote access problems you might run into.

Problems with a VPN Due to the Internet Service Provider

ISPs such as America Online (AOL), Microsoft Network (MSN), Earthlink, and the hundreds of other international, national, and local ISPs can present some special challenges to anyone supporting VPN users. Fortunately, identifying issues is a fairly simple process: You just need to start from the client and work your way out.

In the old days, everyone connected to their ISPs through a dial-up modem, so many of the issues were related to modem connections. Although modem connections still make up a significant number of Internet connections, we now also have high-speed broadband such as xDSL and cable modem to contend with. Here we do not cover troubleshooting the ISP connections themselves but rather specific VPN-related ISP issues.

If you are unable to establish a VPN connection across your ISP connection, ask yourself the following questions:

1. **Do you have a connection to the Internet?** You can check this by attempting to access a Web site. If you can access a generic Internet Web site such as www.microsoft.com, try accessing a Web site from your corporate Internet connection, if it's available. This will allow you to not only test Internet connectivity but also connectivity from the remote network to the corporate network. If you are unable to access the Internet, you need to check with your ISP's technical support people. If you can access the Internet but

not your corporate network, check with your own technical support staff and verify that there are no connectivity issues at the other end of the connection.

2. **If you have Internet access, have you successfully connected before?** If you have connected, think about what could have changed on your connection. Have you upgraded your modem, installed a firewall, or made any changes that could prevent a VPN connection from being established? If there have been no changes on your end or if this is the first time you have tried to connect, check with your ISP to ensure that its network supports the VPN protocol you are attempting to use. We discuss NAT issues later in this section, but that is a potential problem.

3. **Anything else?** Other ISP-related issues can be firewall configurations, the use of transparent proxy servers, or, in some isolated networks, the lack of router support for either PPTP or L2TP/IPSec. This last issue is very rare these days, but it was common when these protocols were introduced.

These are the main areas you need to be concerned with when you're dealing with ISP-related issues. When in doubt, try to simplify the local network as much as possible, to immediately eliminate that as a source of trouble. If you have an extensive home network, with wireless and a firewall, try connecting your computer directly to the ISP network connection, and verify that you don't have local configuration issues before you involve technical support in resolving your issues.

Client Computer Operating System Issues

Once you have ruled out the ISP as a source of trouble, you need to check the configuration of the client computer. Again, following our methodology, once you have established that this is an issue with just your system, look to see what changed. Some common places to check for potential changes that could impact your connection are these:

- Verify that your user account and password are correct. Sometimes a client connection issue can be a stuck Caps Lock key.

- Installation of new applications such as a personal firewall or a security update can potentially impact the stability of your client environment. If you have made such a change, try removing the new software or update, and see if it corrects your issue.

- When in doubt, delete your VPN connection and reinstall it.

If none of these steps corrects your issue, you should engage your technical support team to verify that your client configuration matches the configuration of the VPN server at the other end.

Network Address Translation Devices

Before we discuss the issues associated with NAT, we need to talk about what exactly NAT is. As you are undoubtedly aware, the Internet relies on the TCP/IP protocol for communications. In order for two systems to communicate using TCP/IP, each system must have a unique IP address; without a unique address, the network cannot deliver the packet to your system. This concept is fairly straightforward until we discuss the size of the Internet.

In the early days of the Internet, when IP addressing was being developed, the 32-bit addressing scheme (known as IPv4) was considered more than adequate for any potential network growth. Theoretically, 4,294,967,296 unique addresses were available using 32-bit addresses; even discounting the reserved ranges, there were still over 3 billion possible addresses. At the time, that was enough addresses to provide an address for every person on the planet, including children.

Unfortunately, the designers of the addressing scheme dramatically underestimated the explosive growth of the Internet as well as the popularity of TCP/IP in business and home networks. There are no longer enough addresses to go around. As a result, a new addressing scheme is under development. IPv6 is an addressing scheme that allows for a dramatically larger pool of addresses but is enjoying very limited deployment on the Internet today. This is in large part due to the use of NAT. (For more information on NAT, see RFC 3022, *Traditional IP Network Address Translator (Traditional NAT)*, January 2001.)

NAT is an Internet standard that allows you to use one set of IP addresses on your internal LAN and a second set of IP addresses for the Internet connection. A device (usually a router or firewall) between the two connections provides NAT services, managing the translation of internal addresses to external addresses. This allows companies to use large numbers of unregistered internal addresses while only needing a fraction of that number of addresses on the Internet, thus conserving the addresses.

There are two main types of NAT:

- **Static NAT** This version of NAT maps an unregistered IP address on the private network to a registered IP address on the public network on a one-to-one basis. This type is typically used when the translated device needs to be accessible from the public network. For example, a Web server on your private network might have an unregistered address of 10.10.10.10 but a NAT address of 12.2.2.123. A user trying to connect to that Web site can enter 12.2.2.123, and the router or firewall at the other end will translate that address to 10.10.10.10 when the packet reaches it.

- **Dynamic NAT** This version of NAT maps an unregistered IP address to a registered IP address from a group of registered IP addresses. This version is more commonly used when large pools of systems on the internal network need to access the Internet and don't have a requirement for a static address. The workstation's address is translated to the next available registered address as soon as it initiates a connection to the public network.

This high-level overview of NAT is useful, but the critical thing to remember about NAT is that due to limitations in the first version of the IPSec standard, IPSec cannot traverse a translated network. IPSec requires that both the VPN client and the VPN server have static, untranslated addresses on the public network in order to connect. What this means from a practical perspective is that if you are trying to connect and NAT is anywhere in the network architecture, you cannot use an L2TP/IPSec VPN. (*Note:* This situation is expected to change with the release of .NET Server 2003, but the released version of the Microsoft L2TP/IPSec client/server VPN will not work.) The PPTP protocol does not suffer from this limitation. So, if you are using NAT, plan to use PPTP for the near future, until the IPSec standard matures.

Damage & Defense...

NAT and the End User's Home Network

It is very easy to say "IPSec doesn't support NAT; use PPTP instead," but how does this impact you in the real world? In most environments, NAT-related issues arise from end users' home network connections. As a general rule, companies that provide ISP access for their employees still provide dial-up Internet access. Not only is it cost-effective compared with high-speed access, it can be used not only from home offices but also while traveling. This makes it a great solution for mobile users, and because almost all major ISPs provide Internet-routable (not translated) addresses for their dial-up users, NAT-related issues are almost nonexistent.

Not so with high-speed home networks. Most broadband providers rely on NAT to ensure that they have enough IP addresses to support all their users. To make matters worse, even if you do find a provider that is using Internet-routable addresses, now you run into the users who want to hook up their kid's PC while connecting their own home PC and company laptop to the Internet over the same connection. They run out to buy a low-cost router and start doing their own NAT.

The net result of these complications is that unless you are able to mandate the use of a dial ISP with Internet-routable addresses, you need to rely on PPTP for all your VPN connections. L2TP/IPSec will not work for the majority of your high-speed users.

Routing and Remote Access Server Issues

We've looked at ISP issues, NAT issues, and client issues. Let's take a look at some of the possible problems with the server. When you have a server issue, it will generally affect a specific population of users. These issues break down into three main types:

- **Single-user issues** Some common server-related issues that can cause a server to not allow a single user to connect include:
    - Not having enough PPTP or L2TP ports enabled. You can enable more ports if needed or check to verify that the ports are not locked up or otherwise not available.
    - Not having the correct combination of user permissions and remote access policies enabled to permit the user to connect. You need to correctly configure the user's permissions to correct this issue.
    - The user's account is completely disabled. To fix this issue, you should enable the user's account.
    - User's client and server are not configured to utilize the same authentication or VPN protocol. To correct this issue, you generally need to reconfigure the client's authentication. You should never reconfigure the server to address a single-user issue, unless you are sure the change won't have any side effects that might impact other users.
    - If the user credentials (user ID, password, and domain) are correct, you might have a DHCP issue. Check to make sure that you haven't run out of addresses. If you have, you need to allocate additional addresses.

- **Group-related issues** Although these issues are similar to the issues seen with a single user, having a group of users (not *all* users, which we discuss in the next section) can make troubleshooting the issue a little easier. Some common things you can do to help narrow down the source of the problem include:
    - Check for common factors. If the users are all in the same Active Directory container or group, a permissions or remote access policy conflict could be preventing the users from connecting.
    - If the users are all configured to use PPTP and they don't work, but the L2TP/IPSec does (or vice-versa), check the appropriate group of ports and any associated authentication or encryption setting used by those ports. In the event of the issue being with L2TP/IPSec only, you might have an issue with the machine certificate used by that system.

- **Serverwide issues** On a particularly bad day you will run into an issue in which the entire system is unavailable for remote users. If this is the issue, check the following:
    - Is the Routing and Remote Access service started on the VPN server? If it's not, try to start it.
    - Are your PPTP and/or L2TP/IPSec ports enabled for inbound requests? If they're not, enable them.
    - Are the correct authentication protocols still enabled?
    - Is the user domain available? You might have an issue with your Active Directory or Windows NT domain. If you have configured RADIUS authentication, your issue could also lie with the RADIUS server connection.
    - You could have a routing issue. The routing table on the server could be corrupted or you could not have the correct routes on your network for the DHCP addresses configured on your server. If this is the case, users will connect but will be unable to access any resources. You can correct this situation by updating the routes on your network or by changing the DHCP addresses to addresses that are already routable on the network. Avoid having your remote access server participate in any dynamic routing; the security issues associated with that kind of dynamic network access are numerous.
    - Another issue that could prevent users either from connecting or from reaching a remote network are the IP filters. If your IP filters are configured improperly, they can be dropping tunnel traffic. An easy test for this issue is to document your filters and then delete them, to see if the issue is resolved.

These are just a sample of the issues you can run into while working in a remote access/VPN environment. Due to the dispersed nature of the user population, diverse (in most environments) system operating systems and configurations, and the intricacies of the Internet's addressing and routing architecture, troubleshooting issues with this infrastructure represent a major test of your troubleshooting skills.

Firewall Issues

Finally, you will also encounter firewall issues when you work with VPNs. These issues break down into two main categories: VPN server-side issues and VPN client-side issues.

Server-side issues are typically the more difficult to work on, since you cannot disable the firewall to see if the issue goes away. So, on the server side you have to deal with any firewall issues between your production network and the VPN client, without the luxury of trying to connect without the firewall to rule out other issues. Some companies put their VPN servers directly on the Internet, but doing so can be a security problem, and you are almost always better off placing them behind a firewall. This situation raises two issues. First, is the firewall also doing any NAT? If it is, you will only be able to use PPTP for VPN connections, or you will have to rearchitect the connection to the Internet. Next, are the correct ports open to allow the clients to connect to the firewall? PPTP uses the GRE protocol or protocol 47 to make the connection, whereas L2TP/IPSec needs protocol 50 (for ESP), 51 (for AH), plus UDP port 500 for the Internet Key Exchange (IKE).

On the client side, you have essentially the same potential issues, but you should always remove the firewall from the equation when you're troubleshooting. Connecting the client directly to the Internet and trying to connect quickly confirms or rules out a client-side firewall issue.

Once you have confirmed it is a firewall issue (by being able to connect from the direct connection), you need to reexamine your network for the use of NAT on the firewall and verify that the appropriate ports are opened.

Summary of Exam Objectives

Now that we have completed the chapter, let's review the exam objectives. Windows 2000 supports several authentication protocols, including the Password Authentication Protocol (PAP), the Challenge Handshake Authentication Protocol (CHAP), the Microsoft Challenge Handshake Authentication Protocol (MS-CHAP) and MS-CHAP version 2, and finally, the Extensible Authentication Protocol (EAP). These protocols are used in conjunction with the Windows 2000 Routing and Remote Access Service (RRAS) to provide authentication for both remote dial-in and remote VPN users. A server running the Windows 2000 RRAS can act as a dial-in server, allowing users to connect directly with a modem using the PPP protocol or as a VPN server, supporting VPN access using the PPTP or L2TP/IPSec protocols.

All configuration for remote access using Windows 2000 is done via the Routing and Remote Access Service console, a Microsoft Management Console snap-in. Be sure you are familiar with this tool, since you will need it to configure and manage both your dial-in and VPN ports, server configuration, and server policies.

PPTP and L2TP/IPSec are both supported for VPN connections. PPTP can be used to tunnel any Windows 2000 supported protocol and can traverse a network using Network Address Translation (NAT). This is also considered a proprietary Microsoft protocol, and widespread adoption of the standard has not occurred. The L2TP/IPSec protocol is based on Cisco Systems L2F and the standards-based IPSec protocol.

Once there framework is installed, you need to set up your access policies. Remote access policies are a set of conditions and connection settings that determine connection permissions. With a remote access policy, you can configure Grant or Deny permissions based on the time of day or day of the week, by Windows 2000 group, by protocol or VPN protocol, by connection type, and a number of other factors. You can also use the remote access profile portion of the policy to set idle timeouts, maximum session times, authentication protocols, encryption strengths, and several other connection parameters.

One part of the remote access policy that you need to be familiar with is the remote access profile. A remote access profile lets you configure dial-in constraints, IP characteristics, multilink parameters, authentication protocols, encryption protocols, and advanced configurations settings.

There are three ways to administer permissions in a Windows 2000 RRAS environment. They are:

- **Access by user** In this model, remote access permissions are determined by the remote access permission on the Dial-in tab of the user account, much as they were in the pre-Windows 2000 RAS environment. Remote access permissions are set on a per-user basis by setting the remote access permission to either Allow access or Deny access.

www.syngress.com

- **Access by policy in a Windows 2000 native-mode domain** In this model, the remote access permission on every user account is set to control access through Remote Access Policy.

- **Access by policy in a Windows 2000 mixed-mode domain** In this model, every user account's remote access permission is set to Allow access, the default remote access policy is deleted, and separate remote access policies are created for each type of connections that is allowed.

When configuring a secure client for a VPN connection, remember that this capability is built into Windows 2000 and Windows XP, but for other Windows operating systems, you need to download the Microsoft L2TP/IPSec VPN Client.

The Connection Manager Administration Kit (CMAK) is used to configure a service profile, the set of files required to configure remote user's connection details bundled into a self-installing executable file that you distribute to users who need remote access. This service profile works on any 32-bit Windows platform and requires, in all, about 1MB free hard disk space. Users must have the Connection Manager v1.2 software installed in order to use your configuration options, which can be included in the service profile. If users already have this software installed, the hard disk space required is greatly reduced (requires about 200KB).

Finally, you need to recall how to troubleshoot these connections. Keep in mind the generic troubleshooting methodology we covered in the chapter:

1. Identify the symptoms.
2. Determine the problem scope; how big is this problem?
3. Look for changes.
4. Try the most likely solution; fix it already!
5. Is it fixed?
6. Did you break anything else?
7. Write it down.

Next, you need to consider the different areas in which you might encounter issues with your connection. If you are unable to establish a VPN connection across your ISP connection, check the following:

1. Do you have a connection to the Internet?
2. If you have Internet access, have you successfully connected before? If you have, think about what might have changed on your connection.

3. Other ISP-related issues can be firewall configurations, the use of transparent proxy servers, or, in some isolated networks, the lack of router support for either PPTP or L2TP/IPSec. This last issue is very rare these days, but was common when these protocols were introduced.

On client systems, you need to look for changes to the operating system—have you installed a new application, patch, or update? Have you verified that your user account and password are correct? When in doubt, delete your VPN connection and reinstall it.

Network Address Translation, or NAT, allows a single device, usually a router or firewall, to act as an intermediary between a public network and a private. This intermediary converts the private addresses, which can be duplicated in other locations on other private networks, to unique public addresses, allowing the private network to communicate across the public network, without any address conflicts. NAT can cause major problems with L2TP/IPSec, due to the limitations of the IPSec protocol. IPSec can't function as written in a NAT environment.

Then we have the Windows 2000 RRAS server issues. These can vary from the service being disabled to not having enough ports or having bad IP filters on an interface. The key to addressing server issues is identifying the scope of the problem. If there is one user with a problem, you should start with that user's machine and work your way back to the network. If a group of users is having trouble, look for common factors. Are they all in the same OU or AD group? Do they all connect using one protocol or the other? Are they all authenticating using the same protocol? Once you have identified the common factors, locating the solution becomes much easier. On the opposite end of the single-user issue is the situation in which the entire server is unavailable. Now you are looking to make sure the server is still connected to the network, that the RRAS service is running, whether you have run out of ports or addresses, or any of the other software, hardware, or configuration issues that could shut down your server.

Finally, we have the firewall issues. Occurring at either end of the connection these days, the key to firewalls is to make sure the ports you need for VPN connectivity are open. Although the process for opening these ports varies from firewall to firewall, the issues are almost always port-related. The one exception to that rule is when the firewall is providing NAT services. L2TP/IPSec won't work in a NAT environment, although Microsoft is hoping to address that shortcoming in the Windows .NET Server 2003 release.

Exam Objectives Fast Track

Remote Access Authentication Methods

- ☑ Windows 2000 RRAS supports the following protocols:
  - **PAP** Password Authentication Protocol
  - **CHAP** Challenge Handshake Authentication Protocol
  - **MS-CHAP** Microsoft Challenge Handshake Authentication Protocol
  - **MS-CHAP v2** Microsoft Challenge Handshake Authentication Protocol Version 2
  - **EAP** Extensible Authentication Protocol

- ☑ The Extensible Authentication Protocol comes in two main types:
  - EAP-MD5 CHAP
  - EAP-TLS

- ☑ EAP also is used to support Smart Cards or X.509 certificate-based authentication.

Configuring a Remote Access Server

- ☑ Windows 2000 RRAS is installed as part of the Windows 2000 Server operating system. You do not need to install it.

- ☑ Configuring a RAS server can be done using the wizard. This process configures five PPTP and five L2TP ports as part of the installation process.

- ☑ Ports can be modified and monitored once the installation is complete using the Routing and Remote Access Service console.

Configuring a Virtual Private Networking Server

- ☑ Configuring a VPN server can be done using the Routing and Remote Access wizard. This process configures 128 PPTP and 128 L2TP ports as part of the installation process.

- ☑ L2TP is a standards-based VPN protocol, but it cannot traverse a NAT environment. It uses one of the IPSec protocols, Encapsulating Security Payload (ESP), for encryption and is commonly referred to as L2TP/IPSec.

- ☑ PPTP is a Microsoft proprietary protocol that supports NAT environments, but it is not widely implemented now that IPSec is available as a standard.

- ☑ Windows 2000 Server RRAS also support IPSec in tunneling mode to provide support for non-Windows operating systems. This setup is not used very frequently, but it is available.

Introduction to Remote Access Policies

- ☑ Remote access policies are sets of conditions and connection settings that determine connection permissions.

- ☑ Remote access policies are stored locally on each Windows 2000 RRAS server. If you want to use centralized policies, you need to utilize RADIUS for policy authentication.

- ☑ Some of the conditions that can be used in a remote access policy include:
  - Time of day or day of the week
  - Windows 2000 group
  - Authentication protocol
  - VPN protocol
  - Connection type

Configuring Clients for Secure Remote Access

- ☑ Windows 2000 and Windows XP ship with the VPN client. All other Microsoft operating systems must download a client.

- ☑ L2TP/IPSec is the default protocol the client will try to use. In a NAT environment, L2TP/IPSec will not work; in that circumstance, you need to use PPTP.

- ☑ Under Windows 2000 and Windows XP, the VPN connection appears as an additional entry in Network and Dial-Up Connections.

Troubleshooting Remote Access Problems

- ☑ For ISP-related problems, make sure that you can connect to the Internet and, if possible, to a server on the same segment as your VPN server, to ensure that you have end-to-end connectivity. Then look for NAT or firewall issues on the ISP's network.

- ☑ For client computer operating system issues, verify user information, check for changes such as patches, updates, or new applications, and don't be afraid to reinstall the VPN client.

- ☑ For NAT devices, NAT (RFC 3022) allows you to use one set of IP addresses on your internal LAN and a second set of IP addresses for the Internet connection. This is a great IP address conservation strategy, but L2TP/IPSec cannot traverse a NAT environment.

- ☑ For Routing and Remote Access Server issues, identify the population of users who have issues:
    - **Single user** Usually related to the user's account or profile.
    - **Group of users** Identify the commonality between the users and start looking there for the source of the issues.
    - **All users** Start checking to make sure all services are running, connectivity is available, and that there have been no global changes to the environment.

Exam Objectives Frequently Asked Questions

The following Frequently Asked Questions, answered by the authors of this book, are designed to both measure your understanding of the Exam Objectives presented in this chapter, and to assist you with real-life implementation of these concepts.

Q: I have done the exercises with the Connection Manager Administration Kit, and although I understand the tool, when would I use it?

A: There are three common uses for the CMAK. First, if you are an ISP and you want to distribute the phone numbers for your POP to your users and automatically update the phone books as numbers change, you could use the CMAK. Second, if you use an ISP for a large number of users and want to develop a custom dialer for that service, you would use the CMAK. You would use the ISP's phone book information and could customize the client with your help desk number, company logo, and so on. Finally, if you have a large RAS environment, you could use the CMAK tool to create a dialer and distribute it to your users so they wouldn't have to manually configure their dial-up connections.

www.syngress.com

Q: I just set up my first Windows 2000 VPN server, but as soon as I finished running the wizard, I lost access to the Internet.

A: This common issue is caused by the default filters applied to the Internet side of the VPN. They are there to protect your system from unwanted users. Review the filters and see which ones you need and which can be deleted. That should address the issue for you.

Q: My manager just asked me to roll out smartcards to our field sales staff so that they can connect to the VPN securely, but I don't even know where to start to figure this out.

A: First, you need to start by enabling the EAP-TLS protocol. Next, you need to do some research. Start at the Microsoft Web site by searching on *smartcards and EAP*, and then go to your smartcard vendor and get as much information on integration with Windows 2000 RRAS as you can. It's easy to buy smartcards, but implementing them will take a lot of hard work.

Q: I have my Windows 2000 server configured as an RAS server, but now I want to add VPN users. How do I do this without rerunning the Routing and Remote Access wizard?

A: Actually, you have five PPTP and five L2TP ports configured already. If you will have more concurrent users, you will need to add ports, which is pretty simple—just up the number of maximum connections in the Port Properties. Then you need to create your VPN remote access policy, and you're ready for connections.

Q: I read the section of this chapter on remote access policy administrative models, but I don't know which one I should use in my environment. Which is the best model to use?

A: There is no "best" model for administration of remote access, because it varies from implementation to implementation. Much of the decision will be driven by the domain model you are using (mixed-mode or native-mode), but the rest is dependent on your environment. Generally, for larger implementations in a native-mode domain, the access by policy model is the best. The extra complexity of managing the profiles is offset by the large number of users that need to be configured individually.

Q: I have my VPN working, but now I need to know how to encrypt the traffic between the VPN server and our internal servers. How can I do this?

A: You need to configure the LAN connection for the internal network to use IP Security by default. This option is located in the Advanced Options of the TCP/IP Properties, under IP Security. Select either Secure Server (Require Security) to make all traffic secure, or Select Server (Request Security) if you want only specific servers to utilize the security. This security would use the Kerberos trust.

Self Test

A Quick Answer Key follows the Self Test questions. For complete questions, answers, and epxlanations to the Self Test questions in this chapter as well as the other chapters in this book, see the Self Test Appendix.

Remote Access Authentication Methods

1. Mary is configuring her first Windows 2000 RRAS server and wants to use strong authentication protocols to keep her network secure. Which protocol(s) should she use?

    A. L2TP/IPSec

    B. PAP

    C. EAP

    D. CHAP

    E. MS-CHAPv2

2. Jim is the security administrator for his company's legal department. The network and remote access solutions are based on Windows 2000 Server, and Legal just purchased smartcards for the entire department so that they can use secure dial-in access. Jim knows he needs to configure EAP-TLS, but he isn't sure where to configure it. He also only wants to change this setting for the legal department, not for all users. Where is this protocol configured?

    A. In the Dial-in profile for the Legal remote access policy.

    B. In the Modem Pool Properties dialog box, under the Legal profile.

    C. Under the Security tab of the Routing and Remote Access server properties.

    D. In the legal department's remote access policy, on the Authentication tab.

3. Jim's manager has asked him to configure the company Windows 2000 VPN server to allow for the use of smartcards for remote access authentication. What protocol does Jim need to use for this?

   A. PPTP

   B. EAP-TLS

   C. L2TP

   D. MS-CHAP v2

   E. PPP

Configuring a Remote Access Server

4. Mary maintains the remote access infrastructure for her company. Previously, Mary maintained a single Windows 2000 RAS server, but over the weekend she added another Windows 2000 RAS server for higher capacity. The two servers are in the same native-mode Active Directory domain, but during testing Mary cannot dial into the new server using her Windows 2000 credentials. What is the most likely problem?

   A. The Windows 2000 RRAS service is not installed on the new server.

   B. The Windows 2000 RRAS service needs to be enabled in the Active Directory.

   C. The Remote Access Profiles are not shared, and need to be recreated on the new server.

   D. Installing more than one Windows 2000 RRAS server into the same Active Directory domain is not permitted.

Configuring a Virtual Private Networking Server

5. Andrea is responsible for her company's Windows 2000 RRAS server, which has been running as an RAS server for several months. She just manually added services to the server so that the 120 sales representatives could connect to the network using VPN instead of modems. All the sales reps are using PPTP. The first five VPN users connect without issue, but then the server denies access to additional VPN users. RAS users seem to be unaffected by the issue. What is the most likely problem?

A. The server doesn't have enough VPN client licenses for more than five concurrent users.

B. The DHCP server is only providing five IP addresses.

C. When you configure the Routing and Remote Access Service for dial-in, it only creates five PPTP ports.

D. Windows 2000 will only support five VPN connections at a time.

6. June is trying to get a job as a network administrator, and she is being quizzed by the department manager on her knowledge of protocols. Her manager is particularly interested in her background in IPSec, so he has asked her to list the protocols used by IPSec. Which of the following are protocols used by IPSec?

A. ESP

B. AH

C. PPTP

D. L2F

E. ISAKMP

Introduction to Remote Access Policies

7. Tom is the administrator of a Windows 2000 RAS server that's being used for dial-in connections to the corporate network. He needs to be sure that no one is connecting to the server from 1:00 A.M. until 2:00 A.M. while the server is being backed up. Tom is using one policy to permit access for all users. What is the easiest way to add this restriction for all users?

A. Create a new Remote Access policy containing the restriction, and make sure it is processed before the default policy.

B. Add a deny access condition to the existing remote access profile.

C. Add a deny access condition to the existing remote access policy.

D. Create a new Remote Access profile containing the restriction, and make sure it is processed before the default policy.

8. Stacey is the system administrator of a Windows 2000 Routing and Remote Access server that permits the use of the Multilink protocol to allow users to connect with multiple dial-up lines. To configure this setup to work as efficiently as possible, Stacey needs to automatically drop a line from the Multilink connection

when it's not being used. What protocol would need to be enabled to accomplish this task?

A. EAP-TLS

B. PAP

C. PPP

D. Multilink

E. BAP

Configuring Clients for Secure Remote Access

9. Tammy is responsible for setting up a new VPN server using Windows 2000 and the Routing and Remote Access Service. She wants to limit access to the VPN by creating a Remote Access Users group in the Active Directory running in native mode, so she creates the group, puts users in it, and creates a Remote Access Policy called VPN User Access. To be sure this is the only way to access the server, she deletes the default remote access policy. Under the Dial-In tab of each user, she sets the Remote Access Permissions to "Control access through Remote Access Policy." What is the last thing Tammy needs to do to limit access to this policy to users in the VPN User Access group?

    A. Edit the VPN User Access policy and add the condition Windows-Groups, selecting the Remote Access Users group as the group for the condition.

    B. Edit the IPSec ports to allow access by the Remote Access Users group.

    C. Edit the VPN User Access policy and limit the protocol to PPTP, and then grant user access to the Remote Access Users group.

    D. Edit the VPN User Access policy and set the permissions on the policy so that the Remote Access Users group has read access. Then delete the Everyone group from the permissions.

10. Jim is the remote access administrator for a medium-sized manufacturing company. He is in the process of rolling out a new Windows 2000 RRAS server, but he knows that the local telephone area code will be changing in six months. He would like to be able to automatically update the users' phone books with the new numbers, so he uses the Connection Manager Administration Kit to create a service profile for the end users. He is putting the new phone book on a server on the internal network. What protocol will be used by the users to get the new phone book?

A. HTTP

B. HTTPS

C. Telnet

D. FTP

11. June is a network administrator supporting 500 mobile users who dial into the company network using several Windows 2000 RAS servers located throughout the country. She is planning to add between 5 and 10 new RAS servers in other offices in the company, so she has created a dynamic phone book using the Phone Book Administrator utility. Now she wants to publish the phone book so she can create a service profile for her users. What is the easiest way for her to create this phone book?

    A. Save the phone book to her local drive and FTP the resulting files to an FTP server running IIS 4.0 or later.

    B. Save the phone book to her local drive and copy the resulting files to a Web server running IIS 4.0 or later.

    C. From the Publish Phone Book screen, select a directory on an FTP server running IIS 4.0 or later, and select Post.

    D. From the Publish Phone Book screen, select a directory on an FTP server running IIS 4.0 or later, and select Publish.

Troubleshooting Remote Access Problems

12. Joan is a help desk specialist for a small manufacturing company that uses a Windows 2000 server for VPN services. Melissa, a sales engineer, is on a sales call and needs to access the company intranet to get some pricing information. Melissa is using a PPTP connection to access the company VPN, and it worked fine from the hotel last night from a dial-up ISP service. She is trying to connect from the customer network, but she's unable to establish a connection, so she has placed a call to Joan to see what's wrong. Which of the following is a possible reason for this problem?

    A. The local network is using NAT.

    B. The company's firewall does not permit the GRE protocol.

    C. The company's firewall does not permit the ESP protocol.

    D. The company's firewall does not use a proxy server.

13. Ted is a help desk specialist for a small printer manufacturing company that uses a Windows 2000 server for VPN services. Jack, a sales engineer, is on a service call and needs to order parts on the company intranet. Jack is using an L2TP/IPSec connection to access the company VPN, and it works fine from Jack's home office, which connects to the Internet through a broadband connection. Unfortunately, Jack cannot connect from the customer's Ethernet network, and he has placed a help desk call for assistance. Which of the following is a possible reason for this problem?

    A. The local network is using NAT.

    B. The company's firewall does not permit the GRE protocol.

    C. The company's firewall does not permit the PPP protocol.

    D. The company's firewall does not support certificates.

14. Tony is the administrator for his company's Windows 2000 RAS server, which uses the corporate Active Directory service for authentication. Joan, an end user in accounting, is trying to connect to the RAS server but keeps getting the message that she is not an authorized user. She can log into the Active Directory without issue when she is connected to the LAN. What might be causing the problem?

    A. The server needs additional PPTP ports configured.

    B. Joan is not using the correct password.

    C. Joan is trying to use her LAN network account instead of her dial-in account.

    D. The user is not using an ID that is authorized to use the dial-in server.

15. Mary is a help desk technician supporting remote users connecting to the company's Windows 2000 RRAS server. She just got a call from Tony, who is using his company laptop and accessing the RRAS server through a PPTP VPN connection. Last week the connection worked fine, but today it is not connecting. When Mary asks if anything has changed, Tony reluctantly admits that his neighbor just installed a freeware encryption application on the system. What is the first step Mary should recommend to address this issue?

    A. Reinstall the VPN client to replace any files that might have been overwritten, and reboot the system.

    B. Reinstall the client operating system to ensure that the system is installed and configured cleanly.

    C. Update the system virus protection and scan the system for viruses.

    D. Remove the new application and reboot the system.

Self Test Quick Answer Key

For complete questions, answers, and epxlanations to the Self Test questions in this chapter as well as the other chapters in this book, see the Self Test Appendix.

1. **C, E**
2. **A**
3. **B**
4. **C**
5. **C**
6. **A, B, E**
7. **C**
8. **E**
9. **A**
10. **D**
11. **C**
12. **B**
13. **A**
14. **D**
15. **D**

MCSE/MCSA 70-214 Part VI

Monitoring and Responding to Security Incidents

Chapter 10

MCSE/MCSA 70-214

Configuring and Using Auditing and the Event Logs

Exam Objectives in this Chapter:

6.1 Configure and manage auditing. Considerations include Windows Events, Internet Information Services (IIS), firewall log files, Network Monitor Log, and RAS log files.

6.1.1 Manage audit log retention.

6.1.2 Manage distributed audit logs by using EventComb.

6.2 Analyze security events. Considerations include reviewing logs and events.

- ☑ Summary of Exam Objectives
- ☑ Exam Objectives Fast Track
- ☑ Exam Objectives Frequently Asked Questions
- ☑ Self Test
- ☑ Self Test Quick Answer Key

Introduction

For the new Microsoft Security exam, you will be heavily tested on auditing techniques and the tools you have available for auditing a system. Once you pass the exam, you can refer back to this guide to help you find specific auditable events and review how to use the tools and procedures listed within to extract and analyze the data.

Auditing is something every security professional should take very seriously. It is very difficult to find a "needle in a haystack," and that's the mentality you should bring to the table when learning to perform system audits. Security auditing is tested very heavily on the Microsoft Security exam, so not only do you need to know how to do audits in the field, you need to master the testable auditing-based objectives for the exam.

Attack and exploitation of your systems are inevitable. Unfortunately, you cannot close every entrance to your network—if you could, you would not be able to send e-mail, browse the Web, or share files with a remote location. Because of the dynamic nature of networking, you can't close every opening, so you need to protect the openings that you do make. If your systems are attacked, you need to know who, when, how, and where. Other factors such as why can be deduced later. More important is nailing the cracker to stop the attack that is occurring or could possibly occur. You might discover that the attacker is merely checking for possible holes in your network before actually making an attack and causing a problem. This is the *proactive approach* to systems auditing.

Understanding the auditing process and intrusion detection in general will help you determine who is (or was) responsible for an attack and when the attack was carried out. You can use the techniques outlined in this chapter to help find patterns of attack, the time you were attacked, how the attack (such as a logon attempt) was carried out, and how to log that attack and analyze it. We also look at how to analyze the Event Viewer (to which the events are logged) as well as to look at Internet Information Services (IIS) auditing and some other tools that do not come with Windows 2000 (but that can easily be obtained) for Event Log filtering and analysis.

Exam Warning

Auditing takes up quite a few questions on the exam. Make sure that you work through all the exercises in this chapter because you need to understand the concepts found within them.

Auditing for Increased Security

You will need to audit your systems for enhanced and increased security. When the people at Microsoft presented this objective, they were most likely thinking about building your security strategy with defense in depth. This strategy is outlined as a way to avoid depending on a single protective measure deployed on your network. You are not secure by simply implementing a firewall on your Internet connection. You should also implement other security measures, such as an intrusion detection system (IDS) and biometrics for access control.

It is essential to understand that you need many levels (hence, defense in depth) of security to be truly safe from potential threats. A defense-in-depth matrix with auditing included could look something like Figure 10.1.

Figure 10.1 Defense in Depth

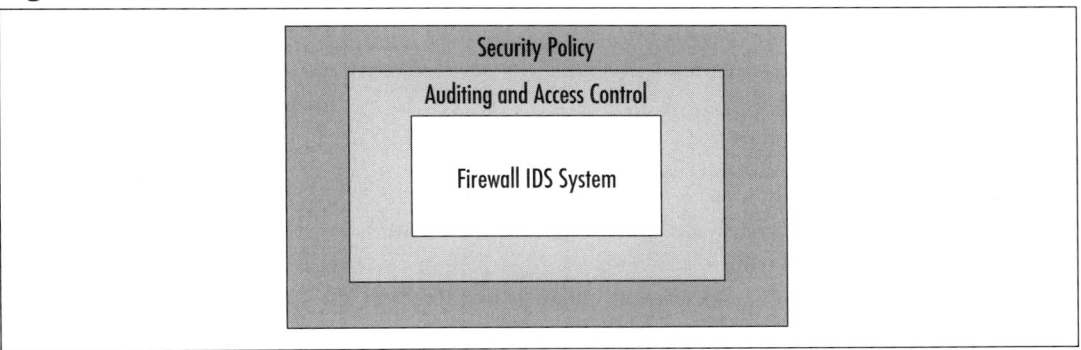

So now that you know why auditing is so important, you could probably benefit from a good definition of the term *auditing*. Auditing is the process of analyzing gathered data for the purpose or intent of determining a possible problem or, in the security arena, an attack or exploit. Auditing is best used on any system that can generate some type of log file that you can save, refer to, and analyze, especially over time.

Your security strategy should implement a strong policy on auditing systems. If you are strapped for time, you should at least implement a policy to audit your most critical systems or systems that are facing the Internet. This way, you can be somewhat informed of possible attack on systems that if rendered inoperable, could put you out of business.

You should try to determine the level of auditing you need to deploy on your systems, because excessive auditing will generate too many events to view and analyze.

When you perform auditing, you can have one of two categories:

- **Success** A success event indicates that a user has successfully gained access to a resource.

- **Failure** A failure event indicates that a user has attempted to gain access to a resource but failed.

These two categories determine many things. If you monitor both, you can find patterns, such as a series of logon failures, which could indicate that someone is trying to log on to a system and failing each time. One of the problems revolving around auditing such as this is, if you have an administrator who forgot a password or has the Cap Lock key on while trying to log on, the administrator could generate a false positive. This result would show up in the Event Log. If you have a series of failures followed by a success, you can see that either the administrator figured out the error or, if it is an attack, the attacker was able to breach the system. This is how both success and failure can be seen working in conjunction with one another.

Notes from the Underground…

Don't Overdo It

When you are preparing to audit your systems, you really need to do some analysis *before* the analysis! Do some research and think about what you are trying to determine using auditing. It is not wise to simply turn on all auditable events without knowing what it is you are enabling. Excessive auditing could actually cause you to lose some logged events if you have the log set to overwrite events as needed. Excessive logging could push an event you might need to see out of the readable log you were going to analyze.

We discuss ways that you can stop this activity in this chapter, but for now remember that if you blindly turn on auditing without thinking about what you want to accomplish, you could actually lose data. There are ways to prevent that from happening. One is to adjust the log size so that it will hold more events. Another way is to set it so that you will only be able to clear the events manually so you don't lose data. Both methods are explained in more detail later in the chapter. You could also use add-on products of third-party tools to accumulate your events in one centralized location, such as Microsoft Operations Manager (MOM), which can help you to gather, filter, and analyze massive amounts of events on all your systems.

Test Day Tip

For the exam, you need to fully understand the basics of auditing. You will not have to master every aspect of auditing, but you will want to make sure that when you work in a production environment, you fully understand all the concepts of auditing to be successful in tracking problems and issues that occur.

Auditing Windows 2000

Auditing is enabled by doing either a local audit or a Group Policy audit. You can set auditing options on a local Windows 2000 machine by going to the Local Security Policy MMC found in the Administrative Tools folder. We are only concerned with the Audit Policy for now. Here, you can specify what you need to audit and adjust auditing for the following events:

- Logon events
- Account logon events
- Object access
- Directory service access
- Privilege use
- Process tracking
- System events
- Policy change

Windows 2000 Local Auditing

For the exam, you are expected to know practically every detail of auditing Windows 2000. You might not be asked very detailed questions such as "What exact Event ID occurs when you have a password attempt failure?" Instead, you will most likely see scenario-based questions for which you'll need every bit of auditing knowledge you possess to decipher what needs to be accomplished in the given scenario.

Audit Account Logon Events

When using auditing for logon events, you are auditing each instance of a user either logging on or off a system on which the account is validated. When you successfully audit an account logon, you will see an entry in the Event Viewer security log. As you can see in Figure 10.2, you have a logon/logoff event (ID 528) that was successful. You can also get more information from the event as you look deeper into the description pane of the dialog box shown. You can see that there was a successful logon (and a successful audit of that logon) for the user rshimonski using the XP1 workstation on the XP1 domain. The logon ID, Type, and Process fields further identify the logon activity.

Figure 10.2 Viewing Logon Event Auditing

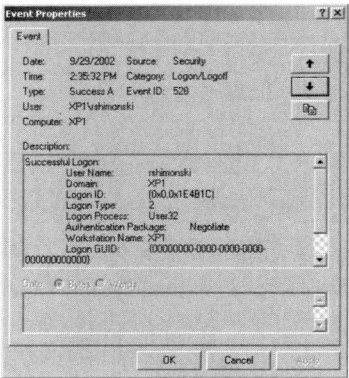

Audit Account Management

When using auditing for account management events, you are auditing each instance of a user doing one of the following:

- A user account or group has been created, altered, or possibly deleted.
- Passwords are changed or set.

When you successfully audit account management, you will see an entry in the Event Viewer Security Log. In Figure 10.3, you have a member add (ID 636) and the event was successful. In the figure shown here, you can see that a group member was added, which triggered the auditing of the event. Here, it is clear that the changes were made where a local group member was added. This caused the audit (account management) to take place and show up in the Event Viewer Security Log. It's a good idea to audit account management if you want to catch users or even administrators adding accounts to groups and giving or getting rights and permissions that they should not have.

Figure 10.3 Viewing Account Management Auditing

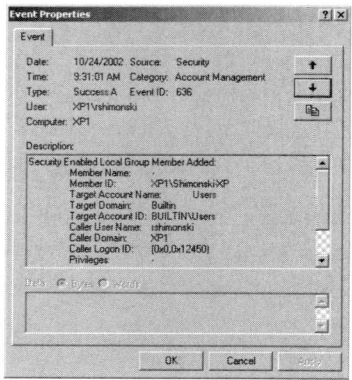

Audit Logon Events

When using auditing for logon events, you are auditing each instance of a user doing one of the following:

- Logging on to this computer
- Logging off this computer
- Making a network connection to this computer

When you successfully audit logon events, you will see an entry in the Event Viewer Security Log. In Figure 10.4, we see a member add (ID 680) and that the event was successful. As you can see, the Event ID is 680. This identifies the account used for the successful logon attempt. This event also indicates the authentication package used to authenticate the account. The authentication package shown in Figure 10.4 has been audited.

Figure 10.4 Viewing an Audit Logon Event

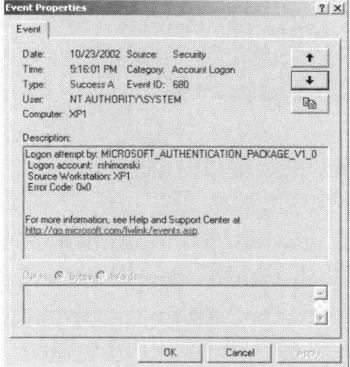

Audit Object Events

When you use auditing for object events, you audit each instance of a user accessing an object—for example, a file, folder, Registry key, printer, and so forth—that has its own system access control list (SACL) specified.

When you successfully audit object events (such as a file, folder, Registry key, printer), you will see an entry in the Event Viewer Security Log. Figure 10.5 shows a member add (ID 562) and that the event was successful.

Audit Policy Change

When using auditing for audit policy events, you audit each instance of an actual policy change on the system. A simple example is shown in Figure 10.6, which shows that auditing is turned on (success and failure based) on multiple items. This was an actual policy change to the system, and the Event Viewer recorded it. This type of audit determines if any type of policy is altered in any way; it is recorded for your analysis to see if anyone is trying to change any policies on the system without permission or perhaps for a malicious reason. The most important thing you need to remember is that whenever you make a change to a policy, as long as you have auditing turned on, you can see if any auditing policies have changed in the Event Viewer.

Figure 10.5 Viewing an Audit Object Event

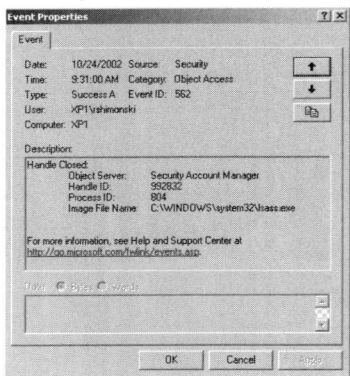

When you successfully audit policy changes, you will see an entry in the Event Viewer Security Log. In Figure 10.6, we have a massive change in our success and failure-based auditing (everything was turned on), which caused a new event ID (ID 612) to generate. Turning on all the auditing options lets you know if someone else is trying to change a policy. If an attacker is able to penetrate the system, the attacker can turn off auditing, make a change, then turn auditing back on. Having all the auditing options turned on determines whether to audit every incidence of a change to user rights assignment policies, audit policies, or trust policies. If you define this policy setting, you can specify whether to audit successes, audit failures, or not audit the event type at all.

Audit Privilege Use

When using auditing for privilege use events, you audit each instance of a user exercising a user right. When you successfully audit privilege use, you see an entry in the Event Viewer Security Log. In Figure 10.7, we have a member add (ID 578), and the event was successful.

Figure 10.6 Viewing an Audit Policy Change Event

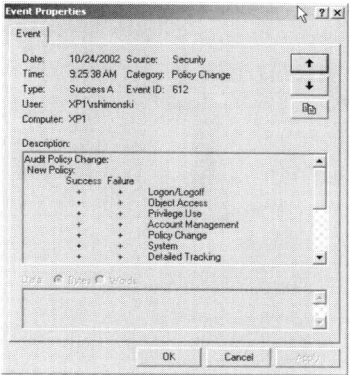

Figure 10.7 Viewing an Audit Privilege Use Event

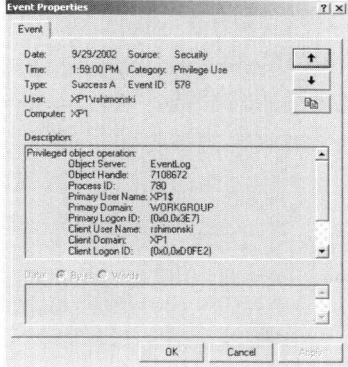

Audit Process Tracking

When using auditing for process-tracking (or detailed tracking) events, you audit for events such as program activation, process exit, handle duplication, and indirect object access. When you successfully audit process-tracking events, you see an entry in the Event Viewer Security Log. In Figure 10.8, we have a member add (ID 593), and the event was successful. It is advisable to audit process if you want to track use of a specific process as shown in Figure 10.8. You might want to see if batch commands are being run on a server where you have none—for example, if you hardened a DMZ-based server and you do not have any batch files running net-based commands such as stopping and starting services on the system.

Figure 10.8 Viewing an Audit Process-Tracking Event

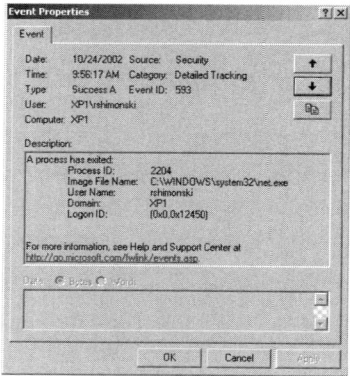

Audit System Events

When using auditing for system events, you audit each instance of a user restarting or shutting down the computer. This auditing also occurs when an event that affects either the system security or the Security Log occurs. Winlogon.exe is an example of a system process that could trigger a system event in the Security Log. When you successfully audit system events, you see an entry in the Event Viewer Security Log. In Figure 10.9, we have a member add (ID 520), and the event was successful. In this example, we changed the system time, which caused the auditing of a system event in the Security Log.

Figure 10.9 Viewing an Audit System Event

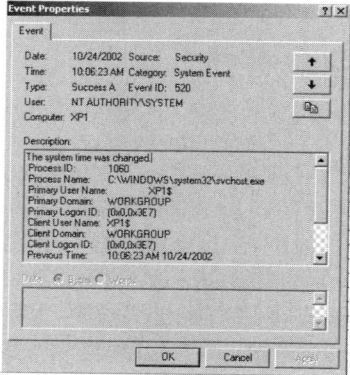

Exam Warning

Memorize everything you can do in the audit policy. You need to recall all this information from memory while working through complex scenarios on the exam.

In Exercise 10.01, you learn how to set basic auditing on a local system. You can also audit with Group Policy. We look at GPO auditing as well later in the chapter, but in Exercise 10.01, you learn how to audit a Windows 2000 system locally.

EXERCISE 10.01

AUDITING WITH LOCAL SECURITY POLICY

1. To edit the local security policy on the machine, go to **Start | Settings | Control Panel | Administrative Tools | Local Security Policy**. You can see the Local Security Policy shown in Figure 10.10.

    Figure 10.10 Opening and Using the Local Security Policy

    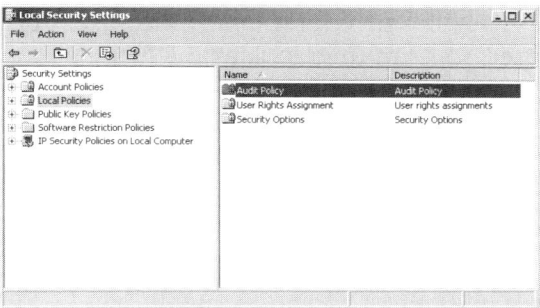

2. Once Local Policies is opened, click the **Audit Policy** folder (see Figure 10.11). Once that folder is opened, double-click the **Audit account logon events policy** found in the right pane of the MMC.

    Figure 10.11 Enabling Auditing on a Local Machine

    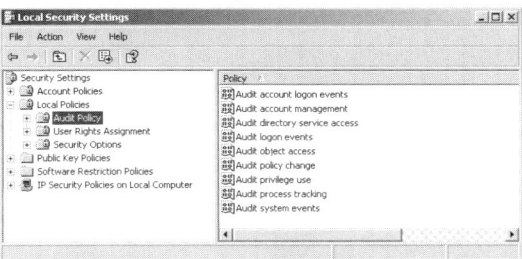

3. Once you double-click it, you will be able to edit the policy. Add a check mark to both the **Success** and **Failure** check boxes, as shown in Figure 10.12.

Figure 10.12 Setting Success- and Failure-Based Auditing

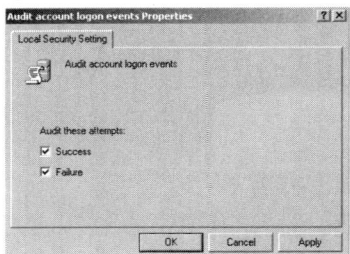

4. Click **OK**, and then close the **Local Security Policy MMC**. You have just successfully configured auditing on your system.

5. Now that you are done, you can go back through the last section and see if you can recreate some of the events described earlier in the chapter. You can then look at the listings of events in the rest of the chapter as a reference to other events you might encounter from time to time during your audits. You can see these events within the Event Viewer.

6. To get to the Event Viewer to display the Security Log, open the **Computer Management** console and drill down to the **Security Log**. If you successfully set up auditing on the system and did something to set off an auditable event, you will see the event listed within the log. A sample of these events is shown in Figure 10.13.

Figure 10.13 Viewing Events Generated within the Security Log

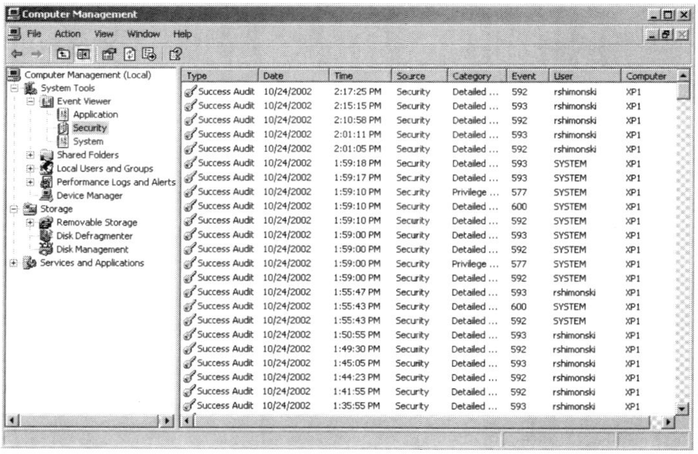

Head of the Class...

Test Your Policies

Always test a newly created policy on a test computer before applying it to your network. Just like anything else you do on a production network, you never want to roll something out without doing a risk analysis on it. Doing a simple risk analysis on your changes will make you look like a superstar. It's astounding how many times changes are pushed out on a production network without proper testing, often with disastrous consequences. Many disasters can be avoided by a little planning. Your polices should be no different. Not much harm can come from a local security policy running with the events being overwritten as necessary, but the most important thing to watch out for is overwriting needed events with excessive events you might not need to know about. This situation, of course, can be fixed by adjusting log size to higher size limits or by frequently checking and saving your logs. By testing your policies, you will know ahead of time what you need to turn on to achieve a desired logging event. Again, this kind of attention to detail makes you look like a professional, not an amateur who only knows how to turn on system auditing.

You have just enabled auditing on all successful logon events as well as failure-based logon events. Although this action might not seem very exciting, you will see how important it is later in the chapter, when we start to check the Event Logs to find and analyze logon attempts to your system. Now that we have completed discussion of local policies, its time to look at the Event Viewer in more detail.

The Event Viewer

The Windows 2000 Security Log can be viewed using the Windows 2000 Event Viewer MMC. We will get into more specific uses of the Event Viewer later in the chapter, but for now let's take a brief look at it and its uses. The Event Viewer (located within the Computer Management Console or in its own separate console located within the Administrative Tools folder) is used to collect and separate system-generated events into specific logs for viewing and analysis. You can filter the logs depending on what you are looking for (only warning-based events, for example), and you can save all recorded event data for future analysis.

EXAM WARNING

The security settings are refreshed every 90 minutes on a workstation or server and every 5 minutes on a domain controller. The settings are also refreshed every 16 hours, whether or not there are any changes.

Auditing with Group Policy

Now that you know the fundamentals of a local security policy audit, let's move on to using Group Policy. For the exam, you will be expected to know both methods, and know them well. Here we look at the fundamentals of GPO-based auditing.

Auditing with Group Policy, you can set the audit on the following levels:

- Site
- Domain
- OU
- Local machine

It is important to remember where you can set auditing, because there are so many places that it can be configured when you're working with Group Policy. Auditing is enabled using Group Policy, at the site, domain, OU, or local machine level. You will find the audit policy settings in the actual GPO that you create. In Figure 10.14, you can see Group Policy set on a site; we have drilled down to the Audit Account Logon events setting. Here we can set the site to be audited for account logon events that turn up as either a success or a failure. It's that easy.

Figure 10.14 Enabling Auditing Using Group Policy

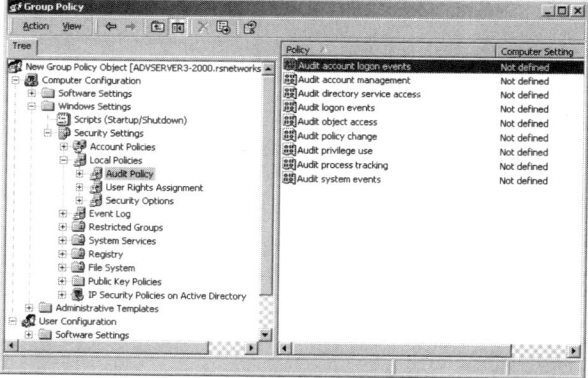

When thinking of proper design, you should set your auditing at the highest possible level in Active Directory to get the highest level of control. The Active Directory is a hierarchical database, so you want to audit from the top down. Doing so allows you to set specific site-level settings for the entire organization.

If you have specific systems that you do not want to audit and you do not incorporate them into the Group Policy audit policy, you can add these later. This can also be done using a Windows 2000 resource kit tool called Auditpol.exe.

> **NOTE**
>
> To access Group Policy for a local machine, start a new MMC (**MMC /a** for author mode) and then add the Group Policy snap-in, making the local computer the focus of the snap-in. Author mode access to a console is used to grant full access to all MMC functionality, including the ability to add or remove snap-ins. You can make a new MMC by going to the Run dialog box and typing and running **MMC**.

Damage & Defense...

Auditing and Your Security Policy

Have you ever worked somewhere and tried to access files on a folder, wondering before you did whether someone would know you tried to get into the folder? If you have ever thought this way, you are taking your first steps into realizing what auditing can do for you. When people are newly hired into a company, it's a good idea to have Human Resources make sure that they read and sign the posted security policy. This policy should include a clause that alerts the new hire to the fact that all data will be mapped to the local machine, so the new hire will not need to browse the network looking for any other data. If he or she does, it's at their own risk, because we are auditing access on file shares throughout the network. If new hires try to access something they shouldn't, they could be caught and reprimanded accordingly.

This policy is not intended to scare new hires but to warn them that the company is auditing the systems it runs, and that the company takes network and systems security very seriously. It also does a good thing; it encourages new hires to trust the network and systems and makes them more apt to save critical and private data to the network (to be secured and backed up) instead of to their local machines, where many end users keep data they don't want anyone to see. The workstation happens to be the easiest place to get the data from—but they might not realize that. Make sure that you incorporate auditing into your security policy because everyone will benefit.

Events to Audit

Windows 2000 provides several categories of auditing for security events. When designing your enterprise audit strategy, you can pick some or all of the following categories:

- Logon events
- Account logon events
- Object access

- Directory service access
- Privilege use
- Process tracking
- System events
- Policy change

Remember, as we mentioned earlier, you need to enable auditing and then watch the events collect in the Event Viewer Security Log. In the following sections, we look at common event IDs that are returned when auditing is enabled for specific categories. It is not only important that you know this information for the exam; you should also be very familiar with the entire process of starting the audit, gathering the collected events, and then using the event IDs to try to figure out what is going on in the system.

Logon Events that Appear in the Event Log

Table 10.1 shows the event IDs that you will see when you audit logon events. This table shows the most common events that you will see in the Security Log.

Table 10.1 Logon Events that Appear in the Event Log

Event	Description
528	A user successfully logged on to a computer.
529	The logon attempt was made with an unknown username or a known username with a bad password.
530	The user account tried to log on outside the allowed time.
531	A logon attempt was made using a disabled account.
532	A logon attempt was made using an expired account.
533	The user is not allowed to log on at this computer.
534	The user attempted to log on with a logon type that is not allowed, such as network, interactive, batch, service, or remote interactive.
535	The password for the specified account has expired.
536	The Net Logon service is not active.
537	The logon attempt failed for other reasons.
538	A user logged off.
539	The account was locked out at the time the logon attempt was made. This event can indicate that a password attack was launched unsuccessfully, resulting in the account being locked out.

Continued

Table 10.1 Logon Events that Appear in the Event Log

Event	Description
540	Successful network logon. This event indicates that a remote user has successfully connected from the network to a local resource on the server, generating a token for the network user.
682	A user has reconnected to a disconnected Terminal Services session. This event indicates that a previous Terminal Services session was connected to.
683	A user disconnected a Terminal Services session without logging off. This event is generated when a user is connected to a Terminal Services session over the network. It appears on the terminal server.

Notes from the Underground...

Hack Alert, Hack Alert!

So you want to be a star auditor of Windows systems. Here is a tip to help you reach your goal. If you turn on success- and failure-based auditing of logon events and event ID 531 starts showing up frequently (as shown in Figure 10.15), you could have a big problem.

Figure 10.15 Event ID 531 Appears Frequently

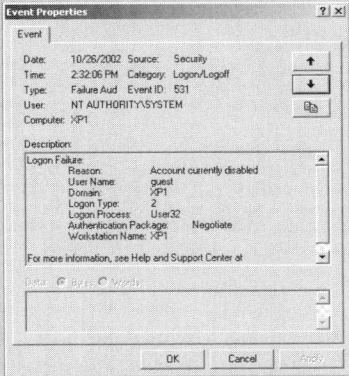

Event ID 531 is a logon attempt on a disabled account. This is a problem if it is the Guest account that was logged on to or the account of an employee that is either away or has been removed. If you find these events, you have a few options available to you. First, if you have accounts on your network that you no longer need, delete them. Next, ensure that your Guest account is still disabled by default. Lastly, if any employee goes on an extended vacation and that person's account has excessive rights, make sure that you watch that account activity closely. See who else knows about this account's excessive

Continued

> rights; you might have a very bad IT professional out there who knows too much for his or her own good.
>   Lastly, the auditing of an account in this fashion is the making of a *honeypot*—a trap you set to nail someone trying to log on with default accounts. Essentially, a honeypot is the system you set up to attract and "trap" attackers who attempt to penetrate your systems. By setting a trap like this, you might find someone trying to crack your systems.

Exam Day Tip

You do not have to memorize every event ID for the exam. However, it serves you best to be familiar with them to help you eliminate the wrong answers from questions you see on the exam.

Local Logon Attempt Failures

You can use the event IDs to start figuring out what's causing a particular problem. For instance, if you think you have a local login attempt, you can monitor for failures. Failed events result in event IDs of 529, 530, 531, 532, 533, 534, and 537. Of these, you could focus on 529 and 534, which could possibly mean that a cracker outside your network is trying to guess at your user account by arbitrarily trying any username and password you have available, such as the Administrator account.

You do, however, want to make sure you use good judgment in suspecting possible attacks. What if a user forgot his or her password and they are just trying to remember it? This could make you believe that a cracker is trying to make an attempt on your systems. The judgment call you need to make is one of frequency. How many times is the attempt occurring? When does it occur? You would be right in being suspicious if, for example, this activity is happening in the middle of the night when nobody should be accessing the systems.

Account Misuse

If you think you are suffering account misuse, you might want to keep an eye on the following events: 530, 531, 532, and 533. These all represent possible issues revolving around account misuse. Either a set of credentials was entered incorrectly (username and password) or something else happened, such as the Cap Lock key being on, for example, that could prevent a user from properly accessing and using an account.

Another form of problem could arise from restrictions on logon hours. Often you set restrictions and then get errors if a user tries to log on to a system outside the allotted times. Figure 10.16 shows you this phenomenon by which a user could log in after 6:00 P.M. to try to download a file or perhaps print a document, and that activity could be construed as misuse. Because the settings were set to deny a logon after 6:00 P.M., an event would be generated as possible misuse of the system. Again, you must use your judgment at times like this.

Figure 10.16 Logon Hours Configuration

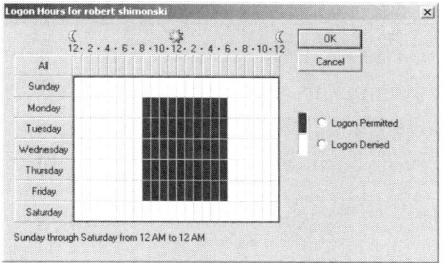

NOTE

Keep on the lookout for event ID 539. ID 539 is an indication that an account has been locked out. This indication could mean that someone using a password-cracking tool might be trying to do a brute-force attack on your systems.

Account Logon Events

Account logon events are audited as logon event IDs, recorded when a user logs on to a system or a domain controller. Table 10.2 shows event IDs that you will see when you audit account logon events. This table shows the most common events that you will see in the Security Log:

Table 10.2 Account Logon Events that Appear in the Event Log

Event	Description
672	An authentication service (AS) ticket was successfully issued and validated.
673	A ticket-granting service (TGS) ticket was granted.
674	A security principal renewed an AS ticket or a TGS ticket.
675	Pre-authentication failed.
676	Authentication ticket request failed.
677	A TGS ticket was not granted.
678	An account was successfully mapped to a domain account.
680	Identifies the account used for the successful logon attempt. This event also indicates the authentication package used to authenticate the account.

Continued

Table 10.2 Account Logon Events that Appear in the Event Log

Event	Description
681	A domain account logon was attempted.
682	A user has reconnected to a disconnected Terminal Services session.
683	A user disconnected a Terminal Services session without logging off.

When auditing account management, you need to look at creating, deleting, and changing properties on user accounts, users, and groups. When these properties are changed, they show up in the Event Viewer Security Log. Table 10.3 shows the event IDs that you will see when you audit account management events. This table shows the most common events that you will see in the Security Log.

Table 10.3 Account Management Events that Appear in the Event Log

Event	Description
624	User account created.
625	User account type change.
626	User account enabled.
627	Password change attempted.
628	User account password set.
629	User account disabled.
630	User account deleted.
631	Security-enabled global group created.
632	Security-enabled global group member added.
633	Security-enabled global group member removed.
634	Security-enabled global group deleted.
635	Security-disabled local group created.
636	Security-enabled local group member added.
637	Security-enabled local group member removed.
638	Security-enabled local group deleted.
639	Security-enabled local group changed.
641	Security-enabled global group changed.
642	User account changed.
643	Domain policy changed.
644	User account locked out.

Auditing Best Practices

You should now be familiar with how to configure auditing, how to look for specific events that an occur, and how to open and look at the Security Log to see the recorded events and their IDs. Let's now take a look at some field tips for better auditing.

The first thing that you should have is an auditing section in your security policy. It should be mandatory that auditing be used on critical systems such as production Web servers and/or any other system on which you absolutely cannot afford a breach of security. More important, you should have a system of checks and balances in place, including administrators being audited as well. Another good idea is to make sure that you do not allow entries to be removed from the Security Log. In Figure 10.17, you can see that we have cleared the Security Log and it was audited as a system event. This is a nice setup because if you audit successful system events, you can catch someone trying to clean out the logs. When the cracker tries to clear this event, it just keeps reproducing the system event that the log was cleared and flags it with an event ID of 517.

Figure 10.17 Viewing Event ID 517 in the Security Log

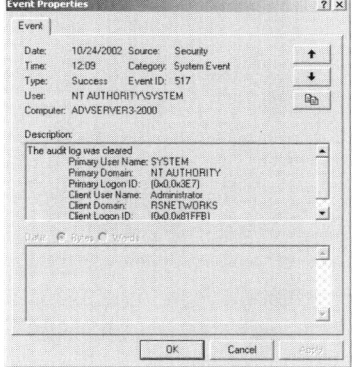

A cracker can also take advantage of your system by deleing the actual log file instead of just clearing it. The way you get around this problem is that you *never* store the actual log files on the same physical server. Instead, have a share on the network on another system that only grants access to you. Store all the *.evt logs on that system. This increases security in case the system you are auditing is compromised at any time.

Exam Warning

Make sure that you are comfortable with Event Log storage. It is not only important for the exam—it's even more so in real-world production scenarios.

Another practice you should get in the habit of is setting up a regular review of these logs. There are tools that can do this for you, such as Microsoft Operations Manager (MOM), but if you don't want to invest the dollars in a product such as that, you must keep yourself on a constant audit schedule. You can only nail an attacker if you perform follow-up work on your initial configurations. Your server will not call you (yet) to tell you it "thinks" it might be under attack. Until this happens, it's up to you, the security analyst, to review and analyze your logs on a constant basis. It is recommended that you do this at least once a week. Here is a list of some other good auditing best practices you can follow:

- You need to know that you can apply more than a single policy to any one computer. Because you have this ability, you could see conflicts within your security policy.

- Make sure that you realize that you have an order or precedence you need to follow. The highest is the OU, then the domain, and then the local computer.

- At the domain level, you can only have one account policy, and it is the default domain policy.

NOTE

By default, all users in a domain can access System and Application Logs. The Security Log is restricted to administrators. Make sure that you keep physical access to the system secure. Lock your systems in the rack, lock the doors to the server farm, lock the consoles with a password—anything you can do to keep the system safe. Lastly, make sure that Terminal Server client access is not abused on the systems, or you can simply audit your system to monitor for it.

Security Analysis

Another best-practice tip is to do a quick self-audit on your system using the tools location within the system. A good tip is to have the system analyze itself. Use **Security Templates** to create a local policy, and then use **Security Configuration and Analysis** to apply the policy. In Figure 10.18, we opened a new MMC (go the **Run** dialog box and type **MMC /a** and then choose **Add snap-ins**) and added the Security Configuration and Analysis snap-in as well as the Security Templates snap-in. We then started a new database and have the system scanning itself.

Figure 10.19 shows a full report of possible problems in our system. Go through the systems analysis and see what you can turn up.

Figure 10.18 Analyzing System Security

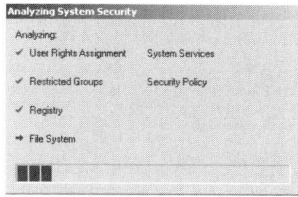

Figure 10.19 Using the Security Configuration and Analysis Tool

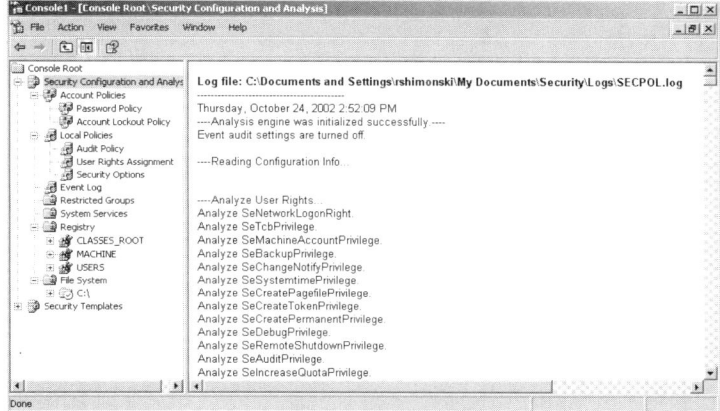

Remember, these are just tips for you to follow to make you a better auditor and to get the most out of your analysis. Now let's look at configuring the Event Viewer Logs for maximum efficiency.

Event Viewer Log Size

By default, the Event Viewer has three logs:

- Application
- Security
- System

These logs have a default size of 512K and will overwrite events as needed within seven days. Make sure that when you're auditing, you set the log file higher (to about 2048KB) and make sure that you are the only person who clears the log, as illustrated in Figure 10.20. This is a good practice because it ties in with our other best-practice tip, which is to visit the system frequently to audit and analyze the logs. Save the logs each week as a way to clear them out. To do this, you only need to right-click the log itself and save it to a safe location. Name the log something that you can refer back to by using a solid log-naming convention such as *date /log type* with the *.evt extension. Here is an example:

```
102402SEC.evt
```

This filename indicates that we saved the Security Log on October 24, 2002 (10/24/02).

Figure 10.20 Adjusting the Security Log Properties

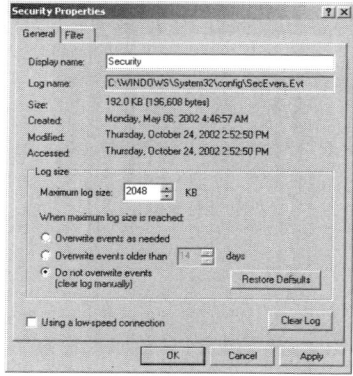

Test Day Tip

You need to know all about log settings for the exam. Make sure that you are comfortable with setting up, saving, and using logs.

Auditing Internet Information Services

Now that you have mastered the process of auditing events and how to navigate the Event Viewer to check these events for analysis, let's look at some other systems you will be responsible for knowing about, not only on the exam but also as a Microsoft Certified Professional dealing with daily security issues on your systems. For the exam, you need to know how to audit Internet Information Services (IIS). IIS is Microsoft's Web services product. IIS 5.0 comes with Windows 2000 Server.

Internet Information Services

IIS creates log files that track connection attempts to Web (HTTP), FTP, NNTP, and SMTP services. If used, each of these services (which can run using IIS) maintains its own log files. In other words, if you don't use the SMTP service, a log file is not generated. In Exercise 10.02, we look at how to set up and view an IIS-based log for the Web service.

… **Configuring and Using Auditing and the Event Logs • Chapter 10** 631

EXERCISE 10.02

CONFIGURING AND VIEWING THE IIS LOG FILES

1. When you set up IIS logging, you need to make sure that you have IIS installed and running. This is easy to do. Go to your **Internet Services Manager (ISM)** console, located within the **Administrative Tools** folder. Open the ISM and make sure your default Web site (or a configured one, if you have it) is running and not stopped. You will see that it is stopped or running, as shown in Figure 10.21.

   Figure 10.21 Viewing the IIS Internet Services Manager

   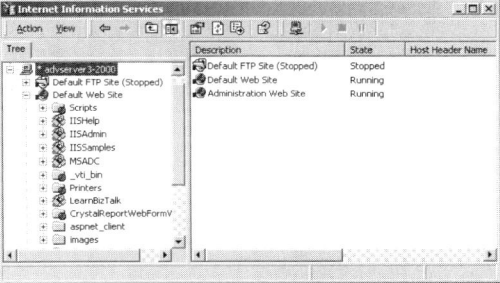

2. Go to the default Web site and right-click it. Go to **Properties**. Choose the **Web Site** properties, and you will by default be on the tab you need (the Web Site tab). On the bottom of the screen you will be able to enable logging, as shown in Figure 10.22. Logging is enabled by default.

   Figure 10.22 Default Web Site Settings

   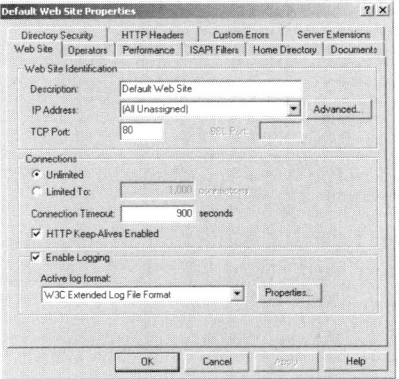

3. You can change the Active Log format (you can configure IIS to store the logs into an ODBC-compliant database, such as Microsoft SQL Server), but for purposes of this exercise, we want to log to a World Wide Web Consortium (W3C) Extended log file format.

4. Click the **Properties** button and you will be presented with the Extended Logging Properties dialog box shown in Figure 10.23. Here, on the bottom of the dialog box, you can see where the log files will be stored. By default, they will be stored in the %WinDir%\System32\Logfiles folder.

Figure 10.23 Viewing the W3C Extended Logging Properties

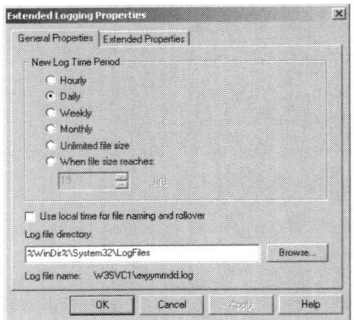

5. Make absolutely sure that you pay attention to the log filename format at the bottom of the dialog box, because you need to know that W3SVC1 is the folder you need to open to see the log files you want to audit. In addition, notice the *exyymmdd.log* format. This format would resemble ex021024.log if it were created on October 24, 2002.

6. Now you can go to **Windows Explorer** and browse to the directory where the log files are stored. Follow the path to the **%WinDir%\System32\Logfiles** folder. Open the **W3SVC1** folder, and open the newest log available. You should see something similar to the following:

```
#Software: Microsoft Internet Information Services 5.0
#Version: 1.0
#Date: 2002-10-24 15:11:51
#Fields: date time c-ip cs-username s-ip s-port cs-method cs-uri-stem
cs-uri-query sc-status cs(User-Agent) 2002-10-24 19:46:40 127.0.0.1 -
127.0.0.1 80 GET /index.htm - 304 Mozilla/4.0+(compatible;+MSIE+6.0;+
Windows+NT+5.0;+.NET+CLR+1.0.3526)
```

7. If you have no entries, you can open a Web browser and go to **http://localhost** (the loopback for the local system at 127.0.0.1). This pulls up the Web site you have configured. If you do not have one, you can make a blank index.htm or default.asp page to put in your Inetpub\wwwroot directory.

8. Refresh the page and audit your log. You should see entries similar to the ones shown in the log that appears in Step 6.

NOTE

You should always make certain that your systems have synchronized clocks, especially systems that create log files. For a file to hold up in a court of law, you must know the time that events happened. Domain synchronization via login script is probably the best way to make sure that all hosts have the correct time. You can use the *Net Time* batch command to perform this operation. Another, more expensive way is to have a device on location that performs time synching through the NTP protocol. You could also set your systems to synchronize with an atomic clock on the Internet, but then you will have to let port 123 through your firewall. Whatever you choose, it's important to do something to keep accurate time. You can see an atomic clock and get the exact time at a site provided by the U.S. government: www.time.gov.

Windows Auditing Tools

In this section of the chapter we look at some of the auditing tools that are not included with Windows 2000 but that you can find online (at www.microsoft.com) and in the Windows 2000 Resource Kit (supplement one). More important, you will be tested on them on the exam. In particular, with auditing in mind, you need to know how to use the Dump Event Log command-line too. (Dumpel.exe) and the EventCombMT GUI-based utility. We discuss both these tools here.

EXAM WARNING

Make sure that you know exactly how to use Dumpel for the exam. You will be expected to know how to use the utility to dump Event Logs.

The Dump Event Log

The Windows 2000 Server Resource Kit has a tool called the Dump Event Log, or Dumpel for short. Dumpel is a command-line tool that's used to dump an Event Log into a tab-separated text file. This file can then be imported into an Excel spreadsheet (because it is tab separated) and/or a database such as Access for storage or future analysis. The tool can also be used for filtering certain event types. Table 10.4 lists the command-line switches you can use with this tool. This table highlights all the functionality that you can perform via the command line.

The dumpel.exe tool uses the following syntax:

```
dumpel -f file [-s \\server] [-l log [-m source]] [-e n1 n2 n3...] [-r]
       [-t] [-d x]
```

Table 10.4 Dumpel Tool Switches

Switch	Details
-f *file*	Specifies the filename for the output file. There is no default for *-f*, so you must specify the file.
-s *server*	Specifies the server for which you want to dump the Event Log. Leading backslashes on the server name are optional.
-l *log*	Specifies the log (system, application, security) to dump. If an invalid log name is specified, the application log is dumped.
-m *source*	Specifies in which source (such as redirector [*rdr*], serial, and so on) to dump records. Only one source can be supplied. If this switch is not used, all events are dumped. If a source is used that is not registered in the Registry, the Application Log is searched for records of this type.
-e *n1 n2 n3*	Filters for event ID *nn* (up to 10 IDs can be specified). If the *-r* switch is not used, only records of these types are dumped; if *-r* is used, all records except records of these types are dumped. If this switch is not used, all events from the specified source name are selected. *Note:* You cannot use this switch without the *-m* switch.
-r	Specifies whether to filter for specific sources or records, or to filter them out.
-t	Specifies that tabs separate individual strings. If *-t* is not used, strings are separated by spaces.
-d *n*	Dumps events for the past *n* days.

TEST DAY TIP

Dumpel can only retrieve content from the System, Application, and Security Log files. This is important because you could have more logs on domain controllers with Active Directory installed. For instance, you will have a File Replication Service, DNS, or Directory Service Logs, and Dumpel will not query content from them. For the exam, you must know what Dumpel can and cannot do.

EventCombMT

If you want a nice GUI-based Event Viewer log manipulation tool for parsing Event Logs, EventCombMT is your tool. What's nice is that you can get this tool online at Microsoft.com. Run a search for it and you will be guided to the tool on Microsoft's site. EventCombMT is a tool that allows you to manage the parsing of many Event Logs from your systems that will be dumped to a text-based file for analysis. This tool allows you to specifically search for event IDs by ID number, or you could search based on many other criteria, such as types of events (warning, informational). Also helpful is the fact that it picks up where Dumpel left off and searches through the logs that Dumpel will not search, such as DNS and Active Directory. EventCombMT also allows you to search within specific time intervals so you can search within specific parameters such as date or by specific month or week. Let's now look at an exercise of using the EventCombMT tool.

EXAM WARNING

Make sure that you are very familiar with the EventCombMT utility. You will find that a great many exam questions revolve around its use as well as how it is inherently different from the Dumpel utility.

EXERCISE 10.03

USING EVENTCOMBMT

1. After you have downloaded the EventCombMT tool from Microsoft.com, you can run the executable without installing it. Since it is self-contained, you could even transport it on a diskette if needed. Put the tool on your local system to prepare to run it.

2. Double-click the executable you downloaded and it will open, as shown in Figure 10.24. As you can see on the dialog box, you can learn a great deal about the proper use of the tool and setup from it. Read this information carefully to see what you need to do to configure the EventCombMT tool.

Figure 10.24 Viewing the EventCombMT Instructions

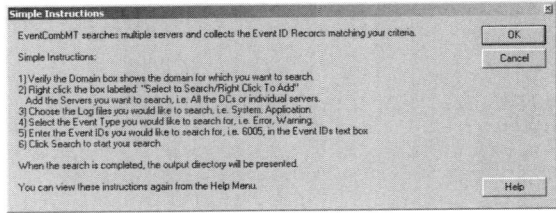

3. Once you click **OK**, you will see the screen shown in Figure 10.25. This is where you can configure your systems to be parsed by EventCombMT.

Figure 10.25 Using the EventCombMT GUI

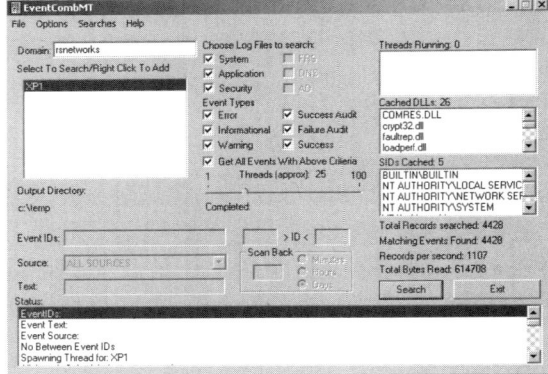

4. In the **Domain** field, enter the domain name that you want the systems to be parsed from. You can click the **Search** button or right-click the left side of the utility (in the blank space) to get a menu. When you see the menu, you will be able to select the **Add servers** option.

5. Add the servers or workstation you want to parse. In Figure 10.25, we added an XP Professional Workstation to be parsed by EventCombMT.

6. After you have added a workstation or server, you can select the search criteria. From the dialog box shown in Figure 10.24, you can see that you can pick from event types or log files to search as well as quite a

few other options, such as specific event IDs or source. We selected a full parse from the XP1 workstation.

7. Once you have finished, you can run the tool (via the **Search** button) and your system will be parsed. Next, you need to navigate to the file to which the data has been consolidated. The file will show up automatically once it is finished, but the path to it will be from the temp directory on your local drive (wherever the Temp path statement is set). Here it is found on C:\Temp.

8. Once you open the file, you will see the code listed in Figure 10.26.

Figure 10.26 Viewing the Temp File Contents

```
578,AUDIT SUCCESS,Security,Thu Oct 24 16:30:26
2002,XP1\rshimonski,Privileged object operation:    Object
Server: EventLog    Object Handle: 11799592      Process ID:
788     Primary User Name: XP1$     Primary Domain: WORKGROUP
Primary Logon ID: (0x0,0x3E7)      Client User Name: rshimonski
Client Domain: XP1      Client Logon ID: (0x0,0x1243A)
Privileges: SeSecurityPrivilege
593,AUDIT SUCCESS,Security,Thu Oct 24 16:30:13
2002,XP1\rshimonski,A process has exited:     Process ID: 3524
Image File Name: C:\WINDOWS\system32\rundll32.exe     User
Name: rshimonski      Domain: XP1     Logon ID: (0x0,0x1243A)
592,AUDIT SUCCESS,Security,Thu Oct 24 16:30:10
2002,XP1\rshimonski,A new process has been created:     New
Process ID: 3524     Image File Name:
C:\WINDOWS\system32\rundll32.exe     Creator Process ID: 552
User Name: rshimonski    Domain:   XP1     Logon ID:
(0x0,0x1243A)
593,AUDIT SUCCESS,Security,Thu Oct 24 16:30:09
2002,XP1\rshimonski,A process has exited:     Process ID: 3104
Image File Name: C:\WINDOWS\system32\notepad.exe      User Name:
rshimonski     Domain:  XP1     Logon ID:  (0x0,0x1243A)
c:\temp\XP1-Security_LOG.txt
```

9. That's it! You have parsed the Event Viewer Log based on your search criteria. Now you can save the log or analyze it further.

Summary of Exam Objectives

In this chapter we looked at many important topics for the Implementing and Administering Security in a Microsoft Windows 2000 Network exam. The most important topics covered were auditing your network for increased security, auditing Windows 2000, auditing IIS, and using Windows auditing tools.

When you're auditing for increased security, it is important to remember what auditing is and why it is needed. Auditing is the process of analyzing gathered data for the purpose or intent of determining a possible problem or, in the security arena, an attack or exploit. We also looked at the need for both success- and failure-based auditable events and the differences between them.

We then covered auditing Windows 2000-based systems. This section of the chapter contained exercises on how to perform an audit and how to analyze events within the Security Log. We looked at how to log auditable events, how to set up success- and failure-based auditing, and how to configure auditing on a local system or through a GPO. We covered many aspects of auditing to include general concepts and auditing-based exercises. Things to remember in detail are how to audit and when to audit for specific events.

Other items of importance are the terminology of defense in depth. The general concept of not relying or depending on a single way to secure your infrastructure or systems (such as having a firewall as the only means of protection) is called *defense in depth*. Memorizing the needs for auditing is also essential. Auditing is the process of analyzing gathered data for the purpose or intent of determining a possible problem or, in the security arena, an attack or exploit. Auditing is best used on any system that can generate some type of log file that you can save, refer to, and analyze. Auditing is the process of logging and analyzing events that occur to proactively find and eliminate problems such as attacks, hacking, or mischief.

We learned that an audit could either be for success or failure of a specific event. Remember, do not just set up failure-based auditing. In reading this chapter, you should have learned that is it more important to first understand what you are auditing because you might be looking for a success as well—such as a successful logon after a series of failures. This activity could constitute not only a password-cracking attempt but a possible breach of your systems.

Windows 2000 comes with the built-in ability to perform system auditing. From the Local Security Policy console, you can choose from many categories, such as auditing for object access of logon events.

Quite a few categories are available to you when you're working with Local Security Policy. You must intimately know all eight of these categories and their uses for the exam. They are logon events, account logon events, object access, directory service access, privilege use, process tracking, system events, and policy change.

You can audit Windows 2000 at the local level (with Local Security Policy) or using Group Policy at the site, domain, or OU level. You will find the audit policy settings in the actual GPO that you create.

We looked at IIS auditing and logging. We covered how to set up logging and how to analyze the log files IIS creates as well as where to find the logs and how to change where the files will log.

Lastly, we looked at two tools that are heavily tested on this exam: Dumpel and EventCombMT. You should know how both tools work.

Exam Objectives Fast Track

Auditing for Increased Security

- ☑ The general concept of not relying or depending on a single way to secure your infrastructure or systems (such as having a firewall as the only means of protection) is called *defense in depth*.

- ☑ Auditing is the process of analyzing gathered data for the purpose or intent of determining a possible problem or, in the security arena, an attack or exploit. Auditing is best used on any system that can generate some type of log file that you can save, refer to, and analyze. Auditing is the process of logging and analyzing events that occur to proactively find and eliminate problems such as attacks, hacking, or mischief.

- ☑ An audit can be for either success or failure of a specific event. Do not just set up failure-based auditing; you should have learned from reading this chapter that is it more important to first understand what you are auditing, because you could be looking for a success as well—such as a successful logon after a series of failures. This could constitute not only a password-cracking attempt but a possible breach of your systems as well.

Auditing Windows 2000

- ☑ Windows 2000 comes with the built-in ability to perform system auditing. In the Local Security Policy console, you can choose from many categories, such as auditing for object access of logon events.

- ☑ Quite a few categories are available to you when you're working with Local Security Policy. You must intimately know all eight of them and their uses for the exam. They are logon events, account logon events, object access, directory service access, privilege use, process tracking, system events, and policy change.

www.syngress.com

- ☑ You can audit Windows 2000 at the local level (with Local Security Policy) or using Group Policy at the site, domain, or OU level. You will find the audit policy settings in the actual GPO that you create.

Auditing IIS

- ☑ Auditing IIS is critical to any system administrator responsible for managing company Web servers. You should audit, monitor, and analyze IIS just the same as Windows 2000 Server.

- ☑ IIS creates log files that track connection attempts to Web (HTTP), FTP, NNTP, and SMTP services. Each of these services (which can run using IIS) maintains its own log files. You can find these log files in the %WinDir%\System32\Logfiles folder.

- ☑ When you log data with IIS, you can log to either W3C Extended format or to ODBC-compliant databases such as SQL Server 2000.

Windows Auditing Tools

- ☑ Dumpel.exe is a command-line tool used to parse Event Logs.

- ☑ Dumpel is used to dump an Event Log into a tab-separated text file. This file can then be imported into an Excel spreadsheet (because it is tab separated) and/or a database such as Access for storage or future analysis.

- ☑ EventCombMT is the GUI-based tool that will allow you to manage the parsing of many Event Logs from your systems that will be dumped to a text-based file for analysis. This tool allows you to specifically search for event IDs by ID number or based on many other criteria.

Exam Objectives Frequently Asked Questions

The following Frequently Asked Questions, answered by the authors of this book, are designed to both measure your understanding of the Exam Objectives presented in this chapter, and to assist you with real-life implementation of these concepts.

Q: Being the administrator of a large Windows 2000 Server-based network, I always wonder if my systems are safe. I have a firewall implemented, so I know I am safe from the outside world, but am I safe on the inside of my network? How do I know?

A: Exactly—you don't know if you are safe or not, so you must do some analysis. First, because you have a firewall implemented means only that your Internet or WAN connection is somewhat safe from exploitation, but because this is the only security you have implemented, you are not using defense in depth, which allows you to have multiple layers of security. Furthermore, you need to set up auditing on your systems. Doing so will clue you in to some of the activities, good and bad, that are occuring on your systems.

Q: I need to parse my Event Logs. I would like to parse my default Event Viewer logs (Security, Application, and System) as well as my DNS Logs. I have the Dumpel.exe command-line tool, but I can't seem to get it to work right. What am I doing wrong?

A: The only thing you are doing wrong is trying to get the DNS Log with a tool that will only parse the Security, Application, and System Logs. You might want to use the EventCombMT tool instead. It will do all the logs you need to parse.

Q: When performing an audit, I would like to log when someone on a server uses the command prompt program successfully. This is known as cmd.exe. How would I audit this event and get it to show up in the Event Viewer Security Log?

A: You need to audit process tracking. Process-tracking events provide you with detailed tracking information for events such as program activation, process exit, handle duplication, and indirect object access. If you turn on success-based auditing for process tracking, when someone uses the command prompt you will get an event in the Event Viewer Security Log.

Q: I would like to audit IIS. I have set up logging, but I am not sure where I need to get the information to log to. I would like to have it saved on the local machine as a text-based log file. Which logging activity should I select?

www.syngress.com

A: Make sure you select W3C Extended logging so that you can look in the %WinDir%\System32\Logfiles folder and find your logs to analyze.

Self Test

A Quick Answer Key follows the Self Test questions. For complete questions, answers, and epxlanations to the Self Test questions in this chapter as well as the other chapters in this book, see the Self Test Appendix.

Auditing for Increased Security

1. Jake is responsible for six Windows 2000 servers in his organization. He has noticed that lately there are multiple login attempts on the main file server. What can Jake do to find out if in fact an attacker is trying to exploit his system? (Choose all that apply.)

    A. Use Dumpel.exe to find the attack IDs numbered 200–600 in the System Event Log. This will indicate a possible attack.

    B. Turn on auditing (success and failure) for logon events. Check the Application Log daily for possible password-cracking attacks.

    C. Set up a Windows 2000 Security Template that will only allow registered IPs to connect to and communicate with the file server.

    D. Configure your router to only let the file server NetBIOS name be authenticated for communication.

2. Stan is the network administrator responsible for 10 Windows 2000 servers and 400 Windows XP Professional workstations, all separated geographically across four sites. Stan is responsible for implementing defense in depth. From the following list, select the options that Stan can implement for a defense-in-depth strategy. (Choose all that apply.)

    A. Set up a and implement a firewall.

    B. Set up and implement auditing.

    C. Set up and implement IDS.

    D. Set up and implement a router ACL.

3. Peter is the administrator for a large Windows 2000 network infrastructure. He is responsible for 10 IIS servers, two Exchange servers, and 20 file and print servers. All 32 servers are internal to the LAN and serve as application, e-mail, file, and print server for over 700 clients in five separate locations. Because of a shortage of staff, Peter needs to make sure that his servers are safe and is giving himself the task of ensuring that auditing takes place so that he can analyze possible mischievous events that could lead to an attack. He turns on auditing for all 32 servers. Peter is also new to auditing, so he turns on auditing for all categories, success and failure based. What is the most logical thing Peter should do now to analyze his servers? (Choose all that apply.)

   A. Peter should plan a time each week to view, archive, and analyze all the events he is receiving.

   B. Peter should analyze all events and start turning off categories he will not need to view in the Security Log.

   C. Peter should adjust his Security Log size to hold more events so that important auditable events are not overwritten.

   D. Peter should use the Dumpel command-line tool in batch format to scan all System Logs in all 32 servers for any event in the 500–600 range.

Auditing Windows 2000

4. Stan is the network administrator responsible for 10 Windows 2000 servers and 400 Windows XP Professional workstations, all separated geographically across four sites. Stan is responsible for auditing two Windows XP Professional workstations. One of the reasons he audits only the two workstations is because the two owners of the workstations are complaining that each time they sit down to work at their workstations, they think someone has tried to log in to them. From the list that follows, what is the most logical way to audit the two workstations so that Stan can analyze whether an attack is actually being attempted?

   A. Use the Local Security Policy on each local workstation and audit logon events (success and failure).

   B. Use the GPO Security Policy on the NY OU and audit logon events (success and failure).

   C. Use the Local Security Policy on the domain controller and audit logon events (success and failure).

   D. Use the Local Security Policy on the domain and audit logon events (success and failure).

5. Jake is responsible for six Windows 2000 servers in his organization. He has noticed that lately there are no events in the Security Log on the main file server. Jake has found a single 517 event in the Security Log. What can Jake do to find out if in fact someone is trying to exploit his system?

   A. The 517 event ID means that an attacker has breached the system and has tried to exploit the lssas.exe process and succeeded.

   B. The 517 event ID is not a valid ID number. The Security Log only looks at event IDs 600 and higher.

   C. The 517 event ID means that an attacker has breached the system and has tried to exploit the cmd.exe process and has failed.

   D. The log has been cleared, and since auditing was turned on, it was caught by the Security Log.

6. Peter is the administrator for a large Windows 2000 network infrastructure. He is responsible for 10 IIS servers, two Exchange servers, and 20 file and print servers. All 32 servers are internal to the LAN and serve as application, e-mail, file, and print servers for over 700 clients in five separate locations. Peter has noticed that there are 10 new events on his main domain controller. The event IDs are showing as Event ID 531. What is possibly happening that Peter should be aware of?

   A. There is a possible attack on the server, whereby someone could be trying to log in with a disabled account.

   B. There is a possible attack on the server, whereby someone could be trying to change the permissions of a group.

   C. There is a possible attack on the server, whereby someone could be trying to change the permissions of a user account.

   D. There is a possible attack on the server, whereby someone could be trying to launch a buffer overflow attack on the server.

Auditing IIS

7. Stan is the network administrator responsible for 10 Windows 2000 servers running IIS 5.0 and 400 Windows XP Professional workstations, all separated geographically across four sites. Stan is responsible for implementing security on his 10 Windows Web-based servers. He would like to set up logging on his systems so he can audit the logs. What type of logging should Stan set up if he wants to log

right to the system in the %WinDir%\System32\Logfiles folder using the default logging the system provides?

A. ODBC logging

B. NCSA Common Log File format

C. W3C Extended Log File format

D. Logging to an Oracle database using SQL Logging

8. Jake is responsible for six Windows 2000 servers in his organization. He has noticed that lately there are multiple login attempts on the main Web server. Jake wants to log to a SQL server so that he can log to a separate server; he also wants to be able to log massive amounts of events. What can Jake do to log all these events to a large SQL database on a separate server so that he can eliminate the threat of being exploited by a possible attacker?

A. ODBC logging

B. NCSA Common Log File format

C. W3C Extended Log File format

D. THD Logging format

Windows Auditing Tools

9. Stan is the network administrator responsible for 10 Windows 2000 servers and 400 Windows XP Professional workstations, all separated geographically across four sites. Stan is auditing all 10 servers and needs a way to parse all Security Logs very quickly from the command prompt. What tool from the list that follows could he use?

A. URLSCAN

B. Dumpel

C. EVENTSWP

D. Net Event

10. Erika is the systems engineer for the London central hub location. The hub location contains over 50 Windows 2000 servers, but only three of them are accessible through the Internet. These three servers are responsible for Web-based services such as FTP and HTTP. All the rest of the servers (all 47 of them) are located within the private LAN protected by a firewall. These 47 servers are used for

applications, file, print, and database purposes. Erika wants to parse all the servers for Event Log information. She wants to collect all the default logs found on all Windows 2000 systems as well as the FRS, DNS, and Active Directory logs as well. Erika has Dumpel.exe and is having problems using it to parse all the logs. What is the problem Erika is running into?

A. Erika is using dumpel.exe and it is corrupted. She needs a new version, and then it will work.

B. Erika is using dumpel.exe and it is never going to be able to parse anything but the default System Logs. It will not parse the FRS, DNS, and ADS logs.

C. Erika is using dumpel.exe and it is not going to work without net1.exe. A batch file must be created to run the tool accurately.

D. Erika is using dumpel.exe and it is not going to work without the use of the Task Scheduler or AT command.

11. Jake is responsible for six Windows 2000 servers in his organization. Jake has been made aware that there could be a problem with his DNS servers on the DMZ. He is concerned that a Zone Transfer attack or DNS poisoning could be attempted. He wants to use a tool that will parse all the DNS and Security Logs. What tool from the list that follows will allow Jake to quickly get all the DNS and Security Logs from his DNS servers?

A. Dumpel

B. EventCombMT

C. EVENTSWP

D. UrlScan

12. Rob is the network engineer responsible for 10 Windows 2000 servers and 400 Windows XP Professional workstations, all separated geographically across four sites. Rob is responsible for getting all Event Logs in all servers across the network. One issue is that getting the Active Directory logs is essential to trying to find NTDS directory shutdowns. What tool should Rob use to get this information?

A. EventCombMT

B. Dumpel

C. EVENTSWP

D. UrlScan

13. Peter is the network administrator responsible for performing security audits on Windows 2000 servers. Peter has a new assignment: to use the EventCombMT utility to search specifically for event ID number 682 because some kind of Terminal Server access problem is being reported. From the answers that follow, is the solution with the EventCombMT utility possible?

   A. Yes, you can use the EventCombMT utility, but it will only search for one ID at a time.

   B. No, you can't use the EventCombMT utility, because it will not search by a single ID, only in groups.

   C. Yes, you can use the EventCombMT utility to search for one or multiple IDs at a time.

   D. No, you can't use the EventCombMT utility, because it doesn't search for specific event IDs.

14. EventCombMT allows you to scan and filter through many types of events. Jane, a network administrator, needs to find out what EventCombMT will filter for her. From the options that follow, what can she filter through using EventCombMT? (Choose all that apply.)

   A. Error

   B. Informational

   C. Warning

   D. Critical

15. Sandra is a systems engineer who has been asked to search and parse Event Viewer Logs. She has acquired and will use the Dumpel utility. Using Dumpel, what option could Sandra use to specify the filename for the output file?

   A. -f

   B. -s

   C. -q

   D. -g

Self Test Quick Answer Key

For complete questions, answers, and epxlanations to the Self Test questions in this chapter as well as the other chapters in this book, see the Self Test Appendix.

1. **B**
2. **A, B, C, D**
3. **A, B, C**
4. **A**
5. **D**
6. **A**
7. **C**
8. **A**
9. **B**
10. **B**
11. **B**
12. **A**
13. **C**
14. **A, B, C**
15. **A**

Chapter 11

MCSE/MCSA 70-214

Responding to and Recovering from Security Breaches

Exam Objectives in this Chapter:

6.3 Respond to security incidents. Incidents include hackers, viruses, denial-of-service (DoS) attacks, natural disasters, and maintaning chains of evidence.

6.3.1 Isolate and contain the incident. Considerations include preserving the chain of evidence.

6.3.2 Implement counter measures.

6.3.3 Restore services.

☑ Summary of Exam Objectives

☑ Exam Objectives Fast Track

☑ Exam Objectives Frequently Asked Questions

☑ Self Test

☑ Self Test Quick Answer Key

Introduction

In Chapter 10 we discussed the process of auditing and trying to find breaches on your system. We went over exactly what you need to do to try to catch an attack or exploit with the tools Microsoft provides you in Windows 2000. In this chapter we look at actual security incidents and how to respond to them, with a focus on the material that you can expect to see on the exam.

In a Microsoft world, you must get used to dealing with attacks, bugs, viruses, worms, and any other type of incident. Not only is Microsoft the leading provider of services worldwide, it is also the most exploited as well. This is not necessarily because Microsoft provides poorly designed software; it is because Microsoft products are the most used and distributed products in the world. Solaris, Linux, Apple, Novell, and Cisco IOS code all suffer the same types of problems, but Microsoft is the most widely used and therefore the most widely attacked. It also doesn't help that most of the attacks on Microsoft systems exploit the same areas over and over again, such as Visual Basic scripting and macro hacks, unchecked buffers and buffer overflows, and massive world-wide exploitation of system bugs and weaknesses not fixed by service packs or hotfixes. These factors, taken together, can cause any systems administrator massive headaches when his or her network is hacked. This being said, it is very important that you know not only how to audit your systems but to be aware of issues waiting around the corner in the form of malware and DoS attacks (the most common on a Microsoft network).

We end this chapter with a very in-depth look at how to perform solid incident response quickly, efficiently, and effectively.

Exam Warning

Make sure that you are very comfortable with working through incident response issues for the exam. This chapter highlights what you need to know to work through incident-related questions; make sure you study this topic very thoroughly.

Security Incidents

Let's finish this book with some specific information on security, incidents, and problems you could have on your Microsoft network. In considering security incidents, you should ask yourself these questions:

- In your current environment, do you have an incident response plan? In other words, will your staff become raving stressed-out lunatics filled with anxiety and anguish when your next incident occurs, or do they know the proper procedure to follow to resolve security incidents?

- If you do have a plan of action, is your current staff up to the challenge? Can they handle the problems that occur, and are they trained to deal with any problem in a systematic way?

- Can you lead your staff, or do you have a team leader who can guide everyone, during the next incident as it occurs?

If you answer "No" to any of these questions, you could be in trouble sometime in the near future. Let's look at how to deal with each incident and what you need to be responsible for.

NOTE

If you want to become the know-it-all guru of dealing with security incident response, you need to visit the Cert.org site for more information on the subject. CERT will show you how to build a plan for a Computer Security Incident Response Team (CSIRT) in detail. Check out the site at www.cert.org/csirts/csirt_faq.html.

Other sites you can visit for more information are CERT (www.cert.org) and FIRST (www.first.org).

Minimizing Security Incidents

One of the most pertinent strategies you can implement is to minimize the number and severity of security incidents. One of the biggest issues for security infrastructures is the fact that not a great deal of effort is put into the possibility that there could be a problem. In fact, most times when we come to an organization to resolve issues, the company's IT organization hasn't given security much thought. For that reason, many security problems linger in the darkness of the networks in question. It is your role as a security analyst to truly look at these possible problems and attack them head-on, one by one, in a process of identification and elimination, so that you can minimize the problems before they occur.

Damage & Defense...

Proactive versus Reactive Security Management

Too often, security problems are only dealt with as they occur. Without naming names (for legal purposes), we came in contact with an enterprise that worked in reactive mode, only dealing with issues as they arose. Reacting to problems as they come up never really fixes anything. Doing so is similar to placing a Band-Aid on a chest wound. You never fully learn what the initial underlying problems were, and worse, you never have the chance to head potential problems off at the pass. Consider the differences between reactive and proactive management:

- **Reactive management** When a problem occurs, you simply react to it. The problem was never truly rooted out before it occurred; you might even have prevented the problem had you or your staff identified the possibility that it could occur. This management style is commonly nicknamed *firefighting*.

- **Proactive management** With proactive thinking, you try to eliminate the *possibility* of the problem before it occurs in the first place. You strive to think of problems that *could* occur and implement safeguards to try to stop them before they do so.

You want to work proactively every day to eliminate problems before they occur. In a security sense, this strategy results in auditing of your systems and creating an incident response plan.

Because incidents do in fact occur (it's a fact of life), you need to train yourself to accurately deal with problems and incidents. On a Microsoft-based network, or any network for that matter, you should think of the following items, which we call a *top 10 incident prevention list*. This list will aid you in minimizing the impact, damage, and stress caused by any security incident that occurs:

1. **Create policies that are written down and backed by management** These can include a security policy, a disaster recovery policy, and a business continuity plan. Any plan you create needs to be written down, read by employees, backed by management, and updated constantly. Without these policies, you are missing the backbone of all security enforcement for your organization.

2. **Test everything** Now that you have plans and policies, do they work? In other words, if you have a disaster recovery policy that talks about utilizing a hot site, have you actually tried it? Is there a specific time frame in which you want to be operational again, and if so, have you tested or timed your recovery? Most

times the answer to these questions is "No." It is essential that you test all your plans and policies to make sure they work *before* disaster strikes.

3. **Audit and assess your network, systems, and staff on a constant basis** Do you know who is accessing your systems? Do you know when they are accessing systems? Do you know who exactly has administrative rights over your entire Active Directory? Who has been delegated rights? You need to know all these things. You need to audit your systems to make sure that you have control over what people can do on them. A good rule of thumb is to audit your critical systems on a weekly basis, at least. After you've done that for a few weeks, you can get an idea of how often you need to audit based on baselined preliminary activity.

4. **Verify your backup and restore solution** You should be aware of where backups are maintained, who can access them, and your procedures for data restoration and system recovery. Make sure that you regularly verify backups and media by selectively restoring data. If you don't have verifiable backups, why were you doing them in the first place?

5. **Implement defense in depth** If you think slapping up a firewall on the network is your key to security success, you are seriously mistaken and most likely your network is in grave danger. A firewall is probably one of the most important protections on a network, but it is by no means the only piece of the puzzle that you need to implement.

6. **Implement change management solutions** You need total control over your network and systems. As a security analyst responsible for your business's infrastructure security, prepare yourself now to bump heads and make enemies. Make sure that every change on the network is documented, and back it up with a backout plan. You would be surprised how many times incidents happen based on your own people making mistakes or covering things up.

7. **Security training is key to continued excellence** Establishing security-training programs for both IT staff and end users is essential to keep your networks safe. There is a danger in people knowing more than you might like them to, but that's the point. Educate your users and staff, but make sure you are on top of things as well. Some of the best security personnel worked their way up the ranks from all areas of networking, systems, support, and development.

8. **When you are completely locked down, do an independent audit** When you have all your systems to your liking, call in an independent auditor. Have an outside team come in and test your security. This is an important element of your security plan. If you know that a group of security auditors

couldn't get through your systems, you have done your job well. If they do get through, you'll gain some starting points for where you need to improve your security.

9. **Build an incident response plan** It is essential to create a plan in case everything falls apart. Let's say you lose a file server due to an attacker breaking into the system and deleting the contents of your hard disks. Now what? Make sure that you have a documented plan accessible by the right people (your team) when an incident does in fact occur.

10. **Create a CSIRT** A CSIRT is a group of people or a team that you build and give responsibilities for dealing with any security incident. Your CSIRT should consist of members whose duties are clearly defined to ensure that no area is left uncovered in your response. The link provided earlier in the chapter will aid you in building a CSIRT if you are interested in starting one.

TEST DAY TIP

The preceding list is a feature created for this book. It is not something you will have to master for the exam, but it helps you to think about what you need to do as a Microsoft Certified Professional and a security analyst working on Microsoft (or any other) technology. Because of the scenarios you will see on the exam, an understanding of the fundamentals of network security and analysis is expected; knowing this type of information will help you to figure out what a scenario question is asking. It will also help you to eliminate incorrect answers.

When reading over the top 10 list, you might start to think about new areas you might want to consider. That's good—it means that your thought processes have been stimulated and motivated toward network security.

One other idea you might want to think about is getting local law enforcement agencies involved when creating your incident response team for minimizing security risks. Remember, you are trying to minimize the *possibility* of security risks, and by having law enforcement visibly on your side, you could deter attackers from even thinking about trying something. This is especially true if you're trying to thwart internal threats, which are more common than external ones. When internal users think that a company might prosecute for damages resulting from an attack, you would be surprised at how quickly games and shenanigans on the network and its systems cease. It also helps to know how the law enforcement agencies operate so that when a problem does occur, you are "in the know" about their polices and procedures, which could speed things considerably.

Hackers

Hackers are not necessarily the cyberterrorists you think they are. The term *hacker* is actually an incorrect one when used to describe a cybercriminal. The media has come to use the term *hacker* in a negative way. You should be aware of the proper meaning of the word. A hacker is someone who constantly works on systems, tweaks them, and tries to exploit them for the benefit of higher knowledge and repair. The normal hacker is mainly a network and systems geek. You could say that all who were involved with this book are hackers in the purest sense of the word. You, the reader, could quite easily call yourself a hacker—hopefully the type who can be called a *good hacker*.

Bad hackers are those who learn tremendous amounts of information about systems and how to exploit them with tools already made or quite possibly with tools they make themselves. The difference between the two types of hacker is what they actually *do* with their knowledge. Someone who is highly malicious, with an intention to do bad things (such as take down Yahoo.com and cost the business a great deal of revenue) for any reason is not the hacker you want to be affiliated with. Even though that person is obviously very knowledgeable about systems and networks, their malicious side causes them to squander all their knowledge on pranks, mischief, and creating problems for people. These hackers simply want to crack someone else's system or otherwise use their expert programming or system and networking knowledge to cause disruption and harm.

Hacker Jargon

Now that you know what the term *hacker* truly means, you need to understand some of the different types of hackers:

- **Cracker** A *cracker* is another name for a bad hacker. A cracker is a malicious person out to do harm or cause problems. Most security folk prefer the work *cracker* to *hacker* to refer to such people.

- **Attacker** An *attacker* is another name for a hacker with bad intentions.

- **Script kiddie** A *script kiddie* is a malicious person who does not possess in-depth system skills. Script kiddies are knowledgeable to an extent, but they're not experienced enough to build their own hacking tools. Script kiddies do not have a deep understanding of the systems they are trying to exploit, but they are able to obtain tools that superior hackers have built. They use downloadable tools and scripts from the Internet and are very good at creating problems with them.

- **Click kiddie** A *click kiddie* is a step below the script kiddie. Click kiddies do not have a deep knowledge of systems, but they are able to use simple malicious tools that they can operate with a mouse pointer (hence the term *click* kiddie).

- **Black hat** A *black hat* is simply another name for a malicious hacker, cracker, or attacker—in other words, a bad guy.

- **White hat** A *white hat* is what you are striving to be, thus it is the most important term for you to know. A white hat is a security analyst who learns the techniques of crackers to better protect their own systems. A security analyst for a company is considered a white-hat hacker.

- **Gray hat** A *gray hat* falls between the white hat and the black hat. The black hat finds a vulnerability and exploits it with malicious intent. A white hat finds an exploit and notifies vendors of the problem. A gray hat finds the exploit and does not exploit it him- or herself, but unlike the white hat who takes the problem to the vendor, the gray hat makes the exploit publicly known so others can exploit it.

NOTE

No need to worry too much about these terms for the exam. We've included them here so you know what the lingo on the exam means. You can learn more about white-hat hacking at the following site: www.whitehats.com/.

Unfortunately, the terminology can become even more distorted. There are other terms out there, such as *phreakers*. Stay aware of the jargon because it will in fact become your language in all the meetings, conferences, and day-to-day work-related events you participate in.

You might be asking, "If this material is not on the exam, why is it in this book?" The reasons it is so important that you know this information are:

- Each term is used on the test within the scenarios. You are not going to have to repeat verbatim the difference between a good hacker and a bad hacker, but the term *hacker* is used, and you need to understand it.

- Once you are done studying for and have taken (and passed) the exam, you will have become an MCP, and more important, a well-rounded expert on working with Microsoft Network Security implementations. This will enable you to obtain a position in which "walking the walk" and "talking the talk" will become everyday expectations for you.

NOTE

Make no mistake—you should not be looking at this exam in any way other than wanting to be an expert at deploying security solutions on a Microsoft network. This desire is important to both passing the test and truly learning the trade. This being the case, our goal is to fully prepare yourself not just to pass an elective exam and earn the MCP title, but also to be able to appropriately act and function as a security analyst on a Microsoft network. Business clients, bosses, and peers will hold you in higher regard when you know your technical jargon as well as the technology behind it. Practice the fundamentals of knowing your trade (walking the walk), but also know how to intelligently discuss it with others (talking the talk).

Malware Issues

Knowledge of Microsoft systems and malware should go hand in hand. One of the most common problems with Microsoft-based systems on a network is that they are constantly attacked with malware. Malware, code that has been written specifically to be malicious, has existed for quite some time, even before the days of the Internet. Since the world has embraced the Internet, malware has become more common and has been able to spread more effectively than ever. In this section, we look at common forms of malware and its effects on not only systems in general, but Microsoft systems in particular.

For years Microsoft has been under the gun to tighten up its systems to make them less prone to attack. The many bugs inherent in Microsoft systems were such a problem in terms of security that not even a flurry of hotfixes, updates, and service packs could contain them. Microsoft listened to users' complaints, and things have changed. Some anti-Microsoft users will disagree with this statement, but the truth is that nowadays there are no more problems with Microsoft systems than with any other systems. In fact, Cisco and Linux systems have recently been found to be just as potentially susceptible to malware as Microsoft's systems are. Because of Microsoft's recent interest in improving security, successful malware attacks against Microsoft systems have in fact dropped dramatically in number. The important thing to remember here is that Microsoft *is* dealing with malware, bugs, and other problems, and for the exam you need to be aware of what the company has done to counter these problems.

In this section of the chapter we cover viruses, worms, and Trojan horses and look at how they affect Microsoft systems. When we discuss Trojan horses, we talk about some of the Trojans that you might expect to see or find as well as take a look at why they are so dangerous. We also talk about what happens to your systems if they are breached and cover DoS attacks in detail. In discussing these types of problems, we also take a look at some tools such as SMBdie and Back Orifice 2000.

Viruses

A computer *virus* is defined as a self-replicating computer program that interferes with a computer's hardware, operating system, or application software. Viruses are designed to replicate and to elude detection. Like any other computer program, a virus must be executed (loaded into the computer's memory) to function and then the computer must follow the virus's instructions. Those instructions are referred to as the *payload* of the virus. The payload can disrupt or change data files, display a message, or cause the operating system to malfunction.

Using that definition, let's explore exactly what a virus does and what its potential dangers are. Viruses spread when the instructions (executable code) that run programs are transferred from one computer to another. A virus can replicate by writing itself to diskettes, hard drives, legitimate computer programs, or even across networks. The positive side of a virus is that a computer attached to an infected computer network or one that downloads an infected program does not necessarily become infected. Remember, the code has to actually be *executed* before your machine can become infected. On the downside, chances are good that if you download a virus to your computer and do not execute it, the virus can probably trick your operating system into running the viral program. Other viruses have the ability to attach themselves to otherwise legitimate programs. This could occur when programs are created, opened, or even modified. Then when that program is run, so is the virus.

Some types of viruses can modify or interfere with your code. Unfortunately, developers can do little to prevent these attacks. A developer cannot write tighter code to protect against a virus. It is simply not possible. Developers can, however, detect modifications that have been made or perform a forensic investigation. They can also use encryption and other methods to protect your code from being accessed in the first place. Let's take a closer look at the six different categories that a virus could fall into and the definitions of each:

- **Parasitic** *Parasitic viruses* infect executable files or programs in the computer. This type of virus typically leaves the contents of the host file unchanged but appends to the host in such a way that the virus code is executed first.

- **Bootstrap sector** *Bootstrap sector viruses* live on the first portion of the hard disk, known as the *boot sector*. (This also applies to diskettes.) This virus replaces either the programs that store information about the disk's contents or the programs that start the computer. This type of virus is most commonly spread via the physical exchange of diskettes.

- **Multipartite** *Multipartite viruses* combine the functionalities of the parasitic virus and the bootstrap sector virus by infecting either files or boot sectors.

- **Companion** Instead of modifying an existing program, a *companion virus* creates a new program with the same name as an already existing legitimate program. It then tricks the OS into running the companion program.

- **Link** *Link viruses* function by modifying the way the OS finds a program, tricking it into first running the virus and then the desired program. This virus is especially dangerous because entire directories can be infected. Any executable program accessed within the directory will trigger the virus.

- **Data file:** A *data file virus* can open, manipulate, and close data files. Data file viruses are written in macro languages and automatically execute when the legitimate program is opened.

Worms

A *worm* is a self-replicating program that does not alter files but resides in active memory and duplicates itself by means of computer networks. Worms use the facilities of an operating system that are meant to be automatic and invisible to the user. It is common for worms to be noticed only when their uncontrolled replication consumes system resources, which then slows or halts other tasks. Some worms are not only self-replicating but also contain a malicious payload.

Worms can be transmitted in one of two ways: either by e-mail or through an Internet chat room. The most famous worm, the "I Love You" bug, originated in May 2000. The swiftness with which this bug moved caused migraines in more than a few network administrators. The "I Love You" worm was first detected in Europe and then in the United States. The initial analysis of the bug quickly determined that it was Visual Basic code that came as an e-mail attachment named Love-Letter-For-You.txt.vbs. When a user clicked the attachment, the virus used Microsoft Outlook to send the virus to everyone in the user's address book. The virus then contacted one of four Web pages in the Philippines. From the contacted Web page, a Trojan horse file, WIN-BUGSFIX.EXE, was then downloaded and collected usernames and passwords stored them on the user's system. It then sent all the usernames and passwords to an e-mail address. The bug quickly spread throughout the United States within 12 hours after it first manifested itself in Europe. The "I Love You" bug bit an estimated half million computers. This is the most legendary example of a worm-based malware attack.

Trojan Horses

A *Trojan horse* (or *Trojan* for short) closely resembles a virus but is actually in a category of its own. The Trojan horse is often referred to as the most elementary form of malicious code. A Trojan horse is used in the same manner as it was in Homer's Iliad; it is a program containing malicious code that appears on the outside to be harmless data or programming. It is most often disguised as something fun, such as a cool game such as elf bowling. The malicious program is hidden, and when called to perform its functionality, it can actually ruin your hard disk or disable your system by deleting or altering files. More vicious Trojans lie dormant until called on to perform evil deeds such as turning your system into one of thousands of "zombies" to partake in an Internetwide attack on an unsuspecting victim in a distributed DoS attack! (More on this subject later in the chapter.)

Not all Trojan horses are that malicious in content, but they can be, and the intent of the program is usually to cause as much damage as possible. One saving grace of a Trojan horse, if there is one, is that it does not propagate itself from one computer to another. Such self-replication is the charming way of the worm.

A common way for you to become the victim of a Trojan horse is for someone to send you e-mail with an attachment claiming to do something it can't or be something it is not. It could be a screen saver (most common with a *.scr extension) or a computer game, or even something as simple as a macro quiz. With the naked eye, it will most likely not be clear that anything untoward has happened when the attachment is launched or executed. However, the reality is that the Trojan has been installed (or initialized) on your system. In Figure 11.1, we purposely installed a Trojan on the system; it is hidden as a screen saver so you can see it running. We sent it to ourselves from a POP3 account so you could see what it would look like as an e-mail with an attachment.

Figure 11.1 Getting the Trojan Payload in an E-Mail

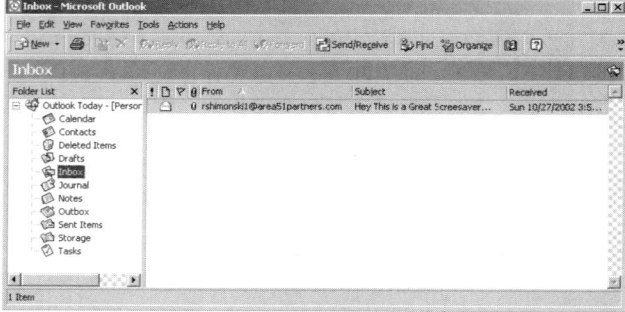

Unfortunately, time has not made people any wiser to the ways of predators on the Internet. We usually spend 5 minutes a week constructing an e-mail that we send to the everyone in the corporation we work for to kindly remind them that if they get e-mails from people they don't know (such as u903jlkf@spazmail.com), they probably should not open the message. If they do, we also educate them that they really are not supposed to download or install anything that came in over the Internet. Most people tell me that as long as you block and filter at the firewall, proxy, and e-mail level, you will be fine, but the people who say this obviously don't know users all that well. If there is a will, there is a way, and users will find it. There are quite a few workarounds to bypassing enterprise-level security, and for that reason, we still like to send out a "user education" e-mail alerting users to possible social engineering attacks or malware that can damage the machines at work. Most of these users forward the email home so they can protect their home machines, too. The point is, it's a great idea to make people aware of the dangers lurking in their e-mailbox.

As you saw in Figure 11.1, we received an e-mail from a potentially dangerous individual. Now, if we were smart, we would not open this e-mail, because it just looks like a malware attack. But what about Betty in Sales who just *loves* new screen savers? Chances are, she can't stop herself from opening this e-mail! So let's pretend for a minute that Betty does in fact open this e-mail.

Betty opens the e-mail and it says, "Double-click on the screen saver to see beautiful flowers and a waterfall." Betty double-clicks. Nothing happens. Because Betty figures it's a dud, she deletes the e-mail and forgets about it.

Figure 11.2 shows you what really happened behind the scenes. A nice piece of malware now resides on the system, waiting for its master (the attacker) to call on it to do its bidding.

Figure 11.2 An Executed, Running, and Able Agent of Destruction

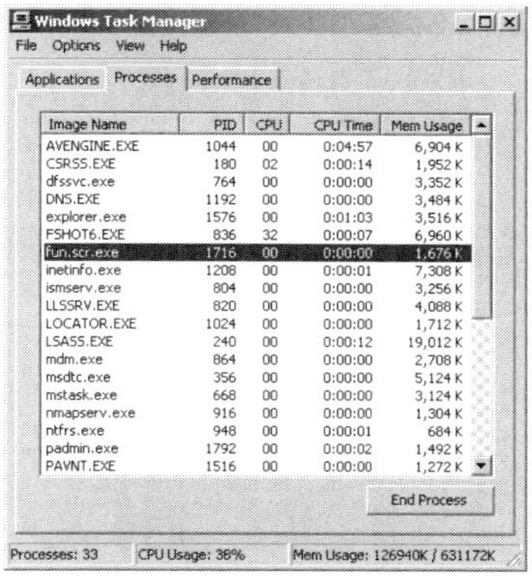

Problems like this happen all too often. Taking a hard look in your Task Manager, as shown in Figure 11.2, will show you running a server object for a tool such as Back Orifice—or any other available Trojan, for that matter. At this point, all that matters is that you are infected.

One way to protect your system from becoming infected in this manner is to have solid enterprisewide antivirus software running on your network and systems. This is a must. Most times, outbreaks and contagions can be eliminated that way. The problem is, you would be surprised at the number of companies that still think security is simply a buzzword to strike fear into the minds of nonsecurity personnel, or, worse yet, a means of attacking their bloated pocketbooks. Such attacks are not a game but a worldwide cancer that can consume your systems and infrastructure.

NOTE

On the Internet, we have found items such as HP Jet Direct cards on remote systems that are willing and able to accept my commands, NetBIOS-enabled systems telling me everything about those systems, and, worse, routers with nothing more than a password of *Cisco*. Be afraid, be very afraid.

To continue with our discussion of Microsoft security, let's look at a tweak you can perform that will make it obvious when a Trojan is in your e-mail or on your system. This is done by simply making sure that your system is configured not to hide anything from you. Because Microsoft feels that you shouldn't see things by default, it configures programs that end in specific extensions, such as .com, .exe, and .bat, to be hidden from you. For that reason, an .exe program won't show up if the Trojan is named fun.scr. In this case, the .exe would be hidden by default. If we looked at the file in the Task Manager, this would not in fact be the case. Most end users at least have enough common sense to know what an .exe file is, because they have probably installed software a few times at home. Figure 11.3 shows how to adjust your system so you can see almost anything that sneaks up on you. To make these adjustments, go to **Start | Programs | Accessories | Windows Explorer**. Once you have opened Windows Explorer, go to the **Tools** Menu and select **Folder Options**. Select the **View** tab, as shown in Figure 11.3. Click the radio button **Show hidden files and folders**, then click the **Apply to All Folders** button at the top of the screen.

Figure 11.3 Removing the Options to Have All Your Files Hidden from You

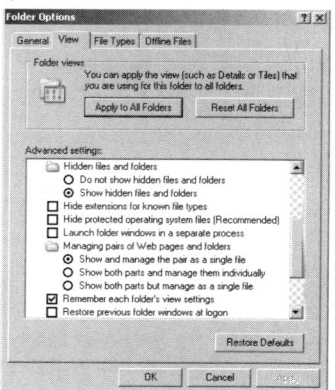

In general, this concept is something that you as a MCP should definitely master. It is integral to your system's security. Be aware that Trojans (and malware in general) can cause your systems a great deal of harm.

Now that we have looked at how Trojans make their way into your network and onto your systems, let's think about what could happen if they were not caught. What makes this type of attack scary is that it contains the possibility that it is a remote control program that could be used to attack or take over your system. After you have launched this attachment, anyone who uses the Trojan horse as a remote server can now connect to your computer. Hackers have advanced tools to determine what systems are running remote control Trojans. After using a specially designed port scanner to find your system, all your files are open to that hacker. Two common Trojan horse remote control programs are Back Orifice and NetBus.

Trojan Awareness

A Trojan can cause massive damage to you and your systems and, worse yet, could turn your system into a virtual killing machine as well! Let's look at Back Orifice specifically so we can highlight the reasons that a tool like this can get ugly if it is installed on your systems.

Back Orifice consists of two key pieces: a client application and a server application. Back Orifice works like this: The client application runs on one machine and the server application runs on a different machine. The client application connects to another machine using the server application. The confusing part here is the fact that the server is what is installed on the victim. Many people confuse this because it doesn't seem logical, but that's how it works. The only way for the server application of Back Orifice to be installed on a machine is for it to be deliberately installed. Obviously, the Trojan does not come with a default installation of Windows 2000, so the attacker must find a way to get the victim to install it. Think of our discussion of how Betty installed that beautiful screen saver that was obviously (to you, if not to her) the BO2K.exe server. In Figure 11.4 you can see the server configuration object configured with snap-ins.

Figure 11.4 Working with the BO2K Server Configuration

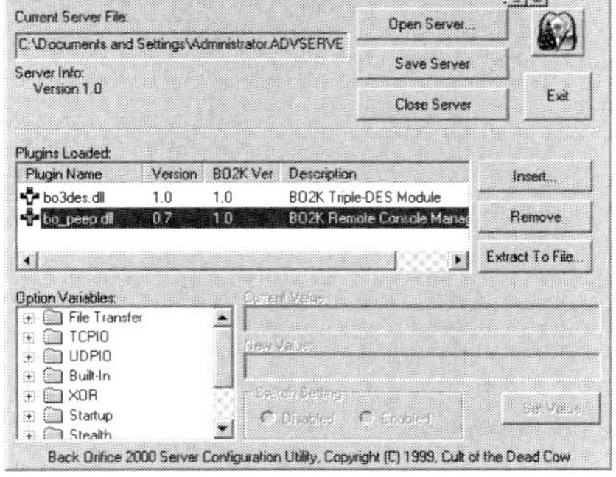

Newer versions of the server executable are downright sneaky. The executables don't show up, because they are transparent. This is an evolving tool—evolving into total stealth mode for any attacker to take advantage of your systems. You really need to be aware of not only this tool but also any Trojan like it. BO2K just happens to be one of the most popular and well known. Figure 11.5 shows you that the tool is highly configurable and intuitive. Knowledge of C++ programming and shell scripting is not needed here! This makes it one of the script kiddies' favorite tools to deploy and use to cause mischief.

Figure 11.5 Adding Servers to the Server List

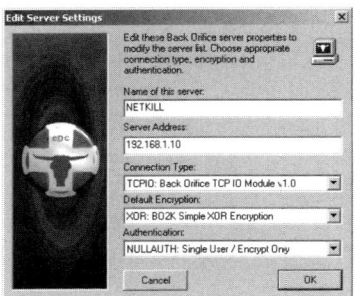

The attacker either has to install the server application on the target machine him- or herself or trick the user of the target machine into doing so—it's more likely that it will be a trick. This is the reason that the server application (BO2K.exe) is commonly disguised as a Trojan horse. After the server application has been installed, the client machine can transfer files to and from the target machine, execute an application on the target machine, restart or lock up the target machine, and log keystrokes from the target machine. All these operations are of value to a hacker.

The server application is a single executable file, just over 122KB in size. The application creates a copy of itself in the Windows system directory and adds a value containing its filename to the Windows Registry under the key:

HKEY_LOCAL_MACHINE\SOFTWARE\Microsoft\Windows\CurrentVersion\RunServices

The specific Registry value that points to the server application is configurable. That way, the server application always starts whenever Windows starts, so it is always functioning. One additional benefit of Back Orifice is that the application will not appear in the Windows task list, rendering it invisible to the naked eye. After first being initialized, it does its owner a favor and drops out of sight. Sneaky, huh?

Another common remote control Trojan horse is named the *Subseven* Trojan. This Trojan is also sent as an e-mail attachment, and after it is executed, it can display a customized message that is intended to mislead the victim. This particular program allows someone to have nearly full control of a victim's computer with the ability to delete folders and/or files. It also uses a function that displays something like a continuous screen cam, which allows the hacker to see screen shots from the victim's computer.

In general, be aware of the types of malware and how they can get on your systems. For the exam, be aware of the general malware concepts. In everyday system security, make sure that you are very aware of the damage that malware can cause your Microsoft systems.

Notes from the Underground…

Back Orifice

The Back Orifice Trojan horse server creates hell for any network, but it takes a little network knowledge to get it operational. The makers of Back Orifice, Cult of the Dead Cow (CDC, whose logo is shown in Figure 11.6), made the tool to exploit the Windows-based operating system, plain and simple, with the possible intent of it being a useful tool. Many could argue in the days of Back Orifice's inception that it was nothing more than a remote access tool, but if you think about the tool's functionality and where it came from, it was more than merely a tool for remote access—it was a wakeup call to Microsoft that its systems were just as susceptible to UNIX-based Root Kit type of applications. All it took was a little know-how and the tool, and attackers were in business.

Figure 11.6 The Logo of Cult of the Dead Cow, Makers of Back Orifice

There are some limitations, though. Possibly the two most critical limitations to the Back Orifice Trojan horse are that the attacker must know the IP address of the target machine and that there cannot be a firewall between the target machine and the attacker. A firewall makes it virtually impossible for the two machines to communicate, most likely because the firewall is blocking a port that the B02K Trojan would be operational on. Newer versions of the tool are known to operate on a wider range of ports, but that goes back to our initial discussion on how most companies haven't invested in their networks' security, nor do they have people on staff who know this information. That's really where the problem stems from. As you can see in Figure 11.7, this is not

Continued

a cheesy tool—it's a GUI-based hacking nightmare. It even has wizards that walk you through initial configuration. How can it get easier than that?

Figure 11.7 The Back Orifice Configuration Wizard

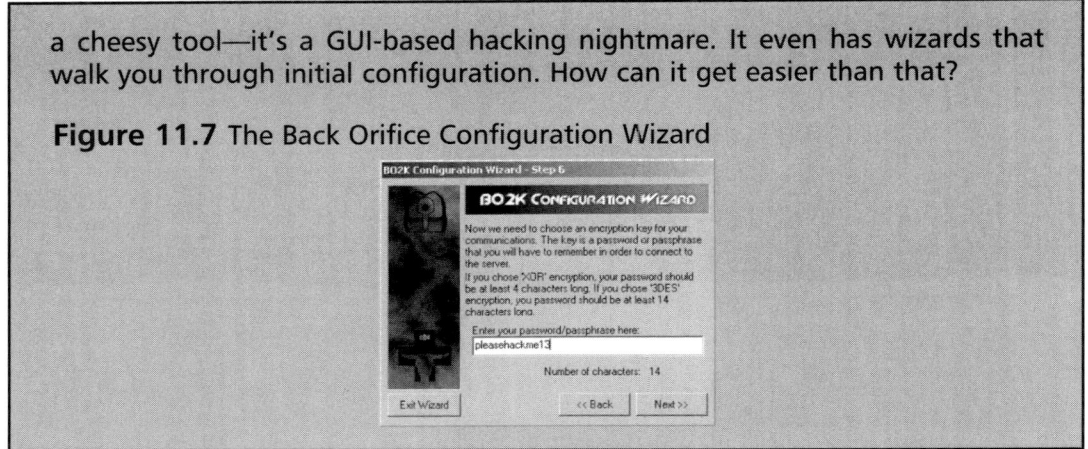

Denial of Service

In this section we cover DoS attacks and their distributed form, the DDoS. DDoS stands for *distributed denial of service*. A DoS attack is simply the denial of available network and systems services from clients by an attacker with malicious intent. This attack is usually launched from a single system. The distributed form of the attack (DDoS) involves using many systems to carry out the same attack, thereby making it a stronger attack coming from many sources instead of just one.

To understand a DDoS attack and its consequences, we first need to grasp the fundamentals of DoS attacks. The progression from understanding DoS to DDoS is quite elementary, although the distinction between the two is important. Given its name, it should not come as a surprise that a DoS attack is aimed squarely at ensuring that the service a computing infrastructure usually delivers is negatively affected in some way. This type of attack does not involve breaking into the target system. Usually a successful DoS attack reduces the quality of the service delivered by some measurable degree, often to the point where the target infrastructure of the DoS attack cannot deliver a service at all.

A common perception is that the target of a DoS attack is a server, but this is not always the case. The fundamental objective of a DoS attack is to degrade service, whether it be hosted by a single server or delivered by an entire network infrastructure.

A DoS attack attempts to reduce a site's ability to service clients, whether physical users or logical entities such as other computer systems. This goal can be achieved by either overloading the ability of the target network or server to handle incoming traffic or by sending network packets that cause target systems and networks to behave unpredictably. Unfortunately for the administrator, unpredictable behavior usually translates into a hung or crashed system.

Numerous forms of DoS attack exist, some of which can be difficult to detect or deflect. Within weeks or months of the appearance of a new attack, subtle copycat variations along the same theme begin appearing elsewhere. By this stage, defenses be deployed for the primary attack as well as its more distant cousins.

Many DoS attacks take place across a network, with the perpetrator seeking to take advantage of the lack of integrated security within the current iteration of Internet Protocol (IP), IP version 4 (IPv4). Hackers are fully aware that security considerations have been passed on to higher-level protocols and applications. An attempt to rectify this problem has resulted in IP version 6 (IPv6), which includes a means of validating the source of packets and their integrity using an authentication header. You don't need IPv6 to implement simple AH, but it is made easier in this version of the IP protocol. Although the continuing improvement of IP is critical, it does not resolve today's problems, because IPv6 is not in widespread use.

DoS attacks not only originate from remote systems, they are also local to the machine. Local DoS attacks are generally easier to locate and rectify because the parameters of the problem space are well defined (local to the host). A common example of a local-based DoS attack includes fork bombs that repeatedly spawn processes to consume system resources.

Although DoS attacks do not in themselves generate a risk to confidential or sensitive data, they can act as an effective tool to mask other, more intrusive activities that could take place simultaneously. Although administrators and security officers attempt to rectify what they perceive to be the main problem, the real penetration could be happening elsewhere. In the confusion and chaos that accompanies system crashes and integrity breaches, experienced hackers can slip in undetected.

The financial and publicity implications of an effective DoS attack are hard to measure—at best they are embarrassing and at worst, a deathblow. In the world of e-commerce, a customer's allegiance is fleeting. If a site is inaccessible or unresponsive, an alternate virtual shop front is only a few clicks away. Companies reliant on Internet traffic and e-purchases are at particular risk from DoS and DDoS attacks. The Web site is the engine that drives e-commerce, and customers are won or lost on the basis of the site's availability and speed. A hacker, regardless of motive, knows that the real place to hurt an e-business is to affect its Internet presence in some way. Unfortunately, DoS attacks can be an efficient means of achieving this end. The next sections cover two elemental types of DoS attacks: resource consumption attacks (such as SYN flood attacks and amplification attacks) and malformed packet attacks. SYN is the bit setting for TCP and stands for *synchronize*, when a system is doing a three-way handshake to establish communications with another system.

In Exercise 11.01 we look at performing a DoS attack on a Windows 2000 server with a tool called SMBdie. This exercise shows you how easy it is for a script kiddie to render your servers completely unusable with the click of a mouse.

> **Notes from the Underground...**
>
> ### BSOD with SMBdie
>
> So, you want to truly create some mischief? Of course you don't, because of your white-hat status, but that won't stop all the kiddies on the network from playing games with *you*! If you start seeing your servers *blue screen*—which occurs when you see only the BSOD, or *blue screen of death*—without reason, you should be aware of some of the downloadable click-kiddie "aggravation-ware" that is freely available on the Internet! Yes, you too can download SMBdie, the Windows-based operating system crasher we examine in Exercise 11.01. Just run an Internet search on it and there it is. This tool, when executed on a network, provides the attacker with a way to send specially crafted packets to your systems to crash them. This is, of course, the very nature of a DoS attack; if the servers aren't up and serving, no service is provided to your network clients. Fortunately for you, good enterprise-level antivirus software will find and quarantine this little monster for you. The problem is, you have to ensure that every device on the network has antivirus software on it. Test this theory by sneaking into a network closet with some open hub ports and a laptop. Within minutes, the servers are down. As an MCP and a white-hat security analyst, you must be aware of problems such as this one.

EXERCISE 11.01

PERFORMING A DOS WITH SMBDIE

1. Download the SMBdie tool by either searching for it on the Internet or from the following link: http://packetstorm.decepticons.org/filedesc/SMBdie.zip.html.
2. Once you open the tool, you can run it as is. Simply double-click the executable to use the tool. (You might want to turn off your antivirus software because it could quarantine the tool.)
3. Enter the IP address of the system you want to launch the attack on in the **Computer (IP address)** field of the tool, as shown in Figure 11.8.
4. Enter the NetBIOS name of the system you want to launch the attack on in the **NETBIOS name** field, as shown in Figure 11.8.

Figure 11.8 Using the SMBdie Tool

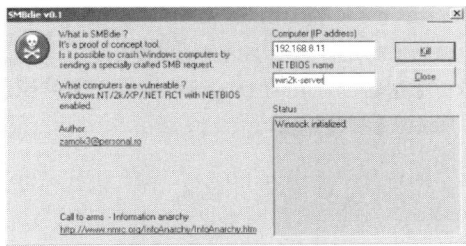

5. Once you have added all appropriate information, launch the attack by clicking the **Kill** button. That's it. You will see the server on which you launch the attack via a screen dump (BSOD).

To continue our discussion of DoS, we need to look at the resources on your system and how Trojans and attackers executing and launching attacks can eat up all the resources on your servers. Computing resources are by their very nature finite (although we wish it could be otherwise!). Administrators around the world bemoan the fact that their infrastructure lacks network bandwidth, CPU cycles, RAM, and secondary storage. Invariably the lack of these resources leads to some form of service degradation that the computing infrastructure delivers to the clients. The reality of having finite resources is highlighted even further when an attack is orchestrated to consume these precious resources.

The consumption of resources (and in this instance, bandwidth is considered a resource) involves the reduction of available resources, whatever their nature, using a directed attack. One of the more common forms of DoS attack targets network bandwidth. In particular, Internet connections and the supporting devices are a prime target of this type of attack due to their limited bandwidth and visibility to the rest of the Internet community. Very few businesses are in the fortunate position of having too much Internet bandwidth. (Does such a thing exist?) When a business relies on the ability to service client requests quickly and efficiently, a bandwidth consumption attack can drive home how effectively that bandwidth can be used to bring the company to its knees.

Launching a Distributed DoS

DDoS attacks advance the DoS conundrum one more painful step forward. DoS attacks have evolved beyond single-tier (SYN flood) attacks, in which the attack comes from one source, and two-tier (Smurf) attacks, where you have redirection of attacks. Modern attack methodologies have now embraced the world of distributed multitier computing. One of the significant differences in methodology of a DDoS attack is that it consists of two distinct phases. During the first phase, the perpetrator compromises computers scattered across the Internet and installs specialized software on these hosts to aid in the attack. In the second phase, the compromised hosts, referred to as *zombies,* are then instructed through intermediaries (called *masters*) to commence the attack. In Figure 11.9 we look at the simplified explanation of a DDoS attack, which generally follows this pattern:

1. The cracker plans his or her attack. The first step is to recruit zombies to do the dirty work.
2. The cracker then crafts a Trojan (like the one we looked at earlier) that can be planted on unsuspecting machines. E-mails are sent and machines are infected; once infected, these machines are recruited into the zombie horde.
3. The cracker plans an attack once the army has been built. An unsuspecting victim site is chosen. In our example scenario, www.hackme.com is the unlucky site.
4. The cracker launches a flood of traffic to hackme.com, which is so flooded with bogus traffic from hundreds of machines that it can't serve up requests for any real visitors to the site. This attack can vary from SYN floods to pings of death; it doesn't matter what the attack is, the point is mapping out that this single person just planted all these Trojans, launched a massive attack, and sat back and watched it happen from the safety of his or her own home.

Figure 11.9 A View of Recruiting Zombies

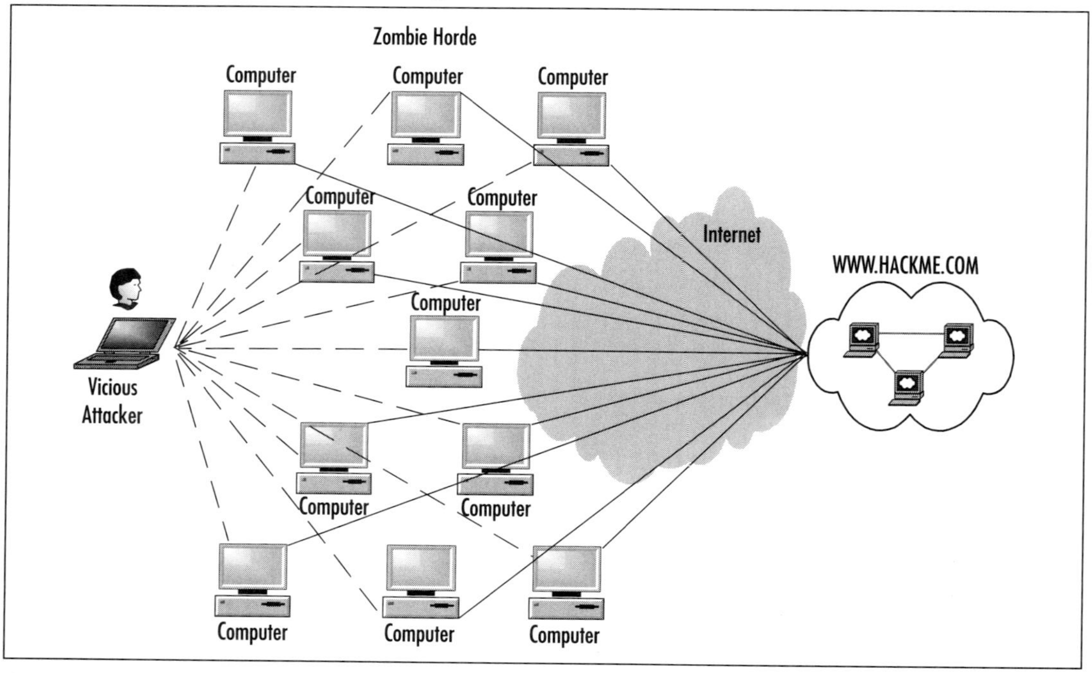

Thanks to the zombie horde, the cracker walks away free of any worry that he or she will be caught, because a packet never left the attacker's machine to attack hackme.com.

Hundreds, possibly thousands, of zombies can be co-opted into the attack by diligent hackers. Using the control software, each of these zombies can then be used to mount its own DoS attack on the target. The cumulative effect of the zombie attack is to either overwhelm the victim with massive amounts of traffic or exhaust resources such as connection queues.

Additionally, this type of attack obfuscates the source of the original attacker: the commander of the zombie hordes. The multitier model of DDoS attacks and their ability to spoof packets and to encrypt communications can make tracking down the real offender a tortuous process. Even worse, it's almost impossible to be able to defend against the attack, which can be a ping flood unless you use certain systems (such as Cisco equipment) that can actually notice an ICMP flood starting and shut itself down.

The command structure supporting a DDoS attack can be quite convoluted, and it can be difficult to determine a terminology that describes it clearly. One of the more understandable naming conventions for a DDoS attacks structure and the components involved is detailed here.

Software components involved in a DDoS attack include:

- **Client** The control software used by the hacker to launch attacks. The client directs command strings to its subordinate hosts.
- **Daemon** Software programs running on a zombie that receives incoming client command strings and acts on them accordingly. The daemon is the process responsible for actually implementing the attack detailed in the command strings.

Hosts involved in a DDoS attack include:

- **Master** A computer from which the client software is run.
- **Zombie** A subordinate host that runs the daemon process.
- **Target** The recipient of the attack.

In sum, as a Microsoft Certified Professional responsible for a network's security, you should be very aware of these issues. You could face massive problems and embarrassment when it is found out that your 30 IIS 5.0 Web servers took part in the activity of taking Yahoo.com out of service. It does happen if you are not aware of what your systems are doing.

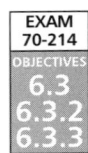

Incident Response

Incident response is the process of identifying and then responding to a problem as it occurs. For the Microsoft exam, you need to know the underlying concepts behind incident response. In this section of the chapter, we look at all the underpinnings of incident response, chain of custody, and how to deal with a problem that occurs on a Microsoft-based network.

Defining an Incident Response Plan

Now that you know what an incident response plan is, you need to know why it is important. Problems will occur, and if an incident does crop up, you and your staff need to know how to deal with it appropriately. You should consider the following actions and incorporate them into your plan:

- **Making an initial assessment** Making an initial assessment is critical to the plan's success. You need to know how to see an incident and assess whether it is an incident or not. Take initial steps to determine if you are dealing with an actual incident or a false positive. Your initial assessment should be very brief.

- **Communicating the incident** Communicating the incident is probably one of the most important steps in the process. Make sure that if an incident occurs, you get this fact to the leader of the team so that the incident plan can be put in action.

- **Containing the damage and then minimizing the risk** Containing the damage and minimizing the risk are critical to tackling an incident. For instance, if the incident in your initial assessment is a worm that is self-replicating across your network, you can contain the damage by unplugging the affected workstation from the switch or hub. This steps contains the damage and minimizes the risk.

- **Identifying the type and severity of the compromise** Identifying the type and severity of the compromise is essential to see the kind of resources you need to put on it. If you have a very large problem that costs the company millions (or worse yet, puts it out of business), you need to label it as such and give it a severity level such as High Priority. You should attempt to determine the exact nature of the attack. In addition, try to determine the attack point of origin—where exactly it is coming from. Directly after, try to identify the systems that have been compromised.

- **Protecting evidence** Protecting evidence is essential for a couple of reasons. For one, you never want to contaminate the evidence yourself. You might also want to make sure that someone else doesn't damage it intentionally.

- **Notifying external agencies** Notifying external agencies such as law enforcement is something you need to plan for. Hopefully it doesn't need to come to this, but if it does, you need to know how to deal with it and whom to contact. Most law enforcement agencies these days are either building or have built some form of cybercrimes division.

- **Recovering systems** Recovering systems is one of the most critical incident plan steps you can perform. After the incident; you have to get your systems back online.

- **Assessing incident damage and cost** Assessing incident damage and cost is something you need to do for your company. Especially with companies that are held publicly by stockholders, if a major loss occurs, this data will be very critical. This step needs to be done by a leader in the incident response team.

- **Reviewing the response and updating policies** Reviewing the response and updating policies on a constant or regular basis is something you need to implement as part of your strategy. Planning is no good unless it's up to date and well prepared. Updating a plan after an actual response is also a good idea so that you can assess the plan itself and how you might have been able to do things better.

NOTE

It is very important that you thoroughly test your incident response process before an incident occurs. Without thorough testing, you cannot be confident that the measures you have in place will be effective in responding to incidents.

Forensics

When certain incidents occur, you need to fix the immediate problem, but you will also need to investigate the person and cause behind it. Companies can find their Web sites or networks hacked by outside parties, receive threats via e-mail, or fall victim to any number of cybercrimes. In other cases, an administrator could discover that people internal to the organization are committing crimes or violating policies. Once systems are secure from further intrusion, you'll need to acquire information that's useful in finding and prosecuting the culprit responsible. Because any facts you acquire could become evidence in court, *computer forensics* must be used.

Computer forensics is the application of computer skills and investigation techniques for the purpose of acquiring evidence. It involves collecting, examining, preserving, and presenting evidence that is stored or transmitted in an electronic format. Because the purpose of computer forensics is its possible use in court, strict procedures must be followed for evidence to be admissible.

Even when an incident isn't criminal in nature, forensic procedures are important to follow. You could encounter incidents in which employees have violated policies. For example, an employee might have violated a company's acceptable use policy and spent considerable time viewing Internet pornography sites during work hours. Using forensic procedures to investigate the incident, you can create a tighter case against the employee. Because every action you took followed established guidelines and acquired evidence properly, the employee will have a more difficult time arguing against the facts. In addition, if during your investigation you find evidence of illegal activities (such as the employee possessing child pornography), the internal investigation could become a criminal one. Any actions you took in your investigation would be scrutinized, and anything you found could be used as evidence in court.

As we'll see in the sections that follow, a number of standards must be met to ensure that evidence isn't compromised and information has been obtained correctly. If forensic procedures aren't followed, judges may deem evidence inadmissible, defense lawyers may argue its validity, and the case could be damaged significantly. In many cases, the only evidence available is that which exists in a digital format. This could mean that the ability to punish an offender rests with *your* abilities to collect, examine, preserve, and present evidence.

Conceptual Knowledge

Computer forensics is a relatively new field that emerged in law enforcement in the 1980s. Since then, it has become an important investigative practice for both police and corporations. It uses scientific methods to retrieve and document evidence located on computers and other electronic devices. This retrieved information could be the only evidence available to convict a culprit, or it could enhance more traditional evidence obtained through other investigative techniques.

Computer forensics uses specialized tools and techniques that have been developed over the years and are accepted in court. Using these tools, you can retrieve digital evidence in a variety of ways. Electronic evidence could reside on hard disks and other devices, have been deleted so it is no longer visible through normal functions of the computer, or hidden in other ways. Although that evidence is invisible through normal channels, forensic software can reveal this data and restore it to a previous state.

TEST DAY TIP

Forensics has four basic components: Evidence must be *collected, examined, preserved,* and *presented*. The tasks involved in forensics either fall into one of these groups or can be performed across most or all of them. A constant element is the need for documentation so that every action in the investigation is recorded. When taking the exam, remember the four basic components and that everything *must* be documented.

Your Role

Law enforcement agencies perform investigations and gather evidence with the understanding that their goal is to find, arrest, prosecute, and convict a suspect, but the investigator's motivation isn't always clear in business cases. A network administrator's job is to ensure that the network gets back up and running after an incident; similarly, a Webmaster works to get an e-commerce site resuming business. Why would computer forensics be important to these jobs? The reason is that if a hacker takes down a Web site or network, he or she could continue to do so until they're caught. Identifying and dealing with threats is a cornerstone of security, whether those threats are electronic or physical in nature.

Even when police have been called in to investigate a crime, a number of company employees will be involved. Members of the IT staff assigned to an incident response team will generally be the first people to respond to the incident; they will then work with investigators to provide expertise and access to systems. Senior staff should be notified to deal with the effect of the incident and any resulting inability to conduct normal business.

If police aren't called in and the matter is to be handled internally, members of the incident response team will have a much broader range of roles. Not only will they deal with the initial response to the incident, they will conduct the investigation and provide evidence to an internal authority. This authority could be senior staff or, in the case of law enforcement, an internal affairs department. Even if no police are involved in the situation, the procedures used in the forensic examination should be the same.

When conducting the investigation, a person must be designated as being in charge of the scene. This person should be knowledgeable in forensics and directly involved in the investigation. In other words, just because the owner of the company is available, she should not be in charge if she's computer illiterate and/or unfamiliar with procedures. The person in charge should have authority to make final decisions on how the scene is secured and how evidence is searched, handled, and processed.

There are three specific roles that employees perform when conducting an investigation. The *first responder* is the first person to arrive at a crime scene. This doesn't mean the janitor who notices a server is making funny noises, but rather someone who has the knowledge and skill to deal with the incident. The first responder may be an officer, security personnel, a member of the IT staff or incident response team, or any number of other individuals. The first responder is responsible for identifying the scope of the crime scene, securing it, and preserving fragile evidence.

Identifying the scope of a crime scene refers to establishing its scale. What is affected, and where could evidence exist? When arriving on the scene, it is the first responder's role to identify the systems that have been affected, because these will be used to collect evidence. If these systems are located in one room, the scope of the crime scene is the room itself. If it is a single server in a closet, the closet is the crime scene. If a system of networked computers is involved, the crime scene could extend to several buildings.

Once the crime scene has been identified, the first responder must then establish a perimeter and protect it. Protecting the crime scene requires cordoning off the area where evidence resides. Until it is established what equipment can be excluded, everything in an area should be considered a possible source of evidence. This includes functioning and nonfunctioning workstations, laptops, servers, handheld personal digital assistants (PDAs), manuals, and anything else in the area of the crime. Until the scene has been processed, no one should be allowed to enter the area, and the first responder should document a list of people who were in the area at the time of the crime.

The first responder shouldn't touch anything within the crime scene. Depending on how the crime was committed, traditional forensics, such as fingerprint analysis, might also be used to determine the identity of the person behind the crime. In the course of the investigation, police could collect DNA, fingerprints, hair, fibers, or other physical evidence. In terms of digital evidence, too, it is important for the first responder not to touch anything, since doing so could alter, damage, or destroy data or other identifying factors.

Preserving fragile evidence is another important duty of the first responder. If a source of evidence, such as a server, is on, the first responder should take steps to preserve and document relevant data so it isn't lost. For example, a computer that could contain evidence might have been left on and have programs opened on the screen. If a power outage occurred, the computer would shut down and any unsaved information in memory would be lost. Photographing the screen or documenting what appeared on it would provide a record of what was displayed and could be used later as evidence.

When investigators arrive on the scene, it is important that the first responder provide as much information to them as possible. If the first responder touched anything, it is important that the investigator be notified so that information can be added to the report. Any of the first responder's observations should be mentioned because this information might provide insight into resolving the incident.

The investigator could be a member of law enforcement or the incident response team. If a member of the incident response team arrives first and collects some evidence, and the police arrive or are called later, it is important that the person in charge of the team hand over all evidence and information dealing with the incident. If more than one member of the team was involved in the collection of evidence, documentation dealing with what each person saw and did must be provided to the investigator.

A chain of command should be established when the person investigating the incident arrives at the scene. The investigator should make it clear that he or she is in charge so that he or she is told of important decisions that have been made. A chain of custody should also be established, documenting who handled or possessed evidence during the course of the investigation. Once the investigation begins, anyone handling the evidence is required to sign it in and out, so that there is a clear understanding and record of who possessed the evidence at any given time.

Even if the first responder has conducted an initial search for evidence, the investigator will need to establish what constitutes evidence and where it resides. If additional evidence is discovered, the perimeter securing the crime scene may be changed. Once the scene is established, the investigator will have crime scene technicians either begin to process the scene or perform the duties of a technician. The investigator or a designated person in charge remains at the scene until all evidence has been properly collected and transported.

Crime scene technicians are individuals who have been trained in computer forensics and have the knowledge, skills, and tools necessary to process a crime scene. The technician is responsible for preserving evidence and will take great efforts to do so. The technician may acquire data from a system's memory, make images of hard disks before shutting them down, and ensure that systems are properly shut down before transport. Before transporting, all evidence will be sealed in bags and/or tagged to identify it as particular pieces of evidence. The information identifying the evidence is added to a log so that a proper inventory of each piece exists. Evidence is further packaged to reduce the risk of damage, such as from electrostatic discharge or jostling during transport. Once transported, the evidence is then stored under lock and key to prevent tampering until such time that it can be properly examined and analyzed.

As you can see, the roles involved in an investigation have varying responsibilities and require special knowledge to perform properly. This section provides an overview of what's involved, but we still need to look at the specific tasks to understand how certain duties are carried out. Understanding these aspects of forensic procedure are not only vital to an investigation—you need to understand them for success in the exam.

Exam Warning

You need to understand the fundamentals of forensics for the exam. You must understand your role as a Microsoft Certified Professional and security analyst.

Chain of Custody

Because of the importance of evidence, it is essential that its continuity is maintained and documented. Toward this end, a *chain of custody* must be established to show how evidence made it from the crime scene to the courtroom. The chain of custody proves where a piece of evidence was at any given time and who was responsible for it. By documenting this information, you can establish that the integrity of your evidence wasn't compromised.

If the chain of custody is broken, it could be argued in court that the evidence fell into the wrong hands and might have been tampered with or other evidence substituted. This brings the value of evidence into question and could make it inadmissible in court. To avoid this situation, you must adhere to established policies and procedures dealing with the management of evidence.

Evidence management begins at the crime scene, where the evidence is bagged and/or tagged. When the crime scene is being processed, each piece of evidence should be sealed inside an *evidence bag*. An evidence bag is a sturdy bag with two-sided tape that allows it to be sealed shut. Once the bag is sealed, the only way to open it is to damage the bag, such as by ripping or cutting it open. The bag should then be marked or a tag should be affixed to it, showing the person who initially took it into custody. The tag provides such information as a number to identify the evidence, a case number (which shows the case with which the evidence is associated), the date and time the evidence was collected, and the name or badge number of the person taking it into custody.

Information on the tag is also written in an *evidence log*, which is a document that inventories all evidence collected in a case. In addition to the data available on the tag, the evidence log includes a description of each piece of evidence, serial numbers, identifying marks or numbers, and other information that's required by policy or local law.

The evidence log also provides a details of the chain of custody. This document will be used to describe who had possession of the evidence after it was initially tagged, transported, and locked in storage. To obtain possession of the evidence, a person needs to sign evidence in and out. Information is added to a chain of custody log to show who had possession of the evidence and for how long. The chain of custody log specifies the person's name, department, date, time, and other pertinent information.

In many cases, the investigator will follow the evidence from crime scene to court, documenting who else had possession along the way. Each time possession is transferred to another person, it is written in the log. For example, the log would show that the investigator had initial custody, while the next line in the log shows that a computer forensic examiner took ownership on a particular date and time. Once the forensic examination is complete, the next line in the log would show that the investigator again took custody. Even though custody is transferred back to the investigator, this fact is indicated in the log so that there is no confusion over who was responsible on any date or time.

Evidence Collection

Collection is a practice consisting of the identification, processing, and documentation of evidence. When collecting evidence, you start by identifying the evidence that is present and where it is located. For example, if someone broke into the server room and changed permissions on the server, the room and server would be where you would find evidence. When establishing this fact, you would secure the scene, preventing others from entering the area and accessing the evidence. If the area wasn't secured, suspects could enter the area and alter or corrupt evidence. For example, if fingerprints were being taken to determine who broke into the server room, someone merely touching the door and other items would distort any findings. Maybe the person left the fingerprints when he broke in, or maybe they were left when the crime scene was insecure? Such confusion can corrupt your attempt to find the culprit responsible for the crime.

Once you've identified the evidence that is present, you are then able to identify how the evidence can be recovered. Evidence on computers can be obtained in a variety of ways, from viewing log files to recovering the data with special software. If data recovery is required, you'll need to identify the operating system being used and/or the media used to store the evidence. Once you've determined this information, you can then decide on the methodology and tools needed to recover the data.

Processing the crime scene also requires preventing any data from being damaged or lost before it can be examined and recorded. This involves taking precautions mentioned in the section dealing with preservation of evidence. Someone should take photographs of the screen of the computer, so that any information displayed there can be analyzed at a later time. Photographs should also be taken of any other evidence and the scene itself. These pictures will provide a visual record that may also be presented as evidence.

Photographs should also be made of how the equipment is set up. When technicians have transported the equipment to a lab and are ready to begin examining it, they will need to set it up exactly as it was at the crime scene. After the case is completed, the original setup information could also be required if the equipment is returned to the owner. To ensure that the equipment is set up properly, photograph the front and back of the machine as it was found. Photographs or diagrams should be made, showing how cables and wires were attached.

It is important that you document everything possible. Identify all persons who were present at the crime scene previous to securing it or at the time of the incident. These people might be able to provide crucial information that they witnessed, or they could be suspects themselves. You should also document any comments that were made, anything you witnessed, and any actions that were performed.

When evidence is collected, it is important that each piece is tagged with an identifying number and that information about the evidence is added to a log. The evidence also needs to be bagged properly to preserve it. For example, hard disks are stored in antistatic bags to prevent damage and data corruption. Once placed in an antistatic bag, hard disks should then be placed in a sealed bag to ensure that no one can tamper with them. The evidence should then be placed in a locked storage facility so that access to the evidence can be properly controlled.

Head of the Class…

Forensic Procedures

Forensics is a science in which the examined evidence could identify or convict a culprit. Because of the weight this evidence could present in a trial or an internal investigation, you must ensure that the evidence hasn't been compromised in any way. If evidence is compromised, it can mean that someone who you're certain committed a crime cannot be convicted or an employee who threatened your company's security will go unpunished.

A commonality in forensics is practicing due care. You need to be extremely careful how evidence is handled and make sure that every action is documented and accountable. At no time should there be any confusion as to who had possession of evidence or what was done to that evidence during that time. By taking precautions to protect the data, you will ensure that it isn't compromised in any way.

Summary of Exam Objectives

In this chapter we covered a number of problems that might occur on a Microsoft-based network. When responding to and recovering from security breaches, you need to understand the types of attack incidents you are vulnerable to and what you can do to protect yourself from them.

We discussed security incidents in this chapter. In dealing with security incidents, one of the most pertinent strategies you can implement is one of minimizing the number and, of course, the severity of security incidents. You always want to ensure that you are limiting your exposure to incidents and have properly planned to deal with them. Another big issue related to security infrastructure is the fact that there is not a great deal of effort put into the possibility that there could be a problem. You have to plan for an attack and be prepared to deal with it after it has been tried—or worse, executed successfully.

Remember your terminology. There are many nicknames for malicious and nonmalicious security professionals. Crackers are people who perform malicious cybercrimes on systems with the purpose of doing harm or causing havoc. We looked at malware-based attacks, since they are so common on Microsoft networks.

A computer virus is a self-replicating computer program that interferes with a computer's hardware, operating system, or application software. Viruses are designed to replicate themselves and elude detection. Like any other computer program, a virus must be executed (loaded into the computer's memory) to function, and then the computer must follow the virus's instructions. Those instructions are referred to as the *payload* of the virus. A worm is a self-replicating program that does not alter files but resides in active memory and duplicates itself by means of computer networks. A Trojan horse (or Trojan, for short) closely resembles a virus but is actually in a category of its own. The Trojan horse is often referred to as the most elementary form of malicious code. Make sure that you are very familiar with these types of viruses for the exam.

We reviewed the fundamentals of DoS attacks and why they are so easy to perform but hard to defend against. We also covered the difference between a DoS attack and a DDoS attack and the components of a DDoS attack such as client, daemon, master, and zombie. We looked at the damage a tool like Back Orifice can do if it is not detected on your systems.

We tied up the chapter with a discussion on incident response—what to do when an incident occurs. We looked at the field of forensics, which combines investigative techniques and computer skills for the collection, examination, preservation, and presentation of evidence. Information acquired through forensic procedures can be used in the investigation of internal problems or for criminal or civil cases. Awareness should be promoted so that users in an organization know to contact the incident response team when incidents such as hacking occur and so management will support any investigations conducted by the team. Because any evidence acquired in an investigation may be used in court proceedings, it is vital that strict procedures be followed in any forensic investigation.

Exam Objectives Fast Track

Security Incidents

- ☑ One of the most pertinent strategies you can implement is one of minimizing the number and, of course, the severity of security incidents.

- ☑ One of the biggest issues related to security infrastructure is the fact that there is not a great deal of effort put into the possibility that there could be a problem.

- ☑ Hackers, also called crackers, are technically proficient people who perform malicious cybercrimes on systems with the purpose of doing harm or causing havoc.

Malware Issues

- ☑ A computer virus is a self-replicating computer program that interferes with a computer's hardware, operating system, or application software.

- ☑ Viruses are designed to replicate and elude detection. Like any other computer program, a virus must be executed (loaded into the computer's memory) to function, and then the computer must follow the virus's instructions. Those instructions are referred to as the *payload* of the virus.

- ☑ A worm is a self-replicating program that does not alter files but resides in active memory and duplicates itself by means of computer networks.

- ☑ A Trojan horse (or Trojan, for short) closely resembles a virus but is actually in a category of its own. The Trojan horse is often referred to as the most elementary form of malicious code.

Incident Response

- ☑ Incident response involves identifying and responding to a problem that has occurred.

- ☑ When certain incidents occur, you might need to fix the immediate problem as well as investigating the person behind it.

- ☑ Because of the importance of evidence, it is essential that its continuity be maintained and documented.

- ☑ A chain of custody must be established to show how evidence made it from the crime scene to the courtroom. The chain of custody proves where a piece of evidence was at any given time and who was responsible for it. By documenting this information, you can establish that the integrity of the evidence wasn't compromised.

- ☑ Collection is a practice consisting of the identification, processing, and documentation of evidence. When collecting evidence, you start by identifying the evidence that is present and where it is located.

Exam Objectives Frequently Asked Questions

The following Frequently Asked Questions, answered by the authors of this book, are designed to both measure your understanding of the Exam Objectives presented in this chapter, and to assist you with real-life implementation of these concepts.

Q: As a Microsoft Certifed Professional, I am concerned that I am not protecting my systems to the best of my ability. What do you suggest I do besides installing antivirus software on my systems?

A: You need to make sure that you update your system with hotfixes and service packs. In addition, make sure that you are trying to block malware from entering your network in the first place. You can also educate your users so that they are aware of the implications of downloading malware onto their machines.

Q: I am bothered by the fact that there are so many freely available tools on the Internet that users in my company can get to. What can I do to protect myself and my organization?

A: Quite simply, you can run the latest antivirus software on your systems. This will find most Trojans and quarantine them from your systems. You can also block access to a lot of Web sites that are inappropriate to the business climate. The latter step is easy for users to get around, though, so your best bet is have updated antivirus software on your systems.

Q: I am confused about the whole hacker thing. Can you please explain the correct terminology?

A: This is a very common issue with new security analysts. Hackers, also called crackers, are knowledgeable people who perform malicious cybercrimes on systems with the purpose of doing harm or causing havoc. The true definition of the term *hacker* is simply a person who really likes to tinker with computer systems; when this activity gets malicious, the term *hacker* acquires a bad meaning.

Q: What exactly is the difference among a virus, a worm, and a Trojan horse? I thought they were all the same thing. What are the main differences among them?

A: When discussing a virus, you should remember that it is really just a simple program written to exploit something on your system. You generally have to invite the virus onto your system, and when you do, it usually is contained on the system unless you spread it yourself. A worm is much more devious. Remember that a worm does the same thing as a virus except it can self-replicate all over your network. A Trojan horse is the same as a virus or a worm, except the Trojan is usually a virus or worm hidden within something else so that you are deceived into running the program on your system.

Q: I am new to incident response and am fairly confused about what a chain of custody is. Can you shed some light on it so that I know what it is and why I need to consider it?

A: A chain of custody must be established to show how evidence made it from a crime scene to the courtroom. The chain of custody proves where a piece of evidence was at any given time and who was responsible for it. You need to consider keeping a chain of custody because if you need to present evidence in a court of law, you will have the documentation to prove that nothing went wrong with the evidence you collected and that it wasn't tampered with.

Self Test

A Quick Answer Key follows the Self Test questions. For complete questions, answers, and epxlanations to the Self Test questions in this chapter as well as the other chapters in this book, see the Self Test Appendix.

Security Incidents

1. Jake is responsible for six Windows 2000 servers in his organization. Jake has noticed that lately there are multiple login attempts on the main file server at about 8:00 P.M., which is after hours. How should Jake classify this issue when he brings this problem up with Sara, his CIO?

    A. Call the CEO immediately because the company might be expected to lose money very shortly.

    B. Bring it up as a hacker breaking into the system. It's after hours, so it must be a hacker doing it.

    C. Bring it up as a possible security incident, but more analysis needs to be done quickly to make sure.

    D. Ignore it; there are always login attempts on the server at this time.

2. Stan is the network administrator responsible for 10 Windows 2000 servers and 400 Windows XP Professional workstations, all separated geographically across four sites. Stan would like to implement two new firewalls, auditing. and enforcement of desktop lockdown procedures. What is the first step Stan should accomplish from the following?

    A. Create policies that are written down and backed by management.

    B. Implement the firewalls only; he needs management's approval to do auditing and lockdown of desktops.

    C. Lock down the desktops and have the network engineer work on the firewalls.

    D. Lock down the servers, and don't worry about the desktops; they will be okay if the servers are addressed.

3. Stacy is the systems engineer for the London central hub location. The hub location contains over 50 Windows 2000 servers, but only three of them are accessible through the Internet. These three servers are responsible for Web-based services such as FTP and HTTP. All the rest of the servers (all 47 of them) are located within the private LAN protected by a firewall. These 47 servers are used for applications, file, print, and database purposes. Stacy is responsible for making sure that the nightly backups are completed. What is the most important thing Stacy should think about so she can avoid a massive problem when or if a security incident arises?

    A. Having an operational hot site so that data is never lost

    B. Implementing a 99.999 percent uptime policy so that she only loses a few hours downtime each year

    C. Verifying her backup and restore solution

    D. Making sure that she uses DXT2 tapes instead of DLT or DAT tapes for extra redundancy

4. Peter is the administrator for a large Windows 2000 network infrastructure. He is responsible for 10 IIS servers, two Exchange servers, and 20 file and print servers. All 32 servers are internal to the LAN and serve as application, e-mail, file, and print servers for over 700 clients in five separate locations. Every week, Peter has a few changes he needs to make on the systems he administers. To minimize the possibility of an incident, what should Peter do from the following list of answers?

    A. Implement the changes and then log them.

    B. Implement the changes and then have his staff look them over.

    C. Implement only one change at a time until he knows its okay.

    D. Implement a change management solution.

5. Tom is the systems administrator for his company. Tom manages 10 Windows 2000 servers and all the applications installed on them to include antivirus and backup software. Tom is plagued with system crashes and has made his management team aware of the fact that they need to spend more time repairing some of the systems and scaling their hardware requirements up to current performance needs. Management does not allow for the upgrade at this time. Tom is still forced to deal with the repetitive systems crashes on a weekly basis. What form of system management does this scenario describe?

www.syngress.com

A. Proactive management

B. Reactive management

C. Disaster management

D. Business management

Malware Issues

6. Jake is responsible for six Windows 2000 servers in his organization. Yesterday, he noticed that a problem is spreading across the enterprise. It is very hard to contain, and Jake is concerned that it could spread all over his network via a malware program with self-replication features. What type of problem are you dealing with?

    A. Worm

    B. Virus

    C. Trojan

    D. Bug

7. Peter is the administrator for a large Windows 2000 network infrastructure. He is responsible for 10 IIS servers, two Exchange servers, and 20 file and print servers. All 32 servers are internal to the LAN and serve as application, e-mail, file, and print servers for over 700 clients in five separate locations. Peter has received a call from a panicky executive who is asking him what the problem is with his machine—it won't boot anymore. When Peter asks the executive what he did just before the machine wouldn't boot, he said he had downloaded a new screen saver from the Internet and when he tried to install it, it didn't seem to install. After that, the PC never seemed the same. Now it won't boot anymore. What could be the issue here, and what is the most logical problem based on this scenario?

    A. Faulty screen saver

    B. Buggy code

    C. Trojan horse

    D. Denial of service attack

8. Jack is the systems engineer for ABC Corporation. One part of Jack's responsibilities is to make sure that any additions to the network are managed and that a system of quality assurance is implemented so that if the new addition to the network is a failure, the network itself is not negatively impacted. From the answers that follow, what step should Jack implement to make sure that the new addition to the network doesn't do harm and, if it does, that it is quickly and easily reversed to put the network back into its original state?

   A. Change the plan to reflect a secondary disaster recovery plan.

   B. Implement change management solutions.

   C. Test his last tape backup.

   D. Implement a new business continuity plan.

9. Patty needs to implement systems security in the form of virus protection on 40 Windows 2000 servers and 3,000 Windows 2000 Professional clients. While installing the antivirus software on the first 10 servers, Patty found a virus. On researching it, she quickly determined that this virus has qualities that allow it to leave the contents of the host file it infected unchanged but append itself to the host in such a way that the virus code is executed first. What type of virus has Patty found?

   A. Data file

   B. Companion

   C. Bootstrap sector

   D. Parasitic

10. Mike needs to implement systems security in the form of virus protection on 40 Windows 2000 servers and 3,000 Windows 2000 Professional clients. While installing the antivirus software on the first 10 servers, Mike finds a virus. On researching it, Mike quickly determines that this virus has qualities that allow it to combine the functionalities of the parasitic virus and the bootstrap sector virus by infecting either files or boot sectors. What type of virus has Mike found?

    A. Multipartite

    B. Bootstrap sector

    C. Companion

    D. Link

Incident Response

11. Stan is the network administrator responsible for 10 Windows 2000 servers running IIS 5.0 and 400 Windows XP Professional workstations, all separated geographically across four sites. Stan is responsible for implementing security on his 10 Windows Web-based servers. Stan notices what he thinks are attacks on his IIS servers. Due to the nature of this problem, Stan assumes that this could be the beginning of a security incident. What should be Stan's first step in this case?

    A. Make an initial assessment of the problem.

    B. Act on the problem immediately and close all ports on the firewall.

    C. Contact the CEO so that she knows what is going on.

    D. Strike back against the attacker with a ping of death.

12. Kristy is responsible for 30 Windows 2000 servers in her organization. She is part of the incident response team for the Windows 2000 environment. In one incident that recently occurred, evidence was mishandled, and that cost them to lose the whole case for the incident in court. When dealing with evidence, what is the most important thing to do so that this does not become a problem?

    A. Make sure that the CIO is always watching what the rest of the team is doing.

    B. The team leader needs to micromanage the rest of the team when taking evidence.

    C. When the evidence is computer related, it is inadmissible in court, so it doesn't really matter.

    D. A chain of custody must be established to show how evidence made it from the crime scene to the courtroom.

13. You are the network administrator responsible for 10 Windows 2000 servers and 400 Windows XP Professional workstations, all separated geographically across four sites. In one of the remote sites, a system was exploited and data was lost. The system is thought to have been attacked from an internal resource. At the scene of the incident, a PDA is lying next to the system that was breached. It doesn't seem to belong to anyone. What is the first thing that should be done with evidence on site?

    A. When collecting evidence, you start by identifying the evidence that is present and where it is located.

    B. Pick up the evidence and take it with you.

    C. Remove the evidence from the scene quickly, before the attacker realizes you know its there.

    D. Move the evidence to another part of the room, away from the system. Document it.

14. Erika is the systems engineer for the Toronto central hub location. The hub location contains over 50 Windows 2000 servers, but only three of them are accessible through the Internet. These three servers are responsible for Web-based services such as FTP and HTTP. All the rest of the servers (all 47 of them) are located within the private LAN protected by a firewall. These 47 servers are used for applications, file, print, and database purposes. The manager at a remote site has phoned Erika claiming that all systems seem to have a virus. The remote site manager is worried because all but two of their systems have become inoperable. They are connected directly to the core network from a Frame Relay link. Erika needs to deal with this problem immediately. What should be her first step from the following list?

    A. Call the CIO and arrange a meeting.

    B. Contain the problem immediately by having the remote site manager power down infected machines.

    C. Have the remote site manager call local law enforcement and tell them that there is a security breach they need to deal with.

    D. Fly down to handle the problem; make travel arrangements as soon as possible.

15. Paul is the network administrator for his company. He manages systems and network security on 10 Windows 2000 servers and the Cisco switches that connect them to the network. If Paul plans to keep his policies up to date and well prepared, which of the following answers provides the step to accomplish this task?

   A. Ask the CIO what needs to be updated.

   B. After an incident, just update the logs so the incident is recorded.

   C. Review the response and updating policies.

   D. Move all systems to another location after an attack.

Self Test Quick Answer Key

For complete questions, answers, and epxlanations to the Self Test questions in this chapter as well as the other chapters in this book, see the Self Test Appendix.

1. **C**
2. **A**
3. **C**
4. **D**
5. **B**
6. **A**
7. **C**
8. **B**
9. **D**
10. **A**
11. **A**
12. **D**
13. **A**
14. **B**
15. **C**

MCSE/MCSA 70-214
Part VII

Appendixes

Appendix A

MCSE/MCSA 70-214

Utilities for the White Hat

Topics Discussed in this Appendix:

- ☑ White Hat Vulnerability Testing
- ☑ White Hat Protection Tools

Introduction

Appendix A looks at some of the tools security analyst's can use to help test and secure their networks. For the exam, it is important to be comfortable with using tools that test systems and protect them from exploitation.

NOTE

You do not need to know how to use these tools for the exam; however, you should know how to use them if you work in the security field.

Following are some of the terms used in this appendix:

- **White Hat** As functional security analyst's working to defend and protect the systems they administer from attack and exploitation, White Hats test hacking tools in a controlled environment. Think of a White Hat as a "good guy" when it comes to network security.

- **Black Hat** Black Hats create tools to manipulate weaknesses within running systems for the purpose of causing harm. Black Hats are usually highly skilled in networking and programming and can create most of the tools they use themselves. These are the most *dangerous* of the "bad guys" in network security.

- **Gray Hat** Falling somewhere in the middle of White Hats and Black Hats, Gray Hats are hackers who are not as malicious as Black Hats, but do not necessarily share the White Hat's beliefs that security breaches should be reported to vendors for repair.

- **Script Kiddies** Script Kiddies are Black Hat wannabe's who find tools online to use to cause harm to networks. Most of the "hacker" population today falls under this category.

- **Click Kiddies** Click Kiddies are the newest version of Script Kiddies who use simple tools that are pre-canned and ready to be executed via the click of a mouse. As more pre-made Malware programs become available online, the number of Click Kiddies will grow.

NOTE

Be aware that as a Microsoft Certified Professional (MCP) operating under good, solid ethics, you should be a White Hat-type of security analyst.

It is important to learn how to use tools of this nature in a controlled environment so that you can learn how to defend against them. Each section of this appendix shows a tool, how to get it, its basic configuration, and why you should be aware of its existence. This information will also help you understand many of the concepts learned within the book such as Public Key Infrastructure (PKI), encryption, ports, and exploitable services that are not shut down or disabled. Exam-specific content is indicated throughout this appendix.

The following sections look at how to test a system's vulnerability with specific tools made to scan and sniff systems and networks looking for exploitable vulnerabilities.

NOTE

It is imperative that you *do not* run these tools on a production network without receiving permission from management first. You never know what will happen so you must be very careful when using these tools, especially if downloading and using them for the first time.

The testing tools covered are:

- LANguard Network Scanner (vulnerability scanner)
- NmapWin (port scanner)
- Ethereal (packet sniffer/protocol analyzer)

There are also tools available that can be used to protect systems from attack and exploitation. Most times, you are using services on the network from the Transmission Control Protocol/Internet Protocol (TCP/IP) protocol suite such as Telnet, and SMTP for e-mail. Because of the massive vulnerabilities that exist with these protocols (such as credentials like username and password being sent in cleartext instead of protected ciphertext), you might want to use alternative tools and services to help remove or diminish the possibility of attack. These tools are:

- Secure Shell (SSH) (encryption for in band terminal emulation)
- Pretty Good Privacy (PGP) (encryption for e-mail protection)

Lastly, it is important to understand that downloading freeware tools from the Internet incurs its own set of possible risks. You may inadvertently download a Trojan or virus. One solution is to connect an old machine to the Internet to download the tools to. Then run antiviral software on the tools to make sure they are clean and then burn them to CD-ROM. Once on CD-ROM, the tools can be used anywhere. Also, the virus definitions on the target machine should be updated so that the most current signatures are available.

NOTE

Some virus scanning tools will flag a possible tool as a virus although it is not affecting the machine. For example, when downloading and testing BackOrifice 2000 (see Chapter 11) on a test lab, most antivirus solutions flag the actual executable (such as Bo.exe) as a Trojan/virus, so you may have to take your chances. Hence why I left tools of this nature out of this appendix.

White Hat Vulnerability Testing

Security analysts use vulnerability scanners to test their system's infrastructure and vulnerability to attack and exploitation. It is imperative that the proper tools are used to take a good hard look at a system's weaknesses so they know how to either remove or repair the problems so that they are no longer exploitable.

LANguard Network Scanner

The "LANguard Network Scanner, marketed by a company called GFI," is by far one of the better free scanners on the market today. Once vulnerabilities are found, this scanner can aid in closing them. .

NOTE

You can download the LANguard Network Scanner for free from the GFI Web site: http://www.gfi.com/downloads/downloads.asp?pid=8&lid=1

Once download, installation is very easy. Once the installation is completed, open the LANguard Network Scanner by either double-clicking the desktop icon it creates or finding it in the Programs menu. Once opened, you will see that the scanner is ready to be used. Figure A.1 shows the Scanner already populated with a Windows 2000 Server.

Figure A.1 Viewing the GFI LANguard Network Scanner

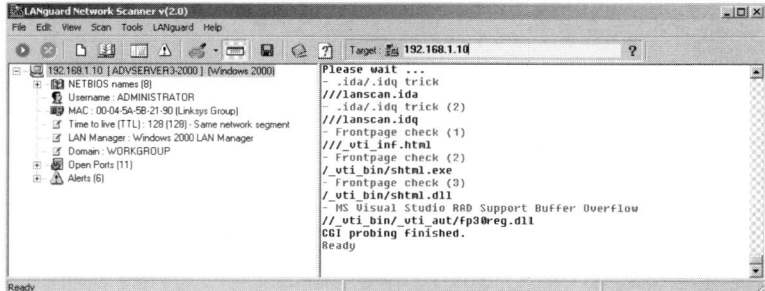

In the figure, you can see that all you need to do is scan via an IP address (or range of IP addresses) to connect to a host and check it for problems. You can also scan via hostname, but for these purposes, we will stay with the basics. A single Windows 2000 Server on the network has been selected for testing. This server was installed and *not* updated with the latest hot fixes from Microsoft.

NOTE

It is critical for the exam and as a MCP that you know everything about service packs and hot fixes. The security of your systems depends greatly on your having this knowledge.

Following are issues you may need to contend with to secure your Windows 2000 Server. Lets look at this in steps:

1. Open the scanner and pick a server. (I selected a server with the IP address of 192.168.1.10.)

2. Scan the server by clicking on the **Start Scanning** icon in the tool bar.

3. Once started, the right-hand pane of the scanner gives feedback on the scan that is taking place. The left-hand pane is where the node (192.168.1.10) will show up if it exists. You will then see a list of services.

4. Figure A.2 shows the final result of the services listed.

   Figure A.2 Scanning and Reviewing the Results of a Windows 2000 Server

5. As can be seen in the figure, there are quite a few items of interest. First, look at the services running on the server. It may be necessary to investigate

whether there is the need for Internet Information Services (IIS [for Web publishing]) to be running on a server being used for file shares.

NOTE

For the exam, you MUST know how to disable services that are unwanted or unnecessary. The IIS Web Publishing Service is at the top of the list! If you are not running a Web site or an intranet, disable this service.

6. The FTP service is also running. You probably do not want this service running on a production server. All a hacker would need to do to is open a Web browser and type: ftp://192.168.1.10. Once opened, they may be able to place warez (files and junk) on the server without your knowing.

NOTE

If protected with appropriate permissions, the system is probably safe. The point is that you may not even have known that this vulnerability existed in the first place and using this scanner may have helped you see it.

7. Another important fact is that there are many services and protocols running on this server that you may not be using. and POP3 are running for e-mail services. If they are not needed, they should be disabled. Since this is an Active Directory Server, DNS must be running, as it is the DNS server for this domain. This tool gives some insight as to what is running and gives an opportunity to see what services and protocols may or may not be needed.

8. Figure A.3 clearly shows that you are being alerted to issues on your Windows 2000 Server that need your immediate attention.

Figure A.3 Viewing CGI Abuses

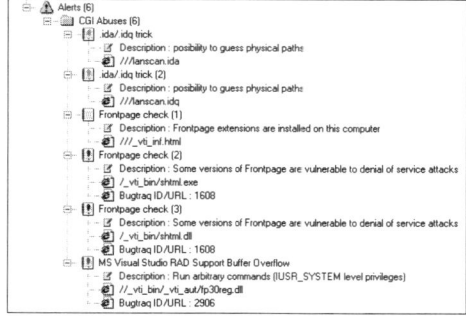

Many of the alerts seen here are fixed by way of hot fixes and service packs but nonetheless, the point of showing them to you is to help you understand how to use this tool, what it shows you, and how to stimulate yourself into further research. Following is a listing for an IIS 5.0 FrontPage Server Extension problem currently listed in the alerts in Figure A.3:

```
Problem: IIS 5.0 cross site scripting vulnerability using .shtml files or
/_vti_bin/shtml.dll
Detail: Using specially designed URLs, IIS 5.0 may return user specified
content to the browser. This poses great security risk, especially if the
browser is JavaScript enabled and the problem is greater in IE. By
clicking on links or just visiting hostile web pages the target IIS server
may return user defined malicous active content. This is a bug in IIS
5.0, but it affects end users and is exploited with a browser.
```

Without using the scanner, you may never have known that the Windows 2000 Server was vulnerable to this type of problem. To sum up the use of this scanner, remember… a scanner only provides you with information that you need to act on. The LANguard Network Scanner test your system for vulnerabilities and show you what it finds. It is up to the security analyst to research the problems further to help solve any problems. Microsoft TechNet, the Microsoft Knowledge Base, and NTBUG-TRAQ can be used to help research any problems found with the scanner.

NOTE
You can visit the NTBUGTRAQ and search the archives at the following URL: http://ntbugtraq.ntadvice.com/default.asp?pid=36&sid=1&S1=ntbugtraq

Network Mapper and Network Mapper for Windows

No White Hat's arsenal would be complete without Network Mapper (Nmap), the UNIX tool of choice for port scanning. A port scanner is a type of vulnerability tester. It is "lightweight" compared to LANguard, but is a very flexible command line-based tool that can be used on any UNIX-based system available. It is also free, and easy to learn and use. Figure A.4 shows Nmap running on a Linux server.

Nmap is an open source utility for network exploration or security auditing. There is also a newer version of Nmap called NmapWin, which is the Windows version of the original Nmap tool.

Figure A.4 Running a Scan with the Linux-based Nmap

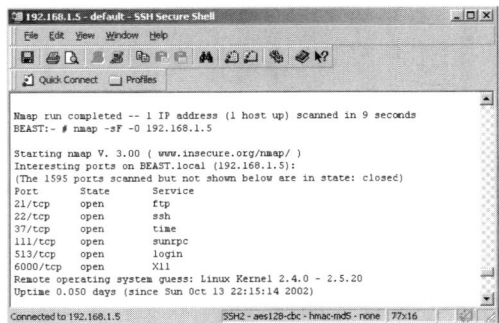

Nmap and NmapWin were developed with high-speed scanning in mind. Following are the high points of the tool:

- It is free and easy to use
- It can rapidly scan both very large networks and/or single systems
- It can accurately figure out what hosts are available on a network
- It can find services and ports available on a system
- It can scan to find which version of what operating system is running

Nmap and NmapWin are very easy to download and install. Once installed, you can use the Help files to find the options needed to scan your network. For the most part, if you simply install it, open it, and add a subnet to it (for example, 192.168.1.0/24), you can scan that entire subnet for hosts.

Figure A.5 shows that NmapWin is used with a Graphical User Interface (GUI). It is the same tool as Nmap, but is not ported to Windows systems by way of a Win32 interface.

To download, install, and use NmapWin, follow these steps:

1. Go to the Web site and download the Windows version called NmapWin.
2. Make sure you download and install WinPcap, which is the Windows-based packet capture architecture that is needed in tandem with NmapWin. (Both links are provided in this appendix.)
3. Download and install both packages. Follow the defaults and select where you want the files to be installed on your system.
4. Make sure you reboot your system before using the software.
5. Once rebooted, open NmapWin and start scanning either individual hosts (as seen in Figure A.5) or entire subnets. Read the downloadable documentation to learn the ins and outs of using the tool.

Figure A.5 Using the Windows-based Version of NmapWin

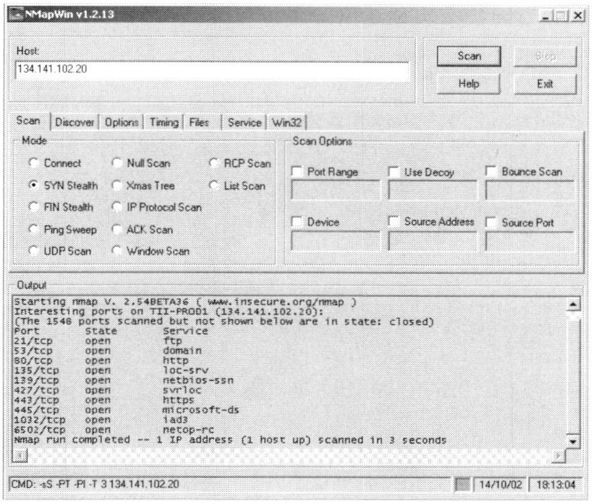

NOTE

Nmap in both the Unix and Windows Win32 version can be found online for free at : http://www.insecure.org/nmap/ and http://winpcap.polito.it/

Ethereal

If you want to "'sniff" your network for free, you may want to download a copy of "Ethereal." Packet sniffers such as Ethereal allow security analyst's to perform a test of their systems to see if they are susceptible to eavesdropping attacks.

Ethereal is a tool that can be used to passively analyze a network to see the kinds of conversations being sent to and from hosts on the network. It can capture NetBIOS Master Browser elections, see which hosts have the Server service or File and Print Sharing enabled or, even capture credentials such as username and password from users on the network perhaps using Telnet for an in-band connection to a device. This being said, in order to know these vulnerabilities exist, a Sniffer should be running on the network to find out exactly is going on inside the wire.

Figure A.6 shows the use of Ethereal on a network where I wanted to make sure that only TCP/IP was running. After running a scan on a local subnet and searching for Internetwork Packet Exchange/Sequenced Packet Exchange (IPX/SPX), unnecessary services and protocols were found running that are using up bandwidth and central processing unit (CPU) cycles on the wide area network (WAN) links and devices, respectively.

Figure A.6 Using Ethereal to Perform Passive Attacks

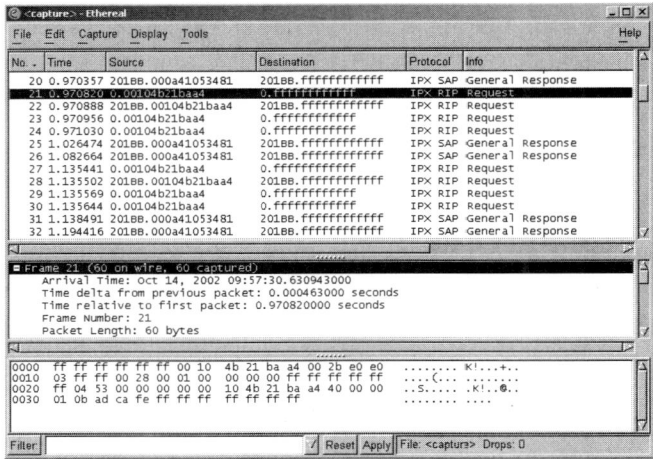

There is a second module to Ethereal that must be installed on the system in order to get it to work. To install Ethereal, do the following:

1. Go to the Web site and download Ethereal.

2. Make sure you download and install WinPcap, which is the Windows-based packet-capture architecture that is needed in tandem with Ethereal. (Both links are provided in this appendix.)

3. Download and install both packages. Follow the defaults and select where you want the files to be installed on your system.

4. Make sure you reboot your system before using the software.

5. Once rebooted, open Ethereal and start sniffing your network (as seen in Figure A.6). Read the downloadable documentation to learn the ins and outs of using the tool.

NOTE

You can get a copy of Ethereal free form the following URLs: http://www.ethereal.com/download.html and http://winpcap.polito.it/

White Hat Protection Tools

This section looks at how to protect a system from exploitation. The two most popular tools used for this purpose are SSH and PGP. Both are free and very helpful in securing known vulnerabilities (which are unfixable based on the way that the underlying protocols work) and network transmissions.

SSH

What type of White Hat would you be if you did not use SSH? SSH is the security analyst's tool of choice for establishing safe connections to systems instead of using Telnet. Telnet is the most unsecure and most widely used protocol for remote connectivity to devices such as routers, switches, firewalls, servers, and more. What is worse is that even though it is a known vulnerability, it is still highly ignored.

The alternative is SSH. It is free, simple to use, and secure. Most people fail to use SSH because it works on a different port than Telnet (port 23) and you must know how to configure the device you want to connect to remotely (router, UNIX server) to use the SSH port (port 22). Read the documentation of the device you want to configure or call their technical support to figure out how to set the device you want to make SSH capable. Once that is done, the rest is easy.

SSH can be seen in Figure A.7. The Windows-based application can be opened up on the desktop and, instead of using Telnet (which is unsecured), SSH can be used so that the transmission is encrypted and safe.

Figure A.7 Using Secure Shell to Work with Remote Systems

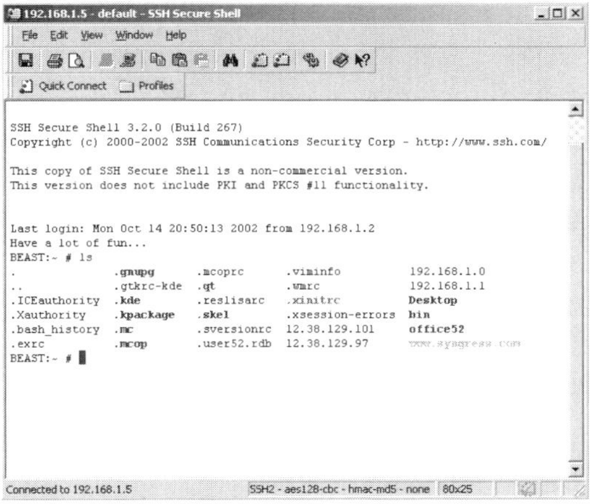

To install and use SSH, do the following:

1. Go to the Web site and download SSH.

2. Download and install the SSH FTP package. Follow the defaults and select where you want the files to be installed on your system.

3. Make sure you reboot your system before using the software.

4. Once rebooted, open SSH and start connecting to the remote devices on your network (seen in Figure A.7).

5. Read the downloadable documentation to learn the ins and outs of using the tool

NOTE

To download and use a free version of Secure Shell (SSH), go to: http://www.ssh.com/

PGP

PGP is the White Hat's answer to personal e-mail security. PGP is a popular program used to encrypt and decrypt e-mail over the Internet. It is by installed snapped into your favorite (and compatible) e-mail program such as Outlook or Outlook Express. Once you learn how to use this tool comfortably, you can encrypt e-mails sent from one place to another without worry of interception and exploitation.

Created by Philip R. Zimmermann in 1991, PGP is widely known, accepted, and used for e-mail-based encryption and security. As a White Hat security analyst or MCP, it is imperative that your e-mail is secureKeep in mind that if you are using PGP inside a corporate network, PGP-encrypted mail may be dropped by administrators trying to stop the egress of confidential information via SMTP.

PGP is used to send an encrypted digital signature that lets the person receiving the message verify the sender's identity and know that the message was not changed while in transit. Like the other tools listed in this appendix, it is also free for personal use, but a small fee is attached for production use.

The PGP tool uses a variation of the PKI system discussed in this book. Figure A.8 shows the Key Ring being used with PGP.

To install and use PGP, do the following:

1. Go to the Web site and download PGP.

2. Download and install PGP and the two recommended hot fixes for your system.

3. Follow the defaults and select where you want the files to be installed on your system.

4. Make sure you reboot your system before using the software.
5. Once rebooted, you can open Outlook and view the Snap-ins for the PGP you can use. It is recommended that you download any documentation you can to learn how to install and use this product, as it is a bit difficult to understand without some reading and practice.

Figure A.8 Using the PGP Key Ring

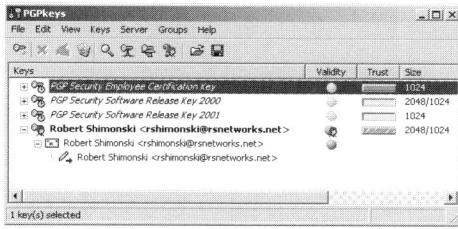

NOTE
To download and use a free version of PGP, go to: http://www.pgpi.org/products/pgp/versions/freeware/win2k/

Summary
All of these tools will help you accomplish the testing of your systems for vulnerabilities and help better protect your systems. This appendix introduces you, the MCP, to the tools used by White Hat security analysts. Please note that you will have to do more research and testing with these tools to truly master them and what they have to offer you.

Appendix B

MCSE/MCSA 70-214

Port Numbers and Associated Attacks

Topics Discussed in this Appendix:

- ☑ Port Numbers

Introduction

Appendix B covers the basic fundamentals of ports, port numbers, and attacks associated with using ports. While this appendix does not cover every port number created, it does cover the most commonly used ones and includes the definition of a port, where to get more information about ports, how they are used, and which ones attackers exploit most.

Port Numbers

A port number is a number assigned to a service. Ports operate at the transport layer of the Open Systems Interconnect (OSI) model and allow communication to be accomplished using specific services such as:

- Telnet (port 23)
- Simple Mail Transfer Protocol (SMTP) (port 25)
- Post Office Protocol 3 (POP3) (port 110)
- Hypertext Transfer Protocol (HTTP) (port 80)

HTTP is the protocol used by the World Wide Web (WWW). Every time URL information is entered into a web browser (as seen in Figure B.1), the HTTP service is being used across the Internet to access web pages on web servers. This service corresponds to a specific port assigned by way of the following standards organizations:

- http://www.iana.org/
- http://www.icann.org/

Figure B.1 Viewing a Web Browser Using the HTTP Service

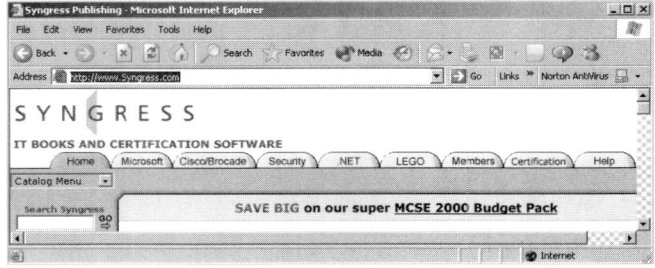

Think of the process this way:

1. At your web browser enter **http://www.syngress.com**.
2. HTTP (layer 7 of the OSI model) uses Transmission Control Protocol (TCP) port 80 (layer 4 of the OSI model). The port number is set by convention. Web servers are not required to listen for HTTP requests on TCP port 80.

3. Because the Web server is listening on port 80, a connection is made.

4. Before making the connection, the browser must resolve the name www.syngress.com to an Internet Protocol (IP) address. This is accomplished by sending a query to a Domain Name System (DNS) server requesting that www.syngress.com be resolved to an IP address. The DNS server sends back the IP address: 216.238.8.44

5. The connection is made via the IP address and TCP port number to create a "socket." A socket is a combination of the transport layer protocol, the port, and the IP address.

6. A socket is denoted as the IP and the port is: 216.238.8.44:80

NOTE
Most Web servers have their ports set to 8080. Where this is the case, the correct socket connection would be: 216.238.8.44:8080

Think of the IP address and port number as being the street address and apartment number, respectively. If not for apartment numbers, it would be difficult to know whom in an apartment building a particular letter was for. This is the same concept behind IP addresses and port numbers. The port number is used by a particular service. When a request is made, the port number tells the computer which service it wants to talk to. The port number defines the endpoints of a connection. The Internet Corporation for Assigned Names and Numbers (ICANN) is responsible for managing port numbers.

There are three ports ranges equaling a total of 65535 ports:

- Well-known port numbers range from 0 to 1023 (equaling 1024 ports in total)
- Registered port numbers range from 1024 to 49151
- Dynamic and private port numbers range from 49152 to 65535

NOTE
There are 1024 total ports available for use. It is easy to forget that the range starts with "0". The values 0 through 1023 inclusive makes 1024 ports available.

There are three categories of ports:

- **Well-Known Port Numbers** Most systems use the well-known port numbers to run system processes or privileged programs such as HTTP, SMTP, FTP and POP3.

- **Registered Port Numbers** Registered port numbers are not controlled by ICANN. They are commonly used with non-system processes or nonprivileged programs, such as an ordinary user running a program.

- **Dynamic/Private Port Numbers** Used for either privately or dynamically assigned ports. Dynamic means that programs simply select an available port from the range. Also, these port numbers can be specified for use because they are not registered.

Table B.1 presents the following:

- Port number
- TCP/User Datagram Protocol (UDP) or both
- A description of the service
- Common attacks

NOTE
This is just a small selection of commonly attacked ports. All network services are at risk from some type of attack.

Table B.1 Well-Known Port Numbers

Port Number	Protocol	Description	Attacks
19	TCP, UDP	Character Generator	One of the most common attacks—the Chargen attack—can be run from a host allowing for connection via port 19. Simply run a Telnet connection to the device via port 19 to run the attack. (Telnet 10.0.0.1 19)
20	TCP, UDP	FTP (Default Data)	FTP can be exploited because the credentials (username and password) are sent in cleartext. If eavesdropping is taking place (packet sniffing),

Continued

Table B.1 Well-Known Port Numbers

Port Number	Protocol	Description	Attacks
21	TCP, UDP	FTP (Control)	credentials can be found and used, thus opening the door for the attacker. FTP can be exploited because the credentials (username and password) are sent in cleartext. If eavesdropping is taking place (packet sniffing), credentials can be found and used, thus opening the door for the attacker.
22	TCP, UDP	Secure Shell (SSH) Remote Login Protocol	SSH is the alternative to Telnet. It is used to create an encrypted connection for terminal emulation
23	TCP, UDP	Telnet	Telnet can be exploited because the credentials (username and password) are sent in cleartext. If eavesdropping is taking place (packet sniffing), credentials can be found and used, thus opening the door for the attacker.
25	TCP, UDP	SMTP	SMTP can be manipulated via Telnet. You can Telnet to the SMTP service and run commands on the server you connect to. Simply run a Telnet connection to the device via port 25 to run the attack. (Telnet 10.0.0.1 25)
53	TCP, UDP	DNS	DNS is highly susceptible to zone transfers via TCP. This is unfortunate because an attacker can take DNS information and learns massive amounts of information about a system via this gathered data. You must be extra careful with this port when configuring DNS on your DMZ.
69	TCP, UDP	Trivial File Transfer Protocol (TFTP)	TFTP is highly dangerous as it allows for the upload and download of data without the checking of credentials.
79	TCP, UDP	Finger	Finger is and old service that provides information on people who are users of a given computer. This port is usually left open by default and can be easily hacked by either the command "finger" or via Telnet to port 79.

Continued

Table B.1 Well-Known Port Numbers

Port Number	Protocol	Description	Attacks
80	TCP, UDP	WWW HTTP	HTTP can be manipulated very easily. Because of the free-willing nature of the Internet, most traffic is passed on port 80. The problem with this is, unless you specifically search for and stop data coming over the Internet, harmful applets and code can be downloaded to a users web browser via HTTP.
109	TCP, UDP	Post Office Protocol - Version 2 (POP2)	POP2 can be manipulated via Telnet. You can Telnet to the POP2 service and run commands on the server you connect to. Simply run a Telnet connection to the device via port 109 to run the attack. (Telnet 10.0.0.1 109)
110	TCP, UDP	Post Office Protocol - Version 3 (POP3)	POP3 can be manipulated via Telnet. You can Telnet to the POP3 service and run commands on the server you connect to. Simply run a Telnet connection to the device via port 110 to run the attack. (Telnet 10.0.0.1 110)
137	TCP, UDP	Network Basic Input/ Output System (NetBIOS) Name Service	NetBIOS should not be allowed to function on any server facing the Internet. This allows Internet-based attackers to see file share information as well as computer names and other important information about the machine.
138	TCP, UDP	NetBIOS Datagram Service	NetBIOS should not be allowed to function on any server facing the Internet. This allows Internet-based attackers to see file share information as well as computer names and other important information about the machine.
139	TCP, UDP	NetBIOS Session Service	NetBIOS should not be allowed to function on any server facing the Internet. This allows Internet-based attackers to see file share information as well as computer names and other important information about the machine.

Continued

Table B.1 Well-Known Port Numbers

Port Number	Protocol	Description	Attacks
156	TCP, UDP	Structured Query Language (SQL) Service	Knowing that an SQL service is running is an open invitation to attacks on database systems.
161	TCP, UDP	Simple Network Management Protocol (SNMP)	SNMP is used to allow for the management of network and system Management Information Bases (MIBs) by a network management system. Since SNMP sends information in cleartext (like community string credentials), you should consider this protocol open to attack. Another common attack is when an attacker uses the default public and private community strings that are assigned by default and very rarely changed, to gain management of the systems.

Appendix C

MCSE/MCSA 70-214

Self Test Questions, Answers, and Explanations

This appendix provides complete Self Test Questions, Answers, and Explanations for each chapter.

Chapter 1: Basic Windows 2000 Security: Using Security Templates

Windows 2000 Active Directory Review

1. One of the advantages of Windows 2000 Active Directory over previous versions of Windows NT is that two-way transitive trusts are automatically created between which objects? (Choose all correct answers.)

    A. Between root domains in an Active Directory forest

    B. Between parent domains and child domains

    C. Between child domains at the same level within the tree

    D. Between Windows 2000 and Windows NT 4.0 domains

    ☑ **A, B.** Windows 2000 automatically creates two-way transitive trusts between root domains in the forest. Additionally, two-way transitive trusts are created between parent and child domains in Windows 2000.

    ☒ **C, D.** Two transitive trusts are not automatically created between child domains or between Windows 2000 domains and Windows NT 4.0 domains, although you can manually create a shortcut trust if you desire. (See Chapter 8 for a full discussion on Windows 2000 trusts.) Thus Answers **C** and **D** are incorrect.

2. The schema serves what function in Active Directory?

    A. Provides a listing, or index, of all the objects within Active Directory

    B. Defines the types of objects that can be stored in Active Directory

    C. Organizes objects, such as users or computers, into a location designed for easier management and assignment of permissions

    D. Provides for name resolution on the network

    ☑ **B.** The schema defines the types of objects that can be stored in Active Directory as well as the attributes each object is allowed to possess.

    ☒ **A, C, D.** The Global Catalog (GC) provides an easily searchable index of all objects contained within Active Directory, thus Answer **A** is incorrect. Organizational Units (OUs) are used to organize objects for easier management, thus Answer **C** is incorrect. Domain Naming System (DNS) and Windows Internet Naming System (WINS) are the commonly used name resolution services on Windows networks, thus Answer **D** is incorrect.

The Basic Windows 2000 Security Tools

3. Hannah wants to increase the security on the member servers in her network, but she does not want to interfere with the normal network communications between the servers and other computers on the network. What would be the best security template for her to apply to these member servers?

   A. hisecdc.inf
   B. securews.inf
   C. basicsv.inf
   D. securedc.inf

   ☑ **B.** The secure templates increase the level of security for Account Policy, certain Registry keys, and Auditing. Permissions for file system objects are not affected by this configuration. Two secure templates are provided: securedc.inf for domain controllers and securews.inf for workstations and member servers. The secure templates provide a medium level of security, stricter than the basic templates but not as secure as the highly secure templates.

   ☒ **A, C, D.** The hisecdc.inf template is a highly secure template for domain controllers, thus Answer **A** is incorrect. The basicsv.inf template is the default template for member servers (and is mostly likely the currently installed template on these servers), thus Answer **C** is incorrect. The securedc.inf template is the secure template for domain controllers, not member servers, thus Answer **D** is incorrect..

4. You are the network administrator for a medium-sized company. The HR department has asked you to help interview candidates for the position of assistant security administrator for your Windows 2000 network. During the interview of one of the candidates, you ask the following question: "What can the secedit.exe utility be used for?" What answers do you expect to hear? (Choose all that apply.)

   A. It can be used to list the current Group Policy in effect for a specific user and computer.
   B. It can be used to analyze the security settings of a system.
   C. It can be used to refresh the applied security settings of a system.
   D. It can be used to validate the syntax of chosen security template.
   E. It can be used to edit group membership and permissions for a user or group.
   F. It can be used to remotely monitor privilege use.
   G. It can be used to configure system security settings.
   H. It can be used to export the values stored in a database to a .inf file.

☑ **B, C, D, G, H.** The secedit.exe utility can be used to analyze system security, configure system security, refresh security settings, export security settings, and validate the syntax of a security template. Refer back to the "Using Secedit.exe" section in this chapter for a thorough review of the functions and switches of the secedit.exe tool.

☒ **A, E, F.** The secedit.exe utility does not list current Group Policy settings that have been applied to a user or computer. That can be done using the gpresult.exe tool, thus Answer **A** is incorrect. Group membership and permissions for users and groups is not done using the secedit.exe utility, thus Answer **E** is incorrect. Furthermore, secedit does not perform remote monitoring of privilege usage, therefore Answer **F** is also incorrect.

5. Andrew must increase the security on the workstations in his network at any cost, preferably achieving the most secure configuration possible. What would be the best template to apply to his workstations the to provide maximum amount of security, and what negative side effects can he expect to see from the application of the chosen template? (Chose two correct answers.)

    A. hisecdc.inf

    B. securews.inf

    C. basicsv.inf

    D. securedc.inf

    E. hisecws.inf

    F. He should expect no adverse effects to occur except for potentially increased login and logoff times due to extra policy processing invoked by the more secure template.

    G. He should expect to lose network connectivity with all other computers that do not support IPSec.

    H. He should expect to have to configure Active Directory integrated zones for his DNS servers to support the newly configured workstations.

    ☑ **E, G**. Highly secure configurations add security to network communications. IPSec will be configured for these machines and will be required for communications. Two highly secure templates are provided: hisecdc.inf for domain controllers and hisecws.inf for workstations and member servers. The highly secure templates provide the highest level of preconfigured security available but will cause communications problems with legacy clients due the requirement of IPSec for network communications.

☒ **A, B, C, D, F, H.** The hisecdc.inf security template is for domain controllers, thus Answer **A** is incorrect. The securews.inf security template is for workstations and member servers, thus Answer **B** is incorrect. The basicsv.inf security template is the default template for member servers, thus Answer **C** is incorrect. The securedc.inf security template is for applying the Secure settings to domain controllers, thus Answer **D** is incorrect. As noted, the primary effect of applying highly secure templates will be a loss of network connectivity to computers that are not running IPSec, so it is essential that all computers requiring communications be configured for IPSec, such as domain controllers and member servers that the IPSec configured workstations will be contacting, thus Answers **F** and **H** are also incorrect.

6. You are preparing to deploy some custom security templates across your organization in an effort to increase the overall security of the network. You plan to deploy your security templates via Group Policy. What is the correct processing order for Group Policy in Windows 2000?

    A. Local, domain, site, Organizational Unit

    B. Local, site, domain, Organizational Unit

    C. Site, domain, Organizational Unit, local

    D. Domain, site, Organizational Unit, local

    ☑ **B.** The correct Group Policy application order in Windows 2000 is local, site, domain, Organizational Unit. Remember that later Group Policy objects overwrite GPOs that have been applied earlier.

    ☒ **A, C, D.** The correct Group Policy application order in Windows 2000 is local, site, domain, Organizational Unit, thus Answers **A**, **C**, and **D** are incorrect.

Configuring Basic Windows 2000 Security with Templates

7. Chris wants to configure her network so that users attempting to log on by guessing passwords will be prevented from gaining access to the system. She proposes to perform the following actions. Which actions will have a positive effect on preventing password-guessing users from gaining access to her network? (Choose all that apply.)

A. Set the Minimum Password Length to 10 characters.

B. Set the Account Lockout Threshold to 0 invalid login attempts.

C. Set the Account Lockout Duration to 60 minutes.

D. Set the Enforce Password History to 25 passwords.

☑ **A, C, D.** Setting the Minimum Password Length to 10 characters will make passwords longer (and thus more complex), which in turn makes a password much more difficult to guess. Setting the Account Lockout duration to a value such as 60 minutes (or even higher) will prevent that user account from being used again for the time value configured. This serves to deter password guessing, because the user needs to know a username in order to guess a password to gain access to the network. Configuring the Enforce Password History will increase overall network security by forcing users to not reuse a password that has been recently used, thus making it much more difficult for a password-guessing individual to gain access by attempting passwords that might be preferred by users. Additionally, you can configure the Password Must Meet Complexity Requirements setting to make passwords stronger by forcing them to contain a mixture of letters, numbers, and characters. The Account Lockout Duration and Reset Account Lockout After settings are configured by default when you configure the Account Lockout Threshold setting.

☒ **B.** Setting the Account Lockout Threshold to 0 invalid attempts in effect disables this setting, thus preventing the system from locking out the user account when a series of incorrect passwords have been entered, thus Answer **B** is incorrect.

8. Jon, the CTO of your company, asks you what can be done to protect certain areas of the Registry from modification by unauthorized users. What do you tell him?

A. Use the secedit.exe utility with the /*validate* switch to set security settings on the Registry keys of concern.

B. Use the regedit application to set security settings on the Registry keys of concern.

C. Use the Security templates and Security Configuration and Analysis snap-ins to configure, analyze, and implement security settings on the Registry keys of concern.

D. Use Windows Explorer to mark the Registry files as read only.

E. Use Windows Explorer to set NTFS permissions on the Registry files so that only authorized users may access them.

☑ **C.** You use the Security templates snap-in to edit the settings of a template and configure the security settings you require. You can then use the Security Configuration and Analysis snap-in to analyze and deploy the settings.

☒ **A, B, D, E.** Using *secedit* with the */validate* switch instructs *secedit* to perform a validation of a template before importing it onto a computer, thus Answer **A** is incorrect. Using the regedit application will not allow you to protect the keys from modification, thus Answer **B** is incorrect. Marking the Registry files as read only or changing their NTFS permissions will most likely cause your computer to operate erratically or stop functioning properly altogether and is not recommended, thus Answers **D** and **E** are also incorrect.

9. You want to configure auditing for the workstations in a specific OU in your network. You have opened Security Configuration and Analysis and selected the basicwk.inf template. What section of the template contains the options that you need to configure to enable auditing?

    A. Local Policies
    B. Account Policies
    C. Event Log
    D. Registry

    ☑ **A.** The Local Policies node contains three areas, one of which is the Audit Policies area. Inside the Audit Policies area is where you will configure audit options in this template.

    ☒ **B, C, D.** The Account Policies node pertains to account issues such as password aging and length, thus Answer **B** is incorrect. The Event Log node contains settings that allow you to configure the Event Log, thus Answer **C** is incorrect. The Registry node contains settings that allow you set key-level security settings in the Registry, thus Answer **D** is incorrect.

Deploying Security Templates

10. Austin has been delegated administrative responsibility for several OUs in his department. How can he most easily make the same changes to the security settings applied to his OUs?

A. Austin should configure and test a template on a local machine using Security Configuration and Analysis. When he gets the configuration established that he requires, he should export the template and then import it into the specific OU Group Policy objects he is responsible for.

B. Austin should use the Security Configuration and Analysis snap-in and target it at the specific OU he wants to work with to make the changes.

C. Austin should edit the Group Policy objects directly for each of the OUs he is responsible for.

D. Austin should ask a domain administrator to apply the desired settings at the domain level and let them propagate down to his OUs.

☑ **A.** The best way to ensure that the changes Austin makes are identical on all his OUs is for him to configure and analyze an incremental security template using the Security Configuration and Analysis snap-in. Once he has gotten the required settings configured to his liking, he can export the security template and subsequently import it into a Group Policy object in each of the OUs he is responsible for.

☒ **B, C, D.** The Security Configuration and Analysis snap-in cannot be targeted at any level other than the local machine, so using it and targeting it toward an OU is not possible, thus Answer **B** is incorrect. Although editing the Group Policy object for each OU he is responsible for is a viable solution, this solution introduces the possibility of making different configuration settings in the various OUs, thus making this a bad choice for Austin, so Answer **C** is incorrect. Applying the settings at the domain level is unnecessary since Austin only needs the settings applied to his specific OUs. Additionally, settings applied at the domain level may be overwritten by Group Policy objects that are at the OU level, thus Answer **D** is also incorrect.

11. You have configured and tested two custom security templates for use on your corporate network, corpserver.inf and corpdesktop.inf. Your network is running all Windows 2000 computers and is fragmented into three distinct sections due to the extremely high cost of establishing WAN links between your three geographical locations. You do have dial-up connectivity between the sites using standard plain old telephone service (POTS) lines, but these lines have proven unreliable at best. How can you deploy these templates to the other two sites in your network?

A. You need to deploy them to two extra domain controllers and then ship one each to your other two sites.

B. You need to export them from Security Configuration and Analysis and send the .inf files to your other two remote sites. Once there, the other two sites can import them into the required Group Policy object.

C. You need to establish a Frame Relay connection between all three sites at the same time and push the templates across the WAN link.

D. You need to make a RDP connection to each domain controller in the remote sites and apply the template to them.

☑ **B**. By exporting the templates from Security Configuration and Analysis, you can send them by any available means to a remote location for application on the network.

☒ **A, C, D**. Shipping fully functional domain controllers is not a very good idea for a number of reasons, not limited to damage or theft, thus Answer **A** is incorrect. Establishing a Frame Relay WAN link just for the purpose of applying a couple of extremely small security templates is an extremely large waste of resources that can be avoided. Additionally, you still need to apply the templates to the other sites in the same fashion, regardless of how you get them there, so Answer **C** is incorrect. Making a Remote Desktop Protocol (RDP) connection to each remote site does not seem likely, since we were never told about having this capability as well as the fact that connectivity does not appear to exist, thus Answer **D** is incorrect.

Analyzing Your Security Configuration

12. Andrea is the network administrator of 55 workstations, 10 member servers, and four domain controllers. She would like to perform a security analysis on all her computers without having to physically visit each one. How can Andrea accomplish this task?

    A. This cannot be done at the current time. Andrea will need to sit in front of each machine and use the Security Configuration and Analysis snap-in to perform the analysis.

    B. Andrea can target a remote computer by right-clicking **Security Configuration and Analysis** and selecting **Connect to another computer**.

    C. Andrea can create a script or batch file using the secedit.exe utility with the /*analyze* switch that has an entry for each computer that she wants to analyze.

    D. Andrea can create a script or batch file using the secedit.exe utility with the /*analyze* switch that calls on a prepopulated text file containing the list of computers to be analyzed.

    ☑ **C**. The easiest way to perform the analysis on a large number of remote computers is to create a custom script or batch file using *secedit /analyze*. There should be an entry in the file for each computer that is to be configured, including the database to use or create, the template to use, and the log file to use or create. Each entry should specify an absolute location using UNC file locations; it is recommended to create the database and log files in a central location for easier viewing later.

☒ **A, B, D.** Andrea will be able to perform the required security analysis easily using the *secedit* tool, thus Answer **A** is incorrect. The **Connect to another computer** option, available in tools such as the Computer Management console, is not available for use in the Security Configuration and Analysis snap-in, thus Answer **B** is incorrect. Secedit cannot use an external text file that contains the scan parameters, thus Answer **D** is incorrect.

13. Christopher is an assistant network administrator working for Andrea. Christopher has been given the task of examining the results of the *secedit /analyze* script that Andrea ran over the network the previous night. How can Christopher most easily examine the analysis results to determine items that require a follow-up?

    A. Christopher must visit each computer locally and view the database contents using the Security Configuration and Analysis snap-in.

    B. Christopher must use the gpresult.exe tool from the Windows 2000 Resource Kit to be able to easily examine the analysis results.

    C. Christopher can read through the text log from the analysis and identify any mismatches as areas requiring a follow-up.

    D. Christopher can load each database file into the Security Configuration and Analysis snap-in that is running on his computer and identify any mismatches as areas requiring a follow-up.

    ☑ **D.** The easiest method of examining the analysis results is to load each database into the Security Configuration and Analysis snap-in and look for mismatches using the GUI.

    ☒ **A, B, C.** Visiting each computer locally to perform the examination is also a valid solution, but it does meet the requirement of needing the least effort, thus Answer **A** is incorrect. The gpresult.exe tool is not used in this fashion but instead provides you with information on applied Group Policy objects, the last time policy was applied, and several other user and computer statistics, thus Answer **B** is incorrect. You can sift through the text file and even use a search tool such as Windows Grep, but the text file method is not as indicative or intuitive as using the GUI, thus Answer **C** is also incorrect.

14. Luanda is attempting to use the Security Configuration and Analysis snap-in to perform an analysis of one of her member servers. The member server is currently configured with the default settings. She wants to compare its settings with those

in the securewk.inf security template. What is the correct order of steps to perform the analysis?

Step 1: Right-click **Security Configuration and Analysis** and select **Analyze computer now**.
Step 2: Right-click **Security Configuration and Analysis** and select **Open database**.
Step 3: Select the security template to be used in the analysis.
Step 4: Select the log file to be used in the analysis.
Step 5: Right-click **Security Configuration and Analysis** and select **Configure computer now**.
Step 6: Select the database to be used in the analysis.

A. 2, 1, 3, 6, 4

B. 1, 6, 4, 5, 3

C. 2, 6, 4, 3, 1

D. 2, 6, 3, 1, 4

E. 1, 6, 3, 2, 4

☑ **D.** The correct order to perform a security analysis using the Security Configuration and Analysis snap-in is select **Open database**, select the database to be used, select the security template to be used, select **Analyze computer now**, and select the log file to be used. You do not need to select **Configure computer now** until you are ready to apply the database settings to the computer.

☒ **A, B, C, E.** The correct order to perform a security analysis using the Security Configuration and Analysis snap-in is select **Open database**, select the database to be used, select the security template to be used, select **Analyze computer now**, and select the log file to be used. You do not need to select **Configure computer now** until you are ready to apply the database settings to the computer. Thus, Answers **A**, **B**, **C**, and **E** are incorrect.

15. You have just completed an analysis of your local computer using Security Configuration and Analysis. Looking at the analysis results, you notice several icons have a green check mark on them. You are concerned that your settings do not match those of the template you compared your computer to. What do icons with green check marks mean?

    A. A discrepancy exists between the database settings and the computer setting.

    B. No analysis was performed for this item because it was not configured in the database.

    C. The database setting and the computer setting match.

D. No analysis was performed for this item because it is not applicable to the computer.

☑ **C.** A green check mark indicates the database setting and the computer setting match.

☒ **A, B, D.** A discrepancy between the database and the computer settings is marked with a red *X*, thus Answer **A** is incorrect. When an analysis is not performed because no settings were configured in the database, a generic icon is displayed, thus Answer **B** is incorrect. When an analysis is not performed because the setting is not applicable to the computer, an exclamation point or question mark is displayed, thus Answer **D** is incorrect.

Chapter 2: Advanced Security Template and Group Policy Issues

Configuring Role-Based Server Security

1. Chris is having difficulty getting the securews.inf template to apply properly on a client workstation. She suspects that the computer was an upgrade from a previous installation of Windows NT 4.0. What two things can she do to correct this problem?

    A. Perform another upgrade installation of Windows 2000; the first one must not have taken properly.

    B. Apply the setup security.inf template to the computer.

    C. Perform a clean installation of Windows 2000 on the computer.

    D. Enforce the desired security settings using a System Policy.

    ☑ **B, D.** Although it is generally preferred to perform a clean installation (upgrade installations are known to have many and varied problems), sometimes that is not an option. In these cases, applying the setup security.inf template should correct the problem with the Windows NT 4.0 style Registry and File System ACLs that are most likely blocking the application of the security template Chris is trying to deploy.

    ☒ Performing another upgrade installation will not correct the problem, so Answer **A** is incorrect. Applying the security settings via a System Policy, although possible, does not solve the problem in an effective manner, so Answer **C** is also incorrect.

2. Rob is responsible for six Windows 2000 IIS servers in his organization. What can Rob do to harden his Windows 2000 IIS servers and prevent their vulnerability to attack? (Choose all that apply.)

   A. Use the IIS Lockdown tool to remove unnecessary IIS settings and configuration options.

   B. Use the Movetree tool to set security settings on the IIS server.

   C. Install the URLScan ISAPI filter to prevent certain types of HTTP requests from being served by the IIS server.

   D. Remove his IIS servers from the Active Directory domain and make them standalone member servers.

   ☑ **A, C, D**. Rob should use the IIS Lockdown tool and install the URLScan ISAPI filter to help harden his IIS servers. Additionally, he should consider using the MBSA tool and the HFNetChk tool as well as implementing a stronger security template to these IIS servers. By removing member servers from the Active Directory domain, you can mitigate the risk to your network should the IIS server be compromised.

   ☒ The Movetree tool is for Active Directory migration and management and is not applicable here, thus Answer **B** is incorrect.

3. Jeff has just performed a default installation of the URLScan ISAPI filter on his IIS server. Looking at the site that corresponds to his Web site, he cannot see the filter in place. What is the most likely problem?

   A. ISAPI filters are only installed on domain controllers running IIS. Jeff will need to install the ISAPI filter there.

   B. ISAPI filters can only be seen by IIS Admin; Jeff's user account is probably not a member of the IIS Admins group.

   C. Jeff must not have Domain Admin privileges on the network; Domain Admin privileges are required to install any ISAPI filter.

   D. The URLScan ISAPI filter is applied at the global level and is thus not shown at the site level.

   ☑ **D**. The URLScan ISAPI filter is applied at the global level, thus applying it to all sites on the server, and it will not be seen on each individual site on the server.

   ☒ ISAPI filters are not installed only on domain controllers; they are installed on the IIS servers that require them, thus Answer **A** is incorrect. Being the IIS Admin is not a requirement to be able to see the applied ISAPI filters, thus Answer **B** is incorrect. Possessing Domain Admin privileges is not required to be able to see the applied ISAPI filters, thus Answer **C** is incorrect.

4. Andrea is responsible for 25 client workstations and five servers in her Windows 2000 network. Her servers consist of two domain controllers, one Exchange server, and two file and print servers. How many different security configurations should she have on her network, at the minimum?

   A. 30
   B. 5
   C. 4
   D. 2

   ☑ **C.** Andrea should ideally have a minimum of four different security configurations: one for her desktop clients, one for her domain controllers, one for her Exchange server, and one for her file and printer servers. The general rule is that you should have a security policy in effect for each type of role that a computer performs. In this case, Andrea has four distinctly different roles on the network. She could configure more security configurations if warranted, such as if some of her client computers are in kiosks in the lobby of the company or otherwise open to anonymous users.

   ☒ Since Andrea has four different groups of computers for which to configure security, Answers **A**, **B**, and **D** are all incorrect.

5. Christopher is making preparations to deploy the hisecdc.inf template to his domain controllers. What things should Christopher do before he deploys this template on his production network? (Choose all that apply.)

   A. Christopher should ensure that he understands the implications and effects of deploying this template on his network.
   B. Christopher should perform a complete backup of his domain controllers.
   C. Christopher should develop a deployment plan that details how the template deployment process will work.
   D. Christopher should write down a list of all administrative usernames and passwords.

   ☑ **A, B, C.** Christopher will want to ensure that he completely understands the effects and implications of applying the template to his domain controllers. It would not do to simply rush into the deployment and create new problems. Furthermore, Christopher should ensure that a recent backup of the System State exists, because a backup can be used to restore a domain controller if the deployment does not go well and causes problems that cannot be fixed otherwise. Using a deployment plan will help ensure that the template is installed properly and in a controlled manner, which can help prevent problems from occurring.

- ☒ Recording the usernames and passwords of all administrator accounts is not a wise idea and certainly will not help Christopher deploy the hisecdc.inf template, thus Answer **D** is incorrect.

6. Crazy Mike, your assistant security administrator, has been given the task of installing the URLScan ISAPI filter on all of your organization's IIS servers. What two ways are available to install the URLScan ISAPI filter?

    A. Extract the URLScan files from the IIS Lockdown Wizard with the **iislockd /c command** and then executing URLScan setup.

    B. Install the URLScan ISAPI filter using the MBSA tool.

    C. Install the URLScan ISAPI filter by downloading it from Windows Update.

    D. Install the URLScan ISAPI filter from within the IIS Lockdown Wizard.

    - ☑ **A, D**. URLScan can be installed with or without using the IIS Lockdown Wizard.

    - ☒ The MBSA tool does not install URLScan, thus Answer **B** is incorrect. Windows Update does not provide you with a means to install the URLScan ISAPI filter, thus Answer **C** is incorrect.

7. You are the network administrator for your organization. You have been charged with creating and implementing a strong network security plan for all your servers and client workstations. How should you go about configuring security for your network? You plan on configuring and testing security templates and their applications in a test environment that mimics your production environment. (Choose all that apply.)

    A. Configure very specific security templates for use on each Organizational Unit that contains a specific group of member servers, such as the Exchange Server OU and the SQL Server OU.

    B. Configure a basic domain-level security template that provides basic security needs such as password and account policies across the entire domain.

    C. Configure a specific security template for the client computers in your network and apply it to a workstation-specific OU, such as Workstations OU.

    D. Configure one security template for all member servers, such as Exchange and SQL servers, and apply it to each OU that contains any of these member servers.

    - ☑ **A, B, C**. Configuring a security template that is specific to each type of role on the network is the best course of action. In this case, you would want to configure and properly deploy templates for domain controllers, Exchange servers, SQL servers, and client computers.

☒ Attempting to use a security template for multiple types of computer roles (such as SQL Server, Exchange Server, etc.) is not a good practice, because each type of server has its own unique needs and vulnerabilities that must be addressed, thus Answer **D** is incorrect.

Creating Secure Workstations

8. Lyman has a portable Windows 2000 computer that he travels with to various customer locations and sales presentations. In the event that Lyman's computer is stolen, what can you as the administrator do to prevent someone decrypting his EFS encrypted files?

   A. Remove the Data Recovery Agent certificate from the portable computer.

   B. Do not allow Lyman to place any sensitive information on the portable computer.

   C. Only allow L2TP connections when Lyman dials into the VPN server for remote access.

   D. Force Lyman to use a password that is extremely complex, consisting of numbers, letters, and characters and that is at least 42 characters long.

   ☑ **A.** Removing the Data Recovery Agent certificate and keys from the portable computer will prevent anyone from using them to decrypt any EFS encrypted documents on the portable computer's hard drive, should it become lost or stolen. This practice is helpful because, in many instances, it is easier to gain access to the built-in local administrative account on the computer than any other account. The default Data Recovery Agent for a computer is the local administrative account.

   ☒ Not allowing Lyman to place any sensitive data on the computer would not make good business sense and does not have any effect on preventing decryption of his encrypted files, thus Answer **B** is incorrect. Allowing only L2TP (with IPSec) VPN connections is a great security measure but is not applicable in this instance, thus Answer **C** is incorrect. Forcing Lyman to use a 42-character password that consists of numbers, letters, and characters still does nothing to prevent the issue of the local administrative account being used to decrypt EFS encrypted files—it will most likely serve to upset Lyman to some degree, however, thus Answer **D** is also incorrect.

9. Austin is seeking to export the certificate and private keys for his portable computer to a removable storage medium. When he opens the Local Security Console and starts the procedure to export the certificate and keys, he cannot select the Yes, export the private key option because it is grayed out and unavailable for

selection. Austin is using the Administrator account. What is the most likely reason for this issue?

A. He does not have the required permissions because he is not a part of the Administrators group.

B. He does not have the required permissions because he is not a part of the Domain Admins group.

C. He is logged into the domain instead of the local computer.

D. He is logged into the local computer instead of the domain.

☑ **C**. In order to export the Data Recovery Agent certificate, you must be logged in using the built-in Administrator account on the local computer. In 99 percent of the cases where this option is grayed out, you are probably logged into the domain instead of the local computer or trying to use another account that is a member of the Administrators group instead of the built-in administrator account.

☒ Being a member of the Administrators group will not help you complete this action, since you must be using the built-in Administrator account, thus Answer **A** is incorrect. Being a member of the Domain Admins group will not automatically grant you the required permissions; you must be using the local built-in Administrator account, thus Answer **B** is incorrect. Being logged into the local computer is the desired effect when attempting to export the local computer Data Recovery Agent certificate and private keys, thus Answer **D** is also incorrect.

10. Matt travels extensively with his Windows 2000 portable computer. What things can you easily do to enhance the security of his portable computer? (Choose all that apply.)

A. Install Windows 98 on the portable computer.

B. Remove the default Data Recovery Agent certificate and private key.

C. Enforce strong passwords for user accounts on the portable computer.

D. Rename the built-in Administrator account and remove it from the Administrators group.

☑ **B, C, D**. Removing the default Data Recovery Agent certificate and private key will prevent the decryption of EFS encrypted files and folders on the computer, should it become lost or stolen. Enforcing strong passwords on all accounts on the portable computer will make it more resistant to brute-force hacking attempts. Renaming the built-in administrator account and removing it from the Administrators group will also enhance security of the portable computer. (Note that you cannot remove the built-in administrative account.)

☒ Installing Windows 98 on Matt's portable computer will most definitely not increase security on it—it would greatly *decrease* the security of the computer, thus Answer **A** is incorrect.

Security Template Application Issues

11. Hannah is confused as to why the security settings she has configured for the computers in her domain are not being applied to five computers. The five computers are a mixture of Windows NT 4.0 Workstation and Windows 98 clients. What is the most likely reason for this problem?

    A. She has not installed the Directory Services Client onto these five legacy computers.

    B. Legacy computers cannot receive Group Policy object settings. Hannah will need to configure the settings she requires via System Policies.

    C. The computers are not located in the correct Organizational Unit.

    D. The computers are not located in her domain but are in another domain instead.

    ☑ **B**. Legacy client computers cannot receive Group Policy settings.

    ☒ Although these computers can participate in Active Directory, in a very limited way, by using the Directory Services Client, Group Policy is still not available to them, thus Answer **A** is incorrect. Because these computers cannot receive Group Policy, their OU placement will not cause this type of problem, thus Answer **C** is incorrect. The domain location of these computers is not an issue since they cannot receive Group Policy, thus Answer **D** is also incorrect.

12. Mei Ling has just applied a new template to her Group Policy object. She then forced Group Policy replication through the domain. What event ID should she hope to see that would indicate that the settings in Group Policy were applied correctly without any problems?

    A. 680

    B. 1704

    C. 612

    D. 520

    ☑ **B**. Event ID 1704 will occur when the Group Policy has been successfully applied.

    ☒ Event ID 680 pertains to the auditing of logon events, thus Answer **A** is incorrect. Event ID 612 pertains to the auditing of policy changes, thus Answer **C** is incorrect. Event ID 520 pertains to system evens, thus Answer **D** is incorrect.

13. It has been noted in your organization that sometimes problems occur when administrators attempt to apply incremental security templates to Windows 2000 computers that have been upgraded from Windows NT 4.0. What options do you have to remedy this situation so that you can apply the security templates? (Choose all that apply.)

    A. Revert all computers back to Windows NT 4.0.

    B. Perform clean installations of Windows 2000 instead of upgrades.

    C. Apply the Setup Security.inf template to the upgraded computers before attempting to apply any other incremental template.

    D. Remove the default Data Recovery Agent certificate and private key from each upgraded computer.

    ☑ **B, C.** In this case, you will be best off to simply perform a clean installation of Windows 2000. A clean installation will completely prevent this from being an issue. If this is not possible, you might be able to get around the problem by applying the Setup Security.inf template, which should correct the ACL problems associated with the upgrade process.

    ☒ Reverting all computers back to Windows NT 4.0 will not allow you to apply the incremental security templates, thus Answer **A** is incorrect. Removing the default Data Recovery Agent, although a good idea, will not help you out in this situation, thus Answer **D** is also incorrect.

Securing Server Message Block Traffic

14. Andrea is configuring SMB signing for her network. Which of the following configuration settings will result in client computers being able to connect to servers and use SMB signing? (Choose all that apply.)

    A. Digitally sign client communication (when possible): Not defined
    Digitally sign client communication (always): Not defined
    Digitally sign server communication (when possible): Enabled
    Digitally sign server communication (always): Enabled

    B. Digitally sign client communication (when possible): Enabled
    Digitally sign client communication (always): Enabled
    Digitally sign server communication (when possible): Enabled
    Digitally sign server communication (always): Enabled

    C. Digitally sign client communication (when possible): Disabled
    Digitally sign client communication (always): Enabled
    Digitally sign server communication (when possible): Enabled
    Digitally sign server communication (always): Disabled

D. Digitally sign client communication (when possible): Disabled
Digitally sign client communication (always): Disabled
Digitally sign server communication (when possible): Disabled
Digitally sign server communication (always): Disabled

☑ **B, D**. In order for a client to make a connection to a server using SMB signing, they must both be configured for at least the same minimum setting. If SMB signing is enabled on a server, clients that are also enabled for SMB signing (or require it) will be able to establish a communications session with that server. If SMB signing is required on a server, a client will not be able to establish a session unless it, at the minimum, has SMB signing enabled.

☒ The combinations presented in answers **A** and **C** will not result in communications due to a mismatch in SMB signing settings, thus Answers **A** and **C** are incorrect.

15. Bruno is attempting to configure SMB signing for his network servers and clients. Which of the following statements is true about configuring SMB signing?

    A. As long as all computers have the same maximum configuration level assigned, they will be able to communicate securely using SMB.

    B. As long as all computers have the same minimum configuration level assigned, they will be able to communicate securely using SMB.

    C. Servers should be set for Enabled and clients should be set for Not Defined on the Always options to be able to communicate securely using SMB.

    D. Servers should be set for Not Defined and clients should be set for Enabled on the When Possible options to be able to communicate securely using SMB.

    ☑ **B**. As long as all computers have the same minimum configuration level assigned, they will be able to communicate securely using SMB.

    ☒ All computes require the same minimum configuration level to ensure SMB signed communications occur, thus Answer **A** is incorrect. If any computers have the Not Defined setting, they will not be configured for SMB signing, thus answers **C** and **D** are incorrect.

Chapter 3: Identifying, Installing, and Troubleshooting Required Updates

Identifying Required Updates

1. Andrea is responsible for keeping 550 Windows 2000 computers up to date. She would like to determine what, if any, required updates her computers need on a

weekly basis. What is the best way for her to go about performing this task with the least administrative effort?

A. Andrea needs to visit each computer and run HFNetChk locally.

B. Andrea needs to create a script that runs HFNetChk against her computers and saves the results to a network share for her to examine.

C. Andrea needs to configure a script that runs Windows Update against each of her computers and provides a text file output.

D. Andrea needs to keep a log of installed versus required updates for each computer and check the Microsoft Web site weekly, looking for new updates that might be required.

☑ Answer **B** is correct. Creating a script to run HFNetChk against her computers is the best option for Andrea in this situation. Using a command similar to **hfnetchk –v –d** *domain_name* **–o tab –f hfnetchk_scan.txt**, she can configure a scan of the entire network that creates a text tab-delimited output file that can be easily analyzed in Microsoft Excel or Access to determine the current update status of all her computers. She can then determine the updates that must be applied and the proper order.

☒ Running HFNetChk locally from each computer is most definitely not the way to accomplish this task using the least amount of administrative effort, thus Answer **A** is incorrect. Windows Update cannot be configured to run and produce a text file output in the way that Andrea requires, thus Answer **C** is incorrect. Keeping a log book of installed updates for each computer, although a good practice, is not an effective solution in this situation, thus Answer **D** is incorrect.

2. Austin is trying to run the MBSA tool on one of his member servers when he is prompted to download and install a strange file claiming to be from Microsoft. What will happen if he rejects the download request for the file MSSecureXML file?

A. Nothing. The file is optional and not required to complete the scan using MBSA.

B. Nothing. The download request was obviously a hack attempt from an outside party. Microsoft never needs to download anything to your computer in order to determine its current update status.

C. Nothing. The MBSA tool cannot work without the file.

D. Nothing. As long as Austin knows which updates are and are not installed on his server, MBSA will function properly.

☑ Answer **C** is correct. Without the XML file containing the list of all updates and fixes, the MBSA tool cannot run. The same holds true when you're attempting to use the HFNetChk tool.

☒ The MSSecureXML file is required in order for MBSA to function, thus Answers **A**, **B**, and **D** are all incorrect.

3. Christopher is looking for a tool that can scan all 458 of his network computers from a central location and provide a detailed report of all updates and patches that he needs to apply. He would like to perform this scan with the least amount of administrative effort. What options are available to him? (Choose all correct answers.)

   A. Christopher can use the HFNetChk tool as part of a batch file or script to perform this task.
   B. Christopher can use Software Update Services to perform this task.
   C. Christopher can use the URLScan tool as part of a batch file or script to perform this task.
   D. Christopher can use the MBSA tool from either the command line or the GUI to perform this task.

   ☑ **A, D**. Christopher has a choice of using either (or both) the HFNetChk tool and the MBSA tool. Both will provide him with a report of the update situation on his network. The MBSA tool, however, will also provide Christopher with all sorts of other computer security-related information that he might not be looking for or be responsible for maintaining.

   ☒ Software Update Services, used with the Automatic Updates client, will install the required updates to computers and do not meet the requirements of the question, thus Answer **B** is incorrect. The URLScan tool is used to secure IIS servers, not for scanning computers for missing updates, thus Answer **C** is incorrect.

4. José is creating a script to run the HFNetChk tool on his network to scan for missing updates. What command does he need to use to allow the application to read a text file containing the IP addresses of the computers that he wants to scan?

   A. hfnetchk –h
   B. hfnetchk –i
   C. hfnetchk –fh
   D. hfnetchk –fip

☑ **D.** The *–fip* switch instructs the HFNetChk tool to read a list of IP addresses from a text file. The IP addresses in the file are those of the computers to be scanned by HFNetChk.

☒ The *–h* switch instructs HFNetChk to scan the specified NetBIOS hostname, thus Answer **A** is incorrect. The *–i* switch instructs HFNetChk to scan the specified IP address, thus Answer **B** is incorrect. The *–fh* switch instructs HFNetChk to scan the list of NetBIOS host names specified in the text file, thus Answer **C** is incorrect.

5. Austin has performed several scans of his network using the MBSA tool. Hannah now wants to examine the results of the scans, but she cannot do so. What is the most likely reason for this problem?

   A. Hannah is not a member of the Domain Admins group and thus does not have the proper permissions to access the location to which the scan results have been saved.

   B. Hannah does not have the proper permissions to access files located in Austin's Documents and Settings folder.

   C. Hannah is not connected to the network.

   D. Hannah's computer is not configured to use Kerberos as its authentication protocol.

   ☑ **B.** MBSA, by default, saves all scans in the Documents and Settings\user_name\SecurityScans folder. This is most likely the reason that Hannah cannot access the files, since they are located in Austin's private folders. Austin can allow Hannah to access the files by modifying the NTFS permissions or, alternatively, he can opt to save the scans to a more accessible location in the future.

   ☒ Membership in the Domain Admins group is not required to run the MBSA tool or view the scan results, thus Answer **A** is incorrect. Hannah not having an active connection to the network would certainly have an impact on her ability to access network files, but that is not as likely a scenario as a permissions problem, thus Answer **C** is incorrect. The use of the Kerberos protocol has nothing at all to do with using the MBSA tool or viewing the scan results, therefore Answer **D** is also incorrect.

6. Bruno is responsible for the security of the Windows 2000 computers in his organization. He has several junior administrators who work for him and apply patches and updates to computers as required. What can Bruno do to allow his junior administrators to be able to easily read the MBSA scan results that he generates on a daily basis with the least effort?

A. Have the junior administrators perform their own MBSA scans. This way, the scan results will be in their Documents and Settings folders.

B. Run the MBSA tool and elect for the results to be redirected to a location other than the default.

C. Give the junior administrators the required NTFS permissions to access the scan results in his Documents and Settings folder.

D. E-mail the MBSA results to all junior administrators daily.

☑ **B.** The easiest thing to do, and the only thing that makes sense from a time and effort perspective, is for Bruno to simply change the location where the MBSA scan results are saved from the default location within his Documents and Settings folder. This location should be a network share that is accessible to all junior administrators.

☒ Having each junior administrator perform his or her own scan is a waste of time and network resources, thus Answer **A** is incorrect. Giving each junior administrator the required NTFS permissions for Bruno's Documents and Settings folder is not required and is dangerous, thus Answer **C** is incorrect. E-mailing the MBSA scan results to each junior administrator daily is again time and resource intensive, thus Answer **D** is also incorrect.

Deploying and Managing Updates

7. Lily is responsible for 20 Windows 2000 computers in her organization. All the computers are on one campus, but they are scattered among four different buildings. Lily is the only network administrator in her company. Her network is a Windows 2000 Active Directory network. What is the easiest way for Lily to keep all her clients updated with the patches and updates they need but not to allow any updates or patches to be issued until she is satisfied that they are stable?

A. Lily should use Windows Update on each computer locally to download and install the updates her computers need.

B. Lily should use the Windows Update Catalog to download and install the updates her computers need.

C. Lily should use Software Update Services and the Automatic Updates client to download and install the updates her computers need.

D. Lily should download all the updates she needs and create an integrated installation CD-ROM to distribute to each of the four buildings to install the updates on her computers.

☑ **C.** Using the Software Update Service to download updates to the local computer, Lily can examine each one for applicability (not all updates that are downloaded will be applicable to her network) and test them for stability and compatibility. When she is satisfied with an update, she can add it to the list of approved updates in SUS. Automatic Updates clients, when configured properly in Group Policy to look toward an internal Windows Update server, make available only those updates that have been placed on the approved list within SUS.

☒ Visiting each computer and using Windows Update would be a waste of time and network resources for Lily—especially considering that her 20 computers are spread over four different buildings, thus Answer **A** is incorrect. Using the Windows Update Catalog would enable Lily to selectively download the updates she wants. However, this solution provides no automatic means of update deployment and installation like that offered by the combination of SUS and Automatic Updates, thus Answer **B** is incorrect. Creating an integrated installation CD-ROM is a fantastic solution for deploying new clients—but not a realistic one in this case, since the computers are already in place, thus Answer **D** is incorrect.

8. Hannah needs to locate and download applicable security updates for her network for testing in a lab environment. What are the best ways for her to get these updates as quickly as possible without downloading anything she doesn't want or installing any additional network services? (Choose all that apply.)

   A. Hannah can visit the TechNET security page and download specific updates that she needs.

   B. Hannah can use the Software Update Services to download available updates.

   C. Hannah can use the Windows Update Catalog to download the updates she needs.

   D. Hannah can allow her computers to use Automatic Updates from the Windows Update Web servers.

   ☑ **A, C.** The best way for Hannah to get the files she needs, and nothing else, without installing or configuring any additional software or services is to either visit the TechNET security page and download specific updates or to browse the Windows Update Catalog and download specific updates.

   ☒ Using Software Update Services does not satisfy the requirements of this question in that it requires a new service to be installed and configured on the network, thus Answer **B** is incorrect. Likewise, using Automatic Updates from the Windows Update Web servers does not satisfy the requirements of the question in that unnecessary updates are likely to be downloaded to her computers, therefore Answer **D** is incorrect.

9. Rick is preparing to install eight hotfixes to his file and print servers. What method should Rick use to ensure that all eight hotfixes get applied correctly and the servers have no stability or compatibility issues after he is done, using the least amount of administrative effort?

   A. Rick should use the Qchain.exe tool in conjunction with a batch file or script to install all eight hotfixes in one shot.

   B. Rick should manually install each hotfix, in order from lowest Q article number to highest Q article number, restarting his server after each one to make sure that version conflicts are prevented.

   C. Rick should manually install all eight hotfixes and then restart his server to ensure that the updates are applied.

   D. Rick should extract all the files from the hotfix executables and then copy these over the existing files on his server.

   ☑ **A**. Rick would be wise to use the Qchain.exe tool during the process of deploying his eight hotfixes. Only by using the Qchain.exe tool can he be assured that version conflicts and system stability issues will be avoided in most cases.

   ☒ Although manually installing each hotfix one at a time is a viable solution, it does not meet the specified criteria in that it takes far from the least amount of effort to make it happen, thus Answer **B** is incorrect. Installing all eight hotfixes at one time and then restarting the server is a sure recipe for disaster because version conflicts are likely to occur, therefore Answer **C** is incorrect. Extracting the files and copying them to the server is not a valid solution and should never be done, thus Answer **D** is also incorrect.

10. Cindy is trying to install the Software Update Service on her server computer, but the installation keeps failing. What is the most likely reason for this problem?

    A. Cindy's network does not have Active Directory, which is required for SUS to work.

    B. Cindy is attempting to install SUS onto a domain controller, which is not allowed.

    C. Cindy's network has only Windows XP Professional clients. You must have Windows 2000 clients for SUS to install properly.

    D. Cindy does not have Enterprise Admin credentials.

    ☑ **B**. SUS cannot be installed onto a domain controller. This is the most likely reason that the installation is failing for Cindy.

☒ Active Directory is not required for SUS to function, although it does make configuring the Automatic Updates client behavior much easier, thus Answer **A** is incorrect. The type of network client does not affect the installation of the SUS service, thus Answer **C** is incorrect. SUS does not require Enterprise Admin credentials to install, so Answer **D** is not a valid answer for the problem.

11. Tom has installed and configured the Automatic Updates client on his computer to download updates from an internal server named GREEN42. Automatic Updates was configured to download and install, automatically, any available updates from GREEN42 on a daily basis. After several weeks, Tom noticed that no updates have been applied to his client computer. Given what you know so far, what is the most likely reason that no updates have been received on Tom's computer?

    A. Tom turns his computer off during the update period that has been configured.
    B. GREEN42 is either not running SUS or is not receiving updates from the Windows Update servers.
    C. Tom forgot to accept the supplemental End User License Agreement that is required to make Active Updates function properly.
    D. Tom's copy of Windows 2000 is not properly licensed.

    ☑ **B.** The most likely cause of Tom's problem is that he either does not have or does not have correctly configured an SUS server named GREEN42 on his network. If the server GREEN42 does actually exist and has been configured with SUS, it is likely that GREEN42 has not yet been configured for synchronization with the Windows Update servers—thus no updates are available for download and installation onto Tom's client computer.

    ☒ Tom turning his off during the update period is possible, but nothing was mentioned about this in the question, thus Answer **A** is not correct. There is no supplemental End User License Agreement to accept for Automatic Updates on the client computer, thus Answer **C** is incorrect. The licensing status of Tom's copy of Windows 2000 is not an issue in regard to Automatic Updates (although the Business Software Alliance might be paying him a visit if it's unlicensed), thus Answer **D** is not correct.

12. Catherine is preparing to deploy Windows 2000 Professional to 75 new workstations in her company. She knows that a new service pack has been made available for Windows 2000, but her Windows 2000 Professional Setup CD-ROM only has Service Pack 1. What is the easiest and fastest way for Catherine to get these 75 new clients installed with Windows 2000 Service Pack 3 without placing an undue strain on the network?

A. Visit each client, installing Windows 2000 Professional Service Pack 1. After the installation is complete, install Service Pack 3.

B. Create a slipstreamed installation source using her Windows 2000 Professional Setup CD-ROM and the Service Pack 3 files. Deploy this source to her new clients over the network using the Remote Installation Service.

C. Use RIS to deploy a Windows 2000 Service Pack 1 image. After this process has been completed, use Group Policy and IntelliMirror to deploy Service Pack 3 using the update.msi file.

D. Create a slipstream installation source and burn it back to CD-ROM using her Windows 2000 Professional Setup CD-ROM and the Service Pack 3 files. Visit each machine and install Windows 2000 Professional Service Pack 3 from this slipstreamed CD-ROM.

☑ **B**. Creating a slipstreamed installation source and then turning that into a CD-based RIS image for deployment using the Remote Installation Service is by far the best option of any presented.

☒ Although she can manually install Windows 2000 and then install Service Pack 3 after that, this process is too time consuming and does not satisfy the criterion for fastest method, thus Answer **A** is incorrect. Deploying Windows 2000 Professional Service Pack 1 via RIS and then following up with a Group Policy-based update to Service Pack 3 is a waste of both time and network resources, thus Answer **C** is incorrect. Creating a slipstreamed Service Pack 3 CD-ROM and manually installing Windows 2000 Professional Service Pack 3 on her 75 computers is also too time consuming and thus does not meet the specified criteria for the question, thus Answer **D** is incorrect.

13. Jon is responsible for three client computers that are not part of the corporate network. These computers have Internet connectivity through a broadband DSL connection at their remote site. What is the best way for Jon to keep these three computers up to date without having to travel to this remote location or spend unnecessary money? No users at the remote location are technically competent to perform this task for Jon.

    A. Jon has no other choice but to travel to this location.

    B. Jon should install and configure the Automatic Updates client to get critical updates from the Windows Update servers and automatically install them upon download.

    C. Jon should FTP into the computers and run the HFNetChk tool to check for required updates.

    D. Jon should configure these computers to participate in the corporate network via a leased WAN link.

☑ **B**. By allowing Automatic Updates to download and install updates from the Windows Update Web servers, Jon can be assured that his remote clients are getting the updates they require.

☒ Traveling to this location is a solution, but an unacceptable one, thus Answer **A** is incorrect. Making an FTP connection to the computers is not a viable solution; HFNetChk cannot be run via FTP, thus Answer **C** is incorrect. Leasing a WAN link for these three computers is not economically feasible, thus Answer **D** is incorrect.

Troubleshooting Update Installations

14. You are the network administrator of a medium-sized regional organization that has one central office and six field offices spread out over several states. A user in each field office is performing most of the local administrative functions for you, although these users are not as knowledgeable as you would like them to be and sometimes cause problems that you must correct yourself. Yesterday, one of your "assistant administrators" applied several hotfixes to a Windows 2000 server computer in his office. Today you received a phone call from this "assistant administrator" informing you that the power failed in that location overnight and now the Windows 2000 server will not start properly. What do you suspect is the cause of this problem?

    A. The power supply in the server has been damaged.
    B. The user did not properly apply the hotfixes by restarting the server after each one or by using Qchain.
    C. The server was attacked overnight and the Registry has been damaged by the attacker.
    D. The user did not use the HFNetChk tool to determine the hotfixes that were required.

    ☑ **B**. The most likely scenario here is that the user who applied the hotfixes applied them all, one after another, without a restart following each one. It's also safe to assume that Qchain was not used.

    ☒ Although the server itself could have sustained damage when the power failed, it's not nearly as likely as the issue of hotfixes being applied incorrectly and causing file version conflicts problems, thus Answer **A** is incorrect. The server might very well have been attacked overnight, but we won't know that until a detailed analysis of it can be made. Again, the most likely reason for this problem is that the hotfixes were not applied correctly, thus Answer **C** is incorrect. Use of the HFNetChk tool to determine which hotfixes were required would probably not have prevented this issue, thus Answer **D** is also incorrect.

15. Dom, your assistant administrator, has been in the office all night applying hotfixes to your production servers. Now when he restarts them, they all fail to start properly. You quickly determine that the cause of the problem was his lack of using the Qchain utility. Now you have a problem to deal with. Which of the following documents should you consider using at this point?

    A. Network Acceptable Use Policy (AUP)

    B. Server update plan

    C. Network disaster recovery plan

    D. Windows 2000 Resource Kit

    ☑ **C.** You are now in a disaster recovery situation. Your production servers are down and cannot be successfully restarted—you have no choice but to perform a restoration off the most recent set of backup media.

    ☒ The AUP is a document that details what users are and are not allowed to do on the network, such as not downloading MP3s or not running file-sharing programs such as LimeWire, thus Answer **A** is incorrect. The server update plan is the document that could have helped Dom prevent this situation had he been using it properly, thus Answer **B** is incorrect. The Windows 2000 Resource Kit is an invaluable asset to any Windows 2000 network administrator and you might very well end up using it, but what you really need right now is your disaster recovery plan, thus Answer **D** is also incorrect.

Chapter 4: Installing, Configuring, and Managing Windows 2000 Certificate Authorities

Cryptography and You: What is it All About?

1. What keys are used in public key encryption and what are their functions? (Choose all that apply.)

    A. A public key that can be used by a sender to encrypt data

    B. A public key that can be used by a recipient to decrypt data

    C. A private key that can be used by a recipient to decrypt data

    D. A private key that can be used by a sender to encrypt data

    ☑ Answers **A** and **C** are correct. The public key is made freely available to all and is used to encrypt data being sent to the key's owner. When the data is received, the recipient will use his or her private key to encrypt the message.

☒ Answers **B** and **D** are incorrect because the public key is made freely available to all and is used to encrypt data being sent to the key's owner. When the data is received, the recipient will use his or her private key to encrypt the message.

2. A digital signature provides what assurance? (Choose all that apply.)
   A. The message has not been tampered with during transit.
   B. The message has been protected from capture during transit.
   C. The message has originated from the sender.
   D. The message has not been delayed during transit.

   ☑ Answers **A** and **C** are correct. A digital signature can be used to verify that the message has not been tampered with and the sender is who he or she claims they are.

   ☒ Answer **B** is incorrect because there is no guarantee of the message not having been captured in transit. Answer **D** is incorrect because there is no guarantee that the message has not been delayed in transit.

3. What is used to provide assurance that the public key being used belongs to the entity that owns the corresponding private key?
   A. Active Directory
   B. Digital certificate
   C. Smart card
   D. User name and password

   ☑ Answer **B** is correct. A digital certificate is used to provide assurance that a public key being used belongs to the owner of the matching private key.

   ☒ Answer **A** is incorrect because Active Directory is not responsible for verifying a match between public and private keys. Answer **C** is incorrect because a smart card is part of a multifactor authentication system, but does not verify that a public and private key pair match. Answer **D** is incorrect because a user name and password is not used to verify a match between a public and private key.

Certificate Authorities

4. What type of CAs does Windows 2000 provide support for? (Choose all that apply.)
   A. Enterprise Root CA
   B. Standalone Root CA
   C. Standalone Subordinate CA

D. Enterprise Subordinate CA

☑ Answers **A**, **B**, **C**, and **D** are correct. Windows 2000 supports four types of CAs: The Enterprise Root CA, the Enterprise Subordinate CA, the Standalone Root CA, and the Standalone Subordinate CA.

☒ None.

5. You wish to deploy a certificate services solution for your network, which is not using Active Directory. Your CA will not be required to be on the network continuously, but only for brief periods of time to allow you to issue certificates and publish updated CRLs. You have installed a Trusted Root CA certificate from VeriSign to act as your CA's root. What type of CA should you deploy?

  A. Enterprise Root CA

  B. Standalone Root CA

  C. Standalone Subordinate CA

  D. Enterprise Subordinate CA

  ☑ Answer **C** is correct. In this case, where you do not plan to leave the CA connected to the network continuously and you are using a third-party Root CA certificate as your root, you would most likely want to deploy a Standalone Subordinate CA.

  ☒ Answers **A** and **D** are incorrect because Enterprise CAs require Active Directory. Answer **B** is incorrect because you do not need to configure a Standalone Root CA since you are going to use a third-party CA as your root.

Installing and Managing Windows 2000 CAs

6. Ralph is preparing to implement a PKI solution in his small corporate network. He is currently using Windows 2000 Servers and Windows 2000 Professional computers, but has not deployed Active Directory. Ralph does not currently have any plans for an Active Directory deployment and his users are happy in the peer-to-peer workgroup arrangement that they are currently using. The company that Ralph works for is a small software development firm that would like to be able to digitally sign their downloadable applications to assure customers that they are legitimate and valid downloads. What type of Certificate Services solution can Ralph deploy to meet this need without requiring him to spend too much time or money?

  A. Ralph should configure his network for Active Directory and issue these code-signing certificates from a newly created Enterprise Root CA.

B. Ralph should configure a Stand-alone Subordinate CA that uses a third-party certificate from VeriSign or Thawte as its root, and issue code-signing certificates with this standalone CA.

C. Ralph should configure his network for Active Directory and create an Enterprise Root and Enterprise subordinate CA. He should then install a trusted Root Certificate on the Enterprise Subordinate CA that comes from a trusted third party such as VeriSign or Thawte, and issue code-signing certificates from the Enterprise Subordinate CA.

D. Ralph should purchase an individual code-signing certificate issued by a trusted third party such as VeriSign or Thawte for each of his code developers, and allow them use these certificates to sign code made available for download.

☑ Answer **B** is correct. Ralph can take the easiest (and cheapest path) to the solution configuring a standalone CA that uses a third-party certificate from VeriSign, Thawte, or any other trusted third-party CA as its root. This standalone CA can then issue code-signing certificates that the developers can use to sign code before making it available for public download.

☒ Answer **A** is incorrect because configuring and implementing Active Directory and using an Enterprise CA with a trusted third-party certificate is more work than is required, especially since there are no plans in place to upgrade the peer-to-peer network to Active Directory for any other reason. Answer **C** is incorrect because issuing code-signing certificates from an internal CA with no path back to a trusted third-party source will not go very far towards reassuring customers that the certificate is valid and trustworthy. Answer **D** is incorrect because purchasing certificates for each developer is not a very time or cost effective solution.

7. Allison is attempting to install Certificate Services on one of her member servers. She is unable to complete the installation. What are some of the possible reasons for her inability to install Certificate Services? (Choose all that apply.)

   A. Allison does not have administrative rights on the domain controllers in her organization.

   B. Allison does not have administrative rights on the DNS servers in her organization.

   C. Allison does not have administrative rights on the WINS servers in her organization.

   D. Allison does not have administrative rights on the computer she is attempting to install Certificate Services onto.

E. Allison does not have administrative rights on the RRAS servers in her organization.

F. Allison does not have administrative rights on the Exchange servers in her organization.

☑ Answers **A**, **B**, and **D** are correct. To install Certificate Services, you need to have administrative permissions on the domain controllers, DNS servers, and the local computer on which Certificate Services is being installed. Failure to have any of these permissions will result in a failure.

☒ Answers **C**, **E**, and **F** are incorrect because having administrative permissions on the WINS, RRAS and Exchange servers is not required for installing Certificate Services.

8. Hannah is attempting to install Certificate Services on one of her member servers. From where would Hannah initiate the installation process?

A. Hannah should issue the certsrv.exe command from the command line to initiate the installation.

B. Hannah should perform the installation by using the Windows 2000 Setup CD-ROM menu.

C. Hannah should perform the installation by configuring Certificate Services from the Windows Component Wizard.

D. Hannah should visit the Windows Update Web site to download and install the required updates to Windows 2000 to support Certificate Services—it is not part of a default installation of Windows 2000.

☑ Answer **C** is correct. Certificate Services is installed and removed by using the Windows Component Wizard.

☒ Answers **A**, **B** and **D** are incorrect **because** Certificate Services is installed and removed by using the Windows Component Wizard.

9. Jon wants to create a trust chain for his Root CA from a third-party CA such as VeriSign or Thawte. How can Jon create this trust chain that starts with the third-party CA, goes next to his Root CA, and then on to his subordinate CAs, which in turn are issuing certificates to users in his network?

A. Jon will need to purchase a special Root CA server from the third-party company and physically place that in his network.

B. Jon will need to purchase a certificate from the third-party CA and import it into the trusted root folder of his Root CA. This will make the third-party CA the root of all CAs in his network.

C. Jon will need to set up a VPN from his network to the third party in order for his Root CA to communicate with their CA's to verify chain of trust.

D. Jon will need to co-locate his CA in the third-party company's building and issue certificates from it to his subordinate CA's and users.

☑ Answer **B** is correct. By acquiring and importing a trusted third-party certificate into the trusted root folder of the Root CA, Jon can establish a chain of trust from the third-party through his Root CA, to his subordinate CAs, and finally to his users and computers. All certificates he issues can be validated back to this trusted third-party Root Certificate.

☒ Answer **A** is incorrect because there is no need to actually purchase a CA from a third-party, just to acquire the third-party Root CA certificate Answer **C** is incorrect because a VPN is not part of the solution to this problem. Answer **D** is incorrect because co-locating a CA is not required to solve this problem.

10. The employees in Christopher's organization routinely access an SSL-secured web site. You would like for their computers to automatically be able to verify the certificate being presented to them instead of being prompted to download and install the other organizations root certificate each time. What can you do? (Choose two correct answers.)

    A. Import the Root Certificate into the Trusted Root Certification Authorities folder in the domain Group Policy Object. This will propagate it to all domain computers.

    B. Import the root certificate into the Trusted Root Certification Authorities folder in the local computer certificate store for your Root CA.

    C. Import the Root Certificate manually into the Trusted Root Certification Authorities folder for each user's personal certificate store.

    D. Import the Root Certificate to your domain controller and then export it to a floppy disk for safekeeping.

    ☑ Answers **A** and **B** are correct. By importing the certificate to your Trusted Root Certification Authorities folders in the domain GPO and on your Root CA, you will establish a chain of trust for your organization through your CA to the other organization.

    ☒ Answer **C** is incorrect because importing the certificate manually onto each computer in your network would be too time-consuming. Answer **D** is incorrect because importing the certificate to the domain controller would not accomplish anything (except in the case where it was also a CA, which was not specified here).

11. You have recently revoked 14 certificates that were in use in your organization. What would be the next thing you would likely want to do?

    A. Perform an incremental backup of your system state data.

    B. Publish a new CRL.

    C. Renew the CA's certificate.

    D. Change the KMS password.

    ☑ Answer **B** is correct. In the situation where you have revoked a certificate (or a large number of them in this case), you would next want to publish the CRL so that all users can be informed of the recently revoked certificates.

    ☒ Answer **A** is incorrect because backing up the system state data would not be the next thing to do after revoking a large number of certificates. Answer **C** is incorrect because renewing the CA's certificate is not required until it is coming upon its expiration. Answer **D** is incorrect because changing the KMS password has nothing to do with revoking certificates.

12. Rob is the administrator of a large Windows 2000 PKI implementation, which has several hundred certificates issued and revoked daily. Which of the following presents the best option Rob can perform that will enable his users to always have the most up to date CRL?

    A. Configure the CRL publication interval for 30 minutes.

    B. Manually publishes the CRL every morning at 9 AM.

    C. Configure the CRL publication interval for 60 minutes.

    D. Add additional CDPs to the publication list for his CRLs.

    ☑ Answer **C** is correct. The best option is to configure the CRL publication schedule for 60-minute intervals. This is the smallest publication interval that can be configured and is the best option of the options presented.

    ☒ Answer **A** is incorrect because you cannot configure the CRL publication interval for any time less than 60 minutes. Answer **B** is incorrect because manually publishing the CRL once per day is not the best solution as revocations made throughout the day will not be published until the next morning. Answer **D** is incorrect because adding additional CDPs, while always a good idea to ensure the maximum availability of a CRL, is not the correct solution.

13. You want to perform a backup of your Enterprise Root CA server. What methods are available to you to accomplish this task? (Choose all that apply.)

    A. Perform a system state backup using the NTBACKUP program.

    B. Export all Trusted Root Certificates to removal media.

C. Create a striped disk set on the CA server.

D. Perform a Certificate Services backup from the CA console.

☑ Answers **A** and **D** are correct. The two methods available for backing up your CA include performing a system state backup or performing a backup from within the Certification Authority console.

☒ Answer **B** is incorrect because exporting all Trusted Root Certificates will not perform a complete backup of the CA. Answer **C** is incorrect because creating a striped disk set will not provide a backup.

Advanced Certificate Management Issues

14. Andrea is the Exchange administrator for her organization. She is using Exchange 2000 on Windows 2000 and is using the Exchange Key Management Service for advanced e-mail message security. One of her users, George, recently dropped his laptop in the hotel pool while vacationing. George has been issued a new laptop, complete with Windows 2000 and Microsoft Outlook. He would like to be able to continue to use secure e-mail. What can Andrea do to allow him to continue to be able to use secure e-mail functions?

    A. George's KMS private key is tied to his GUID and cannot be recovered without deleting and recreating his user account.

    B. Andrea will need to delete George's Exchange mailbox and create a new one from the Exchange System Manager.

    C. Andrea will need to login to the KMS and perform a key recovery action on George's account. He will receive an e-mail from the Exchange System Attendant providing him with instructions on how to configure for advanced e-mail security.

    D. Andrea will need to contact Microsoft to get the unlock code for the PID used to install Outlook on George's old laptop. Only with this PID can she reassociate his Exchange mailbox to his new laptop and allow him to use secure e-mail functions again.

    ☑ Answer **C** is correct. In this case, all that needs to be done is for Andrea to perform a recovery action from the KMS server. George will be sent an e-mail with all of the instructions he needs to get configured for secure e-mail once again.

    ☒ Answers **A**, **B**, and **D** are incorrect because, in this case, all Andrea needs to do is perform a recovery action from the KMS server. George will be sent an e-mail with all of the instructions he needs to reconfigure for e-mail.

15. You are the administrator of your organization's small Windows 2000 network. You have just finished configuring a new laptop computer for your CEO who replaced an existing computer. The first time he attempts to digitally sign a message in Outlook, he finds that he does not have the capability to do so. You are using Exchange 2000 as your messaging system and have the Key Management Server in place. What do you need to so that your CEO can digitally sign his e-mail once again? (Choose two answers.)

    A. Use the Key Manager in the ESM.

    B. Open the User Properties page for your CEO in Active Directory Users and Computers.

    C. Recover the lost key and issue your CEO a new enrollment token.

    D. Place a check in the "Password never expires" check box.

    ☑ Answers **A** and **C** are correct. You will need to use the Key Manager in the ESM to recover the lost key and issue a new enrollment token (e-mail message) to your CEO. After this, he can reconfigure for e-mail security in Outlook by following the instructions in the e-mail.

    ☒ Answers **B** and **D** are incorrect because you will not need to modify your CEOs user account properties from the Active Directory Users and Computers console to perform a KMS key recovery.

Chapter 5: Managing and Troubleshooting the Encrypting File System

The Role of EFS in a Network Security Plan

1. Jon uses EFS to encrypt his files on the network file server. By using EFS, has Jon protected his files at all times?

    A. No, because the files are decrypted on the file server and then sent in plaintext across the network.

    B. Yes, because the files are sent in ciphertext across the network and decrypted on his local computer.

    C. Yes, because EFS also provides end-to-end security for data.

    D. No, because EFS cannot be used on network file servers, only on a local computer.

    ☑ **A.** When files are encrypted on a network server using EFS, they are encrypted only while on that server. Files are decrypted on the server and sent across the network in plaintext. Jon would need to implement IPSec on the network to ensure security while in transit.

☒ **B, C, D**. EFS-encrypted files are decrypted on the file server and transmitted in plaintext across the network, thus Answer **B** is incorrect. EFS does not provide end-to-end security; that is a solution provided by IPSec, thus Answer **C** is incorrect. EFS can be used on network servers as long as they have been marked for delegation, thus Answer **D** is incorrect.

2. Andrea is attempting to encrypt a folder on her Windows 2000 Professional computer. When she encrypts the folder, she notices that it is no longer NTFS compressed. Why is this so?

    A. Andrea is not logged in with a domain account. Domain accounts are required to implement both encryption and compression at the same time.

    B. Andrea is not a member of the Administrators group. Only Administrators can implement both encryption and compression at the same time.

    C. EFS encryption and NTFS compression are mutually exclusive. You cannot implement both encryption and compression at the same time.

    D. Extra users have been added to the files contained in the folder. You must not have extra users added to a file in order to apply both encryption and compression to it.

    ☑ **C**. EFS encryption and NTFS compression are mutually exclusive, thus Andrea will not be able to use both at the same time on her folder. She can have some compressed files and some encrypted files within the same folder, but she cannot apply both attributes at the folder level itself.

    ☒ **A, B, D**. EFS encryption and NTFS compression are mutually exclusive. Being logged in with a domain account or an Administrative account will not change this fact, thus Answers **A** and **B** are incorrect. The extra users function is only available in Windows XP and later operating systems. Furthermore, EFS encryption and NTFS compression are mutually exclusive, thus Answer **D** is incorrect.

3. Catherine is the senior member of the accounting department in your company. She has several database files that need to be protected from access by other members of her department who have NTFS permissions allowing them read and write access to the network share where the database files are located. What is the easiest thing you can do to help Catherine secure her database files without adding to your administrative workload or changing any user's NTFS permissions? (Choose all that apply.)

A. Instruct Catherine to create a new folder and place her database documents inside it.

B. Create a batch file for Catherine that uses the *cipher* command to encrypt her files for her in their current folder.

C. Instruct Catherine to configure EFS encryption on the folder itself from Windows Explorer.

D. Remove all the other users in Catherine's department from the OU they are located in and place them in a new OU with different effective NTFS permissions.

☑ **A, C.** By having Catherine create and encrypt a new folder, all documents created or placed in the folder automatically become encrypted. Additionally, any temp files created by the application in this folder will be encrypted as well, further increasing the security of her data.

☒ **B, D.** Creating a batch file using the *cipher* command is not necessary since Catherine can quite easily create the new folder and encrypt it on her own, thus Answer **B** is incorrect. Moving users from one OU to another is not required and is most certainly not the easiest solution to this problem, thus Answer **D** is incorrect.

Using the Encrypting File System

4. Chris wants to use EFS encryption on some of her files that are stored on the network file server. The file server is running Windows NT 4.0 SP6. Will she be able to use EFS encryption? Why or why not?

   A. Yes. SP6 upgrades NTFS v4 to NTFS v5, which is the version used by Windows 2000.

   B. No. EFS encryption cannot be used on a network file server, only on a local computer.

   C. No. EFS encryption can only be used in Windows 2000, Windows XP, and Windows .NET, not in Windows NT 4.0 or any other Windows product.

   D. Yes. As long as her computer is using Windows 2000, it makes no difference what operating system the file server is running.

   ☑ **C.** EFS is not supported on legacy Windows operating systems, such as Windows NT 4.0 or Windows 98. You must be using Windows 2000 or later in order to be able to use EFS encryption.

   ☒ **A, B, D.** You cannot use EFS encryption on any Service Level of Windows NT 4.0, thus Answer **A** is incorrect. EFS encryption can be used on network file servers running Windows 2000 as long as they have been delegated for trust, thus Answer **B** is incorrect. Again, EFS requires that Windows 2000 or later be in use on the file server, thus Answer **D** is incorrect.

5. What is the result of applying a public key to an unencrypted file called?

   A. Plaintext
   B. Encoded
   C. Ciphertext
   D. Signed

   ☑ **C.** After an unencrypted file has been encrypted using a public key, it is known as *ciphertext*.

   ☒ **A, B, D.** *Plaintext* is the data before it has been encrypted, thus Answer **A** is incorrect. *Encoded text* is text that has been transformed into an encoded form (such as Base 64 Web encoding; see Chapter 8) but is not encrypted and can be very easily decoded without a private key, thus Answer **B** is incorrect. *Signing* refers to using a digital certificate to digitally sign a document proving that it is authentic and valid, thus Answer **D** is incorrect.

6. Hannah has several critical payroll files on which she would like to increase security by encrypting them with EFS encryption. The files are named payroll1.pay, payroll2.pay, and payroll3.pay and are located in the Payroll folder on her computer. What does she need to encrypt to ensure maximum security is obtained for these files and the data they contain?

   A. Hannah needs to implement EFS encryption on the payroll1.pay file, the payroll2.pay file, and the Payroll folder.
   B. Hannah needs to implement EFS encryption on the Payroll folder only.
   C. Hannah needs to implement EFS encryption on the payroll1.pay, payroll2.pay, and payroll3.pay files only.
   D. Hannah need to implement EFS encryption on the root of the volume on which the files are stored.

   ☑ **B.** The best solution is to implement encryption at the folder level (making sure that the encryption attribute is set at that time to all files and folders in that folder). By doing so, not only will the payroll files be encrypted, but so will any temp files that are created in that directory. If she only encrypts the files themselves, any new files added to that directory, including temp files, will not be encrypted.

☒ **A, C, D**. Encrypting only two files and the folder might not automatically provide protection for the third file unless Hannah specifies that it is to be encrypted as well, which she can do. This, however, is not the best approach from a security point of view, thus Answer **A** is incorrect. Encrypting only the three payroll files themselves will leave any temp files that her payroll application creates unencrypted and vulnerable to compromise. It's better to encrypt at the folder level, thus Answer **C** is incorrect. Encrypting an entire volume is not advised and not possible if the volume contains system files. EFS will not encrypt system files, thus Answer **D** is incorrect.

User Operations

7. Austin is preparing to copy several hundred EFS encrypted files from one Windows 2000 NTFS folder to another Windows 2000 NTFS folder. All the files are EFS encrypted. The source folder is EFS encrypted. The destination folder is not EFS encrypted. What will be the result of his action to copy these files?

    A. EFS encrypted files cannot be copied, thus nothing will happen. He will need to decrypt them before copying.

    B. The files will become decrypted because the destination folder is not encrypted.

    C. He will be prompted to choose whether or not each file should remain encrypted after the files have been copied to the destination folder.

    D. The files will remain encrypted because the files themselves are encrypted.

    ☑ **D**. If the file to be copied is encrypted and it is being copied from one Windows 2000 NTFS folder to another, it will remain encrypted regardless of the encryption state of the destination folder.

    ☒ **A, B, C**. EFS-encrypted files can be copied just the same as any other file and can retain their encryption status due to improvements in the Windows 2000 copy command, thus Answer A is incorrect. The encryption state of the folder is not important as long as it is a Windows 2000 NTFS folder and the files themselves are encrypted, which they are in this case, so Answer B is incorrect. There will be no prompt asking Austin to choose what the final encryption status is to be, thus Answer C is incorrect. File operations with EFS-encrypted files are done transparently to the user except in the case of intentional encryptions and decryptions.

8. Chan has identified several folders on several of his Windows 2000 file servers that he would like to encrypt using his EFS certificate. Rather than perform the encryption process manually through Windows Explorer, he wants to use the cipher command. He plans to use the cipher command in a script and does not

want it to stop running if an error is encountered during the process. What command should be used on these folders to achieve this result?

A. *cipher /e /d /s* directory

B. *cipher /e /i /s* directory

C. *cipher /d /i /s* directory

D. *cipher /e /f /s* directory

☑ **B**. Christopher will want to use the *cipher /e /i /s* directory command, where *directory* is the name of the directory in which the files to be encrypted are located. The */e* switch specifies that encryption is to occur, and the */i* switch specifies that the process is to continue, even if errors occur.

☒ **A, C, D**. Issuing a *cipher* command with both the */e* and */d* switches is invalid, thus Answer **A** is incorrect. Issuing a *cipher* command with the */d* switch causes the files to become decrypted, thus Answer **C** is incorrect. Issuing a *cipher* command without the */i* switch will not force the *cipher* operation to continue should errors occur, thus Answer **D** is incorrect.

9. On a local computer, who is the default data recovery agent?

    A. There is no default data recovery agent on a local computer.

    B. The first user added to the Administrators group after installation is complete.

    C. The first user to log into the computer after installation is complete.

    D. The built-in administrative account.

    ☑ **D**. On a local computer, one that is not participating in a Windows 2000 Active Directory domain, the built-in local Administrator account is the default data recovery agent. For security reasons, you should rename this account (from Administrator) and consider exporting the EFS recovery certificate and private keys from the computer—especially if it's a portable computer.

    ☒ **A, B, C**. The built-in local Administrator account is the default data recovery agent on a local computer, thus Answers **A**, **B**, and **C** are incorrect.

10. In a Windows 2000 Active Directory domain, who is the default data recovery agent?

    A. The built-in administrative account on each computer.

    B. The built-in domain administrative account.

    C. The first user to be added to the Administrators group after creating the domain.

    D. The user who installs the first Enterprise Root CA in the domain.

☑ **B.** The built-in domain admin account is the default data recovery agent in a Windows 2000 Active Directory domain. This account name should be changed from Administrator and not be used unless absolutely required. You should consider creating a new EFS recovery agent to perform this function.

☒ **A, C, D.** The built-in domain admin account is the default data recovery agent in a Windows 2000 Active Directory domain, thus Answers **A, C,** and **D** are incorrect.

11. You want to create a new data EFS data recovery agent for your Windows 2000 Active Directory domain. From where will you perform this task?

   A. The Certificate Authority console
   B. The Local Computer Security console on the first domain controller
   C. The System applet on the Root CA
   D. The Group Policy object that is applied to the root domain

   ☑ **D.** New EFS recovery agents can be created from the **Computer Configuration | Windows Settings | Security Settings | Public Key Policies | Encrypted Data Recovery Agents** node of the domain GPO. Right-click **Encrypted Data Recovery Agents** and select **Create** from the context menu to start the Certificate Request Wizard, which will help you complete this process.

   ☒ **A, B, C.** New EFS recovery agents can be created from the **Computer Configuration | Windows Settings | Security Settings | Public Key Policies | Encrypted Data Recovery Agents** node of the domain GPO, thus Answers **A, B,** and **C** are incorrect.

12. What is the effect of running the *cipher* command from a directory without specifying any switches?

   A. It will encrypt all files and folders in the directory except for those that are already encrypted.
   B. It will decrypt all files and folders in the directory that are currently encrypted.
   C. It will prompt you for action (encryption or decryption) for every file and folder located in that directory.
   D. It will provide an output showing the encryption status of every file and folder located in that directory.

   ☑ **D.** By executing the *cipher* command with no modifying switches, you can quickly ascertain the encryption status of all files and folders located in the directory you are examining.

☒ **A, B, C.** By executing the *cipher* command with no modifying switches, you can quickly ascertain the encryption status of all files and folders located in the directory you are examining, thus Answers **A**, **B**, and **C** are all incorrect.

EFS Architecture and Troubleshooting

13. You are the data recovery agent for your Windows 2000 Active Directory domain. Pat informs you that she can no longer access files that she had previously encrypted. You discover that her EFS certificate has expired and issue her a new one. She still cannot access the files. What do you need to in order for her to be able to access these files? (Choose all that apply.)

    A. Use Windows Explorer to decrypt the files for Pat.
    B. Delete Pat's Windows user account and recreate it for her.
    C. Place the files in the location where Pat had saved them originally.
    D. Restore the files to a recovery computer that has the recovery certificates installed.

    ☑ **A, C, D.** In this case, you would need to restore the files from a backup to a recovery computer that has the recovery certificates installed. Once this is done, you can decrypt the files and then place them back into the location where Pat had them originally. Pat can the encrypt them using her new EFS certificate.

    ☒ **B.** Deleting Pat's user account will help correct this problem, thus Answer **B** is incorrect.

14. You are the data recovery agent for your Windows 2000 Active Directory domain. Jon informs you that he can no longer access files that he had previously encrypted. You discover that Jon's EFS certificate has expired, so you issue him a new one. Jon still cannot access the files. What do you need to do in order for Jon to be able to access these files? (Choose all that apply.)

    A. Export your recovery certificate.
    B. Restore the encrypted files from a backup tape.
    C. Issue Jon an EFS Recovery Agent certificate.
    D. Import your recovery certificate onto the computer that contains Jon's encrypted files.

    ☑ **A, D.** You can export your recovery agent certificate and then import it onto the computer that has the encrypted files. Once this is done, you will need to decrypt the files using Windows Explorer. After that has been done, the files can be encrypted again using Jon's new EFS certificate, if he desires to do so.

☒ **B, C.** Restore the encrypted files from a backup tape is not required when using this method, thus Answer **B** is incorrect. Issuing Jon an EFS Recovery Agent certificate is probably not a good idea, since he will then be able to decrypt all EFS encrypted data, thus Answer **C** is incorrect.

15. Andrew is one of your traveling salespeople. Andrew has a Windows 2000 portable computer on which he uses EFS encryption. While Andrew was traveling last week, he encrypted several files on his computer. This week when he placed his portable computer in the port replicator and logged into the corporate network, he reports to you that he cannot access these files any longer, although they are still on his computer. What is the most likely reason for this problem?

    A. His EFS certificate expired since last week.
    B. He encrypted the files using his local computer user account.
    C. He encrypted the files using his cached domain user account.
    D. His hard drive is not NTFS formatted.

    ☑ **B.** The most likely reason that Andrew cannot access the files is that he encrypted them when he was logged into the computer locally instead of using a set of cached domain account credentials.

    ☒ **A, C, D.** Although it is possible that Andrew's EFS certificate expired in this period of time, it is unlikely. The most likely reason that he cannot access the files is that he used his local computer account to encrypt them, thus Answer **A** is incorrect. Again, the most likely reason for the problem is that Andrew used his local computer account, not the domain user account he is trying to use now to access the files, thus Answer **C** is incorrect. If Andrew was able to select EFS encryption on his files in the first place, his hard drive was formatted with NTFS, thus Answer **D** is incorrect.

Chapter 6: Configuring and Troubleshooting Windows IP Security

The Need for Network Security

1. Your network currently does not use IPSec to protect internal communications. An attacker could perform what sort of attack on your network to capture valuable information, such as user names and passwords?

    A. Snooping
    B. Spoofing

C. DoS

D. MITM

☑ Answer **A** is correct Snooping, or sniffing, the network can be done using a software application designed for this purpose that can capture all packets transmitted on the network, not just those addressed to the network adapter being used to perform the attack.

☒ Answer **B** is incorrect because a Spoofing attack is one in which an attacker assumes the identity of a trusted computer in order to trick other computers into giving it otherwise unauthorized access. Answer **C** is incorrect because a DoS attack is one in which a network or network service is targeted by a massive stream of traffic, preventing legitimate users from being able to make use of the network or network service. Answer **D** is incorrect because a MITM attack is one in which an attacker sits between two communicating hosts, intercepting traffic and modifying it before transmitting the traffic to the legitimate hosts. In this way, the man in the middle can change and control the conversation.

2. You have detected an unauthorized computer capturing all traffic between two servers on your network. You suspect that this computer has changed some or all of the transmissions that have been sent from both servers. What type of attack are you most likely experiencing?

A. Snooping

B. Spoofing

C. DoS

D. MITM

☑ Answer **D** is correct In this case, you are most likely experiencing a MITM attack. In this type of attack, the attacker sits between two parties who believe they are communicating with each other, when in fact their entire conversation is being captured and most likely modified by the attacker.

☒ Answer **A** is incorrect because snooping, or sniffing, the network can be done using a software application designed for this purpose that can capture all packets transmitted on the network, not just those addressed to the network adapter being used to perform the attack. Answer **B** is incorrect because a spoofing attack is one in which an attacker assumes the identity of a trusted computer in order to trick other computers into giving it otherwise unauthorized access. Answer **C** is incorrect because a DoS attack is one in which a network or network service is targeted by a massive stream of traffic, preventing legitimate users from being able to make use of the network or network service.

IP Security Overview

3. IPSec operates at what layer of the seven-layer open system interconnection (OSI) Model?

   A. Layer 2
   B. Layer 3
   C. Layer 6
   D. Layer 7

   ☑ Answer **B** is correct. IPSec operates at layer 3 of the seven-layer model. Layer 3 is the network layer.

   ☒ Answer **A** is incorrect because layer 2 is the transport layer. Answer **C** is incorrect because layer 6 is the presentation layer. Answer **D** is incorrect because layer 7 is the application layer.

4. Jon is interested in deploying IPSec on his network. What benefits can Jon expect to gain by doing so? (Choose all that apply.)

   A. Integrity of traffic on his network
   B. Confidentiality of traffic on his network
   C. Authentication of traffic on his network
   D. Impersonation of traffic on his network

   ☑ Answers **A**, **B**, and **C** are correct. IPSec can provide Jon with integrity (assurance that the message received is identical to the message that was sent), confidentiality (keeping your private information private), and authentication (establishes the identity of a sender or recipient).

   ☒ Answer **D** is incorrect because impersonation is a form of attack, such as the MITM attack. Using IPSec can prevent attacks such as this.

5. In regards to IPSec, the AH does what for you?

   A. Ensures data integrity and authentication
   B. Prevents capture of packets
   C. Provides confidentiality
   D. Encrypts the packets

   ☑ Answer **A** is correct The AH is one of two protocols implemented in IPSec. AH ensures data integrity and authentication of sender, thus preventing a replay type of attack.

☒ Answer **B** is incorrect because AH does not prevent capture of packets. Packets can be captured if someone is allowed to gain access to a wired or wireless segment of the network. The capture of packets does not automatically mean, however, that the data on the network is unsafe. It does, however, pose a great risk. Answers **C** and **D** are incorrect because AH does not provide confidentiality of data or data encryption. Those functions are provided by the ESP.

6. What is added to a standard IP datagram when the AH is used?

    A. Encryption to protect the contents of the packet

    B. An AH header that provides authentication, anti-replay, and integrity for the entire packet

    C. An AH header that provides assurance of delivery

    D. An AH header and AH trailer that provides a checksum of the packet

    ☑ Answer **B** is correct. AH is just that: a small header that is inserted into an IP datagram after the IP header and before the TCP header that provides authentication, anti-replay, and integrity. In short, AH tells you that the packet is genuine and came from where it claims to have come from.

    ☒ Answers **A**, **C**, and **D** are incorrect because AH does not provide any form of encryption or confidentiality of the packet, nor does it provide delivery assurance of any kind.

7. Andrea is configuring a new IPSec policy for her network. What methods does she have to choose from as far as authentication? (Choose all that apply.)

    A. Digital certificate

    B. SNMP string

    C. Shared secret

    D. Kerberos

    ☑ Answers **A**, **C**, and **D** are correct. Andrea can use any or all of the following: certificate, shared secret or Kerberos. Kerberos is the default selection. The use of a certificate requires that a functional CA be in place on your network. Shared secrets are the least preferred because they can lead to network compromise if learned by an attacker.

    ☒ Answer **B** is incorrect because SNMP is not used for configuring IPSec. SNMP is typically used for network configuration, such as routers and switches, among other items.

8. During the process of starting an IPSec communication between two computers, how many SAs are created?

   A. One
   B. Two
   C. Three
   D. Depends on the IPSec policy requirements

   ☑ Answer **C** is correct. There are three total SAs created between two computers that wish to use IPSec to secure their communications. There is a Phase 1 SA and two Phase 2 SAs, one for inbound traffic and the other for outbound traffic. The Phase 1 SA involves the negotiation of the encryption algorithm and hashing algorithm to be used, followed by the actual authentication process. The Phase 2 SAs involve the negotiation of the IPSec protocol to be used (AH and/or ASP), the encryption algorithm to be used and the hashing algorithm to be used.

   ☒ Answers **A**, **B**, and **D** are incorrect because there are always three SAs formed when two computers initiate an IPSec-secured communication.

9. Chris wants to use IPSec to secure communications between her main office and a remote office over the Internet. What is this called?

   A. Transport mode
   B. Internet mode
   C. Tunnel mode
   D. Transfer mode

   ☑ Answer **C** is correct. When IPSec is used to secure a communication between two gateways, as in the case of from one office to another across the Internet, it is said to be operating in tunnel mode.

   ☒ Answer **B** is incorrect because Transport mode occurs between clients on the same WAN or over a private (not the Internet) WAN link. Answers **A** and **D** are incorrect. because there is no such thing as Internet mode or Transfer mode.

10. You are interviewing a new candidate for the position of assistant network administrator. Bruno, the candidate, is in the process of answering the question "What does message integrity mean?" Which of the following answers should Bruno give you?

    A. The assurance that the message received is identical to the message that was sent.
    B. The assurance that the identity of a sender or recipient is verified.
    C. The assurance that the message is protected from prying eyes and is kept private.

D. The assurance that the receiving user is authorized to receive the message.

☑ Answer **A** is correct. The term *integrity* refers to the assurance that the message received is identical to the message that was sent.

☒ Answer **B** is incorrect because the term *authentication* refers to the assurance that the identity of the sender or recipient is verified. Answer **C** is incorrect because the term *confidentiality* refers to keeping a message safe from prying eyes, thus ensuring the message is kept private. Answer **D** is incorrect because the assurance that a receiving user is authorized to receive the message is not a function of IPSec, but typically is the responsibility of the messaging and operating system.

IP Security Management Tools

11. You have recently configured and deployed an IPSec solution on your network between all computers in the Finance department. What can you use to verify that IPSec is in fact being used by these computers to secure their communications?

    A. IP Security Policies in the Group Policy Editor
    B. IP Security Monitor
    C. Certificates Snap-in
    D. IP Security Policy Agent

    ☑ Answer **B** is correct. The IP Security Monitor (IPSec Monitor) can be used to monitor IPSec on your network and verify that computers are making the desired hard associations.

    ☒ Answer **A** is incorrect because the IP Security Policies in the Group Policy Editor is used to configure and create IPSec policies. Answer **C** is incorrect because the Certificates Snap-in is not used to monitor IPSec directly. Answer **D** is incorrect because the IP Security Policy Agent is used to load and refresh the applied IP Security policy, not to monitor IPSec.

12. You have configured several different IPSec policies for your organization, one for each department within the organization. From where can a configured IPSec policy be selected for use on a computer? (Choose all correct answers.)

    A. IP Security Policies within Group Policy
    B. IP Security Monitor
    C. TCP/IP Advanced Properties
    D. Certificates Snap-in

☑ Answers **A** and **C** are correct. The IP Security Policies folder within Group Policy can be used to configure and select IP Security policies. The TCP/IP Advanced Properties window can be used to select a preconfigured IP Security policy.

☒ Answer **B** is incorrect because the IP Security Monitor is not used to select an IPSec policy for use. Answer **D** is incorrect because the Certificates Snap-in is not used to select an IPSec policy for use.

Deploying and Troubleshooting Windows IP Security

13. Catherine is interested in deploying IPSec on her network to increase network security. She currently uses a NAT device to translate one Public IP address for her 25 internal clients (Windows 2000 Professional and Windows 98) using DHCP. What concerns should Catherine have in this situation? (Choose all that apply.)

    A. No concerns; IPSec is an ideal solution for any size network.

    B. IPSec is not compatible with DHCP; she will need to manually assign the client computer IP addresses.

    C. IPSec is not compatible with NAT devices; she will not be able to create IPSec connections outside of her network.

    D. IPSec is not supported with legacy operating systems such as Windows 98; these computers will not be able to make secure connections or communicate with other computers that require secure communications.

    ☑ Answers **C** and **D** are correct. IPSec cannot be used to create connections through NAT devices, thus Catherine will not be able to make IPSec secured connections outside of her network. This may or may not be a problem for her, but it is something that she should be aware of during the design and planning phase. IPSec is only supported for Windows 2000 and later operating systems, so her Windows 98 computers will not be able to communicate with any computers that require secure connections. She should consider upgrading these computers to Windows 2000 Professional.

    ☒ Answers **A** and **B** are incorrect because while IPSec is a good solution for any size network, Catherine still has the concerns related to the NAT device and the legacy Windows 98 clients on her network. IPSec has no bearing on DHCP, nor does DHCP have any bearing on IPSec. The only thing to bear in mind is that if you require secure connections on a server providing network services such as DHCP or DNS, then you must ensure that all clients are configured properly to establish connections to the server. If not, network communications will be impossible.

14. You are creating a new IPSec policy for your network. You have several highly sensitive servers that you do not want to allow any unsecured connections to. You have a mix of Windows 2000 Professional and Windows NT 4.0 client computers. You need all of your client computers to be able to connect securely to these servers. What do you need to do? (Choose all that apply.)

    A. Upgrade the Windows NT 4.0 computers to Windows 2000.

    B. Designate that the Windows NT 4.0 computers are to be trusted for delegation.

    C. Ensure that the servers have their archive bit set to false.

    D. Ensure that the "Do not communicate with computers that do not support IPSec" option is selected when you make your new IPSec policy.

    ☑ Answers **A** and **D** are correct. You will need to upgrade the Windows NT 4.0 computers to be able to use IPSec for those machines. Selecting the "Do not communicate with computers that do not support IPSec" option will prevent any unsecured communications from occurring.

    ☒ Answer **B** is incorrect because trusting a computer for delegation is not part of IPSec and cannot be done to a Windows NT 4.0 client at any rate. You might trust a computer for delegation if it were a file server and you wanted to allow people to be able to use EFS encryption on it. Answer **C** is incorrect because setting the archive bit to false affects how the NTBACKUP.EXE utility will handle that volume, and has no impact on IPSec in any way.

15. Hannah wants to customize the IPSec hash algorithm that is in use in her organization's IPSec policy. What are her choices? (Choose all that apply.)

    A. SHA1

    B. WEP

    C. AES

    D. MD5

    ☑ Answers **A** and **D** are correct. IPSec currently supports the SHA1 and MD5 hash algorithms.

    ☒ Answer **B** is incorrect because Wired Equivalent Privacy (WEP) is a security encryption measure used in 802.11 wireless networks (see Chapter 7 for more discussion on WLAN issues). Answer **C** is incorrect because AES is an emerging encryption standard that is favored by the US Government and is likely to see inclusion in a future 802.11 standard. AES uses the Rijndael symmetric encryption algorithm and is extremely secure.

Chapter 7: Implementing Secure Wireless Networks

Introduction to the Wireless LAN

1. Your supervisor has charged you with determining which 802.11 authentication method to use when deploying the new wireless network. Given your knowledge of the 802.11 specification, which of the following is the most secure 802.11 authentication method?

   A. Shared-key Authentication

   B. EAP-TLS

   C. EAP-MD5

   D. Open authentication

   ☑ **D.** Open authentication is actually more secure than shared-key authentication because it is not susceptible to a known plaintext attack, to which the shared-key authentication method is susceptible.

   ☒ **A, B, C.** Shared-key authentication is susceptible to a known plaintext attack if the attacker can capture the random challenge sent by the AP to the client, as well as the encrypted response from the client. The attacker can then try to brute-force the WEP key by trying to decrypt the encrypted response and comparing it to the random challenge sent by the AP, thus Answer **A** is incorrect. EAP-TLS and EAP-MD5 are authentication methods specified in the 802.1x standard, not the 802.11 standard, thus Answers **C** and **D** are incorrect.

2. What are the two WEP key sizes available in 802.11 networks?

   A. 64-bit and 104-bit keys

   B. 24-bit and 64-bit keys

   C. 64-bit and 128-bit keys

   D. 24-bit and 104-bit keys

   ☑ **C.** The 802.11 specification calls for 64-bit keys for use in WEP. Later the specification was amended to allow for 128-bit keys as well.

   ☒ **A, B, D.** The actual key size of the secret key is 40 bits and 104 bits. When added to the 24-bit IV, you wind up with WEP key sizes of 64 bits and 128 bits, thus Answers **A**, **B**, and **D** are incorrect.

3. Which of the following is a weakness in WEP related to the initialization vector (IV)? (Choose all that apply.)

   A. The IV is a static value, which makes it relatively easy for an attacker to brute-force the WEP key from captured traffic.

   B. The IV is transmitted in plaintext and can be easily seen in captured traffic.

   C. The IV is only 24 bits in size, which makes it possible that two or more data frames will be transmitted with the same IV, thereby resulting in an IV collision that an attacker can use to determine information about the network.

   D. There is no weakness in WEP related to the IV.

   ☑ **B, C.** The IV is transmitted in plaintext because the AP or the other ad hoc participants in the network must know its value in order to be able to recreate the WEP key to decrypt traffic. Because of the small size of the IV, space allows for the potential of IV collisions, which an attack can use to XOR out the key stream used to encrypt the traffic and thereby possibly recover information such as IP address information from packets.

   ☒ **A, D.** The IV is not a static value, it is randomly determined, thus Answer **A** is incorrect. Some weaknesses associated with WEP are directly attributable to the short length of the IV, as mentioned previously, thus Answer **D** is incorrect.

4. Bill, the network administrator, wants to deploy a wireless network and use open authentication. His problem is that he also wants to make sure that the network is not accessible by anyone. How can he authenticate users without a shared-key authentication mechanism? (Choose the best answer.)

   A. Use MAC address filters to restrict which wireless network cards can associate to the network.

   B. Deploy a RADIUS server and require the use of EAP.

   C. Set a WEP key on the APs and use it as the indirect authenticator for users.

   D. Use IP filters to restrict access to the wireless network.

   ☑ **C.** Use the WEP key as an indirect authenticator for open networks. Unlike shared-key authentication, open authentication does not provide for a challenge/response exchange and therefore does not expose the WEP key to a known plaintext cryptographic attack.

   ☒ **A, B, D.** MAC filtering does not absolutely authenticate a user, since MAC addresses are easily spoofed. In addition, MAC filtering is an administrative burden, thus Answer **A** is incorrect. Deploying RADIUS server or IP filters are both beyond the scope of the question, thus Answers **B** and **D** are incorrect.

5. The 802.1x standard specifies a series of exchanges between the supplicant and the authentication server. Which of the following is not part of the 802.1x authentication exchange?

   A. Association request
   B. EAPoL start
   C. RADIUS-access-request
   D. EAP-success

   ☑ **A.** The association request is part of the 802.11 standard, not the 802.1x standard.

   ☒ **B, C, D.** The EAPoL start, RADIUS-access-request, and EAP-success messages are all part of the 802.1x authentication exchange, thus Answers **B**, **C**, and **D** are incorrect.

6. 802.1x provides for mutual authentication of the supplicant and the authenticator. Which of the following 802.1x methods support mutual authentication?

   A. EAP-MD5
   B. EAP-PWD
   C. EAP-RC4
   D. EAP-TLS

   ☑ **D.** EAP-TLS provides for mutual authentication through the use of certificates.

   ☒ **A, B, C.** EAP-MD5 does not provide for mutual authentication of the supplicant and the authenticator, thus Answer **A** is incorrect. EAP-PWD and EAP-RC4 are not EAP authentication methods, thus Answers **B** and **C** are incorrect.

Wireless LAN Security Issues

7. The 802.1x standard requires the use of an authentication server to allow access to the wireless LAN. You are deploying a wireless network and will use EAP-TLS as your authentication method. What is the most likely vulnerability in your network?

   A. Unauthorized users accessing the network by spoofing EAP-TLS messages.
   B. Denial of service attacks occurring because 802.11 management frames are not authenticated.
   C. Attackers cracking the encrypted traffic.
   D. None of the above.

- ☑ **B.** One of the biggest problems identified in a paper discussing 802.1x security is the lack of authentication in the 802.11 management frames and that 802.1x does not address this problem.

- ☒ **A, C, D.** Spoofing EAP-TLS is not possible, because the attacker needs the user's certificate and passphrase, thus Answer **A** is incorrect. Cracking encrypted traffic is possible but unlikely, since EAP-TLS allows for WEP key rotation, thus Answer **C** is incorrect. The lack of authentication in 802.11 is the most likely vulnerability, thus Answer **B** is incorrect.

8. The tool NetStumbler detects wireless networks based on what feature?

    A. SSID

    B. WEP key

    C. MAC address

    D. CRC-32 checksum

    - ☑ **A.** NetStumbler detects wireless networks by looking for SSIDs.

    - ☒ **B, C, D.** NetStumbler does identify networks with WEP enabled but does not use that fact in identifying the network, thus Answer **B** is incorrect. NetStumbler does detect clients and APs based on their MACs but does not use this information for identifying wireless networks, thus Answer **C** is incorrect. CRC-32 checksums are of no concern to NetStumbler, thus Answer **D** is incorrect.

9. Some DoS attacks are unintentional. Your wireless network at home has been having sporadic problems. The wireless network is particularly susceptible in the afternoon and the evenings. This is most likely due to which of the following possible problems?

    A. The AP is flaky and needs to be replaced.

    B. Someone is flooding your AP with traffic in a DoS attack.

    C. The wireless network is misconfigured.

    D. Your cordless phone is using the same frequency as the wireless network, and whenever someone calls or receives a call, the phone jams the wireless network.

    - ☑ **D.** The most likely problem is that a cordless phone (or a microwave or one of many other wireless devices) is jamming the wireless signal because it uses the same frequency. This problem is becoming more and more common as cordless phone manufacturers use the 2.4 GHz frequency.

    - ☒ **A, B, C.** Bad hardware is something to be concerned with but should not be considered the sole reason for problems until further investigation has been done to determine the source of the problem, thus Answer **A** is incorrect. It is possible, but not likely, that someone is launching a DoS attack against you, thus Answer **B** is incorrect. If a device is not configured properly, it wouldn't work at all, not just sporadically, thus Answer **D** is incorrect.

10. You suspect that someone is stealing data from your company due to the fact that your closest competitor routinely seems to get its products to market weeks before you on every product you introduce. You have conducted sweeps of your organization's campus looking for surreptitious users and user actions but have yet to locate anything out of the ordinary. What type of wireless network attack are you most likely being subjected to?

    A. Spoofing
    B. Jamming
    C. Sniffing
    D. Man in the Middle

    ☑ **C.** You are being subjected to a sniffing attack whereby an attacker can simply sit passively and capture your wireless network traffic without giving an indication of suspicious activity. You would, in this case, need to investigate strong wireless network security, starting with the implementation of WEP and immediately followed with a solution such as TKIP and LEAP.

    ☒ **A, B, D.** Spoofing attacks are those in which the attacker tricks the network hardware into thinking that he or she is an authorized user, such as MAC spoofing, thus Answer **A** is incorrect. Jamming attacks are those in which high-power RF waves are targeted at a wireless network installation with the hope of knocking it out of operation by overpowering it, thus Answer **B** is incorrect. A man-in-the-middle attack is one in which an attacker sits between two communicating parties, intercepting and manipulating both sides of the transmission to suit his or her own needs, thus Answer **D** is incorrect.

11. Your wireless network does use WEP to authorize users. You do, however, use MAC filtering to ensure that only preauthorized clients can associate with your APs. On Monday morning, you reviewed the AP association table logs for the previous weekend and noticed that the MAC address assigned to the network adapter in your portable computer had associated with your APs several times over the weekend. Your portable computer spent the weekend on your dining room table and was not connected to your corporate wireless network during this period of time. What type of wireless network attack are you most likely being subjected to?

    A. Spoofing
    B. Jamming

C. Sniffing

D. Man in the middle

☑ **A.** You are the victim of a MAC spoofing attack whereby an attacker has captured valid MAC addresses by sniffing your wireless network. The fact that you have no other protection in place has made becoming associated with your APs an easy task for this attacker.

☒ **B, C, D.** Jamming attacks are those in which high-power RF waves are targeted at a wireless network installation with the hope of knocking it out of operation by overpowering it, thus Answer **B** is incorrect. Although your network has been sniffed previously to obtain the valid MAC address, you are currently being attacked using a spoofing attack, thus Answer **C** is incorrect. A man-in-the-middle attack is one in which an attacker sits between two communicating parties, intercepting and manipulating both sides of the transmission to suit his or her own needs, thus Answer **D** is incorrect.

12. The major weakness of WEP has to do with the fact that there are only a limited number of what available?

    A. IVs
    B. Packets
    C. Frames
    D. Beacons

    ☑ **A.** Only 2^{24} IVs are available, which might seem like a lot until you realize that every frame or packet requires a unique IV. The entire stock of IVs could be exhausted in a short amount of time—perhaps just several hours—on a busy wireless network. This gives an attacker the opportunity to capture multiple frames using the same numerical IV, which is a large first step toward cracking the WEP key.

    ☒ **B, C, D.** Only 2^{24} IVs are available, which might seem like a lot until you realize that every frame or packet requires a unique IV. The entire stock of IVs could be exhausted in a short amount of time—perhaps just several hours—on a busy wireless network. This gives an attacker the opportunity to capture multiple frames using the same numerical IV, which is a large first step toward cracking the WEP key, thus Answers **B**, **C** and **D** are incorrect.

Configuring Windows Client Computers for Wireless LAN Security

13. In Windows 2000, how do you configure WEP protection for a wireless client?

    A. Open the network adapter Properties page and configure WEP from the Wireless Networks tab.

    B. Install the high-security encryption pack from Microsoft.

    C. Issue the computer a digital certificate from a Windows 2000 Certificate Authority.

    D. Use the utilities provided by the manufacturer of the network adapter.

    ☑ **D.** Windows 2000 does not provide integrated control and management of wireless network adapters, so you will need to perform all configuration using the vendor-supplied utilities.

    ☒ **A, B, C.** Windows 2000 does not have a Wireless Networks tab in the network adapter Properties page, thus Answer **A** is incorrect. Installing the high encryption pack from Microsoft just raises the encryption strength supported by the computer itself to 128 bits, thus Answer **B** is incorrect. Issuing the computer a digital certificate will not configure it for WEP protection in a wireless network, thus Answer **C** is incorrect.

14. In Windows XP, how do you configure WEP protection for a wireless client?

    A. Open the network adapter Properties page and configure WEP from the Wireless Networks tab.

    B. Install the high-security encryption pack from Microsoft.

    C. Issue the computer a digital certificate from a Windows 2000 Certificate Authority.

    D. Use the utilities provided by the manufacturer of the network adapter.

    ☑ **A.** In about 95 percent or better of the cases, Windows XP integrates control and management of wireless network adapters into the network adapter Properties page.

    ☒ **B, C, D.** Installing the high encryption pack from Microsoft just raises the encryption strength supported by the computer itself to 128 bits, thus Answer **B** is incorrect. Issuing the computer a digital certificate will not configure it for WEP protection in a wireless network, thus Answer **C** is incorrect. In about 95 percent or better of the cases, Windows XP integrates control and management of wireless network adapters into the network adapter Properties page, so you cannot configure network adapters using the manufacturer's utilities, thus Answer **D** is incorrect.

15. You are attempting to configure a client computer wireless network adapter in Windows XP. You have installed and launched the utility program that came with the adapter, but you cannot configure the settings from it. What is the source of your problem?

    A. You are not a member of the Network Configuration Operators group.

    B. You do not have the correct Windows Service Pack installed.

    C. You do not configure wireless network adapters in Windows XP through manufacturer's utilities.

    D. Your network administrator has disabled SSID broadcasting for the wireless network.

    ☑ **C**. In Windows XP, you must use the network adapter Properties page to perform wireless network configuration.

    ☒ **A, B, D**. Being a member of the Network Configuration Operators group is not required to make configuration changes to a wireless network adapter properties, thus Answer **A** is incorrect. The Service Pack level has no bearing to being able to configure the network adapter properties, thus Answer **B** is incorrect. Closed networks, those that do not broadcast the SSID, have no effect on being able to configure the network adapter properties, thus Answer **D** is incorrect.

Chapter 8: Configuring Secure Network and Internet Authentication Methods

Network Authentication in Windows 2000

1. You are the administrator of a mixed-mode Windows NT 4.0 domain. You have Windows 2000 and Windows NT 4.0 servers as well as Windows 2000 Professional, Windows NT Workstation, and Windows 95 client computers. What is the best network authentication method that you can reasonably hope for in your network?

    A. NTLM

    B. Kerberos

    C. Challenge-Handshake Authentication Protocol (CHAP)

    D. NTLMv2

☑ Answer **D** is correct. In this sort of situation, the best form of network authentication that you can hope for is NTLMv2. All legacy clients can be upgraded to support NTLMv2 by installing the dsclient. Windows 2000 supports NTLMv2 for backwards compatibility with legacy clients.

☒ Answer **A** is incorrect because while NTLM is natively available for network authentication by all of your clients and servers, it is not the best method available to you. Answer **B** is incorrect because Kerberos can only be used in Windows 2000 Active Directory domains by Windows 2000 clients. Answer **C** is incorrect because CHAP is a dial-up networking authentication protocol and thus is not used for network authentication.

2. You are the administrator of a Windows 2000 Active Directory domain. Your clients consist of Windows 2000 Professional, Windows NT 4.0, Windows 95, and Windows 3.11 clients. What form of network authentication will your Windows 2000 Professional clients use in this situation?

   A. NTLM
   B. Kerberos
   C. CHAP
   D. NTLMv2

   ☑ Answer **B** is correct. Windows 2000 clients in a Windows 2000 Active Directory domain will use the Kerberos protocol, by default, for network authentication.

   ☒ Answers **A** and **D** are incorrect because Windows 2000 clients in a Windows 2000 Active Directory domain will use the Kerberos protocol, by default, for network authentication. Answer **C** incorrect because CHAP is a dial-up networking authentication protocol and thus is not used for network authentication.

Kerberos Overview

3. Kerberos provides two services to the network. What are the services that are provided to the network? (Choose two that apply.)

   A. TGS—issues individual session tickets that can be used to gain access to network resources.
   B. STS—issues individual session tickets that can be used to gain access to network resources.
   C. AS—authenticates users in the KDC's database and issues them a TGT.
   D. AS—authorizes users in the KDC's database and issues them a TGT.

☑ Answers **A** and **C** are correct. Kerberos provides the TGS and the authentication service to the network.

☒ Answer **B** is incorrect because session tickets are issues by the TGS. Answer **D** is incorrect because Kerberos does not perform authorization, only authentication.

4. When using forwarded tickets, who acquires the session ticket for a client to access a back-end resource?

    A. The client
    B. The front-end server
    C. The back-end server
    D. The KDC

    ☑ Answer **B** is correct. When using forwarded tickets (the type supported in Windows 2000), the front-end server acts as a proxy for the client requesting session tickets to access back-end servers and resources.

    ☒ Answers **A**, **C**, and **D** are incorrect because when using forwarded tickets (the type supported in Windows 2000), the front-end server acts as a proxy for the client requesting session tickets to access back-end servers and resources.

Kerberos in Windows 2000

5. The Kerberos protocol in Windows 2000 runs as a service on all domain controllers, thus all domain controllers are KDCs. What does the KDC use as its account database in Windows 2000?

    A. Active Directory
    B. Security Accounts Manager
    C. LSA
    D. HOSTS

    ☑ Answer **A** is correct. Kerberos in Windows 2000 uses the Active Directory as its user database.

    ☒ Answer **B** is incorrect because the Security Accounts Manager is the local computer security database used in Windows 2000 for logons to the local computer only. Answer **C** is incorrect because the LSA is not a user account database but is instead a security process that runs on Windows 2000 computers. Answer **D** is incorrect because the HOSTS file is used to provide pre-configured IP address to host name mappings for TCP/IP.

6. You have several services that run in a front-end/back-end configuration on your network. All of your computers run Windows 2000 Server or Windows 2000 Professional. The back-end services run in the context of the local system account on the back-end servers. What do you need to do to enable forwarded authentication to occur so that your clients can authenticate to the services running on the back-end server? (Choose all that apply.)

   A. Select the **Account is trusted for delegation** check box on the client's domain user account properties page.

   B. Deselect the **Account is sensitive and cannot be delegated** check box on the client's domain user account properties page.

   C. Select the **Trust computer for delegation** check box on the back-end server's domain computer account properties page.

   D. Select the **Account is trusted for delegation** check box on the domain user account properties page that the services run under.

   ☑ Answers **B** and **C** are correct. In order for a client to be able to use a forwarded ticket, their user account must not be marked as sensitive. The services all run on the local system account, thus the computer must be trusted for delegation.

   ☒ Answers **A** and **D** are incorrect because you do not trust a client account for delegation—you trust a computer or a service account.

7. In Windows 2000, what type of DNS record does a client use to locate a KDC?

   A. PTR
   B. A
   C. SRV
   D. MX

   ☑ Answer **C** is correct Clients query DNS for a SRV (service location) to locate a KDC.

   ☒ Answer B is incorrect because a PTR (pointer) record is used for reverse lookups in DNS. Answer **B** is incorrect because an A (host) record is used for normal lookups in DNS. Answer **D** is incorrect because an MX (mail exchange) record is used to point incoming mail traffic to the messaging server.

Configuring Kerberos Trusts

8. Hannah needs to configure a new external trust to a Windows NT 4.0 domain. How can she perform this task? (Choose all that apply.)

A. She can configure the trust by using the Netdom command.

B. She can configure the trust by using the Active Directory users and computers console.

C. She can configure the trust by using the Netsh command.

D. She can configure the trust by using the Active Directory domains and trusts console.

☑ Answers **A** and **D** are correct. Hannah can use either the Netdom command or the Active Directory domains and trusts console to create, edit, verify, and remove trusts between domains.

☒ Answer **B** is incorrect because the Active Directory users and computers console cannot be used for administering domain trusts, it is used instead for working with Active Directory objects such as users, computers, OUs, groups, and group policy objects. Answer **C** is incorrect because the Netsh command is used for configuring network interface properties from the command line, not for working with domain trusts.

9. What type of trust does Kerberos create between domains in Windows 2000?

A. One-way non-transitive manual

B. Two-way non-transitive automatic

C. Two-way transitive automatic

D. Two-way transitive manual

☑ Answer **C** is correct. Kerberos automatically creates two-way transitive trusts between all domains at the root of a forest and between a parent and child domain.

☒ Answers A, B and D are incorrect because Kerberos automatically creates two-way transitive trusts between all domains at the root of a forest and between a parent and child domain. NTLM trusts in Windows NT 4.0 were manually created one-way non-transitive trusts.

Configuring User Authentication

10. Christopher is the network administrator of his company's Windows 2000 network, which consists of Windows 2000 Servers, Windows 2000 Professional clients, and Windows 98 clients. Christopher wants to ensure that only secure NTLM authentication occurs between his servers and clients. What must be done to make the Windows 2000 computers use NTLMv2 only?

A. Christopher will need to install the DSClient on his Windows 2000 computers to enable NTLMv2.

B. Christopher will need to install a security certificate on each of the Windows 2000 computers to enable NTLMv2.

C. Christopher cannot use NTLMv2 on his Windows 2000 computers without installing at least one Windows .NET Server Domain Controller on the network with the high-encryption update.

D. Christopher can require NTLMv2 via group policy and apply this to the entire domain.

☑ Answer **D** is correct. Christopher will need to require NTLMv2 via Group Policy and apply it at the domain level (or over multiple OUs as applicable) in order to force all of his Windows 2000 computer to use only NTLMv2.

☒ Answer **A** is incorrect because the DSClient is for usage on legacy clients and can be used to enable support for NTLMv2. Answer **B** is incorrect because installing certificates on the computers will not allow Christopher to use NTLMv2. Answer **C** is incorrect because NTLMv2 does not require the presence of Windows .NET Server on the network in order to be used—it is built-in in Windows 2000.

11. Christopher is the network administrator of his company's Windows 2000 network, which consists of Windows 2000 Servers, Windows 2000 Professional clients, and Windows 98 clients. Christopher wants to ensure that only secure NTLM authentication occurs between his servers and clients. What must be done to make the Windows 98 computers use NTLMv2 only?

A. Christopher will need to install the DSClient on his Windows 98 computers to enable NTLMv2.

B. Christopher will need to install a security certificate on each of the Windows 98 computers to enable NTLMv2.

C. Christopher will need to enable the NTLMv2 setting for the OU that contains his Windows 98 computers.

D. Christopher will need to install a Windows 2000-based Remote Authentication Dial-In User Service (RADIUS) server on his network to allow him to use NTLMv2.

☑ Answer **A** is correct. By installing the DSClient on his Windows 98 computers, Christopher will be able to have them use NTLMv2 for network authentication.

☒ Answer **B** is incorrect because installing certificates on the computers will not allow him to use NTLMv2. Answer **C** is incorrect because enabling the

NTLMv2 setting in the GPO that corresponds to the OU the Windows 98 belong to will not have any effect—legacy clients cannot take advantage of Group Policy Objects. Answer **D** is incorrect because installing a RADIUS server has nothing to do with enabling NTLMv2—it would be used to authenticate dial-up connections to the Remote Access Service (RAS) server from remote clients.

Configuring Web Authentication

12. You have configured digest authentication for your Web servers. Jon, one of your user's who needs to authenticate to the Web servers, cannot do so. You have checked Jon's user account properties and found that the "Store Passwords Using Reversible Encryption" option has been checked but Jon still cannot authenticate. What is the most likely reason for his troubles?

    A. Jon's user account is disabled. You should enable it from Active Directory users and computers.

    B. Jon did not change his password after the "Store Passwords Using Reversible Encryption" option was enabled for his account.

    C. Jon changed his password after the "Store Passwords Using Reversible Encryption" option was enabled for his account, which disabled this setting.

    D. Jon's computer that he is attempting to make the connection with does not have the 128-bit high encryption patch applied.

    ☑ Answer **B** is correct. If the "Store Passwords Using Reversible Encryption" option is selected and Jon still cannot use digest authentication, it is highly likely that he has not changed his password since it was enabled. Changing his password will correct this situation.

    ☒ Answer **A** is incorrect because if Jon's account were disabled, he would not be able to use it at all, which is not the case here. Answer **C** is incorrect because changing Jon's password after enabling reversible encryption is just the fix needed for this situation. Answer **D** is incorrect because applying the high encryption patch is not a factor in this situation.

13. Andrew is the network administrator for a small Windows 2000 Active Directory domain. He has configured Integrated Windows authentication for users attempting to authenticate to the Web server. Andrew's network is protected from the Internet by a Cisco PIX firewall. Users attempting to authenticate using Integrated Windows authentication complain that they cannot authenticate. What is the most likely cause of the troubles?

A. Andrew has not configured the user's account properties with the "Store Passwords Using Reversible Encryption" option.

B. Integrated Windows authentication fails when access is through a firewall due to the fact that the firewall places its IP address in the hash, thus rendering the authentication request invalid.

C. Andrew has not configured for Integrated Windows authentication in the group policy object that covers the IIS server's computer account.

D. Andrew has not configured for Integrated Windows authentication in the group policy object that covers the user's accounts.

☑ Answer **B** is correct. One of the weaknesses with Integrated Windows authentication is that it does not work through a firewall. The firewall places its IP address in the Integrated Windows authentication hash, thus making the authentication request invalid.

☒ Answer **A** is incorrect because configuring reversible encryption is for digest authentication, not Integrated Windows authentication. Answers **C** and **D** are incorrect because Integrated Windows authentication is not configured via group policy, but instead via the Web site "Properties" page.

14. Catherine is the administrator of a Windows 2000 network. She has configured anonymous authentication for her Web servers. Users attempting to use anonymous authentication complain to her that they cannot access the site and instead receive a 401 error "Unauthorized: Logon failed" when they attempt to access the Web site. Catherine has checked her IIS servers and they show no unusual conditions. What is the most likely reason for this problem?

A. The IIS server is hung. A restart of the server will clear the problem up.

B. The anonymous account is either missing, misconfigured, or does not have the permissions required.

C. The users do not have user accounts on the IIS server.

D. The users are not using Internet Explorer 5.5 or later.

☑ Answer **B** is correct. Anonymous authentication is a very simple means to "corral" all Web site users into the permissions and privileges assigned to the IUSR_servername account. In most cases, you will want to leave this built-in local account as the anonymous authentication account. Anonymous authentication requires no authentication on the user's end—they are simply allowed access to the Web site and all is well. If this account is missing, misconfigured, or does not have the required permissions, then anonymous authentication will fail most likely resulting in the 401 error.

☒ Answer **A** is incorrect because if the IIS server were hung or otherwise not responding, you would likely get a 404 or 500 error instead of a 401 error—401 errors are specific to logon problems. Answer **C** is incorrect because specific user accounts are not required for anonymous authentication, only the existing of a properly configured anonymous authentication account. Answer **D** is incorrect because anonymous authentication works with all browsers, so the version of IE in use is not an issue here.

15. You have enabled SSL on your Web site but now users complain to you that they cannot establish secure connections on port 80. You know that port 80 is the standard HTTP port, not the secure HTTP port. What port should they be attempting to connect to?

    A. 8080
    B. 443
    C. 25
    D. 110

    ☑ Answer **B** is correct. SSL makes connections on port 443 using URLs starting with https://.

    ☒ Answer **A** is incorrect because port 8080 is typically used by proxy servers. Answer **C** is incorrect because port 25 is used for SMTP. Answer **D** is incorrect because port 110 is used by POP3.

Chapter 9: Configuring and Troubleshooting Remote Access and Virtual Private Networking Authentication

Remote Access Authentication Methods

1. Mary is configuring her first Windows 2000 RRAS server and wants to use strong authentication protocols to keep her network secure. Which protocol(s) should she use?

    A. L2TP/IPSec
    B. PAP
    C. EAP
    D. CHAP
    E. MS-CHAPv2

☑ **C, E.** EAP provides the ability to use smartcards for authentication and provides a strong authentication solution. MS-CHAPv2 provides the strongest authentication available for use with user ID and password.

☒ **A, B, D.** L2TP/IPSec is not an authentication protocol. Both PAP and CHAP are older protocols and provide either no protection or very weak protection of the information being passed.

2. Jim is the security administrator for his company's legal department. The network and remote access solutions are based on Windows 2000 Server, and Legal just purchased smartcards for the entire department so that they can use secure dial-in access. Jim knows he needs to configure EAP-TLS, but he isn't sure where to configure it. He also only wants to change this setting for the legal department, not for all users. Where is this protocol configured?

    A. In the Dial-in profile for the Legal remote access policy
    B. In the Modem Pool Properties dialog box, under the Legal profile
    C. Under the Security tab of the Routing and Remote Access server properties
    D. In the legal department's remote access policy, on the Authentication tab

    ☑ **A.** If you want to configure specific conditions for a group of users, including the authentication protocol, you use a remote access policy. The specific location in the policy in this case is in the profile.

    ☒ **, B, C, D.** There is no Modem Pool in the Windows 2000 RRAS. Changing the RRAS server properties would impact the entire server, not just the legal department, although you can set the protocol there as well. There is no Authentication tab under the remote access policy; it is in the remote access profile.

3. Jim's manager has asked him to configure the company Windows 2000 VPN server to allow for the use of smartcards for remote access authentication. What protocol does Jim need to use for this?

    A. PPTP
    B. EAP-TLS
    C. L2TP
    D. MS-CHAP v2
    E. PPP

    ☑ **B.** EAP-TLS is the protocol needed for smartcard deployments.

☒ **A, C, D, E.** PPTP and L2TP are VPN protocols and do not apply to authentication. MS-CHAP v2 is an authentication protocol but does not support smartcards, and PPP is a transport protocol.

Configuring a Remote Access Server

4. Mary maintains the remote access infrastructure for her company. Previously, Mary maintained a single Windows 2000 RAS server, but over the weekend she added another Windows 2000 RAS server for higher capacity. The two servers are in the same native-mode Active Directory domain, but during testing Mary cannot dial into the new server using her Windows 2000 credentials. What is the most likely problem?

    A. The Windows 2000 RRAS service is not installed on the new server.

    B. The Windows 2000 RRAS service needs to be enabled in the Active Directory

    C. The Remote Access Profiles are not shared, and need to be recreated on the new server.

    D. Installing more than one Windows 2000 RRAS server into the same Active Directory domain is not permitted.

    ☑ **C.** Profiles are stored locally and need to be recreated on the new server before users will be able to authenticate.

    ☒ **A, B, D.** RRAS is installed automatically as part of Windows 2000 Server. It does not need to be enabled in the Active Directory, and you can have more than one Windows 2000 RRAS server in the same domain.

Configuring a Virtual Private Networking Server

5. Andrea is responsible for her company's Windows 2000 RRAS server, which has been running as an RAS server for several months. She just manually added services to the server so that the 120 sales representatives could connect to the network using VPN instead of modems. All the sales reps are using PPTP. The first five VPN users connect without issue, but then the server denies access to additional VPN users. RAS users seem to be unaffected by the issue. What is the most likely problem?

    A. The server doesn't have enough VPN client licenses for more than five concurrent users.

    B. The DHCP server is only providing five IP addresses.

C. When you configure the Routing and Remote Access Service for dial-in, it only creates five PPTP ports.

D. Windows 2000 will only support five VPN connections at a time.

☑ **C**. When you use the Dial-In wizard to configure the RRAS server, it will only create five PPTP and five L2TP ports. If the server had been configured for VPN the first time, 128 ports would have been configured.

☒ **A, B, D**. Windows 2000 doesn't require licenses for VPN connections. The DHCP server issue would impact VPN and RAS users.

6. June is trying to get a job as a network administrator, and she is being quizzed by the department manager on her knowledge of protocols. Her manager is particularly interested in her background in IPSec, so he has asked her to list the protocols used by IPSec. Which of the following are protocols used by IPSec?

   A. ESP

   B. AH

   C. PPTP

   D. L2F

   E. ISAKMP

   ☑ **A, B, E**. ESP, AH, and ISAKMP are all protocols used by IPSec.

   ☒ **C, D**. PPTP and L2F, although tunneling protocols, are not used by IPSec.

Introduction to Remote Access Policies

7. Tom is the administrator of a Windows 2000 RAS server that's being used for dial-in connections to the corporate network. He needs to be sure that no one is connecting to the server from 1:00 a.m. until 2:00 a.m. while the server is being backed up. Tom is using one policy to permit access for all users. What is the easiest way to add this restriction for all users?

   A. Create a new Remote Access policy containing the restriction, and make sure it is processed before the default policy.

   B. Add a deny access condition to the existing remote access profile.

   C. Add a deny access condition to the existing remote access policy.

   D. Create a new Remote Access profile containing the restriction, and make sure it is processed before the default policy.

   ☑ **C**. You can easily add the deny access restriction to the policy by editing the policy properties and adding the condition.

☒ **A, B, D**. Answer A would work, but it would not be the easiest way to do it. You cannot add a deny access condition to a remote access profile. A remote access profile is part of the remote access policy and cannot be used on its own this way.

8. Stacey is the system administrator of a Windows 2000 Routing and Remote Access server that permits the use of the Multilink protocol to allow users to connect with multiple dial-up lines. To configure this setup to work as efficiently as possible, Stacey needs to automatically drop a line from the Multilink connection when it's not being used. What protocol would need to be enabled to accomplish this task?

   A. EAP-TLS
   B. PAP
   C. PPP
   D. Multilink
   E. BAP

   ☑ **E**. Bandwidth Allocation Protocol (BAP) monitors the utilization on a multilink connection and dynamically reduces the number of connected lines if the user's utilization drops below a certain amount.

   ☒ **A, B, C, D**. EAP-TLS, PAP, and PPP do not apply to the Multilink connections. Multilink is used to support the multiple connections, but it doesn't monitor utilization.

Configuring Clients for Secure Remote Access

9. Tammy is responsible for setting up a new VPN server using Windows 2000 and the Routing and Remote Access Service. She wants to limit access to the VPN by creating a Remote Access Users group in the Active Directory running in native mode, so she creates the group, puts users in it, and creates a Remote Access Policy called VPN User Access. To be sure this is the only way to access the server, she deletes the default remote access policy. Under the Dial-In tab of each user, she sets the Remote Access Permissions to "Control access through Remote Access Policy." What is the last thing Tammy needs to do to limit access to this policy to users in the VPN User Access group?

   A. Edit the VPN User Access policy and add the condition Windows-Groups, selecting the Remote Access Users group as the group for the condition.
   B. Edit the IPSec ports to allow access by the Remote Access Users group.

C. Edit the VPN User Access policy and limit the protocol to PPTP, and then grant user access to the Remote Access Users group.

D. Edit the VPN User Access policy and set the permissions on the policy so that the Remote Access Users group has read access. Then delete the Everyone group from the permissions.

☑ **A.** Access by group is controlled by setting the Windows-Groups condition in the policy.

☒ **B, C, D.** You cannot tie ports to groups. You don't need to limit access to PPTP for this question, and you can't grant access through the group without using the Windows-Groups condition. You cannot set permissions as described in **D**.

10. Jim is the remote access administrator for a medium-sized manufacturing company. He is in the process of rolling out a new Windows 2000 RRAS server, but he knows that the local telephone area code will be changing in six months. He would like to be able to automatically update the users' phone books with the new numbers, so he uses the Connection Manager Administration Kit to create a service profile for the end users. He is putting the new phone book on a server on the internal network. What protocol will be used by the users to get the new phone book?

A. HTTP

B. HTTPS

C. Telnet

D. FTP

☑ **D.** The automatic phone book update tool uses the FTP protocol to update the phone books.

☒ **A, B, D.** None of these protocols can be used by the update tool.

11. June is a network administrator supporting 500 mobile users who dial into the company network using several Windows 2000 RAS servers located throughout the country. She is planning to add between 5 and 10 new RAS servers in other offices in the company, so she has created a dynamic phone book using the Phone Book Administrator utility. Now she wants to publish the phone book so she can create a service profile for her users. What is the easiest way for her to create this phone book?

A. Save the phone book to her local drive and FTP the resulting files to an FTP server running IIS 4.0 or later.

B. Save the phone book to her local drive and copy the resulting files to a Web server running IIS 4.0 or later.

C. From the Publish Phone Book screen, select a directory on an FTP server running IIS 4.0 or later, and select Post.

D. From the Publish Phone Book screen, select a directory on an FTP server running IIS 4.0 or later, and select Publish.

☑ **C.** The Phone Book Administration utility allows you to post phone books to the appropriate server using the Post command in the Publish Phone Book screen.

☒ **A, B, D.** While A would allow remote users to download this directory, maintaining a manual process like this is much more difficult than the correct answer. B wouldn't work, since the service profile uses FTP to download files. D is not correct because there is not a Publish option available from that menu.

Troubleshooting Remote Access Problems

12. Joan is a help desk specialist for a small manufacturing company that uses a Windows 2000 server for VPN services. Melissa, a sales engineer, is on a sales call and needs to access the company intranet to get some pricing information. Melissa is using a PPTP connection to access the company VPN, and it worked fine from the hotel last night from a dial-up ISP service. She is trying to connect from the customer network, but she's unable to establish a connection, so she has placed a call to Joan to see what's wrong. Which of the following is a possible reason for this problem?

    A. The local network is using NAT.

    B. The company's firewall does not permit the GRE protocol.

    C. The company's firewall does not permit the ESP protocol.

    D. The company's firewall does not use a proxy server.

    ☑ **B.** In order for a client to communicate with the Windows 2000 VPN server using PPTP, it must be able to connect using the GRE protocol. This protocol is frequently blocked on corporate firewalls.

    ☒ **A, C, D.** PPTP will work across a NAT network. The ESP protocol is used in L2TP/IPSec, not PPTP. A proxy server is not needed for a successful VPN connection.

13. Ted is a help desk specialist for a small printer manufacturing company that uses a Windows 2000 server for VPN services. Jack, a sales engineer, is on a service call and needs to order parts on the company intranet. Jack is using an L2TP/IPSec connection to access the company VPN, and it works fine from Jack's home office, which connects to the Internet through a broadband connection. Unfortunately,

Jack cannot connect from the customer's Ethernet network, and he has placed a help desk call for assistance. Which of the following is a possible reason for this problem?

A. The local network is using NAT.

B. The company's firewall does not permit the GRE protocol.

C. The company's firewall does not permit the PPP protocol.

D. The company's firewall does not support certificates.

☑ A. The IPSec portion of the L2TP/IPSec protocol will not support NAT.

☒ B, C, D. The GRE protocol is not used in conjunction with L2TP/IPSec. The PPP protocol is not used on an Ethernet network. Certificate support is not needed on the local firewall.

14. Tony is the administrator for his company's Windows 2000 RAS server, which uses the corporate Active Directory service for authentication. Joan, an end user in accounting, is trying to connect to the RAS server but keeps getting the message that she is not an authorized user. She can log into the Active Directory without issue when she is connected to the LAN. What might be causing the problem?

A. The server needs additional PPTP ports configured.

B. Joan is not using the correct password.

C. Joan is trying to use her LAN network account instead of her dial-in account.

D. The user is not using an ID that is authorized to use the dial-in server.

☑ D. Before an account can be used to connect to the RAS server, it needs to be authorized through a combination of remote access policy and/or account permissions.

☒ A, B, C. PPTP ports are not used with RAS. Since the RAS server uses Active Directory for authentication, an incorrect password would prevent Joan from logging in at work. This also means that her network account is the same as her RAS account—they are both her Active Directory account.

15. Mary is a help desk technician supporting remote users connecting to the company's Windows 2000 RRAS server. She just got a call from Tony, who is using his company laptop and accessing the RRAS server through a PPTP VPN connection. Last week the connection worked fine, but today it is not connecting. When Mary asks if anything has changed, Tony reluctantly admits that his neighbor just installed a freeware encryption application on the system. What is the first step Mary should recommend to address this issue?

A. Reinstall the VPN client to replace any files that might have been overwritten, and reboot the system.

B. Reinstall the client operating system to ensure that the system is installed and configured cleanly.

C. Update the system virus protection and scan the system for viruses.

D. Remove the new application and reboot the system.

☑ **D.** The first thing that should be tried is undoing the changes made between the time the VPN worked and now—especially if the application is loaded on a company system and is not a standard application.

☒ **A, B, C**. Reinstalling the VPN client shouldn't be the first step; you should remove the application first. There are several other steps that should be taken before resorting to a complete system rebuild. There is no indication that this issue is virus-related. Updating virus protection is never a bad idea, but it will probably not address this issue.

Chapter 10: Configuring and Using Auditing and the Event Logs

1. Jake is responsible for six Windows 2000 servers in his organization. He has noticed that lately there are multiple login attempts on the main file server. What can Jake do to find out if in fact an attacker is trying to exploit his system? (Choose all that apply.)

    A. Use Dumpel.exe to find the attack IDs numbered 200–600 in the System Event Log. This will indicate a possible attack.

    B. Turn on auditing (success and failure) for logon events. Check the Application Log daily for possible password-cracking attacks.

    C. Set up a Windows 2000 Security Template that will only allow registered IPs to connect to and communicate with the file server.

    D. Configure your router to only let the file server NetBIOS name be authenticated for communication.

    ☑ **B.** You want to set up auditing on your server and make sure you check the logs frequently, looking for possible attacks.

    ☒ **A** is incorrect because Dumpel is used to parse Event Viewer Logs and the security-related events will be logged in the Security Log, not the System Log. **C** is incorrect because a template will not work in this fashion. Security templates have nothing to do with looking for registered IPs. **D** is incorrect because routers cannot be configured to authenticate Windows-based NetBIOS names.

2. Stan is the network administrator responsible for 10 Windows 2000 servers and 400 Windows XP Professional workstations, all separated geographically across four sites. Stan is responsible for implementing defense in depth. From the following list, select the options that Stan can implement for a defense-in-depth strategy. (Choose all that apply.)

   A. Set up a and implement a firewall.
   B. Set up and implement auditing
   C. Set up and implement IDS.
   D. Set up and implement a router ACL.

   ☑ **A, B, C,** and **D** are all correct.

   ☒ When setting up a defense-in-depth strategy, you should set up a layered solution for security. Make sure that you implement more than just a firewall to lock the gates; you will want to include auditing, IDS, and router ACLs, among other things.

3. Peter is the administrator for a large Windows 2000 network infrastructure. He is responsible for 10 IIS servers, two Exchange servers, and 20 file and print servers. All 32 servers are internal to the LAN and serve as application, e-mail, file, and print server for over 700 clients in five separate locations. Because of a shortage of staff, Peter needs to make sure that his servers are safe and is giving himself the task of ensuring that auditing takes place so that he can analyze possible mischievous events that could lead to an attack. He turns on auditing for all 32 servers. Peter is also new to auditing, so he turns on auditing for all categories, success and failure based. What is the most logical thing Peter should do now to analyze his servers? (Choose all that apply.)

   A. Peter should plan a time each week to view, archive, and analyze all the events he is receiving.
   B. Peter should analyze all events and start turning off categories he will not need to view in the Security Log.
   C. Peter should adjust his Security Log size to hold more events so that important auditable events are not overwritten.
   D. Peter should use the Dumpel command-line tool in batch format to scan all System Logs in all 32 servers for any event in the 500–600 range.

   ☑ **A, B,** and **C**. Peter needs to closely look at what he is auditing so he can start turning things off that he doesn't need and so he doesn't fill up all his logs. **B** is also correct because when Peter turned on auditing for all events, he was trying to get an idea of what is going on within the network on his systems. **C** is also correct because during this period of auditing events, the logs will fill up past the default of 512K, so in order to not have events overwritten, the Security Logs default parameters need to be adjusted.

☒ **D** is incorrect because it's the Security Log that you need to be concerned about. This question is meant to be misleading.

Auditing Windows 2000

4. Stan is the network administrator responsible for 10 Windows 2000 servers and 400 Windows XP Professional workstations, all separated geographically across four sites. Stan is responsible for auditing two Windows XP Professional workstations. One of the reasons he audits only the two workstations is because the two owners of the workstations are complaining that each time they sit down to work at their workstations, they think someone has tried to log in to them. From the list that follows, what is the most logical way to audit the two workstations so that Stan can analyze whether an attack is actually being attempted?

   A. Use the Local Security Policy on each local workstation and audit logon events (success and failure).

   B. Use the GPO Security Policy on the NY OU and audit logon events (success and failure).

   C. Use the Local Security Policy on the domain controller and audit logon events (success and failure).

   D. Use the Local Security Policy on the domain and audit logon events (success and failure).

   ☑ **A** is the correct answer. The most logical way to audit this issue is to use the Local Security Policy on each local workstation and audit logon events (success and failure).

   ☒ **B, C**, and **D** are not going to work because either Stan will be auditing too much or it will take more work to audit the events he needs. Since it is two specific workstations, the easiest, most logical way is to just audit the two workstations with the Local Security Policy MMC.

5. Jake is responsible for six Windows 2000 servers in his organization. He has noticed that lately there are no events in the Security Log on the main file server. Jake has found a single 517 event in the Security Log. What can Jake do to find out if in fact someone is trying to exploit his system?

A. The 517 event ID means that an attacker has breached the system and has tried to exploit the lssas.exe process and succeeded.

B. The 517 event ID is not a valid ID number. The Security Log only looks at event IDs 600 and higher.

C. The 517 event ID means that an attacker has breached the system and has tried to exploit the cmd.exe process and has failed.

D. The log has been cleared, and since auditing was turned on, it was caught by the Security Log.

☑ **D** is the correct answer. When someone (possibly an attacker who has breached the system) is malicious in their attempts to erase the Security Logs, if you have auditing set up correctly (as you learned in this chapter) you can catch the clearing of the logs with the 517 event. The only possible problem is that if the attacker knew enough to get into the system, he or she could also know how to turn off auditing, and then they wouldn't see this event unless they refreshed the Security Log.

☒ **A** and **C** are both incorrect and misleading. Object access has nothing to do with the 517 event ID or the clearing of the Security Log. Answer **B** is also incorrect. The Security Log will, of course, pick up and show events numbered in the 500 range as well.

6. Peter is the administrator for a large Windows 2000 network infrastructure. He is responsible for 10 IIS servers, two Exchange servers, and 20 file and print servers. All 32 servers are internal to the LAN and serve as application, e-mail, file, and print servers for over 700 clients in five separate locations. Peter has noticed that there are 10 new events on his main domain controller. The event IDs are showing as Event ID 531. What is possibly happening that Peter should be aware of?

   A. There is a possible attack on the server, whereby someone could be trying to log in with a disabled account.

   B. There is a possible attack on the server, whereby someone could be trying to change the permissions of a group.

   C. There is a possible attack on the server, whereby someone could be trying to change the permissions of a user account.

   D. There is a possible attack on the server, whereby someone could be trying to launch a buffer overflow attack on the server.

   ☑ **A** is correct. Event ID 531 showing up in the Event Log is a scary thing. This means that a logon attempt was made using a disabled account. It could mean that either the person for whom you disabled the account has tried it again, or worse yet, someone else is trying to use the account. It could also be an attempt on the Guest account, which is disabled by default.

☒ Answers **B** and **C** are both incorrect and misleading. They both look at a change of permissions, which will not be indicated by a 531 ID. Only the use of a disabled account will generate this ID number if auditing is turned on. Answer **D** is incorrect because a buffer overflow or DoS attack will not generate an ID event like this.

Auditing IIS

7. Stan is the network administrator responsible for 10 Windows 2000 servers running IIS 5.0 and 400 Windows XP Professional workstations, all separated geographically across four sites. Stan is responsible for implementing security on his 10 Windows Web-based servers. He would like to set up logging on his systems so he can audit the logs. What type of logging should Stan set up if he wants to log right to the system in the %WinDir%\System32\Logfiles folder using the default logging the system provides?

   A. ODBC logging
   B. NCSA Common Log File format
   C. W3C Extended Log File format
   D. Logging to an Oracle database using SQL Logging

   ☑ Answer **C** is correct. Auditing IIS is critical to any system administrator responsible for managing company Web servers. You should audit, monitor, and analyze IIS just the same as Windows 2000 Server. When using default logging, you use the W3C Extended Log File format.

   ☒ Answers **A**, **B**, and **D** are incorrect. Answer **A** is listed as ODBC logging which is not correct. Answer **B** is NCSA Common Log File Format, which is also incorrect. Answer **D** is wrong as well; we don't want logging to a separate database.

8. Jake is responsible for six Windows 2000 servers in his organization. He has noticed that lately there are multiple login attempts on the main Web server. Jake wants to log to a SQL server so that he can log to a separate server; he also wants to be able to log massive amounts of events. What can Jake do to log all these events to a large SQL database on a separate server so that he can eliminate the threat of being exploited by a possible attacker?

A. ODBC logging
B. NCSA Common Log File format
C. W3C Extended Log File format
D. THD Logging format

☑ Answer **A** is correct. IIS creates log files that track connection attempts to Web (HTTP), FTP, NNTP, and SMTP services. Each of these services (which can run using IIS) maintains its own log files. You can find these log files in the %WinDir%\System32\Logfiles folder. If you want to log to a separate database that is ODBC compliant (such as SQL 2000), you can use ODBC logging.

☒ All other answers are incorrect. Answers **B** and **C** are the two other log file formats, neither of which is ODBC compliant. Answer **D** is not a log file format at all.

Windows Auditing Tools

9. Stan is the network administrator responsible for 10 Windows 2000 servers and 400 Windows XP Professional workstations, all separated geographically across four sites. Stan is auditing all 10 servers and needs a way to parse all Security Logs very quickly from the command prompt. What tool from the list that follows could he use?

   A. URLSCAN
   B. Dumpel
   C. EVENTSWP
   D. Net Event

   ☑ Answer **B** is correct. Dumpel.exe is used to dump an Event Log into a tab-separated text file. This file can then be imported into an Excel spreadsheet (because it is tab separated) and/or a database such as Access for storage or future analysis.

   ☒ All other answers are incorrect. **A** is a valid tool, but not for parsing Event Logs, and **C** and **D** are not tools at all.

10. Erika is the systems engineer for the London central hub location. The hub location contains over 50 Windows 2000 servers, but only three of them are accessible through the Internet. These three servers are responsible for Web-based services such as FTP and HTTP. All the rest of the servers (all 47 of them) are located within the private LAN protected by a firewall. These 47 servers are used for applications, file, print, and database purposes. Erika wants to parse all the servers

for Event Log information. She wants to collect all the default logs found on all Windows 2000 systems as well as the FRS, DNS, and Active Directory logs as well. Erika has Dumpel.exe and is having problems using it to parse all the logs. What is the problem Erika is running into?

A. Erika is using dumpel.exe and it is corrupted. She needs a new version, and then it will work.

B. Erika is using dumpel.exe and it is never going to be able to parse anything but the default System Logs. It will not parse the FRS, DNS, and ADS logs.

C. Erika is using dumpel.exe and it is not going to work without net1.exe. A batch file must be created to run the tool accurately.

D. Erika is using dumpel.exe and it is not going to work without the use of the Task Scheduler or AT command.

☑ Answer **B** is correct. Dumpel is used to dump an Event Log into a tab-separated text file. This file can then be imported into an Excel spreadsheet (because it is tab separated) and/or a database such as Access for storage or future analysis. Dumpel will only parse the default System Logs. It will not parse the ADS, DNS, and FRS logs.

☒ **A**, **C**, and **D** are incorrect. **A** is incorrect because the real problem is that Dumpel will not parse all logs, only the default System Logs. **C** and **D** are incorrect because Dumpel can in fact be run from the command prompt; both C and D imply that you need to automate this tool to get it to work, which is not true.

11. Jake is responsible for six Windows 2000 servers in his organization. Jake has been made aware that there could be a problem with his DNS servers on the DMZ. He is concerned that a Zone Transfer attack or DNS poisoning could be attempted. He wants to use a tool that will parse all the DNS and Security Logs. What tool from the list that follows will allow Jake to quickly get all the DNS and Security Logs from his DNS servers?

A. Dumpel
B. EventCombMT
C. EVENTSWP
D. UrlScan

☑ Answer **B** is correct. EventCombMT is the GUI-based tool that allows you to manage the parsing of many Event Logs from your systems that will be dumped to a text-based file for analysis. This tool allows you to specifically search for event IDs by ID number, or you could search based on many other criteria. EventCombMT works with the DNS Logs, whereas Dumpel does not.

☒ Answer **A** is incorrect because Dumpel will not parse the DNS Logs. Answers **C** and **D** are incorrect as well. UrlScan is a valid tool but not to be used for parsing Event Logs, and EVENTSWP is not a tool at all.

12. Rob is the network engineer responsible for 10 Windows 2000 servers and 400 Windows XP Professional workstations, all separated geographically across four sites. Rob is responsible for getting all Event Logs in all servers across the network. One issue is that getting the Active Directory logs is essential to trying to find NTDS directory shutdowns. What tool should Rob use to get this information?

    A. EventCombMT
    B. Dumpel
    C. EVENTSWP
    D. UrlScan

    ☑ Answer **A** is correct. EventCombMT is the GUI-based tool that allows you to manage the parsing of many Event Logs from your systems that will be dumped to a text-based file for analysis. This tool allows you to specifically search for event IDs by ID number, or you could search based on many other criteria. Since EventCombMT is the only tool in the list that allows you to get the Directory Service Logs, you will only be able to use that one.

    ☒ Answer **B** is a log parser, but it's not able to get the ADS Logs. Answer **C** is not a valid tool. Answer **D** is a valid tool but does not parse an Event Log.

13. Peter is the network administrator responsible for performing security audits on Windows 2000 servers. Peter has a new assignment: to use the EventCombMT utility to search specifically for event ID number 682 because some kind of Terminal Server access problem is being reported. From the answers that follow, is the solution with the EventCombMT utility possible?

    A. Yes, you can use the EventCombMT utility, but it will only search for one ID at a time.
    B. No, you can't use the EventCombMT utility, because it will not search by a single ID, only in groups.
    C. Yes, you can use the EventCombMT utility to search for one or multiple IDs at a time.
    D. No, you can't use the EventCombMT utility, because it doesn't search for specific event IDs.

    ☑ **C** is the correct answer. The EventCombMT utility will allow you to search for single or multiple event IDs at a time.

☒ Answers **A**, **B**, and **D** are incorrect. Answer **A** is wrong because EventCombMT is not limited to searching only one ID at a time. Answer **B** is incorrect because you are also not locked down to just searching for groups. Answer **D** is incorrect because EventCombMT will in fact search for IDs.

14. EventCombMT allows you to scan and filter through many types of events. Jane, a network administrator, needs to find out what EventCombMT will filter for her. From the options that follow, what can she filter through using EventCombMT? (Choose all that apply.)

    A. Error
    B. Informational
    C. Warning
    D. Critical

    ☑ **A**, **B**, and **C** are all correct. You can search for error, informational, and warning events.

    ☒ Answer **D** is incorrect. Critical is not an event type.

15. Sandra is a systems engineer who has been asked to search and parse Event Viewer Logs. She has acquired and will use the Dumpel utility. Using Dumpel, what option could Sandra use to specify the filename for the output file?

    A. *-f*
    B. *-s*
    C. *-q*
    D. *-g*

    ☑ **A** is the correct answer. The *–f* switch specifies the filename for the output file. There is no default for *-f*, so you must specify the file.

    ☒ Answers **B**, **C**, and **D** are all incorrect. The *–s* switch specifies the server for which you want to dump the Event Log. Leading backslashes on the server name are optional. The other switches do not exist.

Chapter 11: Responding to and Recovering from Security Breaches

Security Incidents

1. Jake is responsible for six Windows 2000 servers in his organization. Jake has noticed that lately there are multiple login attempts on the main file server at

about 8:00 P.M., which is after hours. How should Jake classify this issue when he brings this problem up with Sara, his CIO?

A. Call the CEO immediately because the company might be expected to lose money very shortly.

B. Bring it up as a hacker breaking into the system. It's after hours, so it must be a hacker doing it.

C. Bring it up as a possible security incident, but more analysis needs to be done quickly to make sure.

D. Ignore it; there are always login attempts on the server at this time.

☑ The correct answer is **C**. Jake should, of course, flag this event as a possible security incident, but because of the possibility of false positives, he will need to quickly assess the situation in detail to figure out if it is in fact a security incident. If it is, Jake should mention it to his superiors.

☒ Answer **A** is incorrect because it assumes the activity is a hack and takes the wrong steps before we know pertinent facts. Answer **B** is incorrect because it might not be a hacker but rather a worker staying late at the office. Answer **D** is incorrect because security analysts should never ignore what they think could be a problem.

2. Stan is the network administrator responsible for 10 Windows 2000 servers and 400 Windows XP Professional workstations, all separated geographically across four sites. Stan would like to implement two new firewalls, auditing. and enforcement of desktop lockdown procedures. What is the first step Stan should accomplish from the following?

A. Create policies that are written down and backed by management.

B. Implement the firewalls only; he needs management's approval to do auditing and lockdown of desktops.

C. Lock down the desktops and have the network engineer work on the firewalls.

D. Lock down the servers, and don't worry about the desktops; they will be okay if the servers are addressed.

☑ Answer **A** is correct. A policy is needed before you implement any security infrastructure. A policy can be a security policy, a disaster recovery policy, or a business continuity plan. Any policy you create needs to be written down, read by employees, backed by management, and updated constantly. Without a policy, you are missing the backbone of all security enforcement for your organization.

☒ Answers **A**, **B**, and **C** are all incorrect. All three answers are misleading because if you don't have a security policy, you are weakening your own security infrastructure.

3. Stacy is the systems engineer for the London central hub location. The hub location contains over 50 Windows 2000 servers, but only three of them are accessible through the Internet. These three servers are responsible for Web-based services such as FTP and HTTP. All the rest of the servers (all 47 of them) are located within the private LAN protected by a firewall. These 47 servers are used for applications, file, print, and database purposes. Stacy is responsible for making sure that the nightly backups are completed. What is the most important thing Stacy should think about so she can avoid a massive problem when or if a security incident arises?

   A. Having an operational hot site so that data is never lost

   B. Implementing a 99.999 percent uptime policy so that she only loses a few hours downtime each year

   C. Verifying her backup and restore solution

   D. Making sure that she uses DXT2 tapes instead of DLT or DAT tapes for extra redundancy

   ☑ Answer **C** is correct. You should be aware of where backups are maintained, who can access them, and your procedures for data restoration and system recovery. Make sure that you regularly verify backups and media by selectively restoring data. If you don't have verifiable backups, why are you doing them in the first place? Make sure that you take care to know that your backups are safe and that they work.

   ☒ Answers **A**, **B**, and **D** are all incorrect. These answers are all very misleading. Answers **A** and **B** are similar; they are just trying to steer you away from **C**. Both are things you could possibly implement, but they are not the appropriate answers. Answer **D** is completely incorrect; there is no such thing as a DXT2 tape.

4. Peter is the administrator for a large Windows 2000 network infrastructure. He is responsible for 10 IIS servers, two Exchange servers, and 20 file and print servers. All 32 servers are internal to the LAN and serve as application, e-mail, file, and print servers for over 700 clients in five separate locations. Every week, Peter has a few changes he needs to make on the systems he administers. To minimize the possibility of an incident, what should Peter do from the following list of answers?

   A. Implement the changes and then log them.

   B. Implement the changes and then have his staff look them over.

C. Implement only one change at a time until he knows its okay.

D. Implement a change management solution.

☑ Answer **D** is correct. Total control is needed over networks and systems. Security analysts must make sure that every change on the network is documented and backed up with a plan. Very often, incidents happen based on your own people making mistakes or covering things up.

☒ Change management will keep Peter from getting in trouble by having his own staff create incidents for him. Answers **A**, **B**, and **C** are all incorrect, and although **C** is a proper way to implement changes, Peter still needs to have a full solution with a backout plan.

5. Tom is the systems administrator for his company. Tom manages 10 Windows 2000 servers and all the applications installed on them to include antivirus and backup software. Tom is plagued with system crashes and has made his management team aware of the fact that they need to spend more time repairing some of the systems and scaling their hardware requirements up to current performance needs. Management does not allow for the upgrade at this time. Tom is still forced to deal with the repetitive systems crashes on a weekly basis. What form of system management does this scenario describe?

   A. Proactive management

   B. Reactive management

   C. Disaster management

   D. Business management

   ☑ Answer **B** is correct. This situation is an example of reactive management. When a problem occurs, Tom simply reacts to it. The problem was never truly rooted out before it occurred and might even have been prevented had Tom or his staff identified the possibility that it could occur. This technique is commonly nicknamed *firefighting*.

   ☒ Answers **A**, **C**, and **D** are all incorrect. Answer **A** is the reverse of reactive management. Proactive management is when you try to fix problems before they occur, not during or after, which is the definition of reactive management. Answers **C** and **D** are incorrect because they are not in the same category as proactive or reactive management.

Malware Issues

6. Jake is responsible for six Windows 2000 servers in his organization. Yesterday, he noticed that a problem is spreading across the enterprise. It is very hard to contain,

and Jake is concerned that it could spread all over his network via a malware program with self-replication features. What type of problem are you dealing with?

A. Worm

B. Virus

C. Trojan

D. Bug

☑ The correct answer is **A**. A worm is a self-replicating program that does not alter files but resides in active memory and duplicates itself by means of computer networks.

☒ Answer **B** is incorrect because a virus doesn't self-replicate. Answer **C** is incorrect because a Trojan is not a worm, although a Trojan can contain a worm. Answer **D** is incorrect because it is just a system bug and not a worm.

7. Peter is the administrator for a large Windows 2000 network infrastructure. He is responsible for 10 IIS servers, two Exchange servers, and 20 file and print servers. All 32 servers are internal to the LAN and serve as application, e-mail, file, and print servers for over 700 clients in five separate locations. Peter has received a call from a panicky executive who is asking him what the problem is with his machine—it won't boot anymore. When Peter asks the executive what he did just before the machine wouldn't boot, he said he had downloaded a new screen saver from the Internet and when he tried to install it, it didn't seem to install. After that, the PC never seemed the same. Now it won't boot anymore. What could be the issue here, and what is the most logical problem based on this scenario?

A. Faulty screen saver

B. Buggy code

C. Trojan horse

D. Denial of service attack

☑ The correct answer is **C**. A Trojan horse closely resembles a virus but is actually in a category of its own. The Trojan horse is often referred to as the most elementary form of malicious code and could be transferred via a downloaded file from the Internet.

☒ All other answers are possible, but based on the scenario, the executive most likely downloaded a Trojan that was made to crash his machine.

8. Jack is the systems engineer for ABC Corporation. One part of Jack's responsibilities is to make sure that any additions to the network are managed and that a system of quality assurance is implemented so that if the new addition to the

network is a failure, the network itself is not negatively impacted. From the answers that follow, what step should Jack implement to make sure that the new addition to the network doesn't do harm and, if it does, that it is quickly and easily reversed to put the network back into its original state?

A. Change the plan to reflect a secondary disaster recovery plan.

B. Implement change management solutions.

C. Test his last tape backup.

D. Implement a new business continuity plan.

☑ Answer **B** is correct. Jack should implement change management solutions. Total control is needed over networks and systems. Make sure that every change on the network is documented, and back it up with a plan.

☒ Answers **A**, **C**, and **D** are all incorrect. Answer **A** has nothing to do with any step feasible for implementing change management; it is simply a distraction. Answer **C** is a good thing to do, but it has nothing to do with implementing change management and a solid backout plan to your change. Answer **D**, much like answer **A**, has nothing to do with change management.

9. Patty needs to implement systems security in the form of virus protection on 40 Windows 2000 servers and 3,000 Windows 2000 Professional clients. While installing the antivirus software on the first 10 servers, Patty found a virus. On researching it, she quickly determined that this virus has qualities that allow it to leave the contents of the host file it infected unchanged but append itself to the host in such a way that the virus code is executed first. What type of virus has Patty found?

A. Data file

B. Companion

C. Bootstrap sector

D. Parasitic

☑ Answer **D** is correct. Parasitic viruses infect executable files or programs in the computer. This type of virus typically leaves the contents of the host file unchanged but appends to the host in such a way that the virus code is executed first, before the host's code.

☒ Answers **A**, **B**, and **C** are incorrect. Answer **A** refers to a data file, not a parasitic malware attack. Answer **B** refers to a companion, not a parasitic malware attack. Answer **C** refers to a bootstrap sector virus, not a parasitic malware attack.

10. Mike needs to implement systems security in the form of virus protection on 40 Windows 2000 servers and 3,000 Windows 2000 Professional clients. While installing the antivirus software on the first 10 servers, Mike finds a virus. On researching it, Mike quickly determines that this virus has qualities that allow it to combine the functionalities of the parasitic virus and the bootstrap sector virus by infecting either files or boot sectors. What type of virus has Mike found?

    A. Multipartite

    B. Bootstrap sector

    C. Companion

    D. Link

    ☑ Answer **A** is correct. Multipartite viruses combine the functionalities of the parasitic virus and the bootstrap sector virus by infecting either files or boot sectors.

    ☒ Answers **B**, **C**, and **D** are all incorrect. Answer **B** refers to a bootstrap sector virus instead of a multipartite virus. Answer **C** refers to a companion malware attack, not multipartite. Answer **D** refers to a link virus, not multipartite.

Incident Response

11. Stan is the network administrator responsible for 10 Windows 2000 servers running IIS 5.0 and 400 Windows XP Professional workstations, all separated geographically across four sites. Stan is responsible for implementing security on his 10 Windows Web-based servers. Stan notices what he thinks are attacks on his IIS servers. Due to the nature of this problem, Stan assumes that this could be the beginning of a security incident. What should be Stan's first step in this case?

    A. Make an initial assessment of the problem.

    B. Act on the problem immediately and close all ports on the firewall.

    C. Contact the CEO so that she knows what is going on.

    D. Strike back against the attacker with a ping of death.

    ☑ **A** is the correct answer. Making an initial assessment is critical to the plan. You need to know how to see an event and assess whether it is an incident or not. Take initial steps to determine if you are dealing with an actual incident or a false positive. Your initial assessment should be very brief.

    ☒ Stan's first move should be to assess the situation. After that, he can do whatever is necessary based on his incident response plan. Answer **B** is not appropriate because Stan is essentially denying his own company service if he does this. Answer **C** is incorrect because Stan hasn't even assessed the problem yet, so he shouldn't call the CEO. Answer **D** is incorrect because Stan shouldn't strike back against an attacker.

12. Kristy is responsible for 30 Windows 2000 servers in her organization. She is part of the incident response team for the Windows 2000 environment. In one incident that recently occurred, evidence was mishandled, and that cost them to lose the whole case for the incident in court. When dealing with evidence, what is the most important thing to do so that this does not become a problem?

    A. Make sure that the CIO is always watching what the rest of the team is doing.

    B. The team leader needs to micromanage the rest of the team when taking evidence.

    C. When the evidence is computer related, it is inadmissible in court, so it doesn't really matter.

    D. A chain of custody must be established to show how evidence made it from the crime scene to the courtroom.

    ☑ Answer **D** is correct. Due to the importance of evidence, it is essential that its continuity be maintained and documented. A chain of custody must be established to show how evidence made it from the crime scene to the courtroom. It proves where a piece of evidence was at any given time and who was responsible for it. By documenting this trail, you can establish that the integrity of evidence wasn't compromised.

    ☒ Answer **A** and **B** are incorrect because Kristy shouldn't have to be micromanaged to do her job. As long as the team knows that to do (follow a chain of custody), that's what would be done. Answer **C** is totally wrong because all evidence in one shape or form should be admissible in court.

13. You are the network administrator responsible for 10 Windows 2000 servers and 400 Windows XP Professional workstations, all separated geographically across four sites. In one of the remote sites, a system was exploited and data was lost. The system is thought to have been attacked from an internal resource. At the scene of the incident, a PDA is lying next to the system that was breached. It doesn't seem to belong to anyone. What is the first thing that should be done with evidence on site?

    A. When collecting evidence, you start by identifying the evidence that is present and where it is located.

    B. Pick up the evidence and take it with you.

    C. Remove the evidence from the scene quickly, before the attacker realizes you know its there.

D. Move the evidence to another part of the room, away from the system. Document it.

☑ Answer **A** is correct. Collection is a practice consisting of the identification, processing, and documentation of evidence. When collecting evidence, you start by identifying the evidence that is present and where it is located.

☒ Answers **B**, **C**, and **D** are incorrect because they imply that you should touch or move the evidence. The first thing you need to do is identify the item as evidence and then document it.

14. Erika is the systems engineer for the Toronto central hub location. The hub location contains over 50 Windows 2000 servers, but only three of them are accessible through the Internet. These three servers are responsible for Web-based services such as FTP and HTTP. All the rest of the servers (all 47 of them) are located within the private LAN protected by a firewall. These 47 servers are used for applications, file, print, and database purposes. The manager at a remote site has phoned Erika claiming that all systems seem to have a virus. The remote site manager is worried because all but two of their systems have become inoperable. They are connected directly to the core network from a Frame Relay link. Erika needs to deal with this problem immediately. What should be her first step from the following list?

    A. Call the CIO and arrange a meeting.
    B. Contain the problem immediately by having the remote site manager power down infected machines.
    C. Have the remote site manager call local law enforcement and tell them that there is a security breach they need to deal with.
    D. Fly down to handle the problem; make travel arrangements as soon as possible.

    ☑ Answer **B** is correct. Containing the damage and minimizing the risk are critical to handling an incident. For instance, if the incident in your initial assessment is a worm that is self-replicating across your network, you can contain the damage by unplugging the affected workstation from the switch or hub. This action contains the damage and minimizes the risk.

    ☒ Answer **A** is incorrect because Erika needs to act on this situation and contain the problem immediately. Answer **C** is incorrect because it's ridiculous to call local law enforcement because of a possible worm. Answer **D** is incorrect because Erika will never be able to contain the problem by flying to the remote site, and it could spread in the meantime.

15. Paul is the network administrator for his company. He manages systems and network security on 10 Windows 2000 servers and the Cisco switches that connect them to the network. If Paul plans to keep his policies up to date and well prepared, which of the following answers provides the step to accomplish this task?

   A. Ask the CIO what needs to be updated.

   B. After an incident, just update the logs so the incident is recorded.

   C. Review the response and updating policies.

   D. Move all systems to another location after an attack.

   ☑ Answer **C** is correct. Reviewing the response and updating policies on constant or regular basis are things you need to implement as part of your strategy. A plan is no good unless its up to date and well prepared. Updating a plan after an actual response is also a good idea so that you can assess the plan and how you might have been able to do things better.

   ☒ Answers **A**, **B**, and **D** are incorrect. Answer **A** is incorrect because Paul should not have to ask his CIO what needs to be updated if he is responsible for the updates. Answer **B** is incorrect because Paul needs to do a lot more than updating logs after an incident; he should make note that its important to review the incident response and update his policies as needed. Answer **D** is incorrect because it is ridiculous to plan system moves because of an incident.

Index

cess control list (ACL), 209, 480
access denied' messages,
    decryption and, 300
cessing encrypted files, 275
cess points (APs), WLAN and,
    385
ccount Lockout, configuring
    settings (fig.), 54
count management auditing,
    viewing (fig.), 612
ccount Policies, 33-35
counts, Guest remote access, 573
tions, filter, 351
ctive Directory
    architecture, 9-11
    certificate authorities and,
        210-211
    components, 481
    as database, 16
    diagnostic event logging, 114-116
    domain controllers, creation of,
        89
    history of Windows directory
        services, 6-9
    legacy computer capabilities using
        DS client, 113-114
    logical structure of, 12-14
    physical structure, 13-19
    publishing certificates in, 241
    Users and Computers Console
        (fig.), 26
    Windows 2000, review, 4
    Windows 2000 domain model
        with forests (fig.), 10
lding EFS recovery agents, 289
dd Recovery Agent Wizard, 290
ddress Range Assignment screen,
    537-539
dministrative group, updates and
    permission problems, 182
ministrative models, remote access
    policy, 571-573
dvanced Encryption Standard
    (AES), 334
DVAP132.DLL, 275
ge policies, password, 35
H (Authentication Header), 559
l IP Traffic filter list, 350
ernating current (AC), 389
alyzing
    local security with Security
        Configuration and Analysis
        snap-in, 64-66
    security configurations, 63-72,
        145-151

security with secedit.exe, 70
updates from the GUI, 147-150
updates with HFNetChk, 143-145
your computers, 137-139
antennas, 390
Antheil, George, 390
antivirus software, installation, 683
application-directed attacks, 327
approvals, automatic, 174
architecture
    Active Directory, 9-11
    EFS, 292
    IPSec, 328
    wireless network, 392
assets
    categorizing corporate (table),
        344
    identifying technology, 343
asymmetric cryptography, 268, 201
asymmetric encryption, 264
atomic clock, 633
attackers described, 655
attacks
    application-directed, 327
    Chargen, 712
    compromised key, 327
    denial of service. See DoS attacks
    DoS. See DoS attacks
    Main-in-the-Middle (MITM),
        118, 200, 326
    on member servers, 92
    passive, using Ethereal to perform
        (fig.), 704
    password compromises, 324-325
    Ping-of-Death, 326
    and removable media, 276
    SMURF, 325
    sniffing networks, 284
    snooping, 321
    SYN flood, 667
    TCP/IP sequence number, 322
    TCP SYN, 325
    teardrop, 326
attributes
    encryption, 273
    of objects, 18
audit
    account management, 612
    Local Policies security options
        (table), 36-37
    policy changes, 613-614, 619
    privilege use, 614
auditing
    best practices, 627-630
    with Group Policy, 620

for increased security, 609-610
Internet Information Services,
    630-633
introduction to, 608
with local security policy,
    617-618
minimizing and preventing
    security incidents, 652
process-tracking events, 615
success- and failure-based (fig.),
    618
Windows 2000, 611-626
Windows tools, 633-637
and your security policy, 621
authentication
    basic, anonymous, 497-498
    certificate-based, 489-490
    combining methods, 502
    configuring user, 488-496
    cross-domain (fig.), 468
    defining LM and NLM, 491
    described, 204-205
    digest, using, 498-499
    encrypted data and, 268
    for external users, 488
    IIS 5.0-supported methods
        (table), 503
    Integrated Windows (IWA), 500
    introduction to, 456
    Kerberos, 332
    message, 330-334
    mutual, 532
    privacy and, 247
    remote access methods, 529-533
    and secure communications, 372
    selecting a protocol (fig.), 362
    site configuration and, 17
    smartcards and, 533
    using forwarded tickets (fig.), 470
    using proxy tickets (fig.), 469
    Web, troubleshooting, 510-511
    Web site, 502
    Windows 2000 network, 456-459
authentication header (AH), 335,
    559
Authentication Methods
    Configuration tab (fig.), 352
authenticator process, Kerberos,
    460-463
automatic approvals, 174
automatic certificate enrollment,
    234-236
Automatic Updates
    downloading required files, 172
    installing, configuring, 177-180
autorooters, 152

B

backing up
 Certificate Services, 237-238
 encrypted files, 275
 Registry before changing, 277
Back Orifice, 661, 663, 665
backup plans, 154
Backup Utility, 275
bandwidth, available, 17
Base Cryptographic Provider, 283, 301
basicdc.inf, 21
basicsv.inf, 21, 92
basicwk.inf, 21
best practices, auditing, 627-630
BIOS password and laptops, 111
black hat described, 656, 696
bootstrap sector viruses, 658
brute-force hacking, 42
BSOD (blue screen of death), 668
buffer overruns, SQL Server 2000, 93
buffers described, 93
bulk data encryption, without prior shared secrets, 206

C

CAB format, and XML files, 140
cache, credentials, 478
Carrier Sense Multiple Access with Collision Detection (CSMA/CD), 392-394
CAs. *See* certification authorities (CAs)
Cerberus, 463
certificate authorities (CAs)
 advanced management issues, 240-246
 backing up, restoring CA server, 237-238
 choosing type (fig.), 214
 configuring automatic certificate enrollment, 234-235
 configuring public key Group Policy, 234
 configuring Trusted Root, 236-237
 described, 208, 332
 identifying information (fig.), 215
 installing certificate services, 213-217
 need for stand-alone, 217
 reasons for support model containing multiple, 210
 selecting database storage, 215
 trust and validation, 212
 types, 209, 216
 Windows 2000, 212-213

Certificate Distribution Lists (CDLs), viewing current, 230
Certificate Distribution Points (CDPs), 229, 231
Certificate Export Wizard, 108-110
certificate hierarchies, 211
Certificate Import Wizard, 226
Certificate Management snap-in, adding for local computer (fig.), 347
certificate mapping, client, 500-502
Certificate Request Wizard, 217, 286
certificate revocation list (CRL), 209, 229-231
certificates
 adding to root store (fig.), 226
 advanced management issues, 240-246
 described, 207
 exporting, importing, 222-226
 hierarchies, 211
 listing issued (fig.), 227
 publishing in Active Directory, 241
 requesting, 217-222
 revoking, 226-229
 smartcards and, 533
 templates, configuring, 231-233
 Windows XP auto-enrollment of, 244-246
 X.509v3 properties (table), 208
Certificate Services
 installing, 213-216
 using Web interface, 220-222
Certificates Snap-in, 341
certificate templates, 231-233
chain of custody, evidence in crimes, 678
Challenge Handshake Authentication Protocol (CHAP), 530
channels, 391
CHAP (Challenge Handshake Authentication Protocol), 530
Chargen attacks, 712
checking connected VPN port status, 561
chips, 391
cipher block chaining (CBC), 334-335
ciphers and compromised key attacks, 327
ciphertext, 201
Cipher Utility
 command switches (table), 281
 summary of, 304
 using in Windows 2000, 280-282

cleartext authentication, 489
click kiddies, 656, 696
client certificate mapping, 500-501
Client (Respond Only) IPSec policy, 348
clients
 legacy, issues, 113-114
 requesting server access (fig.), 465
clocks, synchronizing, 633
CMAK (Connection Manager Administration Kit), 576, 580, 596
Code Red worm, 136, 152, 327
command line
 analyzing updates with MBSA, 150-151
 starting IP Security Monitor at, 338
 tools, 30-31
commands
 cipher, 281-282
 secpol.msc, 108
Common Internet File System (CIFS), 490
companion viruses, 659
compatibility, applications and updates, 182
compatws.inf, 22
compression, encryption and, 309
compromised key attacks, 327
computer forensics, 674
computers
 analyzing your, 137-139
 installing updates on new, 155
 IP Security Policies, 337
Computer Security Incident Response Team (CSIRT), 651, 654
confidentiality
 IP security and, 334
 and secure communications, 372
confidentiality of data, 268
configurations, wireless LAN, 386
configuring
 Account Lockout settings, 54
 anonymous, basic, digest, and integrated Windows Web site authentication, 506
 automatic certificate enrollment, 234
 Automatic Updates, 177-180
 basic Windows 2000 security with templates, 32-52
 certificate templates, 231-233
 domain account service for Kerberos delegation, 477
 domain-level security policy (fig.), 25
 File System security, 51-52
 IIS log files, 631

Index 813

interoperability with legacy
    Windows clients, 490-492
L2TP ports, 561-562
local host service for Kerberos
    delegation, 476
network clients for secure remote
    access, 573-582
Password History setting (fig.), 54
publication of CRLs, 229-231
public key Group Policy, 234-237
Registry Security, 48-50
remote access policies, 562-563
remote access profiles, 567-571
remote access server, 534-541
Restricted Groups, 45-46
role-based server security, 86-107
script maps, 103-104
security for the enterprise (fig.),
    88
security templates, 54-55
servers to require NTLMv2,
    492-493
SMB signing (fig.), 119
Software Update Services,
    173-177
System Services security, 47-48
Trusted Root CAs, 236-237
trusts with Active Directory
    domains and trusts, 486-487
trusts with Netdom, 487-488
UNIX server interoperability, 489
user authentication, 488-496,
    515-516
user for Kerberos delegation
    (fig.), 475
VPN servers, 546-556
Web authentication, 497-511,
    516
Web authentication using SSL,
    508-510
Web site authentication, 502
Windows 9.x clients to use
    NTLMv2, 496
Windows NT 4.0 clients to use
    NTLMv2, 495
Connection Manager
    Administration Kit
    (CMAK), 576, 580, 596
Connection Manager, allowing
    users to use, 582
connections
    making new, 577
    wired network, 385
container objects, described, 17
contiguous namespace, 10
copying encrypted files, 276
cordless phones, 390
corporate assets, categorizing
    (table), 344
Corporate Windows Update, 172

crackers, cracking described, 323,
    655
creating
    dynamic phone books, 579
    EFS recovery agent, 285
    filters, 356-359
    IPSec MMC console, 346
    remote access policies, 563-567
    RIS CD-based installation image,
        162-166
    secure workstations, 107-112
    Security Configuration Tool Set
        user interface, 31
    security console, 32
    security policies, 356-369
    static phone book, 578
credentials cache, 478
crime scenes and forensics, 673-680
cross-domain authentication (fig.),
    468
cryptanalysts, 266
CryptoAPI, 294
Cryptographic Service Provider
    (CSP), 215, 294
cryptography
    described, 200, 264
    function types, 247
    IP security. See IP security
    public key, 201-202
    public key (asymmetric), 268
    secret key algorithm (fig.), 269
    secret key (symmetric), 269
CSIRT (Computer Security
    Incident Response Team),
    651
CSMA/CD and CSMA/CA,
    393-394
Cult of the Dead Cow (CDC), 665
Custom Security Method Settings
    dialog box (fig.), 354
*Cybercrime: Computer Forensics
    Handbook* (Shinder), 264

D

data
    confidentiality of, 268
    encrypting (fig.), 202
Database Security window (fig.), 49
data encryption described, 264
Data Encryption Standard (DES),
    201, 269, 334
Data Encryption Standard
    (DES/CBC/Message Digest
    5 hash, 466
data file viruses, 659
datagrams, after applying AH in
    transport mode (fig.), 336
data integrity and secure
    communications, 372

Data Recovery Agent certificate,
    exporting, 123
data types, categorizing impact of
    risk (table), 345
DC security.inf, 22
DDoS attacks, 666, 669-671
DecryptFek function, 301
decrypting
    EFS information, 123
    files, 279
decryption
    described, 201
    process described, 300-301
Deffie-Hellman, 336
delegation of authentication
    concept explained, 468-469
    Windows 2000 and Kerberos,
        474-475
denial of service attacks. *See* DoS
    attacks
deploying
    IP Security, 343-371
    security templates, 53-62
    security via Group Policy, 57
    security via scripting, 60-61
DES, exporting, 254
desktop workstations, securing,
    107-108
DFS (Distributed file System), 114
diagnostic logging, 114-116
Diffie-Hellman keys, 222
digest authentication, 498-499
Digital Signature Algorithm (DSA),
    222
digital signatures, 203-204, 330, 332
directories
    encrypting, 282
    root, 14
Directory Access Protocol
    (DAP), 14
Directory Information Shadowing
    Protocol (DISP), 14
Directory Information Tree
    (DIT), 14
Directory Operational Binding
    Management Protocol
    (DOP), 14
directory services, introduction to, 7
Directory Services Client. *See*
    DSClient
Directory Services (DS) clients,
    legacy issues, 113-114
Directory System Agent (SSA), 14
Directory System Protocol
    (DSP), 14
direct-sequence spread-spectrum
    (DSSS), 391
disabling unwanted services, 700
disks, encryption and, 276
Distributed File System (DFS), 114

Index

DNS names, 10
   and IPSec security, 349
   Microsoft Kerberos, 478
DNS namespace, 11
documenting security incidents, crime scenes, 675, 680
domain controllers
   described, 17
   securing, 90-91
Domain Controllers OU (fig.), 89
Domain Controllers properties window (fig.), 493
Domain Name System (DNS), 213, 349, 472
domains
   connecting external (fig.), 484
   described, 13
   importing security templates in, 59-60
   Kerberos authentication, 463, 467-468, 482
   NT, 7
   realms and, 467
   securing, 88
   trees and forests (fig.), 482
Domain Security Policy console (fig.), 25
DoS attacks, 325, 666-671
download sites
   Ethereal, 704
   Microsoft L2TP/IPSec VPN Client, 575
   Nmap, 703
   NTBUGTRAQ, 701
   SSH, 706
drivers, EFS, 293, 294, 295
DSClient, 89, 491
Dumpel tool switches (table), 634
Dump Event Log, 633-634
dwell time, 391
dynamic ASP, locking down IIS servers, 103
Dynamic Host Configuration Protocol (DHCP), 349
dynamic/private port numbers, 712

E

EAP (Extensible Authentication Protocol), 532-533
EAP-MD5 CHAP, 532
EAP-TLS, 532-533
echo requests, replies, 325
editing built-in IPSec policies, 353
EFS (Encrypting File System), 108, 210
   architecture of, 292
   callback functions, 294
   components of (fig.), 293
   encrypting files with, 274

encryption process (fig.), 270
file information, 7, 38-47
File System Runtime Library (FSRTL), 293
functionality of, 269-271
information, decrypting, 123
preventing on servers, 277
recovery agents, 283, 285, 289
role in security system, 265-266
troubleshooting, 302-303
user operations, 271
using, 266
EfsRead callback function, 309
EfsRecvr utility, 291, 305
electromagnetic (EM) field, 389
e-mail
   Trojan payload in (fig.), 660
   warning of viruses via, 661
   white hat protection for, 697-706
EM fields, 389-390
Encapsulating Security Payload (ESP), 559
Encrypted Data Recovery Policy (EDRP), 267, 283
encrypted files
   adding users in Windows XP, 278
   copying, 276
   moving, renaming, 278
   preventing on servers, 277
   recovering with EfsRecvr utility, 291
   sharing in Windows XP/.NET, 278
   Windows 2000 steps for, 308
encrypting
   data (fig.), 202
   directories, 282
   files, folders, 272
Encrypting File System. *See* EFS (Encrypting File System)
encryption
   basic file, 304
   compression and, 309
   DES, 269
   described, 201, 264
   enabling (fig.), 272
   fundamentals of, 267
   process described, 295-297
   Secure Shell (SSH) tool, 696, 705-706
   verifying your level, 496
Encryption File System. *See* EFS (Encrypting File System)
Enhanced CryptoPAK, 307
Enterprise Root, Subordinate CAs, 209
enterprise security, configuring (fig.), 88
errors, logging, 114

ESP, protocol described, 336
ESP (Encapsulating Security Payload), 559
Ethereal packet sniffer, 703
EventCombMT, using tool, 635-637
EventCombMT GUI-based utility, 633
event ID 531, appearing frequently, 623
Event Log
   account logon events that appear in, 625-626
   account management events in (table), 626
   analyzing security issues using, 116-117
   logon events that appear in (table), 622
   normal entry (fig.), 115
   policies described, 42-43
   security options (table), 43-44
   use in Windows 2000, 114-116
Event Log node, configuring, 29
event logging, VPN servers, 555
Event Viewer
   auditing and, 619
   log size, 629-630
   Security Log, 614-617
events
   to audit, 621-622
   audit system, 616
   failed, event IDs, 624
evidence collection, security incidents, 676-679
Exchange 2000 Server, securing, 97
Exchange BackEnd Incremental.inf, 99
Exchange Key Management Server (KMS), 241
Exchange System Manager (fig.), 243
exporting
   Administrator File Recovery Certificate and keys (fig.), 109
   certificate and private key, 222-225
   Data Recovery Agent certificate, 123
   DES, 254
   security templates, 55-57
Extensible Authentication Protocol (EAP), 532
Extensible Markup Language (XML), 140
extracting Service Pack files (fig.), 157

F

FEK key, 296, 304
File Encryption Key (FEK), 269, 304
file information, EFS, 7, 38-47
files
  accessing encrypted, 275
  compressed, and encryption, 273
  decrypting, 279
  encrypting, 272
  exported certificate (fig.), 224
  removing options to hide (fig.), 662
File System ACLs, upgrading from Windows NT to Windows 2000, 112
File System node, configuring, analyzing with Security Configuration and Analysis snap-in, 29, 30
File System Security node, 50-52
File Transfer Protocol (FTP), authentication and, 456
filter actions, 351
filter lists, 350
filters, IP Security, 354-355
Filter Wizard, 354-355
Finger service, and attack vunerabilities, 713
firewalls
  configuring for IPSec traffic, 369
  remote access issues, 589
fixes, Web site for download, 153
flexible negotiation policies, 353
folders, encrypting, 272
forensics of security incidents, 673-680
forests
  in Active Directory domain (fig.), 10
  described, 12-13, 481
forwarded tickets, Kerberos delegation, 469-470
freeware tools, 697
frequency-hopping spread-spectrum (FHSS), 391
Fresnel zone, 389
FTP protocol
  attack vulnerabilities, 713
  authentication and, 456
FTP service, disabling, 700

G

GenerateFek function, 296
Generic Routing Encapsulation (GRE), 557
GFI LANguard Network Scanner, 698-699
Global Catalog (GC), 14
gpedit.msc, 337
gpotool.exe, gpresult.exe, 31, 71-72, 114
gray hat described, 656, 696
GRE (Generic Routing Encapsulation), 557
Grep tool, using to search log file, 71
Group Policy
  applying security settings to legacy clients, 122
  auditing, 620
  configuring public key, 234-237
  deploying security via, 57
  issues, summary, 120
  security settings, 23-27
  and security templates, 27
  troubleshooting issues with gpresult.exe tool, 114
Group Policy Editor window (fig.), 493
groups
  described, 15-16
  using to assign specific permissions (fig.), 16
Group Security, security settings (fig.), 58
GTE Cybertrust, 208

H

hackers
  described, 684
  good and bad, 655
  jargon, 655-656
  methods used, 321
  shutting out, 44
hacking, 42, 323
handshakes and TCP SYN attacks, 325
hash functions
  cryptography function, 201
  described, 330
hash message authentication codes (HMAC), 330
hashing
  messages, 330
  password, 530
HFNetChk
  switches (table), 141-142
  using, 96-97, 139-145
hisecdc.inf, 22, 89
hisecws.inf, 22, 92
honeypot, 624
hop time, 391
hosts involved in DDoS attacks, 671
hotfixes, described, 134, 135-136
HTTP
  attack vulnerabilities, 714
  port numbers and, 710
  selecting Web service, 103

I

IAS, securing, 106-107
ICANN, 711
IDS (intrusion detection system), 609
IEEE 8095 standard, and wireless networking technology, 388
IIS
  auditing, 630-631
  password control, 508
  requesting server certificate for server, 504
  securing servers, 99
  stopping, 216
  Unicode translation problems, 101
  updating, importance of, 101
IIS 5.0-supported authentication methods (table), 503
IIS Lockdown tool
  locking down Exchange servers with, 98
  locking down IIS servers with, 102-106
  securing SQL Server with, 93-95
IIS servers
  locking down with IIS Lockdown tool, 102-106
  locking down with URLScan tool, 100-102
IIS Web Publishing Service, disabling, 700
IKE, 336, 372
'I Love You' bug, 659
impersonating users, 295
impersonation, spoofing and, 322
implementing new security policies, 356-359
importing
  certificate from Trust Root CA, 225-226
  security templates, 55-57
  security templates at domain level, 59-60
  security templates at OU level, 57-58
  templates (fig.), 91
incident response plans, 654, 672-673
Industrial, Scientific, and Medical (ISM) band, 390
installations, upgrade, 112
installing
  Automatic Updates, 177-180
  Certificate Services, 213-216
  directory services client, 491
  MBSA, 147-148
  PGP, 706
  remote access server, 535-540

816 Index

RIS, 158-162
Software Update Services, 173-177
SSH, 705
updates on new computers, 155
VPN servers, 547-556
Integrated Services Digital Network (ISDN), 529
Integrated Windows Authentication (IWA), 500
integrity, message, 329
IntelliMirror, 177
interference, multipath, 390
International Telecommunications Union (ITU), X.509v3 standard, 207-208
International Telecommunications Union (ITU-T), 11
Internet, importance of updates, hotfixes, 152
Internet Access Servers. *See* IAS
Internet Control Message Protocol (ICMP), SMURF attacks and, 325
Internet Corporation for Assigned Names and Numbers (ICANN), 711
Internet Engineering Task Force (IETF), 480
Internet Information Services. *See* IIS
Internet Key Exchange (IKE), 558
Internet pornography, 674
Internet Protocol Security (IPSec), 558-559
Internet Security Association Key Management Protocol. *See* ISAKMP/Oakley Protocol
Internet Service Providers. *See* ISPs
interoperability
  configuring UNIX server, 489-490
  configuring with legacy Windows clients, 490-491
intrusion detection system (IDS), 609
IP addresses, port numbers and, 711
IP Filter List dialog box (fig.), 351, 362
IP Filter Wizard, 362
IPSec, Policy Agent, 562
IPSec cryptographic services, 329-333
IPSec (Internet Protocol Security), 558-559
IPSec key management, 335
ipsecmon.exe, 338
IPSec Policies snap-in and tasks (fig.), 338

IPSec Policy Agent service, 340-341
IP security
  authentication header (AH), 335
  compatibility notes, 369
  confidentiality, 334
  custom IPSec Management console (fig.), 347
  deploying with certificates, 342
  DNS names and, 349
  ESP protocol, 336
  filter actions, 351
  flexible negotiation policies, 353
  IPSec cryptographic services, 329
  IPSec policies, built-in (fig.), 348
  message authentication, 331-334
  message integrity, 329-331
  overview, 328
  policies, 337, 341, 345-347
  rules, 350
  security associations and key management procedures, 335-337
  security levels, determining, 345
  Security Log, 342
  TCP/IP Advanced options, 341
  troubleshooting, 343-371
IP Security Filter Action Wizard, 365
IP Security Monitor, 338-340
IP Security Policy Wizard, 359-360
IP spoofing, 322
ISAKMP/Oakley protocol, 558
ISAKMP/Oakley Protocol SA process, 336, 337
ISAKMP SA, 336, 372
ISDN (Integrated Services Digital Network), 529
ISPs, VPN problems due to, 584
IWA. *See* Integrated Windows Authentication (IWC)

K
KDC. *See* Key Distribution Center (KDC)
KDCs, DNS name resolution and, 478
Kerberos
  Account Policies (table), 34
  authentication, 332, 336
  authentication across domain boundaries, 467-468
  authentication method described, 458-459
  authenticator, 460-462
  authorization data, KDC and, 479-480
  concepts, 460-462
  configuring client for delegation, 475

configuring trusts, 480-488
delegation of authentication, 459, 468, 474
DNS name resolution, 478
KDC, 462-464
and L2TP/IPSec, 375
KDC service (fig.), 471
Microsoft, and PAC, 517
overview, 459
preauthentication, 477-478
proxy and forwarded tickets, 469
safe, 472
session ticket (ST), 464
simplified trusts, 459
ticket-granting ticket (TGT), 466
v4 and v5 differences, 462
v5 protocol, 457, 490
Windows 2000, and, 470-474
Kerberos V5 protocol, 361
kernel mode, 305
Key Distribution Center (KDC), 459
keys
  and compromised key attacks, 327
  long-term, 464
  public and private, 201
  public and private (table), 268
  recovering lost KMS, 242-244
KsecDD, 293

L
L2TP/IPSec client for Windows 98, 369
L2TP (Layer 2 Tunneling Protocol), 557
L2TP ports, 558
Lamarr, Hedy, 390
LAN, wireless. *See* wireless LAN
LANguard Network Scanner, 698-699
LAN Manager (LM), authentication and, 457
laptop computers, securing, 111-112
law enforcement, forensics of security incidents, 672-680
Layer 2 Forwarding (L2F) protocol, 557
Layer 2 Tunneling Protocol (L2TP), 557
LDAP, Active Directory and, 12
legacy clients, applying security settings to, 122
Lightweight Directory Access Protocol (LDAP), 9
link viruses, 659
Linux, Nmap scan (fig.), 702
LM
  authentication, 491

Index

compatibility levels (table), 495
Local Group Policy Editor, 337
Local Policies, 36-42
Local Policies node, 29
Local Security Authority (LSA), 471
Local Security Authority Subsystem (LSASS), 293
Local Security Policy, opening console, 108
Local Security Settings Console, using (fig.), 24
locking down
   Exchange Servers with IIS Lockdown tool, 98
   IIS servers with IIS Lockdown tool, 102-106
   IIS servers with URLScan tool, 100-102
   selecting type of server to (fig.), 94
   servers, 92
   SQL Server with IIS Lockdown tool, 93-95
lockout, Account Policies (table), 34
logon
   account events (table), 625-626
   events in Event Log (table), 622
   hours configuration (fig.), 625
   local attempt failures, 624
logons, Windows 2000 Kerberos restrictions, 473
Lucifer cipher, 269

M

Macintosh, encrypted files and, 267
Macintosh Guest Authentication dialog box (fig.), 537
MAC layer, wireless network architecture, 392
maintenance, routine, with HFNetChk tool, 96-97
malware issues, 657
managing updates, 152-181
Man-in-the-Middle (MITM) attacks, 200
many-to-one certificate mapping, 501
mapping, client certificate, 500-501
maximum transmission unit (MTU), 480
MBSA, 93, 95
   analyzing for updates from command line, 150-151
   mbsacli.exe switches (table), 146-147
   results (fig.), 149
   scan results (fig.), 96
   tool described, 123
   using, 145-151

mbsacli.exe, 146
MCC snap-in, for certificate policy, 234
mean transfer unit (MTU), 326
member servers, attacks on, 92
memory, RAM, and Kerberos authentication, 472
Mendax, spoofing utility, 323
message authentication, 331-334
message digest, 204
Message Digest 5 (MD5), 330-331
message integrity, IP security and, 329
messages, hashing, 330
methods, remote access authentication, 529-533
Microsoft
   antitrust lawsuit, 135
   malware issues, 657
   security bulletins, 86, 101
   security issues, 650
Microsoft Base Cryptographic Provider, 283, 301
Microsoft Baseline Security Analyzer. *See* MBSA
Microsoft Certificate Service, 209
Microsoft Challenge Handshake Authentication Protocol (MS-CHAP), 530
Microsoft Encryption File System. *See* EFS
Microsoft Kerberos implementation, 470
Microsoft Knowledge Base, 182
Microsoft Management Console. *See* MMC
Microsoft Network Security Hotfix Checker (HFNetChk), 139-145
Microsoft Operations Manager (MOM), 610, 628
Microsoft Point-to-Point Encryption (MPPE), 557
MITM attacks, 326
Mitnick, Kevin, 323
MMC
   certificates and IPSec authentication, 337
   console, building IPSec with, 346
   grouping with Tool Set components, 20
mobility and wireless LANs, 388
modems, 541
moving, encrypted files, 278
MPPE (Microsoft Point-to-Point Encryption), 557
MS-CHAP, 530
MS-CHAP v2, 531, 553-554
MSSecureXML file, 149
multipartite viruses, 658

multipath interference, 390

N

names
   DNS naming, 10
   IP Security Policy, entering (fig.), 359
namespace
   contiguous, 10
   DNS, 11
NAT (Network Address Translation)
   described, devices, 586-587
   and IPSec, 369
   and L2TP/IPSec tunnels, 375-376
National Institute of Standards and Technology (NIST), 107-108
National Security Agency, 91, 201
NetBEUI, LANs and, 320
NetBIOS, attack vulnerabilities, 714
NETBIOS Extended User Interface. *See* NetBEUI
NetBus, 663
NetDiag.exe, 342
Netdom, configuring trusts with, 487-488
Netdom syntax (table), 485
network, security plans. *See* security plans
Network Address Translation. *See* NAT
network cards, VPN requirements, 547
Network Connection wizard, 577
Network Mapper (Nmap), 701
network monitors, 323
network operating systems, directory services and, 5
network security, 320-328
Network Security Hotfix Checker, 139-145
network sniffers, 321
network-to-network VPNs, 546
networks
   history of, 6
   security plan and EFS, 265-266
   wireless. *See* wireless LAN
New Security Method dialog box (fig.), 354
Nimba worm, 152
NIST (National Institute of Standards and Technology), 107-108
NLM authentication, 491
Nmap, 701
notssid.inf, 23
Novell Directory Service (NDS), 5, 19

818 Index

NTBUGTRAQ, 701
NT domains, 7, 8
NTFS file system
   and EFS, 266
   temp files and, 271
NT LAN Manager. *See* NTLM
NTLM
   authentication, 457
   authentication and, 456
   compared with Kerberos, 457
NTLMv2
   configuring Windows clients to use, 495-496
   deploying, 492
   and legacy client upgrades, 114
   making client use, 494

O

objects described, 18
ocfiless.inf, 23
ocfilesw.inf, 23
one-to-one certificate mapping, 501
Organizational Units (OUs)
   Active Directory tree structure, 11-12
   described, 14-15
   Group Policy security settings, 22

P

packet sniffers, Ethereal, 703
PAP (Password Authentication Protocol), 530
parasitic viruses, 658
Password Authentication Protocol (PAP), 530
password compromise attacks, 323-324
password policies, importance of, 324
Password Policy node, analyzing, 66
passwords
   Account Policies and (table), 33-35
   age policies, 35
   cracking in Windows 2000, 123
   hashing, 530
   IIS control, allowing, 508
   and laptop security, 111
   Windows 2000 and Kerberos authentication, 472
patches, 135, 153
pbainst.exe, 579
permissions
   accessing encrypted files, 275
   remote access, 562
   RRAS administration, 591
   troubleshooting update installations, 182

using groups to assign specific (fig.), 16
PGP. *See* Pretty Good Privacy (PGP)
phone books
   dynamic, 579
   static, 578
phones, cordless, 390
ping flood, 671
Ping-of-Death attacks, 326
PKCS-7, PKCS-10, PKCS-12 standards, 222
PKI described, 248
plaintext, authentication challenge (fig.), 205
planning
   organizational updates, 154
   security requirements, 372
Point-to-Point Protocol (PPP), 529-530
Point-to-Point Tunneling protocol (PPTP), 556-557
policies
   configuring remote access, 562-563
   creating security, 356-369
   disaster recovery, 652
   flexible negotiation, 353
   remote access, 529, 563
POP2, POP3, attack vulnerabilities, 714
pornography, viewing at work, 674
portable computers, securing, 111-112
port numbers, 710-715
Port Properties screen (fig.), 542-543
ports
   checking status, 544
   configuring PPTP and L2TP for inbound access only, 559-561
   L2TP, 558
   RAS, working with, 541-544
   VPN, working with, 556-559
PPP Extensible Authentication Protocol (EAP), 532
PPP (Point-to-Point Protocol), 529-530
PPTP Forum, 556
PPTP (Point-to-Point Tunneling Protocol), 556-557
preauthentication, 477-478
preshared key authentication, 331
Pretty Good Privacy (PGP), using, 697, 706
preventing security incidents, 652-654
primary domain controller (PDC), 7

private keys, compromised, 327-328
Privilege Attribute Certificate (PAC), 479
profiles (wireless LAN cards), 111
proof of possession, 205
protocol analyzer (sniffer), 266, 323
protocols
   See also specific protocol
   IPSec-supported, 558-559
   port numbers and (table), 712-715
proxy tickets, Kerberos delegation, 468-469
public key, encryption and decryption (fig.), 268
public key cryptography, 201-203, 207, 268
public key Group Policy, configuring, 234-237
Public Key Infrastructure (PKI), 11, 200
public keys, compromised, 327-328

Q

Q articles, 153
Qchain.exe, 155, 163, 183
Quick Fix Engineering, 135

R

radio frequency communications, 389-390
radio waves, 386
RADIUS (Remote Authentication Dial-In User Service), 532
RAS
   configuring, 534-541
   introduction to, 528
   passwords, 111
   port configuration, 541-544
   troubleshooting remote access problems, 582
   troubleshooting routing and other issues, 588
   vs. RRAS, 534
RAS servers, reason for use, 545
realm, domain and, 467
recovering key management server-issued keys, 241-244
Recovery Agent certificates, exporting, 108-110
Recovery Agent key, removing local computer, 108-111
recovery agents, EFS. See EFS,
Recovery Agent Wizard, 283
referral tickets, 467
registered port numbers, 712
Registry
   backing up before changing, 277
   configuring security, 48-50

editing to increase logging (fig.), 117
encryption and, 277
Windows NT 4.0, upgrading to Windows 2000, 112
Registry node, configuring, analyzing with Security Configuration and Analysis snap-in, 29
remote access
 configuring network clients for secure, 573-582
 firewall issues, 589
 identifying remote users, 541
 troubleshooting problems, 582-590
remote access authentication methods, 529-533
remote access policies
 administrative models, 571-573
 configuring, 562-563
 user profiles, 566
remote access profiles
 authentication, 570
 dial-in constraints, 567-568
 encryption, 570-571
 IP configuration, 568
 multilink configuration, 569
remote access servers, managing multiple, 539
Remote Access Service. *See* RAS
Remote Authentication Dial-In User Service (RADIUS), 532
Remote Client Protocols screen, 536-537
Remote Installation Service (RIS)
 creating CD-based installation image, 162-166
 installing and configuring, 158-162
 slipstreaming installation media for deployment, 155-158
removing shortcuts to middleware, 135
renaming encrypted files, 278
replay cache in Kerberos v5, 462
requesting certificates, 217
Request Security (Optional) properties dialog box (fig.), 352
restoring, Certificate Services, 239-240
Restricted Groups, configuring, 45-46
Restricted Groups node, 29, 44-45
revoking certificates, 226-229
Rijndael symmetric encryption algorithm, 334

RIS. *See* Remote Installation Service (RIS)
risks, evaluating security, 344
Rivest, Shamir, and Adleman, 203
roaming described, 386
rogue servers, 459
routers, configuring for IPSec traffic, 369
Routing and Remote Access Console (fig.), 535
Routing and Remote Access Service. *See* RRAS
RRAS
 described, 528
 servers, VPN capabilities of, 546
 troubleshooting remote access problems, 582
 vs. RAS, 534
RSA algorithm, 203
rules
 IP Security, 350
 security, creating, 359

S

SACL (system access control list), 613
schema objects, attributes, values (table), 14
schemas described, 13
.scr files, 660
script kiddies, 655, 696
script mapping, configuring (fig.), 104
scripting
 deploying security via, 60-61
 implementing security templates using, 62
 updates, 163-165
scripts, hotfix deployment, 185
secedit.exe, 30, 53
 analyzing security with, 70
 deploying security via scripting, 60-62
 using, 67-70
secpol.msc command, 108
secret key, 206-207, 269
securedc.inf, 22, 89
Secure Hash Algorithm (SHA1), 330-331
Secure Server (Require Security) IPSec policy, 348
Secure Shell (SSH)
 using, 705-706
 white hat tool, 697
Secure Sockets Layer (SSL), 11, 307
securews.inf, 22, 92
securing
 domain controllers, 90-91
 domain level, 88
 Exchange 2000 servers, 97-98

Internet Access Service (IAS) servers, 106-107
portable, laptop computers, 111-112
server SMB traffic, 118-119
SQL Server 2000, 93-96
security
 accessing configuration settings at site level (fig.), 25
 analysis, 628
 analyzing issues with Event Logs, 116-117
 attacks. *See* attacks
 auditing systems for increased, 609-610
 Encryption File System. *See* EFS
 end-to-end, 328
 Group Policy settings, 23-27
 incident response plans, 654
 Microsoft, issues, 650
 network, importance of, 320-328
 password policies, 324
 proactive vs. reactive management, 652
 templates. *See* security templates
 wireless LAN issues, 407-426
security bulletins, Microsoft, 86-87
Security Configuration and Analysis, 27-30
Security Configuration and Analysis snap-in, 63-66
security configurations
 analyzing, 63-72
 analyzing with MBSA, 145-151
Security Configuration Tool Set
 creating user interface, 31
 described, 20
security console, creating, 32
security identifiers (SIDs), 479
security incident response and recovery
 forensics, 673-680
 minimizing, 651-654
 prevention list, 652-654
 response plan definition, 672-673
 security incidents, 650-651
Security Log, 342
 adjusting properties (fig.), 630
 restrictions on access, 628
 shutting out hackers, 44
security parameters index (SPI), 335
security patches, 135
security plans
 EFS in. *See* EFS
 evaluating dangers, 344
 multilayered, 265
security policies
 building with customized IPSec consoles, 345-347

820   Index

creating, 356-369
flexibility of, 347
implementing effectively, 343
Security Policy Setting window
    (fig.), 494
Security Rule Wizard, 356-359, 361
security templates
    See also templates
    described (table), 19-21
    and Group Policy, 27
Select Registry Key window (fig.),
    49
server certificates, requesting for IIS
    server, 504
Server Message Block. *See* SMB
Server (Request Security)
    IPSec policy, 348
    properties dialog box (fig.), 350
servers
    adding to the server list (fig.), 664
    members, 92
    preventing files from being
        encrypted on, 277
    updating considerations, 181
    and workstations, 18
service packs described, 134
service tickets, and session tickets,
    474
Session key Perfect Forward
    Secrecy option, 352
session tickets (ST), and service
    tickets, user tickets, 474
session ticket (ST), 464
setup security.inf, 22
shared key, concept and Kerberos,
    460
shared secret keys, 336
shortcuts, to middleware, removing,
    135
SIDs (security identifiers), 479
signatures
    digital, 203-204, 330, 332
    hash, 330
sites described, 17
slipstreaming
    deployment of updates, 153
    described, 156
    installation media for RIS
        deployment, 155-156
    Windows 2000 Professional with
        Service Pack 3, 156-158
smartcards
    authentication and, 533
    and VPN connections, 597
SMB (Server Message Block), 490,
    496
    configuring, 86
    securing traffic, 118-119
SMBdie, performing DoS with,
    668-669

SMS. *See* Systems Management
    Server (SMS)
SMTP, attack vulnerabilities, 713
SMURF attacks, 325, 669
snap-ins, Certificates, 341
sniffer described, 266
Sniffer Pro, 321
SNMP, attack vulnerabilities, 715
snooping described, 321
social engineering and hacking, 323
Social Security numbers, 323
software involved in DDoS attacks,
    671
Software Update Service, 153
Software Update Services (SUS),
    153, 172
    synchronization schedule,
        configuring (fig.), 175
spoofing, 322-323
Spoofit, 323
spreading ratio, 391
spread-spectrum technology, 390
SQL, attack vulnerabilities, 715
SQL Server 2000
    hardening with MBSA, 95
    securing, 93-96
SRV record, 478
SSH. *See* Secure Shell (SSH)
SSL, configuring Web
    authentication using, 508
Standalone Root, Subordinate CAs,
    209
standards, X.500, 11-12
starting, Certificate Import Wizard,
    226
static phone books, 578
statistics, viewing with
    NetDiag.exe, 342
stopping Certificate Services (fig.),
    239
Subseven Trojan, 664
SUS. *See* Software Update Service
    (SUS)
SUSSetup.msi, 173
switches, Cipher command (table),
    281
symmetric cryptography, 269
symmetric encryption, 334
synchronizing clocks, 633
SYN flood attacks, 667
system access control list (SACL),
    613
system crashes, during encryption,
    308
System Policies, 122
systems auditing. *See* auditing
System Services node, 29, 47-48
Systems Management Server
    (SMS), 153, 156, 180

T
TCP/IP
    communications, 394
    properties, changing IP Security
        Policies through (fig.), 341
    protocol, and port numbers
        (table), 712-715
    sequence number attack, 322
TCP SYN attacks, 325
Teardrop attacks, 326
TechNET security homepage, 105
Telnet, attack vulnerabilities, 713
templates
    adding with Automatic Updates
        (fig.), 178
    application issues, 112-117
    applying setup security, 113
    basicdc.inf, 89
    basicsv.inf, 92
    certificate, summary of, 249
    certificate, user and machine
        (tables), 233
    configuring, 54-55
    configuring basic Windows 2000
        security with, 32-52
    configuring certificate, 231-233
    configuring security settings
        manually, 122
    deploying, 53-62
    Exchange BackEnd
        Incremental.inf, 99
    hisecdc.inf, 89
    hisecws.inf, 92
    IIS incremental, 105
    implementing using scripting, 60
    importing, exporting, 55-57, 91
    importing at domain level, 59-60
    legacy client issues, 113-114
    securedc.inf, 89
    securews.inf, 92
    security. *See* security templates
    SMB signing default settings in
        Windows 2000 (table),
        118-119
    testing and deploying, 117
    Windows 2000 workstation, 92
Template Security Policy Setting
    window (fig.), 50
testing
    audit policies, 619
    incident response plans, 673
    security configurations, 53
    security plans, policies, 652
    updates, 181
    white hat vulnerability, 698
TFTP, attack vulnerabilities, 713
TGTs, necessity of, 518
ticket-granting ticket (TGT),
    466-467

Traditional NAT, 586
training, security, minimizing and preventing security incidents, 653
transference of networking sessions, 387
Transmission Control Protocol (TCP), 480
transport mode, IPSec, 328
trees, 10, 13, 481
Trojan horses, 657, 659-660, 684
troubleshooting
　client computer operating systems issues, 585
　EFS, 302-303
　Group Policy application issues, 71
　Group Policy using gpresult.exe tool, 114
　IP Security, 369-371
　methodology, generic, 583-584
　remote access problems, 582-590
　routing and RAS issues, 588
　update installations, 182-183
　Web authentication, 510-511
Truman, President Harry, 201
Trusted Root CAs, 209, 342
　configuring, 236-237
　examining (fig.), 211
　importing certificate from, 225-226
trusts
　configuring Kerberos, 480-488
　Kerberos, linking between domains, 482-488
　Netdom syntax (table), 485
　shortcut and external (fig.), 484

U

UDP and port numbers (table), 712-715
Unicode, IIS, vulnerabilities in, 101
UNIX
　configuring interoperability, 489
　Network Mapper (Nmap), 701
Unlicensed National Information Infrastructure (UNII) band, 390
update installations, troubleshooting, 112, 182-183
updates
　analyzing for, 143-145
　analyzing using MBSA, 147-150
　deploying and managing, 152-181
　deploying to existing computers, 165-166
　getting using Windows Update Catalog, 169-172
　identifying required, 134-136
　installing in isolated networks, 165
　installing on new computers, 155
　scripting, 163-165
　searching for missing, 145-151
　services. See specific service
　testing, 154-155, 181
　version conflicts, 183
updating
　servers, special considerations, 181
　single computer using Windows Update, 166
upgrading Windows NT PDC to Windows 2000, 9
URLScan, ISAPI filter, 122
URLScan tool, 100-102
User Account Properties window (fig.), 499
user authentication
　configuring, 488-496
User Datagram Protocol (UDP), 369
user operations using file encryption, 271
user profiles, remote access, 566
user rights assignment, Local Policies (table), 37-39
users, impersonating, 296
User State Migration Tool, Web site download, 112
user tickets, changing maximum lifetime, 474

V

verifying your encryption level, 496
VeriSign, 208, 239, 333
viewing
　account management auditing (fig.), 612
　audit logon event (fig.), 613
　audit object event (fig.), 614
　audit policy change event (fig.), 615
　audit privilege use event (fig.), 615
　audit process-tracking event (fig.), 616
　audit system event (fig.), 616
　CGI abuses (fig.), 700
　EventCombMT instructions (fig.), 636
　event ID 517 in Security Log (fig.), 627
　events generated within Security Log (fig.), 618
　IIS Internet Services Manager (fig.), 631
　logon event auditing, 612
　statistics with IPSec Monitor, 339
　statistics with NetDiag.exe, 342
　Web browser using HTTP service (fig.), 710
Virtual Collision Detection (VCD), 393
virtual private networks. See VPNs
viruses
　Code Red, 136
　described, 658-659
　Trojan in e-mail (fig.), 660
　and worms and Trojans, 684
VPN
　connections, authentication and, 375
　passwords and laptops, 111
　ports, working with, 556-559
　problems with ISPs, 584
　servers, 546-556
VPNs
　described, 528
　firewall issues, 589

W

walking the tree, 483
WANs (Wide Area Networks), 9
Web authentication
　configuring, 497-511
　methods, 456
　troubleshooting, 510-511
Web Site Properties, Directory Security Tab (fig.), 506
Web sites
　Active Directory delegation, 16
　Active Directory information, 19
　atomic clock, 633
　authentication and, 456
　certificate enrollment, 245
　Ethereal, 704
　gpresult.exe, gpotool.exe, 31
　Group Policy, tools for troubleshooting, 71
　HFNetChk tool, 96
　Honeynet Project, 152
　IIS Lockdown tool, 93
　installing updates in isolated networks, 165
　IPSec troubleshooting, 371
　LANguard Network Scanner, 698
　Microsoft, role-based security, 87
　Microsoft L2TP/IPSec VPN Client download, 575
　Microsoft Press Pass, 135
　Microsoft update, 134
　mixed-mode versus native-mode domains, 572
　National Security Agency, 91
　NetDiag.exe information, 342
　NIST desktop workstation security, 107-108

NTBUGTRAQ, 701
PPP request for comment, 529
Qchain.exe tool download, 163
RIS installation services, 162
security incident response, 651
Security Operations for Windows 2000 Server, 91, 99
Security Operations Guide for Windows 2000 Server, 23
security patches against application vulnerabilities, 327
SMBdie download, 668
SMS updates, 180
TechNET security homepage, 105, 135
Unicode translation problems, hotfix, 102
updates download, 153
User State Migration Tool, 112
VeriSign security failure, 333
white-hat hacking, 656
Windows Catalog, 154
Windows NT 4.0 directory services client download, 458
Windows Update Catalog, 169-172
white hat described, 656, 696
wide area networks (WANs), described, 9
Windows 2000
 Active Directory, review, 4
 auditing, 611-617
 basic security, summary, 73
 CAs, installing, managing, 212-246
 Cipher Utility, using, 280-282
 domain controllers, securing, 89-92
 encryption features, 264-265
 encryption steps, 308
 Event Log entries, 114-116
 Event Viewer, auditing using, 619
 Internet information Services Servers, 99
 KDC and account database, 471-472
 Kerberos authentication in, 470-475
 Kerberos overview, 514-515
 network authentication in, 456-457
 passwords, cracking, 123
 PKI functions, 200

slipstreaming Professional source files with Service Pack 3, 156-158
updates for, 137
version conflicts, 183
vulnerabilities of, 106
Windows 2000 RRAS, EAP-TLS and, 533
Windows 2000 Server
 Active Directory and, 9-10
 Security Operations for, 99
Windows Catalog, Web site, 154
Windows Grep tool, using to search log file, 69
Windows Internet Naming Service (WINS), 349
Windows .NET Server 2003
 2003 release, 593
 auto-enrollment of certificates, 244
 certificate services, 112
Windows NT, 4.0
 upgrading to Windows 2000, 112
 domains, 7-9
 trust relationships in (fig.), 483
 user security, 200
 and Windows 2000, 4
Windows Update
 licensing agreement, accepting (fig.), 168
 updating existing computers with, 165
 updating single computer using, 166
Windows Update Catalog, getting updates using, 169-172
Windows Update Web site, 135, 137, 138
Windows XP
 auto-enrollment of certificates, 244-246
 IPSec Monitor console (fig.), 340
 and laptop security, 111
Windows XP/.NET, sharing encrypted files in, 278
Wired Equivalent Privacy (WEP), collisions and, 393
wireless LANs
 801x authentication, 403-407
 architecture, 392-394
 cards, 111
 concepts about, 388-392
 configuring Windows client computers for, 427-438
 IEEE 8095 standards, 394-398

introduction to, benefits, 384
radio waves and, 386
security issues, 407-426
spread-spectrum, 391-392
transference of networking sessions, 387
wired equivalent privacy, 398-402
wireless network access zone, 386
wireless networks, communication in, 389-392
Wireless Zero Configuration service, 389
wizards
 Add, 365
 Add Recovery Agent, 290
 Back Orifice Configuration, 666
 Certificate Export, 108-110
 Certificate Import, 226
 Certificate Request, 217-220, 286-288
 CMAK, 576, 580
 Filter, 354-355
 IP Filter, 362
 IP Security Filter Action, 365
 IP Security Policy, 359-360
 Network Connection, 577
 Recovery Agent, 283
 RIS Setup (fig.), 161
 Routing and Remote Access Server Setup (fig.), 536
 Security Rule, 356-359, 361
WLAN. *See* wireless LAN
workstations
 creating secure, 107-112
 servers and, 18
World Wide Web (WWW), connectivity and security, 321
worms
 described, 659
 and viruses and Trojans, 684
WUAU22.msi, 177

X

X.509v3 standard
 certificate properties (table), 208
 described, 207
XML. *See* Extensible Markup Language (XML)

Z

Zimmermann, Philip R., 706
zombies, 670